# The Best Test Preparation for the

# GRE

## GRADUATE
## RECORD
## EXAMINATION

# GENERAL TEST

**Pauline Alexander-Travis, Ph.D.**
Assistant Professor of Reading
Western Oklahoma State University, Weatherford, OK

**David Bell, Ed.D.**
Professor of Education
Arkansas Technical University, Russellville, AR

**Anita Price Davis, Ph.D.**
Chairperson of Education Department
Converse College, Spartanburg, SC

**Lucille M. Freeman, Ph.D.**
Associate Professor of Educational Administration
Kearney State College, Kearney, NE

**Leonard L. Gregory, Ph.D.**
Associate Professor of Educational Administration
Kearney State College, Kearney, NE

**Lutfi A. Lutfiyya, Ph.D.**
Associate Professor of Mathematics
Kearney State College, Kearney, NE

**Donald E. Orlosky, Ed.D.**
Chairperson of Educational Leadership Department
University of South Florida, Tampa, FL

**James S. Malek, Ph.D.**
Chairperson and Professor of English
DePaul University, Chicago, IL

**Jerry R. Shipman, Ph.D.**
Professor and Chairperson of Mathematics
Alabama A&M University, Normal, AL

**Ricardo Simpson-Rivera, M.S.**
Visiting Scientist
Oregon State University, Corvallis, OR

Research and Education Association
61 Ethel Road West
Piscataway, New Jersey 08854

The Best Test Preparation for the
GRADUATE RECORD EXAMINATION (GRE)
GENERAL TEST

REVISED EDITION, 1993

Printed in the United States of America

Library of Congress Catalog Card Number 89-69874

International Standard Book Number 0-87891-631-8

Research & Education Association
61 Ethel Road West
Piscataway, New Jersey 08854

*REA supports the effort to conserve*
*and protect environmental resources*
*by printing on recycled papers.*

# CONTENTS

# Contents

# About Research and Education Association

REA is an organization of educators, scientists, and engineers specializing in various academic fields. REA was founded in 1959 for the purpose of disseminating the most recently developed scientific information to groups in industry, government, high schools and universities. Since then, REA has become a successful and highly respected publisher of study aids, test preps, handbooks and reference works.

REA's Test Preparation series extensively prepares students and professionals for the Medical College Admission Test (MCAT), Graduate Record Examinations (GRE), Graduate Management Admission Test (GMAT), Advanced Placement Exams, and College Board Achievement Tests. **Whereas most Test Preparation books present a limited amount of practice exams and bear little resemblance to the actual exams, REA's series presents six exams which accurately depict the actual exams in both degree of difficulty and types of questions. REA's exams are always based on the most recently administered tests and include every type of question that can be expected on the actual tests.**

REA's publications and educational materials are highly regarded for their significant contribution to the quest for excellence that characterizes today's educational goals. We continually receive an unprecedented amount of praise from professionals, instructors, librarians, parents and students for our published books. Our authors are as diverse as the subjects and fields represented in the books we publish. They are well-known in their respective fields and serve on the faculties of prestigious universities throughout the United States.

# You Can Achieve a Top GRE Score

By reviewing and studying this book, you can achieve a top score on the GRE. The GRE General test is not like any exam you have ever taken in college. It does not test prior knowledge of facts specific to any subject or

field of study. As stated by the Graduate Record Examinations Board, the test is "intended to measure verbal, quantitative, and analytical skills, developed throughout your life." Perhaps the most similar tests you have taken were your general college entrance exams, which also tested verbal and quantitative skills rather than prior knowledge of facts specific to any subject or field of study.

The purpose of our book is to prepare you sufficiently for the GRE by providing six full-length exams that accurately reflect the GRE in both degree of difficulty and types of questions. The exams provided are based on the most recently administered GRE's and include every type of question that can be expected on the GRE. Following each exam is an answer key complete with detailed explanations and solutions designed to clarify the material to the student. Our objective is not only to provide the answers, but also to explain to the student why the answer to a particular question is more acceptable than the other possible choices, and at the same time to review the material most likely to be encountered on the actual GRE. By completing all six exams and studying the explanations which follow, you can discover your strengths and weaknesses and thereby concentrate on the sections of the exam which you find more difficult.

## About the Test Experts

In order to meet our objectives of providing exams that reflect the GRE in both accuracy and degree of difficulty, every exam section was carefully prepared by test experts in the various subject fields. Our authors have spent quality time examining and researching the mechanics of actual GRE General Tests to see what types of practice questions will accurately depict the exam and challenge the student. Our experts are highly regarded in the educational community, having studied at the doctorate level and taught in their respective fields at competitive universities and colleges throughout the United States. They have an in-depth knowledge of the questions they have presented in the book and provide accurate questions which appeal to the student's interest. Each question is clearly explained in order to help the student achieve a top score on the GRE.

# About the Test

The GRE General Test is required by graduate and professional schools, as it is considered a very important criterion for admission to a graduate program. Applicants for graduate school submit GRE test results together with other undergraduate records as part of the highly competitive admission process to graduate school. The exam tests verbal, quantitative and analytical skills and ability which have been found to contribute to successful achievement in a graduate program. It does not test prior knowledge of data or facts specific to any field of study. The GRE General Test is given five times a year: April, June, October, December, and February. The test is administered by the Educational Testing Service under the direction of the Graduate Record Examinations Board. Contact your school counselor or local university for information on applying for the test.

The GRE contains three distinct sections with various types of questions:

- **Verbal Ability Section:** two 38-question sections containing analogies, antonyms, sentence completion, and reading comprehension

- **Quantitative Ability:** two 30-question sections containing arithmetic, algebra, geometry, quantitative comparison, discrete quantitative, and data interpretation

- **Analytical Ability:** two 25-question sections containing analytical and logical reasoning

- **A Trial Section:** one of the sections above (this section is not counted towards your score)

Following this preface, test strategies, numerous examples, and suggested studying techniques illustrate the types of questions mentioned previously.

The Graduate Record Examination consists entirely of multiple-choice questions contained in seven timed sections. The total testing time is three and a half hours. Each question presents five choices except for the Quantitative Ability section which presents four choices. Of the seven sections, the actual test contains a trial section which is not identified or counted towards

your score. The purpose of the trial section is to test new questions on students for future exams. **For practicing purposes, this test preparation book has omitted the trial section and has presented the six counted and scored sample sections for each practice exam.**

# Test Format*

| Section | Number of Questions | Minutes |
|---|---|---|
| 1 Verbal | 11 antonyms, 9 analogies, 7 sentence correction, 11 reading comprehension items | 30 |
| 2 Verbal | 11 antonyms, 9 analogies, 7 sentence correction, 11 reading comprehension | 30 |
| 3 Quantitative | 15 quantitative comparisons, 15 mathematical problems | 30 |
| 4 Quantitative | 15 quantitative comparisons, 15 mathematical problems | 30 |
| 5 Analytical | 19 analytical reasoning, 6 logical reasoning | 30 |
| 6 Analytical | 19 analytical reasoning, 6 logical reasoning | 30 |
| 7 Trial Section | Repeat of one of the sections above | 30 |

Total 3 $1/_2$ hours

| | | |
|---|---|---|
| Verbal | = | 76 |
| Quantitative | = | 60 |
| Analytical | = | 50 |
| Total Questions | = | 186 |

* The actual Exam will repeat one additional section, either verbal, analytical, or quantitative (trial section) which will not be counted toward the final score.

# SCORING THE EXAM

The GRE score is based upon the number of correctly answered questions. The test does not deduct points for incorrect answers. (See "Guessing Strategy" for more information concerning this important fact.)

The raw scores are calculated by adding up the correct answers separately for each section. Then the raw scores can be converted to scaled scores from 200 to 800 by finding the corresponding scaled scores in the chart provided below. Each correct answer is worth about ten points. After you take the actual exam you will receive a scoring report which will contain a "percentile score" for each section (how many people scored lower or higher than you).

# SCALED SCORE CONVERSIONS BASED ON RECENT GRE EXAMS

| Raw Score | Verbal Score | % Below | Quantitative Score | % Below | Analytical Score | % Below |
|---|---|---|---|---|---|---|
| | | Scaled Scores and Percents Below | | | | |
| 72 - 76 | 800 | 99 | | | | |
| 71 | 790 | 99 | | | | |
| 70 | 780 | 99 | | | | |
| 69 | 760 | 99 | | | | |
| 68 | 750 | 98 | | | | |
| 67 | 740 | 98 | | | | |
| 66 | 720 | 96 | | | | |
| 65 | 710 | 96 | | | | |
| 64 | 700 | 95 | | | | |
| 63 | 690 | 94 | | | | |
| 62 | 680 | 93 | | | | |
| 61 | 660 | 91 | | | | |
| 60 | 650 | 89 | 800 | 98 | | |
| 59 | 640 | 88 | 800 | 98 | | |
| 58 | 630 | 86 | 790 | 98 | | |
| 57 | 620 | 85 | 780 | 97 | | |
| 56 | 610 | 84 | 770 | 95 | | |
| 55 | 600 | 82 | 750 | 92 | | |
| 54 | 590 | 80 | 740 | 90 | | |
| 53 | 580 | 78 | 730 | 89 | | |
| 52 | 570 | 75 | 720 | 87 | | |
| 51 | 560 | 73 | 700 | 83 | | |
| 50 | 550 | 71 | 690 | 81 | 800 | 99 |
| 49 | 540 | 68 | 680 | 79 | 800 | 99 |
| 48 | 530 | 65 | 670 | 77 | 800 | 99 |
| 47 | 520 | 63 | 650 | 72 | 790 | 98 |
| 46 | 510 | 60 | 640 | 71 | 770 | 98 |

continued on next page

continued from previous page

| Raw Score | Scaled Scores and Percents Below | | | | | |
|---|---|---|---|---|---|---|
| | Verbal Score | % Below | Quantitative Score | % Below | Analytical Score | % Below |
| 45 | 500 | 57 | 630 | 68 | 760 | 97 |
| 44 | 490 | 55 | 620 | 65 | 740 | 95 |
| 43 | 480 | 52 | 600 | 61 | 730 | 94 |
| 42 | 470 | 49 | 590 | 59 | 710 | 92 |
| 41 | 460 | 45 | 580 | 56 | 700 | 91 |
| 40 | 450 | 43 | 560 | 52 | 680 | 88 |
| 39 | 440 | 40 | 550 | 49 | 670 | 86 |
| 38 | 430 | 37 | 540 | 46 | 650 | 84 |
| 37 | 420 | 34 | 530 | 44 | 640 | 81 |
| 36 | 420 | 34 | 510 | 39 | 620 | 77 |
| 35 | 410 | 31 | 500 | 37 | 610 | 74 |
| 34 | 400 | 28 | 490 | 34 | 590 | 69 |
| 33 | 390 | 26 | 480 | 32 | 580 | 67 |
| 32 | 380 | 24 | 460 | 27 | 560 | 61 |
| 31 | 370 | 22 | 450 | 26 | 550 | 59 |
| 30 | 360 | 18 | 440 | 23 | 530 | 53 |
| 29 | 360 | 18 | 430 | 21 | 520 | 50 |
| 28 | 350 | 17 | 410 | 18 | 500 | 44 |
| 27 | 340 | 15 | 400 | 16 | 490 | 41 |
| 26 | 330 | 13 | 390 | 14 | 470 | 36 |
| 25 | 330 | 13 | 380 | 13 | 460 | 33 |
| 24 | 320 | 11 | 360 | 10 | 440 | 27 |
| 23 | 310 | 10 | 350 | 9 | 430 | 25 |
| 22 | 300 | 8 | 340 | 8 | 410 | 21 |
| 21 | 290 | 7 | 330 | 7 | 400 | 18 |
| 20 | 280 | 6 | 310 | 5 | 380 | 15 |
| 19 | 270 | 4 | 300 | 4 | 370 | 13 |
| 18 | 260 | 3 | 290 | 3 | 350 | 10 |
| 17 | 250 | 3 | 280 | 3 | 340 | 9 |
| 16 | 240 | 2 | 260 | 2 | 320 | 6 |
| 15 | 230 | 1 | 250 | 1 | 310 | 5 |
| 14 | 220 | 1 | 240 | 1 | 300 | 4 |
| 13 | 210 | 1 | 230 | 1 | 280 | 3 |
| 12 | 200 | 0 | 210 | 0 | 270 | 2 |
| 11 | 200 | 0 | 200 | 0 | 250 | 1 |
| 10 | 200 | 0 | 200 | 0 | 240 | 1 |
| 9 | 200 | 0 | 200 | 0 | 220 | 1 |
| 8 | 200 | 0 | 200 | 0 | 210 | 0 |
| 0-7 | 200 | 0 | 200 | 0 | 200 | 0 |

# GRE TEST-TAKING STRATEGIES

## HOW TO BEAT THE CLOCK

Every second counts and you want to use the available test time for each section in the most efficient manner. Here's how:

1.  Memorize the test directions for each section of the test. You do not want to waste valuable time on the day of the exam reading directions. Your time should be spent on answering the questions.

2.  The GRE is comprised of relatively easy, medium, and difficult questions. Answer first the questions you find easier and save the difficult questions for later. Do not spend a great deal of time belaboring a difficult question and possibly miss out on answering questions you find easy.

3.  Pace yourself. Work steadily and quickly. Do not get stuck or spend too much time on any one question.

# GUESSING STRATEGY

1.  If you are uncertain of a question, you should guess at the answer rather than not answer at all. You will not be penalized for answering incorrectly, since wrong answers are not counted. This means that you should never leave a space on your answer sheet blank. Even if you do not have time to guess at an answer, be sure to fill in every space on the answer sheet. Since you will not be assessed a penalty for a wrong answer, you will receive credit for any questions you answer correctly by luck.

2.  You can improve your guessing strategy by eliminating choices you recognize as incorrect. When you eliminate an incorrect choice, cross it out. You are allowed to write in your test booklet, and crossing out incorrect choices will help you focus on the correct answer.

# OTHER MUST-DO STRATEGIES

1.   As you work on the test, make sure your answers correspond with the numbers and letters on the answer sheet.

2.   Feel free to write in this book as you are allowed to write in the test booklet of the actual exam. Do not try to solve difficult problems or questions in your head. Work the problem out in your test booklet. Get in the habit of drawing a small sketch or diagram as this is a proven technique for correctly solving problems.

3.   If you are uncertain of a question, make your best guess using the guessing strategy described above, and circle your answer in the exam booklet instead of leaving it blank. This way, if time runs out before you get to approach the question again, you will have at least marked an answer which may be correct.

# THE TEST SECTIONS

As discussed earlier, the GRE contains three sections: Verbal, Quantitative, and Analytical. The following explains these sections in detail and suggests helpful hints in selecting the correct answer. Also found in this section are examples along with detailed explanations.

# VERBAL ABILITY

The Verbal Ability section tests skills in vocabulary, grammar, word relationship, and reading comprehension. Study the VOCABULARY LIST contained in this book. This list contains the most frequently used words which appear on the GRE.

The questions in the Verbal Ability section contain:

 7 sentence completion
 9 analogies
 11 reading comprehension
 11 antonyms

8

The following material introduces each type of question asked in this section.

# SENTENCE COMPLETION

In addition to testing vocabulary skills, Sentence Completion questions measure the ability to recognize the meaning of the sentence logically and structurally.

> **Directions**: Each of the given sentences has blank spaces which indicate words omitted. Choose the best combination of words which fit into the meaning and structure within the context of the sentence.

## EXAMPLE

1. The _____ habits of the wild hawk caused a serious _____ to develop for the chicken farmer.

   (A)  marauding...emergency       (D)  predatory...predicament

   (B)  parasitic...malady          (E)  meticulous...tête-à-tête

   (C)  saprophytic...insurrection

2. The family left their country to _____ to Utopia and escape _____ because of their beliefs.

   (A)  immigrate...prosecution     (D)  wander...arraignment

   (B)  peregrinate...extortion     (E)  roam...censure

   (C)  emigrate...persecution

---

**Suggested Strategies**

- Read the given sentence through carefully.

- Substitute each choice into the sentence and look for correct grammar, structure, and meaning.

- Pay attention to style  clues which may change the mood of the sentence and  hint at the best choice.  For instance, determine if

---

9

the context sets the mood for the choice word to be "positive" or "negative".

- Pay extra attention to transitional words such as *however, although, despite, unfortunately*, etc. These words will affect the mood of the sentence and will give a clue to the correct choice.

- After choosing an answer, read the sentence through for clarity.

## EXPLANATIONS

1.  (D)

(A) MARAUDING (going about in search of plunder and booty) and EMERGENCY (a sudden and unforeseen crisis, often having the pressure of restrictions) do not fit a sentence about a wild hawk very well. (A) is not the best choice. In (B) PARASITIC (living on others) does not fit the sentence about the hawk very well. Neither does MALADY (a disease, a mental or moral disorder) fit in the second blank. In (C) SAPROPHYTIC (living on decaying organic matter) does not apply to a hawk. INSURRECTION (a rising up, a rebellion) does not fit blank two. In (D) PREDATORY (preying upon other animals) and PREDICAMENT (an unpleasant situation) fit the sentence well; (D) is correct. (E) METICULOUS (extremely careful about small details) and TÊTE-À-TÊTE (a private conversation between two people) do not fit the sentence well.

2.  (C)

In (A) IMMIGRATE is usually accompanied by the preposition *from*; this word does not fit. Neither is it likely that there would be a PROSECUTION (a legal suit against) simply because of beliefs, not actions. In (B) PEREGRINATE means to travel, but EXTORTION (drawing someting from someone by force) does not fit logically in the sentence. (B) is incorrect. In (C) one EMIGRATES to another place; PERSECUTION (torment, abuse) might be typical for one's beliefs. These seem logical choices of words. (C) is correct. In (D) since WANDER implies no set destination, this choice does not fit well. Coupled with the word ARRAIGNMENT (to bring before a court, to charge), (D) is clearly not a suitable choice. In (E) ROAM implies no set destination so this choice does not fit well. CENSURE indicates blame or criticism, but is not acceptable coupled with ROAM.

# ANALOGIES

An analogy consists of a relationship between two words. The analogy questions require recognizing the parallel relationships between the pair of words given. Most of the word relationships found on the GRE test will be:

1.  Degree (DISLIKE:DESPISE)

2.  Cause and effect (SUGAR:CAVITY)

3.  Category and example (VEGETABLE:ARTICHOKE)

4.  Part and whole (SLICE:PIE)

5.  Agent and action (EAR:HEARING)

6.  "to be is not to have" (UNFORTUNATE:LUCK)

---

**DIRECTIONS***: In the following questions, the given pair of words contains a specific relationship to each other. Select the best pair of the choices which expresses the same relationship as the given.

---

## EXAMPLES

1.  MERIDIAN:PARALLEL::

    (A) east:west            (D) map:globe

    (B) north:south          (E) compass:direction

    (C) longitude:latitude


2.  ABORIGINAL:INSERTION::

    (A) native:novel         (D) modern:resumption

    (B) original:habituated  (E) accustomed:recurrence

    (C) source:mouth

11

## Suggested Strategies

- It is important to first establish the kind of relationship which exists between the given pair words.

- If more than one answer choice seems to fit the kind of relationship in the given, return to the given to establish a more specific relationship.

- If more than one answer choice still seems to fit the kind of relationship determined, see if there is another meaning to the given pair of words which may have been overlooked. Words may have many meanings.

- If both words in the given pair are nouns, both words in each choice will be nouns. Whatever part of speech the given pair is, the correct choice will be consistent with it.

- Create a sentence with both given words and then replace each with the answer choices to see which is the best choice.

- Be sure to read all the choices before making a decision.

## EXPLANATIONS

1. **(C)**

The relationship between MERIDIAN and PARALLEL is that between two different types of lines on a map; they are used together to locate a point, compute distance, etc. The two are not just opposite terms; they must be used together for location, computation, etc. In (A) EAST and WEST are opposite directions. They are a plausible answer, but not *the* answer since they do not really work together as do a MERIDIAN and a PARALLEL. In (B) NORTH and SOUTH are opposite compass directions. Again they are a possible answer, but not the *best* answer since they do not really work together as do a MERIDIAN and a PARALLEL. In (C) LONGITUDE and LATITUDE compare well with MERIDIAN and PARALLEL. Through MERIDIANS, one arrives at LONGITUDE. Through PARALLELS, one arrives at LATITUDE. Both LONGITUDE and LATITUDE are used in location as are MERIDIANS and PARALLELS. (C) is the best answer. In (D) a MAP is a drawing representing the earth's surface. A GLOBE is a sphere with a map of

the world on it. The two are not necessarily used together. They do not have the same analogy as do MERIDIAN:PARALLEL. In (E) a compass is used to find direction, so (E) is also a different analogy.

2.    (A)
    ABORIGINAL means original, native. INSERTION implies an introduction to something already existing. The two are opposite in that ABORIGINAL implies coming before the act of adding (INSERTION). In (A) NATIVE means original to an area. NOVEL means different. The two are opposite in the same way that ABORIGINAL is opposite from INSERTION. (A) is the correct answer. In (B) ORIGINAL implies being native or "there first." HABITUATED means accustomed. The relationship is closer to being synonymous than opposite. Since an antonymous relationship is sought, (B) is not the best choice. In (C) the SOURCE of a river is its MOUTH. The relationship between the two is not the opposite relationship sought. In (D) MODERN suggests currency, RESUMPTION suggests beginning again. The relationship between the two is not the antonymous relationship sought. In (E) ACCUSTOMED means usual, customary. RECURRENCE means to occur again. The two are not opposite in relationship.

## READING COMPREHENSION

This section asks interpretive, applicative, and inferential questions based on accompanying reading passages. Detailed knowledge of the passage's topic is not tested. The Reading Comprehension section, which includes two passages followed by questions, measures the ability to understand, analyze, and apply information presented in the passages.

Types of questions asked in this section include the following:

1.    Understanding the main idea or the overall meaning of the passage

2.    Determining and evaluating the important points of an argument

3.    Drawing inferences from facts or reaching a conclusion

4.    Interpreting numerical data to reach a conclusion

5.    Recognizing the tone of the passage

Directions: Each passage is followed by questions based on its content. After reading the passage, choose the best answer to each question. Answer all questions based on what is stated or implied in that passage.

## EXAMPLES

Established firmly in popular culture is the notion that each of the two hemispheres of the brain has specialized functions. The left hemisphere, insist proponents of this theory, controls language and logic; the right hemisphere, espousers contend, is the more creative and intuitive half. Many proponents try to classify a person as "right-brained" or "left-brained," suggesting that the two hemispheres do not work together in the same person and, thus, can be considered independent. Because of the supposed independent functions of the two hemispheres and because of their difference in specializations, an activity might engage one part of the brain while the other part is not used at all, they believe. "Right-brained" individuals are the creative intuitive persons (artists, for instance) of society; "left-brained" persons are the verbal, language-oriented, logical individuals of civilization.

Opponents of the split-brain theory dispute the premise that the hemispheres operate independently simply because of specialized functions; they state that the very fact that the two hemispheres differ in purpose indicates that they must integrate activities and therefore result in processes which are different from and even greater than the processes of either hemisphere. These split-brain theory opponents base their arguments on the fact that when surgery is performed to disconnect the two sides, each can still function well (but not perfectly). They also argue that when a person writes an original story, the left hemisphere works to produce a logical work, but the right hemisphere helps with creativity. The third argument is based on the fact that if a patient has right hemisphere damage, major logical disorders are manifested; in fact, more logical disorders appear than if the left hemisphere suffers damage. The opponents to split-brain theory state that it is impossible to educate one side of the brain without educating the other. They state that there is no evidence that one can be purely right-brained or left-brained.

Educators, then, who seek to modify the curriculum and methods to accommodate the split-brain theory must justify their demands. The burden of proof rests with these innovators who seek to restructure education as it

14

currently exists.

1.  To the assertion that the split-brain theory is accurate, the author would probably respond with which of the following?

    (A)  Unqualified disagreement    (D)  Strong disparagement

    (B)  Unquestioning approval      (E)  Implied uncertainty

    (C)  Complete indifference

2.  Which of the following titles best describes the content of the passage?

    (A)  A Reassertion of the Validity of the Split-brain Theory

    (B)  A Renunciation of the Split-brain Theory

    (C)  Split Opinions on the Split-brain Theory

    (D)  Modifying the Curriculum to Accommodate the Split-brain Theory

    (E)  A New Theory: The Split-brain Theory

3.  The attitude of the author toward proponents' furnishing proof to justify modifying the curriculum to accommodate the split-brain theory could be best described as which of the following?

    (A)  Optimism        (D)  Illogical

    (B)  Pessimism       (E)  Indifference

    (C)  Resignation

---

**Suggested Strategies:**

- Skim the passage and look only for the main ideas.

- Do not to spend too much time deciphering the meaning of words and statements when skimming the passage. Go back over specific parts of the passage for in-depth understanding only after reading each question.

> •    Answer each question one at a time. After reading the question, locate the part of the passage that talks about what is said in the question.
>
> •    Consider leaving the reading comprehension for last as you work on the verbal section since it is the most time-consuming part.

## EXPLANATIONS

1.   (E)

In (A) there is no evidence that the author disagrees so vehemently with the split-brain theory as to respond with UNQUALIFIED DISAGREEMENT. In (B) UNQUESTIONING APPROVAL is not the attitude of the author; rather the writer seems willing to listen to both sides, though more inclined to disagree with the theory. In (C) the very fact that the author wrote the article negates the idea that COMPLETE INDIFFERENCE is the best answer. In (D), although the author seems to disagree with the split-brain theory, STRONG DISPARAGEMENT is not the best answer. In (E) IMPLIED UNCERTAINTY seems to be the best of the choices.

2.   (C)

(A) is incorrect since the split-brain theory is not reasserted by the author in the article. In (B), since the split-brain theory is not renunciated by the author, (B) is not the correct choice. (C) is the best answer since it implies what the article does — present both sides of the theory. In (D), since modifying the curriculum is only one part of the article, (D) is incorrect. In (E), since the split-brain theory is not new, (E) is inaccurate.

3.   (B)

In (A), the writer does not seem convinced that the educators who support the split-brain theory can supply justification for modifying the curriculum. The author does not seem OPTIMISTIC. In (B), the writer does seem PESSIMISTIC and unconvinced that the educators can supply the needed proof. (B) is the best answer. For (C), the author is not RESIGNED to the fact that the proponents can supply the necessary proof. In fact the author seems skeptical that such proof can be provided. For (D), the author does not appear ILLOGICAL. The writer seems willing to listen to proponents if they can

provide the facts. In (E), the very fact that the author wrote about and is willing to listen to facts supporting a modification of the curriculum makes the answer INDIFFERENCE inappropriate.

## ANTONYMS

The antonym questions test vocabulary and the ability to figure out the opposite relationship to the given word. An antonym is a word which is opposite in meaning to another.

**Directions:** Each of the following questions provides a given word in capitalized letters followed by five word choices. Choose the best word which is most _opposite_ in meaning to the given word.

## EXAMPLE

1. CONCORD:
   - (A) succor
   - (B) enmity
   - (C) gripper
   - (D) vigilant
   - (E) ennobling

2. INSIDIOUS:
   - (A) precipitant
   - (B) incendiary
   - (C) decadent
   - (D) conducive
   - (E) imprudent

3. MALEFACTION:
   - (A) affinity
   - (B) subsidy
   - (C) profligation
   - (D) idiosyncratic
   - (E) cognate

---

## Suggested Strategies

- Look for the word most opposite in meaning to the given word.

- If more than one choice seems to be the opposite of the given word, return to the given and determine a more precise definition.

- It is helpful to create a sentence using the given word and substitute each choice.

- It is helpful to use any knowledge of root words, prefixes, or suffixes if you are not sure of the meaning of the given word.

- Do not mark an answer until after all the choices are read.

- A trick in figuring the correct answer is to turn each answer choice into its opposite and then compare it to the capitalized word to see if it means the same thing.

---

## EXPLANATIONS

1. **(B)**

CONCORD is a state of agreement, harmony. In (A), SUCCOR is aid, help. (A) is not an antonym for CONCORD and should not be chosen. For (B), ENMITY is ill will or hatred; it is the opposite of CONCORD. (B) is the correct answer. In (C), a GRIPPER is one who holds a camera or other apparatus. It bears no relation to CONCORD and should not be selected as the correct choice. For (D), VIGILANT means alertly watchful. It is not directly related to CONCORD. It is an inappropriate choice. In (E), ENNOBLING means elevating, raising. It is not the opposite of the key word and should not be selected.

2. **(D)**

INSIDIOUS means wily, sly. For (A), PRECIPITANT means rushing ahead. It is not an antonym for INSIDIOUS. In (B), INCENDIARY means tending to excite or inflame. It should not be selected as the antonym. For (C), DECADENT is deteriorating and declining. It is not the opposite of INSIDIOUS. In (D), CONDUCIVE means helpful. It is the opposite of INSIDIOUS. For (E), IMPRUDENT means lacking in caution, indiscreet. It is not the

opposite of INSIDIOUS.

3.　(B)

A MALEFACTION is an evil deed, an offense. (A) AFFINITY means an attraction, a likeness. It is not the opposite for MALEFACTION. (B) A SUBSIDY is a gift, a form of aid. Certainly a SUBSIDY (aid) would be the opposite of MALEFACTION (an evil deed). (B) is the correct answer. In (C), PROFLIGATION means the act of wasting. It is not the opposite of MALE-FACTION. (D) IDIOSYNCRATIC means peculiar, eccentric. It is not an antonym for MALEFACTION. (E) COGNATE means of a similar nature. Since the term is not directly related to MALEFACTION, it should not be chosen.

# QUANTITATIVE ABILITY

Quantitative Ability questions include quantitative comparison, discrete quantitative, and data interpretation skills. This section measures basic mathematical ability, quantitative reasoning, problem solving, and under-standing of mathematical concepts. These questions require a review of basic arithmetic, algebra, geometry, and familiarity with word problems. Study the MATHEMATICS REVIEW which follows the vocabulary list.

Quantitative Ability questions include:

15 quantitative comparison questions
10 discrete quantity mathematical problems
5 data interpretation questions based on a chart

The following material introduces each type of question asked in the section.

## QUANTITATIVE COMPARISON

The quantitative comparison questions challenge ability to determine accurately and quickly the relative sizes of two quantities. It also measures the ability to see whether enough information is given in order to pick a correct choice.

The directions in this section read as follows:

---

**Numbers:** All numbers are real numbers.

**Figures:** Position of points, angles, regions, etc. are assumed to be in the order shown and angle measures are assumed to be positive.

**Lines:** Assume that lines shown as straight are indeed straight.

**Directions:** Each of the following given set of quantities is placed into either column A or B. Compare the two quantities to decide whether:

    A. the quantity in Column A is greater

    B. the quantity in Column B is greater

    C. the two quantities are equal

    D. the relationship cannot be determined from the information given

**Note:** Do not choose (E) since there are only four choices.

**Common Information:** Information which relates to one or both given quantities is centered above the two columns. A symbol which appears in both columns will indicate the same item in Column A and Column B.

---

## EXAMPLES

| **Column A** | **Column B** |
|---|---|

The length of a ruler is "*L*". This value is is increased by 10%, and then decreased by 10%.

---

1.           *L*                     final length

---

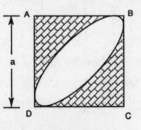

*ABCD* is a square. The un-shaded area represents the intersection of two quadrants.

2.       shaded area         unshaded area

---

## Suggested Strategies:

•   Memorize and understand the directions since it presents abundant information. You will be able to save more time to work on the problems instead of spending time reading the directions.

•   It is better to simplify both given quantities as little as possible to come to a conclusion rather than extensively work out the problem. This will save time and still will allow you to arrive at the correct answer.

•   The answer can be reduced to three choices [(A), (B), or (C)] if both quantities being compared present no variables. If this is the case, the answer can never be (D), which states the relationship **cannot be determined from the information given.**

•   If it is established that (A) is greater when considering certain numbers but (B) is greater when considering other certain numbers, then choose (D) immediately.

---

## EXPLANATIONS

1.   (A)
   The original length = "$L$". When the ruler increases by 10%, the length will be

$$L + 10\% \text{ of } L = L + (10/100)L = 1.1L$$

Then the ruler is decreased by 10%:

$$1.1L - 10\% \text{ of } 1.1L = 1.1L - (10/100)1.1L = .99L$$

**Note:** In the second part, the 10% refers to $1.1L$. Therefore, the final length is $.99L$ and the answer is (A) because $L > .99L$.

2.   (B)
   First, evaluate the shaded area with the following procedure:

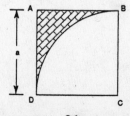

The half-shaded area can be expressed by

half-shaded area = (Sq. area − Quadrant area)

half-shaded area = $a^2 - \pi\, a^2/4 = a^2(1 - \pi/4)$

because the quadrant represents one-fourth of the area of a circle with the radius $a$. Therefore, the shaded area in the problem will be

shaded area = $2a^2(1 - \pi/4) \approx .43a^2$

The unshaded area can be expressed by

unshaded area = (Sq. area − Shaded area)

unshaded area = $a^2 - 2a^2(1 - \pi/4)$

unshaded area = $a^2(\pi/2 - 1) \approx .57a^2$

Therefore, the unshaded area > the shaded area. The answer is (B).

## DISCRETE QUANTITATIVE

Discrete Quantitative questions test the ability to apply given information in an abstract situation in order to solve a problem.

> **Directions**: For the following questions, select the best answer choice to the given question.

### EXAMPLES

1.  Which of the following has the smallest value?

    (A)  $^{1}/_{0.2}$                    (D)  $^{0.2}/_{0.1}$

    (B)  $^{0.1}/_{2}$                    (E)  $^{2}/_{0.1}$

    (C)  $^{0.2}/_{1}$

2.  A square is inscribed in a circle of area $18\pi$. What is the length of a side of the square?

    (A)  6                    (D)  $6\sqrt{2}$

    (B)  3                    (E)  Cannot be determined

    (C)  $3\sqrt{2}$

22

---

**Suggested Strategies:**

- Determine first what form the answer should be put in looking at the forms in the multiple choices.

- If the question requires an approximation, get an idea of the degree of approximation by scanning the multiple choices.

---

## EXPLANATIONS

1. **(B)**

   Note that $\dfrac{.1}{2} = \dfrac{.1 \times 10}{2 \times 10} = \dfrac{1}{20}$ for response (B).

   For choice (A), $\dfrac{1}{.2} = \dfrac{1 \times 10}{.2 \times 10} = \dfrac{10}{2} = 5$ which is larger than $\dfrac{1}{20}$.

   For choice (C), $\dfrac{.2}{1} = \dfrac{.2 \times 10}{1 \times 10} = \dfrac{2}{10} = \dfrac{1}{5}$ which is larger than $\dfrac{1}{20}$.

   For choice (D), $\dfrac{.2}{.1} = \dfrac{.2 \times 10}{.1 \times 10} = \dfrac{2}{1} = 2$ which is larger than $\dfrac{1}{20}$.

   For choice (E), $\dfrac{2}{.1} = \dfrac{2 \times 10}{.1 \times 10} = \dfrac{20}{1} = 20$ which is larger than $\dfrac{1}{20}$.

2. **(A)**

   The formula for the area of a circle is $A = \pi r^2$. Since the area of the square is $18\pi$, then it is true that
   $$\pi r^2 = 18\pi \text{ or } r^2 = 18 \text{ or } r = \sqrt{18} = 3\sqrt{2}.$$
   Then, the diameter of the circle is
   $$2r = 2(3\sqrt{2}) = 6\sqrt{2}.$$
   Using the Pythagorean Theorem:
   $$x^2 + x^2 = (6\sqrt{2})^2$$
   $$2x^2 = 36(2) ; \quad x^2 = 36$$
   $$x = 6 \text{ is the length of the side of the square}$$

## DATA INTERPRETATION

Data interpretation questions test the ability to read graphs and tables and apply information given in order to come to a decision. The questions are based upon graphs or tables. Most of the graphs presented are grid graphs, pie charts, tables, and bar graphs.

---

**Directions:** The following questions refer to the chart and information below. Select the best answer choice to the given question.

---

## EXAMPLE

**Table of Weight Distribution of a 70,000-Gram Man**
**(Weights of some organs given)**

| Organ | Weight in Grams | Organ | Weight in Grams |
|---|---|---|---|
| Skeleton | 10,000 | Muscles | 30,000 |
| Blood | 5,000 | Intestinal tract | 2,000 |
| Liver | 1,700 | Lungs | 1,000 |
| Brain | 1,500 | | |

1. If 40 percent of the weight of the blood is made up of cells, what percent (to the nearest tenth) of the total body weight is made up of blood cells?

    (A)  7.1

    (B)  3.6

    (C)  1.4

    (D)  2.8

    (E)  9.9

2. Which expression represents the total body weight if the weight of the skeleton is represented by $S$ grams?

    (A)  $7S$

    (B)  $70000S$

    (D)  $60S$

    (D)  $S + 6$

    (E)  Cannot be determined

---

**Suggested Strategies:**

• Try not to spend too much time understanding the data. Become more familiar with the data as you read and answer the questions.

• It is more efficient to estimate the average rather than computing it.

---

- When a question seems too involved, it is helpful to break it down into parts.

- Avoid figuring large computations by estimating products and quotients.

- Become familiar with the different types of charts discussed above.

## EXPLANATIONS

1. (D)

Since 40% of the weight of blood is made up of cells, then the weight of the cells is 0.4 times 5000 grams or 2000 grams. So, to find the percent of the total body weight that is made up of blood cells, form the following ratio and change the result to percent.

$$\frac{2,000}{70,000} = \frac{1}{35} = .028 = 2.8\%$$

2. (A)

To find the solution one needs to set up a proportion. Thus, let $x$ denote the total body weight in grams and $S$ denote the weight of the skeleton. Then, the following proportion can be formed.

$$\frac{\text{weight of skeleton}}{\text{total body weight}} = \frac{10,000 \text{ grams}}{70,000 \text{ grams}} = \frac{1}{7} = \frac{S}{x}$$

which implies x = 7S : Total Body Weight

# ANALYTICAL ABILITY

Two types of analytical questions are presented in this section:

Analytical Reasoning and Logical Reasoning

Analytical reasoning questions focus on deducing new information from given data; logical reasoning questions assess understanding of relationships between arguments.

The analytical ability section includes:

19  analytical reasoning questions
6 logical reasoning questions

The following material introduces each type of question asked in this section.

## ANALYTICAL REASONING

The analytical reasoning questions consist of a set of related statements followed by questions which require the process of deduction based on the set of given statements. The questions do not require knowledge of formal logic or mathematics, although they require knowledge of vocabulary and simple computational ability.

---

**Directions:** Each question or group of questions is based on a passage or set of statements. Select the best answer choice.

---

### EXAMPLE

Questions 1 – 3 refer to the following statements.

Debbie, Mary, Joy, and Fred have a Physics final on Friday and they all would like to study together at least once before the test.
Debbie can study only on Monday, Tuesday, and Wednesday nights, and Thursday afternoon and night.
Mary can study only on Monday, Wednesday and Thursday nights, and Tuesday afternoon and night.
Joy can study only on Wednesday and Thursday nights, Tuesday afternoon, and Monday afternoon and night.
Fred can study the afternoons and nights of Tuesday, Wednesday, and Thursday, and on Monday afternoon.

1.    If the group is to study twice, then the days could be

    (A)   Monday and Wednesday

    (B)   Tuesday and Thursday

    (C)   Wednesday and Thursday

    (D)   Monday and Friday

    (E)   Tuesday and Wednesday

2.  If three of them tried to study together when all four could not,

    (A)  this would be possible twice

    (B)  it would have to be on Wednesday night

    (C)  Fred could not attend the three-person groups

    (D)  this could be accomplished on Monday and Tuesday only

    (E)  this would not be possible

3.   If Debbie decided to study every night,

    (A)  she would never be able to study with Fred

    (B)  she would never be able to study with Joy

    (C)  she would have at least two study partners each night

    (D)  she would have to study alone on Monday night

    (E)  she would study with only Mary on Thursday night

---

**Suggested Strategies:**

- Answer first those questions in the group which are less difficult and then return to the more difficult ones. Just because a group looks difficult or complicated does not mean it really is.

- While reading the set of statements, do not introduce assumptions which are not already given.

- Read the set of conditions for face value rather than assuming the statements have hidden meanings.

- Draw a diagram or chart in order to visualize the problem more clearly.

- Do not incorporate any information which is in one question into another question.  Refer only to the set of given statements.

- Answer easier questions first.  This will eliminate time you might spend on a difficult question when an easier one can be answered immediately, adding   points to your score.

- Read all the choices before choosing an answer.

---

# EXPLANATIONS

In answering many of the questions on the analytical part of the GRE it is helpful to construct a chart to examine the options. This can help to visualize or think through the options.

Begin by building the chart.

|        | Mon. | Tues. | Wed. | Thurs. |
|--------|------|-------|------|--------|
| Debbie | N    | N     | N    | AN     |
| Mary   | N    | AN    | N    | N      |
| Joy    | AN   | A     | N    | N      |
| Fred   | A    | AN    | AN   | AN     |

N= night
A= afternoon

You can then answer questions 1 to 3 by examining the information given in the chart.

1.   (C)
You can see from an examination of the chart that Wednesday and Thursday are the only two days this is possible. On Monday Fred could not study at night and the others could not study in the afternoon. On Tuesday Joy could not study at night and the others could not study in the afternoon.

2.   (D)
    This could be accomplished on Monday and Tuesday only. Remember from question one that they could all study together on Wednesday and Thursday. This leaves Monday and Tuesday. Choice (A) is incorrect because they could study together more than twice on those two days. On Tuesday Debbie, Mary, and Fred could study at night and Mary, Joy and Fred could study in the afternoon. Another study session for Debbie, Mary, and Joy would be available Monday night.

3.   (C)
    She would have at least two study partners each night. An examination of the chart indicates that on Monday she could study with Mary and Joy; on

28

Tuesday with Mary and Fred; and on Wednesday and Thursday with the entire group. Choices (A) and (B) are false because Debbie could study with Fred and Joy on Wednesday and Thursday nights. Choice (D) is false because she could study with Mary and Joy and choice (E) is false because she could study with the entire group.

## LOGICAL REASONING

The logical reasoning subsection involves questions which ask for recognizing the point of an argument, identifying assumptions, drawing conclusions from given conditions, finding the missing material from passages, and determining arguments.

> **Directions:** Each question or group of questions is based on a passage or set of statements. Select the best answer choice.

### EXAMPLES

1. Which of the following comes closest to being a factual statement?

    (A) Lawyer: "Our whole political system is corrupt."

    (B) Financial expert: "The price of gold is bound to increase."

    (C) Doctor: "Cigarette smoking may be hazardous to your health."

    (D) Upholsterer: "These are the most comfortable chairs we make."

    (E) Coin Collector: "Fewer than ten of these silver coins were minted in the year 1947."

2. It is immoral to blame people for what they do. They are simply behaving as they have been conditioned to behave and have no choice in the matter. Blaming them will never change their behavior.

    The author undercuts the argument by

    (A) adopting dubious psychological theories

    (B) undermining morality

    (C) attacking human freedom

29

(D)   arguing emotionally

(E)   doing what is argued against

---

**Suggested Strategies:**

•   Read the material carefully, focusing on the argumentative methods employed rather than assessing its truth or falseness.

•   Determine closely what the question is asking for.

•   Read all the choices before choosing an answer.

---

## EXPLANATIONS

1.   (E)

The answer to this question is clearly choice (E). Only the coin collector makes a factual statement — on the number of coins of a specific type minted in a certain year. The remaining people present opinions which, however qualified, cannot be established empirically.

2.   (E)

Though the author argues that blaming people is immoral and futile, the writer blames those who blame others, thus doing just what is argued against. Choice (D) is obviously incorrect, since the author does not appeal to emotion. Choices (A), (B), and (C), even if true, would not constitute undercutting the argument.

# Our GRE Vocabulary List
## The most frequently tested words on the GRE

The verbal sections of the GRE test your abilities in many areas. No area, however, will have a greater impact upon your degree of success on the verbal sections than your vocabulary knowledge. Without a strong, comprehensive vocabulary, it is virtually impossible to score well on the verbal sections. Therefore, in order to be successful on the GRE, you must build your vocabulary and sharpen your skills.

Although this may seem like a tough assignment, it is not as difficult as it sounds. Reading is a simple skill that is also the most effective way to build your vocabulary. Reading increases your familiarity with words and their uses in different contexts. By reading every day, you can increase your chances of recognizing a word and its meaning in a test question.

Remembering the words you read, however, is the tough part. Here is where our GRE Vocabulary List is most helpful. We realize that after a complete undergraduate education, you have naturally formed a fairly strong vocabulary. Therefore, rather than give you an extensive list of thousands of words, we have narrowed down our vocabulary lists to include the one thousand words that most commonly appear on the GRE. The first 600 of these words are frequently appearing words. This means that they have appeared on the GRE over and over again. Our GRE Vocabulary List will give you a strong indication as to the appropriate level of vocabulary that is present on the GRE. In conjunction with reading, our GRE Vocabulary List can aid you in building your vocabulary and sharpening your verbal skills.

The most effective way to utilize the Vocabulary List is to study one section at a time. Make a note of the words with which you are unfamiliar or that are defined in unusual ways. Test yourself on the words by completing the antonym and synonym drills that follow each section. Do the same for the commonly tested words. Any words that you are still unsure about should be studied as much as possible before the day of the test. Although these will not be the only words tested on the GRE, these lists, along with your present vocabulary as a base and lots of reading, will prepare you to be successful on the verbal sections of the GRE.

## Group 1

abase - *v.* - to degrade; humiliate; disgrace
aberration - *n.* - departure from what is right, true, correct
abeyance - *n.* - a state of temporary suspension

abhor - *v*. - to hate

abominate - *v*. - to loathe; to hate

absolve - *v*. - to forgive; to acquit

abstemious - *adj*. - sparingly used or used with temperance

abstinence - *n*. - the act or practice of voluntarily refraining from any action

abstruse - *adj*. - 1. hidden, concealed; 2. difficult to be comprehended

accolade - *n*. - approving or praising mention

accomplice - *n*. - co-conspirator; a partner; partner-in-crime

accretion - *n*. - growth in size by addition or accumulation

accrue - *v*. - collect; build up

acquiesce - *v*. - agree or consent to an opinion

acrid - *adj*. - sharp; bitter; foul smelling

adamant - *adj*. - not yielding; firm

adversary - *n*. - an enemy; foe

advocate - *v*. - 1. to plead in favor of; 2. *n*. - supporter; defender

aesthetic - *adj*. - showing good taste; artistic

aghast - *adj*. - 1. astonished; amazed; 2. horrified; terrified; appalled

alacrity - *n*. - 1. enthusiasm; fervor; 2. liveliness; sprightliness

alleviate - *v*. - to lessen or make easier

allocate - *v*. - set aside; designate; assign

allusion - *n*. - an indirect reference to something

aloof - *adj*. - distant in interest; reserved; cool

altercation - *n*. - controversy; dispute

altruistic - *adj*. - unselfish

amass - *v*. - to collect together; accumulate

ambiguous - *adj*. - not clear; uncertain; vague

ameliorate - *v*. - to make better; to improve

amiable - *adj*. - friendly

amorphous - *adj*. - having no determinate form

analogy - *n*. - similarity; correlation; parallelism; simile; metaphor

anarchist - *n*. - one who believes that a formal government is unnecessary

anomaly - *n*. - abnormality; irregularity; deviation from the regular arrangement

anonymous - *adj*. - nameless; unidentified

antagonism - *n*. - hostility; opposition

antipathy - *n*. - inherent aversion or antagonism of feeling

antiseptic - *adj*. - preventing infection or decay

apathy - *n*. - lack of emotion or interest

appease - *v*. - to make quiet; to calm

apprehensive - *adj*. - fearful; in expectation of evil

arbiter - *n*. - one who is authorized to judge or decide

arbitrary - *adj*. - based on one's preference or judgment

arduous - *adj*. - difficult; laborious

arid - *adj*. - 1. dry; parched; 2. barren; 3. uninteresting; dull

arrogant - *adj*. - acting superior to others; conceited

astute - *adj.* - cunning; sly; crafty
atrophy - *v.* - to waste away through lack of nutrition
audacious - *adj.* - fearless; bold

---

# Drill 1

DIRECTIONS: Match each word in the left column with the word in the right column that is most **opposite** in meaning.

| | *Word* | | | | *Match* | | |
|---|---|---|---|---|---|---|---|
| 1. ___ | audacious | 6. ___ | acrid | A. | hostile | F. | disperse |
| 2. ___ | apathy | 7. ___ | acquiesce | B. | fragrant | G. | enthusiasm |
| 3. ___ | amiable | 8. ___ | arbitrary | C. | selfish | H. | conformity |
| 4. ___ | altruistic | 9. ___ | amass | D. | reasoned | I. | resist |
| 5. ___ | aberration | 10. ___ | adversary | E. | ally | J. | unadventurous |

DIRECTIONS: Match each word in the left column with the word in the right column that is most **similar** in meaning.

| | *Word* | | | | *Match* | | |
|---|---|---|---|---|---|---|---|
| 11. ___ | adamant | 14. ___ | antagonism | A. | afraid | D. | insistent |
| 12. ___ | aesthetic | 15. ___ | altercation | B. | disagreement | E. | hostility |
| 13. ___ | apprehensive | | | C. | tasteful | | |

---

# Group 2

augment - *v.* - to increase or add to; to make larger
auspicious - *adj.* - 1. having omens of success; 2. prosperous; 3. favorable; kind
austere - *v.* - harsh; severe; strict
authentic - *adj.* - real; genuine; trustworthy
awry - *adv.* - 1. crooked(ly); uneven(ly); 2. *adj.* - wrong, askew
axiom - *n.* - an established principle or statement accepted as true
azure - *n.* - the clear blue color of the sky
baleful - *adj.* - sinister; threatening; evil; deadly
banal - *adj.* - common; trivial; trite
baroque - *adj.* - extravagant; ornate
bauble - *n.* - 1. that which is gay or showy; 2. a baby's toy
beget - *v.* - to produce, as an effect
behoove - *v.* - to be advantageous; to be necessary
benefactor - *n.* - one who helps others; a donor
beneficient - *adj.* - doing good
benevolent - *adj.* - kind; generous
benign - *adj.* - mild; harmless
berate - *v.* - scold; reprove; reproach; criticize
bereave - *v.* - to deprive

bereft - *adj.* - deprived; left sad because of someone's death

beseech - *v.* - 1. to ask or pray with urgency; 2. to beg eagerly for

biennial - *adj.* - 1. happening every two years; 2. *n.* - a plant which blooms every two years

blasphemous - *adj.* - irreligious, away from acceptable standards

blatant - *adj.* - 1. obvious; unmistakable; 2. crude; vulgar

blithe - *adj.* - happy; cheery, merry

bombastic - *adj.* - pompous; wordy; turgid

brevity - *n.* - briefness; shortness

brusque - *adj.* - abrupt, blunt, or short in manner or speech

bumptious - *adj.* - impertinent; conceited

burnish - *v.* - to make or become smooth, bright, and glossy

cabal - *v.* - to intrigue or plot; usually in a small group

cache - *n.* - 1. stockpile; store; heap; 2. hiding place for goods

cacophony - *n.* - a jarring or disagreeable sound of words

cajole - *v.* - to flatter; to coax

candid - *adj.* - honest; truthful; sincere

capricious - *adj.* - changeable; fickle

cascade - *n.* - 1. waterfall; 2. *v.* - pour; rush; fall

caustic - *adj.* - burning; sarcastic; harsh

censor - *v.* - to examine and delete objectionable material

censure - *v.* - to criticize or disapprove of

chagrin - *n.* - mortification or disappointment

charisma - *n.* - appeal; magnetism; presence

charlatan - *n.* - an imposter; fake

chastise - *v.* - punish; discipline; admonish; rebuke

chronology - *n.* - the arrangement of events, dates, etc. in a certain order of occurrence

circumlocution - *n.* - an indirect or lengthy way of expressing something

coalesce - *v.* - to combine into a single body or group

coda - *n.* - a musical passage which brings a composition to its definite close

cognizant - *adj.* - being informed or aware

cohesion - *n.* - the act of holding together

---

## Drill 2

DIRECTIONS: Match each word in the left column with the word in the right column that is most **opposite** in meaning.

### Word

### Match

| | | | | | | | |
|---|---|---|---|---|---|---|---|
| 1. ___ | augment | 6. ___ | authentic | A. | permit | F. | malicious |
| 2. ___ | bombastic | 7. ___ | candid | B. | heroine | G. | modest |
| 3. ___ | banal | 8. ___ | circumlocution | C. | directness | H. | mournful |
| 4. ___ | benevolent | 9. ___ | charlatan | D. | diminish | I. | unusual |
| 5. ___ | censor | 10. ___ | blithe | E. | dishonest | J. | counterfeit |

<u>DIRECTIONS</u>: Match each word in the left column with the word in the right column that is most **similar** in meaning.

| *Word* | | *Match* | |
|---|---|---|---|
| 11. ___ baleful | 14. ___ censure | A. harmless | D. ominous |
| 12. ___ benign | 15. ___ capricious | B. reprimand | E. criticize |
| 13. ___ berate | | C. changeable | |

# Group 3

collaborate - *v.* - to work together; cooperate

colloquial - *adj.* - casual; common; conversational; idiomatic

compatible - *adj.* - in agreement with; harmonious

complacent - *adj.* - content; self-satisfied; smug

compliant - *adj.* - yielding; obedient

comprehensive - *adj.* - all-inclusive; complete; thorough

conciliatory - *adj.* - tending to make peace between persons at variance

concise - *adj.* - in few words; brief; condensed

condescend - *v.* - to deal with others in a patronizing manner

condone - *v.* - to overlook; to forgive

conglomeration - *n.* - mixture; collection

conjoin - *v.* - to unite; to combine

conjure - *v.* - 1. to call upon or appeal to; 2. to cause to be, appear, come

connoisseur - *n.* - expert; authority (usually refers to a wine or food expert)

consecrate - *v.* - to sanctify; make sacred; immortalize

consensus - *n.* - unanimity; agreement

consummation - *n.* - the completion; finish

contentious - *adj.* - argumentative; quarrelsome

contrite - *adj.* - regretful; sorrowful

contumacious - *adj.* - insubordinate; rebellious; disobedient

conundrum - *n.* - any question or thing of a perplexing nature

conventional - *adj.* - traditional; common; routine

correlate - *v.* - to bring one thing into mutual relation with another thing

corroborate - *v.* - 1. to strengthen; 2. to confirm; to make more certain

cower - *v.* - crouch down in fear; to shrink and tremble

craven - *adj.* - cowardly; fearful

culpable - *adj.* - blameworthy

cynic - *n.* - one who believes that others are motivated entirely by selfishness

dais - *n.* - a raised platform in a room where tables for honored guests are placed

dank - *adj.* - disagreeably damp or humid

dearth - *n.* - scarcity; shortage

debacle - *n.* - disaster; ruination

debauchery - *n.* - extreme indulgence of one's appetites, especially for sensual pleasure

debilitate - *v.* - deprive of strength

decorous - *adj.* - characterized by good taste

defamation - *n.* - the malicious uttering of falsehood respecting another

deference - *n.* - a yielding in opinion to another

deign - *v.* - condescend

deleterious - *adj.* - harmful to health, well-being

delineate - *v.* - to outline; to describe

demur - *v.* - to object, to take issue

depict - *v.* - to portray in words; present a visual image

deplete - *v.* - to reduce; to empty

depravity - *n.* - moral corruption; badness

deride - *v.* - to ridicule; laugh at with scorn

derision - *n.* - ridicule; mockery

derogatory - *adj.* - belittling; uncomplimentary

desecrate - *v.* - to violate a holy place or sanctuary

desiccate - *v.* - to dry completely

destitute - *adj.* - poor; poverty-stricken

## Drill 3

DIRECTIONS: Match each word in the left column with the word in the right column that is most **opposite** in meaning.

| | *Word* | | | | *Match* | | |
|---|---|---|---|---|---|---|---|
| 1. ___ deplete | | 6. ___ condone | | A. submissive | | F. agree |
| 2. ___ colloquial | | 7. ___ culpable | | B disapprove | | G. beginning |
| 3. ___ concise | | 8. ___ consummation | | C. innocent | | H. sophisticated |
| 4. ___ contumacious | | 9. ___ demur | | D. success | | I. virtue |
| 5. ___ depravity | | 10. ___ debacle | | E. fill | | J. verbose |

DIRECTIONS: Match each word in the left column with the word in the right column that is most **similar** in meaning.

| | *Word* | | | *Match* | |
|---|---|---|---|---|---|
| 11. ___ compatible | | 14. ___ comprehensive | A. portray | | D. thorough |
| 12. ___ depict | | 15. ___ complacent | B. content | | E. common |
| 13. ___ conventional | | | C. harmonious | | |

## Group 4

devoid - *adj.* - lacking; empty

dichotomy - *n.* - division of things by pairs

digress - *v.* - stray from the subject; wander from topic

disavow - *v.* - to deny; to refuse

discerning - *adj.* - distinguishing one thing from another

discomfit - *v.* - 1. to overthrow the plans or expectations of; 2. to confuse

discourse - *n.* - a communication of thoughts by words

disdain - *n.* -1. intense dislike; 2. *v.* - look down upon; scorn

disheartened - *adj.* - discouraged; depressed

disinterested - *adj.* - impartial; unbiased

disparage - *v.* - to belittle; undervalue

disparity - *n.* - difference in form, character, or degree

disperse- *v.* - to scatter; separate

disseminate - *v.* - to circulate; scatter

dissonance - *n.* - discord

diverge - *v.* - separate; split

diverse - *adj.* - different; dissimilar

docile - *adj.* - manageable; obedient

doggerel - *adj.* - trivial; inartistic

dogmatic - *adj.* - stubborn; biased, opinionated

dowdy - *adj.* - drab; shabby

dubious - *adj.* - doubtful; uncertain; skeptical; suspicious

duress - *n.* - force; constraint

earthy - *adj.* - 1. not refined; coarse; 2. simple and natural

ebullient - *adj.* - showing excitement

eccentric - *adj.* - odd; peculiar; strange

eclectic - *adj.* - choosing or selecting from various sources

economical - *adj.* - not wasteful

educe - *v.* - draw forth

effeminate - *adj.* - having qualities generally attributed to a woman

effervescence - *n.* -1. liveliness; spirit; enthusiasm; 2. bubbliness

effigy - *n.* - the image or likeness of a person

effluvium - *n.* - an outflow in the form of a vapor

elusive - *adj.* - hard to catch; difficult to understand

eminence - *n.* - 1. high or lofty place; 2. superiority in position or rank

emulate - *v.* - to strive to equal or excel

engender - *v.* - to create; bring about

enhance - *v.* - to improve; complement; make more attractive

enigma- *n.* - mystery; secret; perplexity

ennui - *n.* - boredom; apathy

ephemeral - *adj.* - temporary; brief; short-lived

epitome - *n.* - model; typification; representation

equivocal - *adj.* - doubtful; uncertain

errant - *adj.* - wandering

erratic - *adj.* - unpredictable; strange

erudite - *adj.* - having extensive knowledge; learned

esoteric - *adj.* - incomprehensible; obscure

ethnic - *adj.* - native; racial; cultural

euphony - *n.* - pleasant sound

evanescent - *adj.* - vanishing; fleeting

## Drill 4

DIRECTIONS: Match each word in the left column with the word in the right column that is most **opposite** in meaning.

### Word

| | | | | |
|---|---|---|---|---|
| 1. ___ dowdy | 6. ___ dubious |
| 2. ___ erudite | 7. ___ disavow |
| 3. ___ ennui | 8. ___ disdain |
| 4. ___ evanescent | 9. ___ docile |
| 5. ___ disheartened | 10. ___ disparage |

### Match

| | | | |
|---|---|---|---|
| A. excitement | F. wild |
| B. certain | G. complement |
| C. acknowledge | H. sanctify |
| D. chic | I. appearing |
| E. uninformed | J. uplifted |

DIRECTIONS: Match each word in the left column with the word in the right column that is most **similar** in meaning.

### Word

| | |
|---|---|
| 11. ___ effervescence | 14. ___ discomfit |
| 12. ___ ethnic | 15. ___ eccentric |
| 13. ___ disseminate | |

### Match

| | |
|---|---|
| A. native | D. liveliness |
| B. distribute | E. odd |
| C. confuse | |

## Group 5

evoke - *v.* - call forth; provoke

exculpate - *v.* - to declare or prove guiltless

exemplary - *adj.* - serving as an example; outstanding

exigent - *n.* - an urgent occasion

exonerate - *v.* - to unload; to release from burden

exorbitant - *adj.* - going beyond what is reasonable; excessive

exotic - *adj.* - unusual; striking

expedient - *adj.* - helpful; practical; worthwhile

expedite - *v.* - speed up

exposition - *n.* - a setting forth of facts or ideas

extol - *v.* - praise; commend

exuberant - *adj.* - overflowing; lavish; superabundant

facade - *n.* - front view; false appearance

facetious - *adj.* - lightly joking

facilitate - *v.* - make easier; simplify

fallacious - *adj.* - misleading

fanatic - *n.* - enthusiast; extremist

fastidious - *adj.* - fussy; hard to please

feasible - *adj.* - reasonable; practical

fecund - *adj.* - fruitful in children; productive

ferret - *v.* - drive or hunt out of hiding

fervor - *n.* - passion; intensity

fickle - *adj.* - changeable; unpredictable

figment - *n.* - product; creation

finesse - *n.* - the ability to handle situations with skill and diplomacy

finite - *adj.* - measurable; limited; not everlasting

flag - *v.* - 1. to send a message by signaling; 2. to become limp

fledgling - *n.* - inexperienced person; beginner

flippant - *adj.* - 1. speaking with ease and rapidity; 2. impertinent

flout - *v.* - to mock; to sneer

fluency - *n.* - smoothness of speech

flux - *n.* - current; continuous change

forbearance - *n.* - patience; self-restraint

fortuitous - *adj.* - accidental; happening by chance; lucky

foster - *v.* - encourage; nurture; support

frenetic - *adj.* - frantic; frenzied

frugality - *n.* - thrift

fulsome - *adj.* - offensive, especially because of excess

furtive - *adj.* - secretive; sly

fustian - *n.* - an inflated style of talking or writing

gaffe - *n.* - a blunder

gainsay - *v.* - to deny or contradict

garbled - *adj.* - mixed up

garner - *v.* - to accumulate

garrulous - *adj.* - talking much about unimportant things

genial - *adj.* - 1. contributing to life and growth; 2. amiable; cordial

genre - *n.* - a kind, sort, or type

germane - *adj.* - pertinent; related; to the point

gerrymander - *v.* - to manipulate unfairly

---

## Drill 5

<u>DIRECTIONS</u>: Match each word in the left column with the word in the right column that is most **opposite** in meaning.

| | *Word* | | | | *Match* | | |
|---|---|---|---|---|---|---|---|
| 1. ___ | facetious | 6. ___ | flippant | A. | combat | F. | denounce |
| 2. ___ | extol | 7. ___ | germane | B. | delay | G. | calm |
| 3. ___ | foster | 8. ___ | garrulous | C. | considerate | H. | solemn |
| 4. ___ | expedite | 9. ___ | genial | D. | rude | I. | immaterial |
| 5. ___ | fastidious | 10. ___ | frenetic | E. | quiet | J. | neglectful |

<u>DIRECTIONS</u>: Match each word in the left column with the word in the right column that is most **similar** in meaning.

| | *Word* | | | | *Match* | | |
|---|---|---|---|---|---|---|---|
| 11. ___ | furtive | 14. ___ | fallacious | A. | enable | D. | worthwhile |
| 12. ___ | expedient | 15. ___ | fickle | B. | stealthy | E. | deceptive |
| 13. ___ | facilitate | | | C. | unpredictable | | |

## Group 6

gibber - *v.* - speak foolishly

gloat - *v.* - brag; glory over

glutton - *n.* - overeater

goad - *v.* - to arouse or incite

grandiose - *adj.* - extravagant; flamboyant

guile - *n.* - slyness; deceit

gullible - *adj.* - easily fooled

hackneyed - *adj.* - commonplace; trite

haggard - *adj.* - tired-looking; fatigued

hamper - *v.* - interfere with; hinder

haphazard - *adj.* - disorganized; random

haughty - *adj.* - proud and disdainful

hedonistic - *adj.* - pleasure seeking

hierarchy - *n.* - body of people, things, or concepts divided into ranks

homeostasis - *n.* - the maintenance of stability or equilibrium

hone - *v.* - sharpen

humility - *n.* - lack of pride; modesty

hypocritical - *adj.* - two-faced; deceptive

hypothetical - *adj.* - assumed; uncertain

iconoclast - *n.* - a breaker or destroyer of images

ideology - *n.* - set of beliefs; principles

idyllic - *adj.* - pleasing and simple

ignoble - *adj.* - shameful; dishonorable

imbue - *v.* - inspire; arouse

immune - *adj.* - protected; unthreatened by

immutable - *adj.* - unchangeable; permanent

impale - *v.* - fix on a stake; stick; pierce

impede - *v.* - to stop in progress

imperious - *adj.* - authoritative

impervious - *adj.* - 1. incapable of being penetrated; 2. not affected or influenced by

impetuous - *adj.* - 1. rash; impulsive; 2. forcible; violent

implement - *v.* - to carry into effect

implication - *n.* - suggestion; inference

implicit - *adj.* - to be understood though not fully expressed

impromptu - *adj.* - without preparation

improvident - *adj.* - lacking foresight and thrift

impudent - *adj.* - shameless; immodest

impugn - *v.* - to contradict

inarticulate - *adj.* - speechless; unable to speak clearly

incessant - *adj.* - constant; continual

inchoate - *adj.* - existing in elementary or beginning form

incisive - *adj.* - cutting into

incognito - *adj.* - unidentified; disguised; concealed
incoherent - *adj.* - illogical; rambling
incompatible - *adj.* - disagreeing; disharmonious
incursion - *n.* - 1. a running in; 2. invasion; raid
indict - *v.* - charge with a crime
indignant - *adj.* - to consider as unworthy or improper
indolent - *adj.* - lazy; inactive
indulgent - *adj.* - lenient: patient

# Drill 6

DIRECTIONS: Match each word in the left column with the word in the right column that is most **opposite** in meaning.

| *Word* | | *Match* | |
|---|---|---|---|
| 1. ___ ignoble | 6. ___ gullible | A. vigorous | F. beneficial |
| 2. ___ haggard | 7. ___ goad | B. cynical | G. admirable |
| 3. ___ gloat | 8. ___ furtive | C. simple | H. organized |
| 4. ___ hedonist | 9. ___ futile | D. deter | I. candid |
| 5. ___ grandiose | 10. ___ haphazard | E. belittle | J. puritan |

DIRECTIONS: Match each word in the left column with the word in the right column that is most **similar** in meaning.

| *Word* | | *Match* | |
|---|---|---|---|
| 11. ___ glutton | 14. ___ hackneyed | A. hinder | D. overeater |
| 12. ___ impale | 15. ___ ideology | B. principles | E. transfix |
| 13. ___ hamper | | C. trite | |

# Group 7

ineluctable - *adj.* - not to be avoided or escaped
inept - *adj.* - incompetent; unskilled
inert - *adj.* - without power to move or to resist an opposite force
infamous - *adj.* - having a bad reputation; notorious
infer- *v.* - form an opinion; conclude
ingenious - *adj.* - gifted with genius; innate or natural quality
inherent - *adj.* - innate; basic; inborn
innate - *adj.* - natural; inborn
innocuous - *adj.* - harmless; innocent
innovate - *v.* - introduce a change; depart from the old
innuendo - *n.* - an indirect remark, gesture or reference
insipid - *adj.* - uninteresting; bland
insolvent - *adj.* - bankrupt; not able to pay debts

intermittent - *adj.* - 1. stopping and starting again at intervals; 2. *n.* - a disease which entirely subsides or ceases at certain intervals

intransigent - *adj.* - refusing to compromise

invective - *n.* - a violent verbal attack

ironic - *adj.* - contradictory; inconsistent; sarcastic

jaded - *adj.* - 1. tired or worn-out; 2. dulled

jeopardy - *n.* - danger

judicious - *adj.* - possessing sound judgement

ken - *n.* - range of knowledge

kinship - *n.* - family relationship

kith - *n.* - acquaintances and relations

knavery - *n.* - dishonesty

labyrinth - *n.* - maze

laconic - *n.* - a brief, pithy expression

laggard - *n.* - a lazy person; one who lags behind

lament - *v.* - to mourn or grieve

languid - *adj.* - weak; fatigued

lascivious - *adj.* - indecent; immoral

latency - *n.* - the condition of being hidden or undeveloped

lax - *adj.* - careless; irresponsible

lecherous - *adj.* - impure in thought and act

lethal - *adj.* - deadly

lethargic - *adj.* - lazy; passive

levee - *n.* - the act or time of rising

levity - *n.* - silliness; lack of seriousness

liaison - *n.* - connection; link

ligneous - *adj.* - consisting of or resembling wood

litigate - *v.* - to contest in a lawsuit

livid - *adj.* - 1. black-and-blue; discolored; 2. enraged; irate

lucid - *adj.* -1. shining; 2. easily understood

lucrative - *adj.* - profitable; gainful

luminous - *adj.* - giving off light; bright

lustrous - *adj.* - bright; radiant

macerate - *v.* - 1. to soften by soaking; 2. to cause to waste away; 3. to torment

magnanimous - *adj.* - forgiving; unselfish

malediction - *n.* - curse; evil spell

malicious - *adj.* - spiteful; vindictive

malleable - *adj.* - that which can be pounded without breaking; adaptable

## Drill 7

DIRECTIONS: Match each word in the left column with the word in the right column that is most **opposite** in meaning.

### Word

| | | | | | | | |
|---|---|---|---|---|---|---|---|
| 1. ___ lamentable | 6. ___ levity | A. | proper | F. | encouraging |
| 2. ___ livid | 7. ___ lax | B. | injurous | G. | compromising |
| 3. ___ lascivious | 8. ___ intransigent | C. | responsible | H. | prudish |
| 4. ___ innocuous | 9. ___ invective | D. | honor | I. | gravity |
| 5. ___ lecherous | 10. ___ magnanimous | E. | blissful | J. | resentful |

### Match

DIRECTIONS: Match each word in the left column with the word in the right column that is most **similar** in meaning.

### Word

| | | | | | |
|---|---|---|---|---|---|
| 11. ___ luminous | 14. ___ languid | A. | bewail | D. | alliance |
| 12. ___ knave | 15. ___ lament | B. | radiant | E. | rogue |
| 13. ___ liaison | | C. | fatigued | | |

### Match

---

# Group 8

mandatory - *adj.* - authoritatively commanded or required

manifest - *adj.* - obvious; clear

maverick - *n.* - person who acts independent of a group

meander - *v.* - wind on a course; go aimlessly

mellifluous - *adj.* - flowing sweetly and smoothly

mentor - *n.* - teacher

mercenary - *n.* - working or done for payment only

metamorphosis - *n.* - change of form

meticulous - *adj.* - exacting; precise

mitigate - *v.* - alleviate; lessen; soothe

molten - *adj.* - melted

morose - *adj.* - moody; despondent

motif - *n.* - theme

motility - *n.* - the quality of exhibiting spontaneous motion

mundane - *adj.* - ordinary; commonplace

munificent - *adj.* - very generous in giving; lavish

myriad - *adj.* - innumerable; countless

nebulous - *adj.* - 1. cloudy; hazy; 2. unclear; vague

neophyte - *n.* - beginner; newcomer

nettle - *v.* - annoy; irritate

nostalgic - *adj.* - longing for the past; filled with bittersweet memories

notorious - *adj.* - infamous; renowned

nullify - *v.* - cancel; invalidate

oaf - *n.* - 1. a misshapen child; 2. a stupid, clumsy fellow

obdurate - *adj.* - stubborn; inflexible

obliterate - *v.* - destroy completely

obsequious - *adj.* - slavishly attentive; servile

obsolete - *adj.* - out of date; passé

occult - *adj.* - mystical; mysterious

ominous - *adj.* - threatening

omniscient - *adj.* - having universal knowledge

opaque - *adj.* - dull; cloudy; nontransparent

opulence - *n.* - wealth; fortune

ornate - *adj.* - elaborate; lavish; decorated

oscillate - *v.* - 1. to swing to and fro; 2. to be indecisive; to fluctuate

ossify - *v.* - to settle or fix rigidly in a practice, custom, attitude, etc.

ostensible - *adj.* - 1. proper to be shown; 2. apparent; declared

ostracize - *v.* - to cast out or banish

palliate - *v.* - 1. to alleviate or ease; 2. to make appear less serious

pallid - *adj.* - sallow; colorless

palpable - *adj.* - tangible; apparent

panegyric - *n.* - a formal speech written in praise of a distinguished person

paradox - *n.* - 1. a statement that seems contradictory but that may actually be true in fact; 2. something inconsistent with common experience

parallel - *adj.* - extending in the same direction and at the same distance apart at every point

paraphernalia - *n.* - equipment; accessories

partisan - *n.* -1. supporter; follower; 2. *adj.* biased; one-sided

passive - *adj.* - submissive; unassertive

pathology - *n.* - part of medicine dealing with the nature of diseases, their causes and symptoms, and the structural and functional changes

pedagogue - *n.* - a dogmatic teacher

penchant - *n.* - a strong liking or fondness

---

## Drill 8

DIRECTIONS: Match each word in the left column with the word in the right column that is most **opposite** in meaning.

### Word

| | | | | | |
|---|---|---|---|---|---|
| 1. ___ ostensible | 6. ___ partisan | A. | aversion | F. | domineering |
| 2. ___ obsolete | 7. ___ obdurate | B. | flexible | G. | distinct |
| 3. ___ nebulous | 8. ___ obsequious | C. | unnoticeable | H. | assertive |
| 4. ___ penchant | 9. ___ palpable | D. | actual | I. | modern |
| 5. ___ neophyte | 10. ___ passive | E. | opponent | J. | veteran |

DIRECTIONS: Match each word in the left column with the word in the right column that is most **similar** in meaning.

### Word

| | | | | |
|---|---|---|---|---|
| 11. ___ nullify | 14. ___ palliate | A. | invalidate | D. threatening |
| 12. ___ ominous | 15. ___ opaque | B. | irritate | E. alleviate |
| 13. ___ nettle | | C. | dull | |

# Group 9

perceptive - *adj.* - full of insight; aware

pensive - *adj.* - reflective; contemplative

percussion - *n.* - the striking of one object against another

peripheral - *adj.* - marginal; outer

perjury - *n.* - the practice of lying

permeable - *adj.* - porous; allowing to pass through

pernicious - *adj.* - dangerous; harmful

perpetual - *adj.* - enduring for all time

pertinent - *adj.* - related to the matter at hand

pervade - *v.* - to occupy the whole of

pessimism - *n.* - seeing only the gloomy side; hopelessness

petulant - *adj.* - 1. forward; immodest; 2. impatient or irritable

philanthropy - *n.*- charity; unselfishness

phlegmatic - *adj.* - without emotion or interest

pinnacle - *n.* - 1. a small turret that rises above the roof of a building; 2. the highest point

pious - *adj.* - religious; devout; dedicated

piquant - *adj.* - 1. agreeably pungent or stimulating to the taste; 2. exciting interest or curiosity

pittance - *n.* - small allowance

placate - *v.* - pacify

placid - *adj.* - serene; tranquil

plethora - *n.* - condition of going beyond what is needed; excess; overabundance

plumb - *v.* - 1. to fall or sink straight down; 2. to hang vertically

polemic - *adj.* - controversial; argumentative

pragmatic - *adj.* - matter-of-fact; practical

preclude - *v.* - inhibit; make impossible

prattle - *v.* - to speak in a childish manner; babble

precipitate - *v.* - 1. to throw headlong; 2. to cause to happen

pristine - *adj.* - still pure or untouched

privy - *adj.* - private; confidential

probity - *n.* - true virtue or integrity; complete honesty

problematic - *adj.* - uncertain

prodigal - *adj.* - wasteful; lavish

prodigious - *adj.* - exceptional; tremendous

prodigy - *n.* - 1. an extraordinary happening; 2. something so extraordinary as to inspire wonder

profound - *adj.* - deep; knowledgeable; thorough

profusion - *n.* - great amount; abundance

progeny - *n.* - children; offspring

propinquity - *n.* - nearness in time or place, relationship, or nature

prosaic - *adj.* - tiresome; ordinary

proselytize - *v.* - to make a convert of

provocative - *adj.* - 1. tempting; 2. irritating

pundit - *n.* - a person of great learning

pungent - *adj.* - sharp; stinging

quandary - *n.* - dilemma

qualify - *v.* - 1. to render fit; 2. to furnish with legal power; 3. to modify

quiescent - *adj.* - inactive; at rest

quirk - *n.* - peculiar behavior; startling twist

rabid - *adj.* - furious; with extreme anger

rampart - *n.* - 1. anything that protects or defends; 2. an embankment of earth that surrounds a fort or castle

rancid - *adj.* - having a bad odor

rant - *v.* - to speak in a loud, pompous manner; rave

## Drill 9

DIRECTIONS: Match each word in the left column with the word in the right column that is most **opposite** in meaning.

| *Word* | | | | *Match* | | | |
|---|---|---|---|---|---|---|---|
| 1. ___ | pristine | 6. ___ | placate | A. | inexperienced | F. | joyous |
| 2. ___ | phlegmatic | 7. ___ | pensive | B. | anger | G. | extraordinary |
| 3. ___ | profound | 8. ___ | peripheral | C. | central | H. | contaminated |
| 4. ___ | qualified | 9. ___ | petulant | D. | cheerful | I. | excited |
| 5. ___ | placid | 10. ___ | prosaic | E. | shallow | J. | turbulent |

DIRECTIONS: Match each word in the left column with the word in the right column that is most **similar** in meaning.

| *Word* | | | | *Match* | | | |
|---|---|---|---|---|---|---|---|
| 11. ___ | provocative | 14. ___ | pious | A. | nearness | D. | flavorsome |
| 12. ___ | pungent | 15. ___ | pragmatic | B. | tempting | E. | practical |
| 13. ___ | propinquity | | | C. | reverent | | |

## Group 10

rationalize - *v.* - to offer reasons for; account for

raucous - *adj.* - disagreeable to the sense of hearing; harsh

realm - *n.* - an area; sphere of activity

rebuff - *n.* - an abrupt, blunt refusal

recession - *n.* - withdrawal; depression

reciprocal - *adj.* - mutual; having the same relationship to each other

recluse - *n.* - solitary and shut off from society

recondite - *adj.* - beyond the grasp of ordinary understanding

redundant - *adj.* - repetitious; unnecessary

refute - *v.* - challenge; disprove

regal - *adj.* - royal; grand

reiterate - *v.* - repeat; to state again

relegate - *v.* - banish; put to a lower position

relevant - *adj.* - of concern; significant

relinquish - *v.* - to let go; abandon

renascence - *n.* - a new birth; revival

render - *v.* - deliver; provide; to give up a possession

replica - *n.* - copy; representation

reprehensible - *adj.* - wicked; disgraceful

reprobate - *adj.* - 1. vicious; unprincipled; 2. *v.* - to disapprove with detestation

repudiate - *v.* - reject; cancel

repugnant - *adj.* - inclined to disobey or oppose

rescind - *v.* - retract; discard

respite - *n.* - recess; rest period

reticent - *adj.* - silent; reserved; shy

retroaction - *n.* - an action elicited by a stimulus

reverie - *n.* - the condition of being unaware of one's surroundings; trance

rhetorical - *adj.* - having to do with verbal communication

ribald - *adj.* - characterized by coarse joking or mocking

rigor- *n.* - severity

rivet - *v.* - to fasten, fix, or hold firmly

rummage - *v.* - search thoroughly

saga - *n.* - a legend; story

sagacious - *adj.* - wise; cunning

salient - *adj.* - noticeable; prominent

salubrious - *adj.* - favorable to health

salvage - *v.* - rescue from loss

sanction - *n.* - 1. support; encouragement; 2. something which makes a rule binding

sanguine - *adj.* - 1. optimistic; cheerful; 2. red

sardonic - *adj.* - bitterly ironical

satiric - *adj.* - indulging in the use of ridicule or sarcasm to expose or attack vice, folly, etc.

saturate - *v.* - soak thoroughly; drench

saturnine - *adj.* - heavy; grave; gloomy

saunter - *v.* - walk at a leisurely pace; stroll

savor - *v.* - to receive pleasure from; enjoy

scrupulous - *adj.* - honorable; exact

seethe - *v.* - to be in a state of emotional turmoil; to become angry

serrated - *adj.* - having a sawtoothed edge

servile - *adj.* - slavish, groveling

shoddy - *adj.* - of inferior quality; cheap

## Drill 10

DIRECTIONS: Match each word in the left column with the word in the right column that is most **opposite** in meaning.

| Word | | Match | |
|------|------|------|------|
| 1. ___ salient | 6. ___ repugnant | A. forward | F. unprincipled |
| 2. ___ reticent | 7. ___ repudiate | B. promote | G. necessary |
| 3. ___ raucous | 8. ___ rebuff | C. pleasant | H. pleasant |
| 4. ___ redundant | 9. ___ scrupulous | D. minor | I. welcome |
| 5. ___ relegate | 10. ___ sanguine | E. affirm | J. pessimistic |

<u>DIRECTIONS</u>: Match each word in the left column with the word in the right column that is most **similar** in meaning.

| Word | | Match | |
|------|------|------|------|
| 11. ___ rescind | 14. ___ sagacious | A. deliver | D. drench |
| 12. ___ reprehensible | 15. ___ saturate | B. blameworthy | E. wise |
| 13. ___ render | | C. retract | |

# Group 11

sinuous - *adj.* - winding; crooked

skulk - *v.* - to move secretly

sojourn - *n.* - temporary stay; visit

solicit - *v.* - ask; seek

soliloquy - *n.* - a talk one has with oneself (esp. on stage)

spendthrift - *n.* - one who spends money carelessly or wastefully

sporadic - *adj.* - rarely occurring or appearing; intermittent

spurious - *adj.* - false; counterfeit

squalid - *adj.* - foul; filthy

stagnant - *adj.* - motionless; uncirculating

stamina - *n.* - endurance

sterile - *adj.* - 1. incapable of producing others; 2. lacking in interest or vitality; 3. free from living microorganisms

stipend - *n.* - payment for work done

stupor - *n.* - a stunned or bewildered condition

suave - *adj.* - effortlessly gracious

subsidiary - *adj.* - subordinate

substantive - *adj.* - 1. existing independently; 2. having a real existence

subtlety - *n.* - 1. understatement; 2. propensity for understatement; 3. sophistication; 4. cunning

succinct - *adj.* - consisting of few words; concise

suffuse - *v.* - to overspread

sullen - *adj.* - 1. showing resentment; 2. gloomy; dismal

sunder - *v.* - break; split in two

superficial - *adj.* - on the surface; narrow-minded; lacking depth

superfluous - *adj.* - unnecessary; extra

surmise - *v.* - draw an inference; guess

surreptitious - *adj.* - done without proper authority

sycophant - *n.* - a person who seeks favor by flattering people of wealth or influence

syllogism - *n.* - reasoning from the general to the particular

synthesis - *n.* - 1. the putting together of two or more things; 2. a whole made up of parts put together

taciturn - *adj.* - reserved; quiet; secretive

tantalize - *v.* - to tempt; to torment

taut - *adj.* - 1. stretched tightly; 2. tense

temerity - *n.* - foolish boldness

temperament - *n.* - 1. a middle course reached by mutual concession; 2. frame of mind

tenacious - *adj.* - persistently holding to something

tepid - *adj.* - lacking warmth, interest, enthusiasm; lukewarm

terse - *adj.* - concise; abrupt

thwart - *v.* - prevent from accomplishing a purpose; frustrate

timbre - *n.* - the degree of resonance of a voiced sound

torpid - *adj.* - lacking alertness and activity; lethargic

toxic - *adj.* - poisonous

tractable - *adj.* - easily led or managed

transitory - *adj.* - of a passing nature; speedily vanishing

transpire - *v.* - to take place; come about

travesty - *n.* - a crude and ridiculous representation

trek - *v.* - to make a journey

trepidation - *n.* - apprehension; uneasiness

tribute - *n.* - expression of admiration

# Drill 11

<u>DIRECTIONS</u>: Match each word in the left column with the word in the right column that is most **opposite** in meaning.

| | Word | | | | Match | | |
|---|---|---|---|---|---|---|---|
| 1. ___ | scrutinize | 6. ___ | tentative | A. | frivolity | F. | skim |
| 2. ___ | skeptic | 7. ___ | thrifty | B. | enjoyable | G. | turbulent |
| 3. ___ | solemnity | 8. ___ | tranquility | C. | prodigal | H. | active |
| 4. ___ | static | 9. ___ | solicit | D. | chaos | I. | believer |
| 5. ___ | tedious | 10. ___ | stagnant | E. | give | J. | confirmed |

<u>DIRECTIONS</u>: Match each word in the left column with the word in the right column that is most **similar** in meaning.

| | Word | | | | Match | | |
|---|---|---|---|---|---|---|---|
| 11. ___ | symmetry | 14. ___ | subtle | A. | understated | D. | fear |
| 12. ___ | superfluous | 15. ___ | trepidation | B. | unnecessary | E. | flatterer |
| 13. ___ | sycophant | | | C. | balance | | |

# Group 12

trite - *adj.* - commonplace; overused

truculent - *adj.* - aggressive; eager to fight

tumid - *adj.* - swollen; inflated

tumult - *n.* - great commotion or agitation

turbulence - *n.* - condition of being physically agitated; disturbance

turpitude - *n.* - shameful wickedness

ubiquitous - *adj.* - ever present in all places; universal

ulterior - *adj.* - buried; concealed

uncanny - *adj.* - of a strange nature; weird

unequivocal - *adj.* - clear; definite

unique - *adj.* - without equal; incomparable

unruly - *adj.* - not submitting to discipline; disobedient

untoward - *adj.* - 1. hard to manage or deal with; 2. inconvenient

unwonted - *adj.* - not ordinary; unusual

urbane - *adj.* - cultured; suave

usury - *n.* - the act of lending money at illegal rates of interest

vacillation - *n.* - fluctuation

vacuous - *adj.* - containing nothing; empty

vantage - *n.* - position giving an advantage

vaunted - *v.* - boasted of

vehement - *adj.* - intense; excited; enthusiastic

veracious - *adj.* - conforming to fact; accurate

veracity - *n.* - 1. honesty; 2. accuracy of statement

verbose- *adj.* - wordy; talkative

versatile - *adj.* - having many uses; multifaceted

vertigo - *n.* - dizziness

vex - *v.* - to trouble the nerves; annoy

vilify - *v.* - slander

vindicate - *v.* - to free from charge; clear

virile - *adj.* - manly, masculine

virtuoso - *n.* - highly skilled artist

virulent- *adj.* - deadly; harmful; malicious

viscous - *adj.* - thick, syrupy, and sticky

visionary - *adj.* - 1. characterized by impractical ideas; 2. not real

vivacious - *adj.* - animated; gay

vogue - *n.* - modern fashion

volatile - *adj.* - changeable; undependable

voluble - *adj.* - fluent

vulnerable - *adj.* - open to attack; unprotected

waive - *v.* - to give up possession or right

wane - *v.* - grow gradually smaller

wanton - *adj.* - unruly; excessive

welter - *v.* - 1. to roll about or wallow; 2. to rise and fall

wheedle - *v.* - try to persuade; coax

whet - *v.* - sharpen

whimsical - *adj.*- fanciful; amusing

winsome - *adj.* - agreeable; charming; delightful

zealot- *n.* - believer, enthusiast; fan

zenith - *n.* - point directly overhead in the sky

zephyr - *n.* - a gentle wind; breeze

# Drill 12

DIRECTIONS: Match each word in the left column with the word in the right column that is most **opposite** in meaning.

| Word | | | Match | |
|------|------|------|-------|------|
| 1. ___ uniform | 6. ___ vigorous | A. amateur | F. support | |
| 2. ___ virtuoso | 7. ___ volatile | B. trivial | G. constancy | |
| 3. ___ vital | 8. ___ vacillation | C. visible | H. lethargic | |
| 4. ___ wane | 9. ___ undermine | D. placid | I. wax | |
| 5. ___ unobtrusive | 10. ___ valid | E. unacceptable | J. varied | |

DIRECTIONS: Match each word in the left column with the word in the right column that is most **similar** in meaning.

| Word | | | Match | |
|------|------|------|-------|------|
| 11. ___ wither | 14. ___ vehement | A. intense | D. possible | |
| 12. ___ whimsical | 15. ___ virulent | B. deadly | E. shrivel | |
| 13. ___ viable | | C. amusing | | |

# COMMONLY TESTED GRE WORDS

abaft - *adv.* - on or toward the rear of a ship

abdicate - *v.* - to reject, denounce, or abandon

abjure - *v.* - to renounce upon oath

abnegation - *n.* - a denial

abscond - *v.* - to go away hastily or secretly; to hide

abstemious - *adj.* - 1. sparing in diet; 2. sparingly used

abysmal - *adj.* - bottomless; immeasurable

acerbity - *n.* - harshness or bitterness

acrimony - *n.* - sharpness

addle - *adj.* - barren; confused

adjure - *v.* - to entreat earnestly and solemnly

adulation - *n.* - praise in excess

adulterate - *v.* - to corrupt, debase, or make impure

agrarian - *adj.* - relating to land and the equal divisions of land

alchemy - *n.* - any imaginary power of transmitting one thing into another

allegory - *n.* - symbolic narration or description

anachronism - *n.* - representation of something existing at other than its proper time

annihilate - *v.* - to reduce to nothing

apocalyptic - *adj.* - pertaining to revelation or discovery

arrogate - *v.* - to claim or demand unduly

artifice - *n.* - skill; ingenuity; craft

askance - *adv.* - sideways; out of one corner of the eye

assay - *n.* - the determination of any quantity of a metal in an ore or alloy

attenuate - *v.* - 1. to make thin or slender; 2. to lessen or weaken

avarice - *n.* - inordinate desire of gaining and possessing wealth

batten - *v.* - to grow fat; to thrive

beholden - *adj.* - obliged; indebted

bellicose - *adj.* - warlike; disposed to quarrel or fight

besmirch - *v.* - to soil or discolor

bestial - *adj.* - having the qualities of a beast

betroth - *v.* - to promise or pledge in marriage

blighted - *adj.* - destroyed; frustrated

bode - *v.* - to foreshow something

boorish - *adj.* - rude; ill-mannered

brindled - *adj.* - streaked or spotted with a darker color

broach - *v.* - 1. to pierce; 2. to introduce into conversation

bucolic - *adj.* - pastoral

burlesque - *v.* - to imitate comically

cadaver - *n.* - a dead body

caliber - *n.* - 1. the diameter of a bullet or shell; 2. quality

callow - *adj.* - immature

calumny - *n.* - slander

canard - *n.* - a false statement or rumor

candid - *adj.* - open; frank; honest

captious - *adj.* - disposed to find fault

carnage - *n.* - slaughter

carte blanche - *n.* - unlimited power to decide

castigate - *v.* - to chastise

cataclysm - *n.* - 1. an overflowing of water; 2. an extraordinary change

catharsis - *n.* - purgation

cavil - *v.* - to find fault without good reason

celibate - *adj.* - unmarried, single; chaste

cessation - *n.* - a ceasing; a stop

chafe - *v.* - to rage; to fret

chaffing - *n.* - banter

chaste - *adj.* - virtuous; free from obscenity

choleric - *adj.* - easily irritated; angry

circumvent - *v.* - to go around

clandestine - *adj.* - secret; private; hidden

cogent - *adj.* - urgent; compelling; convincing

cohort - *n.* - a group; a band

collusion - *n.* - secret agreement for a fraudulent or illegal purpose

comport - *v.* - to agree; to accord

conclave - *n.* - any private meeting or close assembly

connivance - *n.* -passive co-operation

consort - *n.* -1. a companion; 2. *v.* - to be in harmony or agreement

contravene - *v.* - to go against; to oppose

contusion - *n.* - a bruise; an injury where the skin is not broken

copious - *adj.* - abundant; in great quantities

covenant - *n.* - a binding and solemn agreement

coy - *adj.* - 1. modest; bashful; 2. pretending shyness to attract

crass - *adj.* - gross; thick; coarse

cursory - *adj.* - hasty; slight

dally - *v.* - to delay; to put off

dauntless - *adj.* - fearless; not discouraged

debonair - *adj.* - having an affable manner; courteous

decadence - *n.* - a decline in force or quality

deciduous - *adj.* - falling off at a particular season or stage of growth

decry - *v.* - to denounce or condemn openly

defunct - *adj.* - no longer living or existing

deliquesce - *v.* - to melt away

delusion - *n.* - a false statement or opinion

deposition - *n.* - 1. a removal from a position or power; 2. a testimony

depredation - *n.* - a plundering or laying waste

descant - *v.* - to talk at length

despoil - *v.* - to strip; to rob

despotism - *n.* - 1. tyranny; 2. absolute power or influence

desultory - *adj.* - without order or natural connection

dexterous - *adj.* - having or showing mental skill

diffidence - *n.* - 1. lack of self-confidence; 2. distrust

dilapidated - *n.* - falling to pieces or into disrepair

dilettante - *n.* - an admirer of the fine arts; a dabbler

dint - *n.* - a blow; a stroke

disarray - *n.* - 1. disorder; confusion; 2. incomplete or disorderly attire

divulge - *v.* - to become public; to become known

dormant - *adj.* - as if asleep

doting - *adj.* - excessively fond

doughty - *adj.* - brave; valiant

dregs - *n.* - waste or worthless manner

ecclesiastic - *adj.* - pertaining or relating to a church

edify - *v.* - 1. to build or establish; 2. to instruct and improve the mind

efface - *v.* - to erase; to remove from the mind

effrontery - *n.* - impudence; assurance

effusive - *adj.* - pouring out or forth; overflowing

egregious - *adj.* - eminent; remarkable

egress - *v.* - to depart; to go out

elegy - *n.* - a poem of lament and praise for the dead

elucidate - *v.* - to make clear or manifest; to explain

emanate - *v.* - to send forth; to emit

embellish - *v.* - to improve the appearance of

enamored - *adj.* - filled with love and desire

encroach - *v.* - to trespass or intrude

encumber - *v.* - to hold back; to hinder

endue - *v.* - to put on; to cover

enrapture - *v.* - to fill with pleasure

epilogue - *n.* - closing section of a play or novel providing further comment

epiphany - *n.* - an appearance of a supernatural being

epitaph - *n.* - an inscription on a monument, in honor or memory of a dead person

epitome - *n.* - a part that is typical of the whole

equinox - *n.* - precise time when the day and night everywhere is of equal length

equivocate - *v.* - to be purposely ambiguous

eschew - *v.* - to escape from; to avoid

estranged - *adj.* - kept at a distance; alienated

ethereal - *adj.* - 1. very light; airy; 2. heavenly; not earthly

euphemism - *n.* - the use of a word or phrase in place of one that is distasteful

euphoria - *n.* - a feeling of well-being

exhume - *v.* - to unearth; to reveal

expunge - *v.* - to blot out; to delete

exude - *v.* - to flow slowly or ooze in drops

faction - *n.* - a number of people in an organization having a common end view

fallible - *adj.* - liable to be mistaken or erroneous

fathom - *v.* - to reach or penetrate with the mind

fatuous - *adj.* - silly; inane; unreal

fealty - *n.* - fidelity; loyalty

feign - *v.* - to invent or imagine

ferment - *v.* - to excite or agitate

fervid - *adj.* - very hot; burning

fester - *v.* - to become more and more virulent and fixed

fetish - *n.* - anything to which one gives excessive devotion or blind adoration

fidelity - *n.* - faithfulness; honesty

fissure - *n.* - a dividing or breaking into parts

flaccid - *adj.* - 1. hanging in loose folds or wrinkles; 2. lacking force; weak

flamboyant - *adj.* - ornate; too showy

foible - *n.* - a slight frailty in character

foist - *v.* - to put in slyly or stealthily

foray - *v.* - to raid for spoils, plunder

forensic - *adj.* - pertaining to legal or public argument

fortitude - *n.* - firm courage; strength

fractious - *adj.* - rebellious; apt to quarrel

fraught - *adj.* - loaded; charged

froward - *adj.* - not willing to yield or comply with what is reasonable

fulminate - *v.* - to explode with sudden violence

galvanize - *v.* - to stimulate as if by electric shock; startle; excite

gamut - *n.* - 1. a complete range; 2. any complete musical scale

garish - *adj.* - gaudy; showy

gauche - *adj.* - awkward; lacking grace

gauntlet - *n.* - a long glove with a flaring cuff covering the lower part of the arm

germane - *adj.* - closely related; pertinent

glib - *adj.* - smooth and slippery; speaking or spoken in a smooth manner

gnarled - *adj.* - full of knots

gormand - *n.* - a greedy or ravenous eater; glutton

gregarious - *adj.* - fond of the company of others

grisly - *adj.* - frightful; horrible

guffaw - *n.* - a loud, coarse burst of laughter

guise - *n.* - 1. customary behavior; 2. manner of dress; 3. false appearance

halcyon - *adj.* - calm; quiet; peaceful

hapless - *adj.* - unlucky; unfortunate

harangue - *v.* - to speak in an impassioned and forcible manner

heretic - *n.* - one who holds opinion contrary to that which is generally accepted

hiatus - *n.* - an opening or gap; slight pause

hoary - *adj.* - very aged; ancient

homily - *n.* - discourse or sermon read to an audience

hybrid - *n.* - anything of mixed origin

idiosyncrasy - *n.* - any personal peculiarity, mannerism, etc.

igneous - *adj.* - having the nature of fire

ignominious - *adj.* - 1. contemptible; 2. degrading

immaculate - *adj.* - 1. perfectly clean; perfectly correct; 2. pure

imminent - *adj.* - appearing as if about to happen

impasse - *n.* - a situation that has no solution or escape

impenitent - *adj.* - without regret, shame, or remorse

impiety - *n.* - 1. irreverence toward God; 2. lack of respect

impolitic - *adj.* - unwise; imprudent

imprecate - *v.* - to pray for evil; to invoke a curse

imputation - *n.* - attribution

incarcerate - *v.* - to imprison or confine

incommodious - *adj.* - uncomfortable; troublesome

incorporeal - *adj.* - not consisting of matter

incorrigible - *adj.* - not capable of correction or improvement

incubate - *v.* - to sit on and hatch (eggs)

inculcate - *v.* - to impress upon the mind by frequent repetition or urging

indemnify - *v.* - to protect against or keep free from loss

indigenous - *adj.* - innate; inherent; inborn

indomitable - *adj.* - not easily discouraged or defeated

indubitably - *adv.* - unquestionably; surely

inimical - *adj.* - unfriendly; adverse

iniquitous - *adj.* - unjust; wicked

inordinate - *adj.* - not regulated; excessive

intrepid - *adj.* - fearless; brave

inured - *adj.* - accustomed

irascible - *adj.* - easily provoked or inflamed to anger

irreparable - *adj.* - that which cannot be repaired or regained

jettison - *n.* - a throwing overboard of goods to lighten a vehicle in an emergency

jocund - *adj.* - merry; gay; cheerful

lacerate - *v.* - 1. to tear or mangle; 2. to wound or hurt

lambent - *adj.* - giving off a soft radiance

lassitude - *n.* - a state or feeling of being tired or weak

lewd - *adj.* - lustful; wicked

libertine - *n.* - one who indulges his desires without restraint

licentious - *adj.* - disregarding accepted rules and standards

lithe - *adj.* - easily bent; pliable

loquacious - *adj.* - talkative

lucent - *adj.* - shining; translucent

lugubrious - *adj.* - mournful; very sad

lurid - *adj.* - ghastly pale; gloomy

magnate - *n.* - a very influential person in any field of activity

malefactor - *n.* - one who commits a crime

malign - *v.* - to defame; speak evil of

marauder - *n.* - a rover in search of booty or plunder

maudlin - *adj.* - foolishly and tearfully sentimental

mendacious - *adj.* - addicted to deception

mercurial - *adj.* - quick, volatile; changeable

meretricious - *adj.* - alluring by false, showy charms; fleshy

mettle - *n.* - high quality of character

mien - *n.* - manner; external appearance

misanthropy - *n.* - hatred of mankind

mite - *n.* - 1. very small sum of money; 2. very small creature

modulate - *v.* - 1. to regulate or adjust; 2. to vary the pitch of the voice

mollify - *v.* - to soften; to make less intense

moot - *adj.* - subject to or open for discussion or debate

mordant - *adj.* - biting. cutting, or caustic

mutinous - *adj.* - inclined to revolt

nefarious - *adj.* - very wicked; abominable

nemesis - *n.* - just punishment; retribution

nexus - *n.* - a connection

nostrum - *n.* - a quack medicine

noxious - *adj.* - harmful to health or morals

nugatory - *adj.* - trifling; futile; insignificant

obeisance - *n.* - a gesture of respect or reverence

obfuscate - *v.* - to darken; to confuse

objurgate - *v.* - to chide vehemently

obloquy - *n.* - verbal abuse of a person or thing

obtrude - *v.* - to thrust forward; to eject

odious - *adj.* - hateful; disgusting

oligarchy - *n.* - form of government in which the supreme power is placed in the hands of
     a small exclusive group

opalescent - *adj.* - iridescent

opprobrious - *adj.* - reproachful or contemptuous

palatial - *adj.* - large and ornate, like a palace

palindrome - *n.* - a word, verse or sentence that is the same when read backward or forward

paltry - *adj.* - worthless; trifling

pandemonium - *n.* - a place of wild disorder, noise, or confusion

parapet - *n.* - a wall or railing to protect people from falling

pariah - *n.* - an outcast; someone despised by others

parity - *n.* - state of being the same in power, value, or rank

parley - *v.* - to speak with another; to discourse

parry - *v.* - to ward off; to avoid

parsimonious - *adj.* - miserly; stingy

paucity - *n.* - scarcity; small number

peculate - *v.* - to embezzle

pecuniary - *adj.* - relating to money

pellucid - *adj.* - transparent

penury - *n.* - lack of money or property

perdition - *n.* - complete and irreparable loss

peremptory - *adj.* - 1. barring future action; 2. that cannot be denied, changed, etc.

perfidious - *adj.* - violating good faith or vows

perquisite - *n.* - a fee, profit, etc. in addition to the stated income of one's employment

peruse - *v.* - to read carefully and thoroughly

pied - *adj.* - spotted

pinioned - *adj.* - 1. having wings; 2. having wings or arms bound or confined

platonic - *adj.* - 1. idealistic or impractical; 2. not amorous or sensual

plenary - *adj.* - full; entire; complete

plethora - *n.* - the state of being too full; excess

pommel - *n.* - the rounded, upward-projecting front of a saddle

portend - *v.* - to foreshadow

potable - *adj.* - drinkable

prate - *v.* - to talk much and foolishly

precept - *n.* - a rule or direction of moral conduct

precocious - *adj.* - developed or matured earlier than usual

prefatory - *adj.* - introductory

preponderate - *adj.* - to outweigh

prerogative - *n.* - a prior or exclusive right or privilege

prevaricate - *v.* - to evade the truth

prognosis - *n.* - a forecast, especially in medicine

prolific - *adj.* - fruitful

propagate - *v.* - to reproduce or multiply

propitiate - *v.* - to win the good will of

protocol - *n.* - an original draft or record of a document

provident - *adj.* - prudent; economical

proviso - *n.* - conditional stipulation to an agreement

pseudonym - *n.* - a borrowed or fictitious name

puerile - *adj.* - childish; immature

purloin - *v.* - to steal

purview - *n.* - the range of control, activity, or understanding

quaff - *v.* - to drink or swallow in large quantities

quagmire - *n.* - a difficult position, as if on shaky ground

qualm - *n.* - sudden feeling of uneasiness or doubt

quintessence - *n.* - 1. the ultimate substance; 2. the pure essence of anything

quixotic - *adj.* - extravagantly chivalrous

quizzical - *adj.* - odd; comical

ramification - *n.* - the arrangement of branches; consequence

rampant - *adj.* - violent and uncontrollable action

rancor - *n.* - a continuing and bitter hate or ill will

raze - *v.* - to scrape or shave off

recalcitrant - *adj.* - refusing to obey authority

recidivism - *n.* - habitual or chronic relapse

recumbent - *adj.* - leaning or reclining

recusant - *adj.* - disobedient of authority

redolent - *adj.* - sweet-smelling; fragrant

reminiscence - *n.* - a remembering

remonstrate - *v.* - to exhibit strong reasons against an act

rendition - *n.* - a performance or interpretation

repertoire - *n.* - stock of plays which can be readily performed by a company

reprehend - *v.* - to reprimand; to find fault with

reprieve - *v.* - to give temporary relief

resonant - *adj.* - resounding; re-echoing

resplendent - *adj.* - dazzling; splendid

resurgent - *adj.* - rising or tending to rise again

revile - *v.* - to be abusive in speech
risible - *adj.* - able or inclined to laugh
roseate - *adj.* - bright, cheerful, or optimistic
rote - *n.* - a fixed, mechanical way of doing something
rotundity - *n.* - condition of being rounded out or plump
rudimentary - *adj.* - elementary
ruminate - *v.* - to muse on
salutatory - *adj.* - of or containing greetings
sapid - *adj.* - having a pleasant taste
sardonic - *adj.* - bitterly ironical
savant - *n.* - a learned person
schism - *n.* - a division in an organized group
scourge - *v.* - to whip severely
scrutinize - *v.* - to examine closely
scurrilous - *adj.* - using low and indecent language
sedentary - *adj.* - 1. characterized by sitting; 2. remaining in one locality
serendipity - *n.* - an apparent aptitude for making fortunate discoveries accidentally
shoal - *n.* - a great quantity
skeptic - *n.* - one who is always doubtful or questioning
sloth - *n.* - disinclination to action or labor
slovenly - *adv.* - careless in habits. behavior, etc.; untidy
solemnity - *n.* - a deep, reverent feeling often associated with religious occasions
sordid - *adj.* - filthy; foul
specious - *adj.* - appearing just and fair without really being so
spelunker - *n.* - one who explores caves
splenetic - *adj.* - bad-tempered; irritable
staid - *adj.* - sober; sedate
stanch - *v.* - to stop or check the flow of blood
static - *n.* - to remain still, with no movement
stigmatize - *v.* - to characterize or make as disgraceful
stoic - *adj.* - a person who is not easily excited
stolid - *adj.* - unexcitable; dull
striated - *adj.* - marked with fine parallel lines
strident - *adj.* - creaking; harsh; grating
stymie - *n.* - 1. to hinder or obstruct; 2. in golf, an opponent's ball lying in direct line between the player's ball and the hole
succor - *n.* - aid; assistance
sumptuous - *adj.* - involving great expense
sundry - *adj.* - 1. various; miscellaneous; 2. separate; distinct
supplant - *v.* - to take the place of
suppliant - *adj.* - asking earnestly and submissively
surfeit - *v.* - to feed or supply in excess
swathe - *v.* - to wrap around something; envelop
symmetry - *n.* - equal in form on either side of a dividing line
tawdry - *n.* - a gaudy ornament
tedious - *adj.* - wearisome, tiresome
teem - *v.* - 1. to be stocked to overflowing; 2. to pour out; to empty
tenet - *n.* - any principle, doctrine, etc. which a person, school, etc. believes or maintains
tentative - *adj.* - with hesitation; not yet complete
termagant - *n.* - a boisterous, scolding woman; a shrew
terrestrial - *adj.* - pertaining to the earth
tether - *n.* - the range or limit of one's abilities

thrall - *n.* - a slave
thrifty - *adj.* - frugal, careful with money
throe - *v.* - to put in agony
timorous - *adj.* - fearful
tortuous - *adj.* - pertaining to or involving excruciating pain
traduce - *v.* - 1. to exhibit; 2. to slander
tranquility - *n.* - calmness, stillness
transmute - *v.* - to transform
travail - *v.* - to harass; to torment
trenchant - *adj.* - 1. keen; penetrating; 2. clear-cut; distinct
tribunal - *n.* - the seat of judge
troth - *n.* - belief; faith; fidelity
turbid - *adj.* - 1. thick; dense; 2. confused; perplexed
tutelage - *n.* - the condition of being under a guardian or a tutor
umbrage - *n.* - shade; shadow
uncouth - *adj.* - uncultured; crude
undermine - *v.* - to impari, often through subtle means
unfeigned - *adj.* - genuine; real; sincere
uniform - *adj.* - never changing, always with the same standard
unobtrusive - *adj.* - to stay out of the way, to remain quietly in the background
untrowable - *adj.* - incredible
uxoricide - *n.* - the murder of a wife by her husband
vagary - *n.* - 1. an odd action or idea; 2. a wandering
valid - *adj.* - based on good judgment
vantage - *n.* - advantage; gain; profit
vaunt - *v.* - to brag or boast
venal - *adj.* - that can be readily bribed or corrupted
veneer - *n.* - 1. a thin surface layer; 2. any attractive but superficial appearance
verbiage - *n.* - wordiness
verity - *n.* - truthfulness
vertigo - *n.* - a sensation of dizziness
vestige - *n.* - a trace of something that no longer exists
viable - *adj.* - able to live or grow; possible
vicarious - *adj.* - taking the place of another person or thing
vicissitude - *n.* - charges or variation occurring irregularly in the course of something
vigilance - *n.* - watchfulness
vigorous - *adj.* - energetic; strong
visage - *n.* - appearance
vital - *adj.* - extremely important; crucial
vitriolic - *adj.* - extremely biting or caustic
vociferous - *adj.* - making a loud outcry
volition - *n.* - the act of willing
voracious - *adj.* - greedy in eating
vouchsafe - *v.* - 1. to be gracious enough to grant; 2. to guarantee as safe
wan - *adj.* - pale; pallid
wily - *adj.* - cunning; sly
wither - *v.* - to shrivel up; to die
wizened - *adj.* - withered; shrunken
wreak - *v.* - to give vent or free play
wrest - *v.* - 1. to turn or twist; 2. usurp; 3. to distort or change the true meaning of

# VERBAL DRILLS

## ANSWER KEY

### Drill 1

| | | | |
|---|---|---|---|
| 1. | (J) | 9. | (F) |
| 2. | (G) | 10. | (E) |
| 3. | (A) | 11. | (D) |
| 4. | (C) | 12. | (C) |
| 5. | (H) | 13. | (A) |
| 6. | (B) | 14. | (E) |
| 7. | (I) | 15. | (B) |
| 8. | (D) | | |

### Drill 2

| | | | |
|---|---|---|---|
| 1. | (D) | 9. | (B) |
| 2. | (G) | 10. | (H) |
| 3. | (I) | 11. | (D) |
| 4. | (F) | 12. | (A) |
| 5. | (A) | 13. | (B) |
| 6. | (J) | 14. | (E) |
| 7. | (E) | 15. | (C) |
| 8. | (C) | | |

### Drill 3

| | | | |
|---|---|---|---|
| 1. | (E) | 9. | (F) |
| 2. | (H) | 10. | (D) |
| 3. | (J) | 11. | (C) |
| 4. | (A) | 12. | (A) |
| 5. | (I) | 13. | (E) |
| 6. | (B) | 14. | (D) |
| 7. | (C) | 15. | (B) |
| 8. | (G) | | |

### Drill 4

| | | | |
|---|---|---|---|
| 1. | (D) | 9. | (F) |
| 2. | (E) | 10. | (H) |
| 3. | (A) | 11. | (D) |
| 4. | (I) | 12. | (A) |
| 5. | (J) | 13. | (B) |
| 6. | (B) | 14. | (C) |
| 7. | (C) | 15. | (E) |
| 8. | (G) | | |

### Drill 5

| | | | |
|---|---|---|---|
| 1. | (H) | 9. | (D) |
| 2. | (F) | 10. | (G) |
| 3. | (A) | 11. | (B) |
| 4. | (B) | 12. | (D) |
| 5. | (J) | 13. | (A) |
| 6. | (C) | 14. | (E) |
| 7. | (I) | 15. | (C) |
| 8. | (E) | | |

### Drill 6

| | | | |
|---|---|---|---|
| 1. | (G) | 9. | (F) |
| 2. | (A) | 10. | (H) |
| 3. | (E) | 11. | (D) |
| 4. | (J) | 12. | (E) |
| 5. | (C) | 13. | (A) |
| 6. | (B) | 14. | (C) |
| 7. | (D) | 15. | (B) |
| 8. | (I) | | |

## Drill 7

| | | | | |
|---|---|---|---|---|
| 1. | (F) | 9. | (D) |
| 2. | (E) | 10. | (J) |
| 3. | (A) | 11. | (B) |
| 4. | (B) | 12. | (E) |
| 5. | (H) | 13. | (D) |
| 6. | (I) | 14. | (C) |
| 7. | (C) | 15. | (A) |
| 8. | (G) | | |

## Drill 8

| | | | | |
|---|---|---|---|---|
| 1. | (D) | 9. | (C) |
| 2. | (I) | 10. | (H) |
| 3. | (G) | 11. | (A) |
| 4. | (A) | 12. | (D) |
| 5. | (J) | 13. | (B) |
| 6. | (E) | 14. | (E) |
| 7. | (B) | 15. | (C) |
| 8. | (F) | | |

## Drill 9

| | | | | |
|---|---|---|---|---|
| 1. | (H) | 9. | (D) |
| 2. | (I) | 10. | (G) |
| 3. | (E) | 11. | (B) |
| 4. | (A) | 12. | (D) |
| 5. | (J) | 13. | (A) |
| 6. | (B) | 14. | (C) |
| 7. | (F) | 15. | (E) |
| 8. | (C) | | |

## Drill 10

| | | | | |
|---|---|---|---|---|
| 1. | (D) | 9. | (F) |
| 2. | (A) | 10. | (J) |
| 3. | (H) | 11. | (C) |
| 4. | (G) | 12. | (B) |
| 5. | (B) | 13. | (A) |
| 6. | (C) | 14. | (E) |
| 7. | (E) | 15. | (D) |
| 8. | (I) | | |

## Drill 11

| | | | | |
|---|---|---|---|---|
| 1. | (F) | 9. | (E) |
| 2. | (I) | 10. | (G) |
| 3. | (A) | 11. | (C) |
| 4. | (H) | 12. | (B) |
| 5. | (B) | 13. | (E) |
| 6. | (J) | 14. | (A) |
| 7. | (C) | 15. | (D) |
| 8. | (D) | | |

## Drill 12

| | | | | |
|---|---|---|---|---|
| 1. | (J) | 9. | (F) |
| 2. | (A) | 10. | (E) |
| 3. | (B) | 11. | (E) |
| 4. | (I) | 12. | (C) |
| 5. | (C) | 13. | (D) |
| 6. | (H) | 14. | (A) |
| 7. | (D) | 15. | (B) |
| 8. | (G) | | |

# GRE MATH REVIEW

You will be well prepared for the GRE Quantitative Ability sections after you review basic concepts in arithmetic, algebra and geometry. The more familiar you are with these fundamental principles, the better you will do on the GRE Quantitative Ability sections. Our math review represents the various mathematical topics that will appear on the GRE. You will not find calculus, trigonometry, or even imaginary numbers in our math review because these concepts are not tested on the GRE. The mathematical concepts presented on the GRE are ones with which you are already familiar and simply need to review in order to score well.

The topics listed below should be reviewed in order to accurately answer the mathematical GRE sections. See the math review on the following pages.

## ARITHMETIC

1. Integers
2. Fractions & Decimals
3. Real Numbers
4. Ratios
5. Percentages
6. Exponents
7. Mean, Median, Mode

## ALGEBRA

1. Simplifying algebraic expressions
2. Equations
3. Absolute value
4. Inequalities

## GEOMETRY

1. Lines and angles
2. Polygons (convex)
3. Triangles
4. Quadrilaterals
5. Circles
6. Solids
7. Coordinate geometry

## TYPES OF WORD PROBLEMS

1. Rate
2. Work
3. Mixture
4. Interest
5. Discount
6. Profit
7. Sets
8. Geometry
9. Measurement
10. Data Interpretation

# ARITHMETIC

## 1. Integers

If we divide the number line into equal segments called unit lengths, we can then label the boundary points of these segments according to their distance from zero. For example, the point 2 lengths to the left of zero is − 2, while the point 3 lengths to the right of zero is +3 (the + sign is usually assumed, so +3 is written as 3). The number line now looks like this:

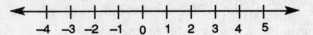

These boundary points represent the subset of the reals known as the integers, denoted $Z$. Some subsets of $Z$ are the natural numbers or positive integers, the set of integers starting with 1 and increasing, $Z^+ = \mathcal{N} = \{1, 2, 3, 4, \ldots\}$; the whole numbers, the set of integers starting with 0 and increasing, $\mathcal{W} = \{0, 1, 2, 3, \ldots\}$; the negative integers, the set of integers starting with − 1 and decreasing: $Z^- = \{-1, -2, -3, \ldots\}$; and the prime numbers, the set of positive integers greater than 1 that are divisible only by 1 and themselves: $\{2, 3, 5, 7, 11, \ldots\}$.

Even integers are integers divisible by 2 and are included in the set $\{\ldots -4, -2, 0, 2, 4, 6, \ldots\}$.

Odd integers are integers not divisible by 2 and are included in the set $\{\ldots, -3, -1, 1, 3, 5, 7, \ldots\}$.

## 2. Fractions and Decimals

In the fraction $r/_1$, the numerator is $r$ and the denominator is 1. The denominator can never be zero since zero divided into a number is not defined.

Equivalent fractions are fractions which represent the same number. For instance, $^6/_8$ and $^3/_4$ are equivalent fractions.

### OPERATIONS WITH FRACTIONS

To understand the operations on fractions, it is first desirable to understand what is known as factoring.

The product of two numbers is equal to a unique number. The two

numbers are said to be factors of the unique number and the process of finding the two numbers is called factoring. It is important to note that when a number in a particular set is factored, then the factors of the number are also in the same set.

e.g., The factors of 6 are

1) 1 and 6 since $1 \times 6 = 6$.

2) 2 and 3 since $2 \times 3 = 6$.

A) The value of a fraction remains unchanged, if its numerator and denominator are both multiplied or divided by the same number, other than zero. e.g.

$$\frac{1}{2} \times \frac{2}{2} = \frac{2}{4} = \frac{1}{2}$$

This is because a fraction $^b/_b$, $b$ any number, is equal to the multiplicative identity, 1.

B) To simplify a fraction is to convert it into a form in which numerator and denominator have no common factor other than 1. e.g.

$$\frac{50}{25} = \frac{50 \div 25}{25 \div 25} = \frac{2}{1} = 2$$

C) The algebraic sum of the fractions having a common denominator is a fraction whose numerator is the algebraic sum of the numerators of the given fractions and whose denominator is the common denominator. e.g.

$$\frac{11}{3} + \frac{5}{3} = \frac{11 + 5}{3} = \frac{16}{3}$$

Similarly, for subtraction,

$$\frac{11}{3} - \frac{5}{3} = \frac{11 - 5}{3} = \frac{6}{3} = 2$$

D) To find the sum of two fractions having different denominators, it is necessary to find the lowest common denominator, (LCD), of the different denominators and convert the fractions into equivalent fractions having the lowest common denominator as a denominator. e.g.,

$$\frac{11}{6} + \frac{5}{16} = ?$$

To find the LCD, we must first find the prime factors of the two denominators.

$$6 \quad = 2 \cdot 3$$
$$16 \quad = 2 \cdot 2 \cdot 2 \cdot 2$$
$$LCD = 2 \cdot 2 \cdot 2 \cdot 2 \cdot 3 = 48$$

Note we do not need to repeat the 2 that appears in both the factors of 6 and 16.

We now rewrite $^{11}/_6$, $^5/_{16}$ to have 48 as their denominator.

$$\frac{11}{6} \cdot \frac{8}{8} = \frac{88}{48} \qquad \frac{5}{16} \cdot \frac{3}{3} = \frac{15}{48}$$

We may now find

$$\frac{11}{6} + \frac{5}{16} = \frac{103}{48}.$$

E) The product of two or more fractions produces a fraction whose numerator is the product of the numerators of the given fractions and whose denominator is the product of the denominators of the given fractions. e.g.,

$$\frac{2}{3} \cdot \frac{1}{5} \cdot \frac{4}{7} = \frac{8}{105}$$

F) The quotient of two given fractions is obtained by inverting the divisor and then multiplying. e.g.,

$$\frac{8}{9} \div \frac{1}{3} = \frac{8}{9} \times \frac{3}{1} = \frac{8}{3}$$

**PROBLEM**

If $a = 4$ and $b = 7$ find the value of $\quad \dfrac{a + \dfrac{a}{b}}{a - \dfrac{a}{b}}.$

**Solution**

By substitution,

$$\frac{a + \dfrac{a}{b}}{a - \dfrac{a}{b}} = \frac{4 + \dfrac{4}{7}}{4 - \dfrac{4}{7}}.$$

In order to combine the terms we convert 4 into sevenths:

$$4 = 4 \cdot 1 = 4 \cdot \frac{7}{7} = \frac{28}{7}.$$

Thus, we have:

$$\frac{\dfrac{28}{7} + \dfrac{4}{7}}{\dfrac{28}{7} - \dfrac{4}{7}} = \frac{\dfrac{32}{7}}{\dfrac{24}{7}}.$$

Dividing by $^{24}/_7$ is equivalent to multiplying by $^7/_{24}$. Therefore,

$$\frac{4 + \dfrac{4}{7}}{4 - \dfrac{4}{7}} = \frac{32}{7} \cdot \frac{7}{24}.$$

Now, the 7 in the numerator cancels with the 7 in the denominator. Thus, we obtain: $^{32}/_{24}$, and dividing numerator and denominator by 8, we obtain: $^4/_3$.

## DECIMALS

If we divide the denominator of a fraction into its numerator, we obtain a decimal form for it. This form attaches significance to the placement of an integer relative to a decimal point. The first place to the left of the decimal point is the units place; the second to the left, is the tens; third, the hundreds, etc. The first place to the right of the decimal point is the tenths, the second the hundredths, etc. The integer in each place tells how many of the values of the place the given number has.

## EXAMPLE

721 has seven hundreds, two tens, and one unit. .584 has five tenths, eight hundredths, and four thousandths.

Since a rational number is of the form $^a/_b$, $b \neq 0$, then all rational numbers can be expressed as decimals by dividing $b$ into $a$. The resulting decimal is either a terminating decimal, meaning that $b$ divides $a$ with remainder 0 after a certain point; or repeating, meaning that $b$ continues to divide $a$ so that the decimal has a repeating pattern of integers.

### EXAMPLES

A)   $^1/_2 = .5$

B)   $^1/_3 = .333...$

C)   $^{11}/_{16} = .6875$

D)   $^2/_7 = .285714285714....$

A) and C) are terminating decimals; B) and D) are repeating decimals. This explanation allows us to define irrational numbers as numbers whose decimal form is non-terminating and non-repeating. e.g.,

$$\sqrt{2} = 1.414...$$
$$\sqrt{3} = 1.732....$$

### PROBLEM

Express $-\,^{10}/_{20}$ as a decimal.

### Solution

$$-\,^{10}/_{20} = -0.5.$$

### PROBLEM

Write $^2/_7$ as a repeating decimal.

### Solution

To write a fraction as a repeating decimal divide the numerator by the denominator, until a pattern of repeated digits appears.

$$2 \div 7 = .285714285714...$$

Identify the entire portion of the decimal which is repeated. The repeating decimal can then be written in the shortened form:

$$^2/_7 = .\overline{285714}$$

## 3. REAL NUMBERS

Most of the numbers used in algebra belong to a set called the real numbers, or reals. This set denoted $\mathcal{R}$, can be represented graphically by the real number line.

Given a straight horizontal line extending continuously in both directions, we arbitrarily fix a point and label it with the number 0. In a similar manner, we can label any point on the line with one of the real numbers, depending on its position relative to 0. Numbers to the right of zero are called positive, while those to the left are called negative. Value increases from left to right, so that if $a$ is to the right of $b$, it is said to be greater than $b$.

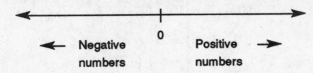

PROBLEM

Classify each of the following numbers into as many different sets as possible. Example: real, integer, rational....

(1)  0

(4)  $^1/_2$

(2)  9

(5)  $^2/_3$

(3)  $\sqrt{6}$

(6)  1.5

SOLUTION

(1)  Zero is a real number and an integer.

(2)  9 is a real, rational, natural number, and an integer.

(3)  $\sqrt{6}$ is an irrational, real number.

(4)  $^1/_2$ is a rational, real number.

(5)  $^2/_3$ is a rational, real number.

(6)   1.5 is a rational, real number, and a decimal.

## POSITIVE AND NEGATIVE NUMBERS

A)   To add two numbers with like signs, add their absolute values and prefix the sum with the common sign. so,

$$6 + 2 = 8, (-6) + (-2) = -8$$

B)   To add two numbers with unlike signs, find the difference between their absolute values, and prefix the result with the sign of the number with the greater absolute value. so,

$$(-4) + 6 = 2, \; 15 + (-19) = -4$$

C)   To subtract a number $b$ from another number $a$, change the sign of $b$ and add to $a$. Examples:

$$10 - (3) = 10 + (-3) = 7 \tag{1}$$

$$2 - (-6) = 2 + 6 = 8 \tag{2}$$
$$(-5) - (-2) = -5 + (+2) = -3 \tag{3}$$

D)   To multiply (or divide) two numbers having like signs, multiply (or divide) their absolute values and prefix the result with a positive sign. Examples:

$$(5)(3) = 15 \tag{1}$$

$$\frac{-6}{-3} = 2 \tag{2}$$

E)   To multiply (or divide) two numbers having unlike signs, multiply (or divide) their absolute values and prefix the result with a negative sign. Examples:

$$(-2)(8) = -16 \tag{1}$$

$$\frac{9}{-3} = -3 \tag{2}$$

According to the law of signs for real numbers, the square of a positive or negative number is always positive. This means that it is impossible to take the square root of a negative number in the real number system.

**PROBLEM**

Find the absolute value for each of the following:

(1)   zero                                    (3)   $-\pi$

(2)   4                                       (4)   $a$, where $a$ is a real number.

**Solution**

The absolute value of a number is represented by 2 vertical lines around the number, and is equal to the given number itself if it is positive, to zero if the number is zero, and to its positive counterpart (its opposite) if it is negative (see section 3 of the Algebra review on Absolute Value).

(1)   $|0| = 0$          (2)   $|4| = 4$          (3)   $|-\pi| = \pi$

(4)   for $a > 0$   $|a| = a$

for $a = 0$   $|a| = 0$

for $a < 0$   $|a| = -a$,

i.e.,   $|a| = \begin{cases} a \text{ if } a > 0 \\ 0 \text{ if } a = 0 \\ -a \text{ if } a < 0 \end{cases}$

**PROBLEM**

Calculate the value of each of the following expressions:

(1)   $||2 - 5| + 6 - 14|$

(2)   $|-5| \cdot 4 + \dfrac{|-12|}{4}$

**Solution**

Before solving this problem, one must remember the order of operations: parenthesis, multiplication and division, addition and subtraction.

(1)   $||-3| + 6 - 14| = |3 + 6 - 14| = |9 - 14| = |-5| = 5$

(2)   $(5 \times 4) + {}^{12}/_4 = 20 + 3 = 23$

## EQUIVALENT FORMS OF A NUMBER

Some problems may call for converting numbers into an equivalent or simplified form in order to make the solution more convenient.

1. Converting a fraction to a decimal:

$$\frac{1}{2} = 0.50$$

Divide the numerator by the denominator:

$$\begin{array}{r} .50 \\ 2\overline{)1.00} \\ \underline{-10} \\ 00 \end{array}$$

2. Converting a number to a percent:

$$0.50 = 50\%$$

Multiply by 100:

$$0.50 = (0.50 \times 100)\% = 50\%$$

3. Converting a percent to a decimal:

$$30\% = 0.30$$

Divide by 100:

$$30\% = \frac{30}{100} = 0.30$$

4. Converting a decimal to a fraction:

$$0.500 = \frac{1}{2}$$

Convert 0.500 to $\frac{500}{1000}$ and then simplify the fraction by dividing the numerator and denominator by common factors:

$$\frac{2 \times 2 \times 5 \times 5 \times 5}{2 \times 2 \times 2 \times 5 \times 5 \times 5}$$

and then cancel out the common numbers to get $\frac{1}{2}$.

**PROBLEM**

> Express
>
> (1)   1.65   as a percentage.
>
> (2)   0.7   as a fraction.
>
> (3)   $-^{10}/_{20}$   as a decimal.
>
> (4)   $^4/_2$   as an integer.

**Solution**

(1)   1.65 x 100 = 165%

(2)   $0.7 = {}^7/_{10}$

(3)   $-{}^{10}/_{20} = -0.5$

(4)   $^4/_2 = 2$

## 4.   RATIOS

The ratio of two numbers $x$ and $y$ written $x : y$ is the fraction $^x/_y$ where $y \neq 0$. A proportion is an equality of two ratios. The laws of proportion are listed below:

If $^a/_b = {}^c/_d$, then

A)   $ad = bc$

B)   $\dfrac{b}{a} = \dfrac{d}{c}$

C)   $\dfrac{a}{c} = \dfrac{b}{d}$

D)   $\dfrac{a+b}{b} = \dfrac{c+d}{d}$

E)   $\dfrac{a-b}{b} = \dfrac{c-d}{d}$

Given a proportion $a{:}b = c{:}d$, then $a$ and $d$ are called the extremes, $b$ and $c$ are called the means and $d$ is called the fourth proportion to $a$, $b$, and $c$.

**PROBLEM**

Solve the proportion $\dfrac{x+1}{4} = \dfrac{15}{12}$.

*Solution*

Cross multiply to determine $x$; that is, multiply the numerator of the first fraction by the denominator of the second, and equate this to the product of the numerator of the second and the denominator of the first.

$$(x+1)\,12 = 4 \cdot 15$$
$$12x + 12 = 60$$
$$x = 4.$$

**PROBLEM**

Find the ratios of $x : y : z$ from the equations

$$7x = 4y + 8z, \quad 3z = 12x + 11\,y.$$

*Solution*

By transposition we have

$$7x - 4y - 8z = 0$$
$$12x + 11y - 3z = 0.$$

To obtain the ratio of $x : y$ we convert the given system into an equation in terms of just $x$ and $y$. $z$ may be eliminated as follows: Multiply each term of the first equation by 3, and each term of the second equation by 8, and then subtract the second equation from the first. We thus obtain:

$$\begin{array}{r} 21x - 12y - 24z \;= 0 \\ -\,(96x + 88y - 24z \;= 0) \\ \hline -75x - 100y \;= 0 \end{array}$$

Dividing each term of the last equation by 25 we obtain

$$-3x - 4y \;= 0$$
$$\text{or,} \qquad -3x \;= 4y.$$

Dividing both sides of this equation by 4, and by $-3$, we have the proportion:

$$^x/_4 = {}^y/_{-3}.$$

We are now interested in obtaining the ratio of $y : z$. To do this we convert the given system of equations into an equation in terms of just $y$ and $z$, by eliminating $x$ as follows: Multiply each term of the first equation by 12, and each term of the second equation by 7, and then subtract the second equation from the first. We thus obtain:

$$
\begin{array}{r}
84x - 48y - 96z = 0 \\
-(84x + 77y - 21z = 0) \\
\hline
-125y - 75z = 0.
\end{array}
$$

Dividing each term of the last equation by 25 we obtain

$$
\begin{aligned}
-5y - 3z &= 0 \\
\text{or,} \quad -3z &= 5y.
\end{aligned}
$$

Dividing both sides of this equation by 5, and by $-3$, we have the proportion:

$$ {}^z/_5 = {}^y/_{-3}. $$

From this result and our previous result we obtain:

$$ {}^x/_4 = {}^y/_{-3} = {}^z/_5 $$

as the desired ratios.

# 5. PERCENTAGES

A percent is a number out of 100. A percent can be defined by fractions with a denominator of 100. Decimals can also represent a percent. For instance,

$$ 56\% = 0.56 \text{ or } {}^{56}/_{100}. $$

**PROBLEM**

Compute the value of

(1)  90% of 400

(3)  50% of 500

(2)  180% of 400

(4)  200% of 4

**Solution**

The symbol % means per hundred, therefore $5\% = {}^5/_{100}$.

(1)  90% of 400 = $^{90}/_{100} \times ^{400}/_1 = 90 \times 4 = 360$

(2)  180% of 400 = $^{180}/_{100} \times ^{400}/_1 = 180 \times 4 = 720$

(3)  50% of 500 = $^{50}/_{100} \times ^{500}/_1 = 50 \times 5 = 250$

(4)  200% of 4 = $^{200}/_{100} \times ^{4}/_1 = 2 \times 4 = 8$

**PROBLEM**

> What percent of   (1)  100 is 99.5?      (2)  200 is 4?

*Solution*

(1)  $99.5 = x \cdot 100$

$99.5 = 100x$

$.995 = x$; but this is the value of $x$ per hundred. Therefore

$x = 99.5\%$.

(2)  $4 = x \times 200$

$4 = 200x$

$.02 = x$.  Again this must be changed to percent, so

$x = 2\%$.

## 6.  EXPONENTS

Given the expression $a^n = b$, where $a$, $n$, and $b \, \varepsilon \, R$, $a$ is called the base, $n$ is called the exponent or power. ($\varepsilon$ denotes "are real numbers.")

In $3^2$, 3 is the base, 2 is the exponent. If $n$ is a positive integer and if $x$ and $y$ are real numbers such that $x^n = y$, then $x$ is said to be an $n$th root of $y$, written

$$x = \sqrt[n]{y} = y^{\frac{1}{n}}.$$

**POSITIVE INTEGRAL EXPONENT:**

If $n$ is a positive integer, then $a^n$ represents the product of $n$ factors each of which is $a$.

## NEGATIVE INTEGRAL EXPONENT:

If $n$ is a negative integer,

$$a^{-n} = \frac{1}{a^n} \qquad a \neq 0$$

so,

$$2^{-4} = \frac{1}{2^4} = \frac{1}{16}$$

## POSITIVE FRACTIONAL EXPONENT:

$$a^{\frac{m}{n}} = \sqrt[n]{a^m}$$

where $m$ and $n$ are positive integers. e.g.

$$4^{\frac{3}{2}} = \sqrt[2]{4^3} = \sqrt{64} = 8$$

## NEGATIVE FRACTIONAL EXPONENT:

$$a^{-\frac{m}{n}} = \frac{1}{a^{\frac{m}{n}}}$$

e.g.,

$$27^{-\frac{2}{3}} = \frac{1}{27^{\frac{2}{3}}} = \frac{1}{\sqrt[3]{27^2}} = \frac{1}{\sqrt[3]{729}} = \frac{1}{9}$$

## ZERO EXPONENT:

$$a^0 = 1, a \neq 0$$

General Laws of Exponents:

A) $a^p a^q = a^{p+q}$

B) $\left(a^p\right)^q = a^{pq}$

C) $\frac{a^p}{a^q} = a^{p-q}, a \neq 0$

D) $(ab)^p = a^p b^p$

E) $\left(\frac{a}{b}\right)^p = \frac{a^p}{b^p}, b \neq 0$

## PROBLEM

Simplify the following expressions:

(1) $-3^{-2}$

(3) $\dfrac{-3}{4^{-1}}$

(2) $(-3)^{-2}$

### Solution

(1) Here the exponent applies only to 3. Since

$$x^{-y} = \frac{1}{x^y}, \; -3^{-2} = -(3^{-2}) = -\frac{1}{3^2} = -\frac{1}{9}.$$

(2) In this case the exponent applies to the negative base. Thus,

$$(-3)^{-2} = -\frac{1}{(-3)^2} = \frac{1}{(-3)(-3)} = \frac{1}{9}.$$

(3)

$$\frac{-3}{4^{-1}} = \frac{-3}{\left(\frac{1}{4}\right)^1} = \frac{-3}{\frac{1^1}{4^1}} = \frac{-3}{\frac{1}{4}}.$$

Division by a fraction is equivalent to multiplication by that fraction's reciprocal, thus

$$\frac{-3}{\frac{1}{4}} = -3 \cdot \frac{4}{1} = -12,$$

and

$$\frac{-3}{4^{-1}} = -12.$$

## PROBLEM

Find the indicated roots.

(1) $\sqrt[5]{32}$

(3) $\sqrt[3]{-125}$

(2) $\pm\sqrt[4]{625}$

(4) $\sqrt[4]{-16}$

### Solution

The following two laws of exponents can be used to solve these problems: (1) $\left(\sqrt[n]{a}\right)^n = \left(a^{1/n}\right)^n = a^1 = a$, and (2) $\left(\sqrt[n]{a}\right)^n = \sqrt[n]{a^n}$.

(1) $\sqrt[5]{32} = \sqrt[5]{2^5} = \left(\sqrt[5]{2}\right)^5 = 2$.

This result is true because $(2)^5 = 32$, that is, $2 \cdot 2 \cdot 2 \cdot 2 \cdot 2 = 32$.

(2) $\sqrt[4]{625} = \sqrt[4]{5^4} = \left(\sqrt[4]{5}\right)^4 = 5$.

This result is true because $(5^4) = 625$, that is, $5 \cdot 5 \cdot 5 \cdot 5 = 625$.

$-\sqrt[4]{625} = -\left(\sqrt[4]{5^4}\right) = -\left[\left(\sqrt[4]{5}\right)^4\right] = -[5] = -5$.

This result is true because $(-5)^4 = 625$, that is, $(-5) \cdot (-5) \cdot (-5) \cdot (-5) = 625$.

(3) $\sqrt[3]{-125} = \sqrt[3]{(-5)^3} = \left(\sqrt[3]{-5}\right)^3 = -5$.

This result is true because $(-5)^3 = -125$, that is, $(-5) \cdot (-5) \cdot (-5) = -125$.

(4) There is no solution to $\sqrt[4]{-16}$ because any number raised to the fourth power is a positive number, that is, $N^4 = (N) \cdot (N) \cdot (N) \cdot (N) =$ a positive number $\neq$ a negative number, $-16$.

## 7. MEAN, MEDIAN, MODE

### MEAN

The mean is the arithmetic average. The sum of the variables divided by the number of variables is the mean. For example:

$$\frac{4 + 3 + 8}{3} = 5$$

### PROBLEM

Find the mean salary for four company employees who make $5/hr., $8/hr., $12/hr., and $15/hr.

*Solution*

The mean salary is the average.

$$\frac{\$5 + \$8 + \$12 + \$15}{4} = \frac{\$40}{4} = \$10/hr.$$

**PROBLEM**

Find the mean length of five fish with lengths of 7.5 in., 7.75 in., 8.5 in., 8.5 in., 8.25 in.

*Solution*

The mean length is the average length.

$$\frac{7.5 + 7.75 + 8.5 + 8.5 + 8.25}{5} = \frac{40.5}{5} = 8.1 \text{ in.}$$

## MEDIAN

The median is the middle value of a set of an odd number of values. There are an equal amount of values larger and smaller than the median. When the set is an even number of values, the average of the two middle values is the median. For example:

The median of (2, 3, 5, 8, 9) is 5.

The median of (2, 3, 5, 9, 10, 11) is $\frac{5 + 9}{2} = 7$.

## MODE

The mode is the most frequently occurring value in the set of values. For example the mode of 4, 5, 8, 3, 8, 2 would be 8.

**PROBLEM**

For this series of observations find the mean, median, and mode.

500, 600, 800, 800, 900, 900, 900, 900, 900, 1000, 1100

*Solution*

The mean is the value obtained by adding all the measurements and dividing by the numbers of measurements.

$$\frac{500+600+800+800+900+900+900+900+900+1000+1100}{11}$$

$$= \frac{9300}{11} = 845.45.$$

The median is the observation in the middle. We have 11, so here it is the sixth, 900.

The mode is the observation that appears most frequently. That is also 900, which has 5 appearances.

All three of these numbers are measures of central tendency. They describe the "middle" or "center" of the data.

## PROBLEM

Nine rats run through a maze. The time each rat took to traverse the maze is recorded and these times are listed below.

1 min., 2.5 min., 3 min., 1.5 min., 2 min.,

1.25 min., 1 min., .9 min., 30 min.

Which of the three measures of central tendency would be the most appropriate in this case?

## Solution

We will calculate the three measures of central tendency and then compare them to determine which would be the most appropriate in describing these data.

The mean is the sum of observations divided by the number of observations. In this case,

$$\frac{1 + 2.5 + 3 + 1.5 + 2 + 1.25 + 1 + .9 + 30}{9} = \frac{43.15}{9} = 4.79 .$$

The median is the "middle number" in an array of the observations from the lowest to the highest.

$$0.9, 1.0, 1.0, 1.25, 1.5, 2.0, 2.5, 3.0, 30.0$$

The median is the fifth observation in this array or 1.5. There are four observations larger than 1.5 and four observations smaller than 1.5.

The mode is the most frequently occurring observation in the sample. In this data set the mode is 1.0.

mean    = 4.79

median  = 1.5

mode   = 1.0

The mean is not appropriate here. Only one rat took more than 4.79 minutes to run the maze and this rate took 30 minutes. We see that the mean has been distorted by this one large observation.

The median or mode seem to describe this data set better and would be more appropriate to use.

# ALGEBRA

## 1. Simplifying Algebraic Expressions

The following concepts are important while factoring or simplifying algebraic expressions.

The factors of an algebraic expression consist of two or more algebraic expressions which when multiplied together produce the given algebraic expression.

Some important formulae, useful for the factoring of algebraic expressions are listed below.

$a(c + d) = ac + ad$

$(a + b)(a - b) = a^2 - b^2$

$(a + b)(a + b) = (a + b)^2 = a^2 + 2ab + b^2$

$(a - b)(a - b) = (a - b)^2 = a^2 - 2ab + b^2$

$(x + a)(x + b) = x^2 + (a + b)x + ab$

$(ax + b)(cx + d) = acx^2 + (ad + bc)x + bd$

$(a + b)(c + d) = ac + bc + ad + bd$

$(a + b)(a + b)(a + b) = (a + b)^3 = a^3 + 3a^2b + 3ab^2 + b^3$

$(a - b)(a - b)(a - b) = (a - b)^3 = a^3 - 3a^2b + 3ab^2 - b^3$

$(a - b)(a^2 + ab + b^2) = a^3 - b^3$

$(a + b)(a^2 - ab + b^2) = a^3 + b^3$

$(a + b + c)^2 = a^2 + b^2 + c^2 + 2ab + 2ac + 2bc$

$(a - b)(a^2 + ab + b^2) = a^3 - b^3$

$(a - b)(a^3 + a^2b + ab^2 + b^3) = a^4 - b^4$

$(a - b)(a^4 + a^3b + a^2b^2 + ab^3 + b^4) = a^5 - b^5$

$(a - b)(a^5 + a^4b + a^3b^2 + a^2b^3 + ab^4 + b^5) = a^6 - b^6$

$(a - b)(a^{n-1} + a^{n-2}b + a^{n-3}b^2 + \ldots + ab^{n-2} + b^{n-1}) = a^n - b^n$

where $n$ is any positive integer $(1, 2, 3, 4, \ldots)$.

$$(a + b)(a^{n-1} - a^{n-2}b + a^{n-3}b^2 - \ldots - ab^{n-2} + b^{n-1}) = a^n + b^n$$

where $n$ is any positive odd integer $(1, 3, 5, 7, \ldots)$.

The procedure for factoring an algebraic expression completely is as follows:

**Step 1:**　First find the greatest common factor if there is any. Then examine each factor remaining for greatest common factors.

**Step 2:**　Continue factoring the factors obtained in Step 1 until all factors other than monomial factors are prime.

## EXAMPLE

Factoring $4 - 16x^2$,

$$4 - 16x^2 = 4(1 - 4x^2) = 4(1 + 2x)(1 - 2x)$$

## PROBLEM

Express each of the following as a single term.

(A)　$3x^2 + 2x^2 - 4x^2$

(B)　$5axy^2 - 7axy^2 - 3xy^2$

## Solution

(A)　Factor $x^2$ in the expression.

$3x^2 + 2x^2 - 4x^2 = (3 + 2 - 4)x^2 = 1x^2 = x^2$.

(B)　Factor $xy^2$ in the expression and then factor $a$.

$$
\begin{aligned}
5axy^2 - 7axy^2 - 3xy^2 &= (5a - 7a - 3)xy^2 \\
&= [(5 - 7)a - 3]xy^2 \\
&= (-2a - 3)xy^2.
\end{aligned}
$$

**PROBLEM**

> Simplify $\dfrac{\frac{1}{x-1} - \frac{1}{x-2}}{\frac{1}{x-2} - \frac{1}{x-3}}$.

**Solution**

Simplify the expression in the numerator by using the addition rule:

$$\frac{a}{b} + \frac{c}{d} = \frac{ad + bc}{bd}$$

Notice $bd$ is the Least Common Denominator, LCD. We obtain

$$\frac{x - 2 - (x - 1)}{(x - 1)(x - 2)} = \frac{-1}{(x - 1)(x - 2)}$$

in the numerator.

Repeat this procedure for the expression in the denominator:

$$\frac{x - 3 - (x - 2)}{(x - 2)(x - 3)} = \frac{-1}{(x - 2)(x - 3)}$$

We now have

$$\frac{\frac{-1}{(x-1)(x-2)}}{\frac{-1}{(x-2)(x-3)}},$$

which is simplified by inverting the fraction in the denominator and multiplying it by the numerator and cancelling like terms

$$\frac{-1}{(x - 1)(x - 2)} \cdot \frac{(x - 2)(x - 3)}{-1} = \frac{x - 3}{x - 1}.$$

## 2. EQUATIONS

An equation is defined as a statement of equality of two separate expressions.

Equations with the same solutions are said to be equivalent equations.

A)  Replacing an expression of an equation by an equivalent expression results in an equation equivalent to the original one. Given the equation below

$$3x + y + x + 2y = 15$$

We know that for the left side of this equation we can apply the commutative and distributive laws to get:

$$3x + y + x + 2y = 4x + 3y.$$

Since these are equivalent, we can replace the expression in the original equation with the simpler form to get:

$$4x + 3y = 15.$$

B) The addition or subtraction of the same expression on both sides of an equation results in an equivalent equation to the original one: E.g., given the equation

$$y + 6 = 10,$$

we can add $(-6)$ to both sides

$$y + 6 + (-6) = 10 + (-6)$$

to get $y + 0 = 10 - 6 \Rightarrow y = 4$. So $y + 6 = 10$ is equivalent to $y = 4$.

C) The multiplication or division on both sides of an equation by the same expression results in an equivalent equation to the original. E.g.,

$$3x = 6 \Rightarrow \frac{3x}{3} = \frac{6}{3} \Rightarrow x = 2.$$

$3x = 6$ is equivalent to $x = 2$.

D) If both members of an equation are raised to the same power, then the resultant equation is equivalent to the original equation. Example:

$$a = x^2y, \quad (a)^2 = (x^2y)^2, \text{ and } a^2 = x^4y^2.$$

This applies for negative and fractional powers as well. E.g.,

$$x^2 = 3y^4.$$

If we raise both members to the $-2$ power we get

$$(x^2)^{-2} = (3y^4)^{-2}$$

$$\frac{1}{(x^2)^2} = \frac{1}{(3y^4)^2}$$

$$\frac{1}{x^4} = \frac{1}{9y^8}$$

If we raise both members to the $\frac{1}{2}$ power which is the same as taking the square root, we get:

$$(x^2)^{\frac{1}{2}} = (3y^4)^{\frac{1}{2}}$$

$$x = \sqrt{3}\, y^2$$

E)   The reciprocal of both members of an equation are equivalent to the original equation. Note: The reciprocal of zero is undefined.

$$\frac{2x+y}{z} = \frac{5}{2} \qquad \frac{z}{2x+y} = \frac{2}{5}$$

## PROBLEM

Solve, justifying each step. $3x - 8 = 7x + 8$.

## Solution

$$3x - 8 = 7x + 8$$

Adding 8 to both members,      $3x - 8 + 8 = 7x + 8 + 8$

Additive inverse property,      $3x + 0 = 7x + 16$

Additive identity property,      $3x = 7x + 16$

Adding $(-7x)$ to both members,      $3x - 7x = 7x + 16 - 7x$

Commuting,      $-4x = 7x - 7x + 16$

Additive inverse property,      $-4x = 0 + 16$

Additive identity property,      $-4x = 16$

Dividing both sides by $-4$,      $x = {}^{16}\!/_{-4}$

$$x = -4$$

Check: Replacing $x$ by $-4$ in the original equation:

$$
\begin{aligned}
3x - 8 &= 7x + 8 \\
3(-4) - 8 &= 7(-4) + 8 \\
-12 - 8 &= -28 + 8 \\
-20 &= -20
\end{aligned}
$$

## LINEAR EQUATIONS

A linear equation with one unknown is one that can be put into the form $ax + b = 0$, where $a$ and $b$ are constants, $a \neq 0$.

To solve a linear equation means to transform it in the form $x = {}^{-b}/_a$.

A) If the equation has unknowns on both sides of the equality, it is convenient to put similar terms on the same sides. E.g.,

$$4x + 3 = 2x + 9$$

$$4x + 3 - 2x = 2x + 9 - 2x$$

$$(4x - 2x) + 3 = (2x - 2x) + 9$$

$$2x + 3 = 0 + 9$$

$$2x + 3 - 3 = 0 + 9 - 3$$

$$2x = 6$$

$${}^{2x}/_2 = {}^6/_2$$

$$x = 3.$$

B) If the equation appears in fractional form, it is necessary to transform it, using cross-multiplication, and then repeating the same procedure as in A), we obtain:

$$\frac{3x + 4}{3} \quad \diagup\!\!\!\!\diagdown \quad \frac{7x + 2}{5}$$

By using cross-multiplication we would obtain:

$$3(7x + 2) = 5(3x + 4).$$

This is equivalent to:

$$21x + 6 = 15x + 20,$$

which can be solved as in A):

$$21x + 6 = 15x + 20$$

$$21x - 15x + 6 = 15x - 15x + 20$$

$$6x + 6 - 6 = 20 - 6$$

$$6x = 14$$

$$x = {}^{14}/_6$$

$$x = {}^7/_3$$

C)   If there are radicals in the equation, it is necessary to square both sides and then apply A)

$$\sqrt{3x + 1} = 5$$

$$\left(\sqrt{3x + 1}\right)^2 = 5^2$$

$$3x + 1 = 25$$

$$3x + 1 - 1 = 25 - 1$$

$$3x = 24$$

$$x = {}^{24}/_3$$

$$x = 8$$

## PROBLEM

Solve the equation $2(x + 3) = (3x + 5) - (x - 5)$.

### Solution

We transform the given equation to an equivalent equation where we can easily recognize the solution set.

$$2(x + 3) = 3x + 5 - (x - 5)$$

Distribute,                  $2x + 6 = 3x + 5 - x + 5$

Combine terms,               $2x + 6 = 2x + 10$

Subtract $2x$ from both sides,     $6 = 10$

Since $6 = 10$ is not a true statement, there is no real number which will make the original equation true. The equation is inconsistent and the solution set is $\phi$, the empty set.

## PROBLEM

Solve the equation $2(^2/_3\, y + 5) + 2(y + 5) = 130$.

## Solution

The procedure for solving this equation is as follows:

$$^4/_3 y + 10 + 2y + 10 \;=\; 130, \quad \text{Distributive property}$$

$$^4/_3 y + 2y + 20 \;=\; 130, \quad \text{Combining like terms}$$

$$^4/_3 y + 2y \;=\; 110, \quad \text{Subtracting 20 from both sides}$$

$$^4/_3 y + {}^6/_3 y \;=\; 110, \quad \begin{array}{l}\text{Converting } 2y \text{ into a fraction with} \\ \text{denominator } 3\end{array}$$

$$^{10}/_3 y \;=\; 110, \quad \text{Combining like terms}$$

$$y = 110 \cdot {}^3/_{10} \;=\; 33, \quad \text{Dividing by } {}^{10}/_3$$

Check: Replace $y$ by 33 in the original equation,

$$2(^2/_3(33) + 5) + 2(33 + 5) \;=\; 130$$

$$2(22 + 5) + 2(38) \;=\; 130$$

$$2(27) + 76 \;=\; 130$$

$$54 + 76 \;=\; 130$$

$$130 \;=\; 130$$

Therefore the solution to the given equation is $y = 33$.

## TWO LINEAR EQUATIONS

Equations of the form $ax + by = c$, where $a, b, c$ are constants and $a, b \neq 0$ are called linear equations with two unknown variables.

There are several ways to solve systems of linear equations in two variables:

**Method 1:** Addition or subtraction – if necessary multiply the equations by numbers that will make the coefficients of one unknown in the resulting equations numerically equal. If the signs of equal coefficients are the same, subtract the equation, otherwise add.

The result is one equation with one unknown; we solve it and substitute the value into the other equations to find the unknown that we first eliminated.

**Method 2**: Substitution — find the value of one unknown in terms of the other, substitute this value in the other equation and solve.

**Method 3**: Graph — graph both equations. The point of intersection of the drawn lines is a simultaneous solution for the equations and its coordinates correspond to the answer that would be found analytically.

If the lines are parallel they have no simultaneous solution.

Dependent equations are equations that represent the same line, therefore every point on the line of a dependent equation represents a solution. Since there is an infinite number of points there is an infinite number of simultaneous solutions, for example

$$\begin{cases} 2x + y = 8 \\ 4x + 2y = 16 \end{cases}$$

The equations above are dependent, they represent the same line, all points that satisfy either of the equations are solutions of the system.

A system of linear equations is consistent if there is only one solution for the system.

A system of linear equations is inconsistent if it does not have any solutions.

Example of a consistent system. Find the point of intersection of the graphs of the equations:

$$x + y = 3,$$

$$3x - 2y = 14$$

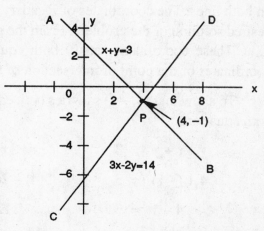

To solve these linear equations, solve for $y$ in terms of $x$. The equations will be in the form $y = mx + b$, where $m$ is the slope and $b$ is the intercept on the $y$-axis.

$$x + y = 3$$

$$y = 3 - x \qquad \text{subtract } x \text{ from both sides}$$

$$3x - 2y = 14 \qquad \text{subtract } 3x \text{ from both sides}$$

$$-2y = 14 - 3x \qquad \text{divide by} - 2.$$

$$y = -7 + \tfrac{3}{2}x$$

The graphs of the linear functions, $y = 3 - x$ and $y = -7 + \tfrac{3}{2}x$ can be determined by plotting only two points. For example, for $y = 3 - x$, let $x = 0$, then $y = 3$. Let $x = 1$, then $y = 2$. The two points on this first line are $(0, 3)$ and $(1, 2)$. For $y = -7 + \tfrac{3}{2}x$, let $x = 0$, then $y = -7$. Let $x = 1$, then $y = -5\tfrac{1}{2}$. The two points on this second line are $(0, -7)$ and $(1, -5\tfrac{1}{2})$.

To find the point of intersection $P$ of

$$x + y = 3 \quad \text{and} \quad 3x - 2y = 14,$$

solve them algebraically. Multiply the first equation by 2. Add these two equations to eliminate the variable $y$.

$$
\begin{array}{r}
2x + 2y = 6 \\
3x - 2y = 14 \\
\hline
5x \quad\;\; = 20
\end{array}
$$

Solve for $x$ to obtain $x = 4$. Substitute this into $y = 3 - x$ to get $y = 3 - 4 = -1$. $P$ is $(4, -1)$. $AB$ is the graph of the first equation, and $CD$ is the graph of the second equation. The point of intersection $P$ of the two graphs is the only point on both lines. The coordinates of $P$ satisfy both equations and represent the desired solution of the problem. From the graph, $P$ seems to be the point $(4, -1)$. These coordinates satisfy both equations, and hence are the exact coordinates of the point of intersection of the two lines.

To show that $(4, -1)$ satisfies both equations, substitute this point into both equations.

| | |
|---|---|
| $x + y = 3$ | $3x - 2y = 14$ |
| $4 + (-1) = 3$ | $3(4) - 2(-1) = 14$ |
| $4 - 1 = 3$ | $12 + 2 = 14$ |
| $3 = 3$ | $14 = 14$ |

Example of an inconsistent system. Solve the equations $2x + 3y = 6$ and $4x + 6y = 7$ simultaneously.

We have 2 equations in 2 unknowns,

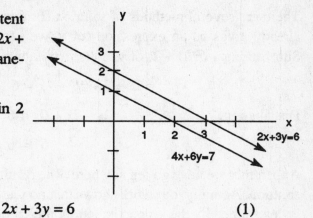

$$2x + 3y = 6 \qquad (1)$$

and

$$4x + 6y = 7 \qquad (2)$$

There are several methods to solve this problem. We have chosen to multiply each equation by a different number so that when the two equations are added, one of the variables drops out. Thus

multiplying equation (1) by 2: $\qquad 4x + 6y = \phantom{-}12 \qquad (3)$

multiplying equation (2) by $-1$: $\qquad \underline{-4x - 6y = \phantom{-}-7} \qquad (4)$

adding equations (3) and (4): $\qquad\qquad\quad 0 = \phantom{-}5$

We obtain a peculiar result!

Actually, what we have shown in this case is that if there were a simultaneous solution to the given equations, then 0 would equal 5. But the conclusion is impossible; therefore there can be no simultaneous solution to these two equations, hence no point satisfying both.

The straight lines which are the graphs of these equations must be parallel if they never intersect, but not identical, which can be seen from the graph of these equations (see the accompanying diagram).

Example of a dependent system. Solve the equations $2x + 3y = 6$ and $y = -\left(\frac{2x}{3}\right) + 2$ simultaneously.

We have 2 equations in 2 unknowns.

$$2x + 3y = 6 \qquad (1)$$

and

$$y = -\left(\frac{2x}{3}\right) + 2 \qquad (2)$$

There are several methods of solution for this problem. Since equation (2) already gives us an expression for $y$, we use the method of substitution. Substituting $-(^{2x}/_3) + 2$ for $y$ in the first equation:

$$2x + 3(-^{2x}/_3 + 2) = 6$$

Distributing, $\qquad\qquad\qquad 2x - 2x + 6 = 6$

$$6 = 6$$

Apparently we have gotten nowhere! The result $6 = 6$ is true, but indicates no solution. Actually, our work shows that no matter what real number $x$ is, if $y$ is determined by the second equation, then the first equation will always be satisfied.

The reason for this peculiarity may be seen if we take a closer look at the equation $y = -(^{2x}/_3) + 2$. It is equivalent to $3y = -2x + 6$, or $2x + 3y = 6$.

In other words, the two equations are equivalent. Any pair of values of $x$ and $y$ which satisfies one satisfies the other.

It is hardly necessary to verify that in this case the graphs of the given equations are identical lines, and that there are an infinite number of simultaneous solutions of these equations.

A system of three linear equations in three unknowns is solved by eliminating one unknown from any two of the three equations and solving them. After finding two unknowns substitute them in any of the equations to find the third unknown.

**PROBLEM**

---

Solve the system

$$2x + 3y - 4z = -8 \qquad\qquad\qquad (1)$$

$$x + y - 2z = -5 \qquad\qquad\qquad (2)$$

$$7x - 2y + 5z = 4 \qquad\qquad\qquad (3)$$

---

*Solution*

We cannot eliminate any variable from two pairs of equations by a

single multiplication. However, both $x$ and $z$ may be eliminated from equations 1 and 2 by multiplying equation 2 by $-2$. Then

$$2x + 3y - 4z = -8 \tag{1}$$

$$-2x - 2y + 4z = 10 \tag{4}$$

By addition, we have $y = 2$. Although we may now eliminate either $x$ or $z$ from another pair of equations, we can more conveniently substitute $y = 2$ in equations 2 and 3 to get two equations in two variables. Thus, making the substitution $y = 2$ in equations 2 and 3, we have

$$x - 2z = -7 \tag{5}$$

$$7x + 5z = 8 \tag{6}$$

Multiply (5) by 5 and multiply (6) by 2. Then add the two new equations. Then $x = -1$. Substitute $x$ in either (5) or (6) to find $z$.

The solution of the system is $x = -1$, $y = 2$, and $z = 3$. Check by substitution.

A system of equations, as shown below, that has all constant terms $b_1$, $b_2$, ..., $b_n$ equal to zero is said to be a homogeneous system:

$$\begin{cases} a_{11}x_1 + a_{12}x_2 + \ldots + a_{1n}x_m = b_1 \\ a_{21}x_1 + a_{22}x_2 + \ldots + a_{2n}x_m = b_2 \\ \quad\vdots \qquad\quad \vdots \qquad\qquad\quad \vdots \qquad\quad \vdots \\ a_{n1}x_1 + a_{n2}x_2 + \ldots + a_{nn}x_m = b_n. \end{cases}$$

A homogeneous system always has at least one solution which is called the trivial solution that is $x_1 = 0$, $x_2 = 0$, ..., $x_m = 0$.

For any given homogeneous system of equations, in which the number of variables is greater than or equal to the number of equations, there are non-trivial solutions.

Two systems of linear equations are said to be equivalent if and only if they have the same solution set.

**PROBLEM**

---

Solve for $x$ and $y$.

$x + 2y = 8$                                     (1)

$3x + 4y = 20$                               (2)

---

*Solution*

Solve equation (1) for $x$ in terms of $y$:

$$x = 8 - 2y \qquad (3)$$

Substitute $(8 - 2y)$ for $x$ in (2):

$$3(8 - 2y) + 4y = 20 \qquad (4)$$

Solve (4) for $y$ as follows:

Distribute:                   $24 - 6y + 4y = 20$

Combine like terms and then subtract 24 from both sides:

$$
\begin{aligned}
24 - 2y &= 20 \\
24 - 24 - 2y &= 20 - 24 \\
-2y &= -4
\end{aligned}
$$

Divide both sides by $-2$:

$$y = 2$$

Substitute 2 for $y$ in equation (1):

$$
\begin{aligned}
x + 2(2) &= 8 \\
x &= 4
\end{aligned}
$$

Thus, our solution is $x = 4$, $y = 2$.

Check: Substitute $x = 4$, $y = 2$ in equations (1) and (2):

$$
\begin{aligned}
4 + 2(2) &= 8 \\
8 &= 8 \\
3(4) + 4(2) &= 20 \\
20 &= 20
\end{aligned}
$$

**PROBLEM**

Solve algebraically:

$$\begin{cases} 4x + 2y = -1 & (1) \\ 5x - 3y = 7 & (2) \end{cases}$$

**Solution**

We arbitrarily choose to eliminate $x$ first.

Multiply (1) by 5: $\qquad\qquad\qquad 20x + 10y = -5 \qquad\qquad (3)$

Multiply (2) by 4: $\qquad\qquad\qquad 20x - 12y = 28 \qquad\qquad (4)$

Subtract (3) − (4): $\qquad\qquad\qquad\qquad 22y = -33 \qquad\qquad (5)$

Divide (5) by 22: $\qquad\qquad\qquad y = -{}^{33}/_{22} = -{}^{3}/_{2},$

To find $x$, substitute $y = -{}^{3}/_{2}$ in either of the original equations. If we use Eq. (1), we obtain $4x + 2(-{}^{3}/_{2}) = -1$, $4x - 3 = -1$, $4x = 2$, $x = {}^{1}/_{2}$.

The solution $({}^{1}/_{2}, -{}^{3}/_{2})$ should be checked in both equations of the given system.

Replacing $({}^{1}/_{2}, -{}^{3}/_{2})$ in Eq. (1):

$$\begin{aligned} 4x + 2y &= -1 \\ 4({}^{1}/_{2}) + 2(-{}^{3}/_{2}) &= -1 \\ {}^{4}/_{2} - 3 &= -1 \\ 2 - 3 &= -1 \\ -1 &= -1 \end{aligned}$$

Replacing $({}^{1}/_{2}, -{}^{3}/_{2})$ in Eq. (2):

$$\begin{aligned} 5x - 3y &= 7 \\ 5({}^{1}/_{2}) - 3(-{}^{3}/_{2}) &= 7 \\ {}^{5}/_{2} + {}^{9}/_{2} &= 7 \\ {}^{14}/_{2} &= 7 \\ 7 &= 7 \end{aligned}$$

(Instead of eliminating $x$ from the two given equations, we could have eliminated $y$ by multiplying Eq. (1) by 3, multiplying Eq. (2) by 2, and then adding the two derived equations.)

## QUADRATIC EQUATIONS

A second degree equation in $x$ of the type $ax^2 + bx + c = 0$, $a \neq 0$, $a, b$ and $c$ are real numbers, is called a quadratic equation.

To solve a quadratic equation is to find values of $x$ which satisfiy $ax^2 + bx + c = 0$. These values of $x$ are called solutions, or roots, of the equation.

A quadratic equation has a maximum of 2 roots. Methods of solving quadratic equations:

A) Direct solution: Given $x^2 - 9 = 0$.

We can solve directly by isolating the variable $x$:

$$x^2 = 9$$

$$x = \pm 3.$$

B) Factoring; given a quadratic equation $ax^2 + bx + c = 0$, $a, b, c \neq 0$, to factor means to express it as the product $a(x - r_1)(x - r_2) = 0$, where $r_1$ and $r_2$ are the two roots.

Some helpful hints to remember are:

a) $r_1 + r_2 = {}^{-b}/_a$.

b) $r_1 r_2 = {}^{c}/_a$.

Given $x^2 - 5x + 4 = 0$.

Since $r_1 + r_2 = {}^{-b}/_a = {}^{-(-5)}/_1 = 5$, so the possible solutions are $(3, 2)$, $(4, 1)$ and $(5, 0)$. Also $r_1 r_2 = {}^{c}/_a = {}^{4}/_1 = 4$; this equation is satisfied only by the second pair, so $r_1 = 4$, $r_2 = 1$ and the factored form is $(x - 4)(x - 1) = 0$.

If the coefficient of $x^2$ is not 1, it is necessary to divide the equation by this coefficient and then factor.

Given $2x^2 - 12x + 16 = 0$

Dividing by 2, we obtain:

$$x^2 - 6x + 8 = 0$$

Since $r_1 + r_2 = {}^{-b}/_a = 6$, the possible solutions are $(6, 0)$, $(5, 1)$, $(4, 2)$, $(3, 3)$. Also $r_1 r_2 = 8$, so the only possible answer is $(4, 2)$ and the expression $x^2 - 6x + 8 = 0$ can be factored as $(x - 4)(x - 2)$.

C)   Completing the Squares:

If it is difficult to factor the quadratic equation using the previous method, we can complete the squares.

Given $x^2 - 12x + 8 = 0$.

We know that the two roots added up should be 12 because $r_1 + r_2 = {}^-$ $^b/_a = {}^{-(-12)}/_1 = 12$. The possible roots are (12, 0), (11, 1), (10, 2), (9, 3), (8,4), (7,5), (6, 6).

But none of these satisfy $r_1 r_2 = 8$, so we cannot use (B).

To complete the square, it is necessary to isolate the constant term,

$$x^2 - 12x = -8.$$

Then take $^1/_2$ coeffocient of $x$, square it and add to both sides

$$x^2 - 12x + \left(\frac{-12}{2}\right)^2 = -8 + \left(\frac{-12}{2}\right)^2$$

$$x^2 - 12x + 36 = -8 + 36 = 28.$$

Now we can use the previous method to factor the left side: $r_1 + r_2 = 12$, $r_1 r_2 = 36$ is satisfied by the pair (6, 6), so we have:

$$(x - 6)^2 = 28.$$

Now extract the root of both sides and solve for $x$.

$$(x - 6) = \pm \sqrt{28} = \pm 2\sqrt{7}$$
$$x = \pm 2\sqrt{7} + 6$$

So the roots are:

$$x = 2\sqrt{7} + 6, \ x = -2\sqrt{7} + 6.$$

**PROBLEM**

Solve the equation $x^2 + 8x + 15 = 0$.

*Solution*

Since $(x + a)(x + b) = x^2 + bx + ax + ab = x^2 + (a + b)x + ab$, we may

factor the given equation, $0 = x^2 + 8x + 15$, replacing $a + b$ by 8 and $ab$ by 15. Thus,

$$a + b = 8, \quad \text{and} \quad ab = 15.$$

We want the two numbers $a$ and $b$ whose sum is 8 and whose product is 15. We check all pairs of numbers whose product is 15:

(a)  $1 \cdot 15 = 15$; thus $a = 1$, $b = 15$ and $ab = 15$.

   $1 + 15 = 16$, therefore we reject these values because $a + b \neq 8$.

(b)  $3 \cdot 5 = 15$, thus $a = 3$, $b = 5$, and $ab = 15$.

   $3 + 5 = 8$. Therefore $a + b = 8$, and we accept these values.

Hence $x^2 + 8x + 15 = 0$ is equivalent to

$$0 = x^2 + (3 + 5)x + 3 \cdot 5 = (x + 3)(x + 5)$$

Hence,    $x + 5 = 0 \ \text{ or } \ x + 3 = 0$

since the product of these two numbers is zero, one of the numbers must be zero. Hence, $x = -5$, or $x = -3$, and the solution set is $x = \{-5, -3\}$.

The student should note that $x = -5$ or $x = -3$. We are certainly not making the statement, that $x = -5$, and $x = -3$. Also, the student should check that both these numbers do actually satisfy the given equations and hence are solutions.

Check: Replacing $x$ by $(-5)$ in the original equation:

$$\begin{aligned}
x^2 + 8x + 15 &= 0 \\
(-5)^2 + 8(-5) + 15 &= 0 \\
25 - 40 + 15 &= 0 \\
-15 + 15 &= 0 \\
0 &= 0
\end{aligned}$$

Replacing $x$ by $(-3)$ in the original equation:

$$\begin{aligned}
x^2 + 8x + 15 &= 0 \\
(-3)^2 + 8(-3) + 15 &= 0 \\
9 - 24 + 15 &= 0 \\
-15 + 15 &= 0 \\
0 &= 0.
\end{aligned}$$

**PROBLEM**

Solve the following equations by factoring.

(a)   $2x^2 + 3x = 0$          (c)   $z^2 - 2z - 3 = 0$

(b)   $y^2 - 2y - 3 = y - 3$          (d)   $2m^2 - 11m - 6 = 0$

*Solution*

(a)   $2x^2 + 3x = 0$. Factoring out the common factor of $x$ from the left side of the given equation,

$$x(2x + 3) = 0.$$

Whenever a product $ab = 0$, where $a$ and $b$ are any two numbers, either $a = 0$ or $b = 0$. Then, either

$$
\begin{aligned}
x = 0 \quad \text{or} \quad 2x + 3 &= 0 \\
2x &= -3 \\
x &= -^3/_2
\end{aligned}
$$

Hence, the solution set to the original equation $2x^2 + 3x = 0$ is: $\{-^3/_2, 0\}$.

(b)   $y^2 - 2y - 3 = y - 3$. Subtract $(y - 3)$ from both sides of the given equation:

$$
\begin{aligned}
y^2 - 2y - 3 - (y - 3) &= y - 3 - (y - 3) \\
y^2 - 2y - 3 - y + 3 &= y - 3 - y + 3 \\
y^2 - 3y &= 0.
\end{aligned}
$$

Factor out a common factor of $y$ from the left side of this equation:

$$y(y - 3) = 0.$$

Thus, $y = 0$ or $y - 3 = 0$, $y = 3$.

Therefore, the solution set to the original equation $y^2 - 2y - 3 = y - 3$ is: $\{0, 3\}$.

(c)   $z^2 - 2z - 3 = 0$. Factor the original equation into a product of two polynomials:

$$z^2 - 2z - 3 = (z - 3)(z + 1) = 0$$

Hence,

$$
\begin{aligned}
(z - 3)(z + 1) = 0; \text{ and } z - 3 &= 0 \text{ or } z + 1 = 0 \\
z = 3 \qquad & \qquad z = -1
\end{aligned}
$$

Therefore, the solution set to the original equation $z^2 - 2z - 3 = 0$ is: $\{-1, 3\}$.

(d) $2m^2 - 11m - 6 = 0$. Factor the original equation into a product of two polynomials:

$$2m^2 - 11m - 6 = (2m + 1)(m - 6) = 0$$

Thus,

$$2m + 1 = 0 \quad \text{or} \quad m - 6 = 0$$
$$2m = -1 \qquad\qquad m = 6$$
$$m = {}^{-1}/_2$$

Therefore, the solution set to the original equation $2m^2 - 11m - 6 = 0$ is: $\{-^1/_2, 6\}$.

## 3. ABSOLUTE VALUE

The absolute value of a real number $A$ is defined as follows:

$$|A| = \begin{cases} A & \text{if } A \geq 0 \\ -A & \text{if } A < 0 \end{cases}$$

**EXAMPLE**

$|5| = 5, |-8| = -(-8) = 8.$

Absolute values follow the given rules:

A) $|-A| = |A|$

B) $|A| \geq 0$, equality holding only if $A = 0$

C) $\left|\dfrac{A}{B}\right| = \dfrac{|A|}{|B|}, B \neq 0$

D) $|AB| = |A| \times |B|$

E) $|A|^2 = A^2$

Absolute value can also be expressed on the real number line as the distance of the point represented by the real number from the point labeled 0.

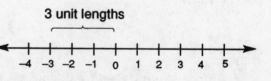

3 unit lengths

So $|-3| = 3$ because $-3$ is 3 units to the left of 0.

**PROBLEM**

Classify each of the following statements as true or false. If it is false, explain why.

(1)  $|-120| > 1$

(4)  $|12 - 3| = 12 - 3$

(2)  $|4 - 12| = |4| - |12|$

(5)  $|-12a| = 12|a|$

(3)  $|4 - 9| = 9 - 4$

*Solution*

(1)  True.

(2)  False,  $\quad |4 - 12| = |4| - |12|$

$$|-8| = 4 - 12$$

$$8 \neq -8$$

In general, $|a + b| \neq |a| + |b|$

(3)  True.

(4)  True.

(5)  True.

**PROBLEM**

Calculate the value of each of the following expressions:

(1)  $||2 - 5| + 6 - 14|$

(2)  $|-5| \cdot |4| + \dfrac{|-12|}{4}$

(3)  $1.6\% + 18\% + 12(26 - (1 - 3) + |-2|)$

(4)  $\frac{1}{6} \times 1.25 - (12.5 + 4\frac{1}{2}) \div 50\%$

*Solution*

Before solving this problem, one must remember the order of operations: parenthesis, multiplication and division, addition and subtraction.

(1) $||-3|+6-14|=|3+6-14|=|9-14|=|-5|=5$

(2) $(5 \times 4) + {}^{12}/_4 = 20 + 3 = 23$

(3) $0.016 + 0.18 + 12(26 - (-2) \div 2)$

$0.016 + 0.18 + 12(26 - (-1))$

$0.196 + 12(27) = 0.196 + 324 = 324.196$

(4) $\dfrac{1.25}{6} - \left(12.5 + \dfrac{9}{2}\right) \div 0.5 = \dfrac{1.25}{6} - \left(\dfrac{34}{2}\right)\left(\dfrac{2}{1}\right)$

$\dfrac{1.25}{6} - 34 = \dfrac{1.25}{6} - \dfrac{204}{6} = -33.792$

## 4. INEQUALITIES

An inequality is a statement that the value of one quantity or expression is greater than (>), less than (<), greater than or equal to (≥) less than or equal to (≤), and not equal to (≠).

**EXAMPLE**

$5 > 4.$

The expression above means that the value of 5 is greater than the value of 4.

A conditional inequality is an inequality whose validity depends on the values of the variables in the sentence. That is, certain values of the variables will make the sentence true, and others will make it false. $3 - y > 3 + y$ is a conditional inequality for the set of real numbers, since it is true for any replacement less than zero and false for all others.

$x + 5 > x + 2$ is an absolute inequality for the set of real numbers, meaning that for any real value $x$, the expression on the left is greater than the expression on the right.

$5y < 2y + y$ is inconsistent for the set of non-negative real numbers. For any $y$ greater than 0 the sentence is always false. A sentence is inconsistent if it is always false when its variables assume allowable values.

The solution of a given inequality in one variable $x$ consists of all values of $x$ for which the inequality is true.

The graph of an inequality in one variable is represented by either a ray or a line segment on the real number line.

The endpoint is not a solution if the variable is strictly less than or greater than a particular value.

## EXAMPLE

$x > 2$

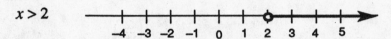

2 is not a solution and should be represented as shown.

The endpoint is a solution if the variable is either (1) less than or equal to or (2) greater than or equal to, a particular value.

## EXAMPLE

$5 > x \geq 2$

In this case 2 is the solution and should be represented as shown.

## PROPERTIES OF INEQUALITIES

If $x$ and $y$ are real numbers then one and only one of the following statements is true.

$$x > y, x = y \text{ or } x < y.$$

This is the order property of real numbers.

If $a$, $b$ and $c$ are real numbers:

A)    If $a < b$ and $b < c$ then $a < c$.

B)    If $a > b$ and $b > c$ then $a > c$.

This is the transitive property of inequalities.

If $a$, $b$ and $c$ are real numbers and $a > b$ then $a + c > b + c$ and $a - c > b - c$. This is the addition property of inequality.

Two inequalities are said to have the same sense if their signs of inequality point in the same direction.

73

The sense of an inequality remains the same if both sides are multiplied or divided by the same positive real number.

**EXAMPLE**

$4 > 3$

If we multiply both sides by 5 we will obtain:

$$4 \times 5 > 3 \times 5$$

$$20 > 15$$

The sense of the inequality does not change.

The sense of an inequality becomes opposite if each side is multiplied or divided by the same negative real number.

**EXAMPLE**

$4 > 3$

If we multiply both sides by $-5$ we would obtain:

$$4 \times -5 < 3 \times -5$$

$$-20 < -15$$

The sense of the inequality becomes opposite.

If $a > b$ and $a$, $b$ and $n$ are positive real numbers, then:

$$a^n > b^n \text{ and } a^{-n} < b^{-n}$$

If $x > y$ and $q > p$ then $x + q > y + p$.

If $x > y > 0$ and $q > p > 0$ then $xq > yp$.

Inequalities that have the same solution set are called equivalent inequalities.

*PROBLEM*

Solve the inequality $2x + 5 > 9$.

### Solution

$$2x + 5 + (-5) > 9 + (-5).$$      Adding − 5 to both sides.

$$2x + 0 > 9 + (-5)$$      Additive inverse property

$$2x > 9 + (-5)$$      Additive identity property

$$2x > 4$$      Combining terms

$$\tfrac{1}{2}(2x) > \tfrac{1}{2} \cdot 4$$      Multiplying both sides by $\tfrac{1}{2}$.

$$x > 2$$

The solution set is

$$X = \{x \mid 2x + 5 > 9\}$$

$$= \{x \mid x > 2\}$$

(that is all $x$, such that $x$ is greater than 2).

### PROBLEM

Solve the inequality $4x + 3 < 6x + 8$.

### Solution

In order to solve the inequality $4x + 3 < 6x + 8$, we must find all values of $x$ which make it true. Thus, we wish to obtain $x$ alone on one side of the inequality.

Add − 3 to both sides:

$$
\begin{array}{r}
4x + 3 < 6x + 8 \\
-3 \qquad -3 \\
\hline
4x < 6x + 5
\end{array}
$$

Add − 6x to both sides:

$$
\begin{array}{r}
4x < \quad 6x + 5 \\
-6x \qquad -6x \\
\hline
-2x < \quad 5
\end{array}
$$

In order to obtain $x$ alone we must divide both sides by $(-2)$. Recall that dividing an inequality by a negative number reverses the inequality sign, hence

$$\frac{-2x}{-2} > \frac{5}{-2}$$

Cancelling $^{-2}/_{-2}$ we obtain, $x > -\,^5/_2$.

Thus, our solution is $\{x : x > -\,^5/_2\}$ (the set of all $x$ such that $x$ is greater than $-\,^5/_2$).

# GEOMETRY

## 1. Lines and Angles

A line in geometry is defined as a straight line.

If $A$ and $B$ are two points on a line, then the line segment $AB$ is the set of points on that line between $A$ and $B$ and including $A$ and $B$, which are called the endpoints. The line segment is referred to as $\overline{AB}$.

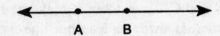

**PROBLEM**

> How many lines can be found that contain (a) one given point (b) two given points (c) three given points?

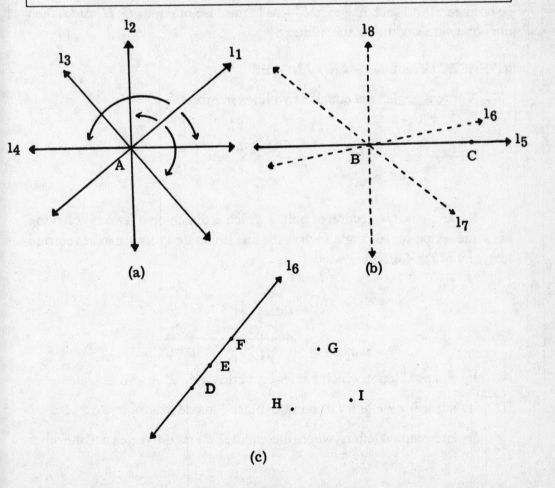

### Solution

(a)   Given one point $A$, there are an infinite number of distinct lines that contain the given point. To see this, consider line $l_1$ passing through point $A$. By rotating $l_1$ around $A$ like the hands of a clock, we obtain different lines $l_2$, $l_3$, etc. Since we can rotate $l_1$ in infinitely many ways, there are infinitely many lines containing $A$.

(b)   Given two distinct points $B$ and $C$, there is one and only one distinct line. To see this, consider all the lines containing point $B$; $l_5$, $l_6$, $l_7$ and $l_8$. Only $l_5$ contains both points $B$ and $C$. Thus, there is only one line containing both points $B$ and $C$. Since there is always at least one line containing two distinct points and never more than one, the line passing through the two points is said to be determined by the two points.

(c)   Given three distinct points, there may be one line or none. If a line exists that contains the three points, such as $D$, $E$, and $F$, then the points are said to be colinear. If no such line exists — as in the case of points $G$, $H$, and $I$, then the points are said to be noncolinear.

## INTERSECTING LINES AND ANGLES

Vertical angles are equal if two lines intersect.

$$\angle a = \angle b$$

An angle is a collection of points which is the union of two rays having the same endpoint. An angle such as the one illustrated below can be referred to in any of the following ways:

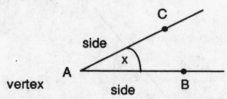

A)   by a capital letter which names its vertex, i.e., $\angle A$;

B)   by a lower-case letter or number placed inside the angle, i.e., $\angle x$;

C)   by three capital letters, where the middle letter is the vertex and the other

two letters are not on the same ray, i.e., ∠ *CAB* or ∠ *BAC*, both of which represent the angle illustrated in the figure.

Two angles with a common vertex and a common side, but no common interior points are called adjacent angles.

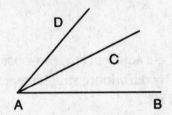

In the above figure, ∠ *DAC* and ∠ *BAC* are adjacent angles; *DAB* and *BAC* are not adjacent angles.

An acute angle is an angle whose measure is larger than 0° but smaller than 90°.

An angle whose measure is 90° is called a right angle.

An obtuse angle is an angle whose measure is larger than 90° but less than 180°.

An angle whose measure is 180° is called a straight angle. Such an angle is, in fact, a straight line.

An angle whose measure is greater than 180° but less than 360° is called a reflex angle.

Complementary angles are two angles, the sum of the measures of which equals 90°.

Supplementary angles are two angles, the sum of the measures of which equals 180°.

Congruent angles are angles of equal measure.

**PROBLEM**

In the figure, we are given $\overleftrightarrow{AB}$ and triangle *ABC*. We are told that the measure of ∠ 1 is five times the measure of ∠ 2. Determine the measures of ∠ 1 and ∠ 2.

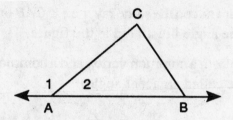

**Solution**

Since ∠ 1 and ∠ 2 are adjacent angles whose non-common sides lie on a straight line, they are, by definition, supplementary. As supplements, their measures must sum to 180°.

If we let $x$ = the measure of ∠2, then, $5x$ = the measure of ∠ 1.

To determine the respective angle measures, set $x + 5x = 180$ and solve for $x$. $6x = 180$. Therefore, $x = 30$ and $5x = 150$.

Therefore, the measure of ∠ 1 = 150 and the measure of ∠ 2 = 30.

## PERPENDICULAR LINES

Two lines are said to be perpendicular if they intersect and form right angles. The symbol for perpendicular (or, is therefore perpendicular to) is ⊥; $\overleftrightarrow{AB}$ is perpendicular to $\overleftrightarrow{CD}$ is written $\overleftrightarrow{AB} \perp \overleftrightarrow{CD}$.

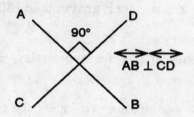

**PROBLEM**

We are given straight lines $\overleftrightarrow{AB}$ and $\overleftrightarrow{CD}$ intersecting at point $P$. $\overleftrightarrow{PR} \perp \overleftrightarrow{AB}$ and the measure of ∠ $APD$ is 170°. Find the measures of ∠ 1, ∠ 2, ∠ 3, and ∠ 4. (See figure on top of next page.)

**Solution**

This problem will involve making use of several of the properties of supplementary and vertical angles, as well as perpendicular lines.

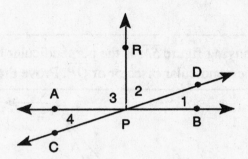

$\angle APD$ and $\angle 1$ are adjacent angles whose non-common sides lie on a straight line, $\overleftrightarrow{AB}$. Therefore, they are supplements and their measures sum to 180°.

$$m \angle APD + m \angle 1 = 180°.$$

We know $m \angle APD = 170°$. Therefore, by substitution, $170° + m \angle 1 = 180°$. This implies $m \angle 1 = 10°$.

$\angle 1$ and $\angle 4$ are vertical angles because they are formed by the intersection of two straight lines, $\overleftrightarrow{CD}$ and $\overleftrightarrow{AB}$, and their sides form two pairs of opposite rays. As vertical angles, they are, by theorem, of equal measure. Since $m \angle 1 = 10°$, then $m \angle 4 = 10°$.

Since $\overleftrightarrow{PR} \perp \overleftrightarrow{AB}$, at their intersection the angles formed must be right angles. Therefore, $\angle 3$ is a right angle and its measure is 90°. $m \angle 3 = 90°$.

The figure shows us that $\angle APD$ is composed of $\angle 3$ and $\angle 2$. Since the measure of the whole must be equal to the sum of the measures of its parts, $m \angle APD = m \angle 3 + m \angle 2$. We know the $m \angle APD = 170°$ and $m \angle 3 = 90°$, therefore, by substitution, we can solve for $m \angle 2$, our last unknown.

$$170° = 90° + m \angle 2$$

$$80° = m \angle 2$$

Therefore, $m \angle 1 = 10°$,         $m \angle 2 = 80°$

$m \angle 3 = 90°$,         $m \angle 4 = 10°$.

**PROBLEM**

> In the accompanying figure $\overline{SM}$ is the perpendicular bisector of $\overline{QR}$, and $\overline{SN}$ is the perpendicular bisector of $\overline{QP}$. Prove that $SR = SP$.

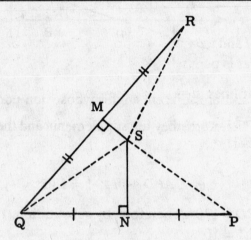

**Solution**

Every point on the perpendicular bisector of a segment is equidistant from the endpoints of the segment.

Since point $S$ is on the perpendicular bisector of $\overline{QR}$,

(I)   $SR = SQ$

Also, since point $S$ is on the perpendicular bisector of $\overline{QP}$,

(II)   $SQ = SP$

By the transitive property (quantities equal to the same quantity are equal), we have:

(III)   $SR = SP$.

**PARALLEL LINES**

Two lines are called parallel lines if, and only if, they are in the same plane (coplanar) and do not intersect. The symbol for parallel, or is parallel to, is ∥; $\overleftrightarrow{AB}$ is parallel to $\overleftrightarrow{CD}$ is written $\overleftrightarrow{AB} \parallel \overleftrightarrow{CD}$.

The distance between two parallel lines is the length of the perpendicular segment from any point on one line to the other line.

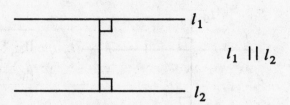

$l_1 \parallel l_2$

Given a line *l* and a point *P* not on line *l*, there is one and only one line through point *P* that is parallel to line *l*.

Two coplanar lines are either intersecting lines or parallel lines.

If two (or more) lines are perpendicular to the same line, then they are parallel to each other.

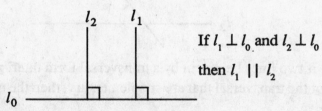

If $l_1 \perp l_0$ and $l_2 \perp l_0$

then $l_1 \parallel l_2$

If two lines are cut by a transversal so that alternate interior angles are equal, the lines are parallel.

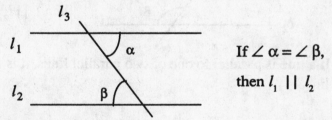

If $\angle \alpha = \angle \beta$,

then $l_1 \parallel l_2$

If two lines are parallel to the same line, then they are parallel to each other.

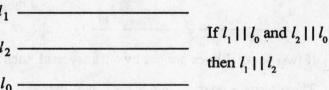

If $l_1 \parallel l_0$ and $l_2 \parallel l_0$

then $l_1 \parallel l_2$

If a line is perpendicular to one of two parallel lines, then it is perpendicular to the other line, too.

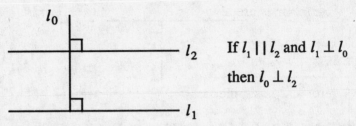

If two lines being cut by a transversal form congruent corresponding angles, then the two lines are parallel.

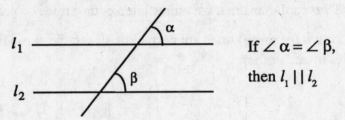

If two lines being cut by a transversal form interior angles on the same side of the transversal that are supplementary, then the two lines are parallel.

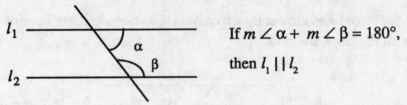

If a line is parallel to one of two parallel lines, it is also parallel to the other line.

If two parallel lines are cut by a transversal, then:

A) The alternate interior angles are congruent.

B) The corresponding angles are congruent.

C) The consecutive interior angles are supplementary.

D) The alternate exterior angles are congruent.

Parallel lines are always the same distance apart.

**PROBLEM**

> Given: $\angle 2$ is supplementary to $\angle 3$.
>
> Prove: $l_1 \parallel l_2$.

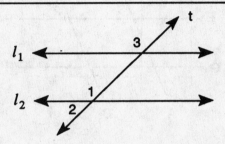

*Solution*

Given two lines intercepted by a transversal, if a pair of corresponding angles are congruent, then the two lines are parallel. In this problem, we will show that since $\angle 1$ and $\angle 2$ are supplementary and $\angle 2$ and $\angle 3$ are supplementary, $\angle 1$ and $\angle 3$ are congruent. Since corresponding angles $\angle 1$ and $\angle 3$ are congruent, it follows $l_1 \parallel l_2$.

| Statement | Reason |
|---|---|
| 1. $\angle 2$ is supplementary to $\angle 3$. | 1. Given. |
| 2. $\angle 1$ is supplementary to $\angle 2$. | 2. Two angles that form a linear pair are supplementary. |
| 3. $\angle 1 \cong \angle 3$ | 3. Angles supplementary to the same angle are congruent. |
| 4. $l_1 \parallel l_2$. | 4. Given two lines intercepted by a transversal, if a pair of corresponding angles are congruent, then the two lines are parallel. |

**PROBLEM**

If line $\overleftrightarrow{AB}$ is parallel to line $\overleftrightarrow{CD}$ and line $\overleftrightarrow{EF}$ is parallel to line $\overleftrightarrow{GH}$, prove that $m \angle 1 = m \angle 2$.

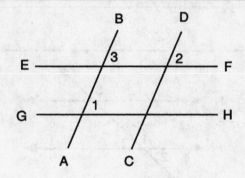

*Solution*

To show $\angle 1 \cong \angle 2$, we relate both to $\angle 3$. Because $\overline{EF} \parallel \overline{GH}$, corresponding angles 1 and 3 are congruent. Since $\overline{AB} \parallel \overline{CD}$, corresponding angles 3 and 2 are congruent. Because both $\angle 1$ and $\angle 2$ are congruent to the same angle, it follows that $\angle 1 \cong \angle 2$.

| Statement | Reason |
|---|---|
| 1. $\overleftrightarrow{EF} \cong \overleftrightarrow{GH}$ | 1. Given. |
| 2. $m \angle 1 = m \angle 3$ | 2. If two parallel lines are cut by a transversal, corresponding angles are of equal measure. |
| 3. $\overleftrightarrow{AB} \parallel \overleftrightarrow{CD}$ | 3. Given. |
| 4. $m \angle 2 = m \angle 3$ | 4. If two parallel lines are cut by a transversal, corresponding angles are equal in measure. |
| 5. $m \angle 1 = m \angle 2$ | 5. If two quantities are equal to the same quantity, they are equal to each other. |

## 2. Polygons (Convex)

A polygon is a figure with the same number of sides as angles.

An equilateral polygon is a polygon all of whose sides are of equal measure.

An equiangular polygon is a polygon all of whose angles are of equal measure.

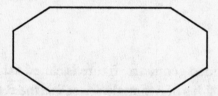

A regular polygon is a polygon that is both equilateral and equiangluar.

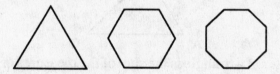

### PROBLEM

Each interior angle of a regular polygon contains 120°. How many sides does the polygon have?

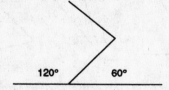

120°    60°

### Solution

At each vertex of a polygon, the exterior angle is supplementary to the interior angle, as shown in the diagram.

Since we are told that the interior angles measure 120 degrees, we can

deduce that the exterior angle measures 60°.

Each exterior angle of a regular polygon of $n$ sides measure $360°/n$ degrees. We know that each exterior angle measures 60°, and, therefore, by setting $360°/n$ equal to 60°, we can determine the number of sides in the polygon. The calculation is as follows:

$$360°/n = 60°$$

$$60°n = 360°$$

$$n = 6.$$

Therefore, the regular polygon, with interior angles of 120°, has 6 sides and is called a hexagon.

## 3. Triangles

A closed three-sided geometric figure is called a triangle. The points of the intersection of the sides of a triangle are called the vertices of the triangle.

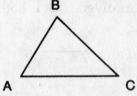

The perimeter of a triangle is the sum of the measures of the sides of the triangle.

A triangle with no equal sides is called a scalene triangle.

A triangle having at least two equal sides is called an isosceles triangle. The third side is called the base of the triangle.

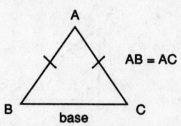

A side of a triangle is a line segment whose endpoints are the vertices of two angles of the triangle.

An interior angle of a triangle is an angle formed by two sides and includes the third side within its collection of points.

An equilateral triangle is a triangle having three equal sides. *AB = AC = BC*

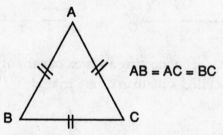

A triangle with one obtuse angle greater than 90° is called an obtuse triangle.

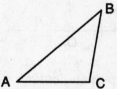

An acute triangle is a triangle with three acute angles (less than 90°).

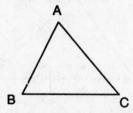

A triangle with a right angle is called a right triangle. The side opposite the right angle in a right triangle is called the hypotenuse of the right triangle. The other two sides are called arms or legs of the right triangle.

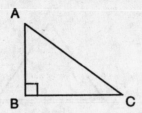

An altitude of a triangle is a line segment from a vertex of the triangle perpendicular to the opposite side.

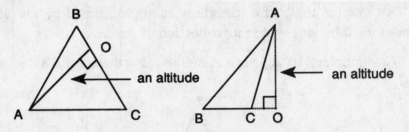

A line segment connecting a vertex of a triangle and the midpoint of the opposite side is called a median of the triangle.

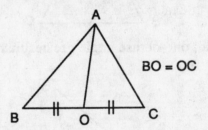

A line that bisects and is perpendicular to a side of a triangle is called a perpendicular bisector of that side.

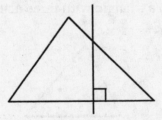

An angle bisector of a triangle is a line that bisects an angle and extends to the opposite side of the triangle.

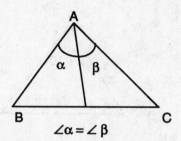

$\angle\alpha = \angle\beta$

The line segment that joins the midpoints of two sides of a triangle is called a midline of the triangle.

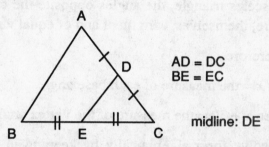

AD = DC
BE = EC

midline: DE

An exterior angle of a triangle is an angle formed outside a triangle by one side of the triangle and the extension of an adjacent side.

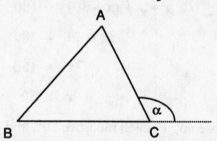

A triangle whose three interior angles have equal measure is said to be equiangular.

Three or more lines (or rays or segments) are concurrent if there exists one point common to all of them, that is, if they all intersect at the same point.

## PROBLEM

The measure of the vertex angle of an isosceles triangle exceeds the measurement of each base angle by 30°. Find the value of each angle of the triangle.

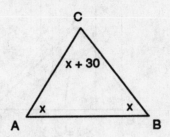

**Solution**

We know that the sum of the values of the angles of a triangle is 180°. In an isosceles triangle, the angles opposite the congruent sides (the base angles) are, themselves, congruent and of equal value.

Therefore,

(1)  Let $x$ = the measure of each base angle.

(2)  Then $x + 30$ = the measure of the vertex angle.

We can solve for $x$ algebraically by keeping in mind the sum of all the measures will be 180°.

$$x + x + (x + 30) = 180$$
$$3x + 30 = 180$$
$$3x = 150$$
$$x = 50$$

Therefore, the base angles each measure 50°, and the vertex angle measures 80°.

**PROBLEM**

Prove that the base angles of an isosceles right triangle have measure 45°.

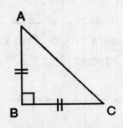

*Solution*

As drawn in the figure, $\triangle ABC$ is an isosceles right triangle with base angles $BAC$ and $BCA$. The sum of the measures of the angles of any triangle is 180°. For $\triangle ABC$, this means

$$m \angle BAC + m \angle BCA + m \angle ABC = 180° \qquad (1)$$

But $m \angle ABC = 90°$ because $ABC$ is a right triangle. Furthermore, $m \angle BCA = m \angle BAC$, since the base angles of an isosceles triangle are congruent. Using these facts in equation (1)

$$m \angle BAC + m \angle BCA + 90° = 180°$$

or $\qquad\qquad 2m \angle BAC = 2m \angle BCA = 90°$

or $\qquad\qquad m \angle BAC = m \angle BCA = 45°.$

Therefore, the base angles of an isosceles right triangle have measure 45°.

# 4.  QUADRILATERALS

A quadrilateral is a polygon with four sides.

## PARALLELOGRAMS

A parallelogram is a quadrilateral whose opposite sides are parallel.

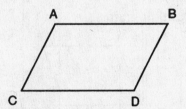

Two angles that have their vertices at the endpoints of the same side of a parallelogram are called consecutive angles.

The perpendicular segment connecting any point of a line containing one side of the parallelogram to the line containing the opposite side of the parallelogram is called the altitude of the parallelogram.

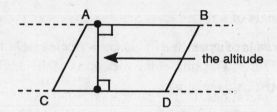

A diagonal of a polygon is a line segment joining any two non-consecutive vertices.

## RECTANGLES

A rectangle is a parallelogram with right angles.

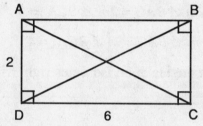

The diagonals of a rectangle are equal.

If the diagonals of a parallelogram are equal, the parallelogram is a rectangle.

If a quadrilateral has four right angles, then it is a rectangle.

## RHOMBI

A rhombus is a parallelogram.

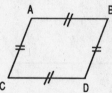

All sides of a rhombus are equal.

The diagonals of a rhombus are perpendicular to each other.

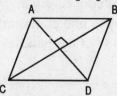

The diagonals of a rhombus bisect the angles of the rhombus.

If the diagonals of a parallelogram are perpendicular, the parallelogram is a rhombus.

If a quadrilateral has four equal sides, then it is a rhombus.

A parallelogram is a rhombus if either diagonal of the parallelogram bisects the angles of the vertices it joins.

## SQUARES

A square is a rhombus with a right angle.

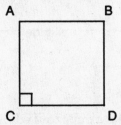

A square is an equilateral quadrilateral.

A square has all the properties of parallelograms, and rectangles.

A rhombus is a square if one of its interior angles is a right angle.

In a square, the measure of either diagonal can be calculated by multiplying the length of any side by the square root of 2.

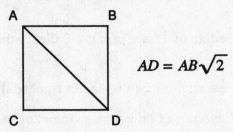

$$AD = AB\sqrt{2}$$

## TRAPEZOIDS

A trapezoid is a quadrilateral with two and only two sides parallel. The parallel sides of a trapezoid are called bases.

The median of a trapezoid is the line joining the midpoints of the non-parallel sides.

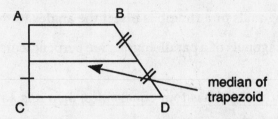

The perpendicular segment connecting any point in the line containing one base of the trapezoid to the line containing the other base is the **altitude** of the trapezoid.

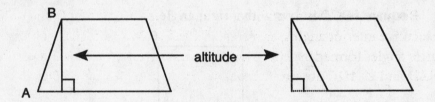

An **isosceles trapezoid** is a trapezoid whose non-parallel sides are equal. A pair of angles including only one of the parallel sides is called a pair of **base angles**.

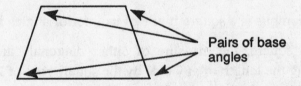

The median of a trapezoid is parallel to the bases and equal to one-half their sum.

The base angles of an isosceles trapezoid are equal.

The diagonals of an isosceles trapezoid are equal.

The opposite angles of an isosceles trapezoid are supplementary.

## PROBLEM

Prove that all pairs of consecutive angles of a parallelogram are supplementary. (See figure.)

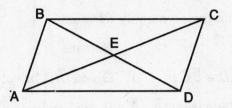

### Solution

We must prove that the pairs of angles $\angle BAD$ and $\angle ADC$, $\angle ADC$ and $\angle DCB$, $\angle DCB$ and $\angle CBA$, and $\angle CBA$ and $\angle BAD$ are supplementary. (This means that the sum of their measures is 180°.)

Because $ABCD$ is a parallelogram, $\overline{AB} \parallel \overline{CD}$. Angles $BAD$ and $ADC$ are consecutive interior angles, as are $\angle CBA$ and $\angle DCB$. Since the consecutive interior angles formed by 2 parallel lines and a transversal are supplementary, $\angle BAD$ and $\angle ADC$ are supplementary, as are $\angle CBA$ and $\angle DCB$.

Similarly, $\overline{AD} \parallel \overline{BC}$. Angles $ADC$ and $DCB$ are consecutive interior angles, as are $\angle CBA$ and $\angle BAD$. Since the consecutive interior angles formed by 2 parallel lines and a transversal are supplementary, $\angle CBA$ and $\angle BAD$ are supplementary, as are $\angle ADC$ and $\angle DCB$.

### PROBLEM

In the accompanying figure, $\triangle ABC$ is given to be an isosceles right triangle with $\angle ABC$ a right angle and $AB \cong BC$. Line segment $\overline{BD}$, which bisects $\overline{CA}$, is extended to $E$, so that $\overline{BD} \cong \overline{DE}$. Prove $BAEC$ is a square.

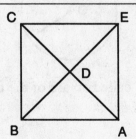

### SOLUTION

A square is a rectangle in which two consecutive sides are congruent. This definition will provide the framework for the proof in this problem. We will prove that $BAEC$ is a parallelogram that is specifically a rectangle with

consecutive sides congruent, namely a square.

| Statement | Reason |
|---|---|
| 1. $\overline{BD} \cong \overline{DE}$ and $\overline{AD} \cong \overline{DC}$ | 1. Given ($\overline{BD}$ bisects $\overline{CA}$). |
| 2. *BAEC* is a parallelogram | 2. If diagonals of a quadrilateral bisect each other, then the quadrilateral is a parallelogram. |
| 3. $\angle ABC$ is a right angle | 3. Given. |
| 4. *BAEC* is a rectangle | 4. A parallelogram, one of whose angles is a right angle, is a rectangle. |
| 5. $\overline{AB} \cong \overline{BC}$ | 5. Given. |
| 6. *BAEC* is a square | 6. If a rectangle has two congruent consecutive sides, then the rectangle is a square. |

## CIRCLES

A circle is a set of points in the same plane equidistant from a fixed point called its center.

A radius of a circle is a line segment drawn from the center of the circle to any point on the circle.

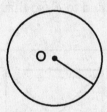

A portion of a circle is called an arc of the circle.

A line that intersects a circle in two points is called a secant.

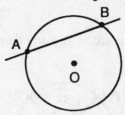

A line segment joining two points on a circle is called a chord of the circle.

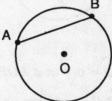

A chord that passes through the center of the circle is called a diameter of the circle.

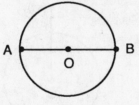

The line passing through the centers of two (or more) circles is called the line of centers.

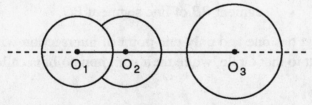

An angle whose vertex is on the circle and whose sides are chords of the circle is called an inscribed angle.

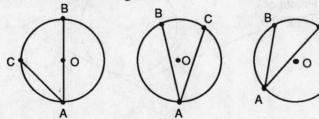

An angle whose vertex is at the center of a circle and whose sides are radii is called a central angle.

The measure of a minor arc is the measure of the central angle that intercepts that arc.

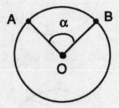

$$m\overarc{AB} = \alpha = m < AOB$$

The distance from a point $P$ to a given circle is the distance from that point to the point where the circle intersects with a line segment with endpoints at the center of the circle and point $P$.

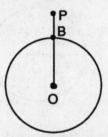

The distance of point $P$ to the diagrammed circle with center $O$ is the line segment $PB$ of line segment $PO$.

A line that has one and only one point of intersection with a circle is called a tangent to that circle, while their common point is called a point of tangency.

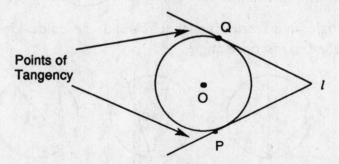

Points of Tangency

Congruent circles are circles whose radii are congruent.

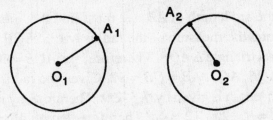

If $O_1A_1 \cong O_2A_2$, then $O_1 \cong O_2$.

The measure of a semicircle is 180°.

A circumscribed circle is a circle passing through all the vertices of a polygon.

Circles that have the same center and unequal radii are called concentric circles.

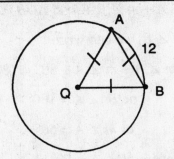

Concentric Circles

**PROBLEM**

> $A$ and $B$ are points on circle $Q$ such that $\triangle AQB$ is equilateral. If length of side $AB = 12$, find the length of arc $\overset{\frown}{AB}$.

## Solution

To find the arc length of $\overset{\frown}{AB}$, we must find the measure of the central angle $\angle AQB$ and the measure of the radius $\overline{QA}$. $\angle AQB$ is an interior angle of the equilateral triangle $\triangle AQB$. Therefore, $m\angle AQB = 60°$. Similarly, in the equilateral $\triangle AQB$, $AQ = AB = QB = 12$. Given the radius, $r$, and the central angle, $n$, the arc length is given by $^n/_{360} \cdot 2\pi r$. Therefore, by substitution, $\angle AQB = {}^{60}/_{360} \cdot 2\pi \cdot 12 = {}^1/_6 \cdot 2\pi \cdot 12 = 4\pi$. Therefore, length of arc $\overset{\frown}{AB} = 4\pi$.

## PROBLEM

In circle $O$, the measure of $\overset{\frown}{AB}$ is 80°. Find the measure of $\angle A$.

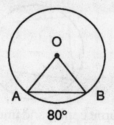

80°

## Solution

The accompanying figure shows that $\overset{\frown}{AB}$ is intercepted by central angle $\angle AOB$. By definition, we know that the measure of the central angle is the measure of its intercepted arc. In this case,

$$m\overset{\frown}{AB} = m\angle AOB = 80°.$$

Radius $\overline{OA}$ and radius $\overline{OB}$ are congruent and form two sides of $\triangle OAB$. By a theorem, the angles opposite these two congruent sides must, themselves, be congruent. Therefore, $m\angle A = m\angle B$.

The sum of the measures of the angles of a triangle is 180°. Therefore,

$$m\angle A + m\angle B + m\angle AOB = 180°.$$

Since $m\angle A = m\angle B$, we can write

$$m\angle A + m\angle A + 80° = 180°$$

$$\text{or } 2m\angle A = 100°$$

$$\text{or } m\angle A = 50°.$$

Therefore, the measure of $\angle A$ is 50°.

# 6. Solids

Solid geometry is the study of figures which consist of points not all in the same plane.

These are some examples of three-dimensional solids:

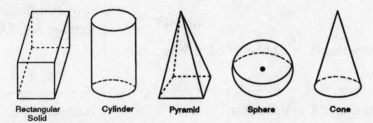

Rectangular Solid     Cylinder     Pyramid     Sphere     Cone

## RECTANGULAR SOLIDS

A solid with lateral faces and bases that are rectangles is called a rectangular solid.

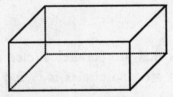

The surface area of a rectangular solid is the sum of the areas of all the faces.

The volume of a rectangular solid is equal to the product of its length, width and height.

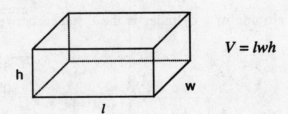

$$V = lwh$$

### PROBLEM

What are the dimensions of a solid cube whose surface area is numerically equal to its volume?

### Solution

The surface area of a cube of edge length $a$ is equal to the sum of the areas of its 6 faces. Since a cube is a regular polygon, all 6 faces are congruent. Each face of a cube is a square of edge length $a$. Hence, the surface area of a cube of edge length $a$ is

$$S = 6a^2.$$

The volume of a cube of edge length $a$ is

$$V = a^3.$$

We require that $A = V$, or that

$$6a^2 = a^3 \quad \text{or} \quad a = 6$$

Hence, if a cube has edge length 6, its surface area will be numerically equal to its volume.

## CYLINDERS

A solid with bases that are parallel circles and with cross sections parallel to the bases that are also circles is called a circular cylinder or a cylinder.

The altitude of a cylinder is the distance between two bases of the cylinder.

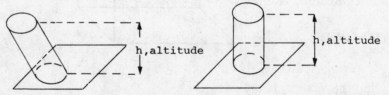

The lateral area of a cylinder is equal to the area of its curved cylindrical surface.

The total area of a cylinder is equal to the sum of its lateral area and the area of its bases.

The volume of any cylinder is the product of the area of its base and the altitude of its cylinder.

$$V = \pi\, r^2 h$$

volume = (area of base) × (height)

## PROBLEM

Find, in terms of $\pi$, the volume of a right circular cylinder if the radius of its base measures 4 in. and its altitude measures 5 in.

## Solution

If we picture the base of the cylinder has having a depth of one unit of measure, we can then calculate the volume by determining the area of the base and multiplying it by the height of the cylinder. In effect, this multiplication amounts to stacking the bases up to the height of the cylinder.

Area of the bases $= \pi\, r^2$, where $r$ is the radius of the circular base. Therefore, the volume is given by

$$V = \pi\, r^2 h.$$

By substitution, $V = \pi\, (4)^2 5$ in.$^3$ = $80\pi$ in.$^3$.

Therefore, volume of the cylinder = $80\pi$ in.$^3$.

## PYRAMIDS

A polyhedron with a polygonal base and with faces that meet at a point (called the vertex) is called a pyramid.

 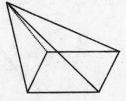

The triangular plane regions of a pyramid are called lateral faces and the intersections of the lateral faces are the lateral edges.

The length of the perpendicular segment from the vertex to the plane of the base of the pyramid is the altitude of the pyramid.

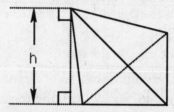

The lateral area of a regular pyramid is equal to one-half the product of its slant height and the perimeter of its base.

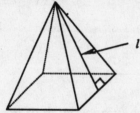

If the perimeter of the pyramid base is $b$, then its lateral area is $A = \frac{1}{2} bl$.

The volume of any pyramid is equal to one-third the product of the area of its base and the measure of its altitude.

$$V = \frac{1}{3} hA$$

## PROBLEM

In a regular square pyramid, the length of each side of the square base is 12 in., and the length of the altitude is 8 in. Find the length of the slant height of the pyramid.

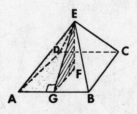

### Solution

Both parts of this example will involve an application of the Pythagorean Theorem in solid geometry. If $h$ is the length of the hypotenuse, and $a$ and $b$ the lengths of the other legs of a right triangle, then, $h2 = a^2 + b^2$.

The slant height is the perpendicular from the vertex of the pyramid to any side of the base. Since each face of a regular pyramid is an isosceles triangle, the slant height bisects the base. To find the slant height, note that slant height $\overline{EG}$ is the hypotenuse of $\triangle EFG$. The altitude of the pyramid, $\overline{EF}$, as shown in the figure, is perpendicular to the plane of the base $ABCD$, by definition. As such, $\overline{EF} \perp \overline{FG}$, because $\overline{FG}$ lies in the plane of the base and intersects $\overline{EF}$ at the latter's point of intersection with the base. The altitude must be drawn to the center of the base. Therefore, $\overline{FG}$ equals one-half the length of a side of the base.

$$FG = \frac{1}{2}\,(12) \text{ in.} = 6 \text{ in.}$$

Since $\triangle EFG$ contains a right angle, it is a right triangle. $\overline{EG}$ is the hypotenuse, or slant height. Therefore,

$$(EG)^2 = (EF)^2 + (FG)^2.$$

By substitution,

$$(EG)^2 = (8 \text{ in.})^2 + (6 \text{ in.})^2 = (64 + 36) \text{ in.}^2$$

$$= 100 \text{ in.}^2$$

$$EG = \sqrt{100} \text{ in.} = 10 \text{ in.}$$

Therefore, the slant height is 10 in.

## SPHERES

A sphere is the set of points in space at a given distance from a given point, called the center of the sphere.

The area of a sphere is equal to the area of its curved spherical surface.

The area of a sphere is equal to four times the area of one of its great circles.

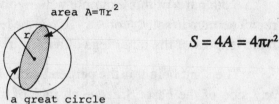

area $A = \pi r^2$

$$S = 4A = 4\pi r^2$$

a great circle

The volume of a sphere is equal to one-third the product of its area and the measure of its radius.

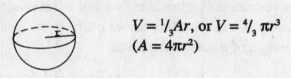

$$V = \tfrac{1}{3}Ar, \text{ or } V = \tfrac{4}{3}\pi r^3$$
$$(A = 4\pi r^2)$$

## PROBLEM

A perfectly spherical planet Sandeep has a diameter of 6000 km.

(a)  Find its area

(b)  Find its volume

### Solution

(a)  $d = 6000$ km.

   $r = \tfrac{d}{2} = \tfrac{6000}{2} = 3000$ km.

   $= 3 \times 10^6 m$

   Area $A = 4\pi r^2$

   $= 4(3.14)(3 \times 10^6)^2$

   $A = 113.04 \times 10^{12} m^2$

(b)  Volume $V = \tfrac{4}{3}\pi r^3$

   $= \tfrac{4}{3}(3.14)(3 \times 10^6)^3$

   $V = 113.04 \times 10^{18} m^3.$

## CONES

A cone is the part of a closed conical surface between the vertex and a plane intersecting one nappe of the conical surface.

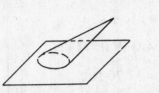 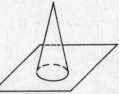

The total area of a cone is equal to the sum of its lateral area and the area of its base.

The volume of any circular cone is equal to one-third the product of the area of its base and the measure of its altitude.

area A

$$V = \frac{1}{3}hA,$$
$$\text{or } V = \frac{1}{3}\pi r^2 h \ (A = \pi r^2)$$

### PROBLEM

(a)  Find the volume of a solid right circular cone whose height is 4 ft. and whose base has radius 3 ft.

(b)  What is the slant height of this cone?

### Solution

The figure shows the cone. $s$ is the measure of the slant height, $h$ is the measure of the height, and $r$ is the measure of the radius of the base.

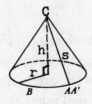

(a)   The volume of a solid right circular cone whose height is $h$, and whose base has radius $r$, is

$$V = \frac{1}{3} \pi r^2 h.$$

In our case, $r = 3$ ft., $h = 4$ ft., and

$$V = (\frac{1}{3}) (\pi) (9 \text{ ft.}^2) (4 \text{ ft.})$$

$$V = 37.70 \text{ ft.}^3.$$

(b)   The slant height of a right circular cone can be calculated by the Pythagorean Theorem. Look at the right triangle with sides $h$, $r$, and $s$, in the above figure. Applying the Pythagorean Theorem to this triangle,

$$s^2 = h^2 + r^2$$

or

$$s = \sqrt{h^2 + r^2}$$

$$s = \sqrt{16 \text{ ft}^2 + 9 \text{ ft}^2} = 5 \text{ ft}$$

## COORDINATE GEOMETRY

Coordinate geometry refers to the study of geometric figures using algebraic principles.

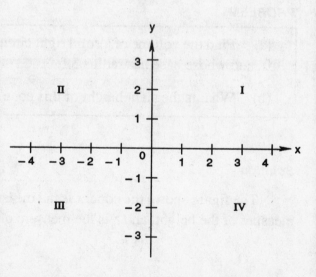

The graph shown is called the Cartesian coordinate plane. The graph consists of a pair of perpendicular lines called coordinate axes. The vertical axis is the $y$-axis and the horizontal axis is the $x$-axis. The point of intersection of these two axes is called the origin; it is the zero point of both axes. Furthermore, points to the right of the origin on the $x$-axis and above the origin on the $y$-axis represent positive real numbers. Points to the left of the origin on the $x$-axis or below the origin on the $y$-axis represent negative real numbers.

The four regions cut off by the coordinate axes are, in counterclockwise direction from the top right, called the first, second, third and fourth quadrant. The first quadrant contains all points with two positive coordinates.

In the graph shown, two points are identified by the ordered pair, $(x, y)$ of numbers. The $x$-coordinate is the first number and the $y$-coordinate is the second number. In this case, point $A$ has the coordinates (4, 2) and the coordinates of point $B$ are $(-3, -5)$.

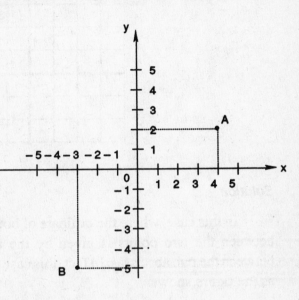

For any two points $A$ and $B$ with coordinates $(X_A, Y_A)$ and $(X_B, Y_B)$, respectively, the distance between $A$ and $B$ is represented by:

$$AB = \sqrt{(X_A - X_B)^2 + (Y_A - Y_B)^2}$$

This is commonly known as the distance formula or the Pythagorean Theorem.

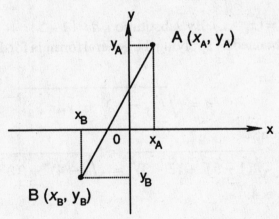

**PROBLEM**

Find the distance between the point $A(1, 3)$ and $B(5, 3)$.

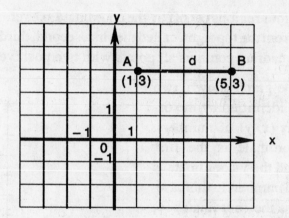

## Solution

In this case, where the ordinate of both points is the same, the distance between the two points is given by the absolute value of the difference between the two abscissas. In fact, this case reduces to merely counting boxes as the figure shows.

Let,  $x_1$ = abscissa of $A$     $y_1$ = ordinate of $A$

   $x_2$ = abscissa of $B$     $y_1$ = ordinate of $B$

   $d$ = the distance.

Therefore, $d = |x_1 - x_2|$. By substitution, $d = |1 - 5| = |-4| = 4$. This answer can also be obtained by applying the general formula for distance between any two points

$$d = \sqrt{(x_1 - x_2)^2 + (y_1 - y_2)^2}$$

By substitution,

$$d = \sqrt{(1-5)^2 + (3-3)^2} = \sqrt{(-4)^2 + (0)^2} = \sqrt{16} = 4.$$

The distance is 4.

# WORD PROBLEMS

## 1. Rate

One of the formulas you will use for rate problems will be:

$$\text{Rate} \times \text{Time} = \text{Distance}$$

### PROBLEM

> If a plane travels five hours from New York to California at a speed of 600 miles per hour, how many miles does the plane travel?

### Solution

Using the formula rate × time = distance, multiply 600 mph × 5 hours = 3000 miles.

The average rate at which an object travels can be solved by dividing the total distance traveled by the total amount of time.

### PROBLEM

> On a 40-mile bicycle trip, Cathy rode half the distance at 20 mph and the other half at 10 mph. What was Cathy's average speed on the bike trip?

### Solution

First you need to break down the problem. On half of the trip which would be 20 miles, Cathy rode 20 mph. Using the rate formula, $^{\text{distance}}/_{\text{rate}} = \text{time}$, you would compute,

$$\frac{20 \text{ miles}}{20 \text{ miles per hour}} = 1 \text{ hour}$$

to travel the first 20 miles. During the second 20 miles, Cathy traveled at 10 miles per hour, which would be

$$\frac{20 \text{ miles}}{10 \text{ miles per hour}} = 2 \text{ hours}$$

Thus, the average speed Cathy traveled would be $^{40}/_{3} = 13.34$ miles per hour.

In solving for some rate problems you can use cross multiplication involving ratios to solve for $x$.

### PROBLEM

> If 2 pairs of shoes cost \$52, then what is the cost of 10 pairs of shoes at this rate?

### Solution

$$\frac{2}{52} = \frac{10}{x}, \quad 2x = 52 \times 10, \quad x = \frac{520}{2}, \quad x = \$260.$$

## 2.  Work

In work problems, one of the basic formulas is

$$\frac{1}{x} + \frac{1}{y} = \frac{1}{z}$$

where $x$ and $y$ represent the number of hours it takes two objects or people to complete the work and $z$ is the total number of hours when both are working together.

### PROBLEM

> Otis can seal and stamp 400 envelopes in 2 hours while Elizabeth seals and stamps 400 envelopes in 1 hour. In how many hours can Otis and Elizabeth, working together, complete a 400-piece mailing at these rates?

### SOLUTION

$$\frac{1}{2} + \frac{1}{1} = \frac{1}{z}, \quad \frac{1}{2} + \frac{2}{2} = \frac{3}{2}, \quad \frac{3}{2} = \frac{1}{z}, \quad 3z = 2$$

$z = {}^2/_3$ of an hour or 40 minutes. Working together, Otis and Elizabeth can seal and stamp 400 envelopes in 40 minutes.

## 3. Mixture

Mixture problems present different products combined and solving for the different parts of the mixture.

**PROBLEM**

A chemist has an 18% solution and a 45% solution of a disinfectant. How many ounces of each should be used to make 12 ounces of a 36% solution?

*Solution*

Let $x$ = Number of ounces from the 18% solution, and

$y$ = Number of ounces from the 45% solution.

(1) $x + y = 12$

(2) $.18x + .45y = .36(12) = 4.32$

Note that .18 of the first solution is pure disinfectant and that .45 of the second solution is pure disinfectant. When the proper quantities are drawn from each mixture the result is 12 ounces of mixture which is .36 pure disinfectant, i.e., the resulting mixture contains 4.32 ounces of pure disinfectant.

When the equations are solved, it is found that

$x = 4$ and $y = 8.$

**PROBLEM**

Clark pays $2.00 per pound for 3 pounds of peanut butter chocolates and then decides to buy 2 pounds of chocolate covered raisins at $2.50 per pound. If Clark mixes both together, what is the cost per pound of the mixture?

*Solution*

The total mixture is 5 pounds and the total value of the chocolates is

$$3(\$2.00) + 2(\$2.50) = \$11.00$$

The price per pound of the chocolates is $^{\$11.00}/_{5\,pounds} = \$2.20$.

## 4. Interest

If the problem calls for computing simple interest, the interest is computed on the principal alone. If the problem involves compounded interest, then the interest on the principal is taken into account in addition to the interest earned before.

### PROBLEM

How much interest will Jerry pay on his loan of $400 for 60 days at 6% per year?

### Solution

Use the formula:

$$\text{Interest} = \text{Principal} \times \text{Rate} \times \text{Time} \ (I = P \times R \times T).$$

$$\$400 \times 6\%/\text{year} \times 60 \text{ days} = \$400 \times .06 \times {}^{60}/_{365}$$

$$= \$400 \times 0.00986$$

$$= \$3.94$$

Jerry will pay $3.94.

### PROBLEM

Mr. Smith wishes to find out how much interest he will receive on $300 if the rate is 3% compounded annually for three years.

### Solution

Compound interest is interest computed on both the principal and the interest it has previously earned. The interest is added to the principal at the end of every year. The interest on the first year is found by multiplying the rate by the principal. Hence, the interest for the first year is

$$3\% \times \$300 = .03 \times \$300 = \$9.00.$$

The principal for the second year is now $309, the old principal ($300) plus the interest ($9). The interest for the second year is found by multiplying the rate by the new principal. Hence, the interest for the second year is

$$3\% \times \$309 = .03 \times \$309 = \$9.27.$$

The principal now becomes $309 + $9.27 = $318.27.

The interest for the third year is found using this new principal. It is

$$3\% \times \$318.27 = .03 \times \$318.27 = \$9.55.$$

At the end of the third year his principal is $318.27 + 9.55 = $327.82. To find how much interest was earned, we subtract his starting principal ($300) from his ending principal ($327.82), to obtain

$$\$327.82 - \$300.00 = \$27.82.$$

## 5. Discount

If the discount problem asks to find the final price after the discount, the answer is solved by multiplying the original price with the discount percent and then subtracting that amount from the original price.

If the problem asks to find what the original price would be if only the discount percentage and the discounted price is given, then the complement of the discount percentage is figured and computed with the discounted price to obtain the original price.

**PROBLEM**

A popular bookstore gives 10% discount to students. What does a student actually pay for a book costing $24.00?

**SOLUTION**

10% of $24 is $2.40 and hence the student pays $24 − $2.40 = $21.60.

### PROBLEM

> Eugene paid $100 for a business suit. The suit's price included a 25% discount. What was the original price of the suit?

*Solution*

Let $x$ represent the original price of the suit and take the complement of .25 (discount price) which is .75.

$.75x = \$100$ or $x = 133.34$. So, the original price of the suit is $133.34.

## 6. Profit

The formula used for the profit problems is

$$\text{Profit} = \text{Revenue} - \text{Cost} \quad \text{or}$$

$$\text{Profit} = \text{Selling Price} - \text{Expenses}.$$

### PROBLEM

> Four high school and college friends started a business of remodeling and selling old automobiles during the summer. For this purpose they paid $600 to rent an empty barn for the summer. They obtained the cars from a dealer for $250 each, and it takes an average of $410 in materials to remodel each car. How many automobiles must the students sell at $1,440 each to obtain a gross profit of $7,000?

*Solution*

$$\text{Total Revenues} - \text{Total Cost} = \text{Gross Profit}$$
$$\text{Revenue} - [\text{Variable Cost} + \text{Fixed Cost}] = \text{Gross Profit}$$

Let $a$ = number of cars

Revenue = $1,440a$

Total Cost [Variable Cost = ($250 + 410)a$
[Fixed Cost = $600

The desired gross profit is $7,000.

118

Using the equation for the gross profit,

$$1{,}440a - [660a + 600] = 7{,}000$$
$$1{,}440a - 660a - 600 = 7{,}000$$
$$780a = 7{,}000 + 600$$
$$780a = 7{,}600$$
$$a = 9.74$$

or to the nearest car, $a = 10$.

**PROBLEM**

> A glass vase sells for $25.00. The net profit is 7%, and the operating expenses are 39%. Find the gross profit on the vase.

**SOLUTION**

The gross profit is equal to the net profit plus the operating expenses. The net profit is 7% of the selling cost; thus it is equal to $7\% \times \$25.00 = .07 \times \$25 = \$1.75$. The operating expenses are 39% of the selling price, thus equal to $39\% \times \$25 = .39 \times \$25 = \$9.75$.

$$
\begin{array}{ll}
\$1.75 & \text{net profit} \\
+ \ \$9.75 & \text{operating expenses} \\
\hline
\$11.50 & \text{gross profit}
\end{array}
$$

# 7. Sets

A set is any collection of well defined objects called elements.

A set which contains only a finite number of elements is called a finite set; a set which contains an infinite number of elements is called an infinite set. Often the sets are designated by listing their elements. For example: $\{a, b, c, d\}$ is the set which contains elements $a, b, c,$ and $d$. The set of positive integers is $\{1, 2, 3, 4, \ldots\}$.

Venn diagrams can represent sets. These diagrams are circles which help to visualize the relationship between members or objects of a set.

Using Venn Diagrams, $A \subset B$ is illustrated by

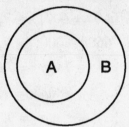

The shaded area represents $A \cup B$ which represents the union of sets $A$ and $B$.

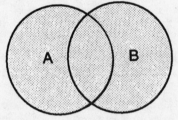

The shaded area represents $A \cap B$ which is the intersection of sets $A$ and $B$.

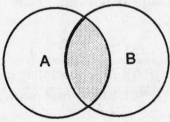

**PROBLEM**

In a certain Broadway show audition, it was asked of 30 performers if they knew how to either sing or dance, or both. If 20 auditioners said they could dance and 14 said they could sing, how many could sing and dance?

**SOLUTION**

Divide the 30 people into 3 sets: those who dance, those who sing and those who dance and sing. $S$ is the number of people who both sing and dance. So $20 - S$ represents the number of people who dance and $14 - S$ represents the number of people who sing.

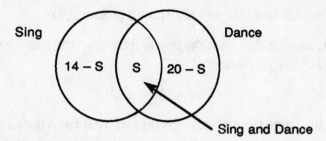

The equation for this problem is as follows:

$$(20 - S) + S + (14 - S) = 30.$$
$$20 + 14 - 30 = S$$
$$34 - 30 = S$$
$$4 = S$$

So, 4 people in the audition both sing and dance.

# 8. Geometry

## PROBLEM

A boy knows that his height is 6 ft. and his shadow is 4 ft. long. At the same time of day, a tree's shadow is 24 ft. long. How high is the tree?

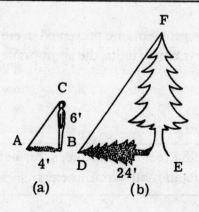

## Solution

Show that $\triangle ABC \approx \triangle DEF$, and then set up a proportion between the

known sides *AB* and *DE*, and the sides *BC* and *EF*.

First, assume that both the boy and the tree are ⊥ to the earth. Then, $\overline{BC}$ ⊥ $\overline{BA}$ and $\overline{EF}$ ⊥ $\overline{ED}$. Hence,

$$\angle ABC \cong \angle DEF.$$

Since it is the same time of day, the rays of light from the sun are incident on both the tree and the boy at the same angle, relative to the earth's surface. Therefore,

$$\angle BAC \cong \angle EDF.$$

We have shown, so far, that 2 pairs of corresponding angles are congruent. Since the sum of the angles of any triangle is 180°, the third pair of corresponding angles is congruent (i.e. $\angle ACB \cong \angle DFE$). By the Angle Angle Angle (A.A.A.) Theorem

$$\angle ABC \approx \angle DEF.$$

By definition of similarity,

$$\frac{FE}{CB} = \frac{ED}{BA}.$$

*CB* = 6', ED = 24', and *BA* = 4'. Therefore,

$$FE= (6') \, (24'/4') = 36'.$$

# 9. Measurement

When measurement problems are presented in either metric or English units which involve conversion of units, the appropriate data will be given in the problem.

### PROBLEM

The Eiffel Tower is 984 feet high. Express this height in meters, in kilometers, in centimeters, and in millimeters.

### Solution

A meter is equivalent to 39.370 inches. In this problem, the height of the

tower in feet must be converted to inches and then the inches can be converted to meters. There are 12 inches in 1 foot. Therefore, feet can be converted to inches by using the factor 12 inches/1 foot.

$$984 \text{ feet} \times 12 \text{ inches/1 foot} = 118 \times 10^2 \text{ inches.}$$

Once the height is found in inches, this can be converted to meters by the factor 1 meter/39.370 inches.

$$11808 \text{ inches} \times 1 \text{ meter/39.370 inches} = 300 \text{ m.}$$

Therefore, the height in meters is 300 m.

There are 1,000 meters in one kilometer. Meters can be converted to kilometers by using the factor 1km/1000 m.

$$300 \text{ m} \times 1 \text{ km/1000 m} = .300 \text{ km.}$$

As such, there are .300 kilometers in 300 m.

There are 100 centimeters in 1 meter, thus meters can be converted to centimeters by multiplying by the factor 100 cm/1 m.

$$300 \text{ m} \times 100 \text{ cm/1 m} = 300 \times 10^2 \text{ cm.}$$

There are 30,000 centimeters in 300 m.

There are 1,000 millimeters in 1 meter; therefore, meters can be converted to millimeters by the factor 1000 mm./1m.

$$300 \text{ m} \times 1,000 \text{ mm/1 m} = 300 \times 10^3 \text{ mm.}$$

There are 300,000 millimeters in 300 meters.

**PROBLEM**

> The unaided eye can perceive objects which have a diameter of 0.1 mm. What is the diameter in inches?

**SOLUTION**

From a standard table of conversion factors, one can find that 1 inch = 2.54 cm. Thus, cm can be converted to inches by multiplying by 1 inch/2.54 cm. Here, one is given the diameter in mm, which is .1 cm. Millimeters are

converted to cm by multiplying the number of mm by .1 cm/1 mm. Solving for cm, you obtain:

$$0.1 \text{ mm} \times .1 \text{ cm}/1 \text{ mm} = .01 \text{ cm}.$$

Solving for inches:

$$0.01 \text{ cm} \times {}^{1 \text{ inch}}/_{2.54 \text{ cm}} = 3.94 \times 10^{-3} \text{ inches}.$$

## 10. Data Interpretation

Some of the problems test ability to apply information given in graphs and tables.

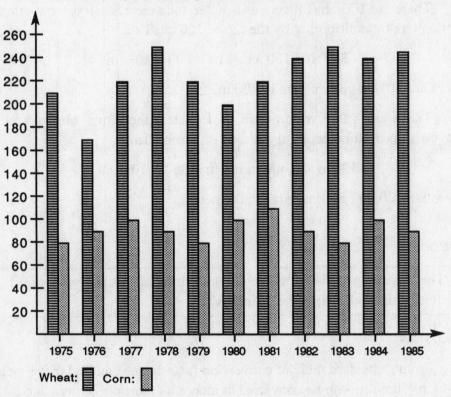

**Number of bushels (to the nearest 5 bushels) of wheat and corn produced by farm RQS from 1975 – 1985**

Wheat: ▨ Corn: ▨

## PROBLEM

> In which year was the least number of bushels of wheat produced?

### Solution

By inspection of the graph, we find that the shortest bar representing wheat production is the one representing the wheat production for 1976. Thus, the least number of bushels of wheat was produced in 1976.

## PROBLEM

> What was the ratio of wheat production in 1985 to that of 1975?

### Solution

From the graph representing wheat production, the number of bushels of wheat produced in 1975 is equal to 210 bushels. This number can be found by locating the bar on the graph representing wheat production in 1975 and then drawing a horizontal line from the top of that bar to the vertical axis. The point where this horizontal line meets the vertical axis represents the number of bushels of wheat produced in 1975. This number on the vertical axis is 210. Similarly, the graph indicates that the number of bushels of wheat produced in 1985 is equal to 245 bushels.

Thus, the ratio of wheat production in 1985 to that of 1975 is 245 to 210, which can be written as $^{245}/_{210}$. Simplifying this ratio to its simplest form yields

$$\frac{245}{210} = \frac{5 \cdot 7 \cdot 7}{2 \cdot 3 \cdot 5 \cdot 7} = \frac{7}{2 \cdot 3} = \frac{7}{6} \text{ or } 7:6$$

# FORMULAS

| DESCRIPTION | FORMULA |
|---|---|
| **AREA ($A$) of a:** | |
| square | $A = s^2$; where $s$ = side |
| rectangle | $A = lw$; where $l$ = length, $w$ = width |
| parallelogram | $A = bh$; where $b$ = base, $h$ = height |
| triangle | $A = \frac{1}{2} bh$; where $b$ = base, $h$ = height |
| circle | $A = \pi r^2$; where $\pi$ = 3.14, $r$ = radius. |
| **PERIMETER ($P$) of a:** | |
| square | $P = 4s$; where $s$ = side |
| rectangle | $P = 2l + 2w$; where $l$ = length, $w$ = width |
| triangle | $P = a + b + c$; where $a$, $b$, and $c$ are the sides |
| circumference (C) of a circle | $C = \pi d$, where $\pi$ = 3.14, $d$ = diameter |
| **VOLUME ($V$) of a:** | |
| cube | $V = s^3$; where $s$ = side |
| rectangular container | $V = lwh$; where $l$ = length, $w$ = width, $h$ = height |
| cylinder | $V = \pi r^2 h$; where $\pi$ = 3.14, $r$ = radius, $h$ = height |
| Pythagorean relationship | $c^2 = a^2 + b^2$; where $c$ = hypotenuse, $a$ and $b$ are legs a right triangle |
| distance ($d$) between two points in a plane | $d = \sqrt{(x_2 - x_1)^2 + (y_2 - y_1)^2}$; where $(x_1, y_1)$ and $(x_2, y_2)$ are two points in a plane |
| slope of a line ($m$) | $m = \dfrac{y_2 - y_1}{x_2 - x_1}$; where $(x_1, y_1)$ and $(x_2, y_2)$ are two points in a plane |
| mean | mean $= \dfrac{x_1 + x_2 + \ldots + x_n}{n}$; where the $x$'s are the values for which a mean is sired, and $n$ = number of values in the series |
| median | median = the point in an ordered set of number: which half of the numbers are above and half of numbers are below this value |
| simple interest ($i$) | $i = prt$; where $p$ = principal, $r$ = rate, $t$ = time |
| distance ($d$) as function of rate and time | $d = rt$; where $r$ = rate, $t$ = time |
| total cost ($c$) | $c = nr$; where $n$ = number of units, $r$ = cost per un |

# GRE
# GENERAL TEST 1
## ANSWER SHEET

**SECTION 1**

1. Ⓐ Ⓑ Ⓒ Ⓓ Ⓔ
2. Ⓐ Ⓑ Ⓒ Ⓓ Ⓔ
3. Ⓐ Ⓑ Ⓒ Ⓓ Ⓔ
4. Ⓐ Ⓑ Ⓒ Ⓓ Ⓔ
5. Ⓐ Ⓑ Ⓒ Ⓓ Ⓔ
6. Ⓐ Ⓑ Ⓒ Ⓓ Ⓔ
7. Ⓐ Ⓑ Ⓒ Ⓓ Ⓔ
8. Ⓐ Ⓑ Ⓒ Ⓓ Ⓔ
9. Ⓐ Ⓑ Ⓒ Ⓓ Ⓔ
10. Ⓐ Ⓑ Ⓒ Ⓓ Ⓔ
11. Ⓐ Ⓑ Ⓒ Ⓓ Ⓔ
12. Ⓐ Ⓑ Ⓒ Ⓓ Ⓔ
13. Ⓐ Ⓑ Ⓒ Ⓓ Ⓔ
14. Ⓐ Ⓑ Ⓒ Ⓓ Ⓔ
15. Ⓐ Ⓑ Ⓒ Ⓓ Ⓔ
16. Ⓐ Ⓑ Ⓒ Ⓓ Ⓔ
17. Ⓐ Ⓑ Ⓒ Ⓓ Ⓔ
18. Ⓐ Ⓑ Ⓒ Ⓓ Ⓔ
19. Ⓐ Ⓑ Ⓒ Ⓓ Ⓔ
20. Ⓐ Ⓑ Ⓒ Ⓓ Ⓔ
21. Ⓐ Ⓑ Ⓒ Ⓓ Ⓔ
22. Ⓐ Ⓑ Ⓒ Ⓓ Ⓔ
23. Ⓐ Ⓑ Ⓒ Ⓓ Ⓔ
24. Ⓐ Ⓑ Ⓒ Ⓓ Ⓔ
25. Ⓐ Ⓑ Ⓒ Ⓓ Ⓔ
26. Ⓐ Ⓑ Ⓒ Ⓓ Ⓔ
27. Ⓐ Ⓑ Ⓒ Ⓓ Ⓔ
28. Ⓐ Ⓑ Ⓒ Ⓓ Ⓔ
29. Ⓐ Ⓑ Ⓒ Ⓓ Ⓔ
30. Ⓐ Ⓑ Ⓒ Ⓓ Ⓔ

31. Ⓐ Ⓑ Ⓒ Ⓓ Ⓔ
32. Ⓐ Ⓑ Ⓒ Ⓓ Ⓔ
33. Ⓐ Ⓑ Ⓒ Ⓓ Ⓔ
34. Ⓐ Ⓑ Ⓒ Ⓓ Ⓔ
35. Ⓐ Ⓑ Ⓒ Ⓓ Ⓔ
36. Ⓐ Ⓑ Ⓒ Ⓓ Ⓔ
37. Ⓐ Ⓑ Ⓒ Ⓓ Ⓔ
38. Ⓐ Ⓑ Ⓒ Ⓓ Ⓔ

**SECTION 2**

1. Ⓐ Ⓑ Ⓒ Ⓓ Ⓔ
2. Ⓐ Ⓑ Ⓒ Ⓓ Ⓔ
3. Ⓐ Ⓑ Ⓒ Ⓓ Ⓔ
4. Ⓐ Ⓑ Ⓒ Ⓓ Ⓔ
5. Ⓐ Ⓑ Ⓒ Ⓓ Ⓔ
6. Ⓐ Ⓑ Ⓒ Ⓓ Ⓔ
7. Ⓐ Ⓑ Ⓒ Ⓓ Ⓔ
8. Ⓐ Ⓑ Ⓒ Ⓓ Ⓔ
9. Ⓐ Ⓑ Ⓒ Ⓓ Ⓔ
10. Ⓐ Ⓑ Ⓒ Ⓓ Ⓔ
11. Ⓐ Ⓑ Ⓒ Ⓓ Ⓔ
12. Ⓐ Ⓑ Ⓒ Ⓓ Ⓔ
13. Ⓐ Ⓑ Ⓒ Ⓓ Ⓔ
14. Ⓐ Ⓑ Ⓒ Ⓓ Ⓔ
15. Ⓐ Ⓑ Ⓒ Ⓓ Ⓔ
16. Ⓐ Ⓑ Ⓒ Ⓓ Ⓔ
17. Ⓐ Ⓑ Ⓒ Ⓓ Ⓔ
18. Ⓐ Ⓑ Ⓒ Ⓓ Ⓔ
19. Ⓐ Ⓑ Ⓒ Ⓓ Ⓔ
20. Ⓐ Ⓑ Ⓒ Ⓓ Ⓔ
21. Ⓐ Ⓑ Ⓒ Ⓓ Ⓔ

22. Ⓐ Ⓑ Ⓒ Ⓓ Ⓔ
23. Ⓐ Ⓑ Ⓒ Ⓓ Ⓔ
24. Ⓐ Ⓑ Ⓒ Ⓓ Ⓔ
25. Ⓐ Ⓑ Ⓒ Ⓓ Ⓔ
26. Ⓐ Ⓑ Ⓒ Ⓓ Ⓔ
27. Ⓐ Ⓑ Ⓒ Ⓓ Ⓔ
28. Ⓐ Ⓑ Ⓒ Ⓓ Ⓔ
29. Ⓐ Ⓑ Ⓒ Ⓓ Ⓔ
30. Ⓐ Ⓑ Ⓒ Ⓓ Ⓔ
31. Ⓐ Ⓑ Ⓒ Ⓓ Ⓔ
32. Ⓐ Ⓑ Ⓒ Ⓓ Ⓔ
33. Ⓐ Ⓑ Ⓒ Ⓓ Ⓔ
34. Ⓐ Ⓑ Ⓒ Ⓓ Ⓔ
35. Ⓐ Ⓑ Ⓒ Ⓓ Ⓔ
36. Ⓐ Ⓑ Ⓒ Ⓓ Ⓔ
37. Ⓐ Ⓑ Ⓒ Ⓓ Ⓔ
38. Ⓐ Ⓑ Ⓒ Ⓓ Ⓔ

**SECTION 3**

1. Ⓐ Ⓑ Ⓒ Ⓓ Ⓔ
2. Ⓐ Ⓑ Ⓒ Ⓓ Ⓔ
3. Ⓐ Ⓑ Ⓒ Ⓓ Ⓔ
4. Ⓐ Ⓑ Ⓒ Ⓓ Ⓔ
5. Ⓐ Ⓑ Ⓒ Ⓓ Ⓔ
6. Ⓐ Ⓑ Ⓒ Ⓓ Ⓔ
7. Ⓐ Ⓑ Ⓒ Ⓓ Ⓔ
8. Ⓐ Ⓑ Ⓒ Ⓓ Ⓔ
9. Ⓐ Ⓑ Ⓒ Ⓓ Ⓔ
10. Ⓐ Ⓑ Ⓒ Ⓓ Ⓔ
11. Ⓐ Ⓑ Ⓒ Ⓓ Ⓔ
12. Ⓐ Ⓑ Ⓒ Ⓓ Ⓔ

13. Ⓐ Ⓑ Ⓒ Ⓓ Ⓔ
14. Ⓐ Ⓑ Ⓒ Ⓓ Ⓔ
15. Ⓐ Ⓑ Ⓒ Ⓓ Ⓔ
16. Ⓐ Ⓑ Ⓒ Ⓓ Ⓔ
17. Ⓐ Ⓑ Ⓒ Ⓓ Ⓔ
18. Ⓐ Ⓑ Ⓒ Ⓓ Ⓔ
19. Ⓐ Ⓑ Ⓒ Ⓓ Ⓔ
20. Ⓐ Ⓑ Ⓒ Ⓓ Ⓔ
21. Ⓐ Ⓑ Ⓒ Ⓓ Ⓔ
22. Ⓐ Ⓑ Ⓒ Ⓓ Ⓔ
23. Ⓐ Ⓑ Ⓒ Ⓓ Ⓔ
24. Ⓐ Ⓑ Ⓒ Ⓓ Ⓔ
25. Ⓐ Ⓑ Ⓒ Ⓓ Ⓔ
26. Ⓐ Ⓑ Ⓒ Ⓓ Ⓔ
27. Ⓐ Ⓑ Ⓒ Ⓓ Ⓔ
28. Ⓐ Ⓑ Ⓒ Ⓓ Ⓔ
29. Ⓐ Ⓑ Ⓒ Ⓓ Ⓔ
30. Ⓐ Ⓑ Ⓒ Ⓓ Ⓔ

## SECTION 4

1. Ⓐ Ⓑ Ⓒ Ⓓ Ⓔ
2. Ⓐ Ⓑ Ⓒ Ⓓ Ⓔ
3. Ⓐ Ⓑ Ⓒ Ⓓ Ⓔ
4. Ⓐ Ⓑ Ⓒ Ⓓ Ⓔ
5. Ⓐ Ⓑ Ⓒ Ⓓ Ⓔ
6. Ⓐ Ⓑ Ⓒ Ⓓ Ⓔ
7. Ⓐ Ⓑ Ⓒ Ⓓ Ⓔ
8. Ⓐ Ⓑ Ⓒ Ⓓ Ⓔ
9. Ⓐ Ⓑ Ⓒ Ⓓ Ⓔ
10. Ⓐ Ⓑ Ⓒ Ⓓ Ⓔ
11. Ⓐ Ⓑ Ⓒ Ⓓ Ⓔ
12. Ⓐ Ⓑ Ⓒ Ⓓ Ⓔ
13. Ⓐ Ⓑ Ⓒ Ⓓ Ⓔ
14. Ⓐ Ⓑ Ⓒ Ⓓ Ⓔ
15. Ⓐ Ⓑ Ⓒ Ⓓ Ⓔ

16. Ⓐ Ⓑ Ⓒ Ⓓ Ⓔ
17. Ⓐ Ⓑ Ⓒ Ⓓ Ⓔ
18. Ⓐ Ⓑ Ⓒ Ⓓ Ⓔ
19. Ⓐ Ⓑ Ⓒ Ⓓ Ⓔ
20. Ⓐ Ⓑ Ⓒ Ⓓ Ⓔ
21. Ⓐ Ⓑ Ⓒ Ⓓ Ⓔ
22. Ⓐ Ⓑ Ⓒ Ⓓ Ⓔ
23. Ⓐ Ⓑ Ⓒ Ⓓ Ⓔ
24. Ⓐ Ⓑ Ⓒ Ⓓ Ⓔ
25. Ⓐ Ⓑ Ⓒ Ⓓ Ⓔ
26. Ⓐ Ⓑ Ⓒ Ⓓ Ⓔ
27. Ⓐ Ⓑ Ⓒ Ⓓ Ⓔ
28. Ⓐ Ⓑ Ⓒ Ⓓ Ⓔ
29. Ⓐ Ⓑ Ⓒ Ⓓ Ⓔ
30. Ⓐ Ⓑ Ⓒ Ⓓ Ⓔ

## SECTION 5

1. Ⓐ Ⓑ Ⓒ Ⓓ Ⓔ
2. Ⓐ Ⓑ Ⓒ Ⓓ Ⓔ
3. Ⓐ Ⓑ Ⓒ Ⓓ Ⓔ
4. Ⓐ Ⓑ Ⓒ Ⓓ Ⓔ
5. Ⓐ Ⓑ Ⓒ Ⓓ Ⓔ
6. Ⓐ Ⓑ Ⓒ Ⓓ Ⓔ
7. Ⓐ Ⓑ Ⓒ Ⓓ Ⓔ
8. Ⓐ Ⓑ Ⓒ Ⓓ Ⓔ
9. Ⓐ Ⓑ Ⓒ Ⓓ Ⓔ
10. Ⓐ Ⓑ Ⓒ Ⓓ Ⓔ
11. Ⓐ Ⓑ Ⓒ Ⓓ Ⓔ
12. Ⓐ Ⓑ Ⓒ Ⓓ Ⓔ
13. Ⓐ Ⓑ Ⓒ Ⓓ Ⓔ
14. Ⓐ Ⓑ Ⓒ Ⓓ Ⓔ
15. Ⓐ Ⓑ Ⓒ Ⓓ Ⓔ
16. Ⓐ Ⓑ Ⓒ Ⓓ Ⓔ
17. Ⓐ Ⓑ Ⓒ Ⓓ Ⓔ
18. Ⓐ Ⓑ Ⓒ Ⓓ Ⓔ

19. Ⓐ Ⓑ Ⓒ Ⓓ Ⓔ
20. Ⓐ Ⓑ Ⓒ Ⓓ Ⓔ
21. Ⓐ Ⓑ Ⓒ Ⓓ Ⓔ
22. Ⓐ Ⓑ Ⓒ Ⓓ Ⓔ
23. Ⓐ Ⓑ Ⓒ Ⓓ Ⓔ
24. Ⓐ Ⓑ Ⓒ Ⓓ Ⓔ
25. Ⓐ Ⓑ Ⓒ Ⓓ Ⓔ

## SECTION 6

1. Ⓐ Ⓑ Ⓒ Ⓓ Ⓔ
2. Ⓐ Ⓑ Ⓒ Ⓓ Ⓔ
3. Ⓐ Ⓑ Ⓒ Ⓓ Ⓔ
4. Ⓐ Ⓑ Ⓒ Ⓓ Ⓔ
5. Ⓐ Ⓑ Ⓒ Ⓓ Ⓔ
6. Ⓐ Ⓑ Ⓒ Ⓓ Ⓔ
7. Ⓐ Ⓑ Ⓒ Ⓓ Ⓔ
8. Ⓐ Ⓑ Ⓒ Ⓓ Ⓔ
9. Ⓐ Ⓑ Ⓒ Ⓓ Ⓔ
10. Ⓐ Ⓑ Ⓒ Ⓓ Ⓔ
11. Ⓐ Ⓑ Ⓒ Ⓓ Ⓔ
12. Ⓐ Ⓑ Ⓒ Ⓓ Ⓔ
13. Ⓐ Ⓑ Ⓒ Ⓓ Ⓔ
14. Ⓐ Ⓑ Ⓒ Ⓓ Ⓔ
15. Ⓐ Ⓑ Ⓒ Ⓓ Ⓔ
16. Ⓐ Ⓑ Ⓒ Ⓓ Ⓔ
17. Ⓐ Ⓑ Ⓒ Ⓓ Ⓔ
18. Ⓐ Ⓑ Ⓒ Ⓓ Ⓔ
19. Ⓐ Ⓑ Ⓒ Ⓓ Ⓔ
20. Ⓐ Ⓑ Ⓒ Ⓓ Ⓔ
21. Ⓐ Ⓑ Ⓒ Ⓓ Ⓔ
22. Ⓐ Ⓑ Ⓒ Ⓓ Ⓔ
23. Ⓐ Ⓑ Ⓒ Ⓓ Ⓔ
24. Ⓐ Ⓑ Ⓒ Ⓓ Ⓔ
25. Ⓐ Ⓑ Ⓒ Ⓓ Ⓔ

# TEST 1

## Section 1

**TIME:** 30 Minutes
38 Questions

**DIRECTIONS:** Each of the given sentences has blank spaces which indicate words omitted. Choose the best combination of words which fit into the meaning and structure within the context of the sentence.

1.   The unmitigated truth is that the author of the essays was _____ in his writing; their publication _____ the teacher's chances for a promotion.

   (A)   abusive...enhanced
   (B)   laconic...obliterated
   (C)   obtuse...obviated
   (D)   profound...diminished
   (E)   prolific...necessitated

2.   The sales associate tried to _____ trade by distributing business cards.

   (A)   elicit
   (B)   solicit
   (C)   illicit
   (D)   elliptic
   (E)   conciliate

3.   Zoologists would use the word _____ to describe a cow and the word _____ to describe a hog.

   (A)   herbivorous...omnivorous
   (B)   omnipotent...scavenger
   (C)   saprophyte...parasite

129

(D) vegetarian…carnivorous

(E) autotrophic…heterotrophic

4. The botanist explained that the plant which is _____ lives more than two years, while the plant which is _____ may store food and grow one year and may reproduce and die in another season.

(A) binary…annual        (D) evergreen…deciduous

(B) perennial …biennial        (E) decennial…triennial

(C) semi-annual…centennial

5. The sociologist interpreted _____ as being socially shared ideas about what is right and _____ as specific models of behaviors for a surrounding environment.

(A) culture…laws        (D) sanctions…folkways

(B) mores…technologies        (E) values…norms

(C) class…caste

6. The enthusiastic teacher described the talented student's clever display as _____.

(A) ingenuous        (D) adroit

(B) incongruous        (E) prosaic

(C) indolent

7. The practiced _____ displayed with _____ three pastes which he represented as costly gems to the buyers.

(A) charlatan…diffidence

(B) mountebank…self-possession

(C) empiric…concern

(D) swindler…aplomb

(E) imposture…assurance

---

**DIRECTIONS:** In the following questions, the given pair of words contains a specific relationship to each other. Select the best pair of choices which expresses the same relationship as the given.

---

8.  CATAPULT:PROJECTILE::

    (A) glacier:ice

    (B) precipice:cliff

    (C) transmit:message

    (D) prototype:replica

    (E) perspiration:emit

9.  PARSIMONIOUS:NIGGARDLY::

    (A) mendicant:benefactor

    (B) avarice:generosity

    (C) convoluted:intricate

    (D) miser:stingy

    (E) penurious:squandering

10. CONVEY:DUCT::

    (A) transport:transfer

    (B) pollute:filter

    (C) decipher:key

    (D) autograph:biography

    (E) falsify:fabricate

11. SUN:SOLAR SYSTEM::

    (A) moon:earth

    (B) island:archipelago

    (C) galaxy:star

    (D) molecule:atom

    (E) verses:poem

12. SOUFFLE:EGGS::

    (A) coconut:macaroon

    (B) pear:nectar

    (C) pigs:truffle

    (D) mousse:cream

    (E) tomato:fruit

131

13.  VACILLATE:DECISION::

  (A)  equivocate:commitment

  (B)  fluctuate:procrastinate

  (C)  conspire:collusion

  (D)  resolve:conclusion

  (E)  ameliorate:resolution

14.  ANTAGONIST:ADVERSARY::

  (A)  opponent:ally          (D)  rival:emulator

  (B)  competitor:auxiliary   (E)  foe:accomplice

  (C)  enemy:confederate

15.  STUPENDOUS:AMAZE::

  (A)  monstrous:bewilder     (D)  confound:atrocious

  (B)  prodigious:perplex     (E)  heinous:astound

  (C)  tremendous:distraction

16.  COVEY:QUAIL::

  (A)  cub:bear               (D)  ewe:sheep

  (B)  pride:lions            (E)  gaggle:ducks

  (C)  stag:deer

---

**DIRECTIONS:** Each passage is followed by questions based on its content. After reading a passage, choose the best answer to each question. Answer all questions based on what is stated or implied in that passage.

---

Dr. Harrison Faigel of Brandeis University has announced to standardized test-takers across the country the results of his experiment to improve the SAT scores of 30 high school students. Faigel was

convinced that student nervousness had affected their scores; to reduce the anxiety of these students who had already been tested, he gave 22 of them a beta blocker before the re-administration of the test. Their scores improved an average of more than 100 points. The other eight (who did not receive the beta blockers) improved only an average of 11 points. Second-time test-takers nationwide improved only an average of 28 points.

Beta blockers are prescription drugs which have been around for 25 years. These medications, which interfere with the effects of adrenalin, have been used for heart conditions and for minor stress such as stage fright—and now for test anxiety. These drugs seem to help test-takers who have low test scores because of test fright, not those who do not "know" the material. Since side effects from these beta blockers do exist, however, some physicians are not ready to prescribe routinely these medications to all test-takers.

17.   The passage suggests which of the following?

(A)   Many researchers will be dissatisfied with Faigel's study because he did not use a control group.

(B)   Second-time test-takers nationwide do fine without help; it is the first-time test-takers who experience anxiety and a lower score.

(C)   Even without study, preparation, and knowledge of the test material, one can experience help by taking the beta blockers before taking a test.

(D)   Adrenalin apparently increases minor stress which may result in lower test scores for already nervous students.

(E)   Adrenalin has long been used for heart conditions and for minor stress such as stage fright — and now for test anxiety.

18.   The passage supplies information for answering which of the following questions?

(A)   Did test anxiety increase the average test scores of our nation?

(B)   Did beta blockers improve the scores of second-time test-

takers nationally?

(C)  Did test fright increase scores of first-time test-takers?

(D)  Does familiarity with the test increase the scores of third-time test-takers?

(E)  Did beta blockers reduce the anxiety and increase the test scores of 30 nervous second-time test-takers?

19.  The passage implies that students' attitudes toward test scores can best be described as which of the following?

(A)  Casual disinterest        (D)  Pessimism

(B)  Resignation                (E)  Concern

(C)  Antagonism

20.  The author mentions speculating on the average standardized test scores. Which of the following logically ensues?

(A)  Retaking the SAT normally results in a significant increase on the scores because of the student's familiarity with the test format.

(B)  The re-administration of tests will be decreased in the future since second-time test-takers routinely increase their average scores significantly.

(C)  The beta blockers, if used routinely by nervous second-time test-takers, may result in an increase in the average standardized test scores for the nation.

(D)  Only competitive students will attempt to utilize beta blockers; average test scores, therefore, will not be significantly affected.

(E)  Competitive students will try to avail themselves of adrenalin; the average scores on standardized tests for the nation will be increased.

21.  Which of the following best summarizes the author's main point?

(A) The study by Faigel indicates to the general public that help for general nervousness is at hand through the use of beta blockers.

(B) Adrenalin increased the performance of 22 second-time test-takers of the SAT.

(C) Beta blockers seem to improve the average scores of second-time takers of the SAT more than 100 points.

(D) Beta blockers should not be used since they may cause side effects.

(E) Nervousness does not seem to affect the test scores of students if they "know" the material in the first place.

22. The author of this article can be best described as which of the following?

   (A) Pessimistic.          (D) Resigned.

   (B) Unconcerned.          (E) Optimistic.

   (C) Indifferent.

23. Recognizing that nervousness may affect test scores and developing a plan to reduce the nervousness and to compare the test results is an example of Faigel's using which of the following?

   (A) Analysis.             (D) Interpretation.

   (B) Synthesis.            (E) Application.

   (C) Deduction.

24. Which function(s) does the first paragraph of this passage perform?

   (A) Present the problem and a possible solution.

   (B) Present the results.      (D) (A) and (B) only.

   (C) Analyze the results.      (E) (A) and (C) only.

135

Amyotrophic lateral sclerosis (ALS) is a debilitating disorder which attacks the body's nervous system and renders muscles useless. The disease, which has no known cause or cure, is that which took the life of Lou Gehrig, a member of baseball's Hall of Fame. Even more perplexing is that three former San Francisco 49ers have also died from ALS, which is usually a rare disease. There exists no corroboration to speculations as to whether pain-killers, steroids, or even the fertilizers used on playing fields triggered the disease. A solution to the enigma of ALS does not seem imminent.

25. The author's attitude toward ALS is best described as which of the following?

   (A) Amusement.

   (B) Indignation.

   (C) Indifference

   (D) Approval.

   (E) Resignation.

26. Which of the following statements is a correct example of deductive reasoning?

   (A) At least four of the victims of the rare ALS have been athletes; the diesease seems to affect active persons more often.

   (B) Four sports figures have died from ALS.

   (C) Since three football players and one baseball player have died from ALS, constant exposure to fertilizers on the playing fields may increase one's chances of developing ALS.

   (D) Three football and one baseball player have died from ALS; the next victim will probably be a ballplayer also.

   (E) All four of the most well-known victims of ALS have been males; the disease seems to affect only men.

27. The topic sentence is which of the following?

   (A) A solution to the enigma of ALS does not seem imminent.

136

(B) The disease, which has no known cause or cure, is that which took the life of Lou Gehrig, a member of baseball's Hall of Fame.

(C) Even more perplexing is that three former San Francisco 49ers have also died from ALS, which is usually a rare disease.

(D) Amyotrophic lateral sclerosis (ALS) is a debilitating disorder which attacks the body's nervous system and renders muscles useless.

(E) There exists no corroboration to speculations as to whether pain-killers, steroids, or even the fertilizers used on playing fields triggered the disease.

---

**DIRECTIONS:** Each of the following questions provides a given word in capitalized letters followed by five choice words. Choose the best word which is most <u>opposite</u> in meaning to the given word.

---

28. MALAPROPOS:

    (A) congruous

    (B) specious

    (C) ponderous

    (D) benign

    (E) propensity

30. UNCOUTH:

    (A) melancholy

    (B) ameliorating

    (C) funereal

    (D) boorish

    (E) urbane

29. ITINERANT:

    (A) illegitimate

    (B) permanent

    (C) idyllic

    (D) gaudy

    (E) felted

31. CORPULENT:

    (A) portly

    (B) vociferate

    (C) becoming

    (D) anorexic

    (E) adverse

32. FERAL:

    (A) voracious

    (B) conscientious

    (C) savage

    (D) exacting

    (E) blithe

33. UNCTUOUS:

    (A) scrupulous

    (B) morose

    (C) ravenous

    (D) agitated

    (E) ingratiating

34. INVIDIOUS:

    (A) repugnant

    (B) obscure

    (C) ransomed

    (D) reconciliable

    (E) perturbed

35. NEBULOUS:

    (A) conclusive

    (B) spurious

    (C) frigate

    (D) saturnine

    (E) ambiguous

36. PROPITIOUS:

    (A) conspicuous

    (B) auspicious

    (C) evanescence

    (D) militant

    (E) aggregative

37. ODYSSEY:

    (A) journey

    (B) errand

    (C) wandering

    (D) voyage

    (E) cruise

38. PUNCTILIOUS:

    (A) somber

    (B) genial

    (C) particular

    (D) negligent

    (E) antagonistic

**STOP**

If time still remains, you may go back and check your work. When the time allotted is up, you may go on to the next section.

# Section 2

---

**TIME:** 30 Minutes
38 Questions

**DIRECTIONS:** Each of the given sentences has blank spaces which indicate words omitted. Choose the best combination of words which fit into the meaning and structure within the context of the sentence.

---

1. The _____ habits of the wild hawk caused a serious _____ to develop for the chicken farmer.

   (A) marauding...emergency

   (B) parasitic...malady

   (C) saprophytic...insurrection

   (D) predatory...predicament

   (E) meticulous...tête-à-tête

2. The family left their country to _____ to Utopia and escape _____ because of their beliefs.

   (A) immigrate...prosecution (D) wander...arraignment

   (B) peregrinate...extortion (E) roam...censure

   (C) emigrate...persecution

3. The frightened mother _____ her young daughter for darting in front of the car.

   (A) implored (D) admonished

   (B) extorted (E) abolished

   (C) exhorted

4. The leaders gave _____ to the members of the Alliance of World Citizens.

   (A)  advise                    (D)  consul

   (B)  council                   (E)  tribune

   (C)  advice

5. She was a perfect receptionist for the complaint department because with her _____ temperament she was not easily aroused.

   (A)  impassive                 (D)  apathetic

   (B)  stoic                     (E)  stolid

   (C)  phlegmatic

6. She responded so quickly with a _____ that it was evident the remark had been _____ until the proper time to use it.

   (A)  repartee...dormant        (D)  humor...camouflaged

   (B)  wit...latent              (E)  sortie...disguised

   (C)  satire...hibernating

7. After reading the letter, she _____ that the manager was attempting to _____ a contract with her.

   (A)  implied...abrogate        (D)  surmised...breech

   (B)  inferred...negotiate      (E)  included...annihilate

   (C)  imposed...nullify

---

**DIRECTIONS:** In the following questions, the given pair of words contains a specific relationship to each other. Select the best pair of choices which expresses the same relationship as the given.

---

8. MERIDIAN:PARALLEL::

 (A) east:west          (D) map:globe

 (B) north:south        (E) compass:direction

 (C) longitude:latitude


9. ABORIGINAL:INSERTION::

 (A) native:novel       (D) modern:resumption

 (B) original:habituated (E) accustomed:recurrence

 (C) source:mouth


10. AVERSION:FONDNESS::

 (A) equivalent:commensurate

 (B) tantamount:equal

 (C) farrier:blacksmith

 (D) execrable:foul

 (E) odious:laudable


11. VITIATE:SPOIL::

 (A) fatuous:asinine     (D) adulterate:cleanse

 (B) contaminate:purge   (E) vicissitude:taint

 (C) abase:corrupt


12. CIRCULATORY:HEART::

 (A) excretory:sweat     (D) digestive:kidney

 (B) neurological:skeleton (E) reproductive:testes

 (C) lungs:respiratory

13. DILETTANTE:TYRO::

    (A) necrology:profession   (D) dabbler:amateur

    (B) ingredient:compound   (E) lawyer:brief

    (C) foible:chaste

14. FRAILTY:VICE::

    (A) felony:misdemeanor

    (B) aggravating:pernicious

    (C) trite:popular

    (D) secreted:veiled

    (E) cloister:monastery

15. QUART:LITER::

    (A) yard:acre   (D) liter:gallon

    (B) yard:meter   (E) mile:kilogram

    (C) ounce:kilowatt

16. FINE:AMERCEMENT::

    (A) loss:gain   (D) lottery:deposit

    (B) forfeiture:reward   (E) contraband:confiscate

    (C) penalty:mulct

---

**DIRECTIONS:** Each passage is followed by questions based on its content. After reading a passage, choose the best answer to each question. Answer all questions based on what is stated or implied in that passage.

---

Established firmly in popular culture is the notion that each of the two hemispheres of the brain has specialized functions. The left hemisphere, insist proponents of this theory, controls language and

logic; the right hemisphere, espousers contend, is the more creative and intuitive half. Many proponents try to classify a person as "right-brained" or "left-brained," suggesting that the two hemispheres do not work together in the same person and, thus, can be considered independent. Because of the supposed independent functions of the two hemispheres and because of their difference in specializations, an activity might engage one part of the brain while the other part is not used at all, they believe. "Right-brained" individuals are the creative intuitive persons (artists, for instance) of society; "left-brained" persons are the verbal, language-oriented, logical individuals of civilization.

Opponents of the split-brain theory dispute the premise that the hemispheres operate independently simply because of specialized functions; they state that the very fact that the two hemispheres differ in purpose indicates that they must integrate activities and therefore result in processes which are different from and even greater than the processes of either hemisphere. These split-brain theory opponents base their arguments on the fact that when surgery is performed to disconnect the two sides, each can still function well (but not perfectly). They also argue that when a person writes an original story, the left hemisphere works to produce a logical work, but the right hemisphere helps with creativity. The third argument is based on the fact that if a patient has right hemisphere damage, major logical disorders are manifested; in fact, more logical disorders appear than if the left hemisphere suffers damage. The opponents to split-brain theory state that it is impossible to educate one side of the brain without educating the other. They state that there is no evidence that one can be purely right-brained or left-brained.

Educators, then, who seek to modify the curriculum and methods to accommodate the split-brain theory must justify their demands. The burden of proof rests with these innovators who seek to restructure education as it currently exists.

17. To the assertion that the split-brain theory is accurate, the author would probably respond with which of the following?

   (A) Unqualified disagreement

   (B) Unquestioning approval

    (C)   Complete indifference

    (D)   Strong disparagement

    (E)   Implied uncertainty

18. Which of the following titles best describes the content of the passage?

    (A)   A Reassertion of the Validity of the Split-brain Theory

    (B)   A Renunciation of the Split-brain Theory

    (C)   Split Opinions on the Split-brain Theory

    (D)   Modifying the Curriculum to Accommodate the Split-brain Theory

    (E)   A New Theory: The Split-brain Theory

19. The attitude of the author toward proponents' furnishing proof to justify modifying the curriculum to accommodate the split-brain theory could be best described as which of the following?

    (A)   Optimism          (D)   Illogical

    (B)   Pessimism        (E)   Indifference

    (C)   Resignation

20. A cause-and-effect relationship could best be illustrated by which of the following true statements?

    (A)   The right hemisphere of the brain controls language and logic; if it is damaged, language may be affected.

    (B)   Since the right hemisphere controls language and logic, educators usually accommodate the right brain.

    (C)   Proponents of the split-brain theory contend that when surgery is performed to disconnect the two sides of the brain, each can still function well (but not perfectly).

    (D)   Educators have modified the curriculum and methods in most schools to accommodate the split-brain theory.

(E) It is impossible to educate one side of the brain without educating the other, according to opponents of the split-brain theory.

21. The most compelling reason that the opponents of the split-brain theory give for their beliefs, according to the author, is which of the following?

   (A) When surgery is performed to disconnect the two sides of the brain, both sides continue to operate well — but not perfectly.

   (B) When a patient has right hemisphere damage, no logical disorders are manifested.

   (C) Because of the independent functions of the two hemispheres, an activity might engage one hemisphere of the brain and not another.

   (D) The hemispheres operate independently because of specialized functions.

   (E) It is impossible to educate one side of the brain without educating the other.

22. According to the passage, the most significant distinction between proponents and opponents of the split-brain theory is which of the following?

   (A) Their beliefs about teaching methods and the curriculum.

   (B) Proponents state that the two hemispheres differ in purpose and, therefore, must integrate activities.

   (C) Opponents state the the hemispheres differ in function and, therefore, can not integrate activites.

   (D) Their beliefs about the functions of the hemispheres of the brain.

   (E) Their beliefs that the brain is divided into hemispheres.

23. Which of the following statements is most compatible with the principles of the split-brain theory?

    (A) The fact that the two hemispheres differ in purpose indicates that they must integrate activities.

    (B) "Right-brained" individuals are the creative, intuitive persons of society; "left-brained" persons are the verbal, language oriented, logical individuals of civilization.

    (C) It is impossible to educate one side of the brain without educating the other.

    (D) More logical disorders appear if the right hemisphere is damaged than if the left hemisphere is damaged.

    (E) When surgery is performed to disconnect the two sides of the brain, each can function well.

24. To an assertion that education curriculum and methods should be altered to accommodate proponents of the split-brain theory, the author would most likely respond with which of the following?

    (A) This is a definite need in our schools today.

    (B) Educators have already made these important modifications.

    (C) Justification for these alterations must be provided by proponents of the split-brain theory.

    (D) It is impossible to educate one side of the brain without educating the other.

    (E) Such alterations might be necessary since "right-brained" persons are the verbal, language-oriented, logical individuals.

Being born female and black were two handicaps Gwendolyn Brooks states that she faced from her birth, in 1917, in Kansas. Brooks was determined to succeed. Despite the lack of encouragement she received from her teachers and others, she was determined to write and found the first publisher for one of her poems when she was eleven.

In 1945 she marketed and sold her first book; national recognition

ensued. She applied for and received grants and fellowships from such organizations as the American Academy of Arts and Letters and the Guggenheim Foundation. Later she received the Pulitzer Prize for Poetry; she was the first black woman to receive such an honor.

Brooks was an integrationist in the 1940's and an advocate of black consciousness in the 1960's. Her writing styles show that she is not bound by rules; her works are not devoid of the truth, even about sensitive subjects like the black experience, life in the ghetto, and city life.

Brooks' reaction to fame is atypical. She continues to work—and work hard. She writes, travels, and helps many who are interested in writing. Especially important to her is increasing her knowledge of her black heritage and encouraging other people to do the same. She encourages dedication to the art to would-be writers.

25. From the article one could say that Brooks could be best described as which of the following?

(A) Humanistic          (D) Craven

(B) Circumspect         (E) Alienated

(C) Obscure

26. The passage implies that Brooks received less credit than she deserved primarily because of which of the following?

(A) She tried to publish too early in her career.

(B) She was aided by funds received through grants.

(C) She was a frequent victim of both racial and gender discrimination.

(D) Her work was too complex to be of widespread interest to others.

(E) She had no interest in the accolades of her colleagues.

27. If the next sentence in the passage were a statement from Brooks, which of the following might most likely be her words?

   (A) "Awards are not important; write what you want to say."

   (B) "Develop a style of your own and do not depart from this art form."

   (C) "*Art* is what the public calls *art*. Find out what this is and 'go for it'."

   (D) "If you sincerely dedicate yourself to your art form, there will be little room left for current events and loneliness."

   (E) "Study the classics before you begin; they are essential elements after which you must pattern your writing if you are to be dedicated to the arts."

---

**DIRECTIONS:** Each of the following questions provides a given word in capitalized letters followed by five choice words. Choose the best word which is most <u>opposite</u> in meaning to the given word.

---

28. CONCORD:

   (A) succor

   (B) enmity

   (C) gripper

   (D) vigilant

   (E) ennobling

29. INSIDIOUS:

   (A) precipitant

   (B) incendiary

   (C) decadent

   (D) conducive

   (E) imprudent

30. MALEFACTION:

   (A) affinity

   (B) subsidy

   (C) profligation

   (D) idosyncratic

   (E) cognate

31. OBDURATE:

   (A) affable

   (B) unsavory

   (C) prevaricating

   (D) credulous

   (E) penitent

32.  RANCOROUS:

    (A)  officious

    (B)  enmity

    (C)  abash

    (D)  nefarious

    (E)  judicious

33.  PERPETUITY:

    (A)  pedantic

    (B)  espouse

    (C)  mortality

    (D)  culpable

    (E)  cybernetics

34.  EXPURGATED:

    (A)  inextirpable

    (B)  sundered

    (C)  venerated

    (D)  expatriated

    (E)  complacent

35.  POSTULATE:

    (A)  mollify

    (B)  conjecture

    (C)  prognosticate

    (D)  corroborate

    (E)  refurbish

36.  CAPRICIOUS:

    (A)  impecunious

    (B)  juxtapositioned

    (C)  scrupulous

    (D)  copious

    (E)  superfluous

37.  NON SEQUITUR:

    (A)  mundane

    (B)  semaphore

    (C)  illogical

    (D)  reasonable

    (E)  fallacious

38.  ZEPHYR:

    (A)  tycoon

    (B)  typhoon

    (C)  coracle

    (D)  taciturn

    (E)  constellation

**STOP**

If time still remains, you may go back and check your work. When the time allotted is up, you may go on to the next section.

# Section 3

**TIME:** 30 Minutes
30 Questions

**NUMBERS:** All numbers are real numbers.

**FIGURES:** Position of points, angles, regions, etc. are assumed to be in the order shown and angle measures are assumed to be positive.

**LINES:** Assume that lines shown as straight are indeed straight.

**DIRECTIONS:** Each of the following given set of quantities is placed into either column A or B. Compare the two quantities to decide whether:

(A)    the quantity in Column A is greater

(B)    the quantity in Column B is greater

(C)    the two quantities are equal

(D)    the relationship cannot be determined from the information given.

**NOTE:** Do not choose (E) since there are only four choices.

**COMMON INFORMATION:** Information which relates to one or both given quantities is centered in the two columns. A symbol which appears in both columns will indicate the same item in Column A and Column B.

**EXAMPLES:**

| Column A | Column B |
|---|---|
| 1.    $5 \times 4$ | $5 + 4$ |

Explanation: The correct answer is (A), since $5 \times 4 = 20$, and $5 + 4 = 9$.

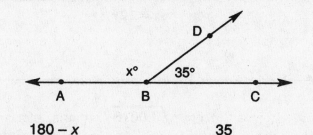

2.        $180 - x$                      35

Explanation: The correct answer is (C). Since Angle *ABC* is a straight angle, its measurement is 180°.

|  | Column A | Column B |
|---|---|---|

$x = 5, y = -3$

1.          $(x + y)^2$              $(x - y)^2$

2.      $\frac{1}{5}$ of 0.2% of \$1000      $(\frac{1}{5})$% of 0.2 of \$1000

$x > 0, y > 0$

3.          $x^2 + y^2$             $(x + y)^2$

Two concentric circles:
Diameter of inner circle is 3.5 units
Diameter of outer circle is 7 units

4.    Circumference of        $\frac{1}{2}$ of circumference of
      inner circle                outer circle

|  | **Column A** | **Column B** |
|---|---|---|

$$4w = 6x = 12y$$

| 5. | $w$ | $y$ |
|---|---|---|

$$1/x = \sqrt{0.0016}\,/5$$

| 6. | $x$ | 12.5 |
|---|---|---|

| 7. | $\dfrac{x-3}{4} + \dfrac{x+7}{3}$ | $\dfrac{7x+19}{7}$ |
|---|---|---|

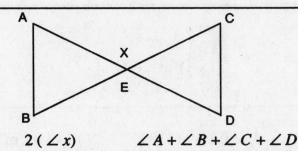

| 8. | $2\,(\angle x)$ | $\angle A + \angle B + \angle C + \angle D$ |
|---|---|---|

$$x^2 = y + 2 = 5$$

| 9. | $x$ | $y$ |
|---|---|---|

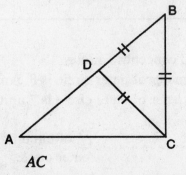

Line segments
$BC = CD = BD$
and $BC \perp AC$

| 10. | $AC$ | $CD$ |
|---|---|---|

152

|              | Column A                                         | Column B                                         |
| ------------ | ------------------------------------------------ | ------------------------------------------------ |
| 11.          | The least common multiple of 20, 24, 32          | The least common multiple of 2, 15, 32           |

Area of a rt. triangle $ABC$ = 60.5 square units
segment $AC$ = segment $CB$

|              | Column A                                         | Column B                                         |
| ------------ | ------------------------------------------------ | ------------------------------------------------ |
| 12.          | Length of $AC$                                   | 11 units                                         |
| 13.          | $\dfrac{13}{16}$                                 | $\dfrac{31}{40}$                                 |

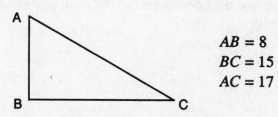

$AB = 8$
$BC = 15$
$AC = 17$

|              | Column A                                         | Column B                                         |
| ------------ | ------------------------------------------------ | ------------------------------------------------ |
| 14.          | Angle $ABC$                                      | 90°                                              |

$w : x = y : z$, $x$ and $z$ are not zero

|              | Column A                                         | Column B                                         |
| ------------ | ------------------------------------------------ | ------------------------------------------------ |
| 15.          | $w + x$                                          | $y + z$                                          |

---

**DIRECTIONS:** For the following questions, select the best answer choice to the given question.

16. What part of three fourths is one tenth?

    (A) $\frac{1}{8}$          (D) $\frac{3}{40}$

    (B) $\frac{15}{2}$         (E) none of these

    (C) $\frac{2}{15}$

17. What is the length of side *BC*?

    (A) 3

    (B) 5

    (C) $\sqrt{34}$

    (D) 7

    (E) none of these

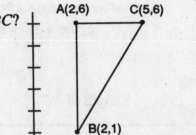

18. A line segment is drawn from the point $(3, 5)$ to the point $(9, 13)$. What are the coordinates of the midpoint of the line segment?

    (A) $(9, 6)$           (D) $(6, 8)$

    (B) $(12, 18)$         (E) $(3, 4)$

    (C) $(6, 9)$

Questions 19 – 23 refer to the graph below.

Portion of Ph.D. Degrees in the Mathematical Sciences
Awarded to U.S. Citizens in 1986

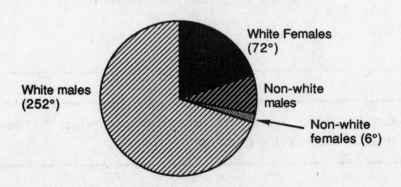

19. What percent of the Ph.D. degrees were awarded in 1986 to non-white males?

    (A) 30

    (B) $8^1/_3$

    (C) $4^1/_6$

    (D) 20

    (E) none of these

20. If 4000 Ph.D.s were awarded in Mathematical Sciences, how many were awarded to white female U.S. citizens?

    (A) 800

    (B) 2880

    (C) 3200

    (D) 1120

    (E) none of these

21. If the 600 white females represent 72° of the figure that depicts the total distribution of Ph.D.s awarded in the Mathematical Sciences in the U.S. in 1986, then how many were awarded to white males?

    (A) 432

    (B) 3000

    (C) about 857

    (D) 2100

    (E) cannot be determined

22. Given the distribution of Ph.D.s awarded in Mathematical Sciences in the U.S. in 1986, what is the ratio of white male's degrees to non-white male's degrees?

    (A) 1 to 5

    (B) 3.5 to 1

    (C) 8.4 to 1

    (D) 42 to 1

    (E) none of these

23. If the non-white female category represents 6° of the distribution of a total of 6000 Ph.D.s awarded in the Mathematical Sciences, then how many Ph.D.s were awarded in this category?

    (A)  50

    (B)  100

    (C)  500

    (D)  1000

    (E)  cannot be determined

24. The solution of the equation $4 - 5(2y + 4) = 4$ is:

    (A)  $-^2/_5$

    (B)  8

    (C)  4

    (D)  $-2$

    (E)  none of these

25. The quotient of $(x^2 - 5x + 3)/(x + 2)$ is:

    (A)  $x - 7 + 17/(x + 2)$

    (B)  $x - 3 + 9/(x + 2)$

    (C)  $x - 7 - 11/(x + 2)$

    (D)  $x - 3 - 3/(x + 2)$

    (E)  $x + 3 - 3(x + 2)$

26. One number is 2 more than 3 times another. Their sum is 22. Find the numbers.

    (A)  8, 14

    (B)  2, 20

    (C)  5, 17

    (D)  4, 18

    (E)  10, 12

27. The value of $B$ in the equation $a = (h/2)(B + b)$ is:

    (A)  $(2a - b)/h$

    (B)  $2h/a - b$

    (C)  $2a - b$

    (D)  $2a/h - b$

    (E)  none of these

28. A box contains 6 red marbles and 4 blue marbles. What is the probability that if 2 marbles are drawn from the box, both will be red?

    (A) $^2/_3$                    (D) $^1/_5$

    (B) $^1/_3$                    (E) $^2/_5$

    (C) $^1/_2$

29. Which of the following integers is the square of an integer for every integer $x$?

    (A) $x^2 + x$                  (D) $x^2 + 2x - 4$

    (B) $x^2 + 1$                  (E) $x^2 + 2x + 1$

    (C) $x^2 + 2x$

30. What is the median of the following group of scores?

    27, 27, 26, 26, 26, 26, 18, 13, 36, 36, 30, 30, 30, 27, 29

    (A) 30                         (D) 27

    (B) 26                         (E) 36

    (C) 25.4

## STOP

If time still remains, you may go back and check your work.
When the time alloted is up, you may go on to the next section.

# Section 4

**TIME:**   30 Minutes
30 Questions

**NUMBERS:** All numbers are real numbers.

**FIGURES:** Position of points, angles, regions, etc. are assumed to be in the order shown and angle measures are assumed to be positive.

**LINES:** Assume that lines shown as straight are indeed straight.

**DIRECTIONS:** Each of the following given set of quantities is placed into either column A or B. Compare the two quantities to decide whether:

(A)   the quantity in Column A is greater

(B)   the quantity in Column B is greater

(C)   the two quantities are equal

(D)   the relationship cannot be determined from the information given.

**NOTE:** Do not choose (E) since there are only four choices.

**COMMON INFORMATION:** Information which relates to one or both given quantities is centered in the two columns. A symbol which appears in both columns will indicate the same item in Column A and Column B.

**EXAMPLES:**

| Column A | Column B |
| --- | --- |
| 1.    $5 \times 4$ | $5 + 4$ |

Explanation:  The correct answer is (A), since $5 \times 4 = 20$, and $5 + 4 = 9$.

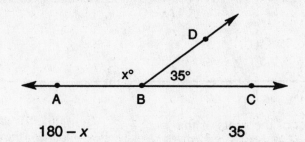

2.              $180 - x$                              35

Explanation: The correct answer is (C). Since Angle *ABC* is a straight angle, its measurement is 180°.

|         Column A         |         Column B         |
| --- | --- |

$$x + y = 6$$
$$3x - y = 4$$

1.            $x - y$                          0

$$w : x = y : z$$
$$x \neq 0, \quad z \neq 0$$

2.            $wz - xy$                          0

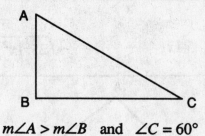

$m\angle A > m\angle B$   and   $\angle C = 60°$

3.            Side *AB*                      Side *BC*

|  | <u>Column A</u> | <u>Column B</u> |
|---|---|---|

$$1/y < 0$$

| 4. | $y$ | $1$ |

| 5. | Product of the roots of the equation $x^2 + 3x + 2 = 0$ | $-1$ |

$$\sqrt{x} = 16, y^3 = 64$$

| 6. | $x$ | $y$ |

| 7. | $(1 - \sqrt{2})(1 - \sqrt{2})$ | $(1 - \sqrt{2})(1 + \sqrt{2})$ |

Given a cube with length of a side equal to $d$ units

| 8. | Surface area of cube | Volume of cube |

$$x > 0$$

| 9. | $5.1x$ | $\sqrt{25.1x^2}$ |

Angle $A = 100°$
Angle $B = 48°$

| 10. | Side $AB$ | Side $BC$ |

| Column A | Column B |
|----------|----------|

**11.** Distance between $A(3, 4)$ and $B(-1, 1)$ | Distance between $C(4, -2)$ and $D(-2, -2)$

Area of triangle plus area of square = 125 and perimeter of square is 40

**12.** Twice the length of line segment $BD$ | The shortest distance from point $A$ to line segment $DE$

$k \mid\mid m$
angle 2 = 60 degrees

**13.** angle 5 | 60 degrees

**14.** The sum of all angles of a polygon whose sides are all equal | The sum of all angles of a square

$$x = 5, y = -3$$

**15.** $(x + y)^2$ | $(x - y)^2$

**DIRECTIONS:** For the following questions, select the best answer choice to the given question.

16. What percent of 260 is 13?

(A) .05%                     (D) .5%

(B) 5%                       (E) 20%

(C) 50%

17. If a triangle of base 6 units has the same area as a circle of radius 6 units, what is the altitude of the triangle?

(A) $\pi$                      (D) $12\pi$

(B) $3\pi$                     (E) $36\pi$

(C) $6\pi$

18. A cube consists of 96 square feet. What is the volume of the cube in cubic feet?

(A) 16                       (D) 96

(B) 36                       (E) 216

(C) 64

19. If the angles of a triangle ABC are in the ratio of 3 : 5 : 7, then the triangle is:

(A) acute                    (D) obtuse

(B) right                    (E) equilateral

(C) isosceles

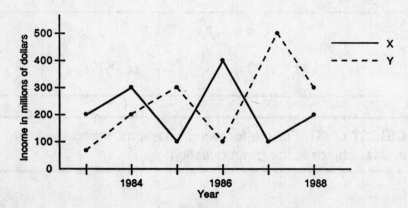

Questions 20 – 24 refer to the previous table.

20. About what was the average income in millions of Y Company between 1986 and 1988?

   (A)  200                        (D)  500

   (B)  300                        (E)  900

   (C)  350

21. By how much was the largest difference between the income earnings of the companies in a given year?

   (A)  100                        (D)  400

   (B)  200                        (E)  500

   (C)  300

22. What was the largest percent of increase in earnings of Y Company?

   (A)  50%                        (D)  300%

   (B)  100%                       (E)  400%

   (C)  200%

23. What was the largest percent of decrease in earnings of the companies?

   (A)  50%                        (D)  75%

   (B)  100%                       (E)  400%

   (C)  200%

24. What was the median income in millions of X Company from 1983 thru 1988?

   (A)  100                        (B)  200

(C)   300

(E)   Can't be determined

(D)   400

25.   If $x$ and $y$ are two different real numbers and $xz = yz$, then what is the value of $z$?

(A)   $x - y$

(D)   $y/x$

(B)   1

(E)   0

(C)   $x/y$

26.   A runner takes 9 seconds to run a distance of 132 feet. What is her speed in miles per hour?

(A)   9

(D)   12

(B)   10

(E)   13

(C)   11

27.   $\dfrac{\left(x^2\right)^{-4}\left(x^{-2}\right)^3}{\left(x^{-3}\right)^{-5}} =$

(A)   $x^5$

(D)   $x^7$

(B)   $1/x^{14}$

(E)   $x^{29}$

(C)   $1/x^{29}$

28.   A wheel with a diameter of 3 feet makes a revolution every 2 minutes. How many feet will the wheel travel in 30 minutes?

(A)   $3\pi$

(D)   $30\pi$

(B)   $6\pi$

(E)   $15\pi$

(C)   $45\pi$

29. A waitress' income consists of her salary and tips. Her salary is $150 a week. During one week that included a holiday her tips were 5/4 of her salary. What fraction of her income for the week came from tips?

(A) 5/8

(B) 5/4

(C) 4/9

(D) 1/2

(E) 5/9

30. Each of the integers $h$, $m$ and $n$ is divisible by 3. Which of the following integers is <u>always</u> divisible by 9?

I. $hm$

II. $h + m$

III. $h + m + n$

(A) I only

(B) II only

(C) III only

(D) II and III only

(E) I, II and III

## STOP

If time still remains, you may go back and check your work.
When the time allotted is up, you may go on to the next section.

# Section 5

TIME:   30 Minutes
        25 Questions

DIRECTIONS: Each question or group of questions is based on a passage or set of statements. Select the best answer choice.

Questions 1 – 4 refer to the following statements.

The state of Texana contains six cities.

F is the westernmost city and south of K.
J and K are south of I.
G and J are west and south of K and south of F.
H is east of I and south of J.
I is east of K.

1.   The northernmost city in Texana is

(A)  G                          (D)  J

(B)  H                          (E)  K

(C)  I

2.   The easternmost city in Texana is

(A)  G                          (D)  J

(B)  H                          (E)  K

(C)  I

3.   The southernmost city in Texana is

(A)  G                          (B)  H

(C)  I                               (E)  K

(D)  J

4.  If the above information is true, all of the following statements EXCEPT which must also be true?

   (A)  G is west of I.

   (B)  F is south and west of I.

   (C)  H is south and east of K.

   (D)  G is east of J.

   (E)  J is west of H.

5.  If your car was manufactured in Sweden after 1980, it has excellent safety features.

   The statement above can be deduced logically from which of the following statements?

   (A)  Some cars made in Sweden before 1980 had excellent safety features.

   (B)  All cars manufactured in Sweden after 1980 have excellent safety features.

   (C)  Swedish laws governing car manufacturing changed radically in 1980.

   (D)  Only if a car was made after 1980 could it have excellent safety features.

   (E)  Excellent safety features were not developed in the United States until 1988.

6.  During January, it always snowed more than two inches in State M whenever the temperature was 32° F or higher. Temperatures in January ranged from 5°F to 40° F.

   Assuming that the statements above are true, which of the following CANNOT be an accurate report of the temperature and snowfall on a January day in State M?

(A)  20° F, 3"          (D)  35° F, 2"

(B)  30° F, 0"          (E)  40° F, 5"

(C)  32° F, 2½"

7.  Opponents of prison reform argue that prisons have not done a good job of rehabilitating criminals, citing the large number of repeat offenders in our prisons — nearly one of every two parolees who have been in prison rehabilitation programs become repeat offenders. Hence they conclude that rehabilitation programs have been ineffective and should be abandoned, and that prisons should be used only for punishment of crimes committed.

Which of the following, if true, most seriously weakens the argument above?

(A)  Some offenders want to be imprisoned; hence imprisonment is not a form of punishment for them.

(B)  Current revenues do not allow the construction of more long-term prisons.

(C)  Studies have shown that over ninety percent of parolees who have not been in prison rehabilitation programs become repeat offenders.

(D)  It is impossible to predict which criminals are most likely to become repeat offenders.

(E)  Studies have shown that the highest percentage of repeat offenders are those who commit serious crimes, such as homicides; whereas the lowest percentage of repeat offenders are those convicted of misdemeanors.

Questions 8 – 13 refer to the following passage.

A landscaping crew will plant ornamental trees, shade trees, evergreen trees, ornamental shrubs, evergreen shrubs, and ornamental grasses on a bare housing site. Planting must be done in five consecutive working days, Monday through Friday, and must conform to all of the following conditions:

168

All evergreens must be planted on the same day.
Ornamentals and evergreens cannot be planted on the same day.
Shade trees must be planted at least one day before evergreen trees.
Ornamental grasses and ornamental trees must be planted on the same day.
Evergreen shrubs must be planted at least one day before ornamental trees.

8. Which of the following can be planted on the same day?

   (A) Evergreen trees and ornamental shrubs

   (B) Ornamental shrubs and evergreen shrubs

   (C) Shade trees and evergreen shrubs

   (D) Shade trees and ornamental grasses

   (E) Ornamental grasses and evergreen trees

9. Which of the following is an acceptable order of planting, from first to last?

   (A) Shade trees, evergreen shrubs, ornamental grasses

   (B) Shade trees, ornamental grasses, evergreen trees

   (C) Shade trees, ornamental trees, evergreen trees

   (D) Evergreen shrubs, shade trees, evergreen trees

   (E) Evergreen shrubs, ornamental grasses, shade trees

10. If the crew plants ornamental grasses on Thursday, it CANNOT plant

   (A) evergreen shrubs on Wednesday

   (B) shade trees on Tuesday

   (C) evergreen trees on Friday

   (D) ornamental shrubs on Friday

   (E) ornamental shrubs on Wednesday

11. If the crew plants evergreen shrubs on Wednesday, it can plant

    (A) ornamental shrubs on Wednesday

    (B) evergreen trees on Friday

    (C) ornamental trees on Tuesday

    (D) shade trees on Monday

    (E) ornamental grasses on Monday

12. If the crew plants ornamental trees on Friday and shade trees on Tuesday, it can plant evergreen shrubs on

    (A) Monday, Tuesday, Wednesday, or Thursday only

    (B) Wednesday or Thursday only

    (C) Tuesday or Thursday only

    (D) Wednesday only

    (E) Thursday only

13. On how many days can the crew plant ornamental shrubs if it plants shade trees on Monday, evergreen shrubs on Wednesday, and ornamental grasses on Friday?

    (A) one                    (D) four

    (B) two                    (E) five

    (C) three

Questions 14 – 17 refer to the following information.

S T U V W X Y and Z weighed in and then competed in a jumping event.

    S weighed more than V and jumped higher than W.
    Z weighed less than X and more than W, and did not jump as high as Y.
    T weighed more than U and less than W, and jumped higher than Y but not as high as U.
    U weighed more than S and did not jump as high as W.

170

14. Which of the following weighed least?

    (A)  S                    (D)  V

    (B)  T                    (E)  Z

    (C)  U

15. Which of the following jumped highest?

    (A)  T                    (D)  Y

    (B)  U                    (E)  Z

    (C)  W

16. Which of the following statements must be true?

    (A)  V weighed less than T and jumped higher than Y.

    (B)  T weighed more than Z and jumped higher than Z.

    (C)  U weighed more than V and jumped higher than S.

    (D)  Y weighed more than Z and jumped higher than Z.

    (E)  W weighed more than S and jumped higher than T.

17. Which of the following statements could be true?

    (A)  X weighed the most and jumped highest of the contestants.

    (B)  W was third heaviest and jumped fifth highest of the contestants.

    (C)  Heavy competitors always jumped higher than lighter ones.

    (D)  Lighter competitors always jumped higher than heavier ones.

    (E)  T was the sixth heaviest and jumped fifth highest of the contestants.

Questions 18-22 refer to the following information.

A state dinner will include a rectangular table for seven that presents several seating problems. The guests are three governors (F, G, H), two senators (J, K), and two congressmen (L, M). Three guests will sit on one side of the table, three directly opposite on the other side, and one at the head of the table. No one will sit at the foot of the table.

Congressmen cannot be seated next to each other.
Senators cannot be seated directly opposite each other.
Governor F cannot be seated next to Senator J.
Governor G must sit immediately on Congressman L's right.
A governor must sit at the head of the table.

18. If H sits at the head of the table, G and J sit immediately to his left and right respectively, and L sits next to K, which guest must sit directly opposite Congressman L?

    (A) F                      (D) L

    (B) G                      (E) M

    (C) J

19. If F sits directly opposite L and between K and M, which guest must sit directly opposite M?

    (A) G                      (D) K

    (B) H                      (E) L

    (C) J

20. If G sits at the head of the table, and F in the middle seat on one side of the table and immediately on K's left, the guest seated directly opposite F must be

    (A) G                      (D) L

    (B) H                      (E) M

    (C) J

172

21. Which of the following is an acceptable seating arrangement starting with one side at the foot of the table, moving toward the head of the table, and continuing around to the opposite foot of the table?

    (A)  J K L F M G H

    (B)  F M L G H K L

    (C)  M J H G L K F

    (D)  J K F H L G M

    (E)  H M J L G F K

22. If F sits directly opposite L, H sits at the head of the table, and G sits immediately on H's left, what is the total number of possible seating arrangements of the guests?

    (A)  one

    (B)  two

    (C)  three

    (D)  four

    (E)  five

23. If it is true that John will be rich if the stock market rises by 20% or more and that Gloria will be rich if the stock market rises by 10% or more, which of the following must be true if the stock market rises by 15%?

    I.    John will be poor.

    II.   Gloria will be rich.

    III.  John will not be rich.

    (A)  I only

    (B)  II only

    (C)  III only

    (D)  I and II only

    (E)  II and III only

24. John swims faster than Carl, but slower than Susan. Laura swims faster than both Susan and John. Richard swims faster than Susan.

    If the statements above are true, one can conclude with certainty that Maria swims faster than John if one knows in addition that

(A)   Maria swims faster than Richard

(B)   Laura swims faster than Maria

(C)   Richard swims as fast as Laura

(D)   Maria swims faster than Carl

(E)   Richard swims faster than Maria

25.   Many more students are placed in remedial mathematics classes at University X than at University Y, even though (a) the median and average mathematical skills test scores of entering freshmen at University X are considerably higher than at University Y, (b) University X enrolls a higher percentage of male students, who generally score higher than female students on mathematical skills tests, than University Y, and (c) University X is much smaller than University Y.

Which of the following, if true, would be most useful in explaining the situation described above?

(A)   Remedial math classes also include transfer students, and the mathematical skills scores of transfer students, who are more numerous at University Y, are only slightly higher at University X.

(B)   The gap between overall test scores of entering freshmen at University X and University Y has narrowed somewhat in the last few years.

(C)   Verbal skills test scores of freshmen and transfer students are actually higher at University Y than at University X.

(D)   University X requires a much higher mathematical skills test score for placement out of remedial and into nonremedial math classes than does University Y.

(E)   University X is much more technologically oriented than University Y; hence it demands a higher level of mathematical skill in its entering freshmen than does University Y.

**STOP**
If time still remains, you may go back and check your work.
When the time allotted is up, you may go on to the next section.

# Section 6

---

**TIME:** 30 Minutes
25 Questions

**DIRECTIONS:** Each question or group of questions is based on a passage or set of statements. Select the best answer choice.

---

Questions 1 – 4 refer to the following passage.

A gardener living in a four-season climate may plant only six different kinds of flowers in her garden. Three are perennials (plants that live from year to year); three are annuals (plants that live for only one growing season). The perennials are white phlox, red astilbe, and yellow coreopsis; the annuals are red salvia, yellow marigolds, and white petunias. Every spring the gardener plants exactly two plants each of three kinds of flowers (a total of six plants per year). One kind must be a perennial; the other two kinds must be annuals. In any year, the gardener can plant no more than one of the annuals she planted the previous year. No annual can be planted in three successive years.

1.  If the gardener plants phlox, marigolds, and petunias the first year, what must she plant the second year to have six white and two red flowering plants in her garden the second summer?

    (A)  petunias and astilbe

    (B)  phlox and salvia

    (C)  phlox and astilbe

    (D)  petunias, astilbe, and salvia

    (E)  phlox, petunias, and salvia

2.  The gardener plants astilbe, petunias, and marigolds the first year; the second year, she plants coreopsis, salvia, and petunias;

175

the third year, she plants astilbe, salvia, and marigolds. What must she plant the fourth year to have exactly four red, six yellow, and two white flowering plants in her garden the fourth summer?

(A)  Coreopsis, marigolds, and petunias

(B)  Coreopsis, salvia, and petunias

(C)  Phlox, salvia, and marigolds

(D)  Astilbe, marigolds, and petunias

(E)  Coreopsis, marigolds, and salvia

3.  Which of the following is a possible sequence of planting combinations if the gardener wishes to have four red, four white, and two yellow flowering plants in her garden the third summer?

(A)  Astilbe, marigolds, petunias; phlox, petunias, salvia; astilbe, marigolds, salvia

(B)  Coreopsis, salvia, petunias; astilbe, marigolds, petunias; phlox, petunias, salvia

(C)  Astilbe, marigolds, petunias; coreopsis, marigolds, salvia; phlox, salvia, petunias

(D)  Phlox, salvia, astilbe; astilbe, marigolds, salvia; astilbe, marigolds, petunias

(E)  Phlox, marigolds, salvia; phlox, petunias, marigolds; astilbe, salvia, petunias

4.  At the end of each year, the gardener makes a record of the number of flowering plants of each color in her garden. At the end of four years, she makes a master record by adding the totals from each year. What is the total number of white flowering plants that would appear on her master record if she planted the following: phlox, petunias, and marigolds in the first year; astilbe, marigolds, and salvia the second year; phlox, petunias, and salvia the third year; coreopsis, marigolds, and petunias the fourth year?

(A)  five                                    (B)  ten

(C)  fourteen          (E)  twenty-four

(D)  eighteen

5.  X freezes at a higher temperature than Y freezes, but at a lower temperature than V freezes.
W freezes at a lower temperature than Y freezes.

If the above statements are true, one can conclude with certainty that Z freezes at a higher temperature than Y freezes if one knows in addition that

(A)  W freezes at a lower temperature than Z freezes

(B)  X freezes at a lower temperature than Z freezes

(C)  V freezes at a higher temperature than Z freezes

(D)  Z freezes at a lower temperature than X freezes

(E)  X freezes at the same temperature that W freezes

6.  Birch trees range in height from ten to forty feet. If a birch tree is over twenty feet tall, it has white bark.

If the statements above are true, which of the following must also be true?

(A)  Ten-foot tall birches do not have white bark.

(B)  Only birches over twenty feet tall have white bark.

(C)  Thirty-foot tall birches have white bark.

(D)  Some ten-foot tall birches have brown bark.

(E)  Twenty-one foot tall birches do not have white bark.

7.  In 1988, the number of prisoners classified as incorrigible in state R exceeds by six times the number of prisoners classified as incorrigible in state S, even though the prison population of state S is nine times greater than the prison population of state R.

Which of the following, if true, would be most helpful in explaining the situation described above?

(A) The number of homicides per thousand population is higher in state R than in state S.

(B) The term incorrigible refers to a broader range of criminals in state R than in state S.

(C) State R is rural, whereas S is an urban state.

(D) In 1988, state R enacted laws imposing longer prison sentences for certain categories of crimes.

(E) State S has a more liberal parole policy than state R.


Questions 8-11 refer to the following passage.

Army intelligence officers must decode the following message by translating all symbols into letters:

$$+ + + * * * \# \ \& \ \% \ \%$$
$$\# \# \$ + + \% \ \phi \ \phi \ ( \ \$$$

The officers know that each symbol represents exactly and only one of the eight letters A E O B G H K M and that each symbol represents the same letter each time the symbol appears. The officers also know that the letter G is represented exactly five times, the letters B and K are each represented exactly three times, and the letters A and M are each represented exactly two times.


8.   If # represents B and % represents 0, then * must represent

(A)  A                           (D)  H

(B)  K                           (E)  M

(C)  E


9.   & can represent only which one of the following?

(A)  B                           (D)  K

(B)  G                           (E)  M

(C)  H

10. If ( represents H, which of the following must represent a vowel?

(A)    &

(B)    $

(C)    #

(D)    %

(E)    *

11. Which of the following is a possible translation of this message?
$ % ¢ $

(A)   A E A M

(B)   M G A M

(C)   A O M M

(D)   MBMA

(E)   AKMA

Questions 12 –15 refer to the following statements.

The tenure and promotion boards must be staffed by eight professors — G, H, I, J, K, L, M, and N. There are two boards of three professors each — one board makes tenure decisions and the other makes promotion decisions.

No professor may serve on both boards in the same year.

At least two members of the tenure board must be tenured. The tenured professors, in descending order of seniority, are M, G, N, and J.

At least two members of the promotion board must be full professors. The full professors, in descending order of seniority, are I, H, K, and L.

Each board must have one professor from each of three disciplinary groups — the humanities, the social sciences, and the natural sciences. The humanities professors are G and K; the social sciences professors are H, M, and N; the natural sciences professors are I, J and L.

The chair of the tenure board must be the most senior tenured professor among the three board members; the chair of the promotion board must be the most senior full professor among the board members.

12. Which of the following could be the promotion board?

(A) J, L, M

(D) G, H, L

(B) G, I, L

(E) H, K, N

(C) I, K, L

13. The two boards must include which of the two following professors?

(A) M and I

(D) H and I

(B) M and K

(E) G and K

(C) I and G

14. If N is the chair of the tenure board, the other two members of the tenure board must be

(A) J and K

(D) G and J

(B) K and L

(E) G and M

(C) H and J

15. If the tenure board consists of G, N, and I, and if H is too ill to serve on either board, which professor must be chair of the promotion board?

(A) I

(D) L

(B) J

(E) M

(C) K

Questions 16 – 22 refer to the following statements.

A twenty-week lawn care contract, beginning on a Monday and ending on a Sunday, has the following provisions:

The lawn will be mowed every Friday unless it rains on Monday or Tuesday, in which case it will be mowed twice a week, on Wednesday and Friday. The lawn will only be mowed on a

Wednesday or a Friday.

The lawn will never be mowed on any day in which it rains.

The lawn will be fertilized on the fifth, tenth, fifteenth, and twentieth Friday regardless of the weather.

The lawn will be weeded three days after each rain, but will never be weeded on a day in which it rains; should it rain on a scheduled weeding day, the weeding will be cancelled and will not be rescheduled.

The lawn will never be weeded and fertilized on the same day; if fertilizing and weeding are scheduled for the same day, weeding will be rescheduled for the day after the lawn has been fertilized.

During the term of the contract, it rained on the third, fifth, fourteenth, and fifteenth Tuesday; the fifth, seventh, tenth, and eleventh Wednesday; and the third, fifth, eleventh, and fourteenth Friday. Assume that all provisions of the contract were honored.

16. How many times was the lawn mowed?

    (A) 16     (D) 23

    (B) 19     (E) 24

    (C) 20

17. How many times was the lawn weeded?

    (A) 8      (D) 12

    (B) 9      (E) 14

    (C) 10

18. On how many Fridays was lawn care performed on the lawn?

    (A) 16     (D) 21

    (B) 17     (E) 24

    (C) 20

19. On how many Saturdays was the lawn weeded?

    (A)  2                          (D)  5

    (B)  3                          (E)  6

    (C)  4

20. If all of the provisions of the contract were observed, which of the following statements is true? During the fifth week, the lawn was

    (A)  mowed and fertilized on Friday and weeded on Saturday

    (B)  mowed, weeded, and fertilized on Friday and weeded on Saturday

    (C)  weeded and fertilized on Friday and mowed on Saturday

    (D)  fertilized on Friday and weeded on Saturday

    (E)  mowed on Friday, fertilized on Saturday, and weeded on Sunday

21. If all of the provisions of the contract were observed, which of the following statements is true? During the fifteenth week, the lawn was

    (A)  mowed and fertilized on Friday, weeded on Saturday only

    (B)  mowed, fertilized,and weeded on Friday, weeded on Saturday

    (C)  mowed and fertilized on Friday, weeded on Monday and Saturday

    (D)  mowed and weeded on Friday, fertilized on Saturday

    (E)  fertilized on Friday, weeded on Saturday, and not mowed this week

22. How many times was the lawn weeded and mowed on the same day?

    (A)  O                          (B) 1

182

(C) 2                                         (E)   4

(D) 3

23.   Some men lose their inhibitions after viewing pornographic
      materials, which leads to an increase in violent crimes against
      women. Hence, laws should be enacted that further restrict the
      sale of pornographic material.

      Which of the following, if true, most weakens the argument
      above?

      (A)   Not all men are moved to violent crime by viewing pornog-
            raphy.

      (B)   Some women invite rape by dressing provocatively.

      (C)   Men who commit violent crimes against women are men-
            tally disturbed.

      (D)   Sales of pornography in urban areas have increased in the
            last decade.

      (E)   Countries that have the most permissive laws or no laws
            regulating the sale of pornography have the lowest rates of
            violent crime against women.

24.   More Americans have read and enjoyed *Valley of the Dolls* than
      *War and Peace*. We can therefore conclude that *Valley of the
      Dolls* is artistically superior to *War and Peace*.

      The argument above assumes that

      (A)   most Americans prefer American novels to Russian novels

      (B)   enjoyment decreases as degree of difficulty increases

      (C)   popularity is a reliable measure of artistic achievement

      (D)   quality is less important than quantity

      (E)   commercial success is more important than critical ac-
            claim

25. John: Students who smoke marijuana tend to have lower GPAs than those who do not, and the more marijuana a student smokes, the lower his or her GPA tends to be. Therefore, smoking marijuana lowers one's grades, perhaps because it has harmful effects on memory.

    Susan: Wrong. Getting poor grades is frustrating, which leads to various forms of escapist behavior, such as getting stoned by smoking marijuana. Hence low grades may lead to marijuana smoking.

    Which of the following best describes the weak point in John's argument on which Susan's response focuses?

    (A) John lacks definite proof that marijuana has harmful effects on memory.

    (B) John lacks exact figures indicating how widespread the smoking of marijuana is among students with low GPAs.

    (C) John does not account for the fact that some marijuana smokers have high GPAs.

    (D) In John's argument, it is possible that the cause he cites actually came after the effect he attributes to it.

    (E) Even if it is true that marijuana has an adverse effect on memory, John does not adequately establish that memory has an important influence on GPAs.

## STOP

If time still remains, you may go back and check your work.

# TEST 1

## ANSWER KEY

### Section 1 — Verbal Ability

| | | | | | | | |
|---|---|---|---|---|---|---|---|
| 1. | (C) | 11. | (B) | 21. | (C) | 31. | (D) |
| 2. | (B) | 12. | (D) | 22. | (E) | 32. | (E) |
| 3. | (A) | 13. | (A) | 23. | (B) | 33. | (D) |
| 4. | (B) | 14. | (D) | 24. | (D) | 34. | (D) |
| 5. | (E) | 15. | (E) | 25. | (E) | 35. | (A) |
| 6. | (D) | 16. | (B) | 26. | (C) | 36. | (D) |
| 7. | (D) | 17. | (D) | 27. | (D) | 37. | (B) |
| 8. | (C) | 18. | (E) | 28. | (A) | 38. | (D) |
| 9. | (C) | 19. | (E) | 29. | (B) | | |
| 10. | (C) | 20. | (C) | 30. | (E) | | |

### Section 2 — Verbal Ability

| | | | | | | | |
|---|---|---|---|---|---|---|---|
| 1. | (D) | 11. | (C) | 21. | (A) | 31. | (E) |
| 2. | (C) | 12. | (E) | 22. | (D) | 32. | (A) |
| 3. | (D) | 13. | (D) | 23. | (B) | 33. | (C) |
| 4. | (C) | 14. | (B) | 24. | (C) | 34. | (A) |
| 5. | (C) | 15. | (B) | 25. | (A) | 35. | (D) |
| 6. | (A) | 16. | (C) | 26. | (C) | 36. | (C) |
| 7. | (B) | 17. | (E) | 27. | (A) | 37. | (D) |
| 8. | (C) | 18. | (C) | 28. | (B) | 38. | (B) |
| 9. | (A) | 19. | (B) | 29. | (D) | | |
| 10. | (E) | 20. | (E) | 30. | (B) | | |

### Section 3 — Quantitative Ability

| | | | | | | | |
|---|---|---|---|---|---|---|---|
| 1. | (B) | 3. | (B) | 5. | (D) | 7. | (D) |
| 2. | (C) | 4. | (C) | 6. | (A) | 8. | (C) |

| 9. | (B) | 15. | (D) | 21. | (D) | 27. | (D) |
|---|---|---|---|---|---|---|---|
| 10. | (A) | 16. | (C) | 22. | (C) | 28. | (B) |
| 11. | (C) | 17. | (C) | 23. | (B) | 29. | (E) |
| 12. | (C) | 18. | (C) | 24. | (D) | 30. | (D) |
| 13. | (A) | 19. | (B) | 25. | (A) | | |
| 14. | (C) | 20. | (A) | 26. | (C) | | |

## Section 4 — Quantitative Ability

| 1. | (B) | 9. | (A) | 17. | (D) | 25. | (E) |
|---|---|---|---|---|---|---|---|
| 2. | (C) | 10. | (B) | 18. | (C) | 26. | (B) |
| 3. | (B) | 11. | (B) | 19. | (A) | 27. | (C) |
| 4. | (B) | 12. | (A) | 20. | (B) | 28. | (C) |
| 5. | (A) | 13. | (C) | 21. | (D) | 29. | (E) |
| 6. | (A) | 14. | (D) | 22. | (E) | 30. | (A) |
| 7. | (A) | 15. | (B) | 23. | (D) | | |
| 8. | (D) | 16. | (B) | 24. | (B) | | |

## Section 5 — Analytical Ability

| 1. | (C) | 8. | (D) | 15. | (C) | 22. | (A) |
|---|---|---|---|---|---|---|---|
| 2. | (B) | 9. | (A) | 16. | (E) | 23. | (B) |
| 3. | (B) | 10. | (C) | 17. | (A) | 24. | (A) |
| 4. | (D) | 11. | (D) | 18. | (E) | 25. | (D) |
| 5. | (B) | 12. | (B) | 19. | (C) | | |
| 6. | (D) | 13. | (D) | 20. | (C) | | |
| 7. | (C) | 14. | (D) | 21. | (D) | | |

## Section 6 — Analytical Ability

| 1. | (E) | 8. | (B) | 15. | (C) | 22. | (A) |
|---|---|---|---|---|---|---|---|
| 2. | (A) | 9. | (C) | 16. | (B) | 23. | (E) |
| 3. | (C) | 10. | (A) | 17. | (B) | 24. | (C) |
| 4. | (D) | 11. | (E) | 18. | (B) | 25. | (D) |
| 5. | (B) | 12. | (D) | 19. | (D) | | |
| 6. | (C) | 13. | (E) | 20. | (D) | | |
| 7. | (B) | 14. | (A) | 21. | (C) | | |

# DETAILED EXPLANATIONS OF ANSWERS

## Section 1–Verbal Ability

1. **(C)**
(A) is incorrect; ABUSIVE means treating badly or harshly. The term does not fit the sentence very well; ABUSIVE writing probably would not ENHANCE one's chance for a promotion. (B) is not an appropriate choice. Since LACONIC means brief and to the point, this type of writing does not seem grounds to OBLITERATE (wipe out) a teacher's chances for promotion. (C) is the correct answer. OBTUSE means blunt, stupid, not sharp. (For instance, an obtuse angle is not sharp, like an acute angle; it is larger than a right angle.) Such writing might OBVIATE (eliminate) one's chances of a promotion. (D) is incorrect; since PROFOUND means not superficial, and clearly marked by intellectual depth, it does not stand to reason that such writing would DIMINISH (or make lsss) one's chances for a promotion. The best answer is not (E). The publication of PROLIFIC (many) writings alone does not make necessary (NECESSITATE) the promotion of a teacher.

2. **(B)**
(A) is not the best choice. ELICIT means to draw out in a skillful way something that is being hidden or held back. Giving business cards is not unique. The best answer is (B). SOLICIT means to ask earnestly, to try to get. Since ILLICIT (C) means illegal, it is an incorrect choice. ELLIPTIC (D) means shaped like an ellipse (with ovals at both ends). CONCILIATE (E) is to win over, to soothe. The word is an inappropriate choice.

3. **(A)**
HERBIVOROUS (HERBA-an herb; VOVARE-to devour) animals, like the cow, subsist on grass and other plants; OMNIVOROUS (OMNIS-all) animals, like the hog, eat any sort of food; (A) is correct. SCAVENGERS eat refuse; OMNIPOTENT (which should not be confused with OMNIVOROUS) means having infinite power. (B) is

not the correct answer. A SAPROPHYTE lives on decaying vegetation; a PARASITE takes what it requires from invading and destroying living plant and animal tissue. Neither term is applicable to the cow or hog, (C) is incorrect. VEGETARIANS eat no meat (and sometimes no animal products) because of health reasons or principles opposing the killing of animals; CARNIVOROUS (CARNIS-flesh) animals are flesh-eating. Cows do not consciously make the choice to be plant-eaters; hogs eat more than just meat. (D) is not the correct choice. AUTOTROPHIC means self-feeding like green plants; HETERO-TROPHIC means fed by others. Since both the cow and the hog are heterotrophic, (E) is not the best answer.

4.    (B)
    BINARY means made of two parts; it does not fit the sentence. ANNUAL is not the correct term for a plant which lives two years. (A) is not the correct answer. Since PERENNIAL (PER-through; AN-NUS-a year) means a plant which lives more than two years and since a BIENNIAL (BI-two) plant continues for two years and then perishes, (B) is the correct answer. (C) SEMI-ANNUAL means two times per year; a CENTENNIAL celebration marks one hundred years, (C) is clearly incorrect. An EVERGREEN is green the year round; a DE-CIDUOUS tree casts its leaves. Answer (D) does not relate directly to the context. DECENNIAL means continuing for ten years; TRIEN-NIAL means continuing for three years. (E) should not be selected.

5.    (E)
    CULTURE is more than just ideas about what is right; CULTURE is all the modes of thought, behavior, and production that are handed down from one generation to another. LAWS are norms that have been enacted through the formal process of government; all moral rules of behavior are not laws. Answer (A) is not appropriate. MORES are strongly sanctioned norms that people consider vital; TECHNOLO-GIES are 1) things and 2) norms for usual things that are found in society. These two sociological terms are not appropriate answers, (B) should not be chosen. CLASS is a social stratum defined primarily by economic criteria like occupation, income and wealth; CASTE is a social stratum into which people are born and in which they must remain for life. (C) is not an appropriate answer. SANCTIONS are rewards and punishments for adhering to or violating rules of behavior;

FOLKWAYS are rules of behavior which are less strongly sanctioned. Neither term is appropriate in this instance, (D) is incorrect. VALUES are ideas about what is right; NORMS are specific models of behavior for a surrounding environment. (E) is the appropriate choice in this instance.

6. (D)
   (A) is not the right answer. The person who chose this answer probably confused the word INGENUOUS (candid, forthright) with INGENIOUS (clever). (B) is incorrect; INCONGRUOUS means not corresponding to what is right and proper. (C) is also incorrect. Since INDOLENT means lazy, it is not suitable in this context. ADROIT (D) means ingenious, an appropriate adjective for the sentence. PROSAIC (E) means dull, tedious or commonplace; it is certainly not correct.

7. (D)
   A CHARLATAN is a quack, a pretender of knowledge and ability; this term comes close but does not exactly describe a person who tries to sell goods which are misrepresented. DIFFIDENCE means unusually shy or timid and certainly does not describe a practiced con artist. (A) is not the best answer. A MOUNTEBANK is synonymous with CHARLATAN; it means a quack, a pretender of knowledge and ability. The term does not aptly describe a con artist in jewels, although SELF-POSSESSION does fit. (B) however, is not the best choice. An EMPIRIC is a quack; the term is best suited to a pretender of knowledge or ability. Neither does CONCERN fit the blank well. (C) is not the best choice. SWINDLER (one who cheats, one who obtains money or property by fraud) fits well, as does APLOMB (self-possession); (D) is correct. A person who selected (E) probably confused IMPOSTURE (a fraudulent item) with IMPOSTOR (one who imposes on others for the sake of deception). ASSURANCE does fit, but IMPOSTURE is incorrect.

8. (C)
   CATAPULT means 1) to throw or 2) to shoot from a weapon. A PROJECTILE is that which has been hurled or shot, as from a sling-shot. A GLACIER is a large mass of ice; ICE is the substance from which the glacier is made. The analogy in (A) is an object-composition

189

relationship — quite different from the analogy existing between CATAPULT and PROJECTILE. A PRECIPICE is a CLIFF; the two are synonyms — (B) is not the type of analogy illustrated by the question. TRANSMIT means to send; a MESSAGE is words sent from one person to another. The analogy between TRANSMIT (to send) and MESSAGE (words sent) is the same as that between CATAPULT and PROJECTILE, (C) is the correct response. A PROTOTYPE is an original; a REPLICA is a copy. The two are opposites, or antonyms, therefore (D) would not be a suitable choice in this instance. The same relationship is present between EMIT (give out) and PERSPIRATION (that which is given out) as between CATAPULT and PROJECTILE, but the order is different. Answer (E) cannot, therefore, be selected.

9.   (C)
PARSIMONIOUS is an adjective (meaning stingy or miserly); NIGGARDLY is an adjective also meaning miserly. The two words are synonymous. A MENDICANT (from the Latin MENDICANS for beggar) means one who begs; a BENEFACTOR is one who gives money or kindly help. These two items, then, are antonyms, or opposites, thus (A) does not fit the sought pattern. AVARICE means greed; GENEROSITY is its opposite. (B) does not fit the synonym pattern desired. PENURIOUS means miserly; SQUANDERING means wasteful. (E) is not an appropriate choice since the parts of speech are not the same as in PARSIMONIOUS:NIGGARDLY. A MISER is one who is stingy; the word is a noun. STINGY means being extremely closefisted or very sparing in spending money; the word is an adjective, therefore (D) does not fit. CONVOLUTED means involved; INTRICATE also means complicated or involved. Even though this is the only choice not related to spending money, (C) is the correct choice. The two words are synonyms, like PARSIMONIOUS:NIGGARDLY.

10.   (C)
CONVEY is a verb which means to carry or transfer; DUCT (coming from the Latin DUCERE which means to lead) is a noun which means a tube or canal for carrying. To CONVEY, or carry something, one might use a DUCT. TRANSPORT (TRANS-across; PORT-to carry) means to carry across. Transfer (TRANS-across; FER-to bear) means to bear across. These two words (A) do not have

the same relationship (analogy) as the verb and noun above. POL-LUTE means to make dirty; a FILTER, on the other hand, can be used to remove dirt. (B) is not analogous to CONVEY and DUCT. To DECIPHER (DE-undo; CIPHER-secret writing) or solve a code, one might use a KEY, which might be an explanation or a book of answers. The relationship between DECIPHER and KEY (C) is the same as that between CONVEY and DUCT. An AUTOGRAPH is a writing (GRAPH) written by one's self (AUTO-); a BIOGRAPHY is a writing (GRAPH) about someone's life (BIO-). These terms (both of which are nouns) do not bear the same analogy as CONVEY and DUCT, (D) is incorrect. FALSIFY is a verb meaning to lie or make false; FABRI-CATE is also a verb meaning to forge or devise falsely. These two verbs are not analogous to the verb and noun CONVEY and DUCT. (E) is a poor choice.

11.  (B)
   The SUN is a part of the SOLAR SYSTEM, along with the group of celestial bodies which revolve around it. The MOON revolves around the EARTH; the MOON is not a part of the earth; therefore (A) is not the best answer. An ISLAND is a part of an ARCHIPELAGO, or group of islands. (B) is the right answer. A GALAXY is formed from STARS, but the order is not the same as in the example. (C) is not correct. A MOLECULE is made from ATOMS; the order MOLE-CULE:ATOMS when compared to SUN:SOLAR SYSTEM would indicate the opposite; (D) is incorrect. (E) is a possible answer, but not the best one for the following reasons. The SUN is one part of the SOLAR SYSTEM; together with other bodies it makes up the whole system. VERSES do make up a poem; there may be only one verse in a poem, however. VERSES is plural in contrast to SUN (singular).

12.  (D)
   A SOUFFLE is usually made from EGGS. COCONUT is often an ingredient in a MACAROON. The order, however, for COCONUT:MACAROON is not the same as for SOUFFLE:EGGS; (A) is not the correct answer. A PEAR does contain NECTAR; a pear, however, is not made from a recipe nor does it contain many added ingredients. (B) is not the right answer. PIGS are trained to find TRUFFLES, an underground fungus. The relationship in (C) obvi-ously is not the same as that between SOUFFLE:EGGS. MOUSSE is

a rich pudding-like dessert which contains CREAM. The analogy between MOUSSE:CREAM (D) and SOUFFLE:EGGS is apparent. A TOMATO is a fruit (not a vegetable), but it is not analogous to SOUFFLE:EGGS. (E) is not the correct choice.

13.   (A)

VACILLATE is a verb meaning to waver. DECISION is a noun meaning the act of committing or deciding. A verb and noun which are opposite in meaning are needed from the choices given. EQUIVO-CATE is a verb meaning to hedge. COMMITMENT is a noun meaning the act of declaring. The analogy in (A) is the same as for VACILLATE:DECISION. FLUCTUATE is a verb meaning to be changing continually. PROCRASTINATION is a noun meaning the act of postponing. (B) is not the appropriate answer. CONSPIRE is a verb meaning to act or plan together secretly; COLLUSION is a noun meaning the act of secretly planning together. The relationship of choice (C) is not the same as that between VACILLATE:DECISION. RESOLVE is a verb meaning to come to a decision; CONCLUSION is a noun meaning the close of an argument, debate, or reasoning. (D) is not the correct answer. AMELIORATE means to lessen, to make mild; RESOLUTION is a noun meaning the act of deciding or determining something. The analogy between AMELIORATE: RESOLUTION (E) and between VACILLATE:DECISION is not the same.

14.   (D)

An ANTAGONIST is an opponent; an ADVERSARY is also an opponent or foe. The two are synonymous. An ALLY is a helper or auxiliary, the opposite of OPPONENT. Answer (A) is not correct. An AUXILIARY is a helper or ally, the opposite of COMPETITOR. Answer (B) should not be chosen. A CONFEDERATE (friend) is the opposite of ENEMY. Answer (C) is incorrect. An EMULATOR is a competitor; it is synonymous with RIVAL. (D) is the right answer. An ACCOMPLICE is an associate in crime; a FOE is a rival; (E) is incorrect.

15.   (E)

STUPENDOUS means astonishingly impressive. AMAZE is to

astonish greatly. MONSTROUS means ugly, fabulous, shocking in wrongness. BEWILDER is to perplex or confuse; it does not imply the surprise seen in AMAZE. Therefore (A) is not the best answer. PRODIGIOUS means a marvelousness beyond belief. PERPLEX is to puzzle, to confuse. PRODIGIOUS behavior does not necessarily result in perplexity; (B) is not the best answer. TREMENDOUS means a power to terrify or inspire awe. DISTRACTION implies diversion, perplexity. DISTRACTION does not have the intensity of AMAZE. (C) involves using knowledge of the degree of words, it is not the best answer. CONFOUND implies a temporary mental paralysis. ATROCIOUS implies such savagery as to excite condemnation. The order is not the same as in the example, (D) is incorrect. HEINOUS implies such flagrant conspicuousness that it excites hatred or horror. ASTOUND stresses shock and surprise. Thus, (E) is the best choice.


16. **(B)**
   A COVEY is a group of QUAIL. A CUB is a young BEAR. The analogy in (A) is not the same as for COVEY:QUAIL. A group of LIONS is a PRIDE; (B) is correct. A STAG is a male DEER. The analogy is not that of COVEY:QUAIL. (C) should not be chosen. A EWE is a female sheep. Again, the analogy is not that of COVEY:QUAIL. (D) is not the correct answer since the group:animal relationship is not there. A GAGGLE is a group of GEESE, not ducks. A person choosing answer (E) probably confused ducks and geese.


17. **(D)**
   A control group of 8 students was used in Faigel's study. (A) is not the best answer; it is false. Second-time test-takers increase only 28 points nationally. (B) is false and not the best answer. The article states that the beta blockers cannot help those who do not "know" the material. (C) is false and should not be selected as the best answer. Adrenalin does increase minor stress and may result in lower test scores; (D) is the best answer. Beta blockers, not adrenalin, have long been used for heart conditions and for minor stress. (E) therefore, is false and not the best answer.


18. **(E)**
   (A) is false. Faigel's study suggests that anxiety reduces test

scores. (B) is also false. Faigel's study is not a national study. Beta blockers have not been tested nationally. (C) should not be chosen. The article suggests that test fright lowers the scores of first-time test-takers — just the opposite of what (C) suggests. (D) is incorrect. No study of third-time test-takers was done by Faigel. The article does not suggest anything about third-time test-takers. (E) is the correct answer since beta blockers do seem to reduce anxiety and increase the test scores of 30 nervous second-time test-takers.

19.   (E)
      CASUAL DISINTEREST (A) does not seem to describe aptly students who become nervous when taking the SAT. RESIGNATION (B) is not the best descriptive adjective for students who continue to take the SAT to try to improve their test scores. ANTAGONISM is not the attitude suggested by the article. No mention is made of students' possessing an antagonistic attitude or of their trying to eradicate standardized testing, (C) is not the best answer. PESSIMISM (D) is not the attitude mentioned in the article or suggested by students who continue to retake a standardized test to improve their grades. CONCERN best describes the attitudes of students who take (and retake) the SAT to try to increase their score and even experience nervousness during the test-taking. (E) seems to be the best answer implied (though not stated) by the article.

20.   (C)
      Second-time test-takers nationwide improve only an average of 28 points — not a significant increase. Statisticians would attribute this insignificant increase to the fact that the test is a *reliable* test; students seem to achieve the same test scores each time it is administered unless they do something different in-between test administrations. (A), therefore, is false and an incorrect answer. The author of the passage makes no speculation on limiting the number of administrations of the SAT. (B) is false and should not be chosen. If beta blockers are used, the article suggests that scores of nervous second-time test-takers may be raised. This, in turn, will raise the national average. (C) is correct and the best choice. Raising test scores of even one group of students will affect the national average. (D), therefore, is false and should not be chosen as the correct answer. Adrenalin has not been shown to increase test scores. (E) should be avoided as the correct answer. It is

beta blockers that seem to reduce nervousness and increase test scores.

21.   (C)

The study by Faigel focuses on SAT test-takers. Faigel does not attempt to make any predictions on how the beta blockers might affect the general public should they take them for nervousness; to the contrary, Faigel cautions that beta blockers do have certain side effects. (A) is certainly not the best answer. It was not adrenalin but beta blockers which increased the performance of second-time takers of the SAT. (B) is an incorrect answer and should not be selected. Since beta blockers do seem to improve the average scores of second-time takers (particularly nervous second-time takers) of the SAT, (C) is a true, appropriate answer. Faigel recognizes that beta blockers do have side effects, but he in no way implies that they should never be used. (D), therefore, is an incorrect answer and should not be chosen. Nervousness *does* seem to affect the test scores of students who "know" the material. Faigel's study suggests by administering beta blockers to help control this nervousness, students can raise their test scores. (E) is not the best answer to this question.

22.   (E)

The author of this article is not PESSIMISTIC (A) in tone; rather the author seems encouraged by the results of Faigel's study. The author of this article does not have an UNCONCERNED attitude toward the study by Faigel. The very fact that the article was written shows some concern on the part of the author. (B) is not an appropriate answer to the question. INDIFFERENT (C) is not the tone of the author's writing. The writer is careful to point out the difference in scores between second-time test-takers who had been administered the beta blockers and second-time test-takers who had not been administered the drugs. The author of this article is not RESIGNED. The author states that the drugs "seem to help test-takers"; on the other hand the writer cautions that side effects do exist. (D) is clearly not to be chosen. The author of the article can best be described as OPTIMISTIC (E). Again, the writer states that beta blockers "seem to help test-takers who have low scores because of test fright."

23.   (B)

ANALYSIS involves separating or breaking down into parts.

Faigel's work primarily involved developing a plan (synthesizing), rather than a separating (ANALYSIS). (A) is not the best answer. SYNTHESIS involves putting together, combining to form a whole. Developing a plan to reduce the nervousness and developing a plan to compare the rest results is certainly a synthesizing. (B) is correct and should be chosen. DEDUCTION (C) involves reasoning from the general to the particular. DEDUCTION does not apply to developing a plan to reduce nervousness and to compare test results. INTERPRETATION is used when one gives an explanation; developing a plan does not necessarily involve INTERPRETATION. Rather, developing a plan is synthesizing. (D) is not the correct answer. APPLICATION means the act of using a particular case or for a particular purpose; Faigel synthesized, rather than applied, when he developed his research plan. (E) is inappropriate.

24. (D)

The first paragraph serves to present the problem (low test scores, possibly because of nervousness of test-takers) and suggest a possible solution (the administration of beta blockers). The paragraph does more than just (A), however. Even though (A) is a possible choice, the test-taker must read further to find the rest of the answer. The author does present the results of the study, but this is done after presenting the problem and the possible solution. (B) is a true answer, but it must be combined with answer (A). The author does not attempt to analyze the results; (C) is an inappropriate answer. (D) is the proper answer because it allows the test-taker to combine (A) (present the problem and a possible solution) with (B) (present the results). Since (C) (analyze the results) was not the correct answer, (E) which combines answer (C) with (A) (present the problem and a possible solution) cannot be correctly selected.

25. (E)

AMUSEMENT is certainly not the author's tone in this passage. (A) should not be chosen. INDIGNATION (B) is not the author's tone. The author has no source upon which to vent indignation in this passage. The very fact that the author bothered to write the passage negates the idea that the author shows INDIFFERENCE. (C) should certainly not be selected as the best answer. APPROVAL is not the best choice for the author's attitude. There is little that a well-meaning

author could approve in this passage. (D) is not an appropriate choice. RESIGNATION (E) is the best choice for the author's attitude. The author is not resigned to never having a cure for ALS; the author admits that there may be a waiting period for this cure, however.

26. (C)
Reasoning from the general to the particular is deduction. In this instance, the victims of ALS who are athletes lead to a generalization that the disease affects active persons more often, therefore (A) is false. Statement (B) is not a deduction; it is simply a restatement of a fact given in the article. (C) is the example of deductive reasoning. One proceeds from the general (the death of four sports figures) to the specific (exposure to fertilizers on the playing field). (D) is incorrect. Looking at the best-known victims of ALS and deducing that the next victim will also be a ballplayer is deduction. However, it is faulty deduction. There have been many victims of ALS who were not ballplayers. If one assumes that the disease ALS affects only men because the article gives four well-known men as victims, this is false reasoning. In addition the reasoning used is generalizing and not deducing. (E) should definitely not be chosen.

27. (D)
The non-imminent solution to ALS is a disturbing fact presented in the passage, but it does not give the topic of the paragraph. (A) should not be selected. Statement (B) gives an important supporting detail from the passage but does not give the topic of the paragraph to the reader. Statement (C) adds additional facts, but it does not give the main subject. (D) informs the reader of the topic of the paragraph. It is the correct choice. Statement (E) is taken from the passage and gives supporting details about the puzzle of ALS; it does not, however, give the topic of the sentence.

28. (A)
MALAPROPOS means not appropriate. (the prefix MAL- means not.) CONGRUOUS means fit, right, suitable; congruous (congruent) angles, for instance, are of the same size and shape. MALAPROPOS and CONGRUOUS are antonyms; (A) is the correct answer. SPECIOUS stresses a clear suggestion of fraud. It does not bear the

opposite relationship to MALAPROPOS sought, (B) should not be selected. PONDEROUS (C) means heavy, dull, bulky, unyieldy. It is certainly not the antonym sought. Since BENIGN means mild, kind, gently, it is not an antonym for a word meaning not appropriate. (D) should not be selected. PROPENSITY (E) means a natural inclination or bent. It does not suggest an opposite relationship to MALAPROPOS.

29.  (B)

ITINERANT is an adjective describing one who travels from place to place. ILLEGITIMATE means that which is illegal or gotten illegally; it is not an opposite (or even seemingly related) to ITINERANT. (A) should not be chosen. PERMANENT means fixed, non-moving. (B) is clearly the antonym for ITINERANT. IDYLLIC means picturesque, simple, pleasing. It is possible that the life of an ITINERANT might be IDYLLIC, but there does not necessarily even have to be a relation between IDYLLIC and ITINERANT. There is certainly no opposite (antonymous) relation; (C) is not the best choice. GAUDY (D) means showy, cheaply brilliant; it is an antonym for the previous selection (IDYLLIC), but it does not have an opposite relation to ITINERANT  and should not be selected as the correct answer. FELTED (E) means matted; hence, it is not the correct choice since it it not an antonym for the key word ITINERANT.

30.  (E)

UNCOUTH means uncultured, crude, boorish, or clumsy. MELANCHOLY is an adjective for gloomy, depressed. Since an UNCOUTH person can be MELANCHOLY, (A) is not an antonym or opposite. AMELIORATING means taking less, making milder. It does not have an opposite relationship to UNCOUTH; (B) is not the correct answer. FUNEREAL is an adjective meaning dismal or mournful; it is not the opposite of UNCOUTH. (C) should not be selected as the correct answer. BOORISH is synonymous with UNCOUTH. (D) is not the correct choice, therefore. URBANE (E) means polite or civil; it is opposite from UNCOUTH and is the correct answer.

31.  (D)

CORPULENT means solid, dense, fleshy, or fat.  PORTLY (A)

means stout, obese, or fat. This synonym should not be selected. VOCIFERATE means to cry out loudly. It bears no relationship to CORPULENT; (B) is incorrect. BECOMING can be used as an adjective meaning befitting or suitable. Since it is not the opposite of CORPULENT, (C) should not be selected as the correct answer. ANOREXIC (D) means suppressing appetite for food and, hence, thin; it is the opposite of CORPULENT and the correct choice. ADVERSE means acting against. Of course corpulence can have an adverse effect on health, but it is not the antonym of ADVERSE; (E) is not the correct choice.

32. (E)
    The adjective FERAL means gloomy. VORACIOUS means excessively eager, immoderate, gluttonous, ravenous. It certainly is not the opposite of FERAL and (A) should not be chosen. CONSCIENTIOUS means influenced by a strict regard to the dictates of conscience. It is seemingly unrelated to FERAL. (B) is wrong. SAVAGE means uncivilized, uncultivated, ferocious. It is not the opposite of FERAL; (C) is an incorrect answer. EXACTING means severe in making demands; it does not bear an opposite relationship to FERAL. (D) is a poor choice. (E) BLITHE means joyous, cheerful, glad. It is the opposite of FERAL; (E) is the correct answer.

33. (D)
    UNCTUOUS means smug characterized by a pretense, especially in trying to persuade or influence others. SCRUPULOUS (A) means careful, exacting. It is not the opposite of UNCTUOUS. MOROSE means gloomy. (B) is not an antonym for UNCTUOUS and should not be selected. RAVENOUS means eager. Since it is not the opposite of UNCTUOUS, (C) is not a suitable choice. AGITATED involves a loss of calmness; there are nervous and emotional signs of emotional excitement. This is quite the opposite of the smug exterior of a unctuous person. (D) is the correct answer. INGRATIATING suggests an attempt to win favor; often the INGRATIATING person uses a servile approach to win favor. A smooth exterior, like that implied with UNCTUOUS, makes the two similar — not opposite. (E) is not the right answer.

34. (D)

INVIDIOUS means likely to give offense, tending to excite ill will. REPUGNANT means distasteful, repellent, hostile; it is more similar than opposite to INVIDIOUS. (A) should not be selected. OBSCURE means not clearly understood. The word does not have the opposite relationship sought; (B) should not be selected. RANSOMED means redeemed, delivered. It is not an antonym for INVIDIOUS. RECONCILABLE means capable of being brought into harmony; it is quite the opposite of INVIDIOUS, which means likely to give offense. (D) is, therefore, the correct answer. PERTURBED (E) means agitated, disturbed, troubled profoundly; it is not the opposite of INVIDIOUS and should not be selected.

35. (A)

NEBULOUS means unclear, vague, and indefinite. Since CONCLUSIVE (A) means leaving no room for doubt, it is the opposite of NEBULOUS and the right answer. SPURIOUS means false, not genuine, counterfeit, illegitimate. (B) is not the antonym sought. A FRIGATE (C) is a ship and, therefore, not the right answer. SATURNINE (D) means heavy, dull, gloomy. It is not the opposite of NEBULOUS. AMBIGUOUS means doubtful or uncertain. (E) is not an antonym for NEBULOUS.

36. (D)

PROPITIOUS means favorably disposed, graciously inclined. CONSPICUOUS (A) means obvious to the eye or mind. The two are not antonyms. AUSPICIOUS is a synonym for PROPITIOUS; both mean favorable, fortunate. (B) is, therefore, not the correct answer. EVANESCENCE (C) means that which dissipates like vapor, vanishes. It is a word that is not related to PROPITIOUS and should not be selected. MILITANT means warlike, fighting. MILITANT is the opposite of PROPITIOUS, or favorably inclined. (D) is the correct answer. AGGREGATIVE means taken together, collective, tending to aggregate. (E) is not a suitable choice as an antonym of PROPITIOUS.

37. (B)

An ODYSSEY is a long series of wanderings. Since a JOURNEY

(A) is a very long trip, it is synonymous with ODYSSEY and an incorrect answer. An ERRAND (B) is a short trip, the opposite of ODYSSEY, and the correct answer. A WANDERING, (C) like an ODYSSEY, is a moving about aimlessly; it is not the opposite of ODYSSEY. A VOYAGE is a long journey by water, much like an ODYSSEY; (D) is not the correct answer. A CRUISE is sailing about from place to place; (E) is very similar to ODYSSEY and should not be selected as the right answer.

38.  (D)
     PUNCTILIOUS means very exact, very careful. SOMBER (A) means melancholy, grave, depressing. It does not have an exactly opposite meaning from PUNCTILIOUS. GENIAL means kindly, cheerful, cheering, of or pertaining to marriage. (B) is clearly not related to PUNCTILIOUS. PARTICULAR is a synonym for PUNC-TILIOUS since it means concerned with or attentive to details. (C) is not the right answer. NEGLIGENT (careless, inattentive, indifferent) is the opposite (synonym) of PUNCTILIOUS (careful, exacting). (D) is, therefore, the correct answer. ANTAGONISTIC (E) means hostile. It is not the opposite of PUNCTILIOUS and should not be selected as the correct answer.

# Section 2–Verbal Ability

1.    (D)
     MARAUDING (going about in search of plunder and booty) and EMERGENCY (a sudden and unforseen crisis, often having the pressure of restrictions) do not fit a sentence about a wild hawk very well. (A) is not the best choice. PARASITIC (living on others) does not fit the sentence about the hawk very well. Neither does MALADY (a disease, a mental or moral disorder) fit in the second blank. (B) should not be selected. SAPROPHYTIC (living on decaying organic matter) does not apply to a hawk. INSURRECTION (a rising up, a rebellion) does not fit blank two. (C) should not be chosen. PREDATORY (preying upon other animals) and PREDICAMENT (an unpleasant situation) fit the sentence well; (D) is correct. (E) METICULOUS (extremely careful about small details and TÉTE-A-TÉTE (a private

conversation between two people) do not fit the sentence well. (E) is wrong.

2.    (C)
IMMIGRATE is usually accompanied by the preposition *from*; this word does not fit. Neither is it likely that there would be a PROSECUTION (a legal suit against) simply because of beliefs, not actions. (A) is not the best answer. PEREGRINATE means to travel, but EXTORTION (drawing something from someone by force) does not fit logically in the sentence. (B) is incorrect. One EMIGRATES to another place; PERSECUTION (torment, abuse) might be typical for one's beliefs. These seem logical choices of words. (C) is correct. Since WANDER implies no set destination, this choice does not fit well. Coupled with the word ARRAIGNMENT (to bring before a court, to charge), (D) is clearly not a suitable choice. ROAM implies no set destination, this choice does not fit well. CENSURE indicates blame or criticism, but is not acceptable coupled with ROAM. Choice (E) is incorrect.

3.    (D)
IMPLORED (A) is a verb meaning begged; it does not fit well into the content of the sentence and is not the right answer. EXTORTED is to draw something (like money) from someone by force; (B) is not the correct answer. EXHORTED means to urge by words of good advice or to caution; since urging is not the issue here, (C) is incorrect. ADMONISHED seems to fit best since it means to warn, to reprove, to caution against specific faults. (D) is the correct answer. ABOL-ISHED (E) means to destroy or put an end to something; this word is too strong for the sentence.

4.    (C)
ADVISE is a verb. (A) is, therefore, not an appropriate choice for a blank requiring a noun. A COUNCIL is an assembly; the person who selected (B) as an answer probably confused the word with *counsel* which means advice. ADVICE is a noun meaning a recommendation or information given. (C) is the correct answer. A CONSUL is a magistrate or an official. The person who chose (D) probably confused CONSUL with *counsel* which means advice. TRIBUNE (E) (not to be

confused with TRIBUTE, which means praise, money, a gift) means an officer or magistrate; it is not an appropriate choice.

5.    (C)
IMPASSIVE implies showing or feeling no emotion or sensation. Showing *no* emotion would not be an asset when working with the public. (A) is not the correct answer. A STOIC is indifferent to pain or pleasure. (B) is not the correct answer since indifference would not be an asset to an employee. PHLEGMATIC implies a temperament or constitution hard to arouse. (C) is the best answer. APATHETIC means lacking normal feeling or interest; indifferent; listless. A person lacking normal feeling or interest would not be an asset for a business. (D) is not the best answer. STOLID means dull — not the best attribute for a complaint department. (E) is not appropriate.

6.    (A)
A REPARTEE is a clever, witty retort; DORMANT suggests inactivity of that which is present. A person who bides her time before giving a statement would hold that retort or REPARTEE DORMANT. (A) is the best answer. WIT suggests the power to evoke laughter by remarks showing quick perception; it is not usually preceded by the article *a*. Only one statement is suggested by the sentence. LATENT stresses concealment. (B) is not the best answer. SATIRE is wit used for the purpose of exposing vice. HIBERNATING is the passing of winter in a lethargic state. These two words of choice (C) are not the best choices for the sentence. HUMOR is an ability to see the absurd and the comical in life's situations; it suggests a series of incidents rather than just one retort. CAMOUFLAGED implies that which is disguised. The sentence suggests not a disguising of the witty statement but rather a concealment of it until the proper moment. (D) is not the best answer. A SORTIE is a mission or an attack. It does not fit the sentence at all. DISGUISED could fit the sentence, but not when printed with SORTIE. (E) is not the best answer.

7.    (B)
IMPLIED is a transitive verb; it must have an object. There is no direct object here so IMPLIED does not fit well. ABROGATE is to annul, to abolish. Because IMPLIED does not fit well, (A) should not

be selected. INFERRED is an intransitive verb in this sentence; it means to draw conclusions from data given. It fits well in this sentence also. NEGOTIATE (procure) fits well in this sentence also. (B) is the correct answer. IMPOSED is to pass off or to obtrude. The word does not fit the meaning of the sentence well at all. NULLIFY (to make or render of no value) fits the sentence but not when coupled with IMPOSED. (C) is not the best choice. SURMISED is to imagine or to guess on slight charges. BREECH is to cover with breeches; the person who selected (D) probably confused BREECH with BREACH (to cancel). INCLUDED means contained; the person who chose (E) probably read the word as concluded, rather than INCLUDED. ANNIHILATE means to make void.

8.    (C)

The relationship between MERIDIAN and PARALLEL is that between two different types of lines on a map; they are used together to locate a point, compute distance, etc. The two are not just opposite terms; they must be used together for location, computation, etc. EAST and WEST are opposite directions. (A) is a plausible answer, but not the best answer since they do not really work together as do a MERIDIAN and a PARALLEL. NORTH and SOUTH are opposite compass directions. Again (B) is a possible answer, but not the *best* answer since they do not really work togehter as do a MERIDIAN and a PARALLEL. LONGITUDE and LATITUDE compare well with MERIDIAN and PARALLEL. Through MERIDIANS one arrives at LONGITUDE; through PARALLELS one arrives at LATITUDE. Both LONGITUDE and LATITUDE are used in locations as are MERIDIANS and PARALLELS. (C) is the best answer. A MAP is a drawing representing the earth's surface; a GLOBE is a sphere with a map of the world on it. The two are not necessarily used together. They do not have the same analogy as do MERIDIAN:PARALLEL. (D) is not the best answer. A COMPASS is used to find DIRECTION. The analogy is not the same as is MERIDIAN:PARALLEL. (E) is not the best answer.

9.    (A)

ABORIGINAL means original, native. INSERTION implies an introduction to something already existing. The two are opposite in that ABORIGINAL implies coming before the act of adding (INSER-

TION). NATIVE means original to an area. NOVEL mean different. The two are opposite in the same way that ABORIGINAL is opposite from INSERTION. (A) is the correct answer. ORIGINAL implies being native or "there first." HABITUATED means accustomed. The relationship is closer to being synonymous than opposite; since an antonymous relationship is sought, (B) is not the best choice. The SOURCE of a river is its MOUTH. The relationship between the two words in (C) is not the opposite relationship sought. MODERN suggests currency; RESUMPTION suggests beginning again. The relationship in (D) is not the antonymous relationship sought. AC-CUSTOMED means usual, customary. RECURRENCE means to occur again. The two are not opposite in the relationship; (E) is incorrect.

10.  (E)

AVERSION means strong dislike; FONDNESS implies attach-ment or affection. The two are opposite. (A) EQUIVALENT and COMMENSURATE are synonyms for equal. (A) is not the right answer. TANTAMOUNT and EQUAL are synonyms for the same, equivalent. (B) is not the best answer. A FARRIER is another name for a BLACKSMITH. The two are the same so (C) is not the best choice. EXECRABLE and FOUL are synonymous terms for very dirty, con-temptible. (D) should not be chosen. ODIOUS means provoking hatred; LAUDABLE is that which can be looked upon with approval. The two are opposites. (E) is the best answer.

11.  (C)

VITIATE (to impair the quality of, to spoil) and SPOIL are synonymous. FATUOUS means without reality; ASININE means stupid. The two are not the best examples of the synonyms sought, (A) is incorrect. CONTAMINATE and PURGE (cleanse) are opposites, hence (B) should not be selected. ABASE is to bring down; it is synonymous with CORRUPT. (C) is the correct answer. ADULTER-ATE is to add, to change, to make worse (usually); CLEANSE is the opposite of ADULTERATE. (D) is not the best answer. VICISSI-TUDE is to change; it can imply regular succession or irregular change. To TAINT is to corrupt, to contaminate. Choice (E) does not have the synonymous relationship sought.

12. (E)

The HEART is a part of the CIRCULATORY system. The part comes before the whole in this analogy. The EXCRETORY system of the body secretes SWEAT, but the analogy is not *whole* to *part*. (A) is incorrect. The NEUROLOGICAL system involves the nervous system. The SKELETON is a part of the skeletal system. (B) is incorrect. The LUNGS are a part of the RESPIRATORY system, but the order is not the same as for CIRCULATORY:HEART. (C) is incorrect. A KIDNEY is not a part of the DIGESTIVE system. (D) is not an appropriate answer. Since the TESTES are a part of the male REPRODUCTIVE system, (E) is the correct answer.

13. (D)

Both DILETTANTE and TYRO are synonymous terms for an amateur, a beginner. A NECROLOGY is a roll of the dead, an obituary notice. The words seems unrelated to PROFESSION. (A) is an incorrect choice. An INGREDIENT is a part of a COMPOUND. (B) does not have the synonymous relationship sought. A FOIBLE is a weak point. CHASTE is unblemished. The two are not synonymous; (C) is incorrect. A DABBLER is an AMATEUR. The two are synonymous. (D) is correct. A LAWYER prepares a BRIEF. The two are not synonymous, (E) is incorrect.

14. (B)

A FRAILITY is an imperfection. The term VICE is used to denote a "serious" imperfection. The difference is in the degree, with a FRAILTY being milder. A FELONY is more serious than a MISDEMEANOR. The analogy is, however, inverted. (A) should not be selected. AGGRAVATING is intensifying, making worse. PERNICIOUS is highly injurious. The degree of PERNICIOUS is greater than that of AGGRAVATING. Their relationship is that of FRAILITY: VICE. (B) is the correct answer. TRITE is overworked, overused. POPULAR is common. The degree of the two is different, but the analogy is different from that of FRAILTY:VICE. (C) is not the correct answer. SECRETED is more carefully hidden than VEILED; again the order is inverted. (D) is incorrect. A CLOISTER implies seclusion from the world. A MONASTERY is a CLOISTER for monks. The relationship between CLOISTER and MONASTERY in choice (E) is not that sought.

**15. (B)**

QUART is the English measure of volume; LITER is the metric volume measure. YARD is the English measure of length; ACRE is an English, not a metric, measurement. (A) is incorrect. YARD is the English measure of length; METER is the metric measure. (B) is correct. OUNCE is an English measure of mass (weight). KILO-WATT is a unit of work. The relationship between the two is not that of measuring the same unit. (C) is incorrect. LITER is the metric unit of volume; GALLON is the English unit. The two are inverted, however, from that of the example. (D) should not be selected. MILE is an English measure of length. KILOGRAM is a metric measurement of mass (weight). The relationship is English to metric, but the thing measured is different. (E) is incorrect.

**16. (C)**

FINE and AMERCEMENT are synonymous for a penalty. LOSS and GAIN are opposites. The person who chose answer (A) probably did not know the meaning of AMERCEMENT, or could not figure out the meaning from using a knowledge of suffixes, prefixes, and root words. FORFEITURE is a fine; REWARD is the opposite. (B) is incorrect since the pair does not have the same relationship as FINE:AMERCEMENT. PENALTY and MULCT are synonymous words. (C) is the correct answer. A LOTTERY is an affair of chance. DEPOSIT as a noun means that which is entrusted to the care of another, a pledge. The relationship between the pair is not the synonymous relationship sought. (D) is incorrect. CONTRABAND is illegal or prohibited commerce; it can also refer to goods or merchandise the importation or exportation of which is forbidden. CONFISCATE is a verb meaning to seize or appropriate; as an adjective it means confiscated or forfeited. The relationship is not that sought. (E) should not be selected.

**17. (E)**

There is no evidence that the author disagrees so vehemently with the split-brain theory as to respond with UNQUALIFIED DISAGREE-MENT. (A) is not the best answer. UNQUESTIONING APPROVAL is not the attitude of the author; rather she seems willing to listen to both sides, though she seems more inclined to disagree with the theory. (B) is not the best answer. The very fact that the author wrote the articles

negates the idea that COMPLETE INDIFFERENCE is the best answer. (C) is not the best choice. Although the author seems to disagree with the split-brain theory, STRONG DISPARAGEMENT is not the best answer, (D) should not be chosen. IMPLIED UNCERTAINTY seems to be the best of the choices. (E) is the best answer.

18. (C)

(A) is incorrect since the split-brain theory is not reasserted by the author in the article. Since the split-brain theory is not renunciated by the author, (B) is not the correct choice. (C) is the best answer since it implies what the article does — present both sides of the theory. Since modifying the curriculum is only one part of the article, (D) is incorrect. Since the split-brain theory is not new, (E) is inaccurate.

19. (B)

The writer does not seem convinced that the educators who support the split-brain theory can supply justification for modifying the curriculum. The author does not seem OPTIMISTIC. (A) is not the best answer. The writer does seem PESSIMISTIC and unconvinced that the educators can supply the needed proof. (B) is the best answer. The author is not RESIGNED to the fact that the proponents can supply the necessary proof; in fact the author seems skeptical that such proof can be provided, thus (C) is incorrect. The author does not appear ILLOGICAL; she seems willing to listen to proponents if they can provide the facts. (D) is not the best choice. The very fact that the author wrote about and is willing to listen to facts supporting a modification of the curriculum makes the answer INDIFFERENCE inappropriate. (E) is not the best answer.

20. (E)

(A) is incorrect since the LEFT hemisphere is believed to control language and logic. Again, the LEFT side is believed to control language and logic, so (B) is incorrect. It is the OPPONENTS (not PROPONENTS) who contend that both hemispheres function well after surgery; (C) is incorrect. At the present time the curriculum and methods have not been generally modified to accommodate the split-brain theory; therefore (D) is incorrect. (E) is the correct answer.

21.  (A)
   (A) is the correct answer. (B) is not the correct answer since damage to the right (as well as the left) side of the brain may result in logical disorders. (C) is not the right answer since it has not been proven to the satisfaction of everyone that one hemisphere may be engaged to the exclusion of the other. The article suggests that the two sides work cooperatively. (D) is, therefore, incorrect. The writer suggests that education involves both (not just one) side of the brain. (E) is incorrect.

22.  (D)
   Proponents and opponents do disagree about methods and curriculum but that is not a fundamental difference; (A) is incorrect. (B) is false; proponents do agree that the purposes of the hemispheres do differ but that the integration of activities is not urged, or even thought possible, by many. Opponents do not always state that the two hemispheres differ significantly in function nor do they always believe that integration of the activities is impossible; (C) is incorrect. The beliefs about the functions of the two hemispheres of the brain are the fundamental differences between proponents and opponents of the split-brain theory; (D) is the correct answer. Both groups agree that the brain is divided into hemispheres; this is not the DISTINCTION between the two groups. (E) is not the correct answer.

23.  (B)
   This statement is one OPPONENTS, not PROPONENTS, of the split-brain theory might espouse; (A) is incorrect. (B) is the correct answer. (C) is incorrect; this is a belief of the OPPONENTS of the split-brain theory. (D) is not the correct choice; this finding is one OPPONENTS of the split-brain theory often make known. Statement (E) is one OPPONENTS of the theory use.

24.  (C)
   The author would disagree with (A). (B) is certainly incorrect; the modifications have neither already been made nor are they on the agenda of most educators. (C) is the correct answer. (D) is incorrect; the author's open-minded point of view is not illustrated by this

statement. The reader should immediately see (E) as erroneous since it reverses the hemisphere associated by proponents of the theory with language and logic.

25. (A)

Brooks can best be described, from the list of words given, as HUMANISTIC. Her concern with integration, black consciousness, would-be writers and her choice of writing topics illustrate why choice (A) is appropriate. (B) is incorrect. Brooks is not afraid to pursue a cause which causes criticism of her from some groups. For those who seek to criticize, she is not CIRCUMSPECT. (C) is false; Brooks is not OBSCURE. She is the most famous black poet writing in our country today. (D) is incorrect; Brooks is not cowardly or CRAVEN. She is not afraid to work for that which she believes is right — even if it might not give her popularity in all circles. (E) is a poor choice. Brooks is not withdrawn or ALIENATED from society. She continues to write and to travel about working with would-be writers.

26. (C)

Brooks was a published writer by eleven; (A) is incorrect. Grants did not lessen, but heighten, her prestige. (B) is incorrect. (C) is the correct answer. After her first book was sold, she received nationwide recognition; (D) is wrong. Brooks takes an interest in others; (E) is incorrect.

27. (A)

Brooks believes in writing what one has to say regardless of whether one is rewarded by others. (A) is a statement similar to what she tells would-be writers on her travels. Brooks does not use just one style of writing; she writes different poems using different styles. She is not bound by tradition. This does not sound like the advice she would give others. (B) is incorrect. (C) Brooks would not believe in writing just to please others. She would believe it more important to please one's self. Brooks would not tell others to write just to sell; (C) is not typical of Brooks. Brooks has always found room for causes and people in her busy life. She would not encourage others to withdraw from life but to experience life. It is from her life experiences that she draws most of her writing ideas; (D) is incorrect. Brooks does not

pattern her writing after one writer; neither does she stick to one style in her works. (E) would not be a suggestion she would make.

28.  (B)
   CONCORD is a state of agreement, harmony. SUCCOR is aid, help. (A) is not an antonym for CONCORD and should not be chosen. ENMITY is ill will or hatred; it is the opposite of CONCORD. (B) is the correct answer. A GRIPPER is one who holds a camera or other apparatus. (C) bears no relation to CONCORD and should not be selected as the correct choice. VIGILANT means alertly watchful. It is not directly related to CONCORD. (D) is an inappropriate choice. ENNOBLING means elevating, raising. (E) is not the opposite of the key word and should not be selected.

29.  (D)
   INSIDIOUS means wily, sly. PRECIPITANT (A) means rushing ahead. It is not an antonym for INSIDIOUS. INCENDIARY means tending to excite or inflame. (B) should not be selected as the antonym. DECADENT is deteriorating, declining. It is not the opposite of INSIDIOUS, (C) is not the correct answer. CONDUCIVE means helpful. (D) is the opposite of INSIDIOUS. IMPRUDENT means lacking in caution, indiscreet. (E) is not the opposite of INSIDIOUS.

30.  (B)
   A MALEFACTION is an evil deed, an offense. AFFINITY means an attraction, a likeness. (A) is not the opposite for MALEFACTION. A SUBSIDY is a gift, a form of aid. Certainly a SUBSIDY (aid) would be the opposite of MALEFACTION (an evil deed). (B) is the correct answer. PROFLIGATION means the act of wasting. It is not the opposite of MALEFACTION. (C) should not be chosen as the correct answer. IDIOSYNCRATIC means (D) peculiar, eccentric. (D) is not an antonym for MALEFACTION. COGNATE means of a similar nature. Since the term is not directly related to MALEFACTION, (E) should not be chosen.

31.  (E)
   OBDURATE means hardened in feeling, unyielding. AFFABLE

(A) means gracious, courteous, sociable, amiable. It is dissimilar from OBDURATE but not the exact opposite. Unsavory means morally offensive. (B) is not an antonym for OBDURATE. PREVARICAT-ING means telling falsehoods. (C) is not directly related to OBDU-RATE and should not be selected as the antonym. CREDULOUS means believable. (D) is not the opposite sought. PENITENT means sorry for sins or faults. It is the opposite of OBDURATE. (E) is the antonym sought.

32.  (A)

RANCOROUS means full of ill will, spite. OFFICIOUS means kind, obliging, dutiful. It is the opposite of RANCOROUS. (A) is the correct answer. ENMITY means having hatred, antagonism. It is not the opposite of RANCOROUS and (B) should not be selected as the correct response. ABASH means to confuse, compound. (C) is not an antonym for the key word. NEFARIOUS means heinously wicked. (D) is synonymous with RANCOROUS and not the antonym sought. JUDICIOUS means wise. (E) does not have the antonymous relation needed for the correct answer.

33.  (C)

PERPETUITY means endless time, an annuity payable forever. A PEDANTIC is one who makes a display of learning. (A) is not an antonym of PERPETUITY. ESPOUSE means to embrace, to adopt as a cause. (B) is not the correct answer. MORTALITY is the condition or quality of being mortal or ending. (C) is the opposite of PERPETU-ITY and the correct answer. CULPABLE means deserving blame or censure. (D) is an incorrect answer. CYBERNETICS (E) is a compara-tive study of the control system formed by the nervous system and brain and mechanical-electrical communication systems.

34.  (A)

EXPURGATED is cleared from anything offensive or erroneous. INEXTIRPABLE means incapable of being erased or corrected. (A) is correct. SUNDERED means cut apart or broken. (B) is not the correct answer. VENERATED means regarded with respect or rever-ence. (C) is incorrect. EXPATRIATED means banished or made an exile of, as a country. (D) is not the antonym sought. COMPLAISANT

(E) means manifesting the desire or disposition to please.

35. **(D)**
    TO POSTULATE is to merely guess or to hypothesize. MOL-LIFY is to appease, to calm. (A) is not the antonym of POSTULATE. CONJECTURE is to guess based on insufficient evidence. (B) is synonymous and not an antonym. PROGNOSTICATE (C) is to guess. It is synonymous with POSTULATE. CORROBORATE is to establish, to confirm. It is the opposite of guessing; (D) is the correct answer. REFURBISH is to brighten or to freshen up. (E) is not directly related to the key word and is not the answer sought.

36. **(C)**
    CAPRICIOUS means fanciful, inconstant, apt to change suddenly. IMPECUNIOUS means poor, habitually without money. (A) does not bear an antonymous relationship to CAPRICIOUS. JUXTAPOSI-TIONED means placed side by side as for the purpose of comparing. (B) is not the correct answer. SCRUPULOUS (C) means to be careful, exact; the dictionary gives it a meaning of faithful, steadfast — the opposite of CAPRICIOUS. COPIOUS means plentiful, abundant. (D) is not the opposite of CAPRICIOUS. SUPERFLUOUS means excessive, more than enough. (E) is not the antonym sought.

37. **(D)**
    A NON SEQUITUR is an inference or conclusion that does not follow from the premise. MUNDANE means earthly; it does not relate to NON SEQUITUR. (A) is not the correct answer. A SEMAPHORE is an apparatus for signaling. (B) does not relate to NON SEQUITUR. ILLOGICAL is a synonym for NON SEQUITUR; (C) is not the best choice. REASONABLE is the opposite of NON SEQUITUR; (D) is the correct answer. FALLACIOUS (E) means logically unsound; it is a synonym for the key word and not the right choice.

38. **(B)**
    A ZEPHYR is a gentle wind. A TYCOON (colloquial) is a wealthy, powerful individual. The individual who chose (A) probably meant to use TYPHOON. A TYPHOON is a violent cyclonic storm,

just the opposite of a ZEPHYR; (B) is the correct choice. A CORACLE (C) is a small boat and obviously not the answer sought. TACITURN is an adjective meaning quiet, soft-spoken. (D) is not the correct choice. A CONSTELLATION is a pattern of stars. (E), like ZEPHYR, is a noun, but it is not the antonym sought.

# Section 3—Quantitative Ability

1.    (B)

To compare $(x + y)^2$ with $(x - y)^2$ set $x = 5$ and $y = -3$ in each expression and calculate. We get

$$(x + y)^2 = (5 + (-3))^2 = (5 - 3)^2 = 2^2 = 4 \text{ and}$$
$$(x - y)^2 = (5 - (-3))^2 = (5 + 3)^2 = 8^2 = 64.$$

Since $64 > 4$ we can conclude that $(x - y)^2$ in Column B is larger than $(x + y)^2$ in Column A for $x = 5$ and $y = -3$.

If response (A) is chosen then perhaps an error was made in the computation after substituting the values for $x$ and $y$, respectively. Or, it was assumed that $(x + y)$ is always greater than $(x - y)$ and thus

$$(x + y)^2 \text{ is greater than } (x - y)^2.$$

Response (C) implies that $(x + y)^2 = (x - y)^2$ for $x = 5$ and $y = -3$ which is not possible. Finally, response (D) as a choice is incorrect.

2.    (C)

First notice that in Column A, $\frac{1}{5}$ of 0.2% of 1000 means that we multiply the values together after 0.2% is changed to the decimal 0.002. Thus, we get $\frac{1}{5} \times 0.002 \times 1000 = 0.4$. In Column B, the expression $(\frac{1}{5})\%$ of 0.2 of 1000 means $(\frac{1}{5})\% \times 0.2 \times 1000 = 0.002 \times 0.2 \times 1000 = 0.4$. Choice of response (B) would probably indicate that $(\frac{1}{5})\%$ in the expression $(\frac{1}{5})\%$ of 0.2 of 1000 was interpreted as 20% instead of 0.2%. Similarly, if choice (A) was selected, then perhaps the decimal equivalent for 0.2% was incorrectly determined in the expression.

3.    (B)

To compare the expression $x^2 + y^2$ in Column A with $(x + y)^2$ one should first assume that these expressions are equal. Then

214

$$x^2 + y^2 = (x + y)^2 \text{ implies } x^2 + y^2 = x^2 + 2xy + y^2. \qquad (1)$$

For $x$ and $y$ both positive their squares are also positive. So, a one-to-one comparison of the expression in Column B with the expression in Column A indicates that Column B is larger since it has an extra term, $2xy$, which is positive. Hence, response (B) is correct.

Response (C) is not possible. To see this add $- x^2$ and $- y^2$, respectively, on both sides of (1). So, one obtains

$$
\begin{aligned}
x^2 + y^2 - x^2 &= x^2 + 2xy + y^2 - x^2 \\
y^2 &= 2xy + y^2 \\
y^2 - y^2 &= 2xy + y^2 - y^2 \\
0 &= 2xy
\end{aligned}
$$

Note that $2xy = 0$ means that either $x = 0$, $y = 0$ or $x = y = 0$. So, the assertion of equality between the two statements leads to a contradiction since the original assumption is that both $x$ and $y$ are positive.

4.  (C)

Recall that the circumference, $C$, or a circle is equal to $\pi$ times the diameter. Thus, for the inner circle one obtains,

$$C = \pi d = \pi(3.5) = 3.5\pi.$$

For the outer circle one obtains,

$$C = \pi d = \pi(7) = 7\pi.$$

One-half of the circumference of the outer circle is $(1/2) (7\pi) = 3.5\pi$. Thus, the quantities in Columns A and B are equal.

5.  (D)

To determine the outcome consider the following:

If $4w = 6x = 12y$ then $4w/4 = 12y/4$ or $w = 3y$. Thus, in general for positive numbers the value of $w$ is always three times as large as the value of $y$. So response (A) would be correct. But, if one substitutes 0 for $w$ then $w$ and $y$ have the same value 0. So, the quantities are equal and response (C) is correct. Finally, if the values of $w$ and $y$ are both negative, then response (B) is correct. (e.g., if $w = - 12$, then $y = - 4$ which is larger then $w$.) Thus, there is not enough information given to make a comparison.

6.   (A)

Observe that $1/x = \sqrt{0.0016}/5$ is a proportion. Thus, the product of the extremes equals the product of the means. So, one gets

$$\sqrt{0.0016}\, x = 5(1) \text{ or } 0.04x = 5 \text{ or } x = 5/0.04 = 125.$$

Hence, $x$ is greater than the 12.5 in Column B.

If one incorrectly finds the square root of 0.0016 to be 0.4, then response (C) would be the outcome.

7.   (D)

First, add the rational expressions in Column A. In order to do this, one needs to find the least common denominator of 4 and 3. Observe that the least common denominator (LCD) is 12 since it is the smallest real number that is divisible by both 4 and 3. So one rewrites the two original rational expressions in Column A as equivalent expressions with 12 as the LCD as follows:

$$\frac{3(x-3)}{3(4)} + \frac{4(x+7)}{4(3)}.$$

Multiplying out the numerator and denominator in each expression and combining or adding the two fractions, the results are:

$$\frac{3x-9}{12} + \frac{4x+28}{12} = \frac{3x-9+4x+28}{12} = \frac{7x+19}{12}$$

So the rational expression in Column A is given by $\frac{7x+19}{12}$ and the

rational expression given in Column B, $\frac{7x+19}{7}$, can now be examined

Compare the numerator of the sum of the rational expressions in Column A with the numerator of the rational expression in Column B. Now suppose $7x + 19$ is a positive value, then the quantity in Column B would be larger. On the other hand, suppose $7x + 19$ is a negative value, then the quantity in Column A would be larger. Hence it is not possible to compare the two columns.

8.   (C)

To explain this answer one needs to first know that the exterior angle of a triangle equals the sum of the measure of both remote interior angles of the triangle. The exterior angle of triangle $CDE$ is angle $x$ and

the remote interior angles are $C$ and $D$. So, the sum of angles $C$ and $D$ equals to angle $x$. Similarly, the exterior angle of triangle $ABE$ is angle $x$ and the remote interior angles are $A$ and $B$. So, the sum of angles $A$ and $B$ equals to angle $x$. Hence, by substitution, one gets that the quantities in the two Columns are equal as follows:

$$\angle x + \angle x = (\angle A + \angle B) + (\angle C + \angle D) \text{ or}$$
$$2(\angle x) = \angle A + \angle B + \angle C + \angle D.$$

9. **(B)**
First one must observe that $x^2 = y + 2 = 5$ means that

(1)   $x^2 = y + 2,$
(2)   $x^2 = 5,$ and
(3)   $y + 2 = 5.$

Now solve equations (2) and (3), respectively, and compare the results. For equation (2) one gets

$$x^2 = 5 \text{ or } x = \sqrt{5} \text{ and } x = -\sqrt{5}.$$

For equation (3) one gets
$$y + 2 = 5 \text{ or } y = 3.$$

Hence, 3 is larger than the positive or negative square root of 5. So, the quantity in Column B is greater.

10. **(A)**
The given information that $BC = CD = BD$ means that triangle $BCD$ is equilateral. Further, this means that each of the three angles in the equilateral triangle is equal to 60 degrees. Since it is also given that $BC \perp AC$, one can deduce from the given figure that:

angle $BCD$ + angle $ACD$ = $60° +$ angle $ACD = 60° + 30° = 90°$,

a right angle.
Now $AC$ lies opposite angle $ADC$ which equals $120°$ since angle $BDC$ is $60°$ and the two angles are supplementary. Also, $CD$ lies opposite angle $DAC$ which must equal 30 degrees. Thus, one can conclude that segment $AC$ in Column A is greater than segment $CD$ in Column B since segment $AC$ is opposite a larger angle than segment $CD$.

11. (C)

The least common multiple (LCM) in Column A is determined by first finding the prime factorization of each of the numbers involved. Then, the product of the unique factors at their highest powers among the numbers is the LCM. Thus, the LCM in Column A is found in the following manner. The prime factorizations of the numbers are:

$$20 = 2 \times 2 \times 5; \quad 24 = 2 \times 2 \times 2 \times 3; \quad 32 = 2 \times 2 \times 2 \times 2 \times 2.$$

Notice that the unique factors among the three numbers are 2, 3, and 5. Now the highest power of 2 among the numbers is $2^5$; the highest power of 3 among the numbers is $3^1$; and the highest power of 5 among the number is $5^1$. Thus, the LCM for Column A is given by:

$$2^5 \times 3^1 \times 5^1 = 32 \times 3 \times 5 = 480.$$

Similarly, since the prime factorizations of the numbers in Column B are:
$$2 = 2^1; \ 15 = 3 \times 5; \ 32 = 2 \times 2 \times 2 \times 2 \times 2$$

and the highest powers among the prime factors are $2^5$, $3^1$, and $5^1$, respectively, the LCM in Column B is given by $2^5 \times 3^1 \times 5^1 = 480$. Thus, the quantities in the two columns are equal.

12. (C)

The formula for the area of a triangle is $A = (1/_2)$ (Base) (Height). So for triangle $ABC$ the lengths of the base and height are given to be equal, that is, segment $AC$ = segment $CB$. Thus, let the variable $x = AC = CB$ and substitute in the area formula to get the following

$$\text{Area} = (1/_2) \, (x) \, (x) = 60.5 \text{ square units}$$

Now solve for $x$,

$$(1/_2)x^2 = 60.5 \text{ square units.}$$
$$x^2 = 121 \text{ square units}$$
$$x = 11 \text{ units}$$

Hence the quantities in the two Columns are equal.

13. (A)

Perhaps the easiest way to approach the comparison of the two quantities is to first find the least common multiple for the denomina-

tors, 16 and 40, which is 80. Then, write equivalent fractions using the LCD. The results are:

$$\frac{13}{16} \times \frac{5}{5} = \frac{65}{80} \text{ and } \frac{31}{40} \times \frac{2}{2} = \frac{62}{80}.$$

Since the numerator, 65, in the equivalent fraction in Column A is greater than the one in Column B, the fraction in Column A is greater.

14.  (C)

To understand this problem first assume that triangle *ABC* is a right triangle. With this assumption the Pythagorean Theorem applies as follows:

$$(AC)^2 = (AB)^2 + (BC)^2.$$

Since the length of the sides of the triangle are given ($AC = 17$, $AB = 8$, $BC = 15$), substitute in the formula and observe whether the result is an equality.

$$(17)^2 = (8)^2 + (15)^2 \text{ or}$$
$$289 = 64 + 225 \text{ or}$$
$$289 = 289.$$

Because the result is an equality, the assumption that the triangle is a right triangle is correct. So, the angle opposite the longest side (angle *ABC*) must be a right angle. The quantities in the two Columns are equal.

15.  (D)

Note that $w : x = w/x$ and $y : z = y/z$. Thus, $w/x = y/z$ is a proportion. Simplify the proportion by recalling that the product of the extremes equal the product of the means. The result is $wz = xy$. Since the values of $w, x, y$ and $z$ are both positive and negative real numbers, there is not enough information that will allow comparison of the quantities $w + x$ and $y + z$.

16.  (C)

First, observe that three fourths is $^3/_4$ and one tenth is $^1/_{10}$. Let $x$ be the unknown part which must be found. Then, one can write from the statement of the problem that the $x$ part of three fourths is given by:

$$\frac{3}{4}x.$$

The equation for the problem is given by $\frac{3}{4}x = \frac{1}{10}$. Multiplying both sides of the equation by the reciprocal of $\frac{3}{4}$ one obtains the following:

$$\frac{4}{3}\frac{3}{4}x = \frac{4}{3}\frac{1}{10} \text{ or } x = \frac{4}{30} \text{ or } x = \frac{2}{15}$$

which is choice (C).

Response (D) is obtained by incorrectly finding the product of $\frac{3}{4}$ and $\frac{1}{10}$ to be the unknown part. Response (B) is obtained by dividing $\frac{3}{4}$ by $\frac{1}{10}$.

17.  (C)

Notice that triangle $ABC$ is a right triangle and that distance $AC = 5 - 2 = 3$ and distance $AB = 6 - 1 = 5$. Use the Pythagoreon Theorem to find the length of side $BC$ as follows:

$$
\begin{aligned}
(BC)^2 &= (AC)^2 + (AB)^2 \\
(BC)^2 &= 3^2 + 5^2 \\
(BC)^2 &= 9 + 25 \\
BC &= \sqrt{34}
\end{aligned}
$$

Response (D) is obtained by simply adding the $y$-coordinates of points $B$ and $C$ which is incorrect. Similarly, response (A) is obtained by finding the difference between the $x$-coordinates for points $B$ and $C$. Also, response (B) is obtained by finding the difference between the $y$-coordinates of points $B$ and $C$.

18.  (C)

In order to find the midpoint of the line segment between two points one must know the formula. It is given by an ordered pair $(x, y)$ where $x$ is formed by the average of the $x$-coordinates and $y$ is formed by the average of the $y$-coordinates of the two points. Thus, the midpoint is

$$x = \frac{3 + 9}{2} = \frac{12}{2} = 6 \text{ and } y = \frac{5 + 13}{2} = \frac{18}{2} = 9$$

or the ordered pair $(6, 9)$.

Response (A) is obtained by incorrectly inter-changing the coordinates. If response (B) is selected then the results are obtained by

simply adding the $x$-coordinates and $y$-coordinates to get (12, 18) which is incorrect. Response (D) is obtained by finding the difference between the $x$-coordinates and $y$-coordinates, respectively. Finally, response (E) is obtained by finding one-half of the difference between the $x$-coordinates and $y$-coordinates, respectively.

19. **(B)**

Since the non-white males category is the only portion (in degrees) not shown in the graph, simply add the given degrees in the circle and subtract the sum from 360 degrees to obtain 30 degrees. Then form the ratio of 30 to 360 and find the percent which is simply $8\frac{1}{3}\%$.

Answer choice (A) indicates that the number of degrees in the circle that represents the non-white males category. Answer choice (D) indicates the percent of the circle that represents the white females category. Answer choice (C) represents only one-half of the correct percent for the non-white males category.

20. **(A)**

Observe that 20% of the total number of Ph.D.s awarded went to white female U.S. citizens, that is, $72/360 = 20\%$. The, multiply 20% (that is 0.20) by 4000 to obtain 800 which is the correct answer.

Answer choice (B) is obtained by incorrectly multiplying 0.72 by 4000 to get 2880. Notice that the portion of the circle representing the white females category is 72 degrees of the whole. One may wrongly consider this as 72/100 or 0.72. Answer choice (C) is obtained by incorrectly subtracting 800 from 4000 and answer choice (D) is obtained by incorrectly subtracting 2880 from 4000.

21. **(D)**

Let $x$ denote the number of Ph.D.s awarded to white males. Then, form ratios 72/600 and 252/x. Then form a proportion $72/600 = 252/x$ and solve for $x$ to obtain the number of Ph.D.s awarded to white males. The result is as follows:

$$\frac{72}{600} = \frac{252}{x} \text{ or } 72x = 600(252) \text{ or } x = 151200 \text{ or } x = 2100.$$

Answer Choice (A) represents a value that is too small. The same is true about answer choice (C) since the white males category represents more than 3 times the area of the white female category.

Answer choice (B) is obtained by dividing 600 by 20% which is incorrect.

22. **(C)**
The ratio of degrees awarded to white males to those awarded to non-white males is given by using 252 to 30, the corresponding portions of the circle representing these categories. So, the ratio is 252/30 or 8.4/1 (that is, 8.4 to 1). Hence, the answer choice is (C).

Answer choice (B) is obtained by finding the ratio of 252 to 72; choice (D) is obtained by finding the ratio of 252 to 6; and choice (A) is illogical.

23. **(B)**
Observe that 6 degrees represent 6/360 of the whole circle. Since the entire circle represents a distribution of 6000 one can find the number of the total that 6 degrees represents as follows:

$$\frac{6}{360} \times 6000 = 100.$$

24. **(D)**
On the left-hand side of the equation apply the distributive property to obtain:

$4 - 10\,y - 20 = 4.$  Then, add 4 and $-20$ to obtain
$-10y - 16 = 4.$  Then, add 16 to both sides of the equation

to get

$-10y = 20.$  Then, divide both sides by $-10$ to get
$y = -2.$

It can be determined that each of the other answer choices is incorrect by simply substituting in the given equation.

25. **(A)**
To find the quotient and the remainder one can either use the long division procedure or the synthetic division procedure. The first procedure should be well-known so the synthetic division procedure is used below. First, take the coefficients and constant term (in order) of the dividend expression and write them as follows:

$$1 \quad -5 \quad 3$$

Next, write the divisor expression in the form $x - a$ and use as the divisor of the three integers above. So, $x + 2 = x - (-2)$. Hence $a = -2$. Thus, one can complete the procedure as follows:

$$
\begin{array}{r|rrr}
-2 & 1 & -5 & 3 \\
  &   & -2 & 14 \\
\hline
  & 1 & -7 & 17
\end{array}
$$

where the first coefficient is simply brought down below the line. The $-2$ under $-5$ (the second coefficient) is obtained by multiplying $-2$ (the divisor value) by the 1 below the line. The 14 under the constant term 3 is obtained by multiplying $-2$ (the divisor value) by the $-7$ below the line. Finally, the quotient is determined by attaching the $x$ variable to 1 since the original dividend was a second degree expression in $x$ and $-7$ becomes the constant term. The remainder is 17 which can be expressed as a fraction $17/(x+2)$. Thus, the complete quotient is given by:

$$1x - 7 + 17/(x+2) \quad \text{or} \quad x - 7 + 17/(x+2)$$

which is choice (A).

The other answer choices are incorrect because they fail in the synthetic division procedure.

26. (C)

Based on the information given in the first sentence of the problem one needs to first represent the unknown numbers. So let $x$ be a number. Then, the other number is given by $3x + 2$, which is two more than 3 times the first number. So the two numbers are: $x$ and $3x + 2$.

Next, form an equation by adding the two numbers and setting the sum equal to 22 and then solve the equation for the two numbers.

$$
\begin{aligned}
x + 3x + 2 &= 22 \\
4x + 2 &= 22 \\
4x &= 20 \\
x &= 5, \text{ one of the numbers. The other}
\end{aligned}
$$

number is given by

$$3x + 2 = 3(5) + 2 = 15 + 2 = 17, \text{ the other number.}$$

Hence, answer choice (C) is correct. The other answer choices fail to satisfy the equation $x + 3x + 2 = 22$.

**27. (D)**

Simplify the equation by first multiplying by 2 on both sides and expand the right-hand side as follows:

$$A = (h/2)(B + b) \text{ or } 2A = 2(h/2)(B + b)$$
$$2A = h(B + b)$$
$$2A = hB + hb$$

Then, solve for $B$ as follows:

$$hB + hb = 2A$$
$$hB = 2A - hb$$
$$B = 2A/h - hb/h$$
$$B = 2A/h - b$$

Hence answer choice (D) is correct. The other choices are incorrect because they are obtained by inappropriately applying algebra techniques.

**28. (B)**

First find the number of different ways of drawing 2 marbles from the box. Use the permutation formula as follows:

$$P(10,2) = \frac{10!}{(10-2)!} = \frac{10!}{8!} = \frac{10(9)(8!)}{8!} = 10(9) = 90 \text{ ways}.$$

Then find the number of different ways of drawing 2 red marbles from the box. Use the permutation formula as follows:

$$P(6,2) = \frac{6!}{(6-2)!} = \frac{6!}{4!} = \frac{6(5)(4!)}{4!} = 6(5) = 30 \text{ ways}.$$

Finally, to get the probability form a ratio of $P(6, 2)$ to $P(10, 2)$. One gets the following:

The probability of drawing 2 red marbles from the box = 30/90 = $\frac{1}{3}$.

**29. (E)**

If $x = 1$ then response (B) is 2, response (A) is 2, response (C) is 3, and response (D) is $-1$. Thus, response (E) is the only response possible. Consider response (E). Notice that by factoring the expression one gets

$$x^2 + 2x + 1 = (x + 1)(x + 1) = (x + 1)^2$$

which is the square of an integer for every integer $x$.

**30. (D)**
The median is defined as the middle score or value when a sequence of numbers are arranged in either ascending or descending order. Thus, when this is done the middle score is 27. The answer choice (B) is the mode, the most frequent score. The other answer choices do not represent the median according to its definition.

## Section 4—Quantitative Ability

**1. (B)**
The given equations form a system which can be easily solved by the elimination method. By elimination one simply adds the two equations together in order to easily eliminate the $y$ variable and solve for the $x$ variable as follows:

$$x + y = 6$$
$$\underline{3x - y = 4}$$
$$4x \quad = 10 \qquad \text{(sum of the equations)}$$

$$\frac{4x}{4} = \frac{10}{4} \quad \text{or} \quad x = 10/4 = 5/2.$$

The next step is to substitute the value of $x$ in $x + y = 6$ and solve for the variable $y$. The result is

$$5/2 + y = 6$$
$$5/2 + y + (-5/2) = 6 + (-5/2)$$
$$y + 0 = 12/2 + (-5/2)$$
$$y = 7/2.$$

Finally, note that $x - y = 5/2 - 7/2 = -1$. Hence, the quantity in Column B is greater than the quantity in Column A.

**2. (C)**
Note that $w : x = w/x$ and $y : z = y/z$. Thus, $w/x = y/z$. Adding the opposite of $y/z$ to both sides of the equation we get

$$w/x + (-y/z) = y/z + (-y/z)$$
$$w/x - y/z = 0.$$

Multiplying through by $xz$, the LCD, we have
$$(xz)\,(w/x) - (xz)\,(y/z) \;=\; (xz)\,(0)$$
$$wz - xy \;=\; 0.$$
Hence, the quantities in both columns are equal.

3.    (B)

Since the measure of angle $C$ equals 60 degrees, then the sum of the measures of angles $A$ and $B$ equals 120 degrees. But, the measure of angle $A$ is given to be larger than the measure of angle $B$. So, Angle $A$ is more than one-half of 120 degrees. But, side $BC$ lies opposite angle $A$ which has a measure of more than 60 (more than 1/2 of 120 degrees). Therefore, side $BC$ is larger than side $AB$ which lies opposite angle $C$ which measures exactly 60 degrees.

4.    (B)

The only way for $1/y$ to be negative is for $y$ to be negative since the numerator is a positive 1. For example, if $y = 2$, then $1/2$ is not less than 0. So, $y$ is always $< 0$. Therefore, 1 in Column B is the larger quantity.

5.    (A)

In Column A find the roots of the given quadratic equation. An easy method of solution is by factoring. Since the left side of the equation

$$x^2 + 3x + 2 \text{ may be factored as } (x + 2)\,(x + 1),$$

then the equation may be written as: $(x + 2)\,(x + 1) = 0$.

Using the zero-factor property (that is, for real numbers $a$ and $b$, if $ab = 0$, then $a = 0$ or $b = 0$), one can write the last equation as two linear equations and solve each to obtain the roots of the original equation. Thus,

$$
\begin{array}{ccc}
x + 2 = 0 & \text{or} & x + 1 = 0 \\
x + 2 + (-2) = 0 + (-2) & & x + 1 + (-1) = 0 + (-1) \\
x + 0 = -2 & & x + 0 = -1 \\
x = -2 & & x = -1
\end{array}
$$

So, the roots of the equation are $-2, -1$. The product is $(-2)\,(-1) = 2$ which is larger than the quantity in Column B.

An easier approach is to recognize that the product of roots of a quadratic equation in standard form $ax^2 + bx + c = 0$ is given by $c/a$.

6.  (A)
    To understand this response, first solve $\sqrt{x} = 16$ for $x$ as follows:

$$(\sqrt{x})^2 = (16)^2$$
$$x = 256.$$

Then, solve the equation $y^3 = 64$ for $y$ as follows:

$$\sqrt[3]{yyy} = \sqrt[3]{64}$$
$$y = 4.$$

Hence, the value of $x = 256 > y = 4$. So, the quantity in Column A is greater.


7.  (A)
    In Column A expand the indicated product by using the foil method or some other method. Thus, the product of

$$(1 - \sqrt{2})(1 - \sqrt{2}) = 1 - \sqrt{2} - \sqrt{2} + (\sqrt{2})(\sqrt{2})$$
$$= 1 - 2\sqrt{2} + \sqrt{4}$$
$$= 1 - 2\sqrt{2} + 2$$
$$= 3 - 2\sqrt{2},$$

which is positive.
    Similarly, in Column B one expands the indicated product to get

$$(1 - \sqrt{2})(1 + \sqrt{2}) = 1 - \sqrt{2} + \sqrt{2} - (\sqrt{2})(\sqrt{2})$$
$$= 1 - \sqrt{4}$$
$$= 1 - 2$$
$$= -1.$$

Thus, the quantity in Column A is larger.


8.  (D)
    The formula for the surface area of a cube is the sum of the area of the 6 faces of the cube. The area of each face is $d(d) = d^2$. Thus, surface area = $6d^2$. On the other hand, the volume of the cube is given by $V = d(d)(d) = d^3$. But since $d$ does not have a particular value it cannot be determined what value is larger. For instance,
    if $d > 6$, then $dd^2 > 6d^2$ or $d^3 > 6d^2$;

if $d = 6$, then $dd^2 = 6d^2$ or $d^3 = 6d^2$ or $6^3 = 6(6)^2$ or $6^3 = 6^3$; and, finally, if $d < 6$, then $dd^2 < 6d^2$ or $d^3 < 6d^2$.

So, no comparison can be made with the given information.

9.  (A)

Notice that $(5.1x)^2 = 26.01x^2$. Thus, one can write

$$\sqrt{(5.1x)^2} = \sqrt{26.01x^2} = 5.1x.$$

But, $25.1x^2 < 26.01x^2$. Hence, $\sqrt{25.1x^2} < \sqrt{26.01x^2} = 5.1x$, which means that the quantity in Column A is larger than the quantity in Column B.

10.  (B)

Recall that triangle $ABC$, as well as any triangle, contains 180 degrees. Thus, the measure of angle $x$ must be the smallest since angle $A$ is 100 degrees and angle $B$ is 48 degrees. That is,

$$
\begin{aligned}
100 + 48 + x &= 180 \text{ degrees} \\
148 + x &= 180 \\
148 + x - 148 &= 180 - 148 \\
x &= 32 \text{ degrees.}
\end{aligned}
$$

Now since angle $A$ (100 degrees) is the largest in triangle $ABC$, then it is a well known theorem that the side $(BC)$ which is opposite this angle is the largest side. Thus, it follows that side $BC$ in Column B is greater than side $AB$ in Column A.

11.  (B)

To determine the comparison one needs to know the formula for finding the distance between two points in the plane. The distance between $A(3, 4)$ and $B(-1, 1)$ is found by using the following formula where the subscript 1 refers to coordinates in point $A$ and subscript 2 refers to coordinates in point $B$.

$$
\begin{aligned}
\sqrt{(x_2 - x_1)^2 + (y_2 - y_1)^2} &= \sqrt{(-1 - 3)^2 + (1 - 4)^2} \\
&= \sqrt{16 + 9} \\
&= \sqrt{25} = 5.
\end{aligned}
$$

The distance between $C(4, -2)$ and $D(-2, -2)$ is found using the same formula as follows where the subscript 1 refers to coordinates in point $C$ and subscript 2 refers to coordinates in point $D$:

$$\sqrt{(-2-4)^2 + (-2-(-2))^2} = \sqrt{(-6)^2 + (0)^2}$$
$$= \sqrt{36} = 6.$$

Hence, the distance from $C$ to $D$ is greater than the distance from $A$ to $B$.

12.　(A)

Observe that each side of the square must be 10 since its perimeter is 40. So the information in Column A yields the value $2(10) = 20$ units, twice the length of line segment $BD$.

In Column B the length of the shortest distance from point $A$ to line segment $DE$ is given by the length of a side of the square plus the height of the triangle. The distance from $DE$ to the base of the triangle is 10 units.

The length of the base of the triangle is also 10 units. In order to find the height of the triangle the area must be known first. The area of the combined figures is given to be 125 square units. But, the

area of the square = $e^2 = (10)^2 = 100$ square units.

Thus, the area of the triangle is 25 square units since the total area of the figures is 125 square units.

The formula for the area of the trianble is $A = (1/2)bh$. Thus, the height of the triangle is given by

$$h = 2A/b = 2(25)/10 = 50/10 = 5 \text{ units.}$$

So, the value of the quantity in Column B is $10 + 5 = 15$ units. Hence, the quantity in Column A is larger.

13.　(C)

By definition angles 4 and 5 are vertical angles and by a theorem vertical angles are equal. Since line segments $k$ and $m$ are parallel, by a theorem the corresponding angles are equal. What are the corresponding angles? They are angles 1 and 3 on the left side of the diagonal $d$ and angles 2 and 4 on the right side of the diagonal. It is

given that angle 2 = 60 degrees. Since angle 4 = angle 2, then angle 4 equals 60 degrees. Finally, since angles 4 and 5 are equal vertical angles then angle 5 equals 60 degrees. So the quantities in both columns are equal.

14.  (D)

Observe that in order to attempt to compare the two statements there is a need to analyze each. The statement in Column B indicates that a representation of the sum of the angles of a square must be made. Since each of the four angles of a square is a right angle, then one can write the sum of the angles as follows:

$$4(90°) = 360°.$$

On the other hand, the statement in Column B indicates that a representation of the sum of all the angles of a polygon whose sides are equal must be made. The sum of all the angles of any polygon with equal sides will vary. Thus, it is not possible to compare the results from the two columns.

15.  (B)

To compare $(x + y)^2$ with $(x - y)^2$ set $x = 5$ and $y = -3$ in each expression and calculate. One gets the following:

$$(x + y)^2 = (5 + (-3))^2 = (5 - 3)^2 = 2^2 = 4 \text{ and}$$
$$(x - y)^2 = (5 - (-3))^2 = (5 + 3)^2 = 8^2 = 64.$$

Since $64 > 4$ we can conclude that $(x - y)^2$ in Column B is larger than $(x + y)^2$ in Column A for $x = 5$ and $y = -3$.

If response (A) is chosen then perhaps an error was made in the computation after substituting the values for $x$ and $y$, respectively. Or, it was wrongly assumed that $(x + y)$ is always greater than $(x - y)$ and thus

$$(x + y)^2 \text{ is greater than } (x - y)^2.$$

Response (C) implies that $(x + y)^2 = (x - y)^2$ for $x = 5$ and $y = -3$ which is not possible. Finally, response (D) is incorrect.

16.  (B)

In order to find what percent of 260 is 13 one needs only to form

the following equation:

$$x\%(260) = 13$$

$$\frac{x(260)}{100} = 13$$

$$260x = 13(100)$$

$$x = 1300/260 = 5 \text{ percent} = 5\%.$$

The other answer choices are incorrect, however. Response (A) is obtained by dividing 13 by 260 and attaching the percent symbol. Response (D) is obtained by again dividing 13 by 260, moving the decimal point one place to the right and attaching the percent symbol. Response (E) is obtained by dividing 260 by 13 and attaching the percent sign. Finally, response (C) is absurd because 50% of 260 is half of 260 which is 130 or 10 times 13.

17. (D)
To find the altitude of the triangle one must recall that the area of a triangle is given by

$$A = (1/2)bh,$$

where $b$ denotes the base and $h$ denotes the altitude. Also, one must recall that the area of a circle is given by

$$A = \pi r^2,$$

where $r$ denotes the radius of the circle.
Since $b = 6$ units then $(1/2)(6)h = 3h = A$, the area of the triangle. In addition, since $r = 6$ units, then $A = \pi r^2 = \pi(6)^2 = 36\pi$, the area of the circle. But the area is the same for both figures. Thus,

$$3h = 36\pi$$
$$h = 12\pi$$

is the altitude of the triangle.
The other answer choices are incorrect and are obtained by inappropriately applying the formulas or committing errors in the calculations.

18. (C)
One needs to first recall that a cube has 6 equal sized faces. Thus,

the area of each face is found by dividing 6 into 96 to obtain 16 square feet. Since each face contains 16 square feet, then one can conclude that each edge of a face is 4 feet long. So, the volume of the cube, given by the formula,

$$V = \text{(length of edge)}^3 \text{ is found to be}$$
$$V = \text{(4 feet)}^3 = 64 \text{ cubic feet.}$$

Response (A) is found by incorrectly choosing the area of a face as the volume; response (B) is found by incorrectly squaring the 6 faces as the volume; response (E) is found by incorrectly cubing 6 as the volume; and, response (D) is found by incorrectly taking 96 as the volume of the cube.

19. (A)

Note that the ratio (3:5:7) of the angles in the triangle *ABC* can be represented as three distinct angles, $3x$, $5x$, and $7x$. Since the total number of degrees in a triangle is 180 degrees, one can write and solve the equation

$$3x + 5x + 7x = 180$$
$$15x = 180$$
$$x = 12.$$

Thus, the measures of the angles in triangle *ABC* are:

$$3x = 3(12) = 36°, 5x = 5(12) = 60°, \text{ and } 7x = 7(12) = 84°,$$

respectively. Since each of the three angles is less than 90°, then triangle *ABC* is an acute triangle.

20. (B)

The average income for *Y* Company is obtained by finding the sum of the income over the years between 1986 and 1988 and dividing by 3. Thus, the result is

$$(100 + 500 + 300) / 3 = \frac{900}{3} \quad 300.$$

The other answer choices are incorrect and are obtained by simply misreading the data from the graph or miscalculating the average.

21.  (D)

By observation one needs only to find the largest spread between corresponding plotted points on the two lines representing the companies. Thus, the largest difference occurred in 1987 where the difference was 400 million (500 – 100). The other answer choices are incorrect as a result of not appropriately observing the largest difference between corresponding plotted points on the graph.

22.  (E)

From the graph notice that the largest increase in earning of $Y$ Company occurred between 1986 and 1987. The amount of the increase was 400 million. Recall that in order to find the percent of increase use the following formula:

$$\text{Percent increase} = \frac{\text{Amount of increase}}{\text{Original amount}} \times 100$$

$$= \frac{400}{100} \times 100 = 400\,\%.$$

The other answer choices are incorrect as a result of either misapplying the formula or not observing the largest increase in earnings of $Y$ Company.

23.  (D)

Of the two companies, $X$ Company had the largest decrease in earnings which occurred between 1986 and 1987. The amount of the decrease was 300 million. Recall that in order to find the percent of decrease one uses the following formula:

$$\text{Percent decrease} = \frac{\text{Amount of decrease}}{\text{Original amount}} \times 100$$

$$= \frac{300}{400} \times 100 = 75\%.$$

The other answer choices are incorrect as a result of misapplying the formula for the percent of decrease or not observing the largest decrease for $X$ Company on the graph.

24.  (B)

The median is the middle annual earnings for $X$ Company arranged in ascending order. Over the indicated years the annual earnings in

millions are 200, 300, 100, 400, 100, 200, respectively. Arranging these values in ascending order and taking the average of the two in the middle gives the value of 200 million for the median.

The other answer choices are incorrect by misapplying the definition of median.

25. (E)

Observe that $xz = yz$ implies that $x = y$ if $z$ is not zero. But $x$ and $y$ are two different real numbers according to the original assumption in the problem. So, the only possible way for the equality to hold is for $z$ to have a value of 0.

26. (B)

First one must determine the equivalent of 132 ft/9 sec. in terms of miles/hour in order to solve the problem. Recall that 1 hour = 60 min. = 3600 sec. and 1 mile = 5280 ft. Thus, one can set up the following proportion:

$$\frac{132 \text{ ft}}{9 \text{ sec}} = \frac{x \text{ ft}}{1 \text{ hr}} = \frac{x \text{ ft}}{3600 \text{ sec}}$$

and solve for $x$. The result is:

$$9x \text{ ft/sec} = 132(3600) \text{ ft/sec}$$
$$x = 475200/9 = 52800 \text{ ft or 10 miles.}$$

Hence, the speed is 10 miles per hour.

27. (C)

First expand $(x^2)^{-4}$ to obtain $x^{-8}$ since the rule is $(x^m)^n = x^{mn}$. Similarly, expand $(x^{-2})^3$ to obtain $x^{-6}$ and $(x^{-3})^{-5}$ to obtain $x^{+15}$. Hence, the original expression may be written as

$$\frac{(x^{-8})(x^{-6})}{x^{15}} \tag{1}$$

By using another of the rules for handling exponents, which states that $x^m x^n = x^{m+n}$, one can determine the results of expression (1) as follows:

$$\frac{(x^{-8})(x^{-6})}{x^{15}} = \frac{x^{-14}}{x^{15}}. \tag{2}$$

Finally, from expression (2) move the numerator, which has a negative exponent, into the denominator by changing the sign of the exponent

and then multiply by the existing denominator to obtain the results as follows:

$$\frac{x^{-14}}{x^{15}} = \frac{1}{(x^{15})(x^{14})} = \frac{1}{x^{29}}.$$

Hence, answer choice (C) is correct. The other answer choices are obtained by not applying correctly the rules of exponents involving multiplication of factors with exponents.

28.　(C)
　　The wheel will travel in 1 revolution (2 minutes) $C = \pi d = \pi(3) = 3\pi$ feet. In 30 minutes it will travel $30/2 = 15$ revolutions. Thus, the wheel will travel $15(3\pi) = 45\pi$ feet in 30 minutes.

29.　(E)
　　Note that tips for the week were $(5/4)(150)$. Thus the total income was as follows:

$$(1)(150 + (5/4)(150) \;\; = (4/4)(150) + (5/4)(150)$$
$$= (9/4)(150).$$

Therefore, tips made up $\dfrac{(5/4)(150)}{(9/4)(150)} = \dfrac{5/4}{9/4} = 5/9$ of her income.

　　Notice that one could figure out the total income in order to arrive at the solution, however, this would be a waste of time.

30.　(A)
　　Since $h$, $m$ and $n$ are divisible by 3, first represent each as follows: $h = 3i$, $m = 3j$, and $n = 3k$, where $i, j, k$ are integers. Now consider the $hm$ as follows:

$$hm = 3i(3j) = 9ij.$$

But clearly, $hm/9 = 9ij/9 = ij$. So, $hm$ is divisible by 9.
　　Using the same technique or by a simple example it is clear that II and III are not possible. Hence, the other answer choices are not possible.

# Section 5—Analytical Ability

**1 – 4.    (C), (B), (B), (D)**

The information provided enables us to draw a map that yields the following information. From north to south, the cities are I, K, F, G/J, H; from west to east, the cities are F, G/J, K, I, H. All cities can be located in relation to each other except G and J, but we know that both are east of F, west of K, north of H, and south of F. Hence the correct answers to questions 1-4 are, respectively, (C), (B), (B), and (D).

**5.    (B)**

The question is which of (A) through (E), if true, would guarantee that a car made in Sweden after 1980 has excellent safety features. Hence statements that deal with conditions before 1980, like (A), or that do not deal with Sweden, like (D) and (E), cannot provide such a guarantee. (C) does not assert that changes in laws guaranteed excellent safety features. Only (B) provides adequate guarantees.

**6.    (D)**

(D) is the correct answer since it violates the conditions of the statement. The temperature was above 32°F; hence it must have snowed *more* than two inches. When the temperature was below 32°F, it might have snowed more or less than two inches; hence (A) and (B) could be accurate reports. (C) and (E) could be accurate reports since the temperature was 32°F or higher, and it snowed more than two inches.

**7.    (C)**

The argument is that prison rehabilitation programs should be abandoned because they are ineffective; evidence of ineffectiveness is the claim that nearly one of two parolees who have been in prison rehabilitation programs become repeat offenders. (C) most seriously weakens the argument by showing indirectly that prison rehabilitation programs *have* been effective if a much higher percentage of prisoners who have not been in such programs become repeat offenders. (A) and (B) do not address the substance of the argument. (D) is neutral; it

could be used either to support or attack the argument. While more relevant than (A) and (B), (E) does not provide support for or weaken the argument, which does not discriminate among kinds of crimes.

8.    (D)
    (D) is correct since planting shade trees and ornamental grasses on the same day does not violate any of the planting conditions. (A), (B), and (E) are incorrect because they violate the condition specifying that ornamentals and evergreens cannot be planted on the same day. (C) is incorrect because it violates the conditions that result when the first and third conditions are combined; shade trees must be planted at least one day before all evergreens (condition three specifies evergreen *trees*, but condition one asserts that evergreen shrubs and evergreen trees must be planted on the same day; hence shade trees must be planted at least one day before evergreen shrubs as well as evergreen trees).

9.    (A)
    Only (A) does not violate any of the planting conditions. (B) violates the fifth condition (evergreen shrubs at least one day before ornamental trees) when that condition is combined with condition one (all evergreens on the same day) and condition four (ornamental grasses and ornamental trees on the same day). (C) violates condition five when it is combined with condition one. (D) violates condition three (shade trees at least one day before evergreen trees) when that condition is combined with condition one (all evergreens on the same day); evergreen shrubs cannot be planted before shade trees if evergreen trees are planted after shade trees. (E) also violates condition three when it is combined with condition one.

10.   (C)
    The crew cannot plant evergreen trees on Friday if it plants ornamental grasses on Thursday because ornamental grasses and ornamental trees must be planted on the same day (Thursday), evergreen shrubs must be planted at least one day before ornamental trees (Wednesday or earlier in the week), and all evergreens, including trees, must be planted on the same day (Wednesday or earlier). Hence evergreen trees cannot be planted on Friday if ornamental grasses are

planted on Thursday. None of the other choices — (A), (B), (D), or (E) — violates planting conditions.

11.  (D)

The crew can plant shade trees on Monday without violating planting conditions (D). (A) violates condition two. (B) violates condition one. (C) violates condition five. (E) violates condition five when it is combined with condition four.

12.  (B)

Evergreen shrubs cannot be planted on Monday or Tuesday if shade trees are planted on Tuesday because shade trees must be planted at least one day before evergreen trees, and all evergreens must be planted on the same day. Planting evergreen shrubs on Wednesday and Thursday does not violate any planting conditions. Hence (B) is correct.

13.  (D)

Only Wednesday is ruled out (ornamentals and evergreens cannot be planted on the same day). Planting the other four days does not violate any planting conditions. Hence (D) is correct.

14 – 15.  (D), (C)

The relationship can be clarified by drawing two diagrams. Weight, from heaviest to lightest: X Z W T U S V. Jumping height, from highest to lowest: S W U T Y Z. Hence the answer to 14 is (D) and the answer to 15 is (C).

16.  (E)

The answer is (E) since we know with certainty that W weighed more than S and jumped higher than T. (A) is incorrect because we do not know how high V jumped. (C) is incorrect because we know T weighed less than Z. (C) is incorrect because we know S jumped higher than U. (D) is incorrect because we do not know how high Y jumped.

17.  (A)

(A) could be true. We know that X weighed more than the other contestants whose weight we know; X might weigh more than those whose weights we do not know. We do not know how high X jumped; X might have jumped higher than all of the others. (B) cannot be true.

We lack information about the jumping heights of two contestants; even if both jumped higher than W, W can finish no lower than fourth. (C) and (D) are incorrect; as the diagrams indicate, some heavy contestants jumped higher than lighter ones and some lighter contestants jumped higher than heavier ones. (E) cannot be true. We lack information about the weight of one contestant; even if that contestant weighs more than T, T cannot be more than fifth heaviest.

18.  (E)
Remembering that L always sits on G's left, one side of the table is G (opposite J), L, K. This leaves only M and F. However, F cannot be directly opposite L because that would place F next to J, a violation of condition three. Hence the correct answer is (E).

19.  (C)
One side of the table is K F M; F is opposite L, who is on G's left. Therefore, H (the only remaining governor) must sit at the head of the table. K and M must sit opposite G and J, but J cannot sit directly opposite K since both are senators. Hence J must sit opposite M, so the correct choice is (C).

20.  (C)
If G sits at the head of the table, L is at his left. F and K must be on the opposite side of the table (F cannot otherwise be on K's left), K farther from the head of the table. J cannot sit directly opposite L since that would place J next to F, nor can J sit directly opposite K since both are senators. Hence J must sit directly opposite F. The answer is (C).

21.  (D)
Only (D) violates none of the conditions. (A) violates condition four (G on L's right). (B) violates condition one (L and M are next to each other). (C) violates conditions two (J and K are directly opposite each other) and four. (E) violates condition five (L is not a governor).

22.  (A)
The question establishes G and L on one side, H at the head of the table, and F in the middle and directly opposite L. It also indirectly establishes J on L's left since J cannot be seated next to F. This leaves only M and K, who must be seated on either side of F and directly

opposite G and J. But K cannot be seated directly opposite J since both are senators. Hence K must be seated opposite G and M opposite J. Thus only one seating arrangement is possible. (A) is correct.

23.  (B)
An "if, then" proposition can yield a valid conclusion only if the conditions in the "if" part of the proposition are affirmed. A 15% rise in the stock market affirms the conditions in the "if" part of the proposition in Gloria's case; hence Gloria will be rich (II). Denying the conditions in the "if" part of the proposition yields no conclusion. A 15% rise in the stock market denies the conditions necessary for us to conclude with certainty that John will be rich, but no conclusion can be drawn. It does not follow that John will be poor or not rich since the "if, then" statement does not deal with John's situation if the stock market does not rise by 20% or more. He could be either rich or poor. Hence the correct answer is (B).

24.  (A)
The information yields the following order, from fastest to slowest swimmers: Laura, Susan, John, Carl. It also tells us that Richard swims faster than Susan (and hence John and Carl). Hence we know that Maria swims faster than John if she swims faster than Richard, who swims faster than John. The answer is (A).

25.  (D)
The question asks us to explain why students with higher mathematical skills test scores are placed in remedial math classes at University X while students with lower mathematical skills test scores at University Y are not. The only answer that accounts for that phenomenon is (D). (A) would contribute to the discrepancy, not explain it. (B) and (C) do not address the phenomenon. (E) deals with entrance scores, but not placement.

## Section 6—Analytical Ability

1.  (E)
Since phlox are perennials, the two phlox plants the gardener

plants the first year will be there the second. To have six white plants, she must plant two more phlox and two petunias the second year, as well as two salvia to have two red plants. Hence the answer is (E).

2. (A)

Before planting in the fourth year, she will have four astilbe (red) and two coreopsis (yellow). In order to have six yellow plants, she must plant coreopsis and marigolds; to have two whites, she must plant petunias (she already has four red plants). Hence the answer is (A).

3. (C)

(C) gives her two red and two yellows before planting in the third year. The addition of phlox, salvia, and petunias gives her a total of four reds (astilbe from the first year, and salvia), four whites (phlox and petunias), and two yellows (coreopsis from the second year). The answer is (C). The other choices either do not yield the correct color totals (A), (E) or violate the planting conditions (B); petunias three successive years, or both, (D).

4. (D)

In the first year, she has four white plants; in the second year, she has two (perennial phlox planted in the first year); in the third year, she has six (phlox and petunias from year three and phlox from year one); in the fourth year, she has six (petunias, plus phlox from years one and three). Hence her totals are 4, 2, 6, and 6, for a master record of 18, (D).

5. (B)

The information yields this relationship, from highest freezing temperature to lowest: V X Y W. If X freezes at a lower temperature than Z, Z is before X, Y, and W on our diagram, freezing at a higher temperature than those three. Hence the answer is (B).

6. (C)

The conditions can be restated as "all birch trees over twenty feet tall have white bark." Hence a thirty-foot birch has white bark (C). Ten-foot birches may or may not have white bark; hence not (A), (B), or (D). (E) is incorrect since twenty-one-foot birches are over twenty

feet and therefore have white bark.

7.　(B)

　　The question asks us to explain why one state classifies many more prisoners as incorrigible than does another state. The best choice is (B). The question does not deal with length of prison sentences (D), or parole policies (E), nor does it link incorrigibility to rural conditions (C), or particular kinds of crimes (A).

8.　(B)

　　The information yields these results: + = G; $ and ¢ = either A or M; B and K must be either #, %, or *. If # is B and % is 0, then * must be K. The answer is (B).

9.　(C)

　　Since we know that B, G, K, and M are represented by symbols that appear more than once, the correct choice must be H.

10.　(A)

　　All of the consonants except H are represented by symbols that appear more than once. If H is represented by (, the only other symbol that appears only once must represent a vowel. That symbol is &.

11.　(E)

　　G is represented by +, so (B) is incorrect. The first and fourth symbol in the message is either A or M; it must be translated by the same letter, whether A or M; (hence (A), (C) and (D) are incorrect. The correct answer is (E). In (E), the first and fourth symbol is translated as A; the third symbol must therefore by translated as M. The second symbol can properly be translated as K.

12.　(D)

　　(D) meets all of the conditions. Two members are full professors (H), (L); one is from the humanities (G), one from the social sciences (H), one from the natural sciences (L). (A) is incorrect because only

one is a full professor; (B) and (C) are incorrect because there is no social sciences representative; (E) is incorrect because there is no natural sciences representative.

13. (E)
Since there are two boards, and each board must include a humanities professor, and since there are only two humanities professors, and since professors cannot serve on more than one board, both humanities professors, (G) and (K) must be included. The answer is (E).

14. (A)
The chair of the tenure board is the most senior tenured member of the board. If N is the chair, the other tenured member on the board must be J, since he is the only other tenured professor with less seniority than N. The other representative must be from the humanities since N is from the social sciences and J from the natural sciences. The humanities representative must be K; it cannot be G, since we know that no tenured professor with more seniority than N can be on the board if N is chairing it.

15. (C)
Only K, L, M, and J are left as possible chairs of the promotion board. Neither M nor J can be chair because neither is a full professor. Of the two full professors, K is senior to L; hence K must be chair of the promotion board.

16. (B)
The lawn was scheduled to be mowed on twenty Fridays, plus four Wednesday mowings following rains on Tuesdays; however, it rained on one Wednesday following a Tuesday rain and on four Fridays. Hence $20 + 4 - 1 - 4 = 19$.

17. (B)
According to the conditions of the contract, the lawn would be scheduled for weeding three days after each rain — i.e., on the fourth Monday, the fifth Friday, the fifth Saturday, the sixth Monday, the seventh Saturday, the tenth Saturday, the eleventh Saturday, the

twelfth Monday, the fourteenth Friday, the fifteenth Monday, and the fifteenth Friday, a total of 12 weedings. However, the weedings scheduled for the third, fifth, and fourteenth Fridays were cancelled because of rain. Hence 12 − 3 = 9.

18.  (B)

The lawn was mowed on sixteen Fridays (on all but the third, fifth, eleventh, and fourteenth, which were rain days), and fertilized on one Friday on which it was not mowed (the fifth). So, 16 + 1 = 17. It was also scheduled for weeding on four Fridays, but three were cancelled because of rain (the third, fifth, and fourteenth) and one was postponed until Saturday (the fifteenth) because of a conflict with fertilizing.

19.  (D)

The lawn was weeded on a regular schedule (three days after rain) on four Saturdays (fifth, seventh, tenth, eleventh). It was also weeded on the fifteenth Saturday when a regularly scheduled weeding on the fifteenth Friday (three days after rain) was postponed for one day because of a fertilizing conflict. Hence the total is five.

20.  (D)

The lawn was fertilized on Friday and weeded on Saturday (three days after a Wednesday rain). The mowing and weeding scheduled for Friday were cancelled because of rain.

21.  (C)

The lawn was routinely mowed and fertilized on Friday as the contract stipulates. It was also weeded on the fifteenth Monday, following rain on the fourteenth Friday. Finally, it was also weeded on Saturday, after the weeding scheduled for Friday was postponed because of fertilizing.

22.  (A)

The lawn was scheduled to be weeded on four Fridays following Tuesday rains (the third, fifth, fourteenth, and fifteenth). On the first three occasions, it was cancelled because of Friday rains. On the fifteenth, it was postponed because of fertilizing. Hence it was never

weeded and mowed on the same day. The answer is (A).

23.   (E)
The argument depends on the assumption that there is a positive correlation between pornography's accessibility and violent crimes against women. Therefore the argument is most seriously weakened by evidence that suggests that such a positive correlation does not exist. Hence (E) is the best answer. (A) does not weaken the argument, which does not extend its claim to all men. (B) and (D) do not address the substance of the argument. (C) may be true, but does not deal with the relationship between pornography and violent crime.

24.   (C)
The argument is independent of considerations of the relationship between degrees of difficulty and pleasure and of Americans' preferences for Russian or American novels, so (A) and (B) can be eliminated. The argument does not separate quality and quantity; rather, it tends to equate them, so (D) can be eliminated. Similarly, the argument tends to confuse or equate commercial success with critical acclaim, so (E) can be eliminated. The best choice is (C); in arguing for the artistic superiority of a popular work to a less popular one simply because the former is more popular, the author assumes that popularity is a reliable measure of artistic merit.

25.   (D)
John has not established whether low grades or marijuana smoking came first. This is the weakness that Susan attacks; her suggestion that low grades cause marijuana smoking is as plausible as John's argument that marijuana smoking causes low grades unless John can provide proof that his cause and effect relationship exists. Hence the answer is (D). John's argument does not depend on proving a relationship between memory and GPA (E) or marijuana and memory (A), since he mentions these only as a possibility. Susan does not attack John's lack of specific statistics (B), nor does she focus on what might be exceptions to John's rule (C).

# GRE
# GENERAL TEST 2
## ANSWER SHEET

### SECTION 1

1. Ⓐ Ⓑ Ⓒ Ⓓ Ⓔ
2. Ⓐ Ⓑ Ⓒ Ⓓ Ⓔ
3. Ⓐ Ⓑ Ⓒ Ⓓ Ⓔ
4. Ⓐ Ⓑ Ⓒ Ⓓ Ⓔ
5. Ⓐ Ⓑ Ⓒ Ⓓ Ⓔ
6. Ⓐ Ⓑ Ⓒ Ⓓ Ⓔ
7. Ⓐ Ⓑ Ⓒ Ⓓ Ⓔ
8. Ⓐ Ⓑ Ⓒ Ⓓ Ⓔ
9. Ⓐ Ⓑ Ⓒ Ⓓ Ⓔ
10. Ⓐ Ⓑ Ⓒ Ⓓ Ⓔ
11. Ⓐ Ⓑ Ⓒ Ⓓ Ⓔ
12. Ⓐ Ⓑ Ⓒ Ⓓ Ⓔ
13. Ⓐ Ⓑ Ⓒ Ⓓ Ⓔ
14. Ⓐ Ⓑ Ⓒ Ⓓ Ⓔ
15. Ⓐ Ⓑ Ⓒ Ⓓ Ⓔ
16. Ⓐ Ⓑ Ⓒ Ⓓ Ⓔ
17. Ⓐ Ⓑ Ⓒ Ⓓ Ⓔ
18. Ⓐ Ⓑ Ⓒ Ⓓ Ⓔ
19. Ⓐ Ⓑ Ⓒ Ⓓ Ⓔ
20. Ⓐ Ⓑ Ⓒ Ⓓ Ⓔ
21. Ⓐ Ⓑ Ⓒ Ⓓ Ⓔ
22. Ⓐ Ⓑ Ⓒ Ⓓ Ⓔ
23. Ⓐ Ⓑ Ⓒ Ⓓ Ⓔ
24. Ⓐ Ⓑ Ⓒ Ⓓ Ⓔ
25. Ⓐ Ⓑ Ⓒ Ⓓ Ⓔ
26. Ⓐ Ⓑ Ⓒ Ⓓ Ⓔ
27. Ⓐ Ⓑ Ⓒ Ⓓ Ⓔ
28. Ⓐ Ⓑ Ⓒ Ⓓ Ⓔ
29. Ⓐ Ⓑ Ⓒ Ⓓ Ⓔ
30. Ⓐ Ⓑ Ⓒ Ⓓ Ⓔ
31. Ⓐ Ⓑ Ⓒ Ⓓ Ⓔ
32. Ⓐ Ⓑ Ⓒ Ⓓ Ⓔ
33. Ⓐ Ⓑ Ⓒ Ⓓ Ⓔ
34. Ⓐ Ⓑ Ⓒ Ⓓ Ⓔ
35. Ⓐ Ⓑ Ⓒ Ⓓ Ⓔ
36. Ⓐ Ⓑ Ⓒ Ⓓ Ⓔ
37. Ⓐ Ⓑ Ⓒ Ⓓ Ⓔ
38. Ⓐ Ⓑ Ⓒ Ⓓ Ⓔ

### SECTION 2

1. Ⓐ Ⓑ Ⓒ Ⓓ Ⓔ
2. Ⓐ Ⓑ Ⓒ Ⓓ Ⓔ
3. Ⓐ Ⓑ Ⓒ Ⓓ Ⓔ
4. Ⓐ Ⓑ Ⓒ Ⓓ Ⓔ
5. Ⓐ Ⓑ Ⓒ Ⓓ Ⓔ
6. Ⓐ Ⓑ Ⓒ Ⓓ Ⓔ
7. Ⓐ Ⓑ Ⓒ Ⓓ Ⓔ
8. Ⓐ Ⓑ Ⓒ Ⓓ Ⓔ
9. Ⓐ Ⓑ Ⓒ Ⓓ Ⓔ
10. Ⓐ Ⓑ Ⓒ Ⓓ Ⓔ
11. Ⓐ Ⓑ Ⓒ Ⓓ Ⓔ
12. Ⓐ Ⓑ Ⓒ Ⓓ Ⓔ
13. Ⓐ Ⓑ Ⓒ Ⓓ Ⓔ
14. Ⓐ Ⓑ Ⓒ Ⓓ Ⓔ
15. Ⓐ Ⓑ Ⓒ Ⓓ Ⓔ
16. Ⓐ Ⓑ Ⓒ Ⓓ Ⓔ
17. Ⓐ Ⓑ Ⓒ Ⓓ Ⓔ
18. Ⓐ Ⓑ Ⓒ Ⓓ Ⓔ
19. Ⓐ Ⓑ Ⓒ Ⓓ Ⓔ
20. Ⓐ Ⓑ Ⓒ Ⓓ Ⓔ
21. Ⓐ Ⓑ Ⓒ Ⓓ Ⓔ

22. Ⓐ Ⓑ Ⓒ Ⓓ Ⓔ
23. Ⓐ Ⓑ Ⓒ Ⓓ Ⓔ
24. Ⓐ Ⓑ Ⓒ Ⓓ Ⓔ
25. Ⓐ Ⓑ Ⓒ Ⓓ Ⓔ
26. Ⓐ Ⓑ Ⓒ Ⓓ Ⓔ
27. Ⓐ Ⓑ Ⓒ Ⓓ Ⓔ
28. Ⓐ Ⓑ Ⓒ Ⓓ Ⓔ
29. Ⓐ Ⓑ Ⓒ Ⓓ Ⓔ
30. Ⓐ Ⓑ Ⓒ Ⓓ Ⓔ
31. Ⓐ Ⓑ Ⓒ Ⓓ Ⓔ
32. Ⓐ Ⓑ Ⓒ Ⓓ Ⓔ
33. Ⓐ Ⓑ Ⓒ Ⓓ Ⓔ
34. Ⓐ Ⓑ Ⓒ Ⓓ Ⓔ
35. Ⓐ Ⓑ Ⓒ Ⓓ Ⓔ
36. Ⓐ Ⓑ Ⓒ Ⓓ Ⓔ
37. Ⓐ Ⓑ Ⓒ Ⓓ Ⓔ
38. Ⓐ Ⓑ Ⓒ Ⓓ Ⓔ

### SECTION 3

1. Ⓐ Ⓑ Ⓒ Ⓓ Ⓔ
2. Ⓐ Ⓑ Ⓒ Ⓓ Ⓔ
3. Ⓐ Ⓑ Ⓒ Ⓓ Ⓔ
4. Ⓐ Ⓑ Ⓒ Ⓓ Ⓔ
5. Ⓐ Ⓑ Ⓒ Ⓓ Ⓔ
6. Ⓐ Ⓑ Ⓒ Ⓓ Ⓔ
7. Ⓐ Ⓑ Ⓒ Ⓓ Ⓔ
8. Ⓐ Ⓑ Ⓒ Ⓓ Ⓔ
9. Ⓐ Ⓑ Ⓒ Ⓓ Ⓔ
10. Ⓐ Ⓑ Ⓒ Ⓓ Ⓔ
11. Ⓐ Ⓑ Ⓒ Ⓓ Ⓔ
12. Ⓐ Ⓑ Ⓒ Ⓓ Ⓔ

13. Ⓐ Ⓑ Ⓒ Ⓓ Ⓔ
14. Ⓐ Ⓑ Ⓒ Ⓓ Ⓔ
15. Ⓐ Ⓑ Ⓒ Ⓓ Ⓔ
16. Ⓐ Ⓑ Ⓒ Ⓓ Ⓔ
17. Ⓐ Ⓑ Ⓒ Ⓓ Ⓔ
18. Ⓐ Ⓑ Ⓒ Ⓓ Ⓔ
19. Ⓐ Ⓑ Ⓒ Ⓓ Ⓔ
20. Ⓐ Ⓑ Ⓒ Ⓓ Ⓔ
21. Ⓐ Ⓑ Ⓒ Ⓓ Ⓔ
22. Ⓐ Ⓑ Ⓒ Ⓓ Ⓔ
23. Ⓐ Ⓑ Ⓒ Ⓓ Ⓔ
24. Ⓐ Ⓑ Ⓒ Ⓓ Ⓔ
25. Ⓐ Ⓑ Ⓒ Ⓓ Ⓔ
26. Ⓐ Ⓑ Ⓒ Ⓓ Ⓔ
27. Ⓐ Ⓑ Ⓒ Ⓓ Ⓔ
28. Ⓐ Ⓑ Ⓒ Ⓓ Ⓔ
29. Ⓐ Ⓑ Ⓒ Ⓓ Ⓔ
30. Ⓐ Ⓑ Ⓒ Ⓓ Ⓔ

## SECTION 4

1. Ⓐ Ⓑ Ⓒ Ⓓ Ⓔ
2. Ⓐ Ⓑ Ⓒ Ⓓ Ⓔ
3. Ⓐ Ⓑ Ⓒ Ⓓ Ⓔ
4. Ⓐ Ⓑ Ⓒ Ⓓ Ⓔ
5. Ⓐ Ⓑ Ⓒ Ⓓ Ⓔ
6. Ⓐ Ⓑ Ⓒ Ⓓ Ⓔ
7. Ⓐ Ⓑ Ⓒ Ⓓ Ⓔ
8. Ⓐ Ⓑ Ⓒ Ⓓ Ⓔ
9. Ⓐ Ⓑ Ⓒ Ⓓ Ⓔ
10. Ⓐ Ⓑ Ⓒ Ⓓ Ⓔ
11. Ⓐ Ⓑ Ⓒ Ⓓ Ⓔ
12. Ⓐ Ⓑ Ⓒ Ⓓ Ⓔ
13. Ⓐ Ⓑ Ⓒ Ⓓ Ⓔ
14. Ⓐ Ⓑ Ⓒ Ⓓ Ⓔ
15. Ⓐ Ⓑ Ⓒ Ⓓ Ⓔ

16. Ⓐ Ⓑ Ⓒ Ⓓ Ⓔ
17. Ⓐ Ⓑ Ⓒ Ⓓ Ⓔ
18. Ⓐ Ⓑ Ⓒ Ⓓ Ⓔ
19. Ⓐ Ⓑ Ⓒ Ⓓ Ⓔ
20. Ⓐ Ⓑ Ⓒ Ⓓ Ⓔ
21. Ⓐ Ⓑ Ⓒ Ⓓ Ⓔ
22. Ⓐ Ⓑ Ⓒ Ⓓ Ⓔ
23. Ⓐ Ⓑ Ⓒ Ⓓ Ⓔ
24. Ⓐ Ⓑ Ⓒ Ⓓ Ⓔ
25. Ⓐ Ⓑ Ⓒ Ⓓ Ⓔ
26. Ⓐ Ⓑ Ⓒ Ⓓ Ⓔ
27. Ⓐ Ⓑ Ⓒ Ⓓ Ⓔ
28. Ⓐ Ⓑ Ⓒ Ⓓ Ⓔ
29. Ⓐ Ⓑ Ⓒ Ⓓ Ⓔ
30. Ⓐ Ⓑ Ⓒ Ⓓ Ⓔ

## SECTION 5

1. Ⓐ Ⓑ Ⓒ Ⓓ Ⓔ
2. Ⓐ Ⓑ Ⓒ Ⓓ Ⓔ
3. Ⓐ Ⓑ Ⓒ Ⓓ Ⓔ
4. Ⓐ Ⓑ Ⓒ Ⓓ Ⓔ
5. Ⓐ Ⓑ Ⓒ Ⓓ Ⓔ
6. Ⓐ Ⓑ Ⓒ Ⓓ Ⓔ
7. Ⓐ Ⓑ Ⓒ Ⓓ Ⓔ
8. Ⓐ Ⓑ Ⓒ Ⓓ Ⓔ
9. Ⓐ Ⓑ Ⓒ Ⓓ Ⓔ
10. Ⓐ Ⓑ Ⓒ Ⓓ Ⓔ
11. Ⓐ Ⓑ Ⓒ Ⓓ Ⓔ
12. Ⓐ Ⓑ Ⓒ Ⓓ Ⓔ
13. Ⓐ Ⓑ Ⓒ Ⓓ Ⓔ
14. Ⓐ Ⓑ Ⓒ Ⓓ Ⓔ
15. Ⓐ Ⓑ Ⓒ Ⓓ Ⓔ
16. Ⓐ Ⓑ Ⓒ Ⓓ Ⓔ
17. Ⓐ Ⓑ Ⓒ Ⓓ Ⓔ
18. Ⓐ Ⓑ Ⓒ Ⓓ Ⓔ

19. Ⓐ Ⓑ Ⓒ Ⓓ Ⓔ
20. Ⓐ Ⓑ Ⓒ Ⓓ Ⓔ
21. Ⓐ Ⓑ Ⓒ Ⓓ Ⓔ
22. Ⓐ Ⓑ Ⓒ Ⓓ Ⓔ
23. Ⓐ Ⓑ Ⓒ Ⓓ Ⓔ
24. Ⓐ Ⓑ Ⓒ Ⓓ Ⓔ
25. Ⓐ Ⓑ Ⓒ Ⓓ Ⓔ

## SECTION 6

1. Ⓐ Ⓑ Ⓒ Ⓓ Ⓔ
2. Ⓐ Ⓑ Ⓒ Ⓓ Ⓔ
3. Ⓐ Ⓑ Ⓒ Ⓓ Ⓔ
4. Ⓐ Ⓑ Ⓒ Ⓓ Ⓔ
5. Ⓐ Ⓑ Ⓒ Ⓓ Ⓔ
6. Ⓐ Ⓑ Ⓒ Ⓓ Ⓔ
7. Ⓐ Ⓑ Ⓒ Ⓓ Ⓔ
8. Ⓐ Ⓑ Ⓒ Ⓓ Ⓔ
9. Ⓐ Ⓑ Ⓒ Ⓓ Ⓔ
10. Ⓐ Ⓑ Ⓒ Ⓓ Ⓔ
11. Ⓐ Ⓑ Ⓒ Ⓓ Ⓔ
12. Ⓐ Ⓑ Ⓒ Ⓓ Ⓔ
13. Ⓐ Ⓑ Ⓒ Ⓓ Ⓔ
14. Ⓐ Ⓑ Ⓒ Ⓓ Ⓔ
15. Ⓐ Ⓑ Ⓒ Ⓓ Ⓔ
16. Ⓐ Ⓑ Ⓒ Ⓓ Ⓔ
17. Ⓐ Ⓑ Ⓒ Ⓓ Ⓔ
18. Ⓐ Ⓑ Ⓒ Ⓓ Ⓔ
19. Ⓐ Ⓑ Ⓒ Ⓓ Ⓔ
20. Ⓐ Ⓑ Ⓒ Ⓓ Ⓔ
21. Ⓐ Ⓑ Ⓒ Ⓓ Ⓔ
22. Ⓐ Ⓑ Ⓒ Ⓓ Ⓔ
23. Ⓐ Ⓑ Ⓒ Ⓓ Ⓔ
24. Ⓐ Ⓑ Ⓒ Ⓓ Ⓔ
25. Ⓐ Ⓑ Ⓒ Ⓓ Ⓔ

# TEST 2

## Section 1

> **TIME:** 30 Minutes
> 38 Questions
>
> **DIRECTIONS:** Each of the given sentences has blank spaces which indicate words omitted. Choose the best combination of words which fit into the meaning and structure within the context of the sentence.

1. A mentally deficient person who has special talents or gifts is correctly referred to as _____; an extraordinary child is referred to as _____.

   (A) proselyte...a progeny

   (B) tainted...prodigious

   (C) a stapes...a progenitor

   (D) a lithographer...portentous

   (E) an idiot savant...a prodigy

2. The domineering male gorilla usually appears _____ in its mating rituals in the wild.

   (A) subjugated          (D) surmounted

   (B) vanquished          (E) imperious

   (C) subdued

3. The sustenance was given so _____ that it did not _____ the patient with new life and vigor.

   (A) infrequently...imbue          (B) uncommonly...infuse

248

    (C)   scarcely...suffuse      (D)   sporadically...inoculate

    (E)   rarely...leaven

4. The cook prepared a particularly rich shellfish purée, or _____, for the honored guests.

    (A)   pottage            (D)   bouillon

    (B)   bisque             (E)   soufflé

    (C)   broth

5. Her constant stealing from the lunch money of others _____ her teacher.

    (A)   annoys           (D) delectates

    (B)   irritates         (E) inconveniences

    (C)   exasperates

6. The words <u>tear</u> (fluid from the eye) and <u>tear</u> (to rip) are examples of _____ ; the words <u>pear</u> and <u>pair</u> are examples of _____ .

    (A)   homographs...homophones

    (B)   homonym...homophones

    (C)   homograph...heteronyms

    (D)   heteronym...homographs

    (E)   homophone...homonyms

7. His walk to return the stolen goods is likely to be _____ by any event since his feeling of _____ toward the coming punishment is so intense.

    (A)   procrastinated...sorrow   (D)   precipitated...woe

    (B)   hastened...grief         (E)   hindered...anguish

    (C)   detained...regret

---

**DIRECTIONS:** In the following questions, the given pair of words contains a specific relationship to each other. Select the best pair of the choices which expresses the same relationship as the given.

---

8.   BESEECH:SUPPLICATE::

   (A)   entreat:carnify

   (B)   beseige:petition

   (C)   solicit:importune

   (D)   beleaguer:estival

   (E)   implore:impede


9.   VITAMIN C:SCURVY::

   (A)   sun:skin cancer

   (B)   niacin:pellagra

   (C)   goiter:iodine

   (D)   rickets:calcium

   (E)   plague:rats


10.   ANALOGOUS:PARALLEL::

   (A)   acidulous:saccharine

   (B)   sinuous:tortuous

   (C)   incongruous:homogeneous

   (D)   pundit:tyro

   (E)   mundane:celestial


11.   A CAPPELLA:ORCHESTRA::

   (A)   profanation:desecration

   (B)   sterile:multiparous

   (C)   proletarian:ignoble

   (D)   emolument:recompense

   (E)   imperious:peremptory


12.   SPLENETIC:IRRITABLE::

   (A)   irascible:peevish

   (B)   propitiating:irresolute

   (C)   cant:culpable

   (D)   spiteful:pacify

   (E)   inflame:appease

13.   ASSUAGE:MELIORATE::

    (A)   mitigate:ameliorate       (D)   allay:inundate

    (B)   equivocate:prognosticate   (E)   mollify:ratiocinate

    (C)   castigate:prevaricate

14.   SPELUNKER:CAVE::

    (A)   conductor:maestro       (D)   numismatist:books

    (B)   prestidigitator:magic     (E)   curator:coins

    (C)   purloiner:parish

15. APOTHEOSIZE:CANONIZE::

    (A)   deprecate:servile       (D) sinecure:aberration

    (B)   smorgasbord:paltry     (E) specious:complaisant

    (C)   permeate:pervade

16. BOY:DIPHTHONG::

    (A)   grass:blend         (D) blend:blind

    (B)   digraph:meat       (E) bird:diphthong

    (C)   digraph:cat

---

**DIRECTIONS:** Each passage is followed by questions based on its content. After reading the passage, choose the best answer to each question. Answer all questions based on what is stated or implied in that passage.

---

Cacti and other succulent plants originate in areas where water is only occasionally available and are, therefore, conditioned to deal with long periods of drought. They possess structural modifications enabling them to store moisture for use in times of scarcity.

Such adaptations may be similar in both groups. (All cacti are succulents but not all succulents are cacti.) Storage areas include thickened leaves, stems, and corms. Leaves, which transpire precious moisture, may be eliminated altogether (with the stem taking over the process of photosynthesis), or the moisture in the leaves may be protected from evaporation by a leathery surface or covered with wiry or velvety hairs, thick spines or even with a powdery coating.

The very shape of many succulents provides the same protection; globular and columnar forms offer the least exposed area to the drying effects of sun and wind.

Many times there are "look-alikes" in the two groups. Certain cacti coming from the New World closely resemble counterparts in the Euphorbias of Africa.

How do we then differentiate between cacti and other succulents? It is not always easy. Presence or absence of leaves can be helpful; size and brilliance of flowers are also helpful, but the real test comes by learning to recognize the areole.

The areole is possessed by cacti alone and consists of cushion-like modification on the body of the cactus from which arise spines, hairs (and the barbed hairs or spines of *Opuntia*), flowers, fruit and often new growth.

The flowers of cacti are usually more conspicuous and most often appear from areoles near the top of the plant. In other succulents they are inclined to be less showy and more likely to emerge from between the leaves or from the base.

In addition, with a very minor possible exception (a form of *Rhipsalis*), all cacti are native to the Western Hemisphere. It is sometimes hard to believe this because of the vast areas of escaped cacti in many parts of the world today.

The majority of other succulents (excluding *Agave, Echeveria, Sedum, Sempervivum* and a few others) are indigenous to Africa and a few scattered areas in the Eastern Hemisphere.

Both cacti and other succulents are excellent subjects for the outdoor garden, greenhouse or windowsill. They require a minimum of care, provided that they have a requisite amount of sunlight and that their condition of hardiness is respected.

17. Which features from the list below best distinguish cacti from other succulents?

    (A) Absence of leaves; presence of areoles; large, brilliant flowers; nativity to the Western Hemisphere.

    (B) Presence or absence of leaves; showy flowers which always appear at the top of the plant; indigenous to Africa and a few scattered areas in the Eastern Hemisphere.

    (C) The areole; presence of leaves; flowers which are likely to emerge from between the leaves or from the base.

    (D) The flowers of cacti are usually more conspicuous and most often appear near the top of the plant; the areole is possessed by cacti alone.

    (E) The majority of other succulents are indigenous to Africa and a few scattered areas in the Eastern Hemisphere.

18. Which of the following is the best title for the passage?

    (A) Succulents and Non-Succulents.

    (B) Regions of the World and their Vegetation.

    (C) Distinguishing Between Succulents and Cacti.

    (D) Subjects for the Outdoor Garden.

    (E) Those Fascinating Cacti and Other Succulents.

19. The attitude of the author toward cacti and succulents is which of the following?

    (A) Cacti are to be chosen over succulents for the home.

    (B) Either are excellent subjects to study in the wild, but to preserve their beauty they should not be removed to the home.

    (C) Both are excellent subjects for botanists to study.

    (D) Both feature interesting adaptations; the cacti is the preferred.

(E) Both are excellent subjects for the outdoor garden, greenhouse or windowsill.

20. A cause-and-effect relationship could best be illustrated by which of the following true statements?

(A) Cacti and succulents have been moved to places where there is only occasional water; they possess structural modifications because of this move which enable them to store moisture.

(B) Moisture transpires from the leaves; leathery surfaces, covered with wiry or velvety hairs, thick spines, or even with a powdery coating have been developed to help prevent this transpiration.

(C) Because of the vast areas of escaped cacti, it is difficult today to believe that most all cacti are indigenous to Africa and a few scattered parts of the Eastern Hemisphere.

(D) The globular and columnar forms of cacti offer a larger exposed area to the sun; photosynthesis is, therefore, increased.

(E) Neither cacti nor other succulents are excellent subjects for the outdoor garden, greenhouse or windowsill since they require constant care.

21. It could logically follow that the first line of the next paragraph would begin with which of the following?

(A) The size and brilliance of the flowers of the cacti are interesting subjects for further attention.

(B) Cacti and other succulents are generally able to withstand rapid changes in temperature.

(C) The globular and columnar shapes of cacti have been frequent topics of study for artists — particularly those of the American Midwest.

(D) Disney's "The Living Desert" is a full-length feature which focuses on cacti.

254

(E) A study of the flowers can tell the researcher much about the original location and structural modifications of the cacti.

22. The most compelling reason for choosing cacti over other succulents for a windowsill would be which of the following?

(A) Cacti require less care than do other succulents.

(B) The shape of the cacti is more appealing than that of the other succulents.

(C) Succulents from the Eastern Hemisphere do not adapt well to the Western Hemisphere.

(D) The flowers of cacti are usually more conspicuous and most often appear between the leaves or at the base.

(E) The flowers of cacti are usually more conspicuous and most often appear from areoles near the top of the plant.

23. The author says that storage areas include thickened leaves, stems, and corms. Which of the following best describes an area called the corm?

(A) A short, bulb-like, upright stem, usually found under-ground.

(B) A bulb-like addition found on the side or top of the plant.

(C) The core of the plant.

(D) An ear-like appendage similar to that of corn.

(E) Another name for the flower.

24. Which of the following would probably best describe the author's reaction to the many laws being enacted to protect the cacti and to prevent their being removed from desert areas or vandalized?

(A) Apathy          (D) Distaste

(B) Confusion       (E) Understanding

(C) Despair

The Jefferson nickel was executed by Felix Schlag, whose design was chosen from among 390 artists' sketches submitted to the Government. This national competition carried with it a prize for $1,000. The Director of the Mint, with the approval of the Secretary of the Treasury, had suggested that Thomas Jefferson's likeness be placed on a U.S. coin as a tribute to his outstanding statesmanship and his record of public service. Schlag's splendid portrayal of our third President appears on the obverse. The reverse has an illustration of Monticello, the magnificent home Jefferson built for himself near Charlottesville, Virginia. The mintmark was on the reverse at the right side of Monticello until 1968. After that date, it was moved to the right of Jefferson's wig, beside the date on the obverse.

Jefferson began building Monticello, his dream house, at the age of 20 and finally finished it forty years later in the twilight of his life. Monticello, pictured in careful detail on the reverse of the nickel, is not an ordinary kind of house. It is rather a revolutionary house for his day. Jefferson was a gadgeteer — a man of creative and inventive genius who put his ideas to practical use. Monticello has an observatory in which Jefferson studied the stars and planets with a telescope. The clock in the main hall not only tells the hour but the days of the week as well, and the gears that drive the hands pass through the wall to a duplicate clock over the porch outside. The house has dozens of other amazing conveniences that have to be seen to be appreciated.

No matter what his talents, Jefferson is remembered as a defender of the human rights of man. He spoke to the world through his pen, preferring to put his thoughts in writing rather than in public speech. In a time when revolution was commonplace in America, Jefferson was asked to write The Declaration of Independence, the ageless announcement of Colonial freedom. His words inspired people and sent out to the world a call to arms in the precious name of liberty:

We hold these Truths to be self-evident, that all men are created equal, that they are endowed by their Creator with certain unalienable Rights, that among these are Life, Liberty and the Pursuit of Happiness.

25. Why was Jefferson called "America's Architect"?

(A) Because he designed Monticello.

(B) Because he designed both Monticello and the University of Virginia.

(C) Because he designed the Jefferson Memorial, a monument which appears on the reverse side of the Jefferson nickel.

(D) Because he not only designed Monticello but also designed the Declaration of Independence.

(E) Because he not only designed Monticello but also the Constitution of the United States.

26. Where would the mintmark appear on a 1969 nickel?

(A) On the obverse side to the right of Monticello.

(B) On the reverse side to the right of Monticello.

(C) On the obverse side to the right of Jefferson's wig.

(D) On the reverse side to the right of Jefferson's wig.

(E) Mintmarks do not appear after 1968.

27. Jefferson referred to "unalienable" rights. Which of the following best describe these rights?

(A) Natural rights not capable of being bought or sold.

(B) Rights of Americans, but rights which do not necessarily apply to aliens who move into the country.

(C) Basic rights of Americans, which he specified to include "...eternal hostility against every form of tyranny over the mind of man."

(D) Basic rights which specifically excluded such intangibles as happiness but which provided for the basic necessities needed for life and well-being.

(E) Basic rights of Americans which specifically included religious freedom.

---

**DIRECTIONS:** Each of the following questions provides a given word in capitalized letters followed by five word choices. Choose the best word which is most <u>opposite</u> in meaning to the given word.

---

28. AVOCATION:

   (A) respite

   (B) profession

   (C) silent

   (D) hobby

   (E) avulsion

29. ADULTERATED:

   (A) ribald

   (B) defiled

   (C) chaste

   (D) infantile

   (E) vicious

30. TACITURN:

   (A) reticent

   (B) appeased

   (C) reserved

   (D) inviegled

   (E) effusive

31. AUGMENTATION:

   (A) constriction

   (B) accession

   (C) expansion

   (D) perturbation

   (E) satiation

32. CANAILLE:

   (A) aggregate

   (B) fulgurant

   (C) fulminant

   (D) bridge

   (E) aristocracy

33. ASININE:

   (A) fatuous

   (B) cunning

   (C) idiosyncratic

   (D) eccentric

   (E) antithetic

34. SAGACIOUS:
    (A) shrewd
    (B) astute
    (C) procumbent
    (D) ductile
    (E) incapable

35. SUBLIMINAL:
    (A) conscious
    (B) subversive
    (C) termagant
    (D) turpitude
    (E) explicit

36. BEATIFIC:
    (A) animalistic
    (B) melancholy
    (C) urbane
    (D) civilized
    (E) similitude

37. TURGID:
    (A) aggressive
    (B) tumid
    (C) bilious
    (D) palpable
    (E) deflated

38. TRANSCENDENT:
    (A) average
    (B) superlunar
    (C) suspension
    (D) vermiculated
    (E) sterling

**STOP**

If time still remains, you may go back and check your work.
When the time allotted is up, you may go on to the next section.

# Section 2

TIME:  30 Minutes
        38 Questions

DIRECTIONS: Each of the given sentences has blank spaces which indicate words omitted. Choose the best combination of words which fit into the meaning and structure within the context of the sentence.

1.  The secret agent's taking the one sheet of _____ had an _____ on the lives of many of her companions.

    (A)  vellum...edict            (D)  parchment...obligation

    (B)  stationary...affect       (E)  bond...effigy

    (C)  stationery...effect

2.  The weekly program on public radio is the most _____ means of educating the public about pollution.

    (A)  proficient                (D)  capable

    (B)  effusive                  (E)  competent

    (C)  effectual

3.  Leaving the research facility unattended, the researcher acted with _____ only to find upon his return that the _____ of the pure water had left all the containers dry.

    (A)  diffidence...generation

    (B)  finesse...magnetization

    (C)  travail...condenscension

    (D)  aplomb...evaporation

    (E)  solicitude...condensation

4. The participant brought upon herself the _____ of being caught cheating in the game and accepted the resulting _____ without murmur.

    (A) ignominy...disqualification

    (B) fame...accolades

    (C) humiliation...elegy

    (D) notoriety...eulogy

    (E) contempt...eminence

5. The speaker said the _____ to the ghost was to _____ that he would have the attention of the children.

    (A) illusion...insure

    (B) elusion...assure

    (C) allusion...ensure

    (D) delusion...construe

    (E) allotment...reassure

6. The accused appeared _____ since she felt certain the male witness would _____ her alibi.

    (A) sanguine...corroborate

    (B) meddlesome...substantiate

    (C) conjugal...revoke

    (D) garbled...authenticate

    (E) concupiscent...abolish

7. The gold-studded costume appeared _____ when compared to the _____ of the flannel suit.

    (A) chaste...gaudiness

    (B) laconic...opulence

    (C) reserved...savoir-faire

    (D) ornate...simplicity

    (E) feudal...raucousness

DIRECTIONS: In the following questions, the given pair of words contains a specific relationship to each other. Select the best pair of the choices which expresses the same relationship as the given.

8.  DISPARAGEMENT:LAUDATION::

    (A)  subtraction:farcical

    (B)  euphemism:defamation

    (C)  prattle:slander

    (D)  eulogy:encomium

    (E)  detraction:commendation

9.  GAUNTLET:HAND::

    (A)  cannon:ball          (D)  lance:shield

    (B)  sword:hand           (E)  armor:body

    (C)  body:shield

10.  DEFICIT:PECULATION::

    (A)  attire:dress         (D)  drought:famine

    (B)  hunger:abstinence    (E)  magistrate:judge

    (C)  appear:manifest

11.  PHOTOTROPISM:TURN::

    (A)  poltroon:valiant

    (B)  thermotropism:temperature

    (C)  photosynthesis:formation

    (D)  lithography:stone

    (E)  bold:impudent

12. PUGILISM:FISTS::
    - (A) lexicographer:animals
    - (B) gynecology:genes
    - (C) nepotism:relatives
    - (D) archeology:fossils
    - (E) pediatrics:aged

13. OBVIOUS:APPARENT::
    - (A) plaintiff:bailiff
    - (B) obtrusive:discernable
    - (C) manifest:evident
    - (D) dim:patent
    - (E) translucent:opaque

14. EDIFICE:FACADE::
    - (A) dorsal:ventral
    - (B) turtle:shell
    - (C) anachronism:chronologic
    - (D) body:skeleton
    - (E) counterfeit:fraudulent

15. FIVE-SIDED:PENTAGON::
    - (A) octagon:eight-sided
    - (B) decagon:ten-sided
    - (C) three-sided:tetragon
    - (D) hectagon:eight-sided
    - (E) dodecagon:twelve-sided

16. LINEN:FLAX::
    - (A) chintz:silk
    - (B) madras:linen
    - (C) rayon:plastic
    - (D) coal:nylon
    - (E) chamois:leather

---

**DIRECTIONS**: Each passage is followed by questions based on its content. After reading the passage, choose the best answer to each question. Answer all questions based on what is stated or implied in that passage.

---

The Lincoln Cent was first struck in 1909 to celebrate the 100th Anniversary of the birth of Abraham Lincoln, our 16th President. Designed by Victor D. Brenner, the coin carried the motto "In God We Trust" — the first time it appeared on this denomination coin. It is interesting that the law for the motto was passed during Lincoln's administration as President.

The obverse has the profile of Lincoln as he looked during the trying years of the War Between the States. Faced with the immense problems of a divided nation, Lincoln had worked long and hard to prevent the split between North and South. "A house divided against itself cannot stand," he warned the nation. With the outbreak of war at Fort Sumter, Lincoln was saddened to see his beloved country caught up in the senseless war in which father fought against son, brother against brother. Throughout America war captured the attention of people: the woman who saved the lives of the wounded, the soldier waiting to go into battle, the bewildered child trying hard to understand the sound of guns. Lincoln stood on the broad, silent battlefield at Gettysburg in 1863 to dedicate the site as a national cemetery. Gettysburg had been the scene of some of the most bitter fighting of the war, and had ended in a Union victory. Lincoln was pleased with the victory but deeply concerned over the deaths of so many soldiers. In his special address at Gettysburg, he called upon the American people to end the war. His words boomed out over the large audience before him:

...It is rather for us [the living] to be here dedicated to the great task remaining before us — that from these honored dead we take increased devotion to that cause for which they gave the last full measure of devotion; that we here highly resolve that these dead shall not have died in vain; that this nation under God, shall have a new birth of freedom; and that government of the people, by the people and for the people, shall not perish from the earth."

Barely a month before the end of the war, Lincoln took the oath of

office a second time as President. With the war still raging, his inaugural address took on added meaning:

> ...With malice toward none, with charity for all, with firmness in the right as God gives us to see the right, let us strive on to finish the work we are in, to bind up the nation's wounds, to care for him who shall have borne the battle and for his widow and his orphan, to do all which may achieve and cherish a just and lasting peace among ourselves and with all nations.

Lincoln himself was a man of humble birth. Born in a log cabin in Kentucky, he studied by candlelight and enjoyed few of the advantages open to most people of his day. With great effort and hard work, he rose to become President of our nation at a difficult time in our history. His portrait on the lowly Cent reminds us that in America, any person willing to work hard can became President.

The reverse side of the Lincoln Cent from 1909 through 1958 has a simple design of two heads of wheat. Wheat can be made into bread which is the basic food of the people of the world.

In this sense, wheat also reminds us of agriculture as the universal symbol of Peace and which is the opposite of War. Wheat also represents abundance, which America offers its people not only in material wealth but in the freedoms and liberties granted by our Constitution.

In 1959, to celebrate the 150th Anniversary of Lincoln's birth, the reverse of the Lincoln Cent was changed and a new design adopted. Created by the mint engraver Frank Gasparro, the new design features the Lincoln Memorial in Washington, DC. The design was selected from a group of 23 models the engraving staff at the U.S. Mint was asked to present for consideration.

Two years after Lincoln died, plans were begun to build a monument to honor the slain President. It was finally decided that a fitting memorial should be erected in our nation's capital at the end of a long mall. Fifty-five years would pass before it was finished. Inside the building, a 19 foot tall statue of Lincoln sitting in a huge chair symbolizes the greatness of the former President.

The Lincoln Memorial was completed and dedicated May 30, 1922, in Potomac Park, Washington, DC. A large impressive structure by architect Henry Bacon, it is supported by 36 columns representing

the 36 states at the time of Lincoln's death. The statue of Lincoln was carved out of Georgia marble by Daniel Chester French.

17. From the tone of Lincoln's Second Inaugural Address the reader can assume that Lincoln's attitude toward the South was which of the following?

    (A)  Discursiveness          (D)  Exculpation

    (B)  Acerbity                (E)  Obtuse

    (C)  Recalcitration

18. From the passage, it can be deduced that Lincoln was assassinated in what year?

    (A)  1863                    (D)  1866

    (B)  1864                    (E)  1867

    (C)  1865

19. The author's attitude toward relieving the problems of the time by fighting the War Between the States can best be described as which of the following?

    (A)  Great admiration        (D)  Dissatisfaction

    (B)  Grudging respect         (E)  Indifference

    (C)  Unbiased objectivity

20. Which best describes the reverse side of the cent minted to celebrate the sesquicentennial of Lincoln's birth?

    (A)  There is a profile of Lincoln as he looked during the trying years of the War Between the States.

    (B)  There is a simple design of two heads of wheat symbolizing bread, peace, and abundance.

    (C)  The Lincoln Memorial at Arlington National Cemetery is engraved there.

(D) The Lincoln Memorial in Washington, DC, graces the reverse side.

(E) The statue of Lincoln seated symbolizes the greatness of the former president on this coin.

21. In his second inaugural address Lincoln did which of the following?

(A) He stated that the living should take increased devotion to the cause for which the honored dead at Gettysburg gave their lives.

(B) He vowed that government of the people, by the people, and for the people should not perish from the earth.

(C) Lincoln explained the symbol of wheat: bread, peace, abundance.

(D) He dedicated the future to binding up the nation's wounds, caring for widows and orphans, and achieving peace.

(E) He warned the people that a house divided against itself cannot stand.

22. Which statement is true of the Lincoln Memorial?

(A) It was built in 1909 to celebrate the centennial anniversary of the birth of Abraham Lincoln.

(B) It was built in 1959 to celebrate the sesquicentennial anniversary of Lincoln's birth.

(C) It was planned two years after Lincoln died to honor the slain President and was dedicated in 1959 to celebrate the sesquicentennial anniversary of Lincoln's birth.

(D) It was dedicated in 1922 as the site of a national cemetery.

(E) It took fifty-seven years to finish and was erected in our nation's capital.

23. The author's reaction to Lincoln's portrait being placed on the lowly cent can best be described as which of the following?

(A) Professional detachment

(B) Slight skepticism

(C) Respectful gratitude

(D) Amused condescension

(E) Bemused speculation

24. With which of the following statements would the author of the article probably agree?

(A) No useful purpose was served by the War Between the States.

(B) The War Between the States served to emancipate the slaves.

(C) The South should be punished for its actions against the Union in the War Between the States.

(D) At Gettysburg, Lincoln urged the people to increase their fighting and subdue the South.

(E) The Five-Dollar Bill with the picture of Lincoln is a more fitting monument to him than the penny.

Public acceptance of wind energy conversion systems is an important consideration in planning for the widespread application of wind energy. Studies have shown that the environmental impact of such systems is relatively small compared to conventional electric power systems. Wind-powered systems do not require the flooding of large land areas or the alteration of the natural ecology, as do hydroelectric systems. Furthermore, they produce no waste products or thermal or chemical effluents, as fossil-fueled and nuclear-fueled systems do.

Conventional wind turbine systems that generate several megawatts of power require large exposed rotors several hundred feet in diameter, located on high towers. The rotors of such systems, being passive, are practically noiseless. However, special precautions will be necessary to prevent them from causing interference with nearby TV or radio receivers, and some safety measures may be required to prevent damage or injury from possible mishaps in cases where there

is danger that the rotors might break or shed ice.

The only other concerns with conventional wind machines are those of esthetics. Large numbers of units and interconnecting transmission lines will be required in the future if such systems are to have any significant impact on U.S. energy demands. Particular attention is being given, therefore, to the development of attractive designs for the towers, rotors, and nacelles of these conventional systems to avoid "visual pollution."

25. The writer's opinion toward wind energy conversion systems can best be described as which of the following?

   (A) Personal dissatisfaction

   (B) Unqualified enthusiasm

   (C) Disinterest

   (D) Negativism

   (E) Open-mindedness

26. The article refers to the *nacelles* of the wind energy conversion systems. Which is the best definition of *nacelles*?

   (A) The part of the system which contains the atomic matter used to generate electricity.

   (B) The enclosed part of the system containing generators.

   (C) The part of the system used to reduce the noise, or nacelle, caused by the generation of electricity.

   (D) The nacelles are a part of the high tower on which the rotors are located.

   (E) The nacelles are the blades of the rotors.

27. The limitations of wind energy conversion systems described by the author are which of the following?

   (A) Interference with television and radio receivers, danger from rotors which break or shed ice, and esthetics.

(B) Esthetics, many transmission lines, and noise.

(C) Safety precautions, the large number of units and interconnecting lines required, and large exposed rotors.

(D) The thermal effluents which are a necessary by-product, the noise from the rotors, and the esthetics.

(E) The visual pollution, the thermal pollution, and the safety precautions mandated.

---

**DIRECTIONS:** Each of the following questions provides a given word in capitalized letters followed by five word choices. Choose the best word which is most <u>opposite</u> in meaning to the given word.

---

28. FACTIOUS:

   (A) bellicose

   (B) desultory

   (C) fortuitous

   (D) fractious

   (E) felicitous

29. CONSONANCE:

   (A) conscience

   (B) conscious

   (C) coalesce

   (D) contention

   (E) consign

30. EFFEMINATE

   (A) tortuous

   (B) virile

   (C) ascetic

   (D) contemptuous

   (E) averse

31. PROBITY:

   (A) aesthetics

   (B) perfidy

   (C) abeyance

   (D) predilection

   (E) complementary

32. FACTITIOUS:
    (A) authentic
    (B) travesty
    (C) pedantic
    (D) mordant
    (E) rapacious

33. STENTORIAN:
    (A) styptical
    (B) egregious
    (C) invidious
    (D) vociferous
    (E) subdued

34. PAUCITY:
    (A) dearth
    (B) loquacious
    (C) sanative
    (D) plethora
    (E) lugubrious

35. AUDACIOUSNESS:
    (A) complaisance
    (B) fastidiousness
    (C) impertinence
    (D) impudence
    (E) insolence

36. VENIAL:
    (A) hedonic
    (B) ineffable
    (C) peccadillo
    (D) implacable
    (E) heinous

37. ABSTRUSE:
    (A) perspicacious
    (B) meretricious
    (C) lugubrious
    (D) insidious
    (E) incongruous

38. PRODIGAL:
    (A) wandering
    (B) tarrying
    (C) spendthrift
    (D) frugal
    (E) lavish

**STOP**
If time still remains, you may go
back and check your work.
When the time allotted is up,
you may go on to the next
section.

# Section 3

TIME:   30 Minutes
           30 Questions

**NUMBERS:** All numbers are real numbers.

**FIGURES:** Position of points, angles, regions, etc. are assumed to be in the order shown and angle measures are assumed to be positive.

**LINES:** Assume that lines shown as straight are indeed straight.

**DIRECTIONS:** Each of the following given set of quantities is placed into either column A or B. Compare the two quantities to decide whether:

(A)   the quantity in Column A is greater

(B)   the quantity in Column B is greater

(C)   the two quantities are equal

(D)   the relationship cannot be determined from the information given.

**NOTE:** Do not choose (E) since there are only four choices.

**COMMON INFORMATION:** Information which relates to one or both given quantities is centered in the two columns. A symbol which appears in both columns will indicate the same item in Column A and Column B.

**EXAMPLES:**

| Column A | Column B |
|----------|----------|
| 1.        5 x 4 | 5 + 4 |

Explanation: The correct answer is (A), since 5 × 4 = 20, and 5 + 4 = 9.

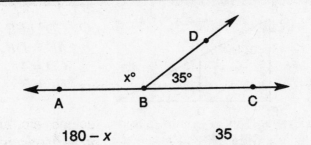

2.                 180 − x                           35

Explanation: The correct answer is (C). Since Angle *ABC* is a straight angle, its measurement is 180°.

|  | **Column A** | **Column B** |
|---|---|---|

$w, x, y$ are positive,
$w + x + y = 20$ and $w = x$

| 1. | $x$ | 10 |
|---|---|---|

| 2. | $\sqrt{9} + \sqrt{7}$ | $\sqrt{16}$ |
|---|---|---|

| 3. | 0 | The largest even integer smaller than 2. |
|---|---|---|

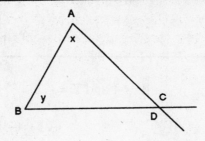

4.                 $\angle y$                        $\angle C - \angle x$

|              | **Column A** | **Column B** |
| ------------ | ------------ | ------------ |

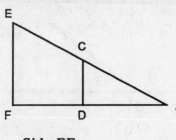

$CD \parallel EF$
$AD = DF$
$CD = 4$
$DF = 3$

5.       Side *EF*           7

---

Given an equilateral triangle
whose perimeter is 30 units.

6.    Area of triangle           $30\sqrt{3}$

---

7.    The values of *y* in      The values of *x* in
      $y^2 + 12y + 27 = 0$       $x^2 - 12x + 27 = 0$

---

8.    An integer $< -1$          Its reciprocal

---

9.       $1 + \dfrac{1}{t}$         $\dfrac{1}{t} \Big/ \dfrac{1}{t+1}$

---

$0.5x - 0.5y = 3$

10.        *x*                *y*

---

$W = 4$ and $Y = -2$

11.      $(2WY)^2$        $(2Y)^2 (4W)$

| **Column A** | **Column B** |
| --- | --- |

$x$ is an integer such that
$$-1 \leq 2x + 1 < 2$$

12.       0                          $x$

$m$ and $n$ are parallel lines.

13.            $\angle b$              $\angle b + \angle c - \angle a$

$BA = BC$

14.            $x$                        $y$

15.    The average of 18, 20, 22, 24, 26        The average of 17, 19, 21, 23, 25, 27

**DIRECTIONS:** For the following questions, select the best answer choice to the given question.

16. Subtract: $4\frac{1}{3} - 1\frac{5}{6}$

   (A)  $3\frac{2}{3}$                          (D)  $2\frac{1}{6}$

   (B)  $2\frac{1}{2}$                          (E)  none of these

   (C)  $3\frac{1}{2}$

17. If the length of a rectangle is increased by 30% and the width is decreased by 20%, then the area is increased by:

   (A)  10%                          (D)  20%

   (B)  5%                           (E)  25%

   (C)  4%

18. What is $t$ equal to if $A = P(1 + rt)$?

   (A)  $A - P - Pr$                    (D)  $(A - P)/Pr$

   (B)  $(A + P)/Pr$                    (E)  none of these

   (C)  $A/P - r$

Questions 19 – 23 refer to the graph below.

**Undergraduate Mathematics Enrollments in the U.S., 1965 – 85**
**(Thousands of enrollments, fall semester)**

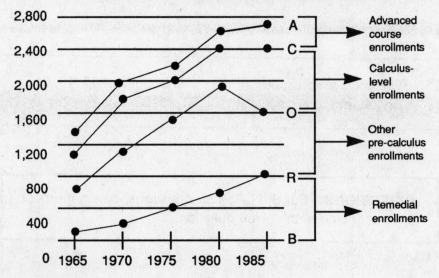

276

(Note: Area between line segments $B$ and $R$ represent remedial enrollments; between line segments $R$ and $O$ represent other precalculus enrollments; between line segments $O$ and $C$ represent calculus enrollments; and, between line segments $C$ and $A$ represent advanced course enrollments.)

19. The total undergraduate mathematics enrollment in the fall of 1975 was about $x$ thousand where $x$ equals about

   (A) 2,800

   (B) 2,000

   (C) 2,400

   (D) 2,200

   (E) 1,500

20. In 1970, the percentage of enrollments in the remedial mathematics category was about:

   (A) 21

   (B) 10.5

   (C) 18

   (D) 79

   (E) 89

21. Between 1970 and 1985 the number of remedial mathematics enrollments:

   (A) increased by about 100%

   (B) increased by about 150%

   (C) increased by about 200%

   (D) increased by about 300%

   (E) increased by about 350%

22. What was the first year when more than 1,600 thousand undergraduate mathematics enrollments were at the precalculus and below levels?

   (A) 1985

   (B) 1975

   (C) 1980

   (D) 1970

   (E) 1965

23. What undergraduate enrollments category was fairly constant over the period of the graph?

    (A) Remedial

    (B) Other precalculus

    (C) Calculus level

    (D) Advanced course

    (E) None of the categories

24. What is the factorization of $x^2 + ax - 2x - 2a$?

    (A) $(x + 2)(x - a)$

    (B) $(x - 2)(x + a)$

    (C) $(x + 2)(x + a)$

    (D) $(x - 2)(x - a)$

    (E) none of these

25. What is the value(s) of $x$ in the equation $(4x - 3)^2 = 4$?

    (A) $^5/_4$

    (B) $^1/_4$

    (C) $^5/_4, ^1/_4$

    (D) $^1/_2, ^5/_2$

    (E) $^5/_2, ^1/_5$

26. What is the product of $(\sqrt{3} + 6)$ and $(\sqrt{3} - 2)$ ?

    (A) $9 + 4\sqrt{3}$

    (B) $-9$

    (C) $-9 + 4\sqrt{3}$

    (D) $-9 + 2\sqrt{3}$

    (E) $9$

27. What is the value of $x$ in the equation $\sqrt{5x - 4} - 5 = -1$?

    (A) $2$

    (B) $5$

    (C) no value

    (D) $4$

    (E) $-4$

28. Jim is twice as old as Susan. If Jim were 4 years younger and Susan were 3 years older, their ages would differ by 12 years. What is the sum of their ages?

278

(A) 19

(D) 57

(B) 42

(E) none of these

(C) 56

29. Joe and Jim together have 14 marbles. Jim and Tim together have 10 marbles. Joe and Tim together have 12 marbles. What is the maximum number of marbles that any one of these may have?

(A) 7

(D) 10

(B) 8

(E) 11

(C) 9

30. The number missing in the series, 2, 6, 12, 20, $x$, 42, 56 is:

(A) 36

(D) 38

(B) 24

(E) 40

(C) 30

## STOP

If time still remains, you may go back and check your work.
When the time allotted is up, you may go on to the next section.

# Section 4

TIME:    30 Minutes
            30 Questions

**NUMBERS:** All numbers are real numbers.

**FIGURES:** Position of points, angles, regions, etc. are assumed to be in the order shown and angle measures are assumed to be positive.

**LINES:** Assume that lines shown as straight are indeed straight.

**DIRECTIONS:** Each of the following given set of quantities is placed into either column A or B. Compare the two quantities to decide whether:

(A)   the quantity in Column A is greater

(B)   the quantity in Column B is greater

(C)   the two quantities are equal

(D)   the relationship cannot be determined from the information given.

**NOTE:** Do not choose (E) since there are only four choices.

**COMMON INFORMATION:** Information which relates to one or both given quantities is centered in the two columns. A symbol which appears in both columns will indicate the same item in Column A and Column B.

**EXAMPLES:**

| Column A | Column B |
|---|---|
| 1.    $5 \times 4$ | $5 + 4$ |

Explanation: The correct answer is (A), since $5 \times 4 = 20$, and $5 + 4 = 9$.

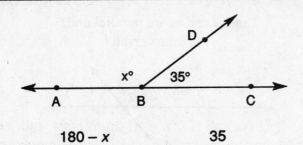

| | | |
|---|---|---|
| 2. | $180 - x$ | 35 |

Explanation: The correct answer is (C). Since Angle *ABC* is a straight angle, its measurement is 180°.

| Column A | Column B |
|---|---|

*x* and *y* are positive integers

| | | |
|---|---|---|
| 1. | $x^2 + y^2$ | $(x + y)^2$ |

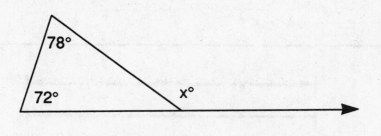

| | | |
|---|---|---|
| 2. | 150 | *x* |

A 30 inches long candle
that burns for 12 minutes
is now 25 inches long

| | | |
|---|---|---|
| 3. | The number of minutes the whole candle burns | 60 minutes |

| Column A | Column B |
|----------|----------|

Lines *l* and *m* are parallel and
*t* is transversal

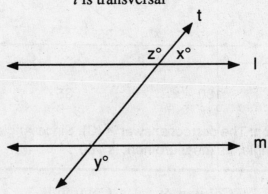

4.  $180 - x°$             $y$

---

$$x - y \neq 0 : y \neq 0$$

5.  $\dfrac{x^2 - y^2}{x^3 - x^2 y}$         $\dfrac{x + y}{y}$

---

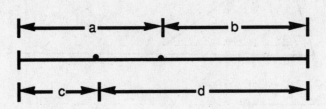

6.  $a + d$             $b + c$

---

$$1 - 2x > x - 5$$

7.  $x$             $2$

|     | Column A | Column B |
| --- | --- | --- |

$x$, $y$ and $z$ are non-zero
integers and $x > y > z$

8. $\dfrac{x}{y}$ $\qquad$ $\dfrac{z}{y}$

---

The average (arithmetic mean) for a set of 28 scores is 80.
Two more students take the test and score 60 and 50.

9. The average for all $\qquad$ $\dfrac{80 + 60 + 50}{3}$
   30 students

---

Quadrilateral $ABCD$ is a parallelogram; segment $\overline{BE}$
is perpendicular to line $\overline{AD}$; the length of $\overline{BE}$ is 8 cm.

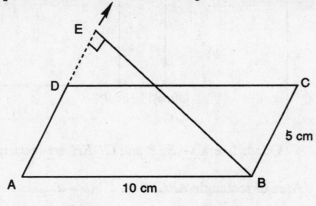

10. Area of $ABCD$ $\qquad$ 40 cm²

---

$a \neq 0$; $b \neq 0$; $b \neq -1$

11. $\dfrac{a}{b}$ $\qquad$ $\dfrac{a + 1}{b + 1}$

---

$x = -4$; $y = 2$

12. 0 $\qquad$ $\dfrac{|x| + 2|y|}{5 + x}$

|  | Column A | Column B |
|---|---|---|
| 13. | $\dfrac{9}{200}$ | 4.5% |

Gail received a 7% raise last year.
Her salary is now $15,515.

| 14. | Gail's salary last year | $14,000 |
|---|---|---|

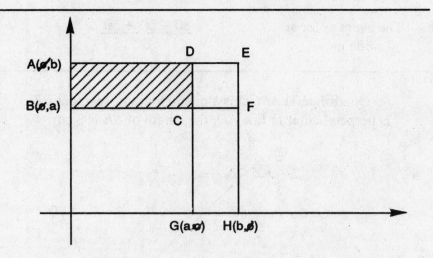

Quadrilaterals *AEFB* and *GDEH* are rectangles

| 15. | Area of rectangle *ABCD* | $b(b - a)$ |
|---|---|---|

---

**DIRECTIONS:** For the following questions, select the best answer choice to the given question.

---

16. Emile receives a flat weekly salary of $240 plus 12% commission of the total volume of all sales he makes. What must his dollar volume be in a week if he is to make a total weekly salary of $540?

(A) $2880          (B) $3600

(C)  $6480                          (D)  $2500

(E)  $2000

17.  If $T = 2\pi \sqrt{\dfrac{L}{g}}$, then $L$ is equal to

(A)  $\dfrac{T^2}{2\pi g}$                    (D)  $\dfrac{T^2 g}{4\pi}$

(B)  $\dfrac{T^2 g}{2\pi}$                    (E)  $\dfrac{T^2}{4\pi^2 g}$

(C)  $\dfrac{T^2 g}{4\pi^2}$

18.  If the measures of the three angles of a triangle are $(3x + 15)°$, $(5x - 15)°$, and $(2x + 30)°$, what is the measure of each angle?

(A)  75°                          (D)  25°

(B)  60°                          (E)  15°

(C)  45°

19.  If $n$ is the first of three consecutive odd numbers, which of the following represents the sum of the three numbers?

(A)  $n + 2$                      (D)  $3n + 6$

(B)  $n + 4$                      (E)  $6(3n)$

(C)  $n + 6$

20.  $1 + \dfrac{y}{(x - 2y)} - \dfrac{y}{(x + 2y)} =$

(A)  0                            (D)  $\dfrac{2x - y}{(x - 2y)(x + 2y)}$

(B)  1                            (E)  $\dfrac{x^2}{(x - 2y)(x + 2y)}$

(C)  $\dfrac{1}{(x - 2y)(x + 2y)}$

285

Questions 21 – 25 refer to the following graphs.

The data represents contributions to federal candidates for public office in the late 1970's.

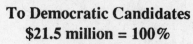

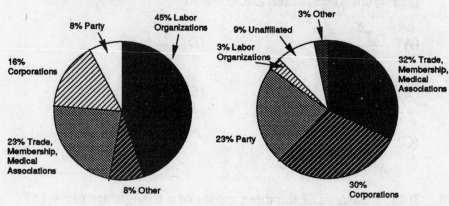

21. What is the average percent of contributions to Republican candidates that come from trade, membership and medical associations?

    (A) 23%                    (D) 9%

    (B) 55%                    (E) 45%

    (C) 32%

22. What is the average dollar amount (in millions) of support for Democratic candidates that come from the party?

    (A) $0.08 million          (D) $5.5 million

    (B) $1.72 million          (E) $1.5 million

    (C) $2.3 million

23. What is the difference (in millions of dollars) between the average dollar amount of support to Democratic candidates and the average dollar amount of support to Republican candidates that come from labor organizations?

    (A) $9.8 million           (B) $9.675 million

286

(C)   $9.08 million          (D)   $8.316 million

(E)   $8.215 million

24.  What is the percent of contributions for Democractic candidates that came from corporations?

(A)   30%                    (D)   14%

(B)   84%                    (E)   16%

(C)   70%

25.  What is the total dollar amount (in millions) of support for both Democratic and Republican candidates that came from corporations?

(A)   $6.608 million        (D)   $9.38 million

(B)   $12.39 million        (E)   $10.049 million

(C)   $5.94 million

26.  Which of the following equations can be used to find a number $x$, if the difference between the square of this number and 21 is the same as the product of 4 times the number?

(A)   $x - 21 = 4x$         (D)   $x + 4x^2 = 21$

(B)   $x^2 - 21 = 4x$       (E)   $x^2 + 21 = 4x$

(C)   $x^2 = 21 - 4x$

27.  In the figure ahown below, line $l$ is parallel to line $m$. If the area of triangle $ABC$ is 40 cm³, what is the area of triangle $ABD$?

(A)   Less than 40 cm³

(B)   More than 40 cm³

(C)   The length of segment $\overline{AD}$ times 40 cm²

(D) Exactly 40 cm³

(E) Cannot be determined from the information given.

28. In the Klysler Auto Factory, robots assemble cars. If 3 robots assemble 17 cars in 10 minutes, how many cars can 14 robots assemble in 45 minutes if all robots work at the same rate all the time?

(A) 357

(B) 340

(C) 705 .

(D) 150

(E) 272

29. If the length of segment $\overline{EB}$, base of triangle $EBC$, is equal to $^1/_4$ the length of segment $\overline{AB}$ ($\overline{AB}$ is the length of rectangle $ABCD$), and the area of triangle $EBC$ is 12 square units, find the area of the shaded region.

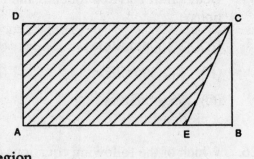

(A) 24 square units

(B) 96 square units

(C) 84 square units

(D) 72 square units

(E) 120 square units

30. A truck contains 150 small packages, some weighing 1 kg each and some weighing 2 kg each. How many packages weighing 2 kg each are in the truck if the total weight of all the packages is 264 kg?

(A) 36

(B) 52

(C) 88

(D) 124

(E) 114

**STOP**

If time still remains, you may go back and check your work.
When the time allotted is up, you may go on to the next section.

# Section 5

TIME:    30 Minutes
          25 Questions

DIRECTIONS: Each question or group of questions is based on a passage or set of statements. Select the best answer choice.

Questions 1-4 refer to the following information.

Mr. Elan always coordinated the color of his sport coat, tie, and trousers. He had four sport coats, six pair of trousers and seven ties. Each sport coat could be worn with two different pairs of trousers and each coat and trouser combination always allowed a choice of three different ties. He always selected his sport coat first.

1.   How many different ways can Mr. Elan wear these three articles of clothing and still conform to his color combinations?

    (A)  9               (D)  12

    (B)  24            (E)  18

    (C)  72

2.   When one of his sport coats is at the cleaners, how many *fewer* combinations of attire does he have?

    (A)  4               (D)  7

    (B)  5              (E)  Cannot determine

    (C)  6

3.   Mr. Elan spilled food on one of his ties and discarded it and also sent one of his sport coats to the cleaners. How many combinations of attire does he now have available?

    (A)  18              (B)  12

(C)  24                          (D)  20

(E)  Cannot determine

4.    If Mr. Elan purchased another sport coat that also coordinated
      with three of his ties and two pairs of his trousers, how
      many additional combinations could he wear that would
      conform to his color requirements?

(A)  6                           (D)  18

(B)  30                          (E)  Cannot determine

(C)  24


Questions 5-8 refer to the following passage.

The quality control department of a clothing manufacturer in-
spected all garments according to four types of flaws: (1) color, (2)
fabric quality, (3) seams, and (4) size. Inspectors forwarded defective
garments to a supervisor to make a final decision. Inspectors attached
tags to garments indicating the type of flaw according to the following:
Type 1 = Red; Type 2 = Blue; Type 3 = Green; Type 4 = Yellow.
Mistakes in color were re-dyed; flaws in fabric went to a "seconds"
outlet; faulty seams were sent to be re-sewn; errors in sizing were sent
to a "re-tag office"; and some were too defective to salvage. The final
decision that a garment could be salvaged was made by Supervisors A,
B, and C. Supervisor A made the decision on color and fabric
problems; Supervisor B made the decision on seam and size problems,
Supervisor C reviewed garments with three or more kinds of defects.
Supervisor D reviewed the recommendations from A, B, and/or C to
make the final decision on all articles to be discarded rather than
repaired.


5.    When a garment has a color blemish that can be corrected, what
      color code will be attached and which of the following people
      will be responsible for detecting the flaw, and making a decision
      about the garment?

(A)  Red, Inspector, Supervisors A and D

(B)  Blue, Inspector, Supervisors A and B

(C)   Red, Inspector, Supervisor A

(D)   Blue, Inspector, Supervisor B

(E)   Red, Inspector, Supervisors B and D

6.   When a garment has inspector tags that are Red, Blue, and Green attached and may not be repairable, which of the following people will be responsible for making a decision about the garment.

(A)   Supervisors A, B, and D

(B)   Supervisors A, C, and D

(C)   Supervisors B, C, and D

(D)   Supervisors C and D

(E)   Supervisors A, B, C, and D

7.   When a garment has a repairable flaw in color and seams what colors will be attached and who will be involved in processing this garment?

(A)   Blue, Yellow, Supervisors A and B

(B)   Red, Green, Inspector, Supervisors A and B

(C)   Red, Yellow, Inspector, Supervisors C and D

(D)   Red, Green, Supervisors A and B

(E)   Red, Blue, Inspector, Supervisors A, B, and C

8.   When a garment has the maximum number of flaws and cannot be repaired, how many people will be involved in the inspection and final decision about this garment?

(A)   1                    (D)   4

(B)   2                    (E)   5

(C)   3

Questions 9-12 refer to the following passage.

The ACME company devised a code to retrieve files from their computer. Their access codes are limited to a total of eight letters or numbers (excluding 0). The letters must appear in alphabetical order and the numbers must appear in descending order. The letters cannot be adjacent to one another but the numbers can be. The code may begin with either a letter or a number but must end with a letter. At least three numbers and three letters must appear in each code.

9.  Which of the following conforms to the requirements for the code?

(A)  8 B 6 H 4 M 2 L          (C)  B K 9 8 M O R 7

(B)  A 7 B 6 4 3 2 F          (D)  8 7 5 L 3 0 1 K

10. Which of the following first three parts of the code could meet the requirements of the code?

(A)  A 7 B . . . . .          (C)  A 2 B . . . . .

(B)  A B 7 . . . . .          (D)  7 A B . . . . .

11. Which of the following last three parts of the code could meet the requirements of the code?

(A)  . . . . . A 7 M          (C)  . . . . . A 2 D

(B)  . . . . . C D 8          (D)  . . . . . C 6 D

12. Which of the following does *not* conform to the requirements for the code?

(A)  B 8 G 6 4 K 2 X          (C)  F H 7 J 6 K 4 L

(B)  5 C 4 G 3 M 2 P          (D)  G 9 J 7 M 5 3 S

Questions 13-16 refer to the following statements.

B, D, E, F, M, and P all ran in a foot race. At the half-way point in the race, the runner who came in first was in fifth place and the runner who was third at the half-way point came in fifth at the end. The runner in last place at the half-way point remained last at the end and the

runner who led at the half-way mark came in second. In the final results M finished two places ahead of E. E finished two places ahead of the runner who was in third at the half-way point. B finished behind M and ahead of E. The runner who was in third at the half-way mark finished three places behind B. F finished two places ahead of D.

13. Who came in first in the race?

   (A) D             (D) M

   (B) E             (E) P

   (C) F

14. Who came in last in the race?

   (A) D             (D) M

   (B) E             (E) P

   (C) F

15. Who came in third in the race?

   (A) D             (D) M

   (B) E             (E) P

   (C) F

16. Who finished two places behind B?

   (A) D             (D) M

   (B) E             (E) P

   (C) F

17. Those who oppose physical punishment as an action for disciplining children state that over 80% of those imprisoned in the United States report physical punishment as a common practice during their own childhood. This argument posed by those who

oppose physical punishment is supported by which of the following assumptions?

(A) There is a positive correlation between physical punishment of children and criminal behavior of those children when they become adults.

(B) Most prisoners are incarcerated for committing a physically violent act.

(C) Small children can be managed without resorting to physical punishment.

(D) Physical punishment does not deter misbehavior of children.

(E) Parents prefer physical punishment as a method to control behavior of their children.

18. Forest fires are often started by natural causes such as lightning, spontaneous combustion or extreme natural heat. Though these fires often seem extremely destructive they actually are nature's way of "cleaning out" the forest and helping it breathe and flourish when the underbrush becomes stifling and the thickness of the forest prevents healthy growth of trees.

Which of the following statements is the most defensible comment to derive from the foregoing passage?

(A) Campers who inadvertently start forest fires are actually helping, rather than hurting, the healthy growth of forests.

(B) Forest fires help preserve a healthy balance of nature for wild animals.

(C) Sometimes the "cleansing" of forests and the conditions that protect wild animal life are contradictory.

(D) More forest fires are started by natural causes than are started by the carelessness of man.

(E) We don't know how many forest fires occur, for lightning and other natural causes start fires in remote areas.

19. When a tree is cut the rings reveal the age of the tree. One ring equals one year. Furthermore, the width of the ring indicates the amount of growth during the year. Often a wide growth ring follows a narrow growth ring which is explained by the slow growth year being a year of drought and the faster growth a consequence of greater rainfall.

    Which of the following statements can be concluded from this passage?

    (A) Analysis of the rings of a felled tree provides information to describe the annual rainfall during each year of the life of the tree.

    (B) When trees survive adverse conditions they become stronger and grow more in subsequent years.

    (C) Trees that grow in arid lands will grow slower than trees that grow in areas with a heavy rainfall.

    (D) Healthy trees can survive long periods of drought.

    (E) Trees that grow in arid areas are harder and make better lumber for building because their rings are closer together.

20. At a Midwestern university an analysis was made of the graduation rate of varsity athletes compared to the graduation rate of members of a fraternity, a sorority, and a dormitory. The rank order, from high to low, of the graduation rates of these four groups was as follows: (1) sorority, (2) dormitory, (3) fraternity, and (4) varsity athletes. Which inference is the most defensible to draw from these findings?

    (A) Serious students do not participate in varsity athletics.

    (B) Varsity athletes do not graduate from college.

    (C) Varsity athletes who join fraternities or sororities increase their likelihood of graduating.

    (D) Distractions and/or time required for varsity athletic participation may make graduation more difficult.

    (E) Dormitory living supports academic pursuits.

21. Careers and job opportunities in computer technology are increasing. Within the next five years careers in the computer industry will exceed the opportunities in any other single field of work. If the preceding statement is true, which of the following implications is the most reliable for young people making a choice about their future occupation and career?

    (A) Only those who prepare for work in the computer industry can expect a reasonable opportunity to find productive employment.

    (B) More people will be working in the computer industry than all other fields of work combined.

    (C) Those who are unskilled or lacking knowledge that is useful in the computer industry will be destined to the lower paying jobs in the economy.

    (D) Those who prepare for employment in the computer industry will most likely find productive employment.

    (E) Those who enjoy high status such as professionals in medicine and law and corporation presidents will be replaced in status by computer experts.

22. There is no reason to rule out the possibility of a cancer cure through experimentation with laser technology. The argument above assumes that:

    (A) Laser technology will provide a cure for cancer.

    (B) Laser technology is our best hope for a cure for cancer.

    (C) If laser technology cured cancer, it would be quickly available since lasers are easily produced.

    (D) The possibility that laser technology may help in curing cancer makes it a worthwhile endeavor for experimentation.

    (E) Laser technology has not been tried as a cure for cancer.

23. John purchased 500 acres of land in an isolated area as an investment. The land was inexpensive and he thought the land would appreciate because people would seek solitude away from the urban areas. Which of the following events is John assuming will *not* happen?

    (A) Access to his property will be unreasonable.

    (B) The taxes and other costs in holding the property will become prohibitive for him.

    (C) The zoning ordinances will prevent development into a profitable enterprise or sale.

    (D) The property will not be damaged by natural causes (flood, fire, erosion, etc.).

    (E) The property will not become valuable before he is too old or deceased.


24. The state legislature commissioned a survey of business and industry leaders to determine their priorities for making public schools more attractive for their employees. The four highest recommendations were (1) higher academic standards, (2) stricter discipline, (3) reduction of the drop-out rate, and (4) lower taxes. Which of the following statements characterizes the four priorities listed?

    (A) The four priorities are consistent with each other.

    (B) The attainment of some of these priorities would militate against the attainment of others.

    (C) If taxes were lowered, they would not expect the other goals to also be met.

    (D) Respondents to the survey expressed satisfaction with the schools.

    (E) The respondents expressed views that are clearly in the best interest of professional educators.

25. Five lobbyists, A, B, C, D, and E agreed to attend meetings of four legislative sub-committees, 1, 2, 3, and 4. They decided to have either 2 or 3 lobbyists attend each committee meeting. They also needed to divide the lobbyists' expertise to assure knowledgeable people would be at each meeting. A and B held similar knowledge; D and C needed to stay together and E could meet with any committee but could not be paired with A.

Which of the following could attend the meeting of sub-committee 1?

(A)  A, B, and C

(B)  A and D

(C)  A, D, and C

(D)  B, D, and E

(E)  A, C, and E

**STOP**
If time still remains, you may go back and check your work.
When the time allotted is up, you may go on to the next section.

# Section 6

**TIME:** 30 Minutes
25 Questions

**DIRECTIONS:** Each question or group of questions is based on a passage or set of statements. Select the best answer choice.

Questions 1 – 5 refer to the following statements.

The parties to an important teacher negotiation meeting are two representatives from the teachers' union, Bell and Green; two representatives from the administration, Kersh and McGee; and the union mediator, Sheets. They are seated at a round table with eight seats.

I. The two representatives of the teachers' union always sit next to each other.

II. The two representatives from the administration always sit with one seat between them.

III. Both sides want to be as close to the union mediator as the other side, but no closer then necessary to the opposing side.

IV. The union mediator wants at least one seat between himself and any of the other negotiators.

1. If conditions I, II, and IV are met which of the following is necessarily true?

   (A) Sheets sits next to one of the teachers' union representatives.

   (B) Bell sits next to one of the administrative representatives.

   (C) One of the administrative representatives will sit next to either Bell or Green.

   (D) Either Kersh or McGee sits next to Sheets.

   (E) None of the above is necessarily true.

299

2. If conditions I, II, and III are met, which of the following is not a possible seating arrangement of the negotiations, starting with Sheets and going clockwise around the table?

   (A) Sheets, Bell, Green, empty, empty, Kersh, empty, McGee.

   (B) Sheets, Green, Bell, empty, empty, McGee, empty, Kersh.

   (C) Sheets, Kersh, empty, McGee, empty, empty, Bell.

   (D) Sheets, McGee, Kersh, empty, empty, empty, Bell.

   (E) All of the above are possible seating arrangements.

3. The superintendent joins the negotiations and sits across the table from the mediator. If all of the conditions are still met as much as possible, which of the following must be true?

   I. An administrative representative will sit next to the superintendent.

   II. A teachers' union representative will sit next to the superintendent.

   III. Both an administrative representative and one from the teachers' union will sit next to the union mediator.

   (A) I only

   (B) II only

   (C) III only

   (D) I and II only

   (E) I, II, and III

4. If the two sides meet without the union mediator and sit so that Bell is seated directly opposite McGee, which of the following is possible?

   (A) Kersh and Green will both be seated to Bell's left and to McGee's right.

   (B) Kersh will be as close to Bell as he is to McGee.

   (C) Green will be separated from Kersh by three seats.

   (D) Green will be separated from McGee by three seats.

   (E) Green and Kersh will be seated directly across from each other.

5.  If Bell's friend joins the negotiations and sits next to him, which of the following is not possible?

    (A) Kersh sits directly opposite Bell.

    (B) Kersh sits directly opposite Bell's friend.

    (C) McGee sits directly opposite Green.

    (D) McGee sits directly opposite Bell's friend.

    (E) Bell's friend sits next to Sheets.

Questions 6-9 refer to the following paragraph.

For a motorist there are three ways of going from Dover to Clarksville. (1) By way of a toll road which is 20 miles long and the toll is $1.25. (2) A causeway between the two cities is a distance of 10 miles and the toll is $1.50 for the vehicle and driver plus 25 cents for each passenger. (3) An interstate without toll goes east for 30 miles to Russellville then northwest for 20 miles to Clarksville.

6.  Which of the following is the shortest route from Clarksville to Russellville?

    (A) directly on the interstate to Russellville

    (B) the toll road

    (C) causeway

    (D) causeway or toll road

    (E) the toll road only if traffic is heavy on the causeway

7.  The most economical way of going from Dover to Russellville, in terms of tolls and distance, is to use the

    (A) causeway

    (B) toll road

    (C) toll road or causeway

    (D) interstate

    (E) depends upon the traffic conditions

8.  David usually drives alone from Clarksville to Dover every work day. Which factor would most probably influence his choice of the toll road or the bridge?

    (A)  whether his wife goes with him

    (B)  traffic conditions on the interstate

    (C)  traffic conditions on the toll road and causeway

    (D)  saving money in tolls

    (E)  price of gasoline consumed in covering the 10 additional miles on the toll road

9.  In choosing between the use of the toll road and the causeway, the chief factors would be

    I.  traffic and road conditions

    II.  number of passengers in the car

    III.  gasoline efficiency of the car

    IV.  desire to save 25 cents

    (A)  I only                    (D)  III and IV only

    (B)  II only                   (E)  I and II only

    (C)  II and III only

Questions 10-14 refer to the following paragraph.

Debbie wants to take four courses this semester. There are only seven courses in which she is interested and that do not conflict with her job: three math courses – algebra, geometry, and trigonometry, and four education courses – human development, educational psychology, learning theory, and teaching methods. To meet college requirements she must take two math courses this semester. There are some scheduling problems, however: human development overlaps both geometry and learning theory, which are sequential; algebra is given at the same time as educational psychology.

10. If Debbie decides she will take human development, what will her other three courses be?

   (A) algebra, trigonometry, and geometry

   (B) algebra, trigonometry, and teaching methods

   (C) algebra, trigonometry, and educational psychology

   (D) trigonometry, geometry, and teaching methods

   (E) trigonometry, teaching methods, and educational psychology

11. If the geometry course is changed to a time which Debbie cannot make, and she decides to take music, which of the following would be her schedule?

   (A) algebra, trigonometry, human development, and learning theory

   (B) algebra, geometry, educational psychology, and learning theory

   (C) algebra, trigonometry, teaching methods, and learning theory

   (D) trigonometry, human development, educational psychology, and learning theory

   (E) trigonometry, teaching methods, human development, and learning theory

12. If Debbie takes four courses this semester she cannot

   I. take educational psychology and not take geometry

   II. take learning theory and not take geometry

   III. take human development and not take trigonometry

   (A) I only            (B) II only

   (C) III only          (D) I and II only

   (E) I and III only

13. Which of the following must always be true?

 I. Debbie must take trigonometry if she takes learning theory

 II. Debbie must take geometry if she takes educational psychology

 III. Debbie must take educational psychology if she takes geometry

 (A) I, II, and III

 (B) II and III only

 (C) I and II only

 (D) III only

 (E) II only

14. If the trigonometry courses are moved to the same time as human development, and Debbie takes trigonometry, what further problem(s) does she face?

 (A) She won't be able to take two math courses

 (B) She won't be able to take algebra

 (C) She won't be able to take teaching methods

 (D) She won't be able to take either algebra or educational psychology

 (E) She won't be able to take four courses which interest her

Questions 15-16 refer to the following passage.

Ms. Franklin: Mr. Green insists that the only way for our company to increase its profits is to double the advertising budget. That obviously is not the answer. Our two major competitors have operations similar to ours. Both are showing increased profits while spending less on advertising than we presently spend.

15. Ms. Franklin's primary method of making either point is to:

 (A) suggest a different underlying cause of the problem

 (B) present evidence which was previously overlooked

 (C) point out a logical flaw in Mr. Green's reasoning

(D) draw an analogy

(E) question Mr. Green's competence

16. Which of the following statements would be Mr. Green's most effective rebuttal to Ms. Franklin's argument?

(A) Our two major competitors do not need to advertise as much as we do, because they are already much better known and have larger shares of the market.

(B) I have been in this business for thirty years, during which time I have repeatedly proven my ability to identify and solve business problems.

(C) The only way for us to increase profits is to sell more of our products; the only way to sell more products is to convince people to buy them; the only way to convince people to buy them is through increased advertising.

(D) You have offered neither statistics to back up your claims nor any proposals for an alternative solution to our problem.

(E) My proposal is not "obviously" wrong. There is only one way to find out if it is wrong, and that is to try it.

Questions 17-18 refer to the following statements.

I. All wheeled conveyances which travel on the highway are polluters.

II. Bicycles are not polluters.

III. Whenever I drive my car on the highway, it rains.

IV. It is raining.

17. If the above statements are all true, which of the following statements must also be true?

(A) Bicycles do not travel on the highway.

(B) Bicycles travel on the highway only if it is raining.

(C)  If my car is not polluting, then it is not raining.

(D)  I am now driving my car on the highway.

(E)  My car is not a polluter.

18.  The conclusion "my car is not polluting" could be logically deducted from statements I – IV if statement

(A)  II was changed to: "Bicycles are polluters."

(B)  II was changed to: "My car is a polluter."

(C)  III was changed to: "If bicycles were polluters, I would be driving my car on the highway."

(D)  IV was changed to: "Rainwater is polluted."

(E)  IV was changed to: "It is not raining."

Questions 19-20 refer to the following passage.

The people do not run the country; neither do elected officials. The corporations run the country. Heads of corporations routinely and imperiously hand down decisions that profoundly affect millions of people. The people affected do not vote on the decision nor for the corporate officers. Yet we are supposed to believe we live in a democracy.

19.  Which of the following statements, if true, would support the author's views?

I.  Corporate lobbies strongly influence the introduction and passage of legislation at all levels of government

II.  Growing numbers of the most talented college graduates are going to work for private corporations rather than for the government.

III.  Few legal requirements are imposed on corporations as to the responsibilities they must fulfill to their employees and their communities.

(A)  I only                                    (B)  II only

(C)   I and III only          (E)     I, II, and III

(D)   II and III only


20.   Which of the following statements most closely parallels the reasoning of the argument above?

(A)   The Police Department just laid off ten patrolmen. Yet we are supposed to believe this is a safe neighborhood.

(B)   He has lied to us many times. Yet we are supposed to believe he is now telling the truth.

(C)   The quality of television programs continues to decline. Yet we are supposed to believe they are still worth watching.

(D)   He has no training or experience in this profession. Yet we are supposed to believe he is qualified for this job.

(E)   We are asked to do nothing but regurgitate facts. Yet we are supposed to believe we are getting an education.


Questions 21-23 refer to the following statement.

Strict gun control laws caused a decrease in violent crimes. In the six months since the city council passed a gun control law, armed robberies in Russellville have dropped by 25%.


21.   All of the following, if true, are valid objections to the argument above except:

(A)   A decrease in crime in one city does not mean that such a decrease would occur anywhere a gun control law was enacted.

(B)   Other factors may have caused the drop in armed robberies.

(C)   Armed robbery is only one category of violent crime that might be affected by a gun control law.

(D)   The gun control law has made it more difficult for citizens to purchase guns for legitimate purposes of self-defense.

(E) Since the law was passed, murders involving guns in Russellville have increased by 33%.

22. Which of the following statements, if true, would strengthen the argument base?

I. Before the law was passed, the number of armed robberies had been steadily increasing.

II. The more severe the punishment mandated for a crime, the less likely that crime is to occur.

III. Three-fourths of all violent crimes involve the use of a gun.

(A) I only

(D) II and III only

(B) III only

(E) I, II, and III

(C) I and II only

23. Which of the following statements, if true, would weaken the argument above?

I. In the six months since the law was passed, 40% more police have been hired.

II. In the six months since the law was passed, accidental deaths by firearms have increased by 10%.

III. Only 30% of those indicted under the new laws have been convicted.

(A) I only

(D) I and III only

(B) III only

(E) II and III only

(C) I and II only

24. Current movies give children a distorted view of the world. Cartoons depict animals as compassionate, loyal, tender souls; while Westerns portray men and women as treacherous, cruel, wanton, hard, uncaring, and deceitful. Children are taught to value animals more highly than human beings.

Which of the following, if true, would weaken the author's conclusion?

I.  Children are not allowed to watch Westerns.

II. The producers of cartoons do not want children to regard animals as higher than human beings.

III. Fables, such as "Androcles and the Lion," tell stories of cooperation between humans and animals, and they usually end with a moral about human virtue.

(A) I only        (D) III only

(B) II only       (E) I, II, and III

(C) I and II

25. Students excused from English composition write better than those who take the course. We can encourage better writing by dropping English composition.

The major flaw in the reasoning used in the argument above is that the author

(A) bases the argument on a purely subjective judgement

(B) does not cite evidence for the statements given

(C) confuses cause and effect

(D) fails to take into account any long-term effects of the course

(E) assumes that all composition courses are essentially alike

**STOP**
If time still remains, you may go back and check your work.

# TEST 2

## ANSWER KEY

### Section 1 — Verbal Ability

| | | | | | | | |
|---|---|---|---|---|---|---|---|
| 1. | (E) | 11. | (B) | 21. | (B) | 31. | (A) |
| 2. | (E) | 12. | (A) | 22. | (E) | 32. | (E) |
| 3. | (A) | 13. | (A) | 23. | (A) | 33. | (B) |
| 4. | (B) | 14. | (B) | 24. | (E) | 34. | (E) |
| 5. | (C) | 15. | (C) | 25. | (D) | 35. | (A) |
| 6. | (A) | 16. | (A) | 26. | (C) | 36. | (B) |
| 7. | (E) | 17. | (D) | 27. | (A) | 37. | (E) |
| 8. | (C) | 18. | (E) | 28. | (B) | 38. | (A) |
| 9. | (B) | 19. | (E) | 29. | (C) | | |
| 10. | (B) | 20. | (B) | 30. | (E) | | |

### Section 2 — Verbal Ability

| | | | | | | | |
|---|---|---|---|---|---|---|---|
| 1. | (C) | 11. | (C) | 21. | (D) | 31. | (B) |
| 2. | (C) | 12. | (C) | 22. | (E) | 32. | (A) |
| 3. | (D) | 13. | (C) | 23. | (C) | 33. | (E) |
| 4. | (A) | 14. | (B) | 24. | (A) | 34. | (D) |
| 5. | (C) | 15. | (C) | 25. | (E) | 35. | (A) |
| 6. | (A) | 16. | (E) | 26. | (B) | 36. | (E) |
| 7. | (D) | 17. | (D) | 27. | (A) | 37. | (A) |
| 8. | (E) | 18. | (C) | 28. | (E) | 38. | (D) |
| 9. | (E) | 19. | (D) | 29. | (D) | | |
| 10. | (B) | 20. | (D) | 30. | (B) | | |

### Section 3 — Quantitative Ability

| | | | | | | | |
|---|---|---|---|---|---|---|---|
| 1. | (B) | 3. | (C) | 5. | (A) | 7. | (B) |
| 2. | (A) | 4. | (C) | 6. | (B) | 8. | (B) |

| | | | | | | | |
|---|---|---|---|---|---|---|---|
| 9. | (C) | 15. | (C) | 21. | (D) | 27. | (D) |
| 10. | (A) | 16. | (B) | 22. | (B) | 28. | (D) |
| 11. | (C) | 17. | (C) | 23. | (D) | 29. | (B) |
| 12. | (D) | 18. | (D) | 24. | (B) | 30. | (C) |
| 13. | (C) | 19. | (D) | 25. | (C) | | |
| 14. | (C) | 20. | (B) | 26. | (C) | | |

## Section 4 — Quantitative Ability

| | | | | | | | |
|---|---|---|---|---|---|---|---|
| 1. | (B) | 9. | (A) | 17. | (C) | 25. | (D) |
| 2. | (C) | 10. | (C) | 18. | (B) | 26. | (B) |
| 3. | (A) | 11. | (D) | 19. | (D) | 27. | (D) |
| 4. | (C) | 12. | (B) | 20. | (E) | 28. | (A) |
| 5. | (D) | 13. | (C) | 21. | (C) | 29. | (C) |
| 6. | (A) | 14. | (A) | 22. | (B) | 30. | (E) |
| 7. | (B) | 15. | (B) | 23. | (C) | | |
| 8. | (D) | 16. | (D) | 24. | (E) | | |

## Section 5 — Analytical Ability

| | | | | | | | |
|---|---|---|---|---|---|---|---|
| 1. | (B) | 8. | (C) | 15. | (B) | 22. | (D) |
| 2. | (C) | 9. | (B) | 16. | (C) | 23. | (E) |
| 3. | (E) | 10. | (A) | 17. | (A) | 24. | (B) |
| 4. | (A) | 11. | (D) | 18. | (C) | 25. | (C) |
| 5. | (C) | 12. | (C) | 19. | (A) | | |
| 6. | (D) | 13. | (D) | 20. | (D) | | |
| 7. | (B) | 14. | (A) | 21. | (D) | | |

## Section 6 — Analytical Ability

| | | | | | | | |
|---|---|---|---|---|---|---|---|
| 1. | (C) | 8. | (C) | 15. | (D) | 22. | (C) |
| 2. | (D) | 9. | (E) | 16. | (A) | 23. | (A) |
| 3. | (A) | 10. | (B) | 17. | (A) | 24. | (A) |
| 4. | (B) | 11. | (C) | 18. | (E) | 25. | (C) |
| 5. | (A) | 12. | (E) | 19. | (C) | | |
| 6. | (A) | 13. | (E) | 20. | (E) | | |
| 7. | (D) | 14. | (E) | 21. | (D) | | |

# DETAILED EXPLANATIONS OF ANSWERS

## Section 1–Verbal Ability

1.    (E)
    For (A), A PROSELYTE (a new convert) does not fit the first blank. PROGENY (offspring) does not fit blank two well. (A) is not an appropriate choice. TAINTED (infected, spoiled) does not fit blank one. PRODIGIOUS means portentous or wonderful, but coupled with TAINTED, (B) is inappropriate. STAPES is the small stirrup-shaped bone in the inner ear; a PROGENITOR is a forefather. (C) is clearly inappropriate. A LITHOGRAPHER is a person who makes lithographs or prints; LITHOGRAPHER clearly does not fit blank one. PORTENTOUS means wonderful, prodigious; it is appropriate for blank two. Coupled with LITHOGRAPHER, however, (D) is not an appropriate choice. (E) Both terms correctly apply. (E) is the best choice.

2.    (E)
    For (A), SUBJUGATED means conquered. (A) is clearly wrong. VANQUISHED means forced into submission. (B) is inappropriate. SUBDUED or conquered does not fit this sentence; (C) is not right. SURMOUNTED means OVERCOME. (D) should not be selected. IMPERIOUS means domineering, lordly. (E) is correct.

3.    (A)
    INFREQUENTLY (at wide intervals) fits the sentence. IMBUE implies giving new life and requires a person or thing as an object; here, *patient* is the object of the vigor so (A) is the correct answer. INFUSE requires that which gives new life and vigor to be the object; it clearly does not fit here since *patient* is the direct object. (B) is not the best choice. SUFFUSE is a spreading through, as of color. (C) is not the best choice. SPORADICALLY implies irregularity; INOCULATE means imbruing a person with something that acts like a disease germ. (D) is incorrect. LEAVEN means to transform a mass, like yeast in dough. (E) is not the best choice.

312

4.    (B)

POTTAGE (or POTAGE) is a thick soup, a kind of stew made of vegetables or meat and vegetables so (A) is not appropriate. BISQUE is a particularly rich puree, often made of shellfish; (B) is the right answer. BROTH is the liquid in which any meat or vegetable has been boiled. BOUILLON is concentrated and clarified broth of beef or vegetables. (D) is incorrect. A SOUFFLE is a dish puffed by cooking; a "rich shellfish purée" would not be puffed. (E) is not a good answer.

5.    (C)

In (A), ANNOYS stresses loss of patience by being forced to endure something unpleasant. (A) is incorrect. (B) IRRITATES emphasizes difficulty in enduring and resulting weariness of spirit. (B) is incorrect. EXASPERATES implies keen and bitter irritation at something not to be endured. (C) is the correct answer. (D) DELEC-TATES (pleases) does not fit the sentence. (D) is not an appropriate choice. (E) INCONVENIENCES is not a strong enough word; (E) is incorrect.

6.    (A)

HOMOGRAPHS and HETERONYMS both are words that are spelled the same but have different pronunciations and meanings. HOMOPHONES are words that sound alike but are different in meaning and spelling. HOMONYMS are words that are spelled and pronounced the same but have different meanings. (A) is the best answer.

7.    (E)

In (A), SORROW is mental suffering and does not fit well in the sentence. It is unlikely that a walk toward punishment would HASTEN the pace. (B) is incorrect. REGRET toward punishment that has not as yet been administered to an individual does not seem appropriate. (C) is incorrect. PRECIPITATED means hastened; (D) does not fit the sentence sense. (E) is the correct choice. ANGUISH implies agony, mental pain toward an event. HINDERED means stalled, retained.

8.    (C)
BESEECH and SUPPLICATE are synonyms for beg or entreat. ENTREAT means to beg; CARNIFY means to make flesh. They are not related. (A) is wrong. BESIEGE (not to be confused with BE-SEECH) is to surround in a hostile manner; PETITION is to beg. (B) is not the correct answer. SOLICIT is to request or beseech; IMPOR-TUNE is also to urge persistently. Since the two are synonyms, (C) is the correct answer. BELEAGUER is to surround, to besiege; ESTI-VAL means belonging to the summer. Clearly (D) is not the right answer. IMPLORE is to beg; IMPEDE is to hinder. (E) is the wrong answer.

9.    (B)
A lack of VITAMIN C causes SCURVY; taking VITAMIN C helps cure SCURVY. (A) The SUN causes SKIN CANCER; care in the SUN can help prevent SKIN CANCER. The analogy is not the same. (B) is the correct answer since NIACIN can prevent PEL-LAGRA. (C) IODINE in the diet can prevent GOITER; the order is not the same as for VITAMIN C:SCURVY. The order for RICKETS:CALCIUM is different than for VITAMIN C:SCURVY. The PLAGUE is carried by fleas on infected RATS; the analogy is not the same as for VITAMIN C:SCURVY.

10.    (B)
ANALOGOUS (similar) and PARALLEL (closely similar) are synonyms. ACIDULOUS (sour) and SACCHARINE (sickeningly sweet) are not synonyms so (A) is incorrect. SINUOUS and TORTU-OUS both mean curving, winding. The two are synonymous and, thus, the right answer. INCONGRUOUS means dissimilar; it is an antonym to HOMOGENEOUS, which suggests similarity. (C) is wrong. A PUNDIT is an expert, while a TYRO is a novice. Since the two are antonyms, (D) is not, therefore, the correct answer. MUNDANE is common, everyday; CELESTIAL refers to heavenly. Because MUNDANE is opposite from CELESTIAL, (E) should not be se-lected.

11.    (B)
A CAPPELLA means without instrumentation — the opposite of ORCHESTRA. PROFANATION (mistreatment of something holy) is similar to DESECRATION. Since the two are synonyms, (A) should

not be selected. STERILE can mean without children; MULTIPA-ROUS means producing many at birth. The two are opposites and, therefore, the right answer. PROLETARIAN (the common people) and IGNOBLE (of low birth) are quite similar in meaning. (C) is, therefore, wrong. EMOLUMENT (profit from a job; a salary; a fee) is closely related to RECOMPENSE (compensation, a return for something done). The two do not have the same analogy as A CAPPELLA:ORCHESTRA. (D) is not the best choice. IMPERIOUS (arrogant, overbearing) and PEREMPTORY (an insistence on an immediate response to one's demands) are quite similar in meaning. (E) is a poor choice.

12.   (A)
SPLENETIC (fretful) and IRRITABLE (very susceptible to anger) are similar. IRASCIBLE (implies an inflammable temper) and PEEVISH (fretful) are similar in meaning. (A) is the correct choice. PROPITIATING (placating for the sake of good will) and IRRESOLUTE (undecided) are not synonyms; (B) is not the correct choice. CANT (to tilt, to slant) bears no apparent relationship to CULPABLE (deserving blame). (C) should not be chosen. SPITEFUL (filled with or showing spite, malicious) and PACIFY (to calm, to appease) are antonyms and should not be selected. INFLAME (to intensify) and APPEASE (to calm, mitigate) are antonyms. (E) is an incorrect choice.

13.   (A)
ASSUAGE and MELIORATE are synonyms meaning to alleviate. In (A), MITIGATE and AMELIORATE both mean to make less; they are synonyms. (A) is the correct answer. EQUIVOCATE (to prevaricate, to lie) and PROGNOSTICATE (to foretell, to foresee) are not synonyms like the analogy sought. (B) should not be selected. To CASTIGATE (to punish, reprove) and to PREVARICATE (to lie, to equivocate) are not synonymous. (C) should not be selected. To ALLAY (to lessen) and to INUNDATE (to cover with, to flood, to overflow) are antonyms. (D) is an incorrect answer. Since MOLLIFY means to lessen and since RATIOCINATE means to reason, (E) should be excluded from the possible answers since the two are not synonymous.

14.   (B)
A SPELUNKER explores CAVES. The analogy is the worker (hobbyist) with the thing he/she explores, works with, or collects. In

(A), since a CONDUCTOR is a MAESTRO, the analogy is not the same as that in SPELUNKER:CAVE. (A) is not the correct answer. A PRESTIDIGITATOR works with MAGIC. (B) is the correct answer. A PURLOINER (one who steals) is not directly related to PARISH. (C) is not the best choice. A NUMISMATIST collects coins — not BOOKS. (D) is incorrect. A CURATOR (an overseer, a keeper, a custodian) is not necessarily related to COINS. (E) should not be selected.

15.   (C)
APOTHEOSIZE (to glorify or deify) and CANONIZE (to glorify, to exalt, to declare a deceased person a saint) are synonymous. To DEPRECATE is to disapprove with regret; SERVILE (of or pertaining to a slave) do not have the synonymous relationship sought so (A) should not be selected. SMORGASBORD suggests an abundance of something — especially food. PALTRY indicates a minimum amount. Since the two are antonyms, (B) should not be selected. PERMEATE and PERVADE are synonyms meaning to spread or diffuse itself through. (C) is, therefore, the correct answer. A SINECURE is a job with little work; an ABERRATION is the act of deviating — especially from what is right. (D) is not the best answer. SPECIOUS (plausible but false) and COMPLAISANT (amiable) do not have the synonymous relationship sought. (E) is not an appropriate choice.

16.   (A)
The -oy in BOY is a DIPHTHONG, two vowels which are both sounded. The word GRASS contains a BLEND (two consonants which come together and which are both sounded). (A) is correct. There is a DIGRAPH (two vowels or consonants which make only one sound) in the word MEAT, but the order is not the same as for BOY:DIPHTHONG. (B) is incorrect. There is no DIGRAPH in CAT. (C) is incorrect. There is a BLEND in BLIND, but the order is not the same as for BOY:DIPHTHONG. (D) is incorrect. Since there is no DIPHTHONG in BIRD, (E) should not be selected.

17.   (D)
Not all cacti are without leaves so (A) is not the correct answer. Cacti are usually without leaves; cacti are indigenous to the Western

316

Hemisphere. (B) is incorrect. Flowers on a cacti usually emerge from the top, not the base. (C) is incorrect. (D) is the correct answer. (E) is a true statement, but it is not a statement that BEST distinguishes cacti from other succulents.

18. (E)
(A) This title is too broad; only cacti and succulents are studied here. (B) This title is not accurate. Regions of the world is not the primary topic of the passage. (C) The passage deals with more than just distinguishing between cacti and succulents. (D) This title limits too much. (E) is the correct answer.

19. (E)
For (A), the writer never implies that cacti are to be chosen over other succulents. The wording of the question ("Cacti are to be chosen over succulents...") implies that cacti are not themselves succulents. (A) is not the best answer. The author does not suggest that they are to be left in the wild; the writer actually states that they are excellent subjects for a garden, greenhouse, or windowsill. (B) is incorrect. The author implies that they are excellent subjects for botanists or the home gardener. (C) is incorrect. Both feature interesting adaptations, but the author does not state that one is preferred over the other. (D) is incorrect. (E) is the correct answer.

20. (B)
In (A), the move itself has not caused cacti and other succulents to possess structural modifications. Again, the wording should be "Cacti and other succulents...." (A) is not the best choice. (B) is the correct answer. Not only does (B) contain a cause-and-effect answer, but also it is a true statement. Since all cacti are not indigenous to Africa and a few scattered parts of the Eastern Hemisphere, this cause-and-effect statement (C) is an incorrect choice. The globular and columnar forms of cacti actually offer a smaller surface area and, hence, lessen the area exposed to the drying effects of the sun and the wind. (D) is incorrect. Since cacti and other succulents require minimum care if they have requisite sunlight and if their condition of hardiness is respected, (E) is false and not the best answer.

21.  (B)

(A) is not the best answer. After a statement about the sunlight and hardiness, it does not logically follow that a section on the flowers would come next. A discussion of the fact that cacti and other succulents are generally able to withstand rapid changes in temperature does logically follow. (B) is a suitable answer. A discussion of artists and their using cacti and other succulents as studies does not seem to flow from the preceding line about hardiness and sunlight. (C) is not an appropriate answer. A reference to a movie does not seem to logically follow after the section on greenhouses, gardens, and hardiness. (D) should not be selected. References to the original location and structural modifications of the cacti do not seem to fit logically at this point. A better place would seem to come earlier in the passage for such an inclusion. (E) is not the best answer.

22.  (E)

For (A), this statement is not implied by the passage; nothing suggests that cacti require less care. The author does not indicate that the shape of cacti is more appealing than that of other succulents. (B) is incorrect. The author does not indicate that succulents from one hemisphere do not adapt well to the other, or vice versa. (C) is not the best answer. The flowers of cacti do not appear between the leaves or at the base. (D) is incorrect. (E) is the correct answer.

23.  (A)

The dictionary definition of corm is (A) — a short, bulblike, upright stem, usually found underground.

24.  (E)

Considering the author's fondness for cacti and other succulents, he would probably view laws to protect them with UNDERSTAND-ING (E).

25.  (D)

(A) is an incomplete answer. Jefferson certainly did design Monticello, but that is not all that he designed. The Declaration of Independence was also designed by him. (A) should not be selected. Again,

the answer is true but it should not be selected because it is only a partial one. (B) is incorrect. Jefferson did not design the Jefferson Memorial. (C) is incorrect. He did, however, design Monticello which appears on the reverse of the Jefferson nickel. (D) is a true answer and the best choice for this question. Jefferson is not given credit in the passage for designing the Constitution of the United States. (James Madison is known as the "Father of the Constitution.") (E) is not, therefore, the best answer.

26. (C)

(C) is the only correct answer. The article states "After that date [1968], it [the mintmark] was moved to the right of Jefferson's wig." Since Jefferson's profile is on the obverse side, (C) is the answer to be chosen. (A) is incorrect since Monticello is on the reverse side. The mintmark is to the right of Jefferson's wig after 1968. Monticello is on the reverse side, but the mintmark is located to the right of Jefferson's wig after 1968. (B) is incorrect. Jefferson is on the obverse (not the reverse) side. (D) is incorrect. (E) is a false statement. Mintmarks appear on all U.S. coins including those minted after 1968. (E) should not be selected.

27. (A)

The dictionary defines unalienable rights as those rights not capable of being bought or sold so (A) is the correct answer. Unalienable rights are those which belong to all, not just Americans. (B) is incorrect. Jefferson believed unalienable rights to be rights of all people — not just Americans. (C) is incorrect. Unalienable rights include life, liberty, and the pursuit of happiness. (D) is not the best answer. Jefferson believed all people had basic rights — not just Americans. These rights he believed to be life, liberty and the pursuit of happiness. (E) is inappropriate.

28. (B)

AVOCATION (not to be confused with VOCATION) means hobby. For (A), a RESPITE is a putting off, a postponement, a delay. It is not the opposite of AVOCATION and (A) should not be selected. A PROFESSION is an occupation, a trade. It is the opposite of AVOCATION and (B) the correct answer. Since SILENT means

quiet, (C) is not the best answer. A hobby is an interest to which one gives spare time. It is synonymous with AVOCATION and (D) should not be selected. An AVULSION is a forcible separation. (E) is not the correct answer.

29.   (C)

ADULTERATED means corrupted, debased, made impure. RIBALD means offensive, irreverent, or vulgar. Since (A) is synonymous with ADULTERATED, it should not be selected. DEFILED means contaminated, corrupt, polluted. Since it is synonymous with ADULTERATED (B) should not be selected. CHASTE means pure in thought and action. It is the opposite of ADULTERATED and is the correct answer. INFANTILE means childish. Since it is not the opposite of ADULTERATED, (D) should not be selected. VICIOUS means spiteful, malicious, evil, wicked. Since it is not the antonym of ADULTERATED, (E) should not be chosen as the correct answer.

30.   (E)

TACITURN means silent, uncommunicative. In (A), RETICENT means habitually silent. Since it is a synonym for TACITURN, (A) is incorrect. APPEASED means satisfied, made calm, quiet. (B) is wrong. RESERVED means restrained, in control, silent; (C) is synonymous and not the right answer. INVEIGLED means enticed. Since it is not the opposite of TACITURN, (D) should not be selected. EFFUSIVE means overly demonstrative, gushing, unrestrained. It is the antonym and should be selected.

31. (A)

AUGMENTATION means expansion, enlargement, dilation. In (A), CONSTRICTION is the antonym and the correct answer. ACCESSION means an increase, an addition. It is synonymous with AUGMENTATION and (B) should not be selected. EXPANSION means the act of increasing in size. It is synonymous with AUGMENTATION and (C) should not be chosen. PERTURBATION is the state of being disturbed. It is not the opposite of AUGMENTATION. (D) is not the correct choice. SATIATION is the act of satisfying fully, glutting. (E) is not the best choice as the opposite of AUGMENTATION.

**32. (E)**
CANAILLE is a mob, a pack, the lowest class of people, the rabble. An AGGREGATE is a mass, a body, a sum total. (A) is not the opposite of CANAILLE. FULGURANT means resembling lightning. (B) is obviously not the opposite of CANAILLE. FULMINATION means the act of attacking suddenly. (C) is not the correct choice. A BRIDGE is a structure built across a river, road, etc. so that people or objects of transportation can get across. (D) is not the right answer. ARISTOCRACY (the upper class) is the opposite of CANAILLE. (E) is correct.

**33. (B)**
ASININE means stupid. FATUOUS means foolish. (A) is synonymous with FATUOUS and should not be chosen. CUNNING is the antonym and (B) the correct answer. IDIOSYNCRATIC means the following of one's own peculiar temperament. (C) should not be chosen as the best answer. ECCENTRIC means diverges from the unusual. (D) is not the best answer. ANTITHETIC means showing clear opposition to; it is not the opposite sought and (E) should not be selected.

**34. (E)**
SAGACIOUS means shrewd. SHREWD is synonymous with SAGACIOUS and (A) should not be selected as the correct answer. ASTUTE means sagacious, shrewd. Since it is a synonym and not an antonym, (B) should not be selected as the correct answer. PROCUMBENT means lying down. (C) is not the antonym sought for SAGACIOUS. DUCTILE is the quality of that which can be drawn out at will. Since it is not an antonym for SAGACIOUS, (D) should not be selected. INCAPABLE means not efficient, not capable, not able. It is the antonym for SAGACIOUS and the correct answer.

**35. (A)**
SUBLIMINAL implies an unawareness. CONSCIOUS means wholly conscious, existing, felt. It is the antonym for SUBLIMINAL and (A) should be selected. SUBVERSIVE is that which ruins or overthrows. It is not an antonym for SUBLIMINAL. (B) is incorrect. A TERMAGANT is a quarrelsome woman; it is unrelated to SUBLIMINAL. (C) should not be chosen. TURPIDITY is depravity. Since

it is not the antonym for SUBLIMINAL, (D) should not be chosen. EXPLICIT means to unfold or explain, which is not the opposite sought.

36.  (B)

BEATIFIC means manifesting bliss, joy. ANIMALISTIC means like an animal. The person who selected (A), this incorrect answer, probably thought erroneously that BEATIFIC comes from the word beast. MELANCHOLY means sad. It is the opposite of BEATIFIC and (B) is the correct answer. URBANE means civilized. The person who chose this as the correct answer probably thought that BEATIFIC came from the word beast. (C) is an incorrect choice. CIVILIZED means educated, refined. It is not the opposite of BEATIFIC and (D) should not be selected. SIMILITUDE means like a copy. (E) is incorrect.

37.  (E)

TURGID implies a fullness, as with air. AGGRESSIVE means having the disposition to dominate. It is not the opposite of TURGID and (A) should not be selected as the correct answer. TUMID, like TURGID, implies having a fullness. It is a synonym for TURGID and (B) is not the antonym sought. BILIOUS means ill-tempered, suffering — as from too much bile. (C) is not the opposite of TURGID. PALPABLE means readily seen, heard, or felt; obvious. Since it is not the opposite of TURGID, (D) should not be selected. DEFLATED is the antonym, or opposite, of TURGID. DEFLATED means reduced the amount of, to let the air out, reduced. (E) is correct.

38.  (A)

TRANSCENDENT implies an above average standing. AVERAGE is the antonym and, hence, (A) the right answer. SUPERLUNAR is being above the moon, not of this world. Since it is not the antonym sought, (B) should not be selected. SUSPENSION means the act of holding for a time, hanging. It is not the opposite and, hence, (C) not an appropriate answer. VERMICULATED means formed with irregular lines or impressions. It is not directly related to TRANSCENDENT and (D) is not the correct choice. STERLING implies an above average standing; it is synonymous with, not an antonym for, TRANSCENDENT. (E) is not the correct choice.

# Section 2–Verbal Ability

**1.   (C)**
VELLUM (a type of paper) fits the sentence, but EDICT (procla-
mation) is not appropriate so (A) should not be selected. STATION-
ARY is an adjective which means not movable; it should not be
confused with the writing paper called STATIONERY. AFFECT is a
verb; it clearly does not fit the second blank which requires a noun. (B)
is incorrect. STATIONERY is a type of writing paper; EFFECT is a
noun meaning result. (C) is the correct answer. PARCHMENT (a type
of paper) fits the sentence, but OBLIGATION appears out of context.
(D) is incorrect. BOND is a type of paper and fits the first blank, but
EFFIGY (statue) does not appear suitable for the second. (E) is wrong.

**2.   (C)**
PROFICIENT implies competency above the average. It is most
often used in describing people so (A) is incorrect. EFFUSIVE means
too emotional; (B) does not fit the sense of the sentence. EFFECTUAL
means having the power to produce the exact effect or result. (C) is
correct. Both CAPABLE and COMPETENT refer to people, not
things. Neither (D) nor (E) are correct.

**3.   (D)**
For (A), DIFFIDENCE suggests timidity — a trait which might not
be characteristic of a researcher who leaves the research facility unattended. Since GENERATION means production, (A) does not logically fit; the production of water would not leave the containers dry.
FINESSE implies skill, cunning. It does not seem to apply to the first
blank. MAGNETIZATION means the act of giving the properties of
a magnet to something. Since it does not reasonably follow that water
can be magnetized with empty containers resulting, (B) is wrong.
TRAVAIL implies labor, pain, toil; the word does not logically fit
blank one. CONDESCENSION (not to be confused with CONDEN-
SATION) does not fit the meaning of the sentence; CONDESCEN-
SION means patronizing or pleasantness to inferiors. (C) is incorrect.
APLOMB implies self-assurance — probably characteristic of a
researcher who leaves his appointed place during an experiment.
EVAPORATION means changing a liquid or solid into vapor; (D) is

correct. SOLICITUDE means excessive care or attention — a descriptive term which does not seem appropriate to describe a researcher who leaves his experiment. CONDENSATION in physics means the act or process of reducing from one form to another and denser form, as steam to water. It does not logically follow that condensation of pure water would result in dry containers. (E) is wrong.

4.    (A)

IGNOMINY (shame, disgrace) and DISQUALIFICATION fit the blanks in the sentence well. (A) is correct. FAME (being very well-known — a positive term) does not fit blank one very well. ACCOLADES (praise and recognition, awards) is not appropriate either. (B) is incorrect. HUMILIATION (mortification) fits well in blank one. It does not follow, however, that an ELEGY (a poem for the dead) would result. (C) is incorrect. NOTORIETY (ill fame) might certainly follow the cheating incident, but a EULOGY (a speech or writing in praise of a person) is not a logical consequence. (D) is not an appropriate choice. EMINENCE (distinction, prominence) does not normally result from cheating. CONTEMPT (disdain) is a somewhat better choice than EMINENCE; nevertheless the pair should not be selected. (E) is incorrect.

5.    (C)

An ILLUSION is an appearance that is not real; INSURE means to make safe. Answer (A) is not the best choice. ELUSION is the act of evading, not to be confused with ALLUSION, which is a reference to something. ASSURE means to make sure or certain. (B) is incorrect. An ALLUSION is a reference to; ENSURE means to make certain. (C) is the right answer. A DELUSION is a false notion; CONSTRUE means to understand. (D) is incorrect. An ALLOTMENT is a share; to REASSURE is to restore to confidence. (E) is incorrect.

6.    (A)

SANGUINE (hopeful) and CORROBORATE (verify) fit the blanks very well. (A) is the correct answer. MEDDLESOME (interfering in others' affairs) does not fit well in blank one — especially to describe an accused person. When coupled with SUBSTANTIATE (confirm), (B) is clearly not the best answer. CONJUGAL (pertaining

to marriage) clearly does not belong in blank one. REVOKE (to repeal) could not, therefore, be chosen as a correct answer. This pair of words should not be selected. GARBLED (scrambled, even deliberately mixed up to achieve a result) might best describe a story, an account, a letter — not a person. Since it would be difficult to AUTHENTI-CATE (verify as true) a garbled "person," (D) is not the best answer. CONCUPISCENT (lustful) and ABOLISH (to do away with) do not fit logically in the sentence. (E) should not be selected.

7.    (D)
GAUDINESS (brightness, showiness) is not a good description of a flannel suit. CHASTE (modest, pure, virtuous) might fit blank one, but when coupled with GAUDINESS, so (A) is not the best choice. LACONIC (brief, as a brief speech which is to the point) is not a good description of a gold-studded suit. OPULENCE (rich, abundant, afflu-ent) does not accurately describe most flannel suits. (B) is incorrect. RESERVED is not the best modifier for a gold-studded costume; neither is SAVOIR-FAIRE (tact — a noun) best for describing a flannel suit. (C) is inappropriate. ORNATE (much adorned, much ornamented) seems an appropriate adjective for a gold-studded cos-tume. SIMPLICITY characterizes most flannel suits. (D) is the best answer. FEUDAL (pertaining to the feudal system) does not accu-rately describe a gold-studded costume; RAUCOUSNESS (hoarse-ness) does not characterize a flannel suit. (E) is wrong.

8.    (E)
DISPARAGEMENT implies the act of detracting from someone. LAUDATION (the act of praising) is its antonym. For (A), SUB-TRACTION (the act of taking away) and FARCICAL (laughable) are not antonyms. Answer (A) is not appropriate. EUPHEMISM (the sub-stitution of a milder phrase or word in place of one which might cause offense) is not an antonym for DEFAMATION (the act of slandering). (B) is not the best answer. PRATTLE is idle talk with no purpose. SLANDER is the act of detracting from reputation. Since the two are not antonyms, (C) is not the best answer. EULOGY (a laudation) is the synonym of ENCOMIUM (warm or high praise). (D) is not the correct answer. CONMENDATION is the act of praising. DETRACTION is the act of taking away one's good name. The two are antonyms and (E) is the correct answer.

9. (E)

A GAUNTLET is a protective device for the HAND. For (A), a CANNON is not a protective device for the BALL. (A) is not the correct answer. A SWORD is not a protective device for the HAND. (B) is an incorrect answer. A SHIELD does protect the BODY, but it is an inverted analogy. (C) is incorrect. A SHIELD is a protection against a LANCE; this is not the analogy sought. (D) is incorrect. ARMOR does protect the BODY. (E) is the correct answer.

10. (B)

A DEFICIT is the result of PECULATION (the act of embezzling). For (A), ATTIRE is synonymous for DRESS, so (A) is not the correct answer. HUNGER is the result of ABSTINENCE. (B) is the correct answer. APPEAR and MANIFEST are synonymous verbs. The analogy is not that sought. (C) is incorrect. FAMINE is the result of DROUGHT; the order is inverted, however. (D) is incorrect. A MAGISTRATE is very similar to a JUDGE; this is not the analogy sought, however. (E) is incorrect.

11. (C)

PHOTOTROPISM means to TURN toward the light. (Notice the second part of the word is given in the last part of the analogy.) For (A), POLTROON (cowardly) and VALIANT (brave) are antonyms — not the relationship sought. (A) is incorrect. Since TEMPERATURE is the meaning of the prefix of THERMOTROPISM (TROPOISM-to turn), the order is not the same as that in PHOTOTROPISM:TURN. (B) is not the best answer. -SYNTHESIS means FORMATION. The analogy is the same as that in PHOTOTROPISM:TURN. (C) is the correct answer. LITHOGRAPHY means writing (-GRAPHY) on STONE (LITHO-). The order is not the same as that in PHOTOTROPISM:TURN; (D) should not be selected. Both BOLD and IMPUDENT imply daring and bravery. They are similar in meaning; their relationship is not, therefore, the same as that of PHOTOTROPISM:TURN. These two synonyms are an inappropriate choice and should not be selected as the correct choice.

12. (C)

PUGILISM means fighting with the FISTS. FISTS are necessary to PUGILISM, In (A), a LEXICOGRAPHER is one who works with

words, one who writes a dictionary. There is no direct relationship between a LEXICOGRAPHER and ANIMALS. (A) is an inappropriate choice. GYNECOLOGY is a branch of medical science that deals with the functions and diseases peculiar to women; it is not directly related to GENES. (B) is inappropriate. NEPOTISM is a term relating to RELATIVES; for instance hiring family to fill positions in a business is called NEPOTISM. (C) is the correct choice. ARCHEOLOGY is a study of the people, customs, and life of ancient times; archeologists may excavate, classify, and study the remains of ancient cities, tools, monuments, or other records that remain. It is paleontology (not archeology) that is a study of FOSSILS. (D) is an incorrect choice. PEDIATRICS is a branch of medicine dealing with children's diseases and the care of babies and children. It is geriatrics which is the science which deals with the study of the AGED and their diseases. (E) is incorrect.

13.   (C)
OBVIOUS and APPARENT are synonyms suggesting something that is evident to the beholder. For (A), the PLAINTIFF brings charges against a defendant. The BAILIFF is an officer, perhaps of the court. The two are not necessarily related. (A) should not be selected. OBTRUSIVE (meddlesome) and DISCERNIBLE (capable of being perceived or seen clearly) do not have the same relationship as the synonyms OBVIOUS:APPARENT. (B) should not be selected. Both MANIFEST and EVIDENT imply being apparent; (C) is correct. DIM means not bright, not clear. PATENT (as in PATENT leather) can mean bright, glossy; the two, then, would be antonyms. Since their relationship is not the same as OBVIOUS:APPARENT, (D) is wrong. TRANSLUCENT means light-penetrable; an OPAQUE substance is unpenetrated by light. The two are antonyms. (E) is an incorrect choice.

14.   (B)
An EDIFICE is a building; a FACADE is the front part of a building or any part that faces a street or other open area. A FACADE, then, is the outer part of an EDIFICE. For (A), DORSAL is on, of, or near the back; VENTRAL is of or having to do with the belly — usually the opposite of DORSAL. Since this opposite relationship is not the same as that between EDIFICE:FACADE, (A) should not be chosen. Since the SHELL is the outer covering of a TURTLE (just as a

FACADE is the outer part of an EDIFICE), (B) is the correct answer. ANACHRONISM is the act of putting some thing, person, or event where it does not belong. CHRONOLOGIC, like chronological, means arranged in the order in which the events happened. The two are opposite in meaning; they do not fit the pattern of EDIFICE:FACADE. (C) is incorrect. A SKELETON is the inner (not the outer) part of the body. (D) should not be selected since the two words do not have the same relationship as do EDIFICE:FACADE. COUNTERFEIT and FRAUDULENT are two words which are synonymous. (E) is incorrect.

15. (C)
   (A) is a correct definition, but the order is not the same as FIVE-SIDED:PENTAGON. (A) should not be selected. Again, a DECAGON is a TEN-SIDED figure, but the order is not the same as for FIVE-SIDED:PENTAGON. (C) is correct. If (D) was selected, the reader probably confused HECTOGON with hexagon — which is a six-sided figure. HECTO- means one hundred, not six. The meaning of (E) is correct, but the order is not the same as in FIVE-SIDED:PENTAGON. (E) is incorrect.

16. (E)
   CHINTZ is made from cotton, not silk, so (A) is incorrect. MADRAS is made from cotton, not LINEN. (B) is wrong. RAYON is not made from PLASTIC but from cellulose. (C) is incorrect. NYLON is made from COAL, but the order does not duplicate LEATHER:FLAX. (D) is incorrect. CHAMOIS is a soft cloth made from LEATHER. (E) is correct.

17. (D)
   DISCURSIVENESS means rambling, shifting from one subject to another. Lincoln was very clear in that he believed that the South should be pardoned and that unity should be restored so (A) is incorrect. ACERBITY implies harshness, severity; this is certainly not the manner in which Lincoln recommended treating the South so that unity could be achieved. (B) is wrong. Since RECALCITRATION implies disobedience, it does not describe Lincoln's attitude toward the South; it is unsuited to the sentence. (C) is incorrect. EXCULPATION means an excusing — exactly the attitude that Lincoln thought best to use toward the South to bring about unity. (D) is correct.

OBTUSE means stupid, slow in understanding, dull; these words seem unfit in describing Lincoln or his attitude toward the problems of a divided nation. (E) is incorrect.

18.  (C)

Question 18 is an interpretive question, the answer to which is not stated but only implied in the passage. The Lincoln Memorial was dedicated in 1922. It took two years after Lincoln died for plans to be begun on a monument to honor the President, the passage tells the reader. Then another 55 years passed before the monument was completed. If one subtracts the two years and the 55 years (the time it took to complete the monument) from 1922 (the year it was dedicated) the answer is 1865. This means that 1865 (C) is the correct answer and the other answers (1863, 1864, 1866, and 1867) should be ignored.

19.  (D)

The author describes the War as "senseless." (A) is false. The "senseless" war merits no respect from the author. (B) is incorrect. The author is not objective toward a "senseless" war in which "father fought son." (C) is not the correct choice. DISSATISFACTION is the best choice. (D) is correct. The writer is not indifferent. (E) is wrong.

20.  (D)

This question is an interpretive question since to figure out the answer one must have knowledge of the word SESQUICENTENNIAL, which means 150 years. In (A), Lincoln's portrait is not on the reverse side. It is on the obverse side. (A) is incorrect. The wheat is not on pennies minted in 1959 and after. (B) is false. The Lincoln Memorial in Washington, DC (not Arlington National Cemetery) graces the reverse side. (C) is inappropriate. (D) is correct. The Lincoln Memorial, not the seated statue of Lincoln, is found on the reverse side. (E) is incorrect.

21.  (D)

This idea came from the Gettysburg Address and not from Lincoln's Second Inaugural Address so (A) is incorrect. This came from the Gettysburg Address. (B) is wrong. The explanation of the wheat symbol came from the article — not Lincoln's Second Inaugural

Address. (C) is incorrect. (D) is true. (E) is not a portion of the address as given in the article.

22.  (E)

To answer this question correctly, one must be able to use the terms CENTENNIAL and SESQUICENTENNIAL since they are used in several of the answers. (A) The article tells the reader the wheat penny was struck to celebrate the 100th anniversary of Lincoln's birth. (A) is wrong. The penny was changed in 1959 to celebrate the 150th anniversary of Lincoln's birth, the article states; (B) is incorrect. The Lincoln Memorial was dedicated in 1922. (C) should not be chosen. The Memorial was not dedicated as the site of a national cemetery. (D) is incorrect.

23.  (C)

For (A), the writer does not use PROFESSIONAL DETACH-MENT in this passage. He seems very pro-Lincoln. He expresses that the face of Lincoln on the lowly Cent is actually inspiring. (A) should not be chosen. SKEPTICISM implies doubt — certainly not an acceptable answer. (B) should not be chosen. The author's attitude toward Lincoln's portrait appearing on the lowly Cent is GRATI-TUDE for the inspiration it provides. (C) is the best answer. The author does not refer to Lincoln or to the portrait appearing on the penny with superiority or CONDESCENSION. (D) is not the best answer. Since the author offers no SPECULATION or forseeing when referring to the portrait on the Cent, (E) should not be selected.

24.  (A)

(A) is correct. (B) is wrong. The author called it a "senseless war." The author seems to admire Lincoln; since Lincoln disagrees with this statement, the author probably would also. (D) is false since Lincoln urged peace. (E) is false because the author believes the lowly Cent is very appropriate.

25.  (E)

(A), PERSONAL DISSATISFACTION toward wind energy con-version systems is not the predominant mood in the passage. The writer

gives both the good and the bad points in using such a system. (A) should not be selected. UNQUALIFIED ENTHUSIASM is not the writer's feeling toward the wind conversion system; the writer keeps an open mind and informs the reader of the strengths and weaknesses of the wind energy conversion system. (B) is not an acceptable answer. The very fact that the writer takes the time to write the passage negates the possibility that DISINTEREST is the prevailing mood in the article. (C) should not be selected. (D) NEGATIVISM is not the tone of the article. Rather, the writer presents an objective view (both good and bad points) of the wind energy conversion system. (E) OPEN-MINDEDNESS is the correct answer since the writer appears completely objective in the treatment and expressed feelings toward the wind energy conversion system.

26. (B)

Since the TOWERS and ROTORS are already mentioned in the sentence, the only part remaining would be the enclosed part which contains the generators; these third parts are called the nacelles. (B) is the only correct answer.

27. (A)

(A) is the correct answer. NOISE (B) is no problem since the rotors are practically noiseless. The MANY LINES are classified under esthetics. SAFETY and ESTHETICS are covered in this answer, but interference with radio and television reception is not mentioned. (C) is incorrect. Since there is no thermal pollution, (D) is incorrect. Again, THERMAL POLLUTION is not applicable; (E) is incorrect.

28. (E)

FACTIOUS means inclined to dispute. BELLICOSE means aggressive. It is not the opposite of FACTIOUS; (A) should not be selected. DESULTORY means without plan. It is not directly related to FACTIOUS and should not be selected as the opposite. FORTUITOUS means accidental. It is not the opposite of FACTIOUS and should not be selected. FRACTIOUS means troublesome. It is similar in meaning (not opposite from) FACTIOUS. FELICITOUS means pleasant. It is the opposite of FACTIOUS. (E) is the correct answer.

29.  (D)

CONSONANCE means agreement. In (A), CONSCIENCE is the sense of the moral goodness of one's own conduct. It is not related to CONSONANCE. (B) CONSCIOUS means aware, sensible. It is unrelated to CONSONANCE. (C) COALESCE is synonymous with BLEND (which suggests a mixing). (D) CONTENTION suggests argument. CONSONANCE suggests harmony, agreement, accordance. CONTENTION is the opposite of CONSONANCE. (D) is the opposite and the correct answer. (E) CONSIGN is to commit, to entrust. It is not related to CONSONANCE and should not be selected.

30.  (B)

EFFEMINATE is marked by weakness, softness, and ease. TORTUOUS means winding. It is not the opposite of EFFEMINATE; (A) should not be selected. VIRILE means masterful, forceful; it is the opposite of EFFEMINATE. (B) is the correct answer. ASCETIC means self-denying. It is not the opposite of EFFEMINATE. (C) should not be selected. CONTEMPTUOUS means scornful. It is not the opposite of EFFEMINATE. (D) is not the correct answer. (E) AVERSE means disinclined. Since it is not the opposite of EFFEMINATE, it should not be selected as the correct answer.

31.  (B)

PROBITY is tried and proven honesty. For (A), AESTHETICS is a sense of beauty. It is not the opposite of PROBITY and should not be selected. (B) PERFIDY is faithlessness. It is the opposite of PROBITY and should be selected as the right answer. (C) ABEYANCE is the act of suspending. It is not the opposite of PROBITY and, hence, should not be chosen. Since (D) PREDILECTION is the act of having positive feelings toward something, it should not be selected as the opposite of PROBITY. (D) is incorrect. (E) COMPLEMENTARY is serving to fill out or complete; it can also mean mutually supplying each other's lack. (E) is not the opposite of PROBITY and should not be selected as the correct answer.

32.  (A)

FACTITIOUS means artificial, a sham. For (A), AUTHENTIC means genuine, real. It is the opposite of FACTITIOUS and, hence, the

correct answer. (B) TRAVESTY is an imitation. It is synonymous with (not an antonym for) FACTITIOUS. (B) should not be selected as the correct answer. (C) PEDANTIC means in a manner that makes a display of learning. Since it is not the opposite of FACTITIOUS, it should not be selected as the correct answer. (D) MORDANT means biting or stinging. It is not directly related to FACTITIOUS and should not be selected as the correct answer. (E) RAPACIOUS means grasping. Since it is not the opposite of FACTITIOUS, it should not be selected as the correct answer.

33. (E)
STENTORIAN means loud. (A) STYPTICAL means producing a contraction of a blood vessel; astringent; stopping bleeding. It is not the opposite of STENTORIAN and should not be selected as the correct answer. (B) EGREGIOUS means of an outside group. It is not directly related to STENTORIAN. (B) should not be selected as the correct answer. (C) INVIDIOUS is used to describe a character such that it cannot be used without causing ill will. Since (C) is not directly related to STENTORIAN, it should not be selected as the right choice. (D) VOCIFEROUS means making a loud outcry. (E) SUBDUED means quiet. It is the opposite of STENTORIAN and is the correct answer.

34. (D)
PAUCITY means a lack. In (A), DEARTH is a scarcity. It is not an antonym for PAUCITY; actually it is more like a synonym. (A) should not be selected as the correct answer. (B) LOQUACIOUS means talkative. It is an incorrect choice. (C) SANATIVE (an adjective) means curative, healing. It is not a correct answer choice. A (D) PLETHORA is a vast amount, a great excess. It is the opposite of PAUCITY and the correct choice. (E) LUGUBRIOUS means mournful. It is not an appropriate choice.

35. (A)
AUDACIOUSNESS means disrespectful. (A) COMPLAISANCE (politeness, courtesy) is the antonym for AUDACIOUSNESS. The correct answer is (A). (B) FASTIDIOUSNESS means the act of being difficult to please, delicate to a fault. The word is not the exact opposite of AUDACIOUSNESS so (B) should not be selected. (C) IMPERTI-

NENCE is the act of exceeding the bounds of propriety. It is more synonymous than antonymous with AUDACIOUSNESS. (C) should not be selected. (D) IMPUDENCE is the act of being bold, blunt, pert; rather than being an antonym for AUDACIOUSNESS, the word is a synonym. (D) should not be chosen as the correct answer. (E) INSOLENCE is the act of being insulting and overbearing. It is definitely not the opposite of AUDACIOUSNESS and should not be chosen as the correct answer.

36.   (E)

VENIAL means excusable. (A) HEDONIC means pertaining to pleasure. It is not antonymous with VENIAL. (B) INEFFABLE means indescribable, difficult to put in words. It should not be selected as the opposite of VENIAL. (C) PECCADILLO means small offense. The person who selected this answer was probably thinking that a PECCADILLO is excusable. The answer sought, however, is the opposite of VENIAL. (C) should not be selected. (D) IMPLACABLE means not of a nature to be placated, appeased easily. It does not fit the pattern sought. (D) is incorrect. HEINOUS means abominable, outrageous. Since it suggests inexcusable behavior, (E) is the correct answer.

37.   (A)

ABSTRUSE means difficult to understand. (A) PERSPICACIOUS means plain to the understanding. It is the opposite of ABSTRUSE and (A) is the correct answer. (B) MERETRICIOUS means in a cheap showy way. It is not the antonym for ABSTRUSE. (B) is wrong. LUGUBRIOUS means looking or sounding profoundly sad. It is not the opposite of ABSTRUSE. (C) is incorrect. INSIDIOUS means alluring but dangerous. (D) should not be selected. INCONGRUOUS means incompatible. (E) is not the right answer.

38.   (D)

PRODIGAL is an adjective meaning given to extravagant expenditures. For (A), WANDERING (roving, roaming) does not relate to PRODIGAL; (A) should not be selected. TARRYING (staying) does not relate to PRODIGAL; (B) is incorrect. SPENDTHRIFT (squandering) is synonymous with PRODIGAL so (C) is incorrect. FRUGAL (saving) is the opposite of PRODIGAL and so (D) is the correct answer. LAVISH (spending with profusion; squandering) is synonymous with PRODIGAL. (E) should not be chosen.

# Section 3—Quantitative Ability

1.  (B)

Notice that $w$, $x$, and $y$ are all positive values and that $w = x$. Now replace $w$ with $x$ in the equation $w + x + y = 20$ and solve for $y$ as follows:

$$
\begin{aligned}
w + x + y &= 20 \\
x + x + y &= 20 \\
2x + y &= 20 \\
y &= 20 - 2x
\end{aligned}
$$

Since $x$ and 10 are being compared, assume that $x$ has a value of 10. Then the expression $y = 20 - 2x$ means that $y = 20 - 2x = 20 - 2(10) = 0$. So, $y = 0$ when $x = 10$ leads to a contradiction since $y$ is given to be positive. Thus, $x$ must be smaller in order for $y$ to be positive. Hence, the quantity in Column B is larger.


2.  (A)

Since $\sqrt{9} = 3$ and $\sqrt{7} > 2$, then it is clear that $\sqrt{9} + \sqrt{7} > 5$. But, $\sqrt{16} = 4$. So, the quantity in Column A is greater than the quantity in Column B.


3.  (C)

Observe that the number 0 is an integer and it is also an even integer because it is divisible by 2. Also, observe that zero is the largest even integer smaller than 2. Thus, the quantities in both columns are equal.


4.  (C)

Consider the triangle $ABD$ and the exterior angle $C$. Recall that one of the basic theorems of geometry indicates the following relation between an exterior angle and certain interior angles of a triangle. That is, the exterior angle of a triangle is equal to the sum of the two nonadjacent interior angles. Note that angles $x$ and $y$ are nonadjacent interior angles relative to angle $C$. So, the following holds:

$$\angle x + \angle y = \angle C \text{ and thus, } \angle y = \angle C - \angle x.$$

Hence, the quantities in both columns are equal.

5.    (A)

Triangles *AEF* and *ACD* are similar since sides *CD* and *EF* are parallel. Thus, corresponding sides are proportional. So, *CD* is to *EF* as *AD* is to *AF* or simply *CD/EF = AD/AF*. Since *AD = DF = 3*, then *AF = 6*. Thus,

$$\frac{CD}{EF} = \frac{AD}{AF} \quad \text{or} \quad \frac{4}{EF} = \frac{3}{6} \quad \text{or} \quad 3EF = 24 \quad \text{or} \quad EF = 8.$$

So the quantity in Column A is greater than the quantity in Column B.

6.    (B)

To determine the area if the equilateral triangle one needs to know the length of one of three equal sides of the triangle and a formula for finding its area. Since the triangle is equilateral with a perimeter of 30 units, then each side, *s*, of the triangle is 10 units.

The formula for finding the area of an equilateral is given by:

$$A = \frac{s^2\sqrt{3}}{4},$$

where *s* denotes the length of a side of an equilateral triangle.

Since *s* = 10 units, then the area of the equilateral triangle (the quantity in Column A) is as follows:

$$A = \frac{10^2\sqrt{3}}{4} = \frac{100\sqrt{3}}{4} = 25\sqrt{3} \text{ units}.$$

So Column B is greater than Column A.

7.    (B)

First factor the left-hand side of each equation as follows:

$$y^2 + 12y + 27 = (y + 9)(y + 3) = 0$$
$$\text{and } x^2 - 12x + 27 = (x - 9)(x - 3) = 0.$$

Notice that the factors are similar except for the signs. However, to compare the values of *y* in Column A with those of *x* in Column B, one needs to solve each of the equations as follows:

$$(y + 9)(y + 3) = 0 \qquad\qquad (x - 9)(x - 3) = 0$$

| $y + 9 = 0$ | $y + 3 = 0$ | $x - 9 = 0$ | $x - 3 = 0$ |
|---|---|---|---|
| $y = -9$ | $y = -3$ | $x = 9$ | $x = 3$ |

Hence, the quantity in Column B will always be greater than the quantity in Column A no matter which value of $y$ or $x$ is chosen.

8.  (B)

Observe that if an integer is less than $-1$ then it is negative and its reciprocal is also a negative rational number. However, the reciprocal is larger than $-1$. For example, consider the integer $-2$. Its reciprocal is $-\frac{1}{2}$ which is larger. Thus, the quantity in Column B is larger than the quantity in Column A.

9.  (C)

One must simplify each of these expressions before a comparison can be made. Thus,

$$1 + \frac{1}{t} = \frac{t}{t} + \frac{1}{t} = \frac{t+1}{t} \text{ and } \frac{1}{t} / \frac{1}{t+1} = \frac{1}{t} \times \frac{t+1}{1} = \frac{t+1}{t}$$

Hence, the quantities in both columns are equal.

10.  (A)

First simplify the equation by multiplying through by 2 to obtain $x - y = 6$. Then, solve the resulting equation for $x$ to obtain $x = 6 + y$. Hence, $x$ has to be the largest value since it is always 6 units greater than $y$. So, the quantity in Column A is greater.

11.  (C)

To determine the value of each quantity one needs only to simplify the expressions and substitute as follows:

$$(2WY)^2 = 2^2 W^2 Y^2 = 4(4)^2 (-2)^2 = 4(16)\,(4) = 256$$
$$\text{and } (2Y)^2\,(4W) = 2^2 Y^2 (4W) = 4(-2)^2(4)\,(4) = 4(4)(4)(4) = 256.$$

Hence, the quantities in both columns are equal.

12.  (D)

Simplify the inequality in order to determine the value of $x$ in Column B. To achieve this one should first add the opposite of 1 throughout the inequality, followed by dividing by 2 throughout the resulting inequality as indicated below.

$$-1 \leq 2x + 1 < 2$$
$$-1 + (-1) \leq 2x + 1 + (-1) < 2 + (-1)$$
$$-2 \leq 2x < 1$$
$$-2/2 \leq 2x/2 < 1/2$$
$$-1 \leq x < 1/2$$

In the last inequality the value of $x$ may be either 0 or $-1$ since $x$ must be an integer. Hence, the quantities in the columns cannot be compared.

13.   (C)

Since $m$ and $n$ are parallel lines cut by the transversal $t$, then angles $a$ and $c$ are corresponding angles. Thus, one can conclude that angle $a$ = angle $c$. Because of this equality, the expression in Column B may be simplified by replacing $\angle a$ with $\angle c$ as follows:

$$\angle b + \angle c - \angle a = \angle b + \angle c - (\angle c) = \angle b + 0 = \angle b.$$

Hence, the quantity in Column B is equal to the quantity in Column A.

14.   (C)

Since line segment $BA$ equals line segment $BC$, triangle $ABC$ is isosceles. Thus, according to a well known theorem the angles $BAC$ and $BCA$ are equal. Since angles $x$ and $y$ are supplementary angles to $BAC$ and $BCA$, respectively, it is clear that

angle $x$ + angle $BAC$ = 180° and angle $y$ + angle $BCA$ = 180°.

But, since angle $BAC$ = angle $BCA$ one can conclude that angle $x$ = angle $y$. So, the quantities in the columns are equal.

15.   (C)

The average of the quantity in Column A is $(18 + 20 + 22 + 24 + 26)/5 = 110/5 = 22$. Also, the average of the quantity in Column B is $(17 + 19 + 21 + 23 + 25 + 27)/6 = 132/6 = 22$. So, the quantities are equal in both columns.

16.   (B)

$$4\frac{1}{3} - 1\frac{5}{6} = 4\frac{2}{6} - 1\frac{5}{6}$$

$$= 3\frac{2+6}{6} - 1\frac{5}{6}$$

$$= 3\frac{8}{6} - 1\frac{5}{6}$$

$$= 2\frac{3}{6} = 2\frac{1}{2}.$$

**17. (C)**

Let $x$ be the length of the rectangle. Then, a 30% increase in the length of the rectangle is given by $x + .3x$. Let $y$ be the width of the rectangle. Then, a 20% decrease in the width of the rectangle is given by $y - .2y$. The original area is given by $A = xy$ and the new area is given by:

$$
\begin{aligned}
A &= (x + .3x)\,(y - .2y) \\
  &= xy - .2xy + .3xy - 0.06xy \\
  &= xy + 0.04xy \\
  &= 1.04xy
\end{aligned}
$$

So, the new area is 104% of the original area which is a $104\% - 100\% = 4\%$ increase, which is answer choice (C). The other answer choices are found by either using the perimeter formula or incorrectly finding the increase and decrease in the length and width, respectively.

**18. (D)**

In the equation or formula one must first apply the distributive property on the right-hand side as follows:

$$
\begin{aligned}
A &= P\,(1 + rt) \\
A &= P + Prt
\end{aligned}
$$

The next step is to add the opposite of $P$ to both sides of the equation as indicated below.

$$
\begin{aligned}
A &= P + Prt \\
A + (-P) &= P + Prt + (-P) \\
A - P &= Prt
\end{aligned}
$$

Finally, divide both sides of the equation by $Pr$ to obtain the value of $t$ as follows:

$$
\begin{aligned}
(A - P)/Pr &= Prt/Pr \\
(A - P)/Pr &= t.
\end{aligned}
$$

Hence, the answer choice (D) is correct. The other answer choices may be obtained by incorrectly applying algebra properties in solving the equation or formula for $t$.

**19.** **(D)**
Examine the graph and observe that the highest plotted point on the graph directly above 1975 is about 2,200.

**20.** **(B)**
Observe that the amount of remedial enrollments in 1970 is 200 thousand. Since the total undergraduate enrollments for 1970 was about 1,900 thousand, one need only form a ratio as follows to find the percent.

$$\frac{200}{1,900} = \frac{2}{19} \text{ or } 10.5\%.$$

**21.** **(D)**
To find the percent of increase one need only to use the following formula:

$$\text{Percent of increase} = \frac{(\text{amount of increase})}{(\text{original amount})} \times 100$$

Thus,

$$\text{Percent of increase} = \frac{(800 - 200)}{(200)} \times 100$$

$$= \frac{600}{200} \times 100$$

$$= 300\%.$$

**22.** **(B)**
Notice that in 1980 the total amount of the precalculus and below enrollments was over the 1,600 thousand level.

**23.** **(D)**
The only category of enrollments in the graph which shows the least amount of variance from year to year is the advanced course enrollments. Notice that the line that represents this category is about

the same distance from the calculus level enrollments for each year in the graph.

24.   (B)
   First, group the expression and then find the monomial factor for each group as follows:

$$(x^2 + ax) + (-2x - 2a) = x(x + a) + (-2)(x + a).$$

Then, the final factorization is formed by using $(x + a)$ and $(x - 2)$. So,

$$x^2 + ax - 2x - 2a = (x - 2)(x + a).$$

Notice that multiplying these two factors together will yield the original algebraic expression. So, (B) is the correct answer choice. The other answer choices are incorrect because when the factors are multiplied together in each case, the results do not yield the original algebraic expression.

25.   (C)
   Take the square root of both sides of the equation to form two first equations and solve each for $x$ as follows:

$$\sqrt{(4x-3)^2} = \sqrt{4} \qquad \text{and} \qquad \sqrt{(4x-3)^2} = -\sqrt{4}$$
$$4x - 3 = 2 \qquad\qquad\qquad 4x - 3 = -2$$
$$4x = 2 + 3 \qquad\qquad\qquad 4x = -2 + 3$$
$$x = \tfrac{5}{4} \qquad\qquad\qquad\qquad x = \tfrac{1}{4}$$

Hence, the values of $x$ are $^5/_4$ and $^1/_4$, respectively, which is answer choice (C). Notice also that answer choices (A) and (B) each satisfy the original equation, but two values of $x$ are required since the equation is quadratic. The values in the other answer choices do not satisfy the original equation.

26.   (C)
   Observe that to find the product the following multiplications should be done.

$$(\sqrt{3} + 6)(\sqrt{3} - 2) = \sqrt{3}(\sqrt{3} - 2) + 6(\sqrt{3} - 2)$$
$$= 3 - 2\sqrt{3} + 6\sqrt{3} - 12$$
$$= -9 + 4\sqrt{3}.$$

27.  (D)
First add 5 to both sides of the equation and then square both sides as follows:

$$\sqrt{5x - 4} - 5 + 5 = -1 + 5$$
$$(\sqrt{5x - 4})^2 = 4^2$$
$$5x - 4 = 16$$
$$5x = 16 + 4$$
$$5x = 20$$
$$x = 4.$$

28.  (D)
The easiest way to determine the result for this problem is to represent the unknown ages, set up an equation, and solve it. Begin by letting $x$ = age of Susan now. Then, $2x$ = the age of Jim now. The next step is to represent Jim's age 4 years ago and Susan's age 3 years from now. Thus, $2x - 4$ = Jim's age 4 years ago. Then, $x + 3$ = Susan's age 3 years from now. Finally an equation can be set up by noting that the age represented by $2x - 4$ differs from the age represented by $x + 2$ by 12 years. So, the equation is given by the following:

$$(2x - 4) - (x + 3) = 12.$$

Solving for $x$ one gets
$$2x - 4 - x - 3 = 12$$
$$x - 7 = 12$$
$$x - 7 + 7 = 12 + 7$$
$$x = 19, \text{ Susan's age now.}$$
$$2x = 38, \text{ Jim's age now.}$$

The sum of their ages (19 + 38) is 57.

29. **(B)**

Let $x$ = Joe's marbles, $y$ = Jim's marbles and $z$ = Tim's marbles. It is given that:

$$x + y = 14 \quad (1)$$
$$y + z = 10 \quad (2)$$
$$x + z = 12 \quad (3)$$

Solve equation (2) for $y$ and equation (3) for $x$. Then substitute their values in equation (1) and solve for $z$.

$$y + z = 10 \implies y + z - z = 10 - z \implies y = 10 - z$$

and

$$x + z = 12 \implies x + z - z = 12 - z \implies x = 12 - z$$

Thus,

$$
\begin{aligned}
x + y = 14 \implies (12 - z) + (10 - z) &= 14 \\
- 2z + 22 &= 14 \\
- 2z + 22 + (-22) &= 14 + (-22) \\
- 2z &= -8 \\
z &= 4, \text{Tim's marbles.}
\end{aligned}
$$

Now substitute the value of $z$ in equations (2) and (3), respectively, and solve. The results are:

$$
\begin{aligned}
y + z = 10 \implies y + 4 - 4 &= 10 - 4 \\
y &= 6, \text{Jim's marbles.}
\end{aligned}
$$

and

$$
\begin{aligned}
y + z = 12 \implies x + 4 - 4 &= 12 - 4 \\
x &= 8, \text{Joe's marbles.}
\end{aligned}
$$

Joe's marbles, 8, is the maximum number of marbles anyone can have.

30. **(C)**

The difference between the first two numbers is 4 $(6 - 2)$; the difference between the second and third numbers is 6 $(12 - 6)$ which is two more than the first difference; the difference between the third and fourth numbers is 8 $(20 - 12)$ which is two more than the second difference; the difference between the fourth and fifth numbers is 10 $(x - 20)$. Thus, the value of $x$ is given by $x - 20 = 10$. Solving for $x$ yields $x = 30$. So, the correct answer choice is (C). Similar analysis of each of the other choices will fail to satisfy the missing value of $x$ such that it is a consistent distance in relation to the other numbers in the series.

# Section 4—Quantitative Ability

**1.    (B)**
    Consider the quantity given in Column B, $(x + y)^2$. Performing the indicated operation yields,

$$(x + y)^2 = (x + y)(x + y)$$
$$= x^2 + 2xy + y^2$$
$$= x^2 + y^2 + 2xy$$

Since both $x$ and $y$ are positive integers it follows that both $xy$ and $2xy$ are positive quantities (positive times positive equals positive). Hence, whatever the value of $x^2 + y^2$ is, the quantity in Column B, $(x + y)^2 = x^2 + y^2 + 2xy$, is greater than the quantity in Column A, $x^2 + y^2$.

**2.    (C)**
    Label the vertices of the given triangle $A, B, C$, and let $y°$ represent the measure of angle $ABC$ (the third interior angle of the given triangle) as shown in the figure.

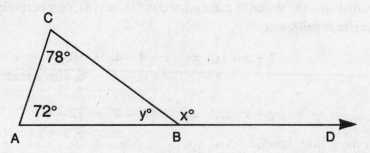

Note that angle $DBC$ is an exterior angle of triangle $ABC$. Since the measure of an exterior angle of a triangle is equal to the sum of the measures of the two non-adjacent angles of the triangle, it follows that

$$x = 78 + 72$$
$$= 150.$$

So the quantities in Columns A and B are equal.
    Another way to attack this comparison problem is to recall that:
    (i)    The sum of the measures of the three interior angles of a triangle is equal to $180°$.
    (ii)    The sum of the measures of two supplementary angles is equal to $180°$.
    In our problem, angles $ABC$ and $DBC$ are supplementary angles. Hence, $x + y = 180$.

Now;

$$78 + 72 + y = 180 \text{ (Note (i) above)}$$
$$150 + y = 180$$
$$x + y = 180 \text{ (Note (ii) above)}$$

Hence, $\qquad$ $150 + y = x + y$ which implies $x = 150$.

3.   (A)

After the 30 inches long candle burns for 12 minutes, it becomes 25 inches long. This means that 5 inches of the candle have burned out in 12 minutes.

To find the total time it takes the whole candle (30 inches long) to burn out, a direct proportion can be used. Let $x$ be the total time the whole candle burns. Then the appropriate proportion is

$$\frac{\text{number of inches burn out } y}{\text{number of inches burn out } x} = \frac{\text{burning time } y}{\text{burning time } x}$$

In this problem, we have

$$\frac{5}{12} = \frac{30}{x}$$

Solving this proportion for $x$, we obtain

$$5x = (30)(12)$$
$$5x = 360$$
$$x = {}^{360}/_5$$
$$x = 72$$

Thus, the whole candle burns out in 72 minutes. So, the quantity in Column A is greater.

4.   (C)

Since $t$ and $l$ are intersecting lines, it follows that $x + z = 180$ (the sum of the measures of two supplementary angles is 180°. Because lines $l$ and $m$ are parallel and $t$ is a transversal, it follows that $z = y$ (corresponding angles have equal measures).

Now:

$$x + z = 180$$
$$y = z$$

Hence, $x + y = 180$. Subtracting $x$ from both sides of this equation yields $y = 180 - x$.

So the two quantities in Columns A and B are equal.

345

5.    (D)

In the quantity, $\dfrac{x^2 - y^2}{x^3 - x^2 y}$, the numerator can be factored as $x^2 - y^2 = (x - y)(x + y)$, and the denominator can be factored as $x^3 - x^2 y = x^2(x - y)$. Hence,

$$\frac{x^2 - y^2}{x^3 - x^2 y} = \frac{(x - y)(x + y)}{x^2(x - y)}$$

$$= \frac{x + y}{x^2} \quad (\text{since } x - y \neq 0).$$

Since no other information is given about the value of $x$ or $y$, the relationship is indeterminate. For example, if $x = 2$ and $y = -3$, then

$$\frac{x + y}{x^2} = \frac{2 + (-3)}{(2)^2} = \frac{-1}{4} = -\frac{1}{4}, \text{ and}$$

$$\frac{x + y}{y} = \frac{2 + (-3)}{-3} = \frac{-1}{-3} = \frac{1}{3}.$$

So the quantity in Column B is greater.

However, if $x = 1$, and $y = -1$, then

$$\frac{x + y}{x^2} = \frac{1 + (-1)}{1} = 0, \text{ and } \frac{x + y}{y} = \frac{1 + (-1)}{-1} = 0$$

So the two quantities in Columns A and B are equal.

6.    (A)

From the diagram in question 6, $a > c, d > b$. Adding these two inequalities, one obtains

$$a + d > b + c.$$

So the quantity in Column A is greater.

7.    (B)

One way to attack this comparison problem is to simply solve the given inequality for the variable $x$. Thus,

$$1 - 2x > x - 5$$
$$1 + 5 > x + 2x$$
$$6 > 3x$$
$$2 > x$$

So the quantity in Column B is greater.

8.    (D)

Since $x$, $y$ and $z$ are integers, it follows that $x$, $y$ and $z$ could be positive or negative. If $y$ is negative, then $z$ is negative, and $x$ could be positive or it could be negative. In either case, we get $^x/_y < ^z/_y$. For example, if $y = -3$, $z = -6$, and $x = 6$, then,

$$x > y > z; ^x/_y = ^6/_{-3} = -2; ^z/_y = -(^6/_3) = 2;$$

and $^x/_y < ^z/_y$. Also, if $y = -6$, $z = -12$, and $x = -3$, then

$$x > y > z; ^x/_y = ^1/_2; ^z/_y = -(^{12}/_6) = 2;$$

and again $^x/_y < ^z/_y$.

However, if $y$ is positive, then $x$ is positive, and $z$ could be positive or negative. In either case, $^x/_y > ^z/_y$. For example, if $y = 10$, $x = 20$, and $z = 5$, then

$$x > y > z; ^x/_y = ^{20}/_{10} = 2; ^z/_y = ^5/_{10} = ^1/_2; \text{ and } ^x/_y > ^z/_y.$$

Thus, since no specific information is given about $x$, $y$ and $z$, the relationship between the two quantities given in Columns A and B is indeterminate.


9.    (A)

The average, $\bar{x}$, of any set of observations (scores) is equal to the sum of all observations divided by the number of observations, $n$.

$$\bar{x} = \frac{\text{sum of all observations}}{n}.$$

In this problem, the average of 28 scores is 80, this means $\bar{x} = 80$ and $n = 28$. Thus,

$$80 = \frac{\text{sum of all 28 scores}}{28}$$

which yields,

$$\text{sum of all 28 scores} = 80 \times 28$$
$$= 2240.$$

If two more students take the test and score 60 and 50, then the number of scores will be $28 + 2 = 30$, and the sum of all 30 scores will be $2240 + 60 + 50 = 2350$. Hence, the average of all 30 scores, $\bar{x}$, is given by

$$\bar{x} = \frac{\text{sum of all 30 scores}}{30}$$

$$= \frac{2350}{30} = 78.333...$$

Now Column A is equal to 78.333..., and the quantity in Column B is equal to

$$\frac{80 + 60 + 50}{3} = 63.333...$$

So the quantity in Column A is greater.

10.  (C)
   Area of a parallelogram is equal to the product of the length of any of its sides and the length of the perpendicular segment drawn from the opposite vertex to that side or the line containing that side.
   In this problem, segment $\overline{AD}$ is one of the sides of the parallelogram $ABCD$, and segment $\overline{BE}$ is perpendicular to line $\overline{AE}$ of which segment $\overline{AD}$ is a subset (line $\overline{AE}$ contains side $\overline{AD}$).
   Hence, area of the parallelogram $ABCD$ is equal to (the length of $\overline{AD}$) × (length of $\overline{BE}$). Thus,

$$\text{Area} = (5 \text{ cm}) \times (8 \text{ cm})$$
$$= 40 \text{ cm}^2.$$

So the two quantities in Columns A and B are equal.

11.  (D)
   With the exception of the restrictions on $a$ and $b$ given in the center, $a \neq -1$, $b \neq 0$, and $a \neq b$, no information is given about the value of $a$ or $b$. Hence, the relationship between the two quantities in Columns A and B in indeterminate. For example, if $a = 2$, and $b = 3$, then,

$$\frac{a}{b} = \frac{2}{3} \quad \text{and} \quad \frac{a+1}{b+1} = \frac{2+1}{3+1} = \frac{3}{4}.$$

In this case, the quantity in Column B is greater. But if $a = 3$, and $b = 2$, then

$$\frac{a}{b} = \frac{3}{2} \quad \text{and} \quad \frac{a+1}{b+1} = \frac{3+1}{2+1} = \frac{4}{3}.$$

In this case, the quantity in Column A is greater.
   So the relationship cannot be determined from the information given.

12.  (B)
   The comparison in this problem can be easily established by

simply evaluating the quantity $\dfrac{|x|+2|y|}{5+(-4)}$, given in Column B, when

$x = -4$, and $y = 2$. This gives

$$\frac{|x|+2|y|}{5+x}=\frac{|-4|+2|2|}{5+(-4)}=\frac{4+4}{5-4}=\frac{8}{1}=8$$

Recall: the absolute value of a real number, $x$, is given by

$$|x|=\begin{cases} x \text{ if } x \geq 0 \\ -x \text{ if } x < 0. \end{cases}$$

Thus, $|-4| = -(-4) = 4$, and $|2| = 2$. So the quantity in Column B is greater.

13. **(C)**
"Percent" means the number of parts per 100. Thus,

$$4.5\% = \frac{4.5}{100} = \frac{45}{1000}.$$

Reducing this fraction $(^{45}/_{1000})$ to its lowest terms yields

$$\frac{45}{1000} = \frac{9}{200}.$$

So the two quantities are equal.

14. **(A)**
One strategy to solve this problem is to calculate Gail's salary this year as compared with her salary last year as follows:

Let $\$x$ represent Gail's salary last year. Since she received a 7% increase over last year's salary, it follows that her salary this year is equal to $\$x + 7\%$ of $\$x$. Thus,

$$\begin{aligned} x + 0.07x &= 15{,}515 \\ 1.07x &= 15{,}515 \\ x &= 15{,}515/1.07 \\ &= 14{,}500. \end{aligned}$$

So the quantity in Column A is greater.

Another strategy that can be used to solve this problem is to take 7% of the quantity in Column B, $14,000, and add it to $14,000. If the final result is $15,515, then the two quantities are equal. If the final result is less than $15,515, then the quantity in Column B is greater.

Thus, 7% of $14,000 + 14,000 = (0.07)(14,000) + 14,000$

$$= 980 + 14,000$$
$$= 14,980.$$

which is less than 15,515. Hence, Gail's salary last year was more than $14,000.

15.  (B)

From the figure in question 15, quadrilateral *ABCD* is a rectangle. Thus, its area is equal to the product of its length, *l*, and its width, *w*.

$$\text{Area} = l \times w$$
$$= a(b - a)$$

But *b* is greater than *a* implies that $b(b-a)$ is greater than $a(b-a)$. So the quantity in Column B is greater.

16.  (D)

Since we do not know Emile's dollar volume during the week in question, we can assign this amount the value of *x*.

Now, Emile's total salary of $540 can be divided into two parts; one part is his flat salary of $240, and the other part is his salary from commissions which amounts to $540 − $240 = $300. This part of his salary is equal to 12% of his dollar volume, x. Thus, 12% of $x = \$300$. This means

$$(0.12)x = 300$$
$$x = 300/0.12 = \$2500.$$

Another way to attack this problem is to test each answer choice as follows:

(A)     (0.12) ($2800)  = $345.60 ≠ $300        (wrong)
(B)     (0.12) ($3600)  = $432 ≠ $300        (wrong)
(C)     (0.12) ($6400)  = $768 ≠ $300        (wrong)
(D)     (0.12) ($2500)  = $300        (correct)
(E)     (0.12) ($2000)  = $240 ≠ $300        (wrong)

17.  (C)

The most direct method for attacking this problem is to solve the equation

$$T = 2\pi \sqrt{\frac{L}{g}}$$

for the variable *L*.

Thus, squaring both sides of this equation yields

$$T^2 = 4\pi^2 \frac{L}{g}$$

Cross multiplication yields

$$T^2 g = 4\pi^2 L$$

$$L = \frac{T^2 g}{4\pi^2}$$

18. **(B)**

This problem can be solved easily by simply using the fact that the sum of the measures of the three interior angles of a triangle is 180°. Thus,

$$
\begin{aligned}
(3x + 15) + (5x - 15) + (2x + 30) &= 180 \\
3x + 5x + 2x + 30 &= 180 \\
10x &= 180 - 30 \\
10x &= 150 \\
x &= 15.
\end{aligned}
$$

This gives us the measure of the
first angle  $= (3x + 15)° = (3 \times 15 + 15)° = 60°$
second angle  $= (5x - 15)° = (5 \times 15 - 15)° = 60°$
third angle  $= (2x + 30)° = (2 \times 15 + 30)° = 60°$.

19. **(D)**

With $n$ being the first odd number, it follows that $n + 2$ and $n + 4$ are the next two odd numbers. This eliminates answer choices (A) and (B) on the basis that each one of them represents only one of the two consecutive odd numbers that follow $n$. Since the sum of the three consecutive odd numbers is $n + (n + 2) + (n + 4) = 3n + 6$, it follows that neither of answer choices (C) and (E) is correct, which leaves answer choice (D) as correct.

20. **(E)**

This problem can be solved easily by performing the indicated operations. The indicated operations are addition and subtraction of rational expressions with unlike denominators. When adding and/or subtracting rational expressions with unlike denominators, we must express all expressions as fractions with the same denominator,

usually called the least common denominator. To find the least common denominator of a set of rational expressions,

(i)  Factor each denominator completely and express repeated factors as powers.

(ii)  Write each different factor that appears in any denominator.

(iii)  Raise each factor in step (ii) to the highest power it occurs in any denominator.

(iv)  The least common denominator is the product of all factors found in step (iii).

In this problem, denominators in factored form are:

$$1 = 1$$
$$x - 2y = (x - 2y)$$
$$x + 2y = (x + 2y)$$

Hence, all the different factors are $1$, $(x - 2y)$, and $(x + 2y)$. This gives us $1(x - 2y)(x + 2y)$ as the least common denominator.

Performing the indicated operations yields:

$$1 + \frac{y}{(x - 2y)} - \frac{y}{x + 2y} =$$

$$= \frac{(x - 2y)(x + 2y)}{(x - 2y)(x + 2y)} + \frac{y(x + 2y)}{(x - 2y)(x + 2y)} - \frac{y(x - 2y)}{(x - 2y)(x + 2y)}$$

$$= \frac{x^2 - 4y^2 + xy + 2y^2 - xy + 2y^2}{(x - 2y)(x + 2y)}$$

$$= \frac{x^2}{(x - 2y)(x + 2y)}$$

21.  (C)

This question can be answered by reading the graph directly. Data about contributions to Republican candidates is given by the pie graph at the right. The graph indicates that 32% of all contributions to Republican candidates came from trade, membership, and medical associations.

22.  (B)

Data about contributions to Democratic dandidates is given by the pie graph below. Reading the graph directly, we find out that 8% of all contributions to Democratic candidates came from the party.

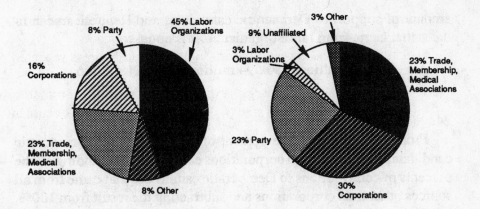

To find the dollar amount of support that corresponds to 8%, we need to calculate 8% of the total dollar amount of support to Democratic candidates. That is, we need to calculate 8% of $21.5 million. Hence, the average dollar amount of support to Democratic candidates that came from the party is equal to

$$(0.08) (\$21.5 \text{ million}) = \$1.72 \text{ million}$$

This eliminates answer choices (A), (C), (D), and (E) and gives answer choice (B) as the correct answer.

23.  (C)
From the pie graph above, the average percent of support to Democratic candidates that came from labor organizations is given as 45%, and from the pie graph at the right, the average percent of support to Republican candidates that came from labor organizations is given as 3%.

Hence, the average dollar amount of support to Democratic candidates that came from labor organizations is equal to

$$45\% \text{ of } \$21.5 \text{ million} = (.45) (\$21.5 \text{ million})$$
$$= \$9.675 \text{ million}$$

and the average dollar amount of support to Republican candidates that came from labor organizations is equal to

$$3\% \text{ of } \$19.8 \text{ million} = (.03) (\$19.8 \text{ million})$$
$$= \$0.594 \text{ million}$$

Thus, the difference, in millions of dollars, between the average dollar

amount of support to Democratic candidates and Republican candidates that came from labor organizations is equal to

$$\$9.675 \text{ million} - \$0.594 \text{ million} = \$9.081 \text{ million}.$$

24. (E)

From the pie graph, the percent of contributions to Democratic candidates that came from corporations can be found by adding all the percents of contributions to Democratic candidates that came from all sources other than corporations and subtracting the result from 100%. Thus,

$$100\% - (45\% + 8\% + 23\% + 8\%) =$$
$$= 1.00 - (0.45 + 0.08 + 0.23 + 0.08)$$
$$= 1.00 - 0.84$$
$$= 0.16 = 16\%.$$

25. (D)

Obviously, the total dollar amount of support for both Democratic and Republican candidates that came from corporations is equal to the sum of the dollar amount of support for Democratic candidates and the dollar amount of support for Republican candidates.

From the pie graph on the left, the percent of contributions to Democratic candidates that came from corporations is given as 16%, and the percent of contributions to Republican candidates that came from corporations is given as 30%.

Hence, the dollar amount of support for Democratic candidates that came from corporations is equal to

$$16\% \text{ of } \$21.5 \text{ million} = (0.16) (\$21.5 \text{ million})$$
$$= \$3.44 \text{ million}$$

and the dollar amount of support for Republican candidates that came from corporations is equal to

$$30\% \text{ of } \$19.8 \text{ million} = (0.30) (\$19.8 \text{ million})$$
$$= \$5.94 \text{ million}.$$

Thus, total dollar amount of support for both Democratic and Republican candidates that came from corporations is equal to

$$\$3.44 \text{ million} + \$5.94 \text{ million} = \$9.38 \text{ million}.$$

26.  (B)
This problem can be easily solved by simply translating the English statements into algebraic expressions. "The difference between the square of this number, $x^2$, and 21" can be written as: $x^2 - 21$. "Is the same as" means equal (=). "The product of 4 times the number" can be written as $4x$. Thus, the information in this problem can be written as follows:

$$x^2 - 21 = 4x.$$

Answer choice (A) is eliminated because the left-hand side of the equation $x - 21 = 4x$, gives the difference between the number $x$ and 21 and not the difference between the square of the number $x$ and 21. Answer choice (C) is eliminated because it gives the difference between 21 and 4 times the number $x$ is equal to the square of the number $x$. In addition, neither of the equations $x + 4x^2 = 21$, and $x^2 + 21 = 4x$ is equivalent to the equation $x^2 - 21 = 4x$, which was obtained by translating the English statements in this problem into algebraic expressions. Thus, answer choices (D) and (E) are also eliminated leaving answer choice (B) as the only correct choice.


27.  (D)
Area of a triangle is equal to one half the product of the length of its base (any one of its sides) and the length of its altitude (the perpendicular segment drawn from the opposite vertex to the base of the triangle or to the line containing the base of the triangle).

In this problem, side $\overline{AB}$ can be taken as the base of triangle $ABC$, and segment $\overline{CE}$ as its altitude. Hence area of triangle $ABC$ is equal to one half the (length of $AB$) × (length of $CE$) = 40 cm². 

In triangle $ABD$, side $\overline{AB}$ can be considered the base of the triangle and segment $\overline{DF}$ can be considered as its altitude. Hence,

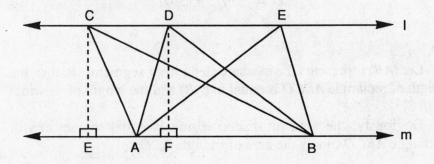

355

Area of triangle $ABD = 1/2$ (length of $\overline{AB}$) × (length of $\overline{DF}$).

Since lines $l$ and $m$ are parallel, and both of segments $\overline{CE}$ and $\overline{DF}$ are perpendicular to lines $l$ and $m$, it follows that $\overline{CE}$ and $\overline{DF}$ have the same length. Thus

Area of triangle $ABD = 1/2$(length of $AB$) × (length of $\overline{CE}$).

But $1/2$(length of $\overline{AB}$) × (length of $\overline{CE}$) = area of triangle $ABC$ which is equal to 40 cm³. Thus, the area of triangle $ABD$ is exactly 40 cm³.


28. **(A)**

One method for attacking this problem is to let $x$ be the number of cars that 14 robots can assemble in 45 minutes. Because the robots work at the same rate all the time, we can express this rate by using the information that 3 robots can assemble 17 cars in 10 minutes.

Now, if 3 robots can assembly 17 cars in 10 minutes, then 3 robots can assemble $^{17}/_{10}$ cars in 1 minute. Consequently, 1 robot assembles $^{1}/_{3}(^{17}/_{10})$ or $^{17}/_{30}$ of a car in 1 minute.

Similarly, if 14 robots assemble $x$ cars in 45 minutes, then the 14 robots assemble $^{x}/_{45}$ cars in 1 minute. Thus, 1 robot assembles $^{1}/_{14}(^{x}/_{45})$, or $^{x}/_{14(45)}$ of a car in 1 minute. Because the rates are equal, we have the proportion

$$\frac{x}{14(45)} = \frac{17}{30}$$

$$\frac{x}{630} = \frac{17}{30}.$$

Solving this proportion for $x$ yields,

$$30x = (630)(17)$$
$$= 10710$$
$$x = {}^{10710}/_{30} = 357.$$


29. **(C)**

Let $(AB)$ represents the measure (length) of segment $\overline{AB}$, then the length of rectangle $ABCD$ is equal to $(AB)$ and the length of its width is $(BC)$.

Obviously, the area of shaded region is equal to the area of rectangle $ABCD$ minus the area of triangle $EBC$.

Recall that the area of a rectangle is equal to the product of the measure of its length and the measure of its width. Thus,

Area of rectangle $ABCD = (AB)\,(BC)$

The area of any triangle is equal to $\frac{1}{2}$ times the measure of its base, (any side of the triangle), times the measure of its altitude (the length of the perpendicular segment drawn from the vertex opposite the base to that base or to the line containing the base). That is, the area of a triangle is equal to $\frac{1}{2}bh$.

Thus,

Area of triangle $EBC = \frac{1}{2}(EB)\,(BC)$.

But $(EB) = \frac{1}{4}(AB)$, hence,

$$\text{Area of triangle } EBC = \frac{1}{2}(\frac{1}{4}(AB))(BC)$$
$$= \frac{1}{8}\,(AB)\,(BC)$$

Since the area of triangle $ABC$ is equal to 12 square units, we have

$$\frac{1}{8}\,(AB)\,(BC) = 12$$

or

$$(AB)\,(BC) = 96.$$

But, $(AB)\,(BC)$ is the area of rectangle $ABCD$. Hence, area of rectangle $ABCD = 96$ square units.

Thus, area of shaded region $= 96 - 12 = 84$ square units.

30.  (E)
One way to attack this problem is to solve it algebraically.

Let $x$ represent the number of packages weighing 2 kg each. Then $(150 - x)$ represents the number of packages weighing 1 kg each.

Therefore,

$$2x + 1(150 - x) = 264$$
$$2x + 150 - x = 264$$
$$x = 264 - 150$$
$$x = 114.$$

Thus, there are 114 packages weighing 2 kg each on the truck.

Another way to solve this problem is to test each of the answer choices (A), (B), (C), (D) and (E). Note that if, for example, the number of packages weighing 2 kg each is 36 (answer choice (A)), then the number of packages weighing 1 kg each will be $(150 - 36) = 114$. Testing the answer choices yields:

(A)       $(36)(2) + (150 - 36)(1) = 72 + 114 = 186$     (wrong)
(B)       $(52)(2) + (150 - 52)(1) = 104 + 98 = 202$     (wrong)
(C)       $(88)(2) + (150 - 88)(1) = 176 + 62 = 238$     (wrong)
(D)      $(124)(2) + (150 - 124)(1) = 248 + 26 = 274$     (wrong)
(E)      $(114)(2) + (150 - 114)(1) = 228 + 36 = 264$     (correct)

# Section 5—Analytical Ability

1.    (B)

Mr. Elan has three decisions to make. Each decision becomes dependent on his previous choice. He can first select any one of 4 sport coats, thus his first decision includes 4 options. Any sport coat selection he makes limits his choice of trousers to 2 options. Thus, the combination of sport coats and trousers he can choose is $4 \times 2 = 8$. After making these first two choices he can then select from 3 ties that will coordinate with his previous two choices. Thus, each of his first two selections (of which there are 8 combinations) has three additional variations. Thus the total number of combinations available to him is $4 \times 2 \times 3 = 24$.

2.    (C)

When one sport coat is not available, then Mr. Elan can select from 3 (sport coats) $\times$ 2 (trousers) $\times$ 3 (ties) = 18. The reduction in combinations of attire is $24 - 18 = 6$. The answer could also be calculated by determining the number of combinations provided by one sport coat; $1 \times 2 \times 3 = 6$.

3.    (E)

No information was provided about the damaged tie to indicate if it coordinated with one or more of the coats remaining in Mr. Elan's closet.

4.    (A)

Adding another sport coat would provide him with a choice of 5 (sport coats) $\times$ 2 (trousers) $\times$ 3 (ties) = 30. He would add $30 - 24 = 6$ new combinations to his wardrobe. Or, you can multiply 1 (sport coat)

× 2 (trousers) × 3 (ties) = 6 to determine the result of adding one sport coat to the wardrobe.

5. (C);  6. (D);  7. (B);  8. (C)

It is important to identify the three stations which garments might pass through during the inspection process. Station 1 is staffed by inspectors who tag defective garments, station 2 is staffed by Supervisors A, B, and C who make salvage decisions, and Supervisor D who is the only one authorized to discard garments. After this understanding is clear, then you can recognize which garments may pass through one station (the inspector) if it is not defective, a second station (the supervisor) if it is defective but is not to be discarded, and a third station (Supervisor D) for a decision about discarding. The color coding will help you decide the routing of defective garments.

9. (B);  10. (A);  11. (D);  12. (C)

The answers in this series require attention to the conditions stipulated in the passage. The best way to answer each question is to examine each option and look for a violation of one or more of the following requirements:

1. Alphabetical order of letters
2. Descending order of numbers
3. Letters cannot be adjacent to each other
4. Code must end with letter
5. At least 3 letters and number in each code.
6. Code must start or end with letters or numbers that conform to the requirements. In item 10 choice C is wrong because the number 2 is the first number in the sequence and it would not be possible to include 3 digits in descending order unless the first number was 3 or higher.

13. (D);  14. (A);  15. (B);  16. (C)

A chart should be developed indicating the position of each runner at the half-way point in the race and their final standings. After constructing such a chart, the letter of the runners can be constructed as follows:

Half-Way  B F P E M D
Finish    M B E F P D

Since E finished two places ahead of the runner who ended in fifth place, E finished third. Since M finished two places ahead of E, M finished first. B finished behind M and ahead of E, therefore E was in second place. Since F finished two places ahead of D, D must be in last place and this leaves P to finish fifth.

17. (A)

Those who use data about criminal behavior to oppose physical punishment of children must establish that a cause-effect relationship exists between these two variables. Though other statements about disciplining children or about may be true and logical, unless the two variables of physical discipline and criminal behavior are related to each other, they do not provide a supporting argument for the position stated in the passage.

18. (C)

The central thrust of the passage is that natural events remove stifling underbrush that would otherwise prevent trees in the forest from reaching their potential growth. Only alternative (C) focuses specifically on this information. All other choices are tangential to or outside the meaning of the paragraph.

19. (A)

The question here is which of the statements can be directly traced to the information provided in the paragraph. If conclusions must be inferred, then their accuracy is diminished. It may be the case that drought causes harder trees or that some trees grow more slowly in arid lands than in rainy areas. However, these are generalizations that extend beyond the information in the paragraph. Only choice (A) can be concluded directly from the paragraph.

20. (D)

The fallacy of over-generalizing is the pitfall in this question. The correct answer (D) avoids the over-generalizing evident in the other responses and also allows for exceptions to the broad categories reported in the passage.

21. (D)

This is a case where a broad generalization may cause stereotyping and inclusion of more people in a category than will actually be the case. The fact that employment in the computer industry will increase does not mean that all other employment opportunities will either disappear or that the status in other positions will be affected.

22. (D)

The passage is an uncluttered statement that laser technology may help with treatment of cancer. The incorrect options all extend the initial passage with assumptions, knowledge, and generalizations that cannot be attributed to the paragraph itself.

23 . (E)

This question can be answered by identifying those events that would prevent John from capitalizing on his investment and deleting them as correct choices. When you read the question from this perspective, all of the choices except (E) would cause John's decision to be a mistake. In alternative (E), he is assuming the property will become valuable while he is still young enough and alive to benefit from the investment. The phrasing of alternative (E) calls for careful reading, however. The question is asked regarding which of the following is *not* supposed to happen and alternative (E) states the property will *not* become valuable until after he is too old or deceased. A good way to read this question is to change both statements to read positively: (1) which of the following is John assuming *will* happen and (2) the property will become valuable before he becomes too old or is deceased.

24. (B)

Only choices (A) and (B) relate directly to the passage. The others are inferences or biases sometimes held but unrelated to the information provided. Thus, the correct answer must indicate that the priorities can all be met or that some of them are in conflict. Since higher standards would make it difficult for more students to succeed in school, priorities 1 and 3 are in conflict. Thus, choice (B) is the best answer to this question.

**25. (C)**

A and B should not both attend the meeting since they have similar knowledge and should not duplicate their knowledge by both attending. D and C need to be at the same meeting, thus alternative C with A, D, and C is the only way to meet the requirements of committee attendance.

# Section 6–Analytical Ability

Questions 1 – 5.

Since all questions are conditional or "if", we can expect the original arrangement will not give a single definite answer. Question 1 uses only part of the information. Solve this first then move on to the others. Conditions I and II set up blocks that can be moved: The teachers' union with two seats and the administration with three, with an empty seat in the middle of the administration. Condition IV sets up three seats for the union mediator, with Sheets having an empty seat on either side.

**1. (C)**

The three conditions result in three blocks of 3,3,2. You cannot identify who is in each seat, but you can note that one administrator will sit next to one teachers' union representative. Choices (A) and (D) fail because IV states that

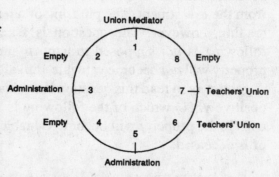

Sheets will have empty seats on either side of him. Option (B) fails because we do not know who will occupy which seat and (E) fails when (C) succeeds.

**2. (D)**

In this problem the union mediator will not have empty seats by him, but since III requires that the two parties be equally near the union mediator, the nearer member of each side will be seated next to the union mediator. Please note they could switch sides, this is significant

as the question asks about the clockwise ordering. The correct choice must violate the rules of I, II, or III. (D) is correct because it has two administrators sitting next to each other in violation of condition II. All of the others satisfy the conditions or rules.

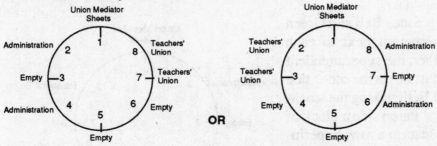

**OR**

3.   (A)

The superintendent sits opposite the union mediator, and all the other conditions apply as much as possible. Rules I and II take precedence because they say "always."

II and III could be met with teachers' union members either next to the union mediator or next to the superintendent. Thus I must be true, but II and III are false.

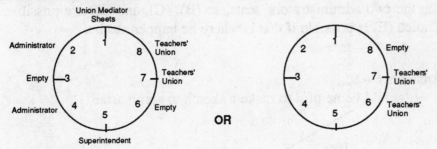

**OR**

4.   (B)

With the union mediator absent, all of the applicable conditions are still in force, which are I and II. III and IV do not apply since the union mediator is absent.

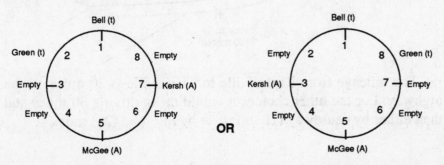

**OR**

363

There are only two possibilities because Kersch and Green would not sit next to each other, eliminating (A).

5.  (A)

Since Bell and Green always sit next to each other, the superintendent must be on the other side of Bell making the teachers' union side a block of 3 seats in a row: Superintendent, Bell, Green. But the superintendent could switch from one side of Bell to the other. With six

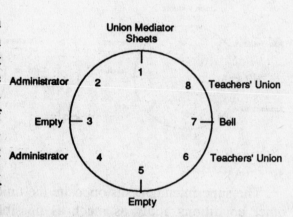

people there are only two empty chairs. One of the empty chairs must be between the two administrators, there cannot be empty chairs on both sides of the union mediator. (A) is not possible because the seat opposite Bell must be empty. The superintendent and Green are opposite the two administrators' seats, so (B), (C), and (D) are possible. Choice (E) is possible if that is where he happens to be.

Answers 6 – 9.

It would be helpful to make a sketch to summarize.

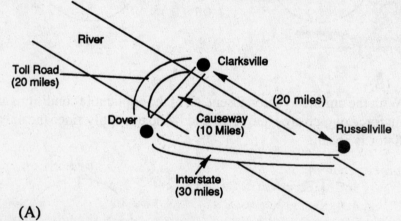

6.  (A)

The mileage from Russellville to Clarksville is 20 miles on the highway. For the other choices it would mean driving 30 miles and then either by causeway (10 miles) or by toll road (20) miles.

**7.    (D)**
The mileage on the interstate from Dover to Russellville is 30 miles. The other choices involve going to Clarksville by toll road or causeway then from Clarksville for 20 miles to Russellville.

**8.    (C)**
The difference in cost between the toll road and the causeway is negligible considering the possible saving in gasoline consumption, thus the most important factor would be traffic conditions.

**9.  (E)**
The extra charge for using the causeway can be compensated by the gasoline consumed on the extra 10 miles when crossing the toll road (IV). The gasoline efficiency can hardly account for the fuel used on 10 miles (III). The driver will be influenced by traffic and road conditions since tolls can be compensated by fuel consumption (I). Many passengers could possibly be a saving of money by using the toll road, if conditions are normal.

**Answers 10 – 14**
A diagram will be useful. List the two groups and connect with lines indicating what sort of connection is being made.

Math (must = 2)                    Education

**10.   (B)**
Work step by step. If Debbie takes human development, then geometry and learning theory are out. If geometry is out, then trigonometry and algebra are the two sciences that she must take. If algebra is scheduled, then educational psychology is out. This leaves choice (B). The other answers will include some subject not possible. (A) is not wrong because it lists the three math subjects, yet is incorrect because it cannot be scheduled with human development.

11.  (C)

If geometry is out, then algebra and trigonometry are required. Algebra precludes educational psychology and learning theory displaces human development, leaving answer choice (C). Choices (A) and (E) are impossible because they have both human development and learning theory. (B) is out because educational psychology cannot be taken with algebra. (D) cannot be scheduled since it has both learning theory and human development which cannot be combined.

12.  (E)

Taking one of the non-math courses eliminates one of the math courses from consideration, thus requiring the other two math courses. II is a trap that says since neither learning theory nor geometry can combine with human development, they must combine with each other. It is possible to have a curriculum of learning theory, trigonometry, algebra, and teaching methods.

13.  (E)

I is the same trick as II in Problem 12. II must be true since educational psychology eliminates algebra, and requires the other two math courses. III need not be true since a curriculum of geometry, algebra, teaching methods, and learning theory is but one example.

14.  (E)

With Debbie taking trigonometry, now scheduled at the same time as human development, she cannot take human development, geometry, or learning theory because they overlap with the new trigonometry time. Only educational psychology may be taken, plus teaching methods. This means that only three courses can be taken (E), though two math courses can still be taken. This eliminates (A). Options (B), (C), and (D) are eliminated by the schedule.

15.  (D)

Ms. Franklin's sole grounds are the example of the two other companies that are like hers, (D). She never suggests the cause of the low profits (A). We do not know that the argument she presents was previously overlooked (B). Mr. Green's reasoning (C) has none of the flaws discussed. Opposing Mr. Green is not the same as questioning his competence (E).

16. (A)

Ms. Franklin uses an analogy. Mr. Green's most effective rebuttal would be to undermine the strength of the analogy. He could point out significant differences between the two situations that are supposed to be alike. This is done in choice (A). In choice (B), this is an assertion of his expertise, and (C) is a statement of his argument. Choice (D) suggests that Ms. Franklin's argument may be weak. Option (E) does not even attempt a rebuttal.

17. (A)

Statements I and II combine to give us (A). If all wheeled conveyances which travel on the highway are polluters, and a bicycle does not travel on the highway, then a bicycle cannot be a polluter. If (A) is correct, (B) must be incorrect because bicycles do not travel on the highways at all. Options (C) and (D) make the same mistake. Choice (E) is false since the car is driven on the highway.

18. (E)

Picking up on our discussion of (C) and (D) in the previous question, changing I or II will not help because they do not discuss the relationship between driving the car and rain. A change in III to deal with pollution still has not made the adjustment between driving and rain, thus (C) must be wrong. Choice (D) is not a good answer because whether rainwater is approved or not has nothing to do with the connection between driving and rain.

19. (C)

The assertion is that corporations, rather than people or elected officials, run the country. The evidence presented is that corporate heads make important decisions without being subject to popular control. Option I strengthens the conclusion by giving evidence of corporate influence in an area not dealt with in the argument. III strengthens by giving additional data suggesting corporate autonomy. II is unrelated to either the evidence or the conclusion.

20. (E)

The original amount has an unstated definition of democracy and

depends on the contrast between this definition (popular control of all decisions affecting our lives) and the facts as alleged by the author. Choice (E) implies that education is merely regurgitation of facts, and depends on the contrasts between this and alleged facts. Choice (A) has no definition of safe neighborhoods. Choices (B), (C), and (D) all involve direct contrasts.

21.   (D)

Gun control laws reduce violent crime is the argument. Presented as evidence is the drop in armed robberies in one city. This is an unwarranted generalization (A) and (C), a failure to consider alternative explanations (B), and a possible failure to look at contrary evidence (E). Option (D) raises an objection not related to the validity of the evidence or the validity of the conclusion in the argument.

22.   (C)

Option I has a partial answer for the objection given in (B). II strengthens the argument in a somewhat more general way. If true, violent crimes committed with a gun will be more strongly deterred by additional punishment mandated for violation of gun control laws. III would strengthen the argument only if the assumption was made that gun control laws make gun crimes less likely.

23.   (A)

An alternative explanation for the drop in the crime rate is given by Option I. II has nothing to do with the crime rate. III does not suggest that gun control law is an ineffective deterrent.

24.   (A)

The point depends upon the assumption that children watch both cartoons and Westerns. If this is untrue, then the conclusion that follows may not be true. It may be true that children get a distorted view of the world from other sources. The claim is that cartoons and Westerns cause this. The intentions of the producers is not relevant, thus II is not useful. That other sources of information would present a proper view does not prove the problem cited, thus III would not weaken the point.

**25. (C)**

It is most likely that students are excused from composition if they demonstrate superior writing ability. Thus, being excused is not a cause of their writing well; but the argument, in assuming that dropping the course will improve everyone's writing, treats it as if it were a cause. Option (A) is incorrect, (B) is incidental and the reasoning would be invalid even if backed by evidence. Choices (D) and (E) focus on incidental features which might be important if the basic reasoning were valid.

# GRE
# GENERAL TEST 3
## ANSWER SHEET

### SECTION 1

1. Ⓐ Ⓑ Ⓒ Ⓓ Ⓔ
2. Ⓐ Ⓑ Ⓒ Ⓓ Ⓔ
3. Ⓐ Ⓑ Ⓒ Ⓓ Ⓔ
4. Ⓐ Ⓑ Ⓒ Ⓓ Ⓔ
5. Ⓐ Ⓑ Ⓒ Ⓓ Ⓔ
6. Ⓐ Ⓑ Ⓒ Ⓓ Ⓔ
7. Ⓐ Ⓑ Ⓒ Ⓓ Ⓔ
8. Ⓐ Ⓑ Ⓒ Ⓓ Ⓔ
9. Ⓐ Ⓑ Ⓒ Ⓓ Ⓔ
10. Ⓐ Ⓑ Ⓒ Ⓓ Ⓔ
11. Ⓐ Ⓑ Ⓒ Ⓓ Ⓔ
12. Ⓐ Ⓑ Ⓒ Ⓓ Ⓔ
13. Ⓐ Ⓑ Ⓒ Ⓓ Ⓔ
14. Ⓐ Ⓑ Ⓒ Ⓓ Ⓔ
15. Ⓐ Ⓑ Ⓒ Ⓓ Ⓔ
16. Ⓐ Ⓑ Ⓒ Ⓓ Ⓔ
17. Ⓐ Ⓑ Ⓒ Ⓓ Ⓔ
18. Ⓐ Ⓑ Ⓒ Ⓓ Ⓔ
19. Ⓐ Ⓑ Ⓒ Ⓓ Ⓔ
20. Ⓐ Ⓑ Ⓒ Ⓓ Ⓔ
21. Ⓐ Ⓑ Ⓒ Ⓓ Ⓔ
22. Ⓐ Ⓑ Ⓒ Ⓓ Ⓔ
23. Ⓐ Ⓑ Ⓒ Ⓓ Ⓔ
24. Ⓐ Ⓑ Ⓒ Ⓓ Ⓔ
25. Ⓐ Ⓑ Ⓒ Ⓓ Ⓔ
26. Ⓐ Ⓑ Ⓒ Ⓓ Ⓔ
27. Ⓐ Ⓑ Ⓒ Ⓓ Ⓔ
28. Ⓐ Ⓑ Ⓒ Ⓓ Ⓔ
29. Ⓐ Ⓑ Ⓒ Ⓓ Ⓔ
30. Ⓐ Ⓑ Ⓒ Ⓓ Ⓔ

31. Ⓐ Ⓑ Ⓒ Ⓓ Ⓔ
32. Ⓐ Ⓑ Ⓒ Ⓓ Ⓔ
33. Ⓐ Ⓑ Ⓒ Ⓓ Ⓔ
34. Ⓐ Ⓑ Ⓒ Ⓓ Ⓔ
35. Ⓐ Ⓑ Ⓒ Ⓓ Ⓔ
36. Ⓐ Ⓑ Ⓒ Ⓓ Ⓔ
37. Ⓐ Ⓑ Ⓒ Ⓓ Ⓔ
38. Ⓐ Ⓑ Ⓒ Ⓓ Ⓔ

### SECTION 2

1. Ⓐ Ⓑ Ⓒ Ⓓ Ⓔ
2. Ⓐ Ⓑ Ⓒ Ⓓ Ⓔ
3. Ⓐ Ⓑ Ⓒ Ⓓ Ⓔ
4. Ⓐ Ⓑ Ⓒ Ⓓ Ⓔ
5. Ⓐ Ⓑ Ⓒ Ⓓ Ⓔ
6. Ⓐ Ⓑ Ⓒ Ⓓ Ⓔ
7. Ⓐ Ⓑ Ⓒ Ⓓ Ⓔ
8. Ⓐ Ⓑ Ⓒ Ⓓ Ⓔ
9. Ⓐ Ⓑ Ⓒ Ⓓ Ⓔ
10. Ⓐ Ⓑ Ⓒ Ⓓ Ⓔ
11. Ⓐ Ⓑ Ⓒ Ⓓ Ⓔ
12. Ⓐ Ⓑ Ⓒ Ⓓ Ⓔ
13. Ⓐ Ⓑ Ⓒ Ⓓ Ⓔ
14. Ⓐ Ⓑ Ⓒ Ⓓ Ⓔ
15. Ⓐ Ⓑ Ⓒ Ⓓ Ⓔ
16. Ⓐ Ⓑ Ⓒ Ⓓ Ⓔ
17. Ⓐ Ⓑ Ⓒ Ⓓ Ⓔ
18. Ⓐ Ⓑ Ⓒ Ⓓ Ⓔ
19. Ⓐ Ⓑ Ⓒ Ⓓ Ⓔ
20. Ⓐ Ⓑ Ⓒ Ⓓ Ⓔ
21. Ⓐ Ⓑ Ⓒ Ⓓ Ⓔ

22. Ⓐ Ⓑ Ⓒ Ⓓ Ⓔ
23. Ⓐ Ⓑ Ⓒ Ⓓ Ⓔ
24. Ⓐ Ⓑ Ⓒ Ⓓ Ⓔ
25. Ⓐ Ⓑ Ⓒ Ⓓ Ⓔ
26. Ⓐ Ⓑ Ⓒ Ⓓ Ⓔ
27. Ⓐ Ⓑ Ⓒ Ⓓ Ⓔ
28. Ⓐ Ⓑ Ⓒ Ⓓ Ⓔ
29. Ⓐ Ⓑ Ⓒ Ⓓ Ⓔ
30. Ⓐ Ⓑ Ⓒ Ⓓ Ⓔ
31. Ⓐ Ⓑ Ⓒ Ⓓ Ⓔ
32. Ⓐ Ⓑ Ⓒ Ⓓ Ⓔ
33. Ⓐ Ⓑ Ⓒ Ⓓ Ⓔ
34. Ⓐ Ⓑ Ⓒ Ⓓ Ⓔ
35. Ⓐ Ⓑ Ⓒ Ⓓ Ⓔ
36. Ⓐ Ⓑ Ⓒ Ⓓ Ⓔ
37. Ⓐ Ⓑ Ⓒ Ⓓ Ⓔ
38. Ⓐ Ⓑ Ⓒ Ⓓ Ⓔ

### SECTION 3

1. Ⓐ Ⓑ Ⓒ Ⓓ Ⓔ
2. Ⓐ Ⓑ Ⓒ Ⓓ Ⓔ
3. Ⓐ Ⓑ Ⓒ Ⓓ Ⓔ
4. Ⓐ Ⓑ Ⓒ Ⓓ Ⓔ
5. Ⓐ Ⓑ Ⓒ Ⓓ Ⓔ
6. Ⓐ Ⓑ Ⓒ Ⓓ Ⓔ
7. Ⓐ Ⓑ Ⓒ Ⓓ Ⓔ
8. Ⓐ Ⓑ Ⓒ Ⓓ Ⓔ
9. Ⓐ Ⓑ Ⓒ Ⓓ Ⓔ
10. Ⓐ Ⓑ Ⓒ Ⓓ Ⓔ
11. Ⓐ Ⓑ Ⓒ Ⓓ Ⓔ
12. Ⓐ Ⓑ Ⓒ Ⓓ Ⓔ

13. Ⓐ Ⓑ Ⓒ Ⓓ Ⓔ
14. Ⓐ Ⓑ Ⓒ Ⓓ Ⓔ
15. Ⓐ Ⓑ Ⓒ Ⓓ Ⓔ
16. Ⓐ Ⓑ Ⓒ Ⓓ Ⓔ
17. Ⓐ Ⓑ Ⓒ Ⓓ Ⓔ
18. Ⓐ Ⓑ Ⓒ Ⓓ Ⓔ
19. Ⓐ Ⓑ Ⓒ Ⓓ Ⓔ
20. Ⓐ Ⓑ Ⓒ Ⓓ Ⓔ
21. Ⓐ Ⓑ Ⓒ Ⓓ Ⓔ
22. Ⓐ Ⓑ Ⓒ Ⓓ Ⓔ
23. Ⓐ Ⓑ Ⓒ Ⓓ Ⓔ
24. Ⓐ Ⓑ Ⓒ Ⓓ Ⓔ
25. Ⓐ Ⓑ Ⓒ Ⓓ Ⓔ
26. Ⓐ Ⓑ Ⓒ Ⓓ Ⓔ
27. Ⓐ Ⓑ Ⓒ Ⓓ Ⓔ
28. Ⓐ Ⓑ Ⓒ Ⓓ Ⓔ
29. Ⓐ Ⓑ Ⓒ Ⓓ Ⓔ
30. Ⓐ Ⓑ Ⓒ Ⓓ Ⓔ

## SECTION 4

1. Ⓐ Ⓑ Ⓒ Ⓓ Ⓔ
2. Ⓐ Ⓑ Ⓒ Ⓓ Ⓔ
3. Ⓐ Ⓑ Ⓒ Ⓓ Ⓔ
4. Ⓐ Ⓑ Ⓒ Ⓓ Ⓔ
5. Ⓐ Ⓑ Ⓒ Ⓓ Ⓔ
6. Ⓐ Ⓑ Ⓒ Ⓓ Ⓔ
7. Ⓐ Ⓑ Ⓒ Ⓓ Ⓔ
8. Ⓐ Ⓑ Ⓒ Ⓓ Ⓔ
9. Ⓐ Ⓑ Ⓒ Ⓓ Ⓔ
10. Ⓐ Ⓑ Ⓒ Ⓓ Ⓔ
11. Ⓐ Ⓑ Ⓒ Ⓓ Ⓔ
12. Ⓐ Ⓑ Ⓒ Ⓓ Ⓔ
13. Ⓐ Ⓑ Ⓒ Ⓓ Ⓔ
14. Ⓐ Ⓑ Ⓒ Ⓓ Ⓔ
15. Ⓐ Ⓑ Ⓒ Ⓓ Ⓔ

16. Ⓐ Ⓑ Ⓒ Ⓓ Ⓔ
17. Ⓐ Ⓑ Ⓒ Ⓓ Ⓔ
18. Ⓐ Ⓑ Ⓒ Ⓓ Ⓔ
19. Ⓐ Ⓑ Ⓒ Ⓓ Ⓔ
20. Ⓐ Ⓑ Ⓒ Ⓓ Ⓔ
21. Ⓐ Ⓑ Ⓒ Ⓓ Ⓔ
22. Ⓐ Ⓑ Ⓒ Ⓓ Ⓔ
23. Ⓐ Ⓑ Ⓒ Ⓓ Ⓔ
24. Ⓐ Ⓑ Ⓒ Ⓓ Ⓔ
25. Ⓐ Ⓑ Ⓒ Ⓓ Ⓔ
26. Ⓐ Ⓑ Ⓒ Ⓓ Ⓔ
27. Ⓐ Ⓑ Ⓒ Ⓓ Ⓔ
28. Ⓐ Ⓑ Ⓒ Ⓓ Ⓔ
29. Ⓐ Ⓑ Ⓒ Ⓓ Ⓔ
30. Ⓐ Ⓑ Ⓒ Ⓓ Ⓔ

## SECTION 5

1. Ⓐ Ⓑ Ⓒ Ⓓ Ⓔ
2. Ⓐ Ⓑ Ⓒ Ⓓ Ⓔ
3. Ⓐ Ⓑ Ⓒ Ⓓ Ⓔ
4. Ⓐ Ⓑ Ⓒ Ⓓ Ⓔ
5. Ⓐ Ⓑ Ⓒ Ⓓ Ⓔ
6. Ⓐ Ⓑ Ⓒ Ⓓ Ⓔ
7. Ⓐ Ⓑ Ⓒ Ⓓ Ⓔ
8. Ⓐ Ⓑ Ⓒ Ⓓ Ⓔ
9. Ⓐ Ⓑ Ⓒ Ⓓ Ⓔ
10. Ⓐ Ⓑ Ⓒ Ⓓ Ⓔ
11. Ⓐ Ⓑ Ⓒ Ⓓ Ⓔ
12. Ⓐ Ⓑ Ⓒ Ⓓ Ⓔ
13. Ⓐ Ⓑ Ⓒ Ⓓ Ⓔ
14. Ⓐ Ⓑ Ⓒ Ⓓ Ⓔ
15. Ⓐ Ⓑ Ⓒ Ⓓ Ⓔ
16. Ⓐ Ⓑ Ⓒ Ⓓ Ⓔ
17. Ⓐ Ⓑ Ⓒ Ⓓ Ⓔ
18. Ⓐ Ⓑ Ⓒ Ⓓ Ⓔ

19. Ⓐ Ⓑ Ⓒ Ⓓ Ⓔ
20. Ⓐ Ⓑ Ⓒ Ⓓ Ⓔ
21. Ⓐ Ⓑ Ⓒ Ⓓ Ⓔ
22. Ⓐ Ⓑ Ⓒ Ⓓ Ⓔ
23. Ⓐ Ⓑ Ⓒ Ⓓ Ⓔ
24. Ⓐ Ⓑ Ⓒ Ⓓ Ⓔ
25. Ⓐ Ⓑ Ⓒ Ⓓ Ⓔ

## SECTION 6

1. Ⓐ Ⓑ Ⓒ Ⓓ Ⓔ
2. Ⓐ Ⓑ Ⓒ Ⓓ Ⓔ
3. Ⓐ Ⓑ Ⓒ Ⓓ Ⓔ
4. Ⓐ Ⓑ Ⓒ Ⓓ Ⓔ
5. Ⓐ Ⓑ Ⓒ Ⓓ Ⓔ
6. Ⓐ Ⓑ Ⓒ Ⓓ Ⓔ
7. Ⓐ Ⓑ Ⓒ Ⓓ Ⓔ
8. Ⓐ Ⓑ Ⓒ Ⓓ Ⓔ
9. Ⓐ Ⓑ Ⓒ Ⓓ Ⓔ
10. Ⓐ Ⓑ Ⓒ Ⓓ Ⓔ
11. Ⓐ Ⓑ Ⓒ Ⓓ Ⓔ
12. Ⓐ Ⓑ Ⓒ Ⓓ Ⓔ
13. Ⓐ Ⓑ Ⓒ Ⓓ Ⓔ
14. Ⓐ Ⓑ Ⓒ Ⓓ Ⓔ
15. Ⓐ Ⓑ Ⓒ Ⓓ Ⓔ
16. Ⓐ Ⓑ Ⓒ Ⓓ Ⓔ
17. Ⓐ Ⓑ Ⓒ Ⓓ Ⓔ
18. Ⓐ Ⓑ Ⓒ Ⓓ Ⓔ
19. Ⓐ Ⓑ Ⓒ Ⓓ Ⓔ
20. Ⓐ Ⓑ Ⓒ Ⓓ Ⓔ
21. Ⓐ Ⓑ Ⓒ Ⓓ Ⓔ
22. Ⓐ Ⓑ Ⓒ Ⓓ Ⓔ
23. Ⓐ Ⓑ Ⓒ Ⓓ Ⓔ
24. Ⓐ Ⓑ Ⓒ Ⓓ Ⓔ
25. Ⓐ Ⓑ Ⓒ Ⓓ Ⓔ

# TEST 3

## Section 1

> **TIME:** 30 Minutes
> 38 Questions
>
> **DIRECTIONS:** Each of the given sentences has blank spaces which indicate words omitted. Choose the best combination of words which fit into the meaning and structure within the context of the sentence.

1. The root, when properly cooked, was converted into a _____ and nutritious food.

   (A) palatable

   (B) dissonant

   (C) savorous

   (D) delightful

   (E) delicious

2. We cannot explain away this deliberate act as due to the _____ of age, or accept the other excuses with which his admirers have sought to _____ it.

   (A) ineptitude...rationalize

   (B) asininity...vindicate

   (C) sagacity...syllogize

   (D) psychosis...exculpate

   (E) garrulity...palliate

3. Fear persisted, and with it persisted an animosity toward the sister; undoubtedly this was the psychological _____ of the incest taboo.

(A) antithesis      (D) variance

(B) impression      (E) correlate

(C) resemblance

4.  She had learned that there was really more than one man in the world, the _____ of knowledge that more than anything else divides a woman from a girl.

(A) disparate       (D) equivalence

(B) portion         (E) correspondence

(C) piece

5.  In the prints of Harunobu there is an intense sympathy with youth, with its shyness, its tremulous _____ .

(A) ecstasy         (D) ardor

(B) fervor          (E) symbolics

(C) spiritualism

6.  Louis Phillipe, so far as was practical, _____ the citizens of foreign states for losses caused by Napoleon.

(A) repartitioned   (D) subscribed

(B) apportioned     (E) subsidized

(C) indemnified

7.  The Greeks had a name for such a mixture of learning and folly, which might be applied to the _____ but poorly read of all ages.

(A) edified         (D) bookish

(B) inerudite       (E) illiterate

(C) omniscient

---

**DIRECTIONS:** In the following questions, the given pair of words contains a specific relationship to each other. Select the best pair of the choices which expresses the same relationship as the given.

---

8.  DUPLICATE:REPLICATE::

    (A)  water:electricity        (D)  felodese:resuscitate

    (B)  earthen:ceramic        (E)  gargantuan:diminutive

    (C)  onomatopoeic:echoic

9.  PREFIX:STRUCTURAL ANALYSIS::

    (A)  ctenophore:jellyfish     (D)  octave:score

    (B)  insect:arthropod       (E)  parang:cleavor

    (C)  harp:arpeggio

10.  LEGION:MULTITUDE::

    (A)  lemming:muskrat       (D)  royalty:farthingale

    (B)  ostrich:falcon         (E)  mirage:illusion

    (C)  fumarole:volcano

11.  PESSIMISTIC:BENEVOLENT::

    (A)  miscellaneous:assorted    (D)  mien:demeanor

    (B)  hemlock:herb         (E)  purloin:revert

    (C)  minimize:derograte

12.  DEMARCATE:CONFOUND::

    (A)  palatable:savory       (D)  pochard:diving duck

    (B)  pithy:sententious      (E)  predilection:objectivity

    (C)  sea:polder

13. ARACHNIDS:ARTHROPOD::

   (A)  particle:atom         (D)  theosophy:monastary

   (B)  spear:aperture       (E)  cornice:furniture

   (C)  rayon:bengaline


14. RACISM:PREJUDICE::

   (A)  neutral:condonation    (D)  diagram:design

   (B)  instigate:provoke      (E)  coquet:pedantism

   (C)  punctilious:fallacious


15. DEPICTIVE:SUGGESTIVE::

   (A)  account:chronicle

   (B)  silk:pongee

   (C)  fecundity:prolificacy

   (D)  protuberance:depression

   (E)  rapacious:benevolent


16. INTOXICATION:INEBRIATION::

   (A)  gluttony:voracity      (D)  plover:sandpiper

   (B)  turban:hat           (E)  peregrine:falcon

   (C)  vim:fatigue


**DIRECTIONS:** Each passage is followed by questions based on its content. After reading the passage, choose the best answer to each question. Answer all questions based on what is stated or implied in that passage.

Père Claude Jean Allouez explored Lake Superior from 1665 to 1667. At his little mission station near the western end of the lake, he heard from the Indians of a great river to the west. Père Jacques Marquette determined to investigate. In 1673, accompanied by Louis Jolliet and five others, he left St. Ignace Mission and ascended the Fox River, which flows into Green Bay, crossed over to the Wisconsin River, and followed it to the upper Mississippi. The party then descended the Mississippi to the mouth of the Arkansas. These Frenchmen were not the first Europeans to sight or travel the Mississippi; De Soto and Moscoso had done so a century and a half before.

The report of the exploration was rushed back to Quebec, where, in 1672, Count Frontenac had arrived as Governor of the province. He and his friend, the remarkable La Salle — who earlier may have penetrated the Ohio River Valley — listened with deep interest. Prior to that time, the two men had been involved in projects to open the Western Lake country to French trade.

17.  Through his exploration, Marquette discovered:

 (A)  he needed to travel north to reach his southern destination.

 (B)  a river he had not expected to find.

 (C)  he was not the first Frenchman to travel the river.

 (D)  a new route for transporting French settlers to the West.

 (E)  French settlements already existed.

18.  Provincial Governor Count Frontenac was deeply interested in Marquette's report because it:

 (A)  allowed him to claim more land for France.

 (B)  confirmed and supported previous reports made by La Salle.

 (C)  supported his own plan to open the Ohio River Valley to French trade.

 (D)  proved the Indians were truthful and could be trusted.

 (E)  made it possible for him to continue in his own project to open the Western Lake country for trade.

19. Frontenac and La Salle had been involved in projects for opening the lake country. The passage implies the projects were related to:

    (A) missionary work.

    (B) agriculture.

    (C) fur trading.

    (D) surveying and exploring.

    (E) water transportation.

20. From the passage, it can be inferred that one of the primary objectives of the French was:

    (A) exploration.

    (B) Christianizing Indians.

    (C) expanding French culture.

    (D) traveling down the Mississippi.

    (E) opening the western lake country to agriculture.

Dr. Robert H. Goddard, at one time a physics professor at Clark University, Worcester, Massachusetts, was largely responsible for the sudden interest in rockets back in the twenties. When Dr. Goddard first started his experiments with rockets, no related technical information was available. He started a new science, industry, and field of engineering. Through his scientific experiments, he pointed the way to the development of rockets as we know them today. The Smithsonian Institute agreed to finance his experiments in 1920. From these experiments he wrote a paper titled "A Method of Reaching Extreme Altitudes," in which he outlined a space rocket of the step (multistage) principle, theoretically capable of reaching the moon.

Goddard discovered that with a properly shaped, smooth, tapered nozzle he could increase the ejection velocity eight times with the same weight of fuel. This would not only drive a rocket eight times faster, but sixty-four times farther, according to his theory. Early in his experiments he found that solid-fuel rockets would not give him the

high power or the duration of power needed for a dependable supersonic motor capable of extreme altitudes. On 16 March 1926, after many trials, Dr. Goddard successfully fired, for the first time in history, a liquid-fuel rocket into the air. It attained an altitude of 184 feet and a speed of 60 mph. This seems small as compared to present-day speeds and heights of missile flights, but instead of trying to achieve speed or altitude at this time, Dr. Goddard was trying to develop a dependable rocket motor.

Dr. Goddard later was the first to fire a rocket that reached a speed faster than the speed of sound. He was first to develop a gyroscopic steering apparatus for rockets. He was the first to use vanes in the jet stream for rocket stabilization during the initial phase of a rocket flight. And he was first to patent the idea of step rockets. After proving on paper and in actual test that a rocket can travel in a vacuum, he developed the mathematical theory of rocket propulsion and rocket flight, including basic designs for long-range rockets. All of this information was available to our military men before World War II, but evidently its immediate use did not seem applicable. Near the end of World War II we started intense work on rocket-powered guided missiles, using the experiments and developments of Dr. Goddard and the American Rocket Society.

21. The passage implies that Dr. Goddard, a physics professor,

    (A)   was the father of the science of rocketry.

    (B)   started a new science, industry, and field of engineering.

    (C)   pointed the way to the development of rockets.

    (D)   outlined the principle of multistage space rockets.

    (E)   was responsible for interest in rockets in the 1920's.

22. One can assume from the article that

    (A)   all factors being equal, a proper shape of the rocket nozzle would increase the ejection velocity and travel distance.

    (B)   solid-fuel rockets would give higher power and duration.

    (C)   blunt nozzle would negatively affect speed and distance.

(D)   supersonic motors are needed for extreme altitudes.

(E)   the first successfully fired liquid fueled rocket was for developing a dependable rocket motor.

23.   Among Dr. Goddard's many achievements, the most far reaching was:

(A)   the development of a rocket stabilizing steering mechanism.

(B)   the development of liquid rocket fuel.

(C)   the development of use of vanes for rocket stabilizing.

(D)   the development of the gyroscope.

(E)   his thesis for multistage rocket design.

24.   It can be inferred from the selection that Goddard's mathematical theory and design are:

(A)   applicable to other types of rocket-powered vehicles.

(B)   includes basic designs for long-range rockets.

(C)   utilizes vanes in jet streams for rocket stabilization.

(D)   tested rocket travel in a vacuum.

(E)   produced gyroscopic steering apparatus.

25.   Dr. Goddard made which of the following assumptions about rockets?

(A)   The amount of fuel had to be in direct proportion to the ejection velocity desired.

(B)   All other factors being equal, the shape of the rocket nozzle increases the ejection velocity and distance to the desired effect.

(C)   A medium of air was not a required component for rocket flight.

(D) Dependability was more important than speed and distance.

(E) Solid rocket fuel failed to deliver high power for an extended duration.

26. Goddard's contribution to World War II lies in:

(A) pre-World War II basic design of rockets.

(B) pre-war multistage principle of flight and propulsion.

(C) developing liquid fuel for aircraft.

(D) providing gyroscopic steering mechanism for submarines.

(E) the availability of his experiments to the military.

27. Interest in rocket development followed Goddard's:

(A) presentation of his paper "A Method of Reaching Extreme Altitudes."

(B) receiving of a grant from the Smithsonian.

(C) experiments with liquid fuel.

(D) use of the gyroscope.

(E) presentation of the mathematical theory of rocket propulsion.

---

**DIRECTIONS:** Each of the following questions provides a given word in capitalized letters followed by five word choices. Choose the best word which is most <u>opposite</u> in meaning to the given word.

---

28. PROCLIVITY:
    (A) penchant
    (B) deflection
    (C) dilatory
    (D) diminish
    (E) procedure

29. REMOTE:
    (A) foreign
    (B) proximate
    (C) parallax
    (D) inapposite
    (E) propinquity

30. ABYSS:
    (A) zenith
    (B) profundity
    (C) interval
    (D) interstice
    (E) depression

31. LENIENT:
    (A) implacable
    (B) indulgence
    (C) perfunctory
    (D) longanimity
    (E) unpunctilious

32. DENSITY:
    (A) obtuseness
    (B) imporosity
    (C) vacuity
    (D) puerility
    (E) levity

33. SOJOURNER:
    (A) suffusion
    (B) inherent
    (C) allocation
    (D) burgess
    (E) luxate

34. ABRIDGMENT:
    (A) epitome
    (B) concision
    (C) laconic
    (D) compendium
    (E) redundant

35. VERTEX:
    (A) exultation
    (B) acme
    (C) eminence
    (D) vortex
    (E) fundamental

36. TREPIDATION:

   (A) apprehension

   (B) sagacity

   (C) perturbation

   (D) agitation

   (E) courage

37. STUBBORNNESS:

   (A) resilient

   (B) precipitation

   (C) tenuous

   (D) viscidity

   (E) subtlety

38. HOMICIDE:

   (A) assize

   (B) annexation

   (C) vitalize

   (D) effectuation

   (E) perpetuation

## STOP

If time still remains, you may go back and check your work.
When the time allotted is up, you may go on to the next section.

# Section 2

TIME: 30 Minutes
38 Questions

DIRECTIONS: Each of the given sentences has blank spaces which indicate words omitted. Choose the best combination of words which fit into the meaning and structure within the context of the sentence.

1. Not all persons whose lives are _____ remain provincial; some have the intellectual and personal characteristics which enable them to develop a/an _____ orientation to life.

   (A) confined...philanthropic

   (B) limited...progressive

   (C) circumscribed...enterprising

   (D) restricted...cosmopolitan

   (E) restrained...hedonistic

2. In an article on "The Present Relations of the Learned Professions to Political Government," the author devoted 1100 words to law, 800 to theology, 375 to education, and 350 to writing; this proportion, it may be _____ , shows his idea of the relative _____ of each in his discussion.

   (A) believed...worth

   (B) assumed...achievements

   (C) supposed...value

   (D) inferred...significance

   (E) determined...merit

3. An "at-risk" student is one, for example, who lives in poverty, whose parents are divorced, whose family provider is unem-

ployed, or whose parents are uneducated; however, _____ variables such as these are not altogether responsible for the high failure rate of at-risk students, whose personal variables such as effort and ability are also factors.

(A) environmental        (D) powerful

(B) critical        (E) endemic

(C) innocuous

4. Committees are ineffective when they cannot agree upon what to do or just how to go about accomplishing it; this situation is a/an _____ of faulty _____ of committee responsibility.

(A) factor...acceptance        (D) part...guidelines

(B) cause...guidelines        (E) example...direction

(C) result...specifications

5. Increasing specialization on the part of workers results in better communication and higher degrees of achievement of goals in relation to the immediate work group or department, but decreases effectiveness of communication among groups or departments and the focus on institutional goals; this presents managers with the problems of increasing _____ and providing _____ .

(A) coordination...vision

(B) supervision...mission

(C) support...direction

(D) re-training...articulation

(E) relationship...orientation

6. As the city grows and more suburbs are annexed, its parks will become _____ for its needs; therefore, land should be purchased to provide _____ parks in the outlying suburbs.

(A) insufficient...updated        (B) depleted...more

(C) deficient...larger      (D) important...new

(E) inadequate...additional

7. Tile manufacturers need high-quality clay; this is why brick yards are invariably located in places where high-quality clay is _____ and can be readily _____ .

  (A) present...verified      (D) abundant...accessed

  (B) evident...procured      (E) visible...utilized

  (C) nearby...obtained

---

**DIRECTIONS:** In the following questions, the given pair of words contains a specific relationship to each other. Select the best pair of the choices which expresses the same relationship as the given.

---

8. DISSONANCE:ASSONANCE::

  (A) redundancy:tautology      (D) prodigious:amazing

  (B) cacophony:melodious      (E) collation:order

  (C) overt:visible

9. MONEY:PHILANTHROPIST::

  (A) convert:missionary

  (B) dexterity:surgeon

  (C) crops:farmer

  (D) students:teacher

  (E) schizophrenics:psychologist

10. DOOR:KEY::

  (A) gem:ring      (B) perfume:aroma

(C)   enigma:clue                     (D)   effort:achievement

(E)   mold:gelatin

11.   INTRIGUE:CONSPIRACY::

(A)   appeal:rebuff                   (D)   sufferance:prohibition

(B)   intrepid:fearless               (E)   individual:many

(C)   printing:writing

12.   CALORIE:HEAT::

(A)   sand:cement                     (D)   caliper:diameter

(B)   succumb:yield                   (E)   retaliation:forgiveness

(C)   metronome:music

13.   TWEETER:WOOFER::

(A)   grade:slope                     (D)   tutelage:protection

(B)   high:low                        (E)   isosceles:equal

(C)   replicate:duplicate

14.   ORNATE:BAROQUE::

(A)   altitude:mountains              (D)   typewriter:computer

(B)   seed:fruit                      (E)   lake:water

(C)   fire:wood

15.   CAUSE:PRECIPITATE::

(A)   facile:difficult                (D)   objective:goal

(B)   latency:maturity                (E)    question:answer

(C)   test:study

16. INDICATIVE:MOOD:

    (A) present:past         (D) declarative:imperative

    (B) pronoun:preposition     (E) future:tense

    (C) sentence:clause

---

**DIRECTIONS**: Each passage is followed by questions based on its content. After reading the passage, choose the best answer to each question. Answer all questions based on what is stated or implied in that passage.

---

The crisis came in the spring of 1775, predictably in Massachusetts. Late on the night of April 18 the Royal Governor, General Thomas Gage, alarmed at the militancy of the rebels, dispatched 600 troops from Boston to seize a major supply depot at Concord. Almost simultaneously the Boston council of safety, aware of Gage's intentions, directed Paul Revere and William Dawes to ride ahead to warn militia units and citizens along the way of the British approach, as well as John Hancock and Samuel Adams, who were staying at nearby Lexington. Forewarned, the two men went into hiding.

About 77 militiamen confronted the redcoats when they plodded into Lexington at dawn. After some tense moments, as the sorely outnumbered colonials were dispersing, blood was shed. More flowed at Concord and much more along the route of the British as they retreated to Boston, harassed most of the way by an aroused citizenry. What had once been merely protest had devolved into open warfare; the War for Independence had begun.

17. In the selection the author was attempting to portray:

    (A) the need for more diplomacy by the colonists before the Revolution began.

    (B) the overaction of the British which started the Revolutionary War.

    (C) the nationalistic attitude of the colonists prior to the Revolutionary War.

(D)  the predictability of the Revolutionary War beginning in Massachusetts.

(E)  the events leading up to the Revolutionary War.

18.  The attitude of the author toward British redcoats could best be described as one of:

(A)  admiration for their excellent fighting ability.

(B)  disrespect for the redcoats.

(C)  lack of military discipline.

(D)  scorn for their readiness.

(E)  sympathy because the British lacked the heart to fight.

19.  From information given in the selection, which of the following statements is the most correct:

(A)  the colonists were better fighters than the British because they were outnumbered.

(B)  there were colonial spies among the British ranks.

(C)  the colonists were well organized to fight a conflict.

(D)  all the revolutionary spokesmen for the colonists were forced to go underground.

(E)  the time for diplomacy had ended.

Michael Faraday, English physicist and chemist, left the world the richest heritage of scientific knowledge since Issac Newton. His significant discoveries include the principle of electromagnetic induction, the field concept that describes the way objects interact, and the two basic laws of electrolysis. He was born in Newington, Surrey, on September 22, 1791, and died in Hampton Court near London on August 25, 1867.

Faraday was one of ten children of a poverty-stricken blacksmith and had little formal education. At 14 he was apprenticed to a bookbinder who allowed the boy to read books and attend scientific

lectures. During a lecture given by Sir Humphry Davy, Faraday took notes, which he sent to the scientist. Because of the excellence of these notes, he later became Davy's assistant at the Royal Institution.

From then on Faraday developed rapidly as a scientist and was awarded many honors. (In 1825 he became Director of the Royal Institution and finally professor of chemistry for life in 1833.) However, he belonged to a religious group, now extinct, which didn't approve of worldly rewards. Because of this he declined knighthood and the presidency of the Royal Society of which he was a member. His religious convictions also made him refuse to prepare poison gas for Britain's use in the Crimean War.

In addition to being a brilliant scientist, Faraday was also a gifted lecturer. He particularly enjoyed giving a special series of scientific lectures for children every year at Christmas.

Faraday was one of the greatest experimental geniuses in the physical sciences. In 1822, impressed by the discovery that an electric current produced a magnetic field, he determined that it was possible to make magnetism produce electricity. He later showed that a movable wire carrying an electric current will rotate around a fixed magnet. Faraday had converted electricity and magnetic forces into mechanical energy, and from this experiment came the principle of the electric motor.

In 1823 he devised methods to liquefy gases. He also produced below-zero temperatures on the Fahrenheit scale in the laboratory for the first time. In 1825 he discovered benzene, a compound important for future work in representing molecular structures in organic chemistry.

His next contribution was in the field of electrochemistry. Davy had produced pure metals by passing an electric current through molten compounds of these metals. Faraday named this process electrolysis and called the compound or solution that could carry an electric current an electrolyte. He gave the name electrodes to the metal rods put into the solution and, at the suggestion of William Whewell, a Cambridge University philosopher, he called the positive rod an anode and the negative rod a cathode.

In 1832 he developed his laws of electrolysis, which stated that the amount of chemical change produced by an electric current is propor-

tional to the total quantity of electricity. The amounts of different elements that can be deposited or dissolved by a specific quantity of electricity are proportional to the chemical equivalent weight of the element. This implies that the same quantity of electricity is required to liberate the equivalent weight of any element by electrolysis. This quantity is now called the faraday. (The chemical equivalent weight of an element is its atomic weight divided by a number, now called the valence, which describes the combining power of the element with other elements.)

20. According to the passage, which of the following was not an accomplishment of Michael Faraday?

    (A) conversion of electricity and magnetic forces into mechanical energy

    (B) devised methods to liquefy gases

    (C) produced pure metals by passing an electric current through molten compounds of these metals

    (D) discovered benzene

    (E) made magnetism-produced electricity

21. The author's attitude toward Michael Faraday is best described as one of:

    (A) admiration              (D) condescension

    (B) disrespect              (E) subjectivity

    (C) distrust

22. Which of the following best states the author's main point?

    (A) Anyone can make a contribution to a field of study with enough desire.

    (B) Michael Faraday made his contributions because he had the opportunities presented to him.

    (C) Michael Faraday made his contributions from the contributions of others, namely Sir Humphry Davy.

(D) It was difficult for Michael Faraday to work in his field because he did not believe in worldly rewards.

(E) Michael Faraday was a self-educated scientific genius.

23. The author provides information that would answer all but which of the following questions?

(A) What is the law of electrolysis?

(B) How does one figure the chemical equivalent weight of an element?

(C) What method was used to liquefy gases?

(D) What is an anode?

(E) What is a faraday?

24. According to the article, which of the following terms was not coined by Faraday in the course of his work?

(A) valence    (D) electrolyte

(B) anode     (E) electrolysis

(C) electrode

25. The author notes that the scientist's religious convictions were responsible for all of Faraday's actions except:

(A) declining knighthood.

(B) declining the position of Director of the Royal Institution.

(C) declining the presidency of the Royal Society.

(D) refusing to prepare poison gas for Britain's use in the Crimean War.

(E) disapproval of worldly rewards.

26. Which of the following had the greatest impact on the future life of Michael Faraday?

(A) birthplace

(B) family

(C) poverty

(D) apprenticeship

(E) association with Sir Humphry Davy

27. Which of the following titles would best describe the author's intent in this selection?

(A) Michael Faraday, His Life and Work

(B) Michael Faraday and the History of Electrolysis

(C) Michael Faraday and his Work at the Royal Institute

(D) Michael Faraday and Sir Humphry Davy

(E) Michael Faraday and Electromagnetic Induction

---

**DIRECTIONS:** Each of the following questions provides a given word in capitalized letters followed by five word choices. Choose the best word which is most <u>opposite</u> in meaning to the given word.

---

28. FORTUITOUS:

(A) sad

(B) unfruitful

(C) unlucky

(D) disenchanted

(E) miserable

29. MYRIAD:

(A) passel

(B) diverse

(C) legion

(D) profuse

(E) individual

30. PARSIMONIOUS:

(A) peculiar

(B) passionate

(C) prodigal

(D) patronizing

(E) pernicious

31. LOQUACIOUS:
    - (A) daring
    - (B) tedious
    - (C) silent
    - (D) wealthy
    - (E) haughty

32. ARCHAIC:
    - (A) exalt
    - (B) modern
    - (C) angelic
    - (D) invisible
    - (E) noble

33. NEFARIOUS:
    - (A) insubordinate
    - (B) good
    - (C) dangerous
    - (D) nervous
    - (E) stubborn

34. AMELIORATE:
    - (A) clarify
    - (B) mandate
    - (C) insist
    - (D) amend
    - (E) worsen

35. INSERT:
    - (A) exude
    - (B) extend
    - (C) extract
    - (D) explore
    - (E) extinguish

36. REQUISITE:
    - (A) alternative
    - (B) futile
    - (C) prerequisite
    - (D) abhorrent
    - (E) superfluous

37. ABJECT:
    - (A) caring
    - (B) joyful
    - (C) empathetic
    - (D) objective
    - (E) rational

38. INSIPID:
    - (A) obtuse
    - (B) humble
    - (C) maternal
    - (D) tasty
    - (E) jealous

**STOP**

If time still remains, you may go back and check your work.
When the time allotted is up, you may go on to the next section.

# Section 3

**TIME:** 30 Minutes
30 Questions

**NUMBERS:** All numbers are real numbers.

**FIGURES:** Position of points, angles, regions, etc. are assumed to be in the order shown and angle measures are assumed to be positive.

**LINES:** Assume that lines shown as straight are indeed straight.

**DIRECTIONS:** Each of the following given set of quantities is placed into either column A or B. Compare the two quantities to decide whether:

(A)   the quantity in Column A is greater

(B)   the quantity in Column B is greater

(C)   the two quantities are equal

(D)   the relationship cannot be determined from the information given.

**NOTE:** Do not choose (E) since there are only four choices.

**COMMON INFORMATION:** Information which relates to one or both given quantities is centered in the two columns. A symbol which appears in both columns will indicate the same item in Column A and Column B.

**EXAMPLES:**

| Column A | Column B |
| --- | --- |
| 1.          $5 \times 4$ | $5 + 4$ |

Explanation: The correct answer is (A), since $5 \times 4 = 20$, and $5 + 4 = 9$.

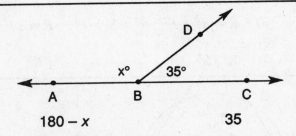

2.    $180 - x$                                       35

Explanation: The correct answer is (C). Since Angle *ABC* is a straight angle, its measurement is 180°.

Column A        Column B

1.      Number of quadrilaterals                    8

Five years ago Tom's age was one-fourth of his father's age. Now it is only one-third.

2.          Tom's age                               20

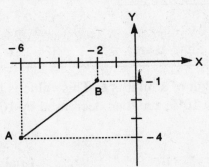

3.      Distance between *A* and *B*               4.5

| Column A | Column B |
|:---:|:---:|

If $R^S = R^2 - S^2$, $S^R = S^2 - R^2$, $R \neq S$

4.      $R^S / S^R$                  $S^R / R^S$

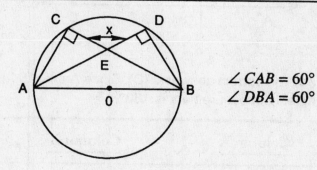

$\angle CAB = 60°$

$\angle DBA = 60°$

5.              $X°$                     $100°$

$$x = -y$$

6.              $x$                      $y$

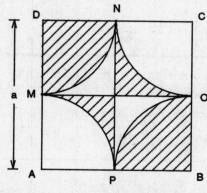

$ABCD$ is a square with side $a$. $M$, $N$, $O$, and $P$ are middle points. $MND$, $MPA$, $POB$, and $ONC$ are four quadrants.

7.      Shaded area           $a^2 / 4$

The length of a ruler is $L$. This value is increased by 10%, and then decreased by 10%.

8.             $L$                 final length

| Column A | Column B |
|---|---|

*ABCD* is a rectangle with *b* > *a*

9.      Shaded area          $\dfrac{bc}{2}$

---

The sum of three consecutive numbers is 3*x*.

10.      The smallest of the three          *X*

---

*ABC* is an equilateral triangle

11.      $\alpha - \beta$          $\gamma$

---

$$x > y > z, \quad z > 0$$

12.      $\dfrac{1}{xy}$          $\dfrac{1}{yz}$

---

*ABCD* is a square. *M, N, O, P* are middle points. The shaded area is formed for 4 quadrants

| Column A | Column B |
|---|---|

---

13. Perimeter of shaded area $\qquad$ $2\pi a$

---

$$0 < X < 2$$

14. $X^2$ $\qquad$ $X^3$

---

$$m > n > 0$$

15. $x^m$ $\qquad$ $x^n$

---

**DIRECTIONS:** For the following questions, select the best answer choice to the given question.

16. What is the value of the following expression: $\dfrac{1}{1 + \dfrac{1}{1 + \frac{1}{4}}}$

    (A) $^9/_5$              (D) 2

    (B) $^5/_9$              (E) 4

    (C) $^1/_2$

17. What is the perimeter of triangle *ABC*?

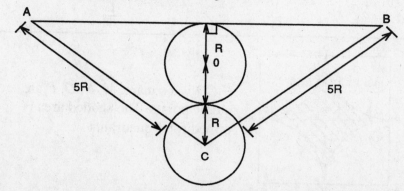

(A)  12$R$         (D)  18$R$

(B)  18$R^2$        (E)  16$R$

(C)  12$R^2$

18.  If $0 < a < 1$ and $b > 1$, which is the largest value?

(A)  $a/_b$         (D)  $(^b/_a)^2$

(B)  $^b/_a$         (E)  cannot be determined

(C)  $(^a/_b)^2$

19.  If $x = 2/\upsilon t$, what is the approximate variation of $x$ when $t$ increases 30% and $\upsilon$ decreases 20%?

(A)  Increase ~ 4%        (D)  Decrease ~ 4%

(B)  Decrease ~ 8%        (E)  Increase 10%

(C)  Increase ~ 8%

20.  Peter bought $n$ compact disks for \$$m$. If in a second purchase he paid \$$q$, what was the increment per compact disk? $(q > m)$

(A)  $(m - q)/n$        (D)  $(q - m)n$

(B)  $(m - q)n$        (E)  $(n - q)/m$

(C)  $(q - m)/n$

Questions 21–25 refer to the table on pages 400 - 401.

21.  What is the relation between kilometers and miles?

(A)  1.609 miles $\doteq$ 1 km        (D)  1.609 km = 1 mile

(B)  1 km = 1 mile        (E)  2 miles = 1 km

(C)  2 km = 1 mile

**United States, Area and Population**

| Division | area * | | population | |
|---|---|---|---|---|
| | sq mi | sq km | 1970 census | 1980 census |
| **Division** | | | | |
| East North Central | 244,366 | 632,905 | 40,253,000 | 41,668,000 |
| | 248,283 | 643,050 | | |
| **States** | | | | |
| Illinois | 55,877 | 144,721 | 11,114,000 | 11,418,000 |
| | 56,400 | 146,075 | | |
| Indiana | 36,189 | 93,729 | 5,194,000 | 5,490,000 |
| | 36,291 | 93,993 | | |
| Michigan | 56,818 | 147,158 | 8,875,000 | 9,258,000 |
| | 58,216 | 150,779 | | |
| Ohio | 41,018 | 106,236 | 10,652,000 | 10,797,000 |
| | 41,222 | 106,764 | | |
| Wisconsin | 54,464 | 141,061 | 4,418,000 | 4,705,000 |
| | 56,154 | 145,438 | | |
| | | | | |
| East South Central | 179,427 | 464,714 | 12,804,000 | 14,663,000 |
| | 181,964 | 471,285† | | |
| **States** | | | | |
| Alabama | 50,851 | 131,703 | 3,444,000 | 3,890,000 |
| | 52,609 | 133,667 | | |
| Kentucky | 39,851 | 103,214 | 3,219,000 | 3,661,000 |
| | 40,395 | 104,623 | | |
| Mississippi | 47,358 | 122,657 | 2,217,000 | 2,521,000 |
| | 47,716 | 123,584 | | |
| Tennessee | 41,367 | 107,140 | 3,924,000 | 4,591,000 |
| | 42,244 | 109,411 | | |
| | | | | |
| Middle Atlantic | 100,426 | 260,102† | 37,199,000 | 36,788,000 |
| | 102,745 | 266,108† | | |
| **States** | | | | |
| New Jersey | 7,532 | 19,508 | 7,168,000 | 7,364,000 |
| | 7,836 | 20,295 | | |
| New York | 47,869 | 123,980 | 18,237,000 | 17,557,000 |
| | 49,576 | 128,401 | | |
| Pennsylvania | 45,025 | 116,614 | 11,794,000 | 11,867,000 |
| | 45,333 | 117,412 | | |
| | | | | |
| Mountain | 856,633 | 2,218,669† | 8,281,000 | 11,369,000 |
| | 863,887 | 2,237,457† | | |
| **States** | | | | |
| Arizona | 113,563 | 294,127 | 1,771,000 | 2,718,000 |
| | 113,909 | 295,023 | | |
| Colorado | 103,794 | 268,825 | 2,207,000 | 2,889,000 |
| | 104,247 | 269,998 | | |
| Idaho | 82,677 | 214,132 | 713,000 | 944,000 |
| | 83,557 | 216,412 | | |
| Montana | 145,603 | 377,110 | 694,000 | 787,000 |
| | 147,138 | 381,086 | | |
| Nevada | 109,889 | 284,611 | 489,000 | 799,000 |
| | 110,540 | 286,297 | | |
| New Mexico | 121,445 | 314,541 | 1,016,000 | 1,300,000 |
| | 121,666 | 315,113 | | |
| Utah | 82,381 | 213,366 | 1,059,000 | 1,461,000 |
| | 84,916 | 219,931 | | |
| Wyoming | 97,281 | 251,957 | 332,000 | 471,000 |
| | 97,914 | 253,596 | | |
| | | | | |
| New England | 62,992 | 163,149† | 11,842,000 | 12,349,000 |
| | 66,608 | 172,514† | | |
| **States** | | | | |
| Connecticut | 4,870 | 12,613 | 3,032,000 | 3,108,000 |
| | 5,009 | 12,973 | | |
| Maine | 30,933 | 80,116 | 992,000 | 1,125,000 |
| | 33,215 | 86,026 | | |
| Massachusetts | 7,833 | 20,287 | 5,689,000 | 5,737,000 |
| | 8,257 | 21,386 | | |
| New Hampshire | 9,033 | 23,395 | 738,000 | 921,000 |
| | 9,304 | 24,097 | | |
| Rhode Island | 1,049 | 2,717 | 947,000 | 947,000 |
| | 1,214 | 3,144 | | |
| Vermont | 9,274 | 24,020 | 444,000 | 511,000 |
| | 9,609 | 24,887 | | |

Britannica Book of the Year (1959), Encyclopedia Britannica, Inc.

## Test 3

| | area * | | population | |
|---|---|---|---|---|
| | sq mi | sq km | 1970 census | 1980 census |
| **Divisions** | | | | |
| Pacific | 892,266 | 2,310,958 | 26,522,000 | 31,797,000 |
| | 916,728 | 2,374,315 | | |
| **States** | | | | |
| Alaska | 566,432 | 1,467,052 | 300,000 | 400,000 |
| | 586,412 | 1,518,800 | | |
| California | 156,537 | 405,429 | 19,953,000 | 23,669,000 |
| | 158,693 | 411,013 | | |
| Hawaii | 6,425 | 16,641 | 769,000 | 965,000 |
| | 6,450 | 16,705 | | |
| Oregon | 96,209 | 249,180 | 2,091,000 | 2,633,000 |
| | 96,981 | 251,180 | | |
| Washington | 66,663 | 172,656 | 3,409,000 | 4,130,000 |
| | 68,192 | 176,616 | | |
| | | | | |
| South Atlantic | 267,352 | 692,438† | 30,671,000 | 36,942,000 |
| | 278,776 | 772,026 | | |
| **States** | | | | |
| Delaware | 1,982 | 5,133 | 548,000 | 595,000 |
| | 2,057 | 5,328 | | |
| District of | 61 | 158 | 757,000 | 638,000 |
| Columbia†† | 67 | 174 | | |
| Florida | 54,136 | 140,212 | 6,789,000 | 9,740,000 |
| | 58,560 | 151,670 | | |
| Georgia | 58,197 | 150,730 | 4,590,000 | 5,464,000 |
| | 58,876 | 152,488 | | |
| Maryland | 9,891 | 25,618 | 3,922,000 | 4,216,000 |
| | 10,577 | 27,394 | | |
| North Carolina | 48,880 | 126,599 | 5,082,000 | 5,874,000 |
| | 52,586 | 136,197 | | |
| South Carolina | 30,280 | 78,425 | 2,591,000 | 3,119,000 |
| | 31,055 | 80,432 | | |
| Virginia | 39,841 | 103,188 | 4,648,000 | 5,346,000 |
| | 40,817 | 105,716 | | |
| West Virginia | 24,084 | 62,377 | 1,744,000 | 1,950,000 |
| | 24,181 | 62,628 | | |
| | | | | |
| West North Central | 508,192 | 1,316,211 | 16,320,000 | 17,183,000 |
| | 517,247 | 1,339,664 | | |
| **States** | | | | |
| Iowa | 56,043 | 145,151 | 2,824,000 | 2,913,000 |
| | 56,290 | 145,790 | | |
| Kansas | 82,056 | 212,524 | 2,247,000 | 2,363,000 |
| | 82,264 | 213,063 | | |
| Minnesota | 78,289 | 205,358 | 3,805,000 | 4,077,000 |
| | 84,068 | 217,735 | | |
| Missouri | 69,046 | 178,828 | 4,677,000 | 4,917,000 |
| | 69,686 | 180,486 | | |
| Nebraska | 76,522 | 198,191 | 1,483,000 | 1,570,000 |
| | 77,227 | 200,017 | | |
| North Dakota | 69,280 | 179,434 | 618,000 | 653,000 |
| | 70,665 | 183,022 | | |
| South Dakota | 75,956 | 196,725 | 666,000 | 690,000 |
| | 77,047 | 199,551 | | |
| | | | | |
| West South Central | 429,284 | 1,111,840† | 19,320,000 | 23,743,000 |
| | 438,884 | 1,136,704 | | |
| **States** | | | | |
| Arkansas | 52,175 | 135,133 | 1,923,000 | 2,286,000 |
| | 53,104 | 137,539 | | |
| Louisiana | 45,155 | 116,951 | 3,641,000 | 4,204,000 |
| | 48,523 | 125,674 | | |
| Oklahoma | 68,984 | 178,668 | 2,559,000 | 3,025,000 |
| | 69,919 | 181,089 | | |
| Texas | 262,970 | 681,089 | 11,197,000 | 14,228,000 |
| | 267,338 | 692,402 | | |
| | | | | |
| Total United States | 3,540,938 | 9,170,987 | 203,212,000 § | 226,505,000 § |
| | 3,615,122 | 9,163,123† | | |

* Where two figures are given, the first is the land area, the second the total area.
† Converted area figures do not add to total given because of rounding.
†† District of Columbia is a federal district.
§ Figures do not add to total given because of rounding.
Source: Official government figures.

22. What are the divisions with the smallest and the largest land areas?

    (A)  New England – Pacific

    (B)  Mountain – New England

    (C)  Pacific – Pacific

    (D)  West North Central – New England

    (E)  Mountain – Middle Atlantic

23. What is the land area in kilometers of the Pacific division?

    (A)  892,266            (D)  2,374,315

    (B)  916,728            (E)  26,522,000

    (C)  2,310,958

24. What percent of the land area represents the Pacific and East North Central divisions?

    (A)  22.1               (D)  25.2

    (B)  32.1               (E)  6.9

    (C)  42.1

25. If in the period 1980 – 1990 the rate of population increase is the same as in the 1970 – 80 period, what will the population of East North Central be in 1990?

    (A)  43,083,000         (D)  43,000,000

    (B)  40,251,160         (E)  43,134,710

    (C)  44,653,060

26. I went to 'Las Vegas' Casino and in the first game I lost one third of my money, in the second game I lost half of the rest. If I still have $1000, how much money did I have when I arrived at the Casino?

(A) $1000      (D) $6000

(B) $2000      (E) $12,000

(C) $3000

27. Which of the following alternatives is correct?

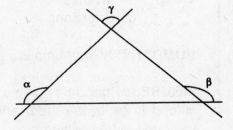

(A) $\alpha + \beta + \gamma = 180°$

(B) $\gamma - \alpha + 180° = \beta$      (D) $\gamma = \alpha + \beta$

(C) $\alpha = \beta + \gamma$      (E) $\alpha = 180° - \beta - \alpha$

28. Given $\dfrac{(\alpha + x) + y}{x + y} = \dfrac{\beta + y}{y}$, $\dfrac{x}{y} = ?$

(A) $\alpha/\beta$      (D) $\alpha/\beta - 1$

(B) $\beta/\alpha$      (E) 1

(C) $\beta/\alpha - 1$

29. The side of a square increases 10% and the area increases
5.25(ft)². What was the original value of the side of the square?

(A) 3 ft      (d) 4 ft

(B) 2 ft      (E) 5 ft

(C) 1 ft

30. If $3^x > 1$ then $x$

(A) $0 < x < 1$      (D) $x > 0$

(B) $x \geq 0$      (E) $x > 1$

(C) $x \geq 1$

**STOP**
If time still remains, you may go back and check your work.
When the time allotted is up, you may go on to the next section.

# Section 4

**TIME:** 30 Minutes
         30 Questions

**NUMBERS:** All numbers are real numbers.

**FIGURES:** Position of points, angles, regions, etc. are assumed to be in the order shown and angle measures are assumed to be positive.

**LINES:** Assume that lines shown as straight are indeed straight.

**DIRECTIONS:** Each of the following given set of quantities is placed into either column A or B. Compare the two quantities to decide whether:

(A)   the quantity in Column A is greater

(B)   the quantity in Column B is greater

(C)   the two quantities are equal

(D)   the relationship cannot be determined from the information given.

**NOTE:** Do not choose (E) since there are only four choices.

**COMMON INFORMATION:** Information which relates to one or both given quantities is centered in the two columns. A symbol which appears in both columns will indicate the same item in Column A and Column B.

**EXAMPLES:**

| Column A | Column B |
|---|---|
| 1. $\quad\quad 5 \times 4$ | $5 + 4$ |

Explanation: The correct answer is (A), since $5 \times 4 = 20$, and $5 + 4 = 9$.

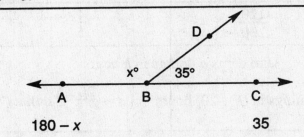

2.       $180 - x$                                    35

Explanation: The correct answer is (C). Since Angle *ABC* is a straight angle, its measurement is 180°.

| Column A | Column B |
| --- | --- |

$$3^x = 81$$

1.                          $x$                                              3

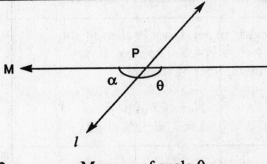

Lines *l* and *m* intersect at point *P* such that the measure of angle θ is 3 times the measure of angle α

2.        Measure of angle θ                        135°

A group of 5 students reported that they earned the following amounts during summer vacation:
$8,000, $9,000, $2,000, $10,000, $6,000.

3.        Average income        Median income

$$x \neq 0; \quad y \neq 0$$

4.              $\left(\dfrac{x}{y}\right)^{10}$                            $\left(\dfrac{y}{x}\right)^{10}$

| Column A | Column B |
|:---:|:---:|

---

**5.** $\dfrac{120}{200}$ $\qquad\qquad$ $\dfrac{4}{5}$

---

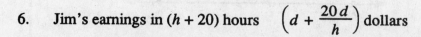

Jim earns $d$ dollars in $h$ hours

**6.** Jim's earnings in $(h + 20)$ hours $\qquad$ $\left(d + \dfrac{20\,d}{h}\right)$ dollars

---

Given triangle $BED$ with $b$ (the measure of side $\overline{ED}$) greater than $e$ (the measure of side $\overline{BD}$).

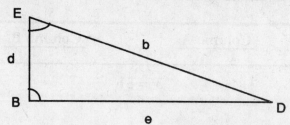

**7.** $\qquad$ Measure of angle $B$ $\qquad$ Measure of angle $E$

---

The ratio of boys to girls in Mr. Good's class is 3:4 and in Ms. Garcia's class is 4:5. The two classes have the same number of students.

**8.** Number of boys in $\qquad$ Number of boys in
$\quad$ Mr. Good's class $\qquad\qquad$ Ms. Garcia's class

---

$$x + 2y > 4$$

**9.** $\qquad\qquad x \qquad\qquad\qquad\qquad y$

---

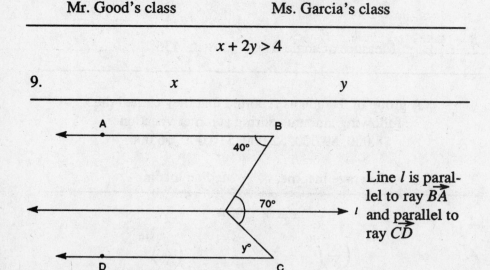

Line $l$ is parallel to ray $\overrightarrow{BA}$ and parallel to ray $\overrightarrow{CD}$

| **Column A** | **Column B** |
|---|---|

(Refer to the previous figure)

10. $y$ | 30°

---

A house that sells for $72,000
requires a 20% down payment.

11. The amount of down payment | $14,000

---

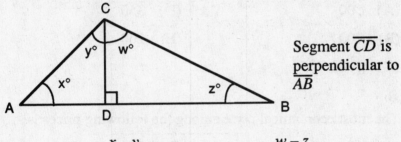

Segment $\overline{CD}$ is perpendicular to $\overline{AB}$

12. $x - y$ | $w - z$

---

$a$ and $b$ are positive integers; $b \geq 2$

13. $\dfrac{a}{b}$ | $\dfrac{a+1}{b-1}$

---

A plane's average speed is 520 miles per hour.

14. The number of minutes it takes the plane to fly 650 miles | 75

---

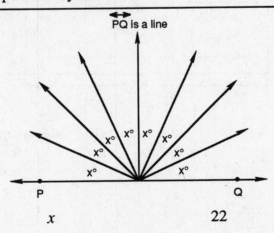

$\overleftrightarrow{PQ}$ is a line

15. $x$ | 22

407

---

**DIRECTIONS:** For the following questions, select the best answer choice to the given question.

---

16. Tickets for a particular concert cost $5 each if purchased in advance and $7 each if bought at the box office on the day of the concert. For this particular concert, 1,200 tickets were sold and the receipts were $6,700. How many tickets were bought at the box office on the day of the concert?

    (A) 500

    (B) 700

    (C) 600

    (D) 350

    (E) 200

17. The most economical price among the following prices is

    (A) 10 oz. for 16¢

    (B) 2 oz. for 3¢

    (C) 4 oz. for 7¢

    (D) 20 oz. for 34¢

    (E) 8 oz. for 13¢

18. In the figure shown, all segments meet at right angles. Find the figure's perimeter in terms of $r$ and $s$.

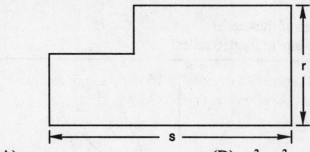

    (A) $r + s$

    (B) $2r + s$

    (C) $2s + r$

    (D) $r^2 + s^2$

    (E) $2r + 2s$

19. If $6x + 12 = 5$, then the value of $(x + 2)$ is

    (A) $-\,{}^{19}\!/_6$            (D) $3\,{}^1\!/_6$

    (B) $-\,1\,{}^1\!/_6$            (E) $1\,{}^1\!/_6$

    (C) ${}^5\!/_6$

20. For non-zero numbers $p$, $q$, $r$, and $s$, ${}^p\!/_q = {}^r\!/_s$. Which of the following statements is true?

    (A) $\dfrac{p + q}{p} = \dfrac{r + s}{r}$      (D) $\dfrac{p - q}{q} = \dfrac{s - r}{r}$

    (B) $\dfrac{p}{r} = \dfrac{q}{r}$          (E) $\dfrac{q}{p - q} = \dfrac{r}{s - r}$

    (C) $\dfrac{r}{s} = \dfrac{q}{p}$

Questions 21 – 25 refer to the chart on the following page. The data represents the sales and advertising for Company B in thousands of dollars (to the nearest ten thousand dollars).

21. From 1981 to 1988 inclusive, what was the amount of the greatest increase in sales from one year to the next?

    (A) $88,000          (D) $65,000

    (B) $110,000        (E) $40,000

    (C) $75,000

22. From 1982 to 1988 inclusive, in which year did sales change by the greatest percent over the previous year?

    (A) 1982           (D) 1986

    (B) 1984           (E) 1988

    (C) 1985

### Sales and Advertising for Company B
### (In thousands of dollars – to the nearest ten thousand dollars)

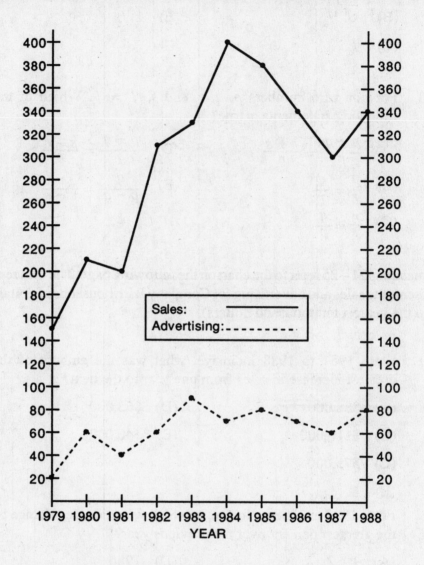

23.  From 1982 to 1988 inclusive, the average (arithmetic mean) advertising for Company B is approximately

(A)  $80,000          (D)  $73,000

(B)  $65,000          (E)  $70,000

(C)  $90,000

24. In how many of the years shown was advertising equal to or greater than 25% of sales?

(A) 6

(D) 3

(B) 5

(E) 2

(C) 4

25. From 1979 to 1988 inclusive, in which year did advertising increase while sales decreased over the previous year?

(A) 1980

(D) 1987

(B) 1983

(E) 1988

(C) 1985

26. Line $AB$ is the perpendicular  bisector of segment $\overline{CP}$ ($P$ is not shown). Then $P$ is the same as which of the following points?

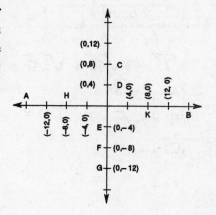

(A) $G$

(B) $F$

(C) $H$

(D) $K$

(E) $D$

27. If $2a + 2b = 1$, and $6a - 2b = 5$, which of the following statements is true?

(A) $3a - b = 5$

(D) $a + b < 3a - b$

(B) $a + b > 3a - b$

(E) $a + b = -1$

(C) $a + b = -2$

28. If $n$ is an integer, which of the following represents an odd number?

   (A)  $2n + 3$                    (D)  $3n$

   (B)  $2n$                         (E)  $n + 1$

   (C)  $2n + 2$

29. A postal truck leaves its station and heads for Chicago, averaging 40 mph. An error in the mailing schedule is spotted and 24 minutes after the truck leaves, a car is sent to overtake the truck. If the car averages 50 mph, how long will it take to catch the postal truck?

   (A)  2.6 hours                   (D)  1.5 hours

   (B)  3 hours                     (E)  1.6 hours

   (C)  2 hours

30. $\sqrt{75} - 3\sqrt{48} + \sqrt{147} =$

   (A)  $3\sqrt{3}$                  (D)  3

   (B)  $7\sqrt{3}$                  (E)  $\sqrt{3}$

   (C)  0

## STOP

If time still remains, you may go back and check your work.
When the time allotted is up, you may go on to the next section.

# Section 5

**TIME:** 30 Minutes
25 Questions

**DIRECTIONS:** Each question or group of questions is based on a passage or set of statements. Select the best answer choice.

1.  Since all ducks I have encountered have been white, it follows that the ducks I will see when I visit the Little Rock Zoo will also be white.

    Which of the following most clearly parallels the reasoning of the preceding argument?

    (A) Some birds are incapable of flight; therefore, ducks are probably incapable of flight.

    (B) Every ballet I have attended has failed to interest me/ so a theatrical production which fails to interest me must be a ballet.

    (C) Since all cases of severe depression I have encountered were susceptible to treatment by chlorpromazine, there must be something in the chlorpromazine which adjusts the patient's brain chemistry.

    (D) Because every society has a word for justice, the concept of fair play must be inherent in the biological makeup of the human species.

    (E) Since no medicine I have tried for my allergy has ever helped, this new product will not work either.

2.  Senator Sheets: No argument for this bill is valid, because no one would argue for this bill without having an ulterior motive; namely, the desire for personal gain.

    The bill's sponsors would be committing the same error in reasoning as Senator Sheets if they responded by saying:

413

(A)  Of course we have ulterior motives. It is perfectly reasonable to support a bill in order to promote our personal interests.

(B)  The fact that passing a bill would benefit its sponsors does not mean that the bill should not be passed.

(C)  The fact that Senator Sheets has substituted a personal attack for a discussion of the merits of the bill leads us to suspect that he can offer no strong arguments against it.

(D)  Senator Sheets has no valid reason for opposing our bill; he is only doing so because we helped defeat his bill last month.

(E)  Everyone is always motivated in part by a desire for personal gain; Senator Sheets is no exception.

3.  Statistics published by the State Department of Traffic and Highway Safety show that nearly 80% of all traffic fatalities occur at speeds under 35 miles per hour and within 25 miles of home.

Which of the following would be the most reasonable conclusion to draw from these statistics?

(A)  A person is less likely to have a fatal accident if he always drives over 35 miles per hour and always at distances greater than 25 miles from his home.

(B)  There is a direct correlation between distance driven and the likelihood of a fatal accident.

(C)  The greater the likelihood that one is about to be involved in a fatal accident, the more likely it is that he is driving close to home at a speed less than 35 miles per hour.

(D)  If it were not the case that a person were about to be involved in a fatal traffic accident, then he would not have been driving at the speed or in the location he was, in fact, driving.

(E)  Most driving is done at less than 35 miles per hour and within 25 miles of home.

4.  Debbie, who had just celebrated her 110th birthday, attributes her longevity to her lifelong habit of drinking a double shot of whiskey each night and smoking three cigars each morning.

    The best way to counter her argument would be to point out that

    (A) smoking has been shown to be a causative factor in several life-threatening diseases.

    (B) other factors besides those mentioned may have caused her to live 110 years.

    (C) not all centenarians drink alcohol and smoke tobacco.

    (D) Debbie should not be consuming the substance mentioned without medical advice.

    (E) alcohol has been shown to kill brain cells.

5.  If Fred graduated from the University after 1965, he was required to take Western Civilization.

    The statement above can be logically deduced from which of the following?

    (A) Before 1965, Western Civilization was not a required course at the University.

    (B) Every student who took Western Civilization at the University graduated after 1965.

    (C) No student who graduated from the University before 1965 took Western Civilization.

    (D) All students graduating from the University after 1965 were required to take Western Civilization.

    (E) Before 1965, no student was not permitted to graduate from the University without having taken Western Civilization.

Questions 6-7 refer to the following statements.

Tracy to Dennis: I'm not going to play with your dog because I'll be sneezing all afternoon if I do. I've played with your dog three times, and each time I've sneezed all afternoon.

6. The argument above is most like which of the following arguments?

   (A) Empiricism must have developed later than rationalism, because it developed as a reaction to rationalism.

   (B) Drug A increases fertility in humans. Every woman given the drug in tests gave birth to more than one child.

   (C) The dumping of chemicals into the lake two months ago caused the present dying of the fish. No fish died in the lakes into which no chemicals were dumped.

   (D) The committee's report must have been valid, because it predicted that a crisis would develop, and that is exactly what has happened.

   (E) David's fiancee must be allergic to roses. Every time he gives her roses, she becomes weepy.

7. Tracy's argument would be most strengthened if it is also true that

   (A) Dennis also sneezes after playing with his cat.

   (B) Tracy never sneezes just before playing with Dennis' dog.

   (C) Tracy also sneezes after playing with David's cat.

   (D) Tracy sneezes only after playing with Dennis' dog.

   (E) Tracy also sneezes after sleeping on a feather pillow.

Questions 8 – 9 refer to the following passage.

Stock market analysts always attribute a sudden drop in the market to some domestic or international political crisis. I maintain, however, that those declines are attributable to the phases of the moon, which also causes periodic political upheavals and increases in tension in world affairs.

8. Which of the following best describes the author's method of questioning the claim of market analysts?

(A) He presents a counter-example.

(B) He presents statistical evidence.

(C) He suggests an alternative causal-linkage.

(D) He appeals to generally accepted beliefs.

(E) He demonstrates that market analysts' reports are unreliable.

9. It can be inferred that the author is critical of the stock market analysts because he

(A) believes that they have oversimplified the connection between political crisis and fluctuation of the market.

(B) knows that the stock market generally shows more gains than losses.

(C) suspects that stock analysts have vested interests in the stock market, and are therefore likely to distort their explanations.

(D) anticipates making large profits in the market himself.

(E) is worried that if the connection between political events and stock market prices becomes well known, unscrupulous investors will take advantage of the information.

Questions 10-13 refer to the following statements.

Seven baseball players are to be honored at a dinner. The players will be seated along one side of a single rectangular table.

Bell and Sheets have to leave the luncheon early and so must be seated at the extreme right end of the table, which is closest to the exit.

Green will receive a trophy and so must be in the center chair to facilitate the presentation.

Berry and Tyler who were bitter rivals for the position of catcher during the season, dislike one another and should be seated as far apart as is convenient.

Moody and Horton are best friends and want to sit together.

417

10.  Which of the following may not be seated at either end of the table?

(A)  Berry

(B)  Tyler

(C)  Sheets

(D)  Horton

(E)  Bell

11.  Which of the following pairs may not be seated together?

(A)  Horton and Tyler

(B)  Green and Tyler

(C)  Moody and Bell

(D)  Sheets and Tyler

(E)  Moody and Berry

12.  Which of the following pairs may not occupy the seats on either side of Green?

(A)  Horton and Tyler

(B)  Tyler and Moody

(C)  Moody and Sheets

(D)  Horton and Berry

(E)  Berry and Moody

13.  If neither Moody nor Tyler is seated next to Green, how many different seating arrangements are possible?

(A)  1

(B)  2

(C)  3

(D)  4

(E)  5

Questions 14- 19 refer to the following passage.

The headmaster of a girl's school is selecting a committee of students to attend a national conference. The students eligible to attend are Joy, Debbie, Edie, Linda, Millie, Pam, and Judy. The committee must be selected given the following considerations.

If Judy is selected, Edie must be selected.
If both Edie and Debbie are selected, then Joy cannot be selected.

If both Debbie and Joy are selected, then Millie cannot be selected

If Joy is selected, then either Linda or Pam must be selected; but Linda and Pam cannot both be selected.

Either Linda or Millie must be selected, but Linda and Millie cannot both be selected.

14. If neither Linda nor Pam is selected, what is the largest number of students who can be selected for the conference?

   (A) 2                        (D) 5

   (B) 3                        (E) 6

   (C) 4

15. If both Joy and Judy are selected, what is the smallest number of students who can be selected for the conference?

   (A) 3                        (D) 6

   (B) 4                        (E) 7

   (C) 5

16. If both Joy and Pam are selected, which of the following must be true?

   (A) Debbie must be selected.     (D) Edie cannot be selected.

   (B) Linda must be selected.      (E) Judy cannot be selected.

   (C) Millie must be selected.

17. Which of the following is an acceptable delegation to the conference if only three students are selected?

   (A) Joy, Debbie, and Linda       (D) Edie, Linda, and Millie

   (B) Joy, Debbie, and Millie      (E) Edie, Linda, and Pam

   (C) Joy, Edie, and Judy

18. If both Joy and Millie are chosen, which of the following cannot be true?

    I.    Edie is chosen

    II.   Debbie is chosen

    III.  Pam is not chosen

    (A)  I, but not II or III        (D)  II and III, but not I

    (B)  II, but not I or III        (E)  I, II, and III

    (C)  III, but not I or II

19. If Pam and three other students are selected, which of the following groups can accompany Pam?

    (A)  Joy, Debbie, and Millie

    (B)  Joy, Edie, and Millie

    (C)  Joy, Debbie, and Judy

    (D)  Joy, Judy, and Linda

    (E)  Edie, Linda, and Judy

Questions 20 – 22 refer to the following passage.

A dachshund, beagle, bassett, and chow win the top four prizes in the dog show. Their owners are Mr. Harriman, Mr. Tyler, Mr. Phillips, and Mr. Berry. The dogs' names are Toby, Rusty, Deuce, and Ace. The owners' and dogs' names are not necessarily in any order.

Mr. Phillips' dog wins neither first nor second prize.
The bassett wins first prize.
Ace wins second prize.
The dachshund is Toby.
Mr. Tyler's dog, the chow, wins fourth prize.
Mr. Berry's dog is Rusty.

20. First prize is won by

    (A)  Mr. Harriman's dog.     (B)  Mr. Berry's dog

(C) Ace

(D) Toby

(E) Deuce

21. Mr. Phillip's dog

(A) is the bassett

(D) wins second prize

(B) is the beagle

(E) is Rusty

(C) is the dachshund

22. Deuce

(A) is owned by Mr. Tyler

(B) is owned by Mr. Harriman

(C) is the beagle

(D) is the bassett

(E) wins third prize

Questions 23 – 25 refer to the following passage.

Mr. and Mrs. Johnson and Dr. and Mrs. Steinmiller each have different tastes in music. One prefers rock and roll, one easy listening, one classical, and the last country music. Of the four, only two have brown hair and one of these likes easy listening best. The wife with brown hair likes country music and her husband likes classical music best. Mrs. Steinmiller has blond hair.

23. What is Mrs. Steinmiller's preferred music?

(A) classical

(D) country

(B) easy listening

(E) cannot be determined

(C) rock and roll

24. What color hair does Dr. Steinmiller have and what music does he prefer?

   (A) brown hair and easy listening

   (B) brown hair and classical music

   (C) brown hair and rock and roll

   (D) blond hair and country music

   (E) blond hair and easy listening

25. Who prefers classical music?

   (A) Mrs. Steinmiller          (D) Mr. Johnson

   (B) Dr. Steinmiller           (E) cannot be determined

   (C) Mrs. Johnson

**STOP**

If time still remains, you may go back and check your work.
When the time allotted is up, you may go on to the next section.

# Section 6

TIME:   30 Minutes
        25 Questions

DIRECTIONS: Each question or group of questions is based on a passage or set of statements. Select the best answer choice.

Questions 1 – 4 refer to the following statements.

A five-member research group is chosen from mathematicians A, B, C, and D and physicists E, F, G and H. At least three mathematicians must be in the research group. However,

A refuses to work with D.
B refuses to work with E.
F refuses to work with G.
D refuses to work with F.

1.  If B is chosen, who else would have to be in the group?

    (A) F                   (D) C

    (B) G                   (E) D

    (C) A

2.  If G is rejected, which other member could not work with the group?

    (A) A                   (D) F

    (B) B                   (E) D

    (C) C

3.  If B and C are chosen, which is necessarily true?

    I.   A is chosen.

    II.   D is chosen.

    III.  Either F or G is chosen.

  (A)  I only               (D)  II and III only

  (B)  II only             (E)  neither I, II nor III

  (C)  III only

4.    If H is chosen, which must be true?

    I.    A must be chosen.

    II.   B must be chosen.

    III.  G must be chosen

  (A)  I only               (D)  II and III only

  (B)  II only             (E)  neither I, II nor III

  (C)  III only

Questions 5 – 9 refer to the following statements.

Five executives of an international company hold a meeting in Atlanta, Georgia.

Mr. Anderson converses in Portuguese and German.
Mr. Bell converses in Portuguese and English.
Ms. Phillips converses in English and German.
Ms. Askew converses in Russian and Portuguese.
Mr. Sheets converses in German and Russian.

5.    Which of the following can act as interpreter when Ms. Phillips and Ms. Askew wish to confer?

  (A)  Mr. Anderson

  (B)  Mr. Bell

  (C)  Mr. Sheets

  (D)  Mr. Anderson or Mr. Bell

  (E)  Any of the other three executives

6. Which of the following cannot converse without an interpreter?

   (A) Mr. Bell and Mr. Sheets.

   (B) Mr. Anderson and Mr. Bell

   (C) Mr. Anderson and Ms. Phillips

   (D) Mr. Bell and Ms. Askew

   (E) Mr. Anderson and Mr. Sheets

7. Besides Mr. Sheets, who can converse with Ms. Askew without an interpreter?

   (A) Mr. Anderson

   (B) Mr. Bell

   (C) Ms. Phillips

   (D) Mr. Anderson and Mr. Bell

   (E) Mr. Anderson, Mr. Bell, and Ms. Phillips

8. A sixth executive, Mr. Fleniken is flown in for the conference. In order to be understood by the maximum number of the executives, he should be fluent in

   (A) English and Russian      (D) German and Portuguese

   (B) German and English       (E) English and Portuguese

   (C) Russian and German

9. Of the languages spoken the two that are least common are

   (A) English and Portuguese    (D) German and English

   (B) English and Russian       (E) Russian and Portuguese

   (C) German and Portuguese

Questions 10 – 13 refer to the following statements.

1) A is older than B and taller than C.
2) D is younger than E, older than C, and shorter than F.
3) G is older than H, younger than C, shorter than H, and taller than F.
4) H is older than A and shorter than C.

10. Which of the following is the youngest?

(A) A  (D) D

(B) B  (E) E

(C) C

11. Which of the following is the tallest?

(A) A  (D) D

(B) H  (E) C

(C) F

12. Which of the following is true?

(A) A is the second oldest and is the third tallest.

(B) C is younger than D and taller than H.

(C) D is the oldest and shortest.

(D) G is older than E and shorter than A.

(E) H is older than B and taller than A.

13. Which statement about the group A, B, C, D, E, F, G, and H is necessarily false?

(A) D is the shortest of the group.

(B) C is the second tallest of the group.

(C) D is the second oldest of the group.

(D)   A is the tallest of the group.

(E)   F is the third oldest of the group.

Questions 14 – 16 refer to the following statements.

1)   Eight physicists P, Q, R, S, T, U, V, W attend a seminar, where they are seated in a row.

2)   Three of these, Q, U, and W, are also biologists.

3)   Four of the eight, P, R, S, and V are also mathematicians.

4)   No scientists who work in the same two fields will be seated next to one another.

14.   Which of the following is a possible seating arrangement?

(A)   Q R U S P T V W

(B)   U P Q R V S T W

(C)   P Q R T S U V W

(D)   P Q R S T U V W

(E)   R Q P T U W S V

15.   To have the proper seating arrangement, which of the following scientists cannot sit next to S?

(A)   Q, V and W only

(B)   R, V only

(C)   P, R, V, T only

(D)   T only

(E)   P, R, V only

16.   If, before all the scientists are seated, there is a vacant seat on each side of P, which two scientists may occupy these seats?

(A)   T and R

(B)   Q and S

(C)   W and T

(D)   R and S

(E)   U and V

Questions 17 – 18 refer to the following statement.

"All actions have consequences. Given this fact, we may wish to play it safe by never doing anything."

17. The speaker implies that:

(A) we may prefer to live safely.

(B) all acts have consequences.

(C) consequentiality is not safe.

(D) not doing anything is not an act.

(E) doing nothing is not an act and keeps us safe from consequences.

18. What conclusion about consequences must we accept if we accept the writer's statements?

(A) Consequences are significant only for active people.

(B) All consequences are dangerous.

(C) There are some acts that do not produce consequences.

(D) Consequences have moral force.

(E) Consequences are always dismal.

Questions 19 – 20 refer to the following statements.

Recent studies indicate that more violent crimes are committed during hot weather than cold weather. Thus, if we could control the weather, the violent crime rate would drop.

19. The argument above makes which of the following assumptions?

I. The relationship between weather conditions and crime rates is merely coincidental.

II. The relationship between weather conditions and the crime rate is causal.

III. The relationship between weather conditions and the crime rate is controllable.

(A) I and II

(B) II and III

(C) I, II and III

(D) I only

(E) none of the above

20. The argument would be strengthened if it is pointed out that

(A) the annual crime statistics for New York are higher than ihose for Los Angeles.

(B) in laboratory tests, increased heat alone accounted for increased aggressive behavior between members of the test group.

(C) poor socioeconomic conditions, more uncomfortable in hot weather than in cold, are the direct causes of increased crime.

(D) weather control will be possible in the near future.

(E) more people leave their doors and windows open during hot weather.

Questions 21 – 22 refer to the following passage.

Leave behind the frantic turmoil of civilization and come back with us to the real America; still the land of the eagle, the buffalo, the mountain lion and elk; still spacious, sprawling, majestic. Experience the freedom and serenity still to be found in _____.

21. For this question choose the completion that best fits the passage.

(A) the natural wonders of our land

(B) our amazing urban centers

(C) the wild jungles of Africa

(D) one's own subconscious

(E) the sprawling cities of the great Southwest

22. In which of the following pamphlets would one least expect to find the preceding passage?

    (A) A Hunter's Guide to the United States

    (B) Exploring the Great Outdoors

    (C) The Quite Beauty of Alaska

    (D) How the Eagle Became Extinct

    (E) Returning to America

Questions 23 – 25 refer to the following passage.

"The older we get, the less sleep we should desire. This is because our advanced knowledge and capabilities are most enjoyable when used; therefore, 'mindless' sleep becomes a waste of time."

23. Which of the following distinctions is not expressed or implied by the author?

    (A) between sleep and wakefulness

    (B) between youth and maturity

    (C) between productivity and waste

    (D) between a desire and a requirement

    (E) between more sleep and less sleep

24. The author of this statement assumes that

    (A) less sleep is not desirable

    (B) sleep advances knowledge and capabilities

    (C) mindlessness coincides with wakefulness

    (D) knowledge and capabilities naturally improve with age

    (E) sleep is only for the young

25. This author's statement might be strengthened if he or she pointed out that

   (A) advanced knowledge is often manifested in creative dreams

   (B) the mind is quite active during sleep

   (C) few empirical studies have concluded that sleep is an intellectual stimulant

   (D) advanced capabilities are not necessarily mind-associated

   (E) dreams teach us how to use waking experiences more intelligently

**STOP**

If time still remains, you may go back and check your work.

# TEST 3

## ANSWER KEY

### Section 1 — Verbal Ability

| | | | | | | | |
|---|---|---|---|---|---|---|---|
| 1. | (A) | 11. | (E) | 21. | (A) | 31. | (A) |
| 2. | (E) | 12. | (E) | 22. | (C) | 32. | (E) |
| 3. | (E) | 13. | (C) | 23. | (E) | 33. | (B) |
| 4. | (C) | 14. | (A) | 24. | (A) | 34. | (E) |
| 5. | (D) | 15. | (A) | 25. | (C) | 35. | (E) |
| 6. | (C) | 16. | (A) | 26. | (E) | 36. | (E) |
| 7. | (D) | 17. | (A) | 27. | (B) | 37. | (A) |
| 8. | (C) | 18. | (B) | 28. | (B) | 38. | (C) |
| 9. | (D) | 19. | (C) | 29. | (B) | | |
| 10. | (E) | 20. | (A) | 30. | (A) | | |

### Section 2 — Verbal Ability

| | | | | | | | |
|---|---|---|---|---|---|---|---|
| 1. | (D) | 11. | (B) | 21. | (A) | 31. | (C) |
| 2. | (D) | 12. | (D) | 22. | (E) | 32. | (B) |
| 3. | (A) | 13. | (B) | 23. | (C) | 33. | (B) |
| 4. | (C) | 14. | (A) | 24. | (A) | 34. | (E) |
| 5. | (A) | 15. | (D) | 25. | (B) | 35. | (C) |
| 6. | (E) | 16. | (E) | 26. | (D) | 36. | (E) |
| 7. | (D) | 17. | (E) | 27. | (A) | 37. | (B) |
| 8. | (B) | 18. | (B) | 28. | (C) | 38. | (D) |
| 9. | (B) | 19. | (E) | 29. | (E) | | |
| 10. | (C) | 20. | (C) | 30. | (C) | | |

### Section 3 — Quantitative Ability

| | | | | | | | |
|---|---|---|---|---|---|---|---|
| 1. | (A) | 3. | (A) | 5. | (A) | 7. | (A) |
| 2. | (B) | 4. | (C) | 6. | (D) | 8. | (A) |

| 9. | (B) | 15. | (D) | 21. | (D) | 27. | (B) |
|----|-----|-----|-----|-----|-----|-----|-----|
| 10. | (B) | 16. | (B) | 22. | (A) | 28. | (D) |
| 11. | (C) | 17. | (D) | 23. | (C) | 29. | (E) |
| 12. | (B) | 18. | (D) | 24. | (B) | 30. | (D) |
| 13. | (B) | 19. | (D) | 25. | (E) | | |
| 14. | (D) | 20. | (C) | 26. | (C) | | |

## Section 4 — Quantitative Ability

| 1. | (A) | 9. | (D) | 17. | (B) | 25. | (C) |
|----|-----|-----|-----|-----|-----|-----|-----|
| 2. | (C) | 10. | (C) | 18. | (E) | 26. | (B) |
| 3. | (B) | 11. | (A) | 19. | (C) | 27. | (D) |
| 4. | (D) | 12. | (D) | 20. | (A) | 28. | (A) |
| 5. | (B) | 13. | (B) | 21. | (B) | 29. | (E) |
| 6. | (C) | 14. | (C) | 22. | (A) | 30. | (C) |
| 7. | (A) | 15. | (A) | 23. | (D) | | |
| 8. | (B) | 16. | (D) | 24. | (E) | | |

## Section 5 — Analytical Ability

| 1. | (E) | 8. | (C) | 15. | (B) | 22. | (A) |
|----|-----|-----|-----|-----|-----|-----|-----|
| 2. | (D) | 9. | (A) | 16. | (C) | 23. | (C) |
| 3. | (E) | 10. | (D) | 17. | (A) | 24. | (A) |
| 4. | (B) | 11. | (C) | 18. | (D) | 25. | (D) |
| 5. | (D) | 12. | (C) | 19. | (B) | | |
| 6. | (B) | 13. | (B) | 20. | (B) | | |
| 7. | (D) | 14. | (C) | 21. | (C) | | |

## Section 6 — Analytical Ability

| 1. | (D) | 8. | (D) | 15. | (E) | 22. | (D) |
|----|-----|-----|-----|-----|-----|-----|-----|
| 2. | (E) | 9. | (B) | 16. | (C) | 23. | (D) |
| 3. | (C) | 10. | (B) | 17. | (E) | 24. | (D) |
| 4. | (B) | 11. | (A) | 18. | (B) | 25. | (C) |
| 5. | (E) | 12. | (B) | 19. | (E) | | |
| 6. | (A) | 13. | (E) | 20. | (B) | | |
| 7. | (D) | 14. | (C) | 21. | (A) | | |

# DETAILED EXPLANATIONS OF ANSWERS

## Section 1–Verbal Ability

1.  (A)

SAVOROUS indicates a particular flavor or smell. DELIGHT-FUL and DELICIOUS have the added implication of sensual gratification. The word "and" suggests the correct choice will be the same part of speech and carry a meaning compatible with NUTRITIOUS. DISSONANT means disagreeable. Only PALATABLE implies acceptability and is the correct choice.

2.  (E)

INEPTITUDE and ASININITY are synonymous and defined as lacking in intelligence. RATIONALIZE and VINDICATE are also synonyms referring to having plausible but untrue reasons for conduct. SAGACITY denotes wisdom, PSYCHOSIS is defined as insanity. The contextual clues of "Explain away" and "other excuses" imply more than one excuse was given. GARRULITY refers to talkativeness. PALLIATE suggests "to cover up." Therefore, GARRULITY and PALLIATE are the correct choices.

3.  (E)

IMPRESSION and RESEMBLANCE refer to a copy. ANTITHESIS means the "opposite of". VARIANCE denotes disagreement. CORRELATE is the correct choice as it alone refers to one thing corresponding to another by looking at it from a different viewpoint.

4.  (C)

EQUIVALENCE and CORRESPONDENCE refer to equality. DISPARATE denotes inequality. PORTION implies a distinct part determined by its size. Only PIECE is unqualified by shape or size. Contextual clue "knowledge" cannot be partitioned into distinctly shaped sizes. PIECE is the correct choice.

434

5.    (D)
    ECSTASY is defined as a state of enjoyment. The word "sympathy" in the passage is contradictory. FERVOR relates to prayer. SPIRITUALISM and SYMBOLICS suggests the occult. The passage does not support this. ARDOR is the correct choice, implying a nondirected passion without regard to a goal.

6.    (C)
    REPARTITIONED and APPORTIONED are synonyms meaning "to divide." SUBSCRIBED and SUBSIDIZED are synonyms meaning "to donate." Only INDEMNIFIED implies reimbursement for loss or damage.

7.    (D)
    INERUDITE and ILLITERATE refer to a lack of knowledge or ability. EDIFIED and OMNISCIENT are the opposite implying abundant knowledge. BOOKISH is the correct choice as it suggests knowledge gained through books alone. The contextual clues of "folly" and "poorly read" indicate a dirth of experiential knowledge.

8.    (C)
    FELODESE and RESUSITATE are antonyms as are GARGANTUAN and DIMINUTIVE. EARTHEN and CERAMIC have a whole-to-part relationship. WATER and ELECTRICITY possess a cause/effect relationship. Therefore only ONOMATOPOEIC and ECHOIC have a synonymous relationship as do the lead words of DUPLICATE and REPLICATE.

9.    (D)
    CTENOPHORE and JELLYFISH are synonyms as are PARANG and CLEAVOR. HARP and ARPEGGIO have a cause/effect relationship, while INSECT and ARTHROPOD are contained in a member-class relationship. OCTAVE and SCORE is the correct choice. They have a part-to-whole relationship as do the lead words of PREFIX and STRUCTURAL ANALYSIS.

10.  (E)

LEMMING and MUSKRAT have a member/member relationship. OSTRICH and FALCON also have a member/member relationship. ROYALTY and FARTHINGALE are contained in a purpose relationship, while FUMAROLE and VOLCANO have a part-to-whole relationship. MIRAGE and ILLUSION is the correct choice since they have the same relationship as the lead words of LEGION and MULTITUDE, which is that of a synonym.

11.  (E)

MISCELLANEOUS and ASSORTED are synonyms as are MINIMIZE AND DEROGRATE. MIEN and DEMEANOR are also synonymous. HEMLOCK and HERB belong to the member/class relationship. Only PURLOIN and REVERT have the same relationship as the lead words, that of antonyms.

12.  (E)

SEA and POLDER are contained in a cause/effect relationship. POCHARD and DIVING DUCK belong to a member/class relationship. PALATABLE and SAVORY as well as PITHY and SENTENTIOUS all belong to the synonymous relationship. The correct choice is (E). PREDILECTION and OBJECTIVITY have the same relationship as the lead words of DEMARCATE and CONFOUND, that of antonyms.

13.  (C)

PARTICLE and ATOM as well as CORNICE and FURNITURE belong to the part-to-whole relationship. THEOSOPHY and MONASTERY possess the relationship of purpose. SPEAR and APERTURE are synonymous. RAYON and BENGALINE are member/class relationship even as ARACHNIDS and ARTHROPOD also belong to the member/class relationship.

14.  (A)

INSTIGATE and PROVOKE, DIAGRAM and DESIGN and COQUET and PEDANTISM all have the synonymous relationship. PUNCTILIOUS and FALLACIOUS contain an antonymous relationship. Only NEUTRAL and CONDONATION have a cause/effect relationship as do the lead words of RACISM and PREJUDICE.

15.  (A)
FECUNDITY and PROLIFICACY, PROTUBERANCE and DEPRESSION, and RAPACIOUS and BENEVOLENT are antonymous relationships. SILK and PONGEE are a cause/effect relationship. ACCOUNT and CHRONICLE are synonymous with DEPICTIVE and SUGGESTIVE.

16.  (A)
PLOVER and SANDPIPER and PEREGRINE and FALCON belong to the member/member relationship. TURBAN and HAT belong to the member/class relationship. VIM and FATIGUE are antonyms. GLUTTONY and VORACITY are synonyms as the lead words of INTOXICATION and INEBRIATION are synonymous.

17.  (A)
(B) is a negative statement. Sentence two states the opposite "he heard from the Indians of a great river to the west." (C) is stated in the last sentence of paragraph one. (D) is an inferred statement. No reference was made to French settlements, therefore leaving (E) as incorrect. (A) is the correct choice; the key contextual words are "ascended" and "descended."

18.  (B)
No reference was made to (A). (C) is incorrect because the passage states that the Governor had previously been involved in projects to open the lake country. (D) is incorrect because the Indians had been truthful but that alone did not necessarily make them trustworthy. (E) is incorrect; no mention was made of the Governor continuing his own project. (B) is the correct choice. The phrase "may have penetrated the Ohio River Valley" supports the statement "confirmed and supported previous reports made by La Salle."

19.  (C)
(A), (B), (D) and (E) are not stated. (C) is the correct choice. The last sentence uses the term "French trade" implying the French traded something to the Indians. The only commodity the Indians had to trade back to the French would have been furs.

20. (A)

(B), (C), (D) and (E) are simply not referred to either explicitly or inferentially. (A) is the correct choice. Paragraph one states that Marquette was determined to "investigate." No other rationale is given for his journey, thereby inferring that exploration was his primary objective.

21. (A)

(B), (C), (D) and (E) are stated in paragraph one. (A) is the correct choice. It is inferred from sentence three, paragraph one "He *started* a new science."

22. (C)

(A) is stated in paragraph two, sentence one. (B) is a negative statement, paragraph two, sentence three states the opposite. (D) Three is an incorrect choice. Paragraph two, sentence four states "a dependable supersonic motor." Paragraph two, the last sentence states (E). (C) is the correct choice. Paragraph two, sentence one states "smooth, tapered nozzle increases velocity by eight times and distance by sixty-four times"; implying that a blunt nozzle negatively affects both speed and distance.

23. (E)

(A), (B), (C) and (D) are stated and share a part-to-whole relationship with (E). Without the whole, the multistage principle contained within Goddard's thesis, the development of the parts would have been directionless, therefore (E) is the correct answer.

24. (A)

(B), (C), (D) and (E) are explicitly stated. (A) is the correct choice. It is inferred from the statement "proving on paper and in actual test that a rocket can travel in a vacuum ... basic designs..."

25. (C)

(A) is a false statement. (B), (D) and (E) are stated in the passage. (C) is the correct choice. "A rocket could travel in a vacuum" suggests that a medium of air is not necessary for rocket flight.

26. (E)

The contribution lies in Dr. Goddard's willingness to make available to the military the experiments and developments.

27. (B)

(A), (C), (D) and (E) were sequential in development following (B) which is the correct choice. "Receiving the grant" came as a result of the interest of the Smithsonian Institute.

28. (B)

PROCEDURE alludes to a particular way of doing something. DIMINISH implies "to reduce" and DILATORY suggests delaying. PENCHANT is synonymous with PROCLIVITY. Only DEFLECTION (B), meaning to turn aside, is the opposite of PROCLIVITY, meaning a strong leaning toward something.

29. (B)

FOREIGN suggests being situated outside a place while PARALLAX indicates an apparent difference in the direction of an object as seen from two perspectives. INAPPOSITE refers to being not relevant. PROPINQUITY denotes a closeness in a relationship as opposed to PROXIMATE (choice (B)) which is nearness in space. (B) is the opposite of REMOTE.

30. (A)

INTERVAL and INTERSTICE both refer to a space of time between two events. DEPRESSION denotes the action of causing one or something to sink to a lower position. PROFUNDITY is a synonym of abyss. (A) ZENITH, defined as the highest point reached in the heavens, is the opposite of ABYSS, the lowest point.

31. (A)

PERFUNCTORY, LONGANIMITY and UNPUNCTILIOUS denote actions related to personal characteristics. INDULGENCE is a synonym of lenient. Only (A), IMPLACABLE, defined as not capable of being appeased, is the opposite of lenient, which means to "take unrestrained pleasure in."

439

32. (E)

IMPOROSITY is synonymous with DENSITY. OBTUSENESS suggests dullness rather than weight. VACUITY refers to an empty space. PUERILITY is unrelated, referring to childish behavior. Only LEVITY (E) denotes lightness of weight, which is the opposite of density.

33. (B)

SUFFUSION denotes an overspreading of something over time. ALLOCATION also refers to being added but includes the suggestion of an assignment for a specific purpose. BURGESS simply implies representation. LUXATE is nearly antonymous meaning to throw out or dislocate. Only (B) INHERENT means the essential character of something as opposed to SOJOURNER which means temporary addition of.

34. (E)

EPITOME, CONCISION, LACONIC and COMPENDIUM are synonyms of abridgment. REDUNDANT (E) has the opposite meaning of "in excess of."

35. (E)

VERTEX and ACME are synonymous, defined as the highest point or summit. EMINENCE is a near synonym of vertex and acme. Although it too, denotes outstanding it does not refer to direction. EXULTATION refers to the extreme but denotes mood rather than direction. VORTEX produces an action of lowering or pulling down. Only FUNDAMENTAL (E) meaning "original source" is the opposite of vertex.

36. (E)

TREPIDATION and APPREHENSION are synonymous, meaning "fear". PERTURBATION refers to the degree of apprehension. AGITATION implies an emotional state accompanied by irregular movement. SAGACITY suggests a part to whole relationship, relating to the mental capacity to discern character. COURAGE, (E) is defined as mental and moral strength as opposed to trepidation, meaning fear.

37.   (A)
    STUBBORNNESS and VISCIDITY imply an unyielding quality. PRECIPITATION is an antonym of TENUOUS, relating to strength or lack of strength. SUBTLETY refers to the ability to make a fine distinction. RESILIENT (A) denotes the ability to adjust to change as opposed to the inability to change.

38.   (C)
    ASSIZE, to produce an ordinance, is a near synonym of EFFEC-TUATION, producing the desired effect. ANNEXATION refers to uniting or joining while PERPETUATION carries the added meaning of lasting indefinitely. VITALIZE, (C) to live, is the opposite of HOMICIDE, to destroy.

## Section 2–Verbal Ability

1.   (D)
    The second term in each pair given describes a particular orientation or outlook on life. Of these, COSMOPOLITAN (free from local, provincial, or national ideas or prejudices) is the only one which is the opposite of provincial (having unsophisticated or narrow points of view). Any of the initial terms given could be appropriately used in the first blank.

2.   (D)
    The author's intent is to identify the degree to which various professions relate to political government. The importance or significance he assigns to each is inferred from the number of words he assigns to each profession. (D) INFERRED…SIGNIFICANCE is the correct answer. Acceptability of alternatives (A), (B), (C), and (E) is counteracted by the second term in each case. WORTH, VALUE, and MERIT have to do with quality of the various professions rather than with their importance or significance in relation to the discussion. The achievements of the professions are likewise distinct from the importance or significance of the profession, in relation to the idea presented here.

441

3.    (A)
The answer is (A) ENVIRONMENTAL. This is the alternative of choice because it is juxtaposed with "personal" variables in the sentence. The transition word, "however" is a clue that what follows will be a qualifier or thought in some way contrary to that previously presented. Alternatives (B) CRITICAL and (D) POWERFUL are wrong because both environmental and personal variables can be critical and powerful. Alternative (C) INNOCUOUS is wrong because it means "harmless" and does not fit the sense of the sentence. Alternative (E) ENDEMIC is wrong because endemic means "prevalent in or restricted to a particular locality." The variables mentioned are not restricted to the at-risk student population. Other persons also have these variables in their lives.

4.    (C)
The correct answer is (C) RESULT...SPECIFICATIONS. The situation described is the predictable result of not specifically identifying a task and the procedure to be followed in attaining the task. The key to selecting the correct answer in this item is to realize that the situation described is more than just a FACTOR, a PART, or an EXAMPLE. This enables the elimination of three alternatives (A), (D), and (E). Of the two remaining (B) and (C), the alternative (B) can be eliminated because the situation is a result rather than a cause.

5.    (A)
The correct answer is (A) COORDINATION...VISION. Facilitating communication among work groups within an organization is specifically a coordination problem. This realization is the key to selecting the correct alternative. Increasing workers' awareness and focus on organization goals, as opposed to goals of individual work groups, could be called a problem of providing VISION (A), or MISSION (B), DIRECTION (C), or ORIENTATION (E).

6.    (E)
Urban parks will become INADEQUATE and additional parks will be needed in the suburbs. (A) is incorrect because parks which do not exist cannot be UPDATED; (B) is incorrect because use of existing parks will not DEPLETE them (use them up); (C) is incorrect because

the parks in the suburbs need not be LARGER than the urban parks; and (D) is wrong because the parks were IMPORTANT for the city even before growth occurred.

7.    (D)

The answer is (D) ABUNDANT...OBTAINED. Tile makers require a great quantity (ABUNDANCE) of high quality clay, and, once found, the clay must be ACCESSIBLE in order for it to be of use. The second term in alternatives (A), (B), (C), and (E) each includes the idea of accessibility. However, of all the alternatives, only (D) includes the idea of high degree of quantity. EVIDENT and NEARBY merely indicate presence.

8.    (B)

DISSONANCE (discord) and ASSONANCE (harmony) are opposites. (B) CACOPHONY (harsh, jarring sounds) and MELODI-OUS are also opposites. The other analogies listed are made up of terms which are synonymous.

9.    (B)

A PHILANTHROPIST is a person who acts on a desire to help mankind by donating money to worthy causes. The relationships between these two terms is possession. The philanthropist must possess money in order to be a philanthropist. The relationship between the terms in alternative (B) is also that of possession. A SURGEON must possess DEXTERITY or he or she cannot perform the duties of surgeon.

In relation to alternatives (A) and (C), the first term in each is the result of the second. CONVERTS are the result of MISSIONARY efforts and crops are the result of the farmer's efforts. In relation to alternatives (D) and (E), the first term identifies those who receive the efforts of the second. PSYCHOLOGISTS help SCHIZOPHRENICS and TEACHERS teach STUDENTS.

10.    (C)

A KEY can be used to unlock a DOOR. This relationship is also evidenced in alternative (C) ENIGMA:CLUE. A CLUE may unlock a riddle. The relationship in (A) GEM:RING is that of use. A GEM may

443

be used in a RING. The relationship in (B) PERFUME:AROMA is that of entity and characteristic. AROMA is characteristic of PERFUME. Alternative (D) EFFORT:ACHIEVEMENT presents the relationship of prerequisite:event. EFFORT is a prerequisite to ACHIEVEMENT. In the final alternative, a MOLD may be used to shape GELATIN.

11.   (B)
INTRIGUE and CONSPIRACY are synonymous. The same relationship is found in alternative (B) INTREPID:FEARLESS. These words are synonyms. The other analogies listed (A), (C), (D), and (E) all include terms which are opposites.

12.   (D)
A CALORIE measures HEAT, and CALIPER measures DIAMETER (D). SAND is an ingredient of CEMENT (A); SUCCUMB and YIELD are synonyms (B); a METRONOME provides a consistent beat for MUSIC (C); and (E) RETALIATION is an opposite of FORGIVENESS.

13.   (B)
A TWEETER is a small loudspeaker for reproducing high-frequency sounds, while a WOOFER is a large loudspeaker for reproducing low-frequency sounds. (B) HIGH:LOW identifies this relationship also. The other alternatives, (A), (C), (D), and (E) all express synonymous relationships.

14.   (A)
BAROQUE art is ORNATE. The first term is characteristic of the second term. This same relationship is found in alternative (A). ALTITUDE is characteristic of MOUNTAINS. In other alternatives, a SEED is in FRUIT (B); WOOD can be used to start a FIRE (C); a TYPEWRITER is a precursor to the COMPUTER (D); and a LAKE holds WATER (E).

15.   (D)
CAUSE and PRECIPITATE mean the same thing. (D) OBJECTIVE and GOAL also mean the same thing. The other alternatives

express opposite relationships.

16. (E)
    This analogy is taken from the general area of English grammar. It is a "part-to-whole" analogy. That is, the initial pair of words has a part-to-whole relationship. There are three "moods" in English; indicative (I study), subjunctive (I might study), and vocative (Study!). The INDICATIVE mood is a sub-set of the concept MOOD. (A) PRESENT and PAST are both tenses and in this regard they share equal status. Neither is a sub-set of the other, as is the case with the analogy given. (B) PRONOUNS and PREPOSITIONS are the names given two different parts of speech. They are both parts of a whole that could be called "parts of speech." (C) is a whole-to-part analogy. A SENTENCE may contain a CLAUSE. This alternative is wrong because the whole (the sentence) is listed before the part (the clause). In the analogy given, the part is listed before the whole. The same order must be present in the answer. Alternative (D) gives two of the four kinds of sentences. Each is in this regard a "part." There is no "whole" mentioned. (E) is the correct answer because it is a part-whole analogy. The FUTURE is one of six parts or sub-sets within TENSE. The others are present, past, present perfect, past perfect, and future perfect.

17. (E)
    The author was attempting to portray the events leading up to the Revolutionary War. In the final sentence, after some detail, the author states "...the War for Independence had begun." In relation to (A), there was no attempt at diplomacy by the Colonists. Answer (B) is incorrect. General Thomas Gage probably did overreact, but that was not the theme of the selection. (C) is incorrect. Even though nationalism had united most colonists, the author does not mention this point. (D) is incorrect. The author does state this premise in the first sentence, but does not enlarge the theme.

18. (B)
    A disrespect for the redcoats can be inferred from information the author presents in relation to the manner in which the soldiers entered Lexington, the numbers of redcoats, and their retreat back to Boston.

445

19. **(E)**

War could not be averted, and the time of mere protest had ended. In relation to (A), there is no statement in the selection that the colonists were better fighters, even though this could be inferred since they were outnumbered and eventually drove the British back to Boston. (B) is wrong because even though the colonists knew of General Gage's intentions almost instantaneously, the author makes no statement about spies. (C) is also incorrect. There was a supply depot at Concord but the author does not comment on the preparation of the colonists and a communications network. (D) is incorrect because there were many colonial spokesmen for the revolution and the author speaks of only two in the area at the time.

20. **(C)**

(C) was not an accomplishment of Faraday. This process was first accomplished by Sir Humphry Davy. (A), (B), (D), (E) were all identified as accomplishments of Michael Faraday in the article.

21. **(A)**

The author begins the article with Faraday's accomplishments in spite of a lack of formal education. The implication here is regard and admiration for this person. In relation to alternatives (B) and (C), the author implies neither disrespect nor distrust. In relation to alternative (E), the selection is written in objective terms without any intellectual or emotional identification with the subject. In relation to alternative (D), the author does not minimize Faraday's accomplishments or imply that any of Faraday's actions was inferior to those of others.

22. **(E)**

The author's main point is that Faraday was a self-educated genius. The author makes a point of discussing his contributions, as well as Faraday's lack of formal education, and the educational opportunities made available to him during his apprenticeship with the bookbinder.

23. **(C)**

The author does not explain that gas is liquified by lowering the temperature. Each of the other questions can be answered with the information given.

24. **(A)**
Valence is a more recent term given to the chemical equivalent weight of an element's atomic weight divided by a number. (B), (C), (D), and (E) were all terms developed by Faraday.

25. **(B)**
Becoming Director of the Royal Institution was a step along Faraday's professional career path. The actions identified in (A), (C), and (E) each involve his disbelief in and declining of worldly rewards as part of his belief system; and alternative (D) presents a clear moral choice again based upon his personal convictions.

26. **(D)**
It was the apprenticeship to the bookbinder that allowed him the opportunity to read and to attend scientific lectures that eventually developed his association with Sir Humphry Davy. (A) is incorrect, his birthplace evidently played little part. (B) and (C) are also incorrect. Being one of ten children and experiencing poverty may have meant that apprenticing family members was forthcoming, but these were not the events that made an impact. (E) is incorrect, the association between the two men came after the interest in science had begun.

27. **(A)**
The selection is a brief history of the life and work of the scientist Michael Faraday. (B) is incorrect, electrolysis is only one part of the selection. (C) is incorrect, it can be assumed that most of the work specifically was done at the Royal Institution, but this was not stated. (E) is incorrect, electromagnetic induction was described but was never referred to by name except in paragraph one.

28. **(C)**
FORTUITOUS is an adjective meaning "lucky," or "happening by chance." It is related in derivation to the word fortunate and fortune through the Latin *fors*, meaning "chance," or luck." The opposite of FORTUITOUS is (C) UNLUCKY. Alternatives (A), (D), and (E) are emotional states of being, while (B) UNFRUITFUL, means unproductive.

29. (E)

MYRIAD (Greek, *myrious,* "countless") carries the meaning of "a great number of persons or things." Its opposite here is (E) INDIVIDUAL, meaning "existing as a separate thing or being," or "relating to a single person or thing." Alternative (A) PASSEL means "a group, especially a fairly large group"; (B) DIVERSE means "different" or "varied"; (C) LEGION means "a large number, a multitude"; and (D) PROFUSE means "giving or given freely and abundantly."

30. (C)

PARSIMONIOUS means excessively frugal. A PARSIMONIOUS person is often referred to as a miserly person, a stingy person, or a tightfisted person. Its opposite is (C) PRODIGAL. A PRODIGAL person is one who is excessively extravagant in relation to money. Alternative (A) PECULIAR means "deviating from the customary"; alternative (B) PASSIONATE means "fired with intense feeling"; alternative (D) PATRONIZING means "treating in an indulgent manner"; and alternative (E) PERNICIOUS means "extremely destructive or harmful."

31. (C)

LOQUACIOUS (Latin, *loqui,* – "speak") means "very talkative." Its opposite is (C) SILENT. Alternative (A) DARING, means "fearless, bold"; (B) TEDIOUS means "long and dull, tiresome," as a "tedious lecture"; (D) WEALTHY means "rich"; and (E) HAUGHTY (French, *haut,* – "high") means "showing great pride in oneself and contempt for others, arrogant."

32. (B)

The adjective ARCHAIC comes from the Greek word for "ancient." Its opposite in the list given is (B) MODERN. Alternative (C) ANGELIC refers to a beautiful, good angel-like person; (D) INVISIBLE means "unable to be seen" or "imperceptible," and (E) NOBLE means "famous" or "renowned."

33. (B)

The adjective NEFARIOUS is derived from the Latin words "ne-" (not) and "fas-" (lawful). The English meaning is "wicked." Its

opposite in the list given is (B) GOOD. (C) DANGEROUS, (D) NERVOUS, and (E) STUBBORN identify other, unrelated personal characteristics.

34. **(E)**
AMELIORATE, from the Latin *melior*, meaning "better," conveys the idea "to make or become better, to improve." Its opposite in the list given is (E) WORSEN. The other alternatives carry unrelated meanings. (A) CLARIFY, to make clear; (B) MANDATE, to order; (C) INSIST, to take a stand and maintain it; and (D) AMEND, to improve.

35. **(C)**
To INSERT (Latin, *serere*, – "join") means "to put or fit into something else." Its opposite is (C) EXTRACT, meaning to draw out, as to extract a tooth. (A) EXUDE means to "ooze" or to "radiate"; (B) EXTEND means to "lengthen," (D) EXPLORE means "to examine carefully," and (E) EXTINGUISH means "to put out" or "destroy," as one might put out a fire. The Latin prefixes "in" and "ex" mean "in" and "out."

36. **(E)**
REQUISITE is an adjective meaning necessary or required. Its opposite is (E) SUPERFLUOUS, meaning unnecessary or excessive. An alternative (A) is one of several possible choices. FUTILE (B) means useless; as in a "futile attempt." A PREREQUISITE (C) is something required beforehand as a necessary condition, for instance, a French I class would be a prerequisite for a French II class. ABHORRENT (D) carries the meaning "detestable," as an "abhorrent action."

37. **(B)**
ABJECT is an adjective which means miserable or wretched. Its opposite in the list given is (B) JOYFUL. CARING (A) is not the opposite. EMPATHETIC (C) means "with emphasis or force," OBJECTIVE (D) means "with bias or prejudice," and RATIONAL (E) means "sensible, or based on reasoning," as, a "rational response."

38. **(D)**
INSIPID is an adjective derived from the Latin word *sapidus*, that

means "savory" and the prefix "in" meaning "not." INSIPID means "without flavor" or "tasteless" in English. Its opposite is (D) TASTY. Alternative (A) OBTUSE means blunt; (B) HUMBLE means unpretentious or moderate; (C) MATERNAL means "like a mother"; and (E) JEALOUS, means resentfully envious.

# Section 3—Quantitative Ability

1.  (A)
   Relabel the figure. Using the letters, $E, F, G, H, I, J, K, L,$ $M, N, O$ and $P$, we have:

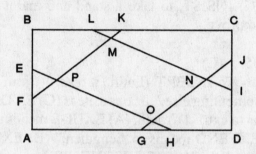

The quadrilaterals are:

$$\begin{matrix} ABCD & FPHA & GOEA & HOJD & INGD \\ JNLC & KMIC & LMFB & EPKB & MNOP \end{matrix}$$

The total number is 10.

2.  (B)

| | Five years ago | Present |
|---|---|---|
| Father | $x - 5$ | $x$ |
| Tom | $\dfrac{x}{3} - 5$ | $\dfrac{x}{3}$ |

Five years ago Tom's age was one-fourth of his father's age.

$$\frac{x}{3} - 5 = \frac{x - 5}{4}$$
$$4x - 60 = 3(x - 5)$$
$$4x - 60 = 3x - 15$$
$$x = 45$$
$$\frac{x}{3} = 15 ,$$

i.e., Tom's age is 15.

3.    (A)

The distance between $B$ and $C$ is 4. The distance between $A$ and $C$ is 3. $\triangle ABC$ is a right triangle. By Pythagorean theorem, the distance between $A$ and $B =$ $\sqrt{3^2 + 4^2} = 5$

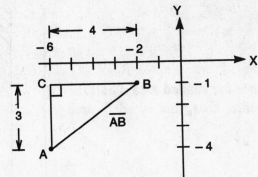

4.    (C)

If

$$R^S = R^2 - S^2$$
$$S^R = S^2 - R^2$$

then

$$R^S / S^R = (R^2 - S^2) / (S^2 - R^2)$$
$$= (R - S)(R + S) / (S - R)(S + R)$$
$$= (R - S) / (S - R)$$
$$= -1.$$

By the similar argument, we have $S^R / R^S = -1$. Thus the values are equal.

5.    (A)

Since $ABC$ and $ABD$ are right triangles,

$$\angle ACB\,(90°) - \angle CAB = 30°$$
$$\angle ADB\,(90°) - \angle DBA = 30°$$

In $\triangle ABE$, $x + 30° + 30° = 180°$, so, $x = 120°$.

6.    (D)

Given that $x = -y$

if $y > 0$,  $x < 0$ and $y > x$
if $y < 0$,  $x > 0$ and $y < x$
if $y = 0$,  $x = 0$ and $y = x$

The relationship cannot be determined from the information given.

7.    (A)

The shaded area can be arranged as presented in the following figure:

451

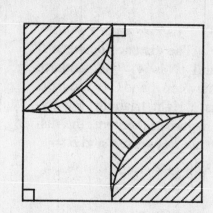

Since the shaded area = half the square area, the shaded area $= \dfrac{a^2}{2}$.

8.  (A)

The original length $= L$. When the ruler increases by 10%, the length will be

$$L + 10\% \text{ of } L = L + 0.1L = 1.1L$$

Then the ruler is decreased by 10%

$$1.1L - 10\% \text{ of } 1.1L = 1.1L - (0.1)1.1L = .99L$$

Therefore, the final length is $.99L$ which is less than the original length. $(L > .99L.)$

9.  (B)

The shaded area is a triangle $AEC$, so

$$\text{shaded area} = \frac{\text{height} \times \text{base}}{2} = \frac{ac}{2}$$

but

$$a < b$$

therefore,

$$\frac{ac}{2} < \frac{bc}{2}$$

10.  (B)

Let $x - 1, x, x + 1$ be three consecutive numbers, then $(x + 1) + x + (x - 1) = 3x$, and the smallest of the three is $x - 1$ which is less than $x$.

11.  (C)

Since $ABC$ is an equilateral triangle, $\angle ACD = 30°$, so,

$$\gamma + 10° = 30°$$
or, $$\gamma = 20°$$
and $$10 + \beta + 90° = 180°$$
$$\beta = 80°$$
$$\alpha + \beta = 180°$$
$$\alpha = 180° - \beta$$
$$\alpha = 100°$$

therefore $\alpha - \beta = 20° = \gamma$.

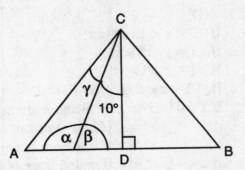

**12. (B)**
To compare $1/_{xy}$ with $1/yz$ is the same as if we compare $1/_x$ with $1/z$ because $y$ appears in both denominators, and we know that $x > z$. Therefore,

$$1/_x < 1/_z \quad \text{and} \quad 1/_{xy} < 1/_{zy}.$$

**13. (B)**
The perimeter (not the area) is equivalent to the circumference of radius $a/2$

$$\text{Perimeter} = 2\pi(^a/_2) = \pi a.$$

**14. (D)**
For any value of $X$ when $X > 1$, $X^2 > X$, and $X^3 > X^2$. As an example,

$$\text{when } x = 2, \quad 2^3 = 8 > 4 = 2^2$$
$$\text{when } x = 3, \quad 3^3 = 27 > 9 = 3^2.$$

We can conclude

$$X^3 > X^2 \text{ when } 1 < X < 2.$$

But in the interval $0 < X < 1$, $X^2 < X$ and $X^3 < X$.
As an example

$$\text{when } x = 0.1, \quad (0.1)^3 = 0.001 < 0.01 = (0.1)^2$$
$$\text{when } x = 0.5, \quad (0.5)^3 = 0.125 < 0.25 = (0.5)^2$$

We can conclude

$$X^3 > X^2 \text{ when } 1 < X < 2$$
$$X^3 < X^2 \text{ when } 0 < X < 1.$$

453

15. (D)

If $0 < x < 1$, $x^m < x^n$

If $x = 1$, $x^m = x^n$

If $1 < x$, $x^m > x^n$

If $-1 < x < 0$, $x^m > x^n$

If $x = -1$, $x^m = x^n$ if $m$ and $n$ are both even or both odd

  $x^m > x^n$ if $m$ is even but $n$ is odd

  $x^m > x^n$ if $n$ is even but $m$ is odd

If $x < -1$, $x^m = x^n$ if $m$ and $n$ are both odd

  $x^m > x^n$ if $m$ and $n$ are both even

  $x^m > x^n$ if $m$ is even but $n$ is odd

  $x^m > x^n$ if $n$ is even but $m$ is odd

Thus, the relationship cannot be determined.

16. (B)

$$\frac{1}{1 + \dfrac{1}{1 + \frac{1}{4}}} = \frac{1}{1 + \dfrac{1}{\frac{1}{4} + 1}} = \frac{1}{1 + \frac{4}{5}} = \frac{5}{5 + 4} = \frac{5}{9}.$$

17. (D)

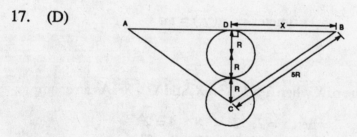

Redraw the figure. It is easy to see that $AC = BC = 5R$. Let $X = BD$, then $AB = 2X$. Using the Pythagorean theorem in triangle $BCD$

$$(3R)^2 + x^2 = (5R)^2$$
$$9R^2 + x^2 = 25R^2$$
$$x^2 = 16R^2$$
$$x = 4R$$

and the perimeter of triangle $ABC$ will be:

$$5R + 5R + 2(4R) = 18R.$$

18. (D)

We need to find the largest value given. Given $0 < a < 1$ and $b > 1$, we know that $a/_b < 1$, $b/_a > 1$, so $b/_a > a/_b$, and $(b/_a)^2 > (a/_b)^2$. Therefore, the choice is between $(b/_a)$ and $(b/_a)^2$. But $(b/_a)^2 > (b/_a)$ since $b/_a > 1$. Thus the largest value is a $(b/_a)^2$.

19. (D)

We will define: $x^1$ = new value of $x$.

$$x^1 = \frac{2}{\underbrace{\left(v - \frac{20}{100}v\right)}_{\text{decreases }20\%}\underbrace{\left(t + \frac{30}{100}t\right)}_{t \text{ increases }30\%}}$$

$$x^1 = \frac{2}{.8v \times 1.3t} = \frac{1}{1.04}\left(\frac{2}{vt}\right)$$

$$x^1 = .96\left(\frac{2}{vt}\right)$$

the variation of $x$ is

$$x^1 - x = .96\left(\frac{2}{vt}\right) - \left(\frac{2}{vt}\right)$$

$$x^1 - x = -.04\left(\frac{2}{vt}\right)$$

$$x^1 - x = \frac{-4}{100}\left(\frac{2}{vt}\right)$$

$$x^1 - x = \frac{-4}{100}(x)$$

Therefore the variation in terms of $x$ is about $-4\%$ or a decrease of 4%.

20. (C)

The first time Peter paid $^m/_n$ dollars/disk and the second time he paid $^q/_n$ dollars/disk. The increment was

$$\frac{q}{n} - \frac{m}{n} = \frac{q-m}{n} = (q-m)/n.$$

21. (D)

If you take the area of any division (or state) you obtain, for example:

| | | |
|---|---|---|
| East North Central | 244,366 miles² | = 632,905 km² |
| find the square root: | 494.33 miles | = 795.55 km |
| | 1 mile | = 1.609 km. |

22. (A)

The largest division is the Pacific — (2.310,958 km² or 892,226 mi²). The New England division has the smallest area — (163,149 km² or 69,992 mi²).

**23. (C)**

For area there are two columns, one in sq. mi. and the second in sq. km. In the latter appear two numbers for Pacific Division.

$$2,310,958$$
$$2,374,315$$

The first one is for land area and the second one for total area.

**24. (B)**

| | | |
|---|---|---|
| Land area (US) | = | 9,170,987 km² |
| Pacific | = | 2,310,958 km² |
| East N. Central | = | 632,905 km² |

$$\text{percentage} = \frac{2,310,958 + 632,905}{9,170,987} \times 100\% = 32.1\%$$

**25. (E)**

First, calculate the rate in the period 1970 – 80 for the East North Central Division. Population 1980 / Population 1970 = 41,668,000/ 40,253,000 = 1.0352. Thus the rate of increase = 3.52%.

$$
\begin{aligned}
\text{Population 1990} &= \text{Population 1980} + (0.352 \times \text{Pop. 1980}) \\
&= 41,668,000 + (0.352 \times 41,668,000) \\
&= 43,134,710.
\end{aligned}
$$

**26. (C)**

Let $x$ = amount of money that I have when I arrive at Casino Las Vegas. After the first game

$$x - \frac{1}{3}x = \frac{2}{3}x$$

After the second game

$$\frac{2}{3}x - \frac{1}{2}\left(\frac{2}{3}x\right) = \frac{1}{3}x$$

and at this moment I have $1000. Therefore

$$1000 = {}^1/_3 x \quad x = 3000.$$

**27. (B)**

Redraw the figure and put the interior angles in the triangle. The

456

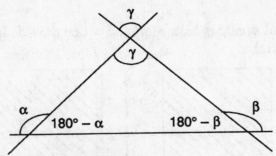

sum of the interior angles is 180°.

$$180° - \alpha + 180° - \beta + \gamma = 180°$$

rearranging and simplifying

$$180° - \alpha + \gamma = \beta, \text{ or } \gamma - \alpha + 180° = \beta.$$

28.  (D)
   We need to find an expression for $^x/_y$ as a function of $\alpha$ and $\beta$

$$\frac{(\alpha + x) + y}{x + y} = \frac{\beta + y}{y}$$

This is the same as

$$\frac{\alpha + (x + y)}{x + y} = \frac{\beta + y}{y}$$

Rearranging

$$\frac{\alpha}{x + y} + \frac{x + y}{x + y} = \frac{\beta}{y} + \frac{y}{y}$$

$$\frac{\alpha}{x + y} + 1 = \frac{\beta}{y} + 1$$

$$\frac{\alpha}{x + y} = \frac{\beta}{y}$$

$$\frac{\alpha}{\beta} = \frac{x + y}{y}$$

$$\frac{\alpha}{\beta} = \frac{x}{y} + \frac{y}{y}$$

$$\frac{\alpha}{\beta} = \frac{x}{y} + 1$$

$$\frac{x}{y} = \frac{\alpha}{\beta} - 1$$

29. (E)

The original square is below left and when the side increases by 10% is below right.

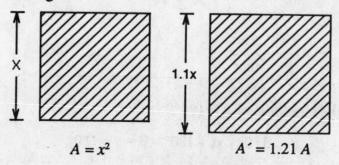

$$A = x^2 \qquad\qquad A' = 1.21\,A$$

The difference in Areas is 5.25 $(\text{ft})^2$, therefore

$$
\begin{aligned}
1.21x^2 - x^2 &= 5.25 \\
.21x^2 &= 5.25 \\
x^2 &= {}^{5.25}\!/_{.21} \\
x^2 &= 25 \\
x &= 5.
\end{aligned}
$$

30. (D)

We need to find the value of $x$, where $3^x > 1$.

$$\text{If } x = 0 \quad \text{then} \quad 3^0 = 1$$
$$\text{If } x = 1 \quad \text{then} \quad 3^1 = 3$$

given that $3^x$ must be bigger than $1$, $x > 0$.

# Section 4—Quantitative Ability

1. (A)

The simplest approach to this problem is to write the right hand side of the center equation as 3 to some power as is the case in the left hand side of the equation. Note that 81 can be factored into its prime factors as

$$
\begin{aligned}
81 &= 3 \cdot 3 \cdot 3 \cdot 3 \\
&= 3^4
\end{aligned}
$$

Thus, the center equation can be written as

$$3^x = 3^4$$

since the bases in both sides of the later equation are the same, it follows that the powers must be the same. Hence, $x = 4$, so the quantity in Column A is greater.

2.    (C)

Let $m \angle \alpha$ represent the measure of angle $\alpha$. Since lines $l$ and $m$ are intersecting at point $P$, it follows that angle $\alpha$ and $\theta$ are supplementary angles. That is, the sum of their measures is 180°. Hence, $m \angle \alpha + m \angle \theta = 180°$.

The center information tells us that $m \angle \theta$ is 3 times the $m \angle \alpha$, that is $m \angle \theta = 3m \angle \alpha$.

Now,

$$
\begin{aligned}
m \angle \alpha + m \angle \theta &= 180° \\
m \angle \alpha + 3m \angle \alpha &= 180° \\
4m \angle \alpha &= 180° \\
m \angle \alpha &= 45°
\end{aligned}
$$

Hence,

$$
\begin{aligned}
m \angle \theta &= 3m \angle \alpha \\
&= 3(45°) \\
&= 135°
\end{aligned}
$$

so the quantities are equal.

3.    (B)

To answer this question, one simply needs to calculate the average (arithmetic mean) and the median of the amounts given in the center information and then compare the two quantities. Recall that

(i)    The average, $\overline{X}$ of a set of numbers is equal to the sum of the numbers divided by the number of numbers, $n$. That is

$$\overline{X} = \frac{\text{sum of the numbers}}{n}$$

(ii)    The median of a set of numbers arranged in an increasing or decreasing order is defined as

(a)    The middle number if the number of numbers is odd.

(b)    The average of the two middle numbers if the number of numbers is even.

In this problem, the numbers are:

$$\$8,000, \$9,000, \$2,000, \$10,000, \$6,000$$

Thus

$$\overline{X} = \frac{8000 + 9000 + 2000 + 10000 + 6000}{5} = \frac{35000}{5} = 7000$$

This means the average of the given numbers is $7,000.

To calculate the median, we need to arrange the given numbers in an increasing or decreasing order. Putting them in an increasing order yields:

$$2,000, \ 6,000, \ 8,000, \ 9,000, \ 10,000.$$

Thus, the median income is $8,000 since 8,000 is the middle number. So the quantity in Column B is greater.

4.    (D)

Performing the indicated operations in Columns A and B yields

$$\left(\frac{x}{y}\right)^{10} = \frac{x^{10}}{y^{10}} \text{ and } \left(\frac{y}{x}\right)^{10} = \frac{y^{10}}{x^{10}}.$$

Since both $x/y$ and $y/x$ are raised to a positive power 10, whatever the values of $x$ and $y$ are, the value of $(x/y)^{10}$ and the value of $(y/x)^{10}$ are both positive. The question now is which is larger: $(x/y)^{10}$ or $(y/x)^{10}$?

Since no information is given about the value of $x$ or $y$, the relationship is indeterminate. For example, if $x = 2$, and $y = 3$, then $(x/y)^{10} = (2/3)^{10}$, and $(y/x)^{10} = (3/2)^{10}$. Since $3/2 > 2/3$, it follows that $(3/2)^{10} > (2/3)^{10}$, and the quantity in Column B is greater. But if $x = 3$ and $y = 2$, then $(x/y)^{10} = (3/2)^{10}$, $(y/x)^{10} = (2/3)^{10}$, and the quantity in Column A is greater.

5.    (B)

The comparison in this problem can be easily established by reducing each fraction to its simplest (lowest) terms. The fraction $4/5$ is already in its simplest form. Thus, we need only to reduce the fraction $120/200$ to its simplest form. This can be achieved by factoring both the numerator and the denominator into their prime factors as follows:

$$\frac{120}{200} = \frac{2 \cdot 2 \cdot 2 \cdot 3 \cdot 5}{2 \cdot 2 \cdot 2 \cdot 5 \cdot 5}$$

Cancelling common factors of the numerator and the denominator yields

$$\frac{120}{200} = \frac{3}{5}$$

So the quantity in Column B is greater.

6.    (C)
Because Jim earns $d$ dollars in $h$ hours, it follows that he earns $d \div h = {}^d/_h$ dollars per hour. If he works $(h + 20)$ hours at the rate of ${}^d/_h$ dollars per hour, then his total earnings will be equal to

$$(h + 20) \cdot \frac{d}{h} \text{ dollars} .$$

Simplifying yields

$$(h + 20) \cdot \left(\frac{d}{h}\right) = h \cdot \frac{d}{h} + \frac{20\,d}{h}$$

$$= d + \frac{20d}{h}$$

Thus, Jim's total earnings in $(h + 20)$ hours can be expressed as

$$\left(d + \frac{20\,d}{h}\right) \text{ dollars} .$$

So the quantities in Columns A and B are equal.


7.    (A)
Let $m \angle x$ denote the measure of angle $x$. In any triangle, if the sides of the triangle are not congruent, then the larger angle lies opposite the longer side.

In this problem, since $b > e$, it follows that the $m \angle B > m \angle e$.

So the quantity in Column A is greater.


8.    (B)
Since Mr. Good's class and Ms. Garcia's class have the same number of students and we do not know this number, we can start by letting x be the number of students in each of the two classes.

From the center information, the ratio of boys to girls in Mr. Good's class is 3:4. This means 3 out of every 7 students in Mr. Good's class are boys. Hence, the ratio of the number of boys in Mr. Good's class is 3:7 or ${}^3/_7$, that is, the number of boys in his class is ${}^3/_7 x = {}^{3x}/_7$.

Similarly, the center information tells us that the ratio of boys to girls in Ms. Garcia's class is 4:5. This implies that 4 out of every 9 students in her class are boys. That is, the number of boys in her class is ${}^4/_9 x = {}^{4x}/_9$.

The question now is, which is larger ${}^{3x}/_7$ or ${}^{4x}/_9$? To answer this question, we need to express both fractions with the same denominator, usually the least common denominator. The least common multiple of 7 and 9 is 63. Hence,

$$\frac{3x}{7} = \frac{9(3x)}{63} = \frac{27x}{63}$$

$$\frac{4x}{9} = \frac{7(4x)}{63} = \frac{28x}{63}$$

Thus, the quantity in Column A is equal to $^{27x}/_{63}$ and the quantity in Column B is equal to $^{28x}/_{63}$.

So the quantity in Column B is greater.

9.   (D)

Since no information about the value of $x$ or $y$ is given, the relationship between the two quantities in Columns A and B is indeterminate. For example, if $x = 3$ and $y = 1$, then $x + 2y = 3 + 2 = 5 > 4$ which implies the quantity in Column A is greater. But if $x = 1$ and $y = 3$, then $x + 2y = 1 + 2(3) = 7 > 4$, and the quantity in Column B is greater.

10.   (C)

Let $m \angle a$ represent the measure of angle $a$; and $E$ and $F$ be points on line $l$ as shown in the figure.

Line $l$ is parallel to ray $\overrightarrow{BA}$ and line $\overleftrightarrow{BE}$ is a transversal, thus, angles $BEF$ and $ABE$ are alternate interior angles which implies that

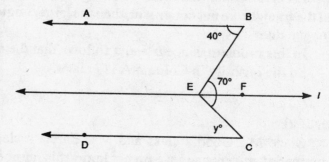

$$m \angle BEF = m \angle ABE = 40°.$$

Note that

$$m \angle BEF + m \angle FEC = 70°$$
$$40° + m \angle FEC = 70°$$
$$m \angle FEC = 30°$$

From the center information, line $l$ is parallel to ray $\overrightarrow{CD}$ and line $\overleftrightarrow{EC}$ is a transversal. Thus $\angle FEC$ and $\angle ECD$ are alternate interior angles. This implies $m \angle ECD = 30°$, or $y = 30$.

So the two quantities in Columns A and B are equal.

11. **(A)**

The simplest approach to attack this comparison problem is to calculate the amount of down payment. From the center information, the down payment is 20% of the sale price of the house, thus,

$$\text{Down payment} = 20\% \text{ of } \$72,000$$
$$= (0.20)\,(\$72,000)$$
$$= \$14,400.$$

So the quantity in Column A is greater.

12. **(D)**

From the center information, $\overline{CD}$ is perpendicular to $\overline{AB}$. Hence, angle $CDB$ and angle $CDA$ are right angles. This means triangles $CBD$ and $CDA$ are right triangles. Since the sum of the measures of the three interior angles of a triangle is 180°, and the measure of a right angle is 90°, it follows that

$$x + y = 90 \text{ and } w + z = 90$$

However, this does not give us any information about the value of $x - y$ or the value of $w - z$. Thus, the relationship is indeterminate from the information given.

13. **(B)**

Comparing two rational expressions generally requires rewriting both of them with the same denominator, usually the least common denominator.

In this problem, the least common denominator of the two denominators, $b$ and $(b-1)$ is $b(b-1)$. Hence, rewriting both expressions with the same denominator, $b(b-1)$ yields,

$$\frac{a}{b} = \frac{a(b-1)}{b(b-1)} = \frac{ab-a}{b(b-1)}$$

and

$$\frac{a+1}{b-1} = \frac{b(a+b)}{b(b-1)} = \frac{ab+b^2}{b(b-1)}$$

From the center information, $b \geq 2$. This implies $b^2 \geq 4$. Hence

$$ab + b^2 > ab - a$$

Thus

$$\frac{a+1}{b-1} > \frac{a}{b}$$

463

so the quantity in Column B is greater.

14.   (C)

The time in hours can be found by dividing the distance of travel in miles by the average speed in miles per hour.

Hence, if $d$ is the distance in miles, $r$ is the average speed in miles per hour, and $t$ is the time of travel in hours, then

$$t = \frac{d}{r}$$

In this problem, $d = 650$ miles, $r = 520$ miles per hour. Thus, substitution of these values in the above equation yields,

$$t = \frac{650}{520} = \frac{5}{4} \text{ hours}.$$

Hence, the time required for the plane to travel 650 miles is $1\frac{1}{4}$ hours.

Since the number of minutes must be found, we change the $1\frac{1}{4}$ hours into minutes by multiplying $1\frac{1}{4}$ by 60.

Thus, $(1\frac{1}{4})(60) = \frac{5}{4}(60) = 5(15) = 75$.

15.   (A)

Since $\overleftrightarrow{PQ}$ is a line, it follows that the measure of the straight angle $PEQ$ is equal to 180°. But from the figure, the measure of angle $PEQ$ is equal to

$x + x + x + x + x + x + x + x = 8x.$

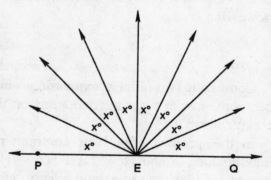

Thus,

$$8x = 180$$
$$x = 22.5.$$

So the quantity in Column A is greater.

16.   (D)

This problem can be solved by creating an algebraic formula in one unknown variable, then solve it for the variable. To do so, let $x$ be the number of tickets that were bought at the box office. Then the number

of tickets that were purchased at the advance sale is $(1200 - x)$. Hence, we can set up the formula as follows:

$$
\begin{aligned}
5(1{,}200 - x) + 7x &= 6{,}700 \\
6{,}000 - 5x + 7x &= 6{,}700 \\
2x &= 6{,}700 - 6{,}000 \\
2x &= 700 \\
x &= 350
\end{aligned}
$$

Hence, the number of tickets that were bought at the box office is 350.

One can also solve this problem by testing each of the answer choices given. If for example the number of tickets that were bought at the box office at $7 each is 500, then the number of tickets that were bought at the advance sale at the rate of $5 each is $(1200 - 500) = 700$. In this case, the total amount of receipts should be $500(\$5) + 700(\$7)$. If the total amount of receipts is $6,700, then the answer choice with the answer 500 is correct. Thus,

(A) $(500)(\$7) + (1{,}200 - 500)(\$5)$
$$
\begin{aligned}
&= 500(\$7) + (700)(\$5) \\
&= \$3{,}500 + \$3{,}500 \\
&= \$7{,}000 \\
&\neq \$6{,}700
\end{aligned}
$$

(B) $(700)(\$7) + (1{,}200 - 700)(\$5)$
$$
\begin{aligned}
&= 700(\$7) + (500)(\$5) \\
&= \$4{,}900 + \$3{,}500 \\
&= \$8{,}400 \\
&\neq \$6{,}700
\end{aligned}
$$

(C) $(600)(\$7) + (1{,}200 - 600)(\$5)$
$$
\begin{aligned}
&= 600(\$7) + (600)(\$5) \\
&= \$4{,}200 + \$3{,}000 \\
&= \$7{,}200 \\
&\neq \$6{,}700
\end{aligned}
$$

(D) $(350)(\$7) + (1{,}200 - 350)(\$5)$
$$
\begin{aligned}
&= 350(\$7) + (850)(\$5) \\
&= \$2{,}450 + \$4{,}250 \\
&= \$6700
\end{aligned}
$$

(E) $(200)(\$7) + (1{,}200 - 200)(\$5)$
$$
\begin{aligned}
&= 200(\$7) + (1{,}000)(\$5) \\
&= \$1{,}400 + \$5{,}000 \\
&\doteq \$6{,}400 \\
&\neq \$6{,}700
\end{aligned}
$$

17. **(B)**
    This problem can be solved as follows:

1. Divide each price by the number of ounces in each price to obtain the following prices per ounce for the given prices in answer choices (A) through (E):

$$\text{(A)}\ \frac{16}{10}\cancel{c}, \text{ (B)}\ \frac{3}{2}\cancel{c}, \text{ (C)}\ \frac{7}{4}\cancel{c}, \text{ (D)}\ \frac{34}{20}\cancel{c}, \text{ (E)}\ \frac{13}{8}\cancel{c}.$$

2. Change each of the prices per ounce obtained in step (1) above to an equivalent fraction having a denominator equal to the least common denominator, 40, we obtain,

$$\text{(A)}\ \frac{16}{10}=\frac{64}{40}; \text{ (B)}\ \frac{3}{2}=\frac{60}{40}; \text{ (C)}\ \frac{7}{4}=\frac{70}{40}; \text{ (D)}\ \frac{34}{20}=\frac{68}{4};$$

and (E) $\frac{13}{8}=\frac{65}{40}$.

Since the smallest of the resulting fractions in step (2) is $^{60}/_{40}$, it follows that the most economical price among the given prices is 2oz. for 3¢.

18. (E)

Label the vertices of the given figure $A, B, C, D, E, F$ and the segment $\overline{DE}$ to meet $\overline{AB}$ at $G$, and let $m\overline{AB}$ denote the length of segment $\overline{AB}$.

Since all the segments in the figure meet at right

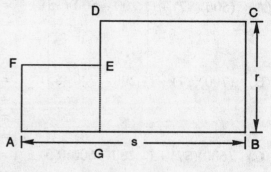

angles, it follows that each of the quadrilaterals $AGEF$ and $GBCD$ is a rectangle. This implies that

$$m\overline{DE} + m\overline{EG} = m\overline{CB} = r$$

But, the $m\overline{EG} = m\overline{AF}$ (since $AGEF$ is a rectangle). Hence,

$$m\overline{AF} + m\overline{ED} = r$$

Also, $m\overline{DC} = m\overline{GB}$ (since $GBCD$ is a rectangle), and the $m\overline{FE} = m\overline{AG}$ (since $AGEF$ is a rectangle). Thus,

$$\begin{aligned} m\overline{DC} + m\overline{EF} &= m\overline{GB} + m\overline{AG} \\ &= m\overline{AB} \\ &= S \end{aligned}$$

Recall that the perimeter of a closed polygon such as the figure given is equal to the sum of the measures of its segments.

Thus, the perimeter of the given figure is equal to

$$m\overline{AB} + m\overline{BC} + m\overline{CD} + m\overline{DE} + m\overline{EF} =$$
$$= m\overline{AB} + m\overline{CB} + (m\overline{DC} + m\overline{EF})$$
$$+ (m\overline{ED} + m\overline{AF})$$
$$= s + r + s + r$$
$$= 2s + 2r.$$

19. (C)

One way to solve this problem is to find the value of $x$ in the equation $6x + 12 = 5$, then substitute the obtained value for $x$ in the quantity $(x + 2)$. Thus,

$$6x + 12 = 5$$
$$6x = 5 - 12$$
$$6x = -7$$
$$x = -\frac{7}{6}$$

Hence,

$$(x + 2) = \frac{-7}{6} + 2$$
$$= \frac{-7 + 12}{6} = \frac{5}{6}.$$

Another way to attack this problem is to factor the left hand side of the equation $6x + 12 = 5$. This gives $6(x + 2) = 5$. Since we need to find the value of $(x + 2)$, we can solve the later equation for $(x + 2)$ directly. This gives us

$$6(x + 2) = 5$$
$$(x + 2) = \frac{5}{6}.$$

20. (A)

In order for any of the statements given in the answer choices (A) through (E) to be true, it has to be equivalent to the proportion $\frac{p}{q} = \frac{r}{s}$.

In general, if $\frac{p}{q} = \frac{r}{s}$, then the following proportions are equivalent, that is, they have the same solutions. This can be justified by cross-multiplication.

$$\frac{p}{q} = \frac{r}{s}, \ \frac{p}{r} = \frac{q}{s}, \ \frac{r}{p} = \frac{s}{q}, \ \frac{q}{p} = \frac{s}{r}.$$

This eliminates answer choices (B) and (C).

Note that if $p/q = r/s$, then any proportion that is equivalent to it must be reducible to the equation $ps = qr$ (cross-multiplication). Testing each of answer choices (A), (D) and (E) yields

(A)   $\dfrac{p+q}{p} = \dfrac{r+s}{r}$ , then $(p+q)r = p(r+s)$

     $pr + qr = pr + ps$

          $qr = ps.$

(D)   $\dfrac{p-q}{q} = \dfrac{s-r}{r}$ , then $(p-q)r = (s-r)q$

     $rp - rq = qs - rq$

         $rp = qs.$

which is not equivalent to $ps = qr$.

(E)   $\dfrac{q}{p-q} = \dfrac{r}{s-r}$ , then $q(s-r) = r(p-q)$

     $qs - qr = rp - rq$

         $qs = rp.$

which is not equivalent to $ps = qr$.

21.   (B)

To answer this question, one needs to use the following information which can be obtained from the sales graph. Note that the graph shows an increase in sales during each of the years 1982, 1983, 1984 and 1988 as follows:

| Year | Increase in sales over the previous year (in thousands of dollars) |
|---|---|
| 1982 | $310{,}000 - 200{,}000 = 110{,}000$ |
| 1983 | $330{,}000 - 310{,}000 = 20{,}000$ |
| 1984 | $400{,}000 - 330{,}000 = 70{,}000$ |
| 1988 | $340{,}000 - 300{,}000 = 40{,}000$ |

Thus, the amount of greatest increase in sales from one year to the next was $110,000.

22.　(A)

This question asks about the percent change over the previous year. Hence, the most direct way to solve this problem is to calculate the percent change of sales for each year over the previous year. However, one does not need to examine the percent change in every year in the graph, only those years that are listed as possible choices. Note that

$$\text{percent change} = \frac{\text{change in sales}}{\text{sales in previous years}}$$

$$= \frac{\text{sales of this year} - \text{sales of previous year}}{\text{sales of previous year}}.$$

Thus, examining the percent change of the years listed as possible answers yields:

(A)　1982　$\dfrac{310,000 - 200,000}{200,000} = \dfrac{110,000}{200,000} = \dfrac{11}{21} \cong 52\%$

(B)　1984　$\dfrac{400,000 - 330,000}{330,000} = \dfrac{70,000}{330,000} = \dfrac{7}{33} \cong 21\%$

(C)　1985　$\dfrac{380,000 - 400,000}{400,000} = \dfrac{-20,000}{400,000} = -\dfrac{2}{4} \cong -5\%$

(D)　1986　$\dfrac{340,000 - 380,000}{380,000} = \dfrac{-40,000}{380,000} = -\dfrac{4}{38} \cong -11\%$

(E)　1987　$\dfrac{340,000 - 300,000}{300,000} = \dfrac{40,000}{300,000} = \dfrac{4}{30} \cong 13\%$

Since we are looking for the greatest percent change, it follows that the correct answer is answer choice (A). In 1982, sales increased by 52% over sales of 1981.

23.　(D)

This question asks about the arithmetic mean of the amounts spent on advertising from 1982 to 1988 inclusive.

Recall that the arithmetic mean of a set of observations, $\overline{X}$, is equal to the sum of all observations, divided by the number of observations, $n$. That is

$$\overline{X} = \frac{\text{sum of all observations}}{n}$$

In this problem, the advertising graph provides us with the following amounts that we need to compute their arithmetic mean.

| Year | Advertising (in thousands of dollars) |
|------|------|
| 1982 | 60 |
| 1983 | 90 |
| 1984 | 70 |
| 1985 | 80 |
| 1986 | 70 |
| 1987 | 60 |
| 1988 | 80 |
| Total | 510 |

Thus,

$$\overline{X} = \frac{510,000}{7} = 73,000.$$

Hence, the average amount of money spent on advertising from 1982 to 1988 inclusive is approximately $73,000 per year.

24. **(E)**

This question can be answered by calculating 25% of the amount of sales for each year, and then comparing the result with the amount of advertising for that year. Equivalently, divide the amount of sales of each year by 4, and compare the result with the amount of advertising during that year.

From the graphs, one obtains the following information:

| Year | Sales (in thousands of dollars) divided by 4 | Advertising (in thousands of dollars) divided by 4 |
|------|------|------|
| 1979 | 37.5 | 20 |
| 1980 | 52.5 | 60 |
| 1981 | 50.0 | 40 |
| 1982 | 77.5 | 60 |
| 1983 | 82.5 | 90 |
| 1984 | 100.0 | 70 |
| 1985 | 95.0 | 80 |
| 1986 | 85.0 | 70 |
| 1987 | 75.0 | 60 |
| 1988 | 85.0 | 80 |

The table indicates that only in two years, advertising is equal to or greater than 25% of sales.

25. (C)
This question can be answered by considering the change in both sales and advertising only in those years listed as possible choices. Thus,

| Year | Change | |
| --- | --- | --- |
| | Sales | Advertising |
| 1980 | Increase | Increase |
| 1983 | Increase | Increase |
| 1985 | Decrease | Increase |
| 1987 | Decrease | Decrease |
| 1988 | Increase | Increase |

The table shows that only in 1985 advertising increased while sales decreased during that year.

26. (B)
Name line $\overleftrightarrow{AB}$ the x-axis and line $\overleftrightarrow{CG}$ the y-axis. Since these two axes are intersecting at the point $(0, 0)$, we have the familiar coordinate plane or the xy-plane.

Using algebraic techniques, we can calculate the exact distance between any 2 points in the plane. Recall that the point $P_1(5, 0)$ is a point on the x-axis, while the point $P_2(0, 5)$ is on the y-axis. In general, given 2 points, $P(x_1, 0)$ and $Q(x_2, 0)$, on the x-axis, the distance between $P$ and $Q$ is defined as

$$PQ = |x_2 - x_1| = |x_1 - x_2|$$

where $|x_2 - x_1|$ reads the absolute value of $x_2 - x_1$ and defined as the non-negative difference of $x_1$ and $x_2$. Similarly, if $S(0, y_1)$ and $R(0, y_2)$ are two points on the y-axis, then the distance between $S$ and $R$ is given as

$$SR = |y_2 - y_1| = |y_1 - y_2|$$

In this problem, since $\overleftrightarrow{AB}$ is the perpendicular bisector of segment $\overline{CP}$,

it follows that the point $P$ must be on the $y$-axis. Thus both points, $C$ and $P$ are on the $y$-axis. Since we do not know the coordinates of the point $P$, let $P$ have the coordinates $(0, y)$. In addition, note that $C$ is where the $x$-axis and $P$ must be below the $x$-axis.

From the above discussion, answer choice (C) is eliminated because the point $H$ lies on the $x$-axis, and answer choice (D) is eliminated for the same reason.

Since the coordinates from the midpoint of segment $\overline{CP}$ are $(0, 0)$, it follows that the distance from $C(0, 8)$ to $M(0, 0)$ is the same as the distance from $M(0, 0)$ to $P(0, y)$. Hence,

$$\begin{aligned} CM &= MP \\ 0 - 8 &= y - 0 \\ -8 &= y \end{aligned}$$

This means that the point $P$ has the coordinates $(0, -8)$. Thus $P$ is the same as point $F$.

27.  (D)

Though there are several methods to solve this problem, one method is to rewrite the equation $2a + 2b = 1$ as $2(a + b) = 1$. Solving this equation for $(a + b)$ yields $(a + b) = \frac{1}{2}$. Similarly, rewriting the equation $6a - 2b = 5$ as $2(3a - b) = 5$ and solving for $(3a - b)$, yields $(3a - b) = \frac{5}{2}$.

Now $(a + b) = \frac{1}{2}$ and $(3a - b) = \frac{5}{2}$ eliminates answer choices (A), (C), and (E) immediately.

Since $\frac{1}{2} < \frac{5}{2}$, it follows that answer choice (B) is eliminated. However, since $\frac{1}{2} < \frac{5}{2}$, it follows that $(a + b) < (3a - b)$.

28.  (A)

$n$ is an integer means $n$ can be an odd number or an even number. If $n$ is odd, then $3n$ is odd (odd $\times$ odd = odd). If $n$ is even, then $3n$ is even (odd $\times$ even = even). This simple discussion eliminates answer choice (D). Answer choice (E) is eliminated because if $n$ is odd, then $(n + 1)$ is even, and if $n$ is even, then $(n + 1)$ is odd.

If $n$ is an integer (odd or even), then $2n$ is even (any integer $\times 2 =$ an even integer), and $(2n + 2)$ is even (since even + even = even). Thus, answer choices (B) and (C) are eliminated.

If $n$ is an integer, then $2n$ is even and $2n + 3$ is odd (even + odd = odd).

**29.   (E)**

This question asks about the time of travel. This requires the use of the formula

$$\text{Distance} = \text{Rate} \times \text{Time}$$

One way to solve this problem is to create an algebraic equation. To do so, let $t$ be the time, in hours, it takes the car to catch up with the postal truck, then the time of travel of the truck should be $(t + {}^{24}\!/_{60})$ hours. (Note that 24 minutes $= {}^{24}\!/_{60}$ hours $= 0.4$ hours).

When the car catches up with the truck, the distance traveled by the truck in $(t + {}^{24}\!/_{60})$ hours at a rate of 40 mph will be the same as the distance traveled by the car at a rate of 50 mph for a period of $t$ hours. Let $d$ denote that distance. Then for the

(i)  Truck:
$$\begin{aligned} d &= \text{Rate} \times \text{Time} \\ &= 40\,(t + 0.4) \\ &= 40t + 16 \end{aligned}$$

(ii)  Car:
$$\begin{aligned} d &= \text{Rate} \times \text{Time} \\ &= (50) \times (t) \\ &= 50t \end{aligned}$$

Hence,
$$\begin{aligned} 50t &= 40t + 16 \\ 50t - 40t &= 16 \\ 10t &= 16 \\ t &= 1.6 \end{aligned}$$

Thus, it takes the car 1.6 hours to catch up with the postal truck.

Another way to solve this problem is to test each of the answer choices given. Remember that if the time of travel of the car is $t$ hours, then the time of travel of the truck is $(t + .4)$ hours, and the distance traveled by the car is the same distance traveled by the truck. Thus, testing the answer choices yields

| Answer choice | Time of Travel (hours) | | Rate of Travel (mph) | | Distance Traveled (miles) | | |
|---|---|---|---|---|---|---|---|
| | Car | Truck | Car | Truck | Car | | Truck |
| (A) | 2.6 | 3 | 50 | 40 | 130 | $\neq$ | 120 |
| (B) | 3.0 | 3.4 | 50 | 40 | 150 | $\neq$ | 136 |
| (C) | 2.0 | 2.4 | 50 | 40 | 100 | $\neq$ | 96 |
| (D) | 1.5 | 1.9 | 50 | 40 | 75 | $\neq$ | 95 |
| (E) | 1.6 | 2.0 | 50 | 40 | 80 | $=$ | 80 |

30. (C)

Certainly, the easiest and the most direct way to solve this problem is to perform the indicated operations.

Performing the indicated operations yields,

$$\sqrt{75} - 3\sqrt{48} + \sqrt{147} = \sqrt{(25)(3)} - 3\sqrt{(16)(3)} + \sqrt{(49)(3)}$$
$$= 5\sqrt{3} - 3(4)\sqrt{3} + 7\sqrt{3}$$
$$= 5\sqrt{3} - 12\sqrt{3} + 7\sqrt{3}$$
$$= (5 - 12 + 7)\sqrt{3}$$
$$= (12 - 12)\sqrt{3}$$
$$= 0.\sqrt{3}$$
$$= 0$$

# Section 5—Analytical Ability

1. (E)

The argument is a generalization. All observed ducks are white. This is like saying: "Some children are not well behaved. All little girls are children. Therefore, all little girls are not well behaved." Option (B) contains a suppressed premise. Choice (C) attempts to take a generalization and explain it by suggesting a causal linkage. Option (D) moves from the universality of the concept of justice to the conclusion that justice is a physical trait of man. Choice (E) is the only option that parallels the original argument.

2. (D)

The claims are made: (1) anyone supporting the bill must have an ulterior motive, and (2) therefore, there are no valid grounds for supporting the bill. Choice (D) makes the same two claims. Option (B) is the best response and does not make the error in reasoning that he makes; Choice (A) grants the claims and does not attack him; while (C) attacks the argument rather than the motives; and (E) attacks Sheets, but does not claim that this discredits his argument.

3. (E)

Common sense dictates that where one is driving in relationship to

his home has little or nothing to do with the safety factor. Intuitively it seems that a person driving under 35 miles per hour is safer than the one driving at 60 miles per hour. The explanation may be then that more driving occurs under the described conditions. Choice (A) is inconsistent with common sense and (B) is incorrect since the statistics mention the location of the accident in terms of the distance from home not how far the driver had driven at the time of the accident. Option (C) compounds the error made by (A). It commits the further error of conditioning the speed of driving on the occurrence of an accident. Choice (D) does the same thing.

4.   (B)

Debbie's argument is flawed because she fails to consider all the possible factors that could explain her longevity; (B) points this out. Choices (A) and (C) do not weaken her argument as they do not prove that whiskey and tobacco have bad effects in all cases. Choice (C) proves only that other factors may explain other survival rates. Option (D) does not address the flaw and we do not know if she has sought medical advice. Choice (E) is not relevant to the argument.

5.   (D)

Note the question stem. Choice (D) works well as it gives us the argument structure: "All post" 1965 students are required... Fred is a post 1965 student. Therefore, Fred is required to take it. Choice (A) addresses the situation before 1965, and (B) fails because we cannot conclude from the fact that all of those who took the course graduated after 1965 and that Fred was one of them. Choice (C) fails for the same reason that (A) fails. Option (E) is a double negative and actually says that before 1965 the course was not required.

6.   (B)

Tracy assumes a causal relationship on the basis of inference. She commits two logical errors: She fails to include alternative causes, and she uses too small a number of tests for a valid conclusion. Option (A) concludes that an event must have occurred after its cause. Choice (C) includes evidence that does tend to rule out alternative explanations, while choice (D) fails to consider alternative explanations, but involves no inference. Choice (E) includes sufficient tests but fails to

consider all possible explanations.

7.    (D)
    Choice (A) is wrong because Dennis could sneeze for a different reason. Choice (B) does strengthen the argument, but not as much as choice (D). Option (C) weakens the argument and (E) implies that Tracy may make herself sneeze.

8.    (C)
    The author ascribes the position of the analysts as always attributing a sudden drop to a crisis. Then he attacks the simple causal explanation by explaining that, though a crisis is followed by a market drop, the reason is not that the crisis causes the drop but that both are the effect of some common cause, the changing of the moon. The task is not to grade the argument, only to describe the structure. Choice (A) is not a proper characterization of that structure because the author never provides a specific example. Option (B) is not applicable since no statistics are produced. Choice (D) is rejected since the author is attacking accepted beliefs rather than appealing to them to support this position. Option (E) will not work because the author wants to draw a different conclusion.

9.    (A)
    The author may be ridiculing the analysts for always attributing a drop in the market to a political crisis. But whether you take the argument in this way or as a serious attempt to explain the fluctuation of the stock market, (A) will be the correct answer. Option (E) goes beyond the factual description as does (D). Choice (C) has no support in the paragraph, for nothing suggests that he wishes to attack the credibility of the source rather than the argument itself. Option (B) is appropriate to the main point of the passage. Whether the market ultimately evens itself out has nothing to do with the causes of the fluctuations.

Questions 10 – 13
    The players must be seated as shown in the following diagram:

| Berry | Moody | Moody | Green | Berry | Bell | Bell |
|-------|-------|-------|-------|-------|------|------|
| or | or | or | | or | or | or |
| Tyler | Horton | Horton | | Tyler | Sheets | Sheets |

Note that all the seats except for the center seat may be occupied by either of two individuals. Take this into account when answering the questions.

10. **(D)**

In order for Horton and Moody to be seated together, they must occupy the second and third seat from the left, in either order. Thus, Horton may not be seated at either end of the table.

11. **(C)**

Since Moody is in either the second or third seat from the left, he cannot be next to Bell, who is in either the first or second seat from the right.

12. **(C)**

Sheets is in one of the two seats nearest the exit, and therefore cannot be on either side of Green.

13. **(B)**

If neither Moody nor Tyler is seated next to Green, then Green must be flanked by Horton on the left and Berry on the right. This means that the table must be seated as follows (left to right) Tyler, Moody, Horton, Green, Berry, and, in the last two seats, Bell and Sheets in either order. The fact that Bell and Sheets may be seated in either order results in the two possible seating arrangements for the table as a whole.

Questions 14 – 19

Begin by arranging the information.
(1)     Judy → Edie
(2)     (Edie & Debbie) → cannot select Joy
(3)     (Debbie & Joy) → cannot select Millie
(4-a)   Joy → (Linda vs Pam)
(4-b)   cannot select (Linda & Pam)

(5-a)  (Linda vs Millie)

(5-b)  cannot select (Linda & Millie)

The numbered statements correspond to the five conditions given in the set. The fourth and fifth are broken down into two statements because each of these conditions is actually two conditions. So (4-a) corresponds to "If Joy is selected, then either Linda or Pam must be selected," and (4-b) corresponds to Linda and Pam cannot both be selected." Statement 5 is treated in a similar fashion.

14.  (C)

If neither Linda nor Pam is selected, then we know by (5-a) that Millie is selected and by (4-a) that Joy is not selected. Thus far we have eliminated Linda and Pam by stipulation and Joy, and we have selected Millie, which leaves Debbie, Edie, and Judy for consideration. Since Joy is not selected, we may include both Edie and Debbie without violating (2). And having chosen Edie, we may include Judy without violating (1). So, on the assumption that neither Linda nor Pam is selected, the largest delegation would consist of Millie, Edie, Debbie, and Pam.

15.  (B)

If Judy is selected, then by (1) Edie must also be selected. Further, if Joy is selected, by (4-a) either Linda or Pam must be selected. But we also have (5-a), and either Linda or Millie must be selected. Since we have both (Linda or Pam) or (Linda or Millie), we will minimize the number selected if we choose Linda rather than Pam or Millie. So the smallest delegation which includes both Joy and Judy will also include Edie and Linda.

16.  (C)

If Joy is selected, then by (4-a) either Linda or Pam must be selected. Since by (4-b) we cannot choose both Linda and Pam, Linda cannot be selected. But we know by (5-a) that either Linda or Millie must be chosen, so we must pick Millie. As for the incorrect answers, this reasoning eliminates (B) as false. As for (A), we cannot choose Debbie, for to choose Debbie along with Joy would mean we could not select Millie (3). But we have already learned that we must choose Millie because Linda cannot be chosen. As for (D) and (E), it is

possible to choose Edie or Judy and Edie. Since Debbie cannot be selected, this effectively isolates Edie and Judy from the other students by breaking the only connection with Edie and Judy, which is (2).

17. **(A)**
Joy, Debbie, and Linda are a possible three-student delegation. Selecting Joy requires that we have either Linda or Pam (4-a), and that condition is satisfied by including Linda. Having Joy and Debbie together means only that we may not have Millie (3), but that can be avoided if we choose Linda to satisfy (5-a). As for (b), Joy, Debbie, and Millie are not a possible delegation, since Debbie and Joy together requires that Millie not be chosen, by (3). As for (C), Joy, Edie, and Judy are not acceptable because, by (5-a), we must have either Linda or Millie. As for (D), Edie, Linda, and Millie are not permissible because this violates (5-b). Finally, (E) is incorrect since the group Edie, Linda, and Pam violates (4-b).

18. **(D)**
If Joy is selected, then either Linda or Pam must also be selected, by (4-a). But if Millie is chosen, then Linda cannot be chosen, by (5-b), which means that Pam must be chosen. So it is not possible that Pam is not chosen. Hence, III must be part of the correct choice. Then, since Millie and Joy are chosen, we cannot choose Debbie, by (3), so II is part of the correct choice. As for statement I, Edie may or may not be chosen.

19. **(B)**
Joy, Edie, and Millie accompanied by Pam will satisfy all of the requirements. Choosing Millie satisfies (5-a). Then, Joy and Pam together satisfies (4-a). We do not have Linda, so both (4-b) and (5-b) are respected. And since we do not have Debbie, (2) and (3) are satisfied. Finally, without Judy, we have no problem with (1). As for (A), Joy and Debbie cannot accompany Millie; that is a violation of (3). As for (C), Judy must be accompanied by Edie, by (1); and (D) can be eliminated on the same grounds. Finally, as for (E), Linda and Pam violates (4-b).

Questions 20 – 22.

A four by four grid listing prizes, breeds, owners, and dog names is needed.

| Prize | Breed | Owner | Name |
|-------|-------|-------|------|
| 1 | bassett | Berry | Rusty |
| 2 | beagle | Harriman | Ace |
| 3 | dachshund | Phillips | Toby |
| 4 | chow | Tyler | Deuce |

**20. (B)**

Once statement (6) identifies the 4th prize winner and you determine that Mr. Phillips' dog therefore won 3rd prize, it follows that since Ace won 2nd prize, Mr. Berry's Rusty was the bassett that won first prize.

**21. (C)**

The same reasoning process used in question 20 makes Mr. Phillips' dog the dachshund that won third prize.

**22. (A)**

This can be read from the diagram.

Questions 23 – 25.

The three questions all stem from "what is it" questions, we know that the situation is one in which the arrangement is stable or fixed. The setup includes three items of information sorted out about four people. In addition, there is the auxiliary relationship in that there are two couples. You can present the information in one chart.

| Name | Mr. J | Mrs. J. | Dr. S. | Mrs. S |
|------|-------|---------|--------|--------|
| Music | Classical | Country | | |
| Hair | | Brown | | Blond |

Now consider the last information.

| Name | Mr. J | Mrs. J. | Dr. S. | Mrs. S |
|------|-------|---------|--------|--------|
| Music | Classical | Country | Easy Listening | Rock and Roll |
| Hair | Not Brown | Brown | Brown | Blond |

All the answers can be read from the diagram.

23.  (C)

Music tastes are fully determined.


24.  (A)

Dr. Steinmiller has brown hair and likes easy listening.


25.  (D)

Mr. Johnson likes classical music.


# Section 6—Analytical Ability

Questions 1 – 4

Three mathematicians from A, B, C, and D must be chosen. The only combinations are:

ABC   ACD   ABD   BCD   ABCD

Since A refuses to work with D, combinations A C D, A B D and A B C D are ruled out. Thus the only combinations with the mathematicians are:

ABC   or   BCD

Since B refuses to work with E, and F refuses to work with G, the mathematicians A B C could only work with F and H or G and H. Thus possible combinations of the five-member group are:

ABCFH   or   ABCGH

Since B refuses to work with E, and D refuses to work with F, the mathematicians B C D could only work with G and H. Thus a possible combination of the group is:

BCDGH

The only possible combinations are therefore:

ABCFH   ABCGH   BCDGH


1.  (D)

It can be seen from the three combinations A B C F H, A B C G H,

and B C D G H that C appears in every possible group.

2.   (E)
   It can be seen from the three combinations A B C F H, A B C G H, and B C D G H that if G is rejected, the group must be A B C F H. Thus D is not in the group.

3.   (C)
   From the set of possible combinations A B C F H, A B C G H, and B C D G H, it can be seen that only statement III is necessarily true.

4.   (B)
   From the set of possible combinations A B C F H, A B C G H, B C D G H, only statement II must be true.

5.   (E)
   When Ms. Phillips and Ms. Askew converse they can use English, German, Russian, and Portuguese between them. Mr. Anderson speaks Portuguese and German. Mr. Bell speaks Portuguese and English. Mr. Sheets speaks Russian and German.

6.   (A)
   Mr. Bell understands Portuguese and English. Mr. Sheets speaks German and Russian.

7.   (D)
   Mr. Anderson and Mr. Bell can both converse in Portuguese.

8.   (D)
   Mr. Anderson, Mr. Bell, and Ms. Askew speak Portuguese. Ms. Phillips and Mr. Sheets speak German.

9.   (B)
   German and Portuguese are spoken by 3, English and Russian by 2.

**Questions 10 – 13**

Let us arrange the letters in two separate categories. The first category will be for age — older and younger. The second category will be for height — taller and shorter.

We represent older with the mathematical "greater than" sign >. We represent taller with a double mathematical "greater than" sign >>.

From the first statement (A is older than B and taller than C), we get this representation:

$$A > B \quad \text{and} \quad A >> C$$

The second statement (D is younger than E, older than C, and shorter than F) translates mathematically as:

$$E > D > C \quad \text{and} \quad F >> D$$

The third statement (G is older than H, younger than C, shorter than H, and taller than F) gives us:

$$C > G > H \quad \text{and} \quad H >> G >> F$$

The fourth statement (H is older than A and shorter than C) gives us:

$$H > A \quad \text{and} \quad C >> H$$

Thus, consolidating, we have:

| | | |
|---|---|---|
| $A > B$ | | $A >> C$ |
| $E > D > C$ | | $F >> D$ |
| $C > G > H$ | and | $H >> G >> F$ |
| $H > A$ | | $C >> H$ |

Again, with the mathematical inequality sign we can further consolidate the above in two separate inequality statements:

$$E > D > C > G > H > A > B$$
$$\text{and}$$
$$A >> C >> H >> G >> F >> D$$

10.   (B)

Since $E > D > C > G > H > A > B$, B must be the youngest of the group because it is the least of all the the given letters.

11. **(A)**

A >> C >> H >> G >> F >> D. Therefore, A must be the tallest because it is the greatest of all the given letters.

12. **(B)**

From the final mathematical representation above, we can see that D > C and C >> H, thus indicating that C is younger than D and taller than H.

13. **(E)**

(Note that the correct choice must be a false choice). We see that the only choices that deal with younger-older people are Choices (C) and (E). Choice (C) is a true statement, so it is incorrect. Now let us go to the shorter-taller choices — that is, Choices (A), (B), and (D). Choice (A) is a true statement, so it is an incorrect choice. Choice (B) is a true statement, so it is an incorrect choice. Choice (D) is a true statement, so it is an incorrect choice. As for Choice (E), we cannot determine whether F is the third oldest of the group because F is not included in the younger-older mathematical representation. However, since the other four choices are incorrect, we can, by a process of elimination, conclude that Choice (E) is the only correct choice.

Questions 14 – 16

The four seating conditions listed allow us to make the following inferences:

**Inference 1** — Because of Conditions 2 and 4, we infer that Q, U, and W, being physicists as well as biologists, must not sit next to each other.

**Inference 2** — Because of Conditions 3 and 4, we infer that P, R, S, and V, being physicists as well as mathematicians, must not sit next to each other.

**Inference 3** — Conditions 1, 2, and 3 allow us to infer that there are no restrictions on where T can sit.

14. **(C)**

Choices (A), (B), (D), and (E) are inconsistent with Inference 2 since in each of these choices at least two of the scientists, P, R, S, and V are seated next to each other.

15.  (E)

Inference 2 tells us that P, R, and V are the only scientists that cannot sit next to S.


16.  (C)

From Inference 2, it is clear that no combination that involves either R, S, or V is possible. W and T may each sit next to P.


17.  (E)

Choices (A) and (B) are not implications; they are explicitly stated. (C) is vague; the meaning of consequentiality is not clear. (D) is incorrect because the author is arguing that doing nothing has no consequences. Choice (E) is correct. This author says that doing nothing keeps us safe from consequences; this could be true only in light of the implication that doing nothing is not an act.


18.  (B)

According to the author, the alternative to experiencing consequences is playing it "safe"; this can mean only that consequences are dangerous.


19.  (E)

The only correct choice is II, it is argued that hot weather causes crime. This is not mere coincidence, and the statement does not state that we can control the weather. (E) must be chosen because no other choice offered II exclusively.


20.  (B)

The argument posits an exclusive relationship between hot weather and crime. (A), (C) and (E) contradict such an exclusive relationship, (D) is irrelevant to the relationship, only (B) provides evidence supporting and strengthening the heat-crime relationship.


21.  (A)

The correct answer to this question is Choice (A). In completing

the passage, we are looking for a phrase which mentions the natural beauty of America, a beauty and serenity not found in the cities or in the cities or in urban centers. Choice (C) is incorrect because it mentions the wild jungles of Africa, whereas we are concerned only with life in these United States.

22. (D)

One could find this passage in any of the described pamphlets except for the one mentioned in Choice (D). The passage clearly states that America is "still the land of the eagle" and therefore a pamphlet discussing how the eagle became extinct would obviously contradict the passage.

23. (D)

The author does not address the distinction between how much sleep we desire and how much our bodies require. Each of the other distinctions is addressed in the passage.

24. (D)

In the passage, becoming older corresponds with "advanced knowledge and capabilities." Choices (A), (B), and (C) should be eliminated because each is contradicted by the assumptions of the passage (the passage suggests that more sleep is undesirable, knowledge and capabilities are connected with wakefulness, and mindlessness is connected with sleep). Choice (E) is a generalization not at all concerned with amount of sleep and therefore not relevant to the passage.

25. (C)

Choices (A), (B), and (E) present information that supports the value of sleep, and (D) dissociates advanced capabilities from the mind, thus damaging the author's mind/mindlessness distinction.

# GRE
# GENERAL TEST 4
## ANSWER SHEET

### SECTION 1

1. Ⓐ Ⓑ Ⓒ Ⓓ Ⓔ
2. Ⓐ Ⓑ Ⓒ Ⓓ Ⓔ
3. Ⓐ Ⓑ Ⓒ Ⓓ Ⓔ
4. Ⓐ Ⓑ Ⓒ Ⓓ Ⓔ
5. Ⓐ Ⓑ Ⓒ Ⓓ Ⓔ
6. Ⓐ Ⓑ Ⓒ Ⓓ Ⓔ
7. Ⓐ Ⓑ Ⓒ Ⓓ Ⓔ
8. Ⓐ Ⓑ Ⓒ Ⓓ Ⓔ
9. Ⓐ Ⓑ Ⓒ Ⓓ Ⓔ
10. Ⓐ Ⓑ Ⓒ Ⓓ Ⓔ
11. Ⓐ Ⓑ Ⓒ Ⓓ Ⓔ
12. Ⓐ Ⓑ Ⓒ Ⓓ Ⓔ
13. Ⓐ Ⓑ Ⓒ Ⓓ Ⓔ
14. Ⓐ Ⓑ Ⓒ Ⓓ Ⓔ
15. Ⓐ Ⓑ Ⓒ Ⓓ Ⓔ
16. Ⓐ Ⓑ Ⓒ Ⓓ Ⓔ
17. Ⓐ Ⓑ Ⓒ Ⓓ Ⓔ
18. Ⓐ Ⓑ Ⓒ Ⓓ Ⓔ
19. Ⓐ Ⓑ Ⓒ Ⓓ Ⓔ
20. Ⓐ Ⓑ Ⓒ Ⓓ Ⓔ
21. Ⓐ Ⓑ Ⓒ Ⓓ Ⓔ
22. Ⓐ Ⓑ Ⓒ Ⓓ Ⓔ
23. Ⓐ Ⓑ Ⓒ Ⓓ Ⓔ
24. Ⓐ Ⓑ Ⓒ Ⓓ Ⓔ
25. Ⓐ Ⓑ Ⓒ Ⓓ Ⓔ
26. Ⓐ Ⓑ Ⓒ Ⓓ Ⓔ
27. Ⓐ Ⓑ Ⓒ Ⓓ Ⓔ
28. Ⓐ Ⓑ Ⓒ Ⓓ Ⓔ
29. Ⓐ Ⓑ Ⓒ Ⓓ Ⓔ
30. Ⓐ Ⓑ Ⓒ Ⓓ Ⓔ

31. Ⓐ Ⓑ Ⓒ Ⓓ Ⓔ
32. Ⓐ Ⓑ Ⓒ Ⓓ Ⓔ
33. Ⓐ Ⓑ Ⓒ Ⓓ Ⓔ
34. Ⓐ Ⓑ Ⓒ Ⓓ Ⓔ
35. Ⓐ Ⓑ Ⓒ Ⓓ Ⓔ
36. Ⓐ Ⓑ Ⓒ Ⓓ Ⓔ
37. Ⓐ Ⓑ Ⓒ Ⓓ Ⓔ
38. Ⓐ Ⓑ Ⓒ Ⓓ Ⓔ

### SECTION 2

1. Ⓐ Ⓑ Ⓒ Ⓓ Ⓔ
2. Ⓐ Ⓑ Ⓒ Ⓓ Ⓔ
3. Ⓐ Ⓑ Ⓒ Ⓓ Ⓔ
4. Ⓐ Ⓑ Ⓒ Ⓓ Ⓔ
5. Ⓐ Ⓑ Ⓒ Ⓓ Ⓔ
6. Ⓐ Ⓑ Ⓒ Ⓓ Ⓔ
7. Ⓐ Ⓑ Ⓒ Ⓓ Ⓔ
8. Ⓐ Ⓑ Ⓒ Ⓓ Ⓔ
9. Ⓐ Ⓑ Ⓒ Ⓓ Ⓔ
10. Ⓐ Ⓑ Ⓒ Ⓓ Ⓔ
11. Ⓐ Ⓑ Ⓒ Ⓓ Ⓔ
12. Ⓐ Ⓑ Ⓒ Ⓓ Ⓔ
13. Ⓐ Ⓑ Ⓒ Ⓓ Ⓔ
14. Ⓐ Ⓑ Ⓒ Ⓓ Ⓔ
15. Ⓐ Ⓑ Ⓒ Ⓓ Ⓔ
16. Ⓐ Ⓑ Ⓒ Ⓓ Ⓔ
17. Ⓐ Ⓑ Ⓒ Ⓓ Ⓔ
18. Ⓐ Ⓑ Ⓒ Ⓓ Ⓔ
19. Ⓐ Ⓑ Ⓒ Ⓓ Ⓔ
20. Ⓐ Ⓑ Ⓒ Ⓓ Ⓔ
21. Ⓐ Ⓑ Ⓒ Ⓓ Ⓔ

22. Ⓐ Ⓑ Ⓒ Ⓓ Ⓔ
23. Ⓐ Ⓑ Ⓒ Ⓓ Ⓔ
24. Ⓐ Ⓑ Ⓒ Ⓓ Ⓔ
25. Ⓐ Ⓑ Ⓒ Ⓓ Ⓔ
26. Ⓐ Ⓑ Ⓒ Ⓓ Ⓔ
27. Ⓐ Ⓑ Ⓒ Ⓓ Ⓔ
28. Ⓐ Ⓑ Ⓒ Ⓓ Ⓔ
29. Ⓐ Ⓑ Ⓒ Ⓓ Ⓔ
30. Ⓐ Ⓑ Ⓒ Ⓓ Ⓔ
31. Ⓐ Ⓑ Ⓒ Ⓓ Ⓔ
32. Ⓐ Ⓑ Ⓒ Ⓓ Ⓔ
33. Ⓐ Ⓑ Ⓒ Ⓓ Ⓔ
34. Ⓐ Ⓑ Ⓒ Ⓓ Ⓔ
35. Ⓐ Ⓑ Ⓒ Ⓓ Ⓔ
36. Ⓐ Ⓑ Ⓒ Ⓓ Ⓔ
37. Ⓐ Ⓑ Ⓒ Ⓓ Ⓔ
38. Ⓐ Ⓑ Ⓒ Ⓓ Ⓔ

### SECTION 3

1. Ⓐ Ⓑ Ⓒ Ⓓ Ⓔ
2. Ⓐ Ⓑ Ⓒ Ⓓ Ⓔ
3. Ⓐ Ⓑ Ⓒ Ⓓ Ⓔ
4. Ⓐ Ⓑ Ⓒ Ⓓ Ⓔ
5. Ⓐ Ⓑ Ⓒ Ⓓ Ⓔ
6. Ⓐ Ⓑ Ⓒ Ⓓ Ⓔ
7. Ⓐ Ⓑ Ⓒ Ⓓ Ⓔ
8. Ⓐ Ⓑ Ⓒ Ⓓ Ⓔ
9. Ⓐ Ⓑ Ⓒ Ⓓ Ⓔ
10. Ⓐ Ⓑ Ⓒ Ⓓ Ⓔ
11. Ⓐ Ⓑ Ⓒ Ⓓ Ⓔ
12. Ⓐ Ⓑ Ⓒ Ⓓ Ⓔ

13. Ⓐ Ⓑ Ⓒ Ⓓ Ⓔ
14. Ⓐ Ⓑ Ⓒ Ⓓ Ⓔ
15. Ⓐ Ⓑ Ⓒ Ⓓ Ⓔ
16. Ⓐ Ⓑ Ⓒ Ⓓ Ⓔ
17. Ⓐ Ⓑ Ⓒ Ⓓ Ⓔ
18. Ⓐ Ⓑ Ⓒ Ⓓ Ⓔ
19. Ⓐ Ⓑ Ⓒ Ⓓ Ⓔ
20. Ⓐ Ⓑ Ⓒ Ⓓ Ⓔ
21. Ⓐ Ⓑ Ⓒ Ⓓ Ⓔ
22. Ⓐ Ⓑ Ⓒ Ⓓ Ⓔ
23. Ⓐ Ⓑ Ⓒ Ⓓ Ⓔ
24. Ⓐ Ⓑ Ⓒ Ⓓ Ⓔ
25. Ⓐ Ⓑ Ⓒ Ⓓ Ⓔ
26. Ⓐ Ⓑ Ⓒ Ⓓ Ⓔ
27. Ⓐ Ⓑ Ⓒ Ⓓ Ⓔ
28. Ⓐ Ⓑ Ⓒ Ⓓ Ⓔ
29. Ⓐ Ⓑ Ⓒ Ⓓ Ⓔ
30. Ⓐ Ⓑ Ⓒ Ⓓ Ⓔ

## SECTION 4

1. Ⓐ Ⓑ Ⓒ Ⓓ Ⓔ
2. Ⓐ Ⓑ Ⓒ Ⓓ Ⓔ
3. Ⓐ Ⓑ Ⓒ Ⓓ Ⓔ
4. Ⓐ Ⓑ Ⓒ Ⓓ Ⓔ
5. Ⓐ Ⓑ Ⓒ Ⓓ Ⓔ
6. Ⓐ Ⓑ Ⓒ Ⓓ Ⓔ
7. Ⓐ Ⓑ Ⓒ Ⓓ Ⓔ
8. Ⓐ Ⓑ Ⓒ Ⓓ Ⓔ
9. Ⓐ Ⓑ Ⓒ Ⓓ Ⓔ
10. Ⓐ Ⓑ Ⓒ Ⓓ Ⓔ
11. Ⓐ Ⓑ Ⓒ Ⓓ Ⓔ
12. Ⓐ Ⓑ Ⓒ Ⓓ Ⓔ
13. Ⓐ Ⓑ Ⓒ Ⓓ Ⓔ
14. Ⓐ Ⓑ Ⓒ Ⓓ Ⓔ
15. Ⓐ Ⓑ Ⓒ Ⓓ Ⓔ

16. Ⓐ Ⓑ Ⓒ Ⓓ Ⓔ
17. Ⓐ Ⓑ Ⓒ Ⓓ Ⓔ
18. Ⓐ Ⓑ Ⓒ Ⓓ Ⓔ
19. Ⓐ Ⓑ Ⓒ Ⓓ Ⓔ
20. Ⓐ Ⓑ Ⓒ Ⓓ Ⓔ
21. Ⓐ Ⓑ Ⓒ Ⓓ Ⓔ
22. Ⓐ Ⓑ Ⓒ Ⓓ Ⓔ
23. Ⓐ Ⓑ Ⓒ Ⓓ Ⓔ
24. Ⓐ Ⓑ Ⓒ Ⓓ Ⓔ
25. Ⓐ Ⓑ Ⓒ Ⓓ Ⓔ
26. Ⓐ Ⓑ Ⓒ Ⓓ Ⓔ
27. Ⓐ Ⓑ Ⓒ Ⓓ Ⓔ
28. Ⓐ Ⓑ Ⓒ Ⓓ Ⓔ
29. Ⓐ Ⓑ Ⓒ Ⓓ Ⓔ
30. Ⓐ Ⓑ Ⓒ Ⓓ Ⓔ

## SECTION 5

1. Ⓐ Ⓑ Ⓒ Ⓓ Ⓔ
2. Ⓐ Ⓑ Ⓒ Ⓓ Ⓔ
3. Ⓐ Ⓑ Ⓒ Ⓓ Ⓔ
4. Ⓐ Ⓑ Ⓒ Ⓓ Ⓔ
5. Ⓐ Ⓑ Ⓒ Ⓓ Ⓔ
6. Ⓐ Ⓑ Ⓒ Ⓓ Ⓔ
7. Ⓐ Ⓑ Ⓒ Ⓓ Ⓔ
8. Ⓐ Ⓑ Ⓒ Ⓓ Ⓔ
9. Ⓐ Ⓑ Ⓒ Ⓓ Ⓔ
10. Ⓐ Ⓑ Ⓒ Ⓓ Ⓔ
11. Ⓐ Ⓑ Ⓒ Ⓓ Ⓔ
12. Ⓐ Ⓑ Ⓒ Ⓓ Ⓔ
13. Ⓐ Ⓑ Ⓒ Ⓓ Ⓔ
14. Ⓐ Ⓑ Ⓒ Ⓓ Ⓔ
15. Ⓐ Ⓑ Ⓒ Ⓓ Ⓔ
16. Ⓐ Ⓑ Ⓒ Ⓓ Ⓔ
17. Ⓐ Ⓑ Ⓒ Ⓓ Ⓔ
18. Ⓐ Ⓑ Ⓒ Ⓓ Ⓔ

19. Ⓐ Ⓑ Ⓒ Ⓓ Ⓔ
20. Ⓐ Ⓑ Ⓒ Ⓓ Ⓔ
21. Ⓐ Ⓑ Ⓒ Ⓓ Ⓔ
22. Ⓐ Ⓑ Ⓒ Ⓓ Ⓔ
23. Ⓐ Ⓑ Ⓒ Ⓓ Ⓔ
24. Ⓐ Ⓑ Ⓒ Ⓓ Ⓔ
25. Ⓐ Ⓑ Ⓒ Ⓓ Ⓔ

## SECTION 6

1. Ⓐ Ⓑ Ⓒ Ⓓ Ⓔ
2. Ⓐ Ⓑ Ⓒ Ⓓ Ⓔ
3. Ⓐ Ⓑ Ⓒ Ⓓ Ⓔ
4. Ⓐ Ⓑ Ⓒ Ⓓ Ⓔ
5. Ⓐ Ⓑ Ⓒ Ⓓ Ⓔ
6. Ⓐ Ⓑ Ⓒ Ⓓ Ⓔ
7. Ⓐ Ⓑ Ⓒ Ⓓ Ⓔ
8. Ⓐ Ⓑ Ⓒ Ⓓ Ⓔ
9. Ⓐ Ⓑ Ⓒ Ⓓ Ⓔ
10. Ⓐ Ⓑ Ⓒ Ⓓ Ⓔ
11. Ⓐ Ⓑ Ⓒ Ⓓ Ⓔ
12. Ⓐ Ⓑ Ⓒ Ⓓ Ⓔ
13. Ⓐ Ⓑ Ⓒ Ⓓ Ⓔ
14. Ⓐ Ⓑ Ⓒ Ⓓ Ⓔ
15. Ⓐ Ⓑ Ⓒ Ⓓ Ⓔ
16. Ⓐ Ⓑ Ⓒ Ⓓ Ⓔ
17. Ⓐ Ⓑ Ⓒ Ⓓ Ⓔ
18. Ⓐ Ⓑ Ⓒ Ⓓ Ⓔ
19. Ⓐ Ⓑ Ⓒ Ⓓ Ⓔ
20. Ⓐ Ⓑ Ⓒ Ⓓ Ⓔ
21. Ⓐ Ⓑ Ⓒ Ⓓ Ⓔ
22. Ⓐ Ⓑ Ⓒ Ⓓ Ⓔ
23. Ⓐ Ⓑ Ⓒ Ⓓ Ⓔ
24. Ⓐ Ⓑ Ⓒ Ⓓ Ⓔ
25. Ⓐ Ⓑ Ⓒ Ⓓ Ⓔ

# TEST 4

## Section 1

---

**TIME:** 30 Minutes
       38 Questions

**DIRECTIONS:** Each of the given sentences has blank spaces which indicate words omitted. Choose the best combination of words which fit into the meaning and structure within the context of the sentence.

---

1. Soulé is five feet five inches tall and inclines toward stoutness, but his erect bearing and quick movements tend to _____ this.

   (A) emphasize

   (B) conceal

   (C) negate

   (D) camouflage

   (E) disavow

2. Ages of fierceness have suppressed what is naturally kindly in the _____ of ordinary men and women.

   (A) condition

   (B) character

   (C) phenomenon

   (D) disposition

   (E) evolution

3. What ever might be in her head, it was neither love, nor romance, nor any of the emotions usually _____ to the young.

   (A) sejunctioned

   (B) segregated

   (C) ascribed

   (D) rescinded

   (E) scissioned

489

4. A man may be moral without being _____ , but he cannot be _____ without being moral.

   (A) devout...pious

   (B) altruistic...veracious

   (C) chaste...precise

   (D) pious...religious

   (E) iniquitous...contrite

5. The rational mind of a _____ and _____ person is by nature guided by his own theories and believes "What must be, will be."

   (A) irresolute...authoritarian

   (B) determined...dogmatic

   (C) doctrinaire...authoritarian

   (D) capricious...dogmatic

   (E) recidivist...vacillating

6. To remain at _____ with his wife seemed to him almost a disaster.

   (A) disparity

   (B) transcendency

   (C) concord

   (D) misogamy

   (E) variance

7. He was eagerly interested and wanted to experiment on himself, although ultimately _____ on account of his age.

   (A) deterred

   (B) accommodated

   (C) reconciled

   (D) dissuaded

   (E) acclimated

**DIRECTIONS:** In the following questions, the given pair of words contains a specific relationship to each other. Select the best pair of the choices which expresses the same relationship as the given.

8. BENEVOLENCE:PHILANTHROPY::

   (A) tolerance:bigotry

   (B) lenity:virulence

   (C) haunt:sporadic

   (D) amiability:complaisant

   (E) penurious:hoarding

9. DESIRE:WANT::

   (A) penchant:partiality

   (B) supineness:propensity

   (C) disdain:inattention

   (D) aspire:seek

   (E) avidity:greed

10. ABYSS:APEX::

   (A) east:west

   (B) horizontal:parallel

   (C) across:beside

   (D) bottom:pinnacle

   (E) under:over

11. AFFABLE:FRIENDLY::

   (A) fun:smile

   (B) amicable:congenial

   (C) hilarious:delight

   (D) speak:conversation

   (E) outspoken:taciturn

12. COURAGE:GALLANTRY::

   (A) cowardice:timidity

   (B) poltroonery:fortitude

   (C) chivalry:pusillanimity

   (D) anxiety:solicitude

   (E) agitation:perturbation

13. PRIDE:HAUGHTINESS::

   (A) arrogance:submission

   (B) abasement:crestless

(C)   affability:supercilious

(D)   vainglory:pomposity

(E)   diplomatic:inconsonant

14.   IMAGINARY:REAL::

(A)   skies:roads

(B)   equator:Mississippi River

(C)   television:telephone

(D)   vitamins:food

(E)   oxygen:breath

15.   WANTED:NEED::

(A)   indigence:exigency

(B)   crave:deprive

(C)   thirst: hunger

(D)   desire:lust

(E)   covet:necessary

16.   ALLUDE:HINT::

(A)   shy:conspicuous

(B)   boisterous:obstreperous

(C)   intelligent:sagacious

(D)   self-conscious:assertive

(E)   infer:deduce

**DIRECTIONS:** Each passage is followed by questions based on its content. After reading the passage, choose the best answer to each question. Answer all questions based on what is stated or implied in that passage.

The major debilitating symptoms of Alzheimer's disease include serious forgetfulness — particularly about recent events — and confusion. At first, the individual experiences only minor and almost imperceptible symptoms that are often attributed to emotional upsets or other physical illnesses. Gradually, however, the person becomes more forgetful and this may be reported by anxious relatives. The person may neglect to turn off the oven, may misplace things, may recheck to see if a task was done, may take longer to complete a chore that was previously routine, or may repeat already answered questions. As the disease progresses, memory loss and such changes in personality, mood, and behavior as confusion, irritability, restlessness, and agitation, are likely to appear. Judgment, concentration, orientation, writing, reading, speech, motor behavior, and naming of objects may also be affected. Even when a loving and caring family is available to give support, the victim of Alzheimer's disease is most likely to spend his or her last days in a nursing home or long-term care institution. At this time, there is no cure.

17. This passage implies that victims of Alzheimer's disease may

    (A) not remember childhood events.

    (B) suffer a gradual worsening of cognitive functions.

    (C) incur personality and behavioral changes.

    (D) spend last days in a long-term care facility.

    (E) retain the ability to perform those skills learned prior to the onset of the disease.

18. Serious forgetfulness is described as being debilitating due to:

    (A) length of time needed to complete a task.

    (B) loss of judgment and concentration.

    (C) lack of ability to live alone.

    (D) extreme amount of care needed for the patient.

    (E) inability to read and write.

19. The passage supplies information for verifying which of the following assumptions?

    (A) The Alzheimer's patient has a specific illness at the onset of the disease.

    (B) Skill mastery is retained after cognitive functioning is diminished.

    (C) Personality changes may be a major symptom of the disease.

    (D) Senility and Alzheimer's disease are synonymous.

    (E) Long-term care is necessary for all patients.

20. The passage suggests:

    (A) Alzheimer's affects only cognitive functioning, therefore the patient lives a normal life span.

    (B) Long-term care is usually viewed as an alternative for the Alzheimer's patient.

    (C) The patient suffers physical symptoms other than cognitive disabilities.

    (D) Recent research yields the prospect of a cure in the near future.

    (E) Alzheimer's can be identified by routine examination.

A submarine was first used as an offensive weapon during the American Revolutionary War. The Turtle, a one-man submersible designed by an American inventor named David Bushnell and hand operated by a screw propeller, attempted to sink a British man-of-war in New York Harbor. The plan was to attach a charge of gunpowder to the ship's bottom with screws and explode it with a time fuze. After repeated failures to force the screws through the copper sheathing of the hull of HMS *Eagle*, the submarine gave up and withdrew, exploding its powder a short distance from the *Eagle*. Although the attack was unsuccessful, it caused the British to move their blockading ships from the harbor to the outer bay.

On 17 February 1864, a Confederate craft, a hand-propelled submersible, carrying a crew of eight men, sank a Federal corvette that was blockading Charleston Harbor. The hit was accomplished by a torpedo suspended ahead of the Confederate Hunley as she rammed the Union frigate Housatonic, and is the first recorded instance of a submarine sinking a warship.

The submarine first became a major component in naval warfare during World War I, when Germany demonstrated its full potentialities. Wholesale sinking of Allied shipping by the German U-boats almost swung the war in favor of the Central Powers. Then, as now, the submarine's greatest advantage was that it could operate beneath the ocean surface where detection was difficult. Sinking a submarine was comparatively easy, once it was found — but finding it before it could attack was another matter.

During the closing months of World War I, the Allied Submarine Devices Investigation Committee was formed to obtain from science and technology more effective underwater detection equipment. The committee developed a reasonably accurate device for locating a submerged submarine. This device was a trainable hydrophone, which was attached to the bottom of the ASW ship, and used to detect screw noises and other sounds that came from a submarine. Although the committee disbanded after World War I, the British made improvements on the locating device during the interval between then and World War II, and named it ASDIC after the committee.

American scientists further improved on the device, calling it sonar, a name derived from the underlined initials of the words <u>so</u>und <u>na</u>vigation and <u>r</u>anging.

At the end of World War II, the United States improved the snorkel (a device for bringing air to the crew and engines when operating submerged on diesels) and developed the Guppy (short for greater underwater propulsion power), a conversion of the fleet-type submarine of World War II fame. The superstructure was changed by reducing the surface area, streamlining every protruding object, and enclosing the periscope shears in a streamlined metal fairing. Performance increased greatly with improved electronic equipment, additional battery capacity, and the addition of the snorkel.

21. According to the passage, the submarine's success was due in part to its ability to:

    (A) strike and escape undetected.

    (B) move swifter than other vessels.

    (C) remain underwater for longer periods of time.

    (D) submerge to great depths while being hunted.

    (E) run silently.

22. The passage states that in the first submarine offensive the submarine:

    (A) encountered and sank German U-boats.

    (B) sank a ship belonging to its own nation.

    (C) torpedoed a British man-of-war.

    (D) sank nothing and exploded its powder away from its target.

    (E) was detected and was itself destroyed.

23. The passage implies that one of the most pressing modifications needed for the submarine was to:

    (A) streamline its shape.

    (B) enlarge the submarine for accommodating more torpedoes and men.

    (C) reduce the noise caused by the submarine.

    (D) modify for staying submerged longer.

    (E) add a snorkel.

24. The passage implies that

    (A) The US improved the snorkel.

    (B) The US developed the Guppy.

    (C) The Guppy is a conversion of the submarine.

(D)   The streamlining of the superstructure increased the ship's performance.

(E)   The submarine became a major component in Naval warfare in 1917.

25.   It is implied that:

(A)   ASDIC was formed to obtain technology for underwater detection.

(B)   ASDIC developed an accurate device for locating submarines.

(C)   the hydrophone was attached to the bottom of the ship.

(D)   the technology of the hydrophone is being used currently.

(E)   ASDIC was formed to develop technology to defend US shipping.

26.   From the passage, one can infer:

(A)   David Bushnell was indirectly responsible for the sinking of the Federal corvette in Charleston Harbor.

(B)   David Bushnell invented the Turtle.

(C)   The Turtle was a one-man submarine.

(D)   The Turtle sank the Eagle on February 19, 1864.

(E)   The design of the Turtle was a response to science fiction.

27.   The passage supplies information relating to SONAR. SONAR not only picked up the sound of submarines moving through the water but also:

(A)   indicated the speed at which the sub was moving.

(B)   gave the location of the submarine.

(C)   indicated the speed of the torpedo.

(D)   placed the submarine within a specified range.

(E)   supplied the depth at which the submarine traveled.

DIRECTIONS: Each of the following questions provides a given word in capitalized letters followed by five word choices. Choose the best word which is most <u>opposite</u> in meaning to the given word.

28. FATIGUE:

   (A) exhaustion

   (B) vestment

   (C) prostration

   (D) enervate

   (E) refection

29. NONEXISTENCE:

   (A) absolute

   (B) nullity

   (C) abeyance

   (D) void

   (E) amorphism

30. CONTRAST:

   (A) antithesis

   (B) foil

   (C) refutative

   (D) adapting

   (E) coalescence

31. APPENDAGE:

   (A) curtail

   (B) severance

   (C) accessory

   (D) adjunct

   (E) adherent

32. PREVALENCE:

   (A) permeate

   (B) currency

   (C) advantage

   (D) subordinate

   (E) penetrate

33. INTERMIXTURE:

   (A) hybrid

   (B) junction

   (C) adulterant

   (D) miscegenation

   (E) homogeneous

34. **RESOLUTION:**
    (A) analysis
    (B) disloyal
    (C) obdurate
    (D) catalysis
    (E) synthesis

35. **HARMONY:**
    (A) euphony
    (B) anomaly
    (C) subordinate
    (D) gradation
    (E) collateral

36. **PRECEDENCE:**
    (A) preliminary
    (B) preference
    (C) consequence
    (D) antecedent
    (E) prefix

37. **DISPERSION:**
    (A) edit
    (B) radiation
    (C) diffusion
    (D) compilation
    (E) educe

38. **GENERIC:**
    (A) general
    (B) analogous
    (C) collective
    (D) specific
    (E) typical

## STOP

If time still remains, you may go back and check your work.
When the time allotted is up, you may go on to the next section.

# Section 2

TIME:   30 Minutes
         38 Questions

DIRECTIONS: Each of the given sentences has blank spaces which indicate words omitted. Choose the best combination of words which fit into the meaning and structure within the context of the sentence.

1.    A storm of _____ swept over the country when _____ at the highest levels of the government became common knowledge.

    (A)   indignation ...corruption

    (B)   protest...cooperation

    (C)   praise...dedication

    (D)   uncertainty...graft

    (E)   indifference...actions

2.    The work of those government officials who must live in hostile foreign countries is full of perils; _____ for their families and _____ for themselves.

    (A)   dangers...dangers        (D)   risks...risks

    (B)   hazards...hazards       (E)   threats...threats

    (C)   perils...perils

3.    It is not the personal qualities of an individual which permit independence and self-sufficiency _____ the myriad of public services which undergird modern life that permit the _____ of independence and self-sufficiency.

    (A)   just...existence         (B)   indeed...reality

(C)  only...presence        (D)  but...illusion

(E)  besides...self-delusion

4.  The hive is constructed so that the bee may work all around each frame and so that the _____ , when full, may be _____ without disturbing the other frames.

(A)  bee...handled        (D)  vessel...destroyed

(B)  latter...removed        (E)  queen...carried off

(C)  hive...taken

5.  This method of analysis will enable school boards to _____ accurate demographic changes over five _____ years.

(A)  anticipate...entire        (D)  project...past

(B)  predict...preceding        (E)  forecast...succeeding

(C)  foretell...passing

6.  You should not praise a man for being incorrupt if he has never had _____ , because in such a case his incorruptibility may be merely a lack of _____ .

(A)  wealth...desire        (D)  power...opportunity

(B)  fame...temptation        (E)  status...necessity

(C)  prestige...purpose

7.  The chairman rapped _____ for order; but owing to the extreme _____ of the audience, he soon gave up the attempt.

(A)  twice...ennui        (D)  timidly...chaos

(B)  vigorously...enthusiasm        (E)  lightly...disharmony

(C)  quickly...interest

DIRECTIONS: In the following questions, the given pair of words contains a specific relationship to each other. Select the best pair of the choices which expresses the same relationship as the given.

8. SOCIABILITY:SOCIOPATH::

   (A) Delusion:Schizophrenic      (D) Illusion:Psychosis

   (B) Sensitivity:Psychic         (E) Calm:Neurotic

   (C) Space:Claustrophobic

9. SAND:DUNE::

   (A) Tree:Forest                 (D) Clamor:Tumult

   (B) Rock:Boulder                (E) Twig:Log

   (C) Shower:Deluge

10. VARIABLE:EQUATION::

   (A) Oxygen:Water                (D) Clay:Sculpture

   (B) Paramecia:Amoeba            (E) Furnace:Heat

   (C) Analysis:Summary

11. QUILL:FOUNTAIN PEN::

   (A) Rural:Urban                 (D) Solo:Quartet

   (B) Young:Old                   (E) Mangle:Iron

   (C) Truce:Peace

12. ARC:CIRCUMFERENCE::

   (A) Moon:Earth                  (D) Exercise:Rest

   (B) Hour:Day                    (E) Knowledge:Wisdom

   (C) Cabin:Mansion

13. EXPURGATE:CENSOR::

 (A) Expunge:Wash
 (B) Arcane:Secret
 (C) Frenetic:French
 (D) Phrenetic:Phoneme
 (E) Wrought:Excited

14. PHYLUM:CLASSIFICATION::

 (A) Cat:Feline
 (B) Commitment:Vow
 (C) Lie:Deceit
 (D) Medal:Honor
 (E) Control:Harness

15. RIB:UMBRELLA::

 (A) Leg:Table
 (B) Stud:Wall
 (C) Shelf:Closet
 (D) Hinge:Door
 (E) Knob:Drawer

16. DECODE:UNDERSTAND::

 (A) Detonate:Explode
 (B) Study:Research
 (C) Destroy:Build
 (D) Skill:Practice
 (E) Sow:Reap

---

**DIRECTIONS:** Each passage is followed by questions based on its content. After reading the passage, choose the best answer to each question. Answer all questions based on what is stated or implied in that passage.

---

Our heritage is richer because of the men and women of France who came to this continent and explored and settled the wilderness. The breadth of their achievements and the depth of the heritage they bequeathed to the United States transcends their small numbers. A substantial part of this heritage was mixed into the mainstream of America through 6,000 unhappy Acadians, who were expelled in 1755

from Acadia (Nova Scotia) by the British, its new rulers under the terms of the Treaty of Utrecht. The Acadians at first scattered throughout the British colonies, from Maine to Georgia, but most of them finally settled in Louisiana. Henry Wadsworth Longfellow's poem *Evangeline*, an epic about the Acadian odyssey, is the most widely known tribute to the French heritage in the United States.

Other persecuted Huguenots, also seeking refuge and religious freedom, contributed another equally important segment of our French heritage. They settled in clusters from Rhode Island to South Carolina, especially in Charleston, and enriched the cultural patterns evolving in the colonies. Therefore, much of the flavor of France in the United States today stems not from areas that once were French colonies but from French settlers in the British colonies.

17. The author gives primary emphasis to:

    (A) Racial persecution by the British.

    (B) Those French who settled in Louisiana.

    (C) Those French who settled in the wilderness.

    (D) An epic of the French odyssey.

    (E) French heritage in America.

18. It can be inferred that the Acadians were:

    (A) British            (D) unhappy

    (B) persecuted         (E) reclusive

    (C) gypsies

19. The author viewed the coming of the French to America as:

    (A) auspicious         (D) unlikely

    (B) unfortunate        (E) foreboding

    (C) inevitable

Pennsylvania was the most successful of the proprietary colonies. Admiral Sir William Penn was a wealthy and respected friend of Charles II. His son, William, was an associate of George Fox, founder of the Society of Friends—a despised Quaker. When the senior Penn died, in 1670, his Quaker son inherited not only the friendship of the Crown but also an outstanding unpaid debt of some magnitude owed to his father by the King. As settlement, in 1681 he received a grant of land in America, called "Pennsylvania," which he decided to use as a refuge for his persecuted coreligionists. It was a princely domain, extending along the Delaware River from the 40th to the 43rd parallel. As Proprietor, Penn was both ruler and landlord. The restrictions on the grant were essentially the same as those imposed on the second Lord Baltimore: colonial laws had to be in harmony with those of England and had to be assented to by a representative assembly.

Penn lost little time in advertising his grant and the terms on which he offered settlement. He promised religious freedom and virtually total self-government. More than 1,000 colonists arrived the first year, most of whom were Mennonites and Quakers. Penn himself arrived in 1682 at New Castle and spent the winter at Upland, a Swedish settlement on the Delaware that the English had taken over; he renamed it Chester. He founded a capital city a few miles upstream and named it Philadelphia — the City of Brotherly Love. Well situated and well planned, it grew rapidly. Within 2 years, it had more than 600 houses, many of them handsome brick residences surrounded by lawns and gardens.

Shiploads of Quakers poured into the colony. By the summer of 1683, more than 3,000 settlers had arrived. Welsh, Germans, Scotch-Irish, Mennonites, Quakers, Jews, and Baptists mingled in a New World utopia. Not even the great Puritan migration had populated a colony so fast. Pennsylvania soon rivaled Massachusetts, New York, and Virginia. In part its prosperity was attributable to its splendid location and fertile soils, but even more to the proprietor's felicitous administration. In a series of laws — the Great Law and the First and Second Frames of Government — Penn created one of the most humane and progressive governments then in existence. It was characterized by broad principles of religious toleration, a well-organized bicameral legislature, and forward-looking penal code.

Another reason for the colony's growth was that, unlike the other colonies, it was not troubled by the Indians. Penn had bought their

lands and made a series of peace treaties that were scrupulously fair and rigidly adhered to. For more than half a century, Indians and whites lived in Pennsylvania in peace. Quaker farmers, who were never armed, could leave their children with neighboring "savages" when they went into town for a visit.

By any measure, Penn's "Holy Experiment" was a magnificent success. Penn proved that a state could function smoothly on Quaker principles, without oaths, arms, or priests, and that these principles encouraged individual morality and freedom of conscience. Furthermore, ever a good businessman, he made a personal fortune while treating his subjects with unbending fairness and honesty.

20. It is implied that:

   (A) High values need not be compromised in order to obtain financial, social, and political success.

   (B) The development of the colony would have taken a much different course if the senior Penn had not died so early.

   (C) All colonies should have been proprietary colonies.

   (D) Colonists in Pennsylvania did not take child care as seriously as those in other colonies.

   (E) Rapid colonization is superior to slow colonization.

21. The author mentions the Holy Experiment as an example of:

   (A) English-Colonial collaboration

   (B) an early bicameral

   (C) a treaty with Indians

   (D) an example of religious toleration

   (E) a reason for establishing a proprietary colony

22. Which of the following was not true of Pennsylvania's colony?

   (A) rapid settlement

(B)    refuge for religious non-conformists

(C)    tolerant state religion

(D)    proprietary government

(E)    laws in harmony with those of England

23.    It can be inferred from the selection that:

(A)    All other colonies would have grown more rapidly if they had been organized in a manner similar to Pennsylvania.

(B)    All colonies should have been in harmony with the laws of England and had a representative assembly.

(C)    Those colonies that were awards for service from the crown were better-administered.

(D)    The Pennsylvania Colony was the first colony to experience a tolerance for a number of nationalities and varied religious groups.

(E)    Life with the Indians would have been much easier in other colonies if land had been purchased and treaties adhered to.

24.    .The "Great Law" and the "First and Second Frames of Government"

(A)    established Penn's political reputation.

(B)    created treaties with the Indians.

(C)    became the basis of a progressive republic form of government.

(D)    placed restrictions on immigration.

(E)    had to be overturned when they became inefficient.

25.    After the summer of 1683 the Pennsylvania Colony could be referred to as:

(A)    A "melting-pot" colony.

(B)   A Quaker Colony.

(C)   The largest American Colony.

(D)   A Colonial Republic.

(E)   The first "democratic" colony.


26.   According to the selection, as religious freedom was guaranteed, all of the following religious sects were mentioned as settlers in Pennsylvania except:

(A)   Catholic.                    (D)   Mennonite.

(B)   Jew.                          (E)   Quaker.

(C)   Baptist.


27.   The author uses which of the following writing techniques?

(A)   syllogistic form

(B)   development of an analogy

(C)   literary allusion

(D)   direct quotation

(E)   supporting facts


---

**DIRECTIONS:** Each of the following questions provides a given word in capitalized letters followed by five word choices. Choose the best word which is most <u>opposite</u> in meaning to the given word.

---

28. CAPRICIOUS:
    (A) Stuffy
    (B) Steadfast
    (C) Scurrilous
    (D) Sagacious
    (E) Sybaritic

29. CORROBORATE:
    (A) Abrogate
    (B) Disclaim
    (C) Contradict
    (D) Disprove
    (E) Doubt

30. REPUDIATE:
    (A) Adore
    (B) Agree
    (C) Advocate
    (D) Admire
    (E) Adopt

31. UNIFORM:
    (A) Asymmetrical
    (B) Confusion
    (C) Chaos
    (D) Disassembled
    (E) Various

32. ADDICT:
    (A) Cease
    (B) Deprive
    (C) Wean
    (D) Alienate
    (E) Estrange

33. UNDERMINE:
    (A) Reinforce
    (B) Reestablish
    (C) Restore
    (D) Consolidate
    (E) Corroborate

34. RELIGIOUS:
    (A) Malevolent
    (B) Secular
    (C) Evil
    (D) Impious
    (E) Unrighteous

35. GLUTTONOUS:
    (A) Voracious
    (B) Fastidious
    (C) Ascetic
    (D) Abstemious
    (E) Austere

36. RUDE:

    (A) Urbane

    (B) Debonair

    (C) Pleasant

    (D) Friendly

    (E) Confident

38. RESERVED:

    (A) Chivalrous

    (B) Affable

    (C) Ingratiating

    (D) Cultivated

    (E) Well-bred

37. UNINTELLIGIBLE:

    (A) Explicable

    (B) Solvable

    (C) Recognizable

    (D) Rational

    (E) Apparent

**STOP**

If time still remains, you may go back and check your work.
When the time allotted is up, you may go on to the next section.

# Section 3

**TIME:**   30 Minutes
              30 Questions

**NUMBERS:** All numbers are real numbers.

**FIGURES:** Position of points, angles, regions, etc. are assumed to be in the order shown and angle measures are assumed to be positive.

**LINES:** Assume that lines shown as straight are indeed straight.

**DIRECTIONS:** Each of the following given set of quantities is placed into either column A or B. Compare the two quantities to decide whether:

(A)   the quantity in Column A is greater

(B)   the quantity in Column B is greater

(C)   the two quantities are equal

(D)   the relationship cannot be determined from the information given.

**NOTE:** Do not choose (E) since there are only four choices.

**COMMON INFORMATION:** Information which relates to one or both given quantities is centered in the two columns. A symbol which appears in both columns will indicate the same item in Column A and Column B.

**EXAMPLES:**

| Column A | Column B |
|----------|----------|
| 1.        $5 \times 4$ | $5 + 4$ |

Explanation: The correct answer is (A), since $5 \times 4 = 20$, and $5 + 4 = 9$.

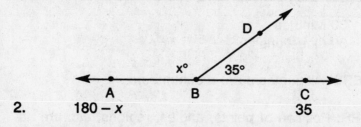

2.      $180 - x$                                                      $35$

Explanation: The correct answer is (C). Since Angle *ABC* is a straight angle, its measurement is 180°.

| Column A | Column B |
|----------|----------|

$$f(x,y) = \frac{2x+y}{y^2}$$

1.              $f(1,1)$                                    $f(1,2)$

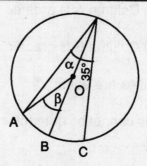

$\overset{\frown}{AB} = \overset{\frown}{BC}$, O is the center of the circle.

2.                  $\beta$                                    $3\alpha$

60% of $x + 2$ is 36.

3.                  $x$                                        $60$

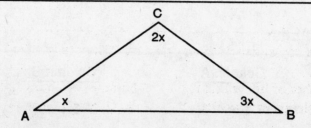

| Column A | Column B |
|----------|----------|

4. $\qquad$ $3X$ $\qquad$ $90°$

The central number of 3 consecutive
even numbers is $2x + 2$

5. $\qquad$ $2x$ $\qquad$ The average of the three even numbers.

$\overline{AB} = \overline{BC} = \overline{AC}$

6. $\qquad$ Number of triangles $\qquad$ 15

$(X, Y)$ is a point in the fourth quadrant.

7. $\qquad$ $X$ $\qquad$ $2Y$

One boy sleeps 14 hours per day (1 month = 30 days).

8. Number of hours that the boy sleeps in 3 weeks. $\qquad$ Number of hours that the boy doesn't sleep in a month.

| **Column A** | **Column B** |
|---|---|

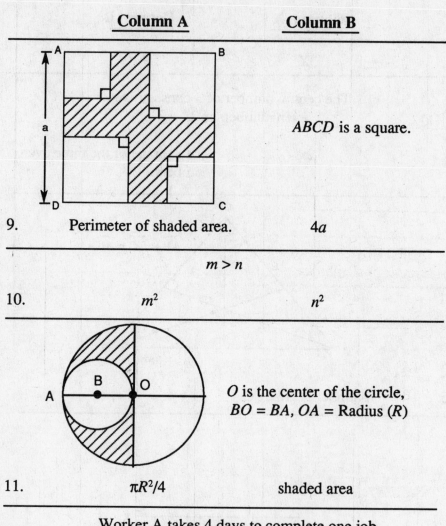

9.      Perimeter of shaded area.      $4a$

---

$m > n$

10.      $m^2$      $n^2$

---

$O$ is the center of the circle,
$BO = BA$, $OA =$ Radius ($R$)

11.      $\pi R^2/4$      shaded area

---

Worker A takes 4 days to complete one job,
and worker B takes 6 days.

12.      time it takes both workers together to complete the job.      2.5 days

---

*ABCD* is a rectangle

13.      $\alpha + \beta$      $180°$

| Column A | Column B |
|----------|----------|

$$0 < X < 1$$

14. $\dfrac{1}{1 + 1/(1 + 1/x)}$ | 1

$$y = ax + b$$
$$\text{where } x > 0, a > 0, b > 0$$

15. $x$ | $y$

---

**DIRECTIONS:** For the following questions, select the best answer choice to the given question.

---

16. $\left[\dfrac{.0003 \times 9 \times 10^{-1}}{18 \times 10^{-4}}\right]^{-1} = ?$

(A) 20/3

(B) 3/20

(C) 3/2

(D) 2/3

(E) 19/3

17. In the figure, *ABC* is an equilateral triangle. What is the value of α if *AT* is the bisector of angle *BAC*?

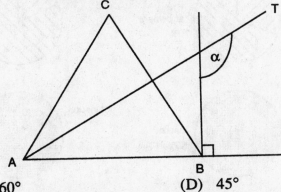

(A) 60°

(B) 90°

(C) 120°

(D) 45°

(E) 135°

18. What is the reciprocal of $1:{}^8/_3$?

    (A) ${}^8/_3$

    (B) ${}^3/_8$

    (C) $1\,{}^8/_3$

    (D) $1\,{}^3/_8$

    (E) $1 + {}^8/_3$

19. If $a * b = 6a - 2bx$ and $9 * 6 = 6$, then $x = ?$

    (A) 2

    (B) 0

    (C) 1

    (D) 4

    (E) 3

20. The perimeter of a square inscribed in the circumference of radius $R$ is ?

    (A) $4R$

    (B) $8R$

    (C) $2R\sqrt{2}$

    (D) $4R\sqrt{2}$

    (E) $8R\sqrt{2}$

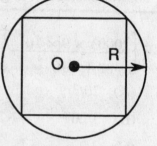

Questions 21 – 25 refer to the following graphs.

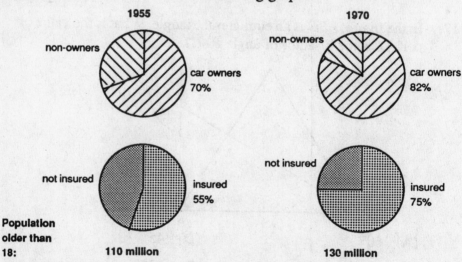

In doing the analysis, consider everyone who is older than 18 as a car owner or a non-car owner.

21. The number of people with car insurance in 1970 was approximately

    (A)  40 million

    (B)  80 million

    (C)  107 million

    (D)  98 million

    (E)  130 million

22. What was the increase in the number of cars with insurance from 1955 to 1970?

    (A)  30.76 million

    (B)  37.65 million

    (C)  30 million

    (D)  37 million

    (E)  29.6 million

23. What is the ratio of cars without insurance in 1970 to cars without insurance in 1955?

    (A)  .55

    (B)  1.81

    (C)  .77

    (D)  1.3

    (E)  1.5

24. What was the percent increase of the number of cars from 1955 to 1970 (approximately)?

    (A)  38.4%

    (B)  27.8%

    (C)  43.8%

    (D)  28.7%

    (E)  12.0%

25. What is the ratio of people who did not own cars in 1970 to those who did not own cars in 1955?

    (A)  1.41

    (B)  0.71

    (C)  0.17

    (D)  5.88

    (E)  0.60

26. A man who is 40 years old has three sons, ages 6, 3, and 1. In how many years will the combined age of this three sons equal 80% of his age?

    (A)  5                      (D)  20

    (B)  10                     (E)  25

    (C)  15

27. Which of the following statements are true, if
    $$x + y + z = 10$$
    $$y \geq 5$$
    $$4 \geq z \geq 3$$

    I.    $x < z$

    II.   $x > y$

    III.  $x + z \leq y$

    (A)  only I                 (D)  I and III

    (B)  only II                (E)  I, II and III

    (C)  only III

28. Two pounds of pears and one pound of peaches cost $1.40. Three pounds of pears and two pounds of peaches cost $2.40. How much is the combined cost of one pound of pears and one pound of peaches?

    (A)  $2.00                  (D)  $.80

    (B)  $1.50                  (E)  $1.00

    (C)  $1.60

29. In a class of 40 students, 30 speak French and 20 speak German. How many speak both French and German?

    (A)  5                      (D)  10

    (B)  20                     (E)  30

    (C)  15

30. $\sqrt{X\sqrt{X\sqrt{X}}} = ?$

(A) $X^{7/8}$

(B) $X^{7/4}$

(C) $X^{15/16}$

(D) $X^{3/4}$

(E) $X^{15/8}$

## STOP

**If time still remains, you may go back and check your work.
When the time allotted is up, you may go on to the next section.**

# Section 4

**TIME:**   30 Minutes
30 Questions

**NUMBERS:** All numbers are real numbers.

**FIGURES:** Position of points, angles, regions, etc. are assumed to be in the order shown and angle measures are assumed to be positive.

**LINES:** Assume that lines shown as straight are indeed straight.

**DIRECTIONS:** Each of the following given set of quantities is placed into either column A or B. Compare the two quantities to decide whether:

(A)   the quantity in Column A is greater

(B)   the quantity in Column B is greater

(C)   the two quantities are equal

(D)   the relationship cannot be determined from the information given.

**NOTE:** Do not choose (E) since there are only four choices.

**COMMON INFORMATION:** Information which relates to one or both given quantities is centered in the two columns. A symbol which appears in both columns will indicate the same item in Column A and Column B.

**EXAMPLES:**

| Column A | Column B |
|----------|----------|
| 1.   $5 \times 4$ | $5 + 4$ |

Explanation: The correct answer is (A), since $5 \times 4 = 20$, and $5 + 4 = 9$.

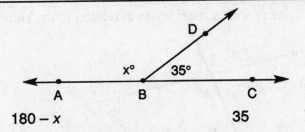

2.       $180 - x$                                    35

Explanation: The correct answer is (C). Since Angle *ABC* is a straight angle, its measurement is 180°.

|  | <u>Column A</u> | <u>Column B</u> |
|---|---|---|

*l, m,* and *n* are lines

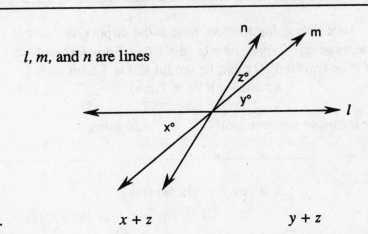

1.              $x + z$                              $y + z$

---

$$2x + y = 6; \ x - y = 4$$

2.              2                                      $y$

---

The total price of 2 shirts and 2 ties is $80.

3.       The price of one shirt       The price of one tie

---

4.              2                            $18 \times 3 + 44 - 84 \div 7$

| <u>Column A</u> | <u>Column B</u> |
|---|---|

Lines *l* and *m* meet when extended to the right.

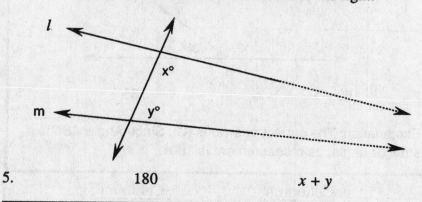

5.            180                 $x + y$

---

Jack was going to meet Jane at the airport. If he traveled 60 mph, he would arrive 1 hour early; and if he traveled 30 mph, he would arrive 1 hour late. (Distance = Rate × Time)

6.     Distance to the airport       120 miles

---

*a, b,* and *c* are integers

7.           $ac$                $bc$

---

For all real numbers *a, b,* and *c,*
$$a * b = a + b - ab$$

8.        − 20             $(-4) * 5$

---

$m\overline{AB}$ represents the measure of segment $\overline{AB}$;
$$m\overline{AY} > m\overline{XZ}$$

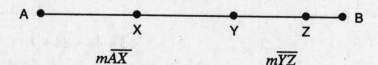

9.       $m\overline{AX}$             $m\overline{YZ}$

|  | Column A | Column B |
|---|---|---|

---

10. The difference between $x$ and $y$, divided by 6 | $\dfrac{x-y}{6}$

---

A car travels 400 miles on 20 gallons of gasoline.

11. Number of gallons of gasoline consumed on a trip of 900 miles. | 40

---

$$3x + y + z = 15$$

12. $x$ | 5

---

The average (arithmetic mean) of
40, 20, 30, 24, 27 and 15 is $\bar{x}$

13. $\bar{x}$ | 26

---

A tree casts a shadow 40 m (meters) long.
At the same time a meter stick casts a 2.5 m shadow.

tree

40 m

1m

2.5 m

14. Height of the tree | 17 m

---

$$\frac{y}{3} + \frac{y}{2} = 6$$

15. 6 | $y$

---

**DIRECTIONS:** For the following questions, select the best answer choice to the given question.

---

16. A used car dealer reduced the price of all the cars on his lot by $300. If a car was originally priced at $1,195, what percent (to the nearest tenth) is the markdown on the sale price?

    (A)  29.3%                    (D)  25.1%

    (B)  8.4%                     (E)  33.5%

    (C)  37.7%

17. If *n* and *k* are even integers, which of the following is an even integer?

    (A)  $n + k + 1$              (D)  $(n - 3)(k + 1)$

    (B)  $(n - 1)(k + 1)$         (E)  $2(n + k) + 1$

    (C)  $2(n + k + 1)$

18. If lines *l*, *m*, and *n* intersect at point *P*, express $x + y$ in terms of *a*.

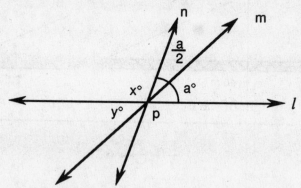

    (A)  $180 - \frac{a}{2}$      (D)  $a - 180$

    (B)  $\frac{a}{2} - 180$      (E)  $180 - a$

    (C)  $90 - \frac{a}{2}$

19. If $x - (4x - 8) + 9 + (6x - 8) = 9 - x + 24$, then $x =$

    (A)  4

    (D)  6

    (B)  2

    (E)  10

    (C)  8

20. If $R$, $S$, and $Q$ can wallpaper a house in 8 hours and $R$ and $S$ can do it in 12 hours, how long will it take $Q$ alone to wallpaper the house?

    (A)  12 hours

    (D)  20 hours

    (B)  24 hours

    (E)  28 hours

    (C)  8 hours

Questions 21 – 25 refer to the following tables.

Table 1 represents the amount of money (to the nearest dollar) spent by 50 state university students in the school's book store during the month of August, 1988 on textbooks. The table is broken down by students' class rank, and Table 2 represents the amount of money spent by the same 50 students in the school's book store during August, 1988 on items other than textbooks.

### Table 1

| | Freshman | Sophomore | Junior | Senior | Graduate |
|---|---|---|---|---|---|
| | $180 | $158 | $179 | $166 | $116 |
| | 195 | 191 | 194 | 189 | 153 |
| | 168 | 202 | 210 | 190 | 98 |
| | 184 | 173 | 203 | 157 | 121 |
| | 205 | 187 | 183 | 203 | 92 |
| | 208 | 212 | 177 | 171 | 118 |
| | 184 | 197 | 192 | 180 | 126 |
| | 178 | 181 | 169 | 164 | 114 |
| | 163 | 166 | 198 | 188 | 119 |
| | 196 | 180 | 204 | 170 | 96 |
| Total | $1,861 | $1,847 | $1,909 | $1,778 | $1,153 |

**Table 2**

| Freshman | Sophomore | Junior | Senior | Graduate |
|---|---|---|---|---|
| $12 | $15 | $13 | $27 | $14 |
| 9 | 13 | 15 | 19 | 10 |
| 12 | 14 | 17 | 23 | 7 |
| 14 | 15 | 24 | 23 | 26 |
| 12 | 13 | 21 | 25 | 14 |
| 14 | 11 | 19 | 16 | 10 |
| 5 | 12 | 15 | 32 | 16 |
| 10 | 14 | 17 | 26 | 17 |
| 13 | 17 | 20 | 23 | 19 |
| 13 | 16 | 19 | 27 | 19 |
| Total $114 | $140 | $180 | $241 | $152 |

21. Among all the students' class ranks, which class shows the greatest relative variation in the amount of money spent in the school's book store on items other than textbooks?

(A) Graduate          (D) Sophomore

(B) Senior            (E) Freshman

(C) Junior

22. Which of the following is the best approximation (to the nearest dollar) of the average amount of money spent by any senior class student in the school's book store in August on textbooks only?

(A) $193          (D) $178

(B) $168          (E) $173

(C) $183

23. Approximately, what is the difference between the average amount of money spent in the school's book store in August by a senior class student and the average amount of money spent by a graduate class student?

(A) $63          (D) $82

(B) $95          (E) $64

(C) $71

526

24. If the freshman class had 3,000 students in it during August, which of the following is the best approximation for the total amount of money spent by the entire freshman class in the school's book store in August?

   (A) $558,000           (D) $585,000

   (B) $566,700           (E) $592,500

   (C) $572,200

25. If state university enrollment in August, 1988 totaled 10,000 students, and the freshman class had 3,000 students in it, approximately what is the percent of the amount of money spent by the freshman class in the school's book store in August on items other than textbooks of the total amount of money spent by the entire student body on items other than textbooks?

   (A) 15%               (D) 33%

   (B) 21%               (E) 39%

   (C) 27%

26. Which of the following equations can be used to find a woman's present age, if she is now 6 times as old as her son, and next year, her age will be equal to the square of her son's age?

   (A) $6w + 1 = w^2 + 1$           (D) $6w + 1 = (w + 1)^2$

   (B) $6(w + 1) = w^2 + 1$         (E) $w + 6 = (w + 1)^2$

   (C) $6(w + 1) = (w + 1)^2$

27. The measure of an inscribed angle is equal to one-half the measure of its inscribed arc. In the figure shown, triangle $ABC$ is inscribed in circle $O$, and line $\overleftrightarrow{BD}$ is tangent to the circle at point $B$. If the measure of angle $CBD$ is 70°, what is the measure of angle $BAC$?

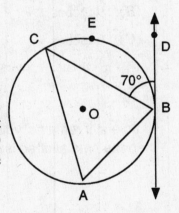

(A) 110°

(D) 35°

(B) 70°

(E) 40°

(C) 140°

28. A counting number with exactly 2 different factors is called a prime number. Which of the following pairs of numbers are consecutive prime numbers?

(A) 27 and 29

(D) 37 and 29

(B) 31 and 33

(E) 41 and 43

(C) 35 and 37

29. If $V = \pi b^2 (r - {}^b/_3)$, then $r$ is equal to

(A) $\dfrac{V}{\pi b^2} + \dfrac{b}{3}$

(D) $V + \dfrac{b}{3}$

(B) $\dfrac{V}{\pi b^2} + \dfrac{b}{3\pi}$

(E) $V + \dfrac{\pi b}{3}$

(C) $\dfrac{V}{\pi b^2} + 3b$

30. An old picture has dimensions 33 inches by 24 inches. What one length must be cut from each dimension so that the ratio of the shorter side to the longer side is $^2/_3$?

(A) $4^1/_2$ inches

(D) $10^1/_2$ inches

(B) 9 inches

(E) 3 inches

(C) 6 inches

## STOP

If time still remains, you may go back and check your work.
When the time allotted is up, you may go on to the next section.

# Section 5

**TIME:** 30 Minutes
25 Questions

---

**DIRECTIONS:** Each question or group of questions is based on a passage or set of statements. Select the best answer choice.

---

Questions 1-4 refer to the following passage.

Salaries for members of the physics department at a mid-sized college are increased annually on the basis of across-the-board, merit and discretionary allotments. There are five members of the department and the chairman must recommend appropriate raises in the merit and discretionary categories. The chairman has been allocated $3600 for merit raises and $2100 for discretionary raises. The minimum discretionary raise he may recommend is $700. Furthermore, he may not recommend discretionary increases to any faculty member unless they have also been recommended for at least a $1000 merit increase.

1.  What is the maximum amount that could be awarded to any one faculty member?

    (A)  $5700

    (B)  $3100

    (C)  $4300

    (D)  $2400

    (E)  $1700

2.  Which of the following distributions would be allowed under these guidelines?

    (A)  3 faculty receive $1700 each and 2 faculty receive $300 each.

    (B)  All 5 faculty receive the same amount – $1140.

    (C)  Divide the $3600 to the two most outstanding faculty equally and divide the $2100 equally among the other three faculty.

529

(D) Divide the merit allocation equally and recommend the discretionary allocation to be divided equally among the three lowest paid faculty.

(E) Give $1000 in merit money to 3 faculty; $600 in merit raise to one faculty; and divide the $2100 in discretionary money equally among all five faculty.

3. What is the lowest amount the chairman could recommend for any single faculty member to receive from the merit and discretionary amounts combined?

(A) $1700          (D) $300

(B) $1000          (E) $0

(C) $700

4. If the chairman wanted to recommend the most equal raises possible within the guidelines, what would be the difference between the highest and lowest paid faculty member if he also recommended expenditure of the entire allocation?

(A) $600          (D) $1700

(B) $900          (E) $2100

(C) $1400

Questions 5-8 refer to the following passage.

The production and quality control departments of a towel and blanket factory voted to change to flex time. The schedule they agreed on was to work a 4-day week of 10 hours each day. Management agreed but stipulated that of the ten workers who comprised these two departments, at least 6 workers must be present each day, that each department have at least 3 people present each day, and that the sequence of work to be done must be followed according to the people who performed certain tasks. The production department included employees A, B, C, D, and E, and the quality control department included employees 1, 2, 3, 4, and 5. The weekly schedule of the employees required that A and B must complete their daily work before 3 and 4 can do theirs, and 1 and 2 must do their daily work before C and D. All other employees can work on any day with anyone else.

530

5.  Which of the following is an acceptable schedule for Monday?

    (A)  A, B, C, D, E and 1, 2, 3, 4, 5

    (B)  A, B, C, D, E and 1, 2, 3, 4

    (C)  C, D, E and 3, 4, 5

    (D)  A, B, E and 1, 2, 5

    (E)  A, B, C, D, E and 1, 2, 3, 4

6.  Which of the following is an acceptable work schedule for A?

    (A)  Tuesday, Wednesday, Thursday, Friday

    (B)  Monday, Tuesday, Wednesday, Thursday

    (C)  Monday, Tuesday, Wednesday, Friday

    (D)  Monday, Tuesday, Thursday, Friday

    (E)  Monday, Wednesday, Thursday, Friday

7.  Which of the following is an acceptable work schedule for 3?

    (A)  Monday, Tuesday, Wednesday, Thursday

    (B)  Monday, Wednesday, Thursday, Friday

    (C)  Monday, Tuesday, Wednesday, Friday

    (D)  Monday, Tuesday, Thursday, Friday

    (E)  Tuesday, Wednesday, Thursday, Friday

8.  Which of the following is an acceptable schedule for Friday?

    (A)  C, D, E and 3, 4, 5

    (B)  A, C, D, E and 3, 4, 5

    (C)  D, E and 3, 4, 5

    (D)  B, D, E and 3, 4, 5

    (E)  C, D, E and 2, 3, 4

Questions 9-12 refer to the following set of statements.

The school superintendent of a large district established an advisory board consisting of school administrators from 3 elementary schools (E), 2 middle schools (M) and 3 high schools (H). Meetings could be held at one school at each level (E, M, or H). The elementary school administrators are E-1, E-2, and E-3; middle school administrators are M-1 and M-2; high school administrators are H-1, H-2, and H-3. Due to schedules, distance and travel arrangements, the following limitations exist with respect to meetings of this group.

> E-1 cannot attend any meetings at M
> H-1 cannot attend any meetings on Tuesday or Thursday
> M-3 cannot attend any meetings at E
> E-2 and M-2 can only attend the same meetings
> E-3 cannot attend any meetings at H
> M-2 cannot meet on Friday
> M-1, H-2, and H-3 can attend any time or place

9. Which of the following could attend a meeting on Friday at H?

   (A)  E-1, E-3, M-1, M-2, H-1

   (B)  E-1, E-2, M-2, H-1, H-2

   (C)  E-1, M-1, H-1, H-2, H-3

   (D)  M-2, M-3, E-1, H-2, H-3

   (E)  E-1, E-2, E-3, M-1, H-3

10. When and where could a meeting be scheduled that would be possible for everyone to attend?

    (A)  Monday at M

    (B)  Tuesday at M

    (C)  Wednesday at E

    (D)  Thursday at H

    (E)  It is impossible for everyone to attend

11. If all elementary school administrators must attend a particular meeting, when and where might that meeting be held?

   (A) Monday at M

   (B) Tuesday at H

   (C) Friday at E

   (D) Wednesday at E

   (E) It is not possible to schedule a meeting for all elementary school administrators

12. If a meeting is scheduled with the least conflicts, how many of the 8 members of the advisory board could attend?

   (A) 8             (D) 5

   (B) 7             (E) 4

   (C) 6

Questions 13-16 refer to the following information.

On a certain day, twenty fines were collected for traffic violations. Fifteen speeders were fined. Ten of those fined were also put in jail. Speeders were each fined $50 if they were jailed and $40 if they were not jailed. Non-speeders were fined $35.

13. What is the least number of speeders who could have been jailed?

   (A) 0             (D) 7

   (B) 3             (E) 10

   (C) 5

14. What is the largest number of speeders who could have been jailed?

   (A) 0             (D) 7

   (B) 3             (E) 10

   (C) 5

15. If the amount of money collected in fines was $845, how many speeders were jailed?

(A) 10                    (D) 7

(B) 9                     (E) 6

(C) 8

16. If all of those jailed were also speeders, how much was collected in fines?

(A) $875                  (D) $860

(B) $900                  (E) $890

(C) $850

17. It is possible for a nation to over-educate its population. The economic institutions depend on a labor force that is content to do menial labor and follow orders. If the level of education for the general population is raised to the point that insufficient numbers are willing to work as laborers and subordinates, the economic system will crumble.

Which of the following assumptions supports the position expressed in this statement?

(A) Technology makes the need for educated people more critical and the future will require more highly educated people.

(B) Just because some people prefer to let others assume leadership roles does not mean they must also be ignorant or under-educated in order to be content.

(C) Education is useful for satisfactory employment but it is even more critical for the productive use of leisure time, therefore a nation should not limit educational levels on the basis of employability only.

(D) Educated people are dissatisfied if they are not employed in work commensurate with their education.

(E) Educated people use their knowledge in all aspects of their lives, not just in their careers.

18. Major social change is never the result of human intervention. Mankind may try to alter society by passing laws, petitioning for change, or introducing new institutions. All of these intrusions will fail or succeed because the subtle and complex elements in the society that must support change have, or have not evolved to a state that will allow change to occur.

Which of the following statements most directly opposes the position stated above?

(A) Micro-changes in the social order can be successfully promulgated, and the sum of these micro-changes will bring about macro-changes over time.

(B) Major changes promoted by mankind are usually destructive and those changes that occur through the evolution of natural cycles are positive and lasting.

(C) Whatever mankind has created and/or can understand, mankind has the ability to change.

(D) Real changes that are good, stable and lasting are the result of the combined efforts of mankind and the fortuitous timeliness of the social context in which change occurs.

(E) Nature is random, unsystematic, illogical, and events that occur "naturally" must be brought under control by mankind or the consequences for society are chaotic and destructive.

19. A tourist who spent three days in Paris and returned to her midwestern social club was asked to describe her impressions of the French. She reported that they had little interest in their own political system, were mostly interested in pursuing personal pleasures, knew very little about the United States, and that we could not count on them as allies if we needed them.

Which of the following most nearly characterizes the fallacy of her remarks?

(A)  She has drawn an irrelevant conclusion in which information of one type is used to draw an inference unrelated to the nature of that information.

(B)  She has appealed to force — which is an appeal to accept her conclusions under threat of severe consequences — the loss of the French as allies.

(C)  She has tried to make her case by offering an opinion based on the popular belief that the French are unresponsive to people from other lands, especially those from the United States.

(D)  She has drawn conclusions on the basis of a brief visit and limited contact with a few people which is an over-generalization.

(E)  She has stated a "false cause" argument which occurs from inferring one event was caused by another, in this case the personal pleasure preference of the French would prevent them from being an ally of the United States.

20.  People are living longer and the number of people in the work force as a proportion of those retired is decreasing. In fact, over a period of about 5 decades from the 1950's to the year 2000, the number of people working for each person retired will shift from about 14 to 3.

Which of the following is the most defendable solution to the social need for the elderly to maintain a reasonable standard of living during retirement and maintain the principles of choice and freedom that typify the culture of the United States?

(A)  Provide incentives for people to have more children to change the ratio of workers to retirees to a more desirable proportion.

(B)  Employ more people in the 60-80 age range to enable them to supplement their retirement income.

(C)  Increase the social security payments made by workers to be able to increase Social Security payments to the retired population.

(D) Assist people to plan for retirement through better financial planning that will allow retirement with more options and dignity.

(E) Create government-subsidized housing for the elderly in exchange for a percent of the estate of the retirees.

21. Some propose that states should link the right to drive with school attendance for those people who are 18 years old or less. Those who graduate from high school before age 18 are exempt from this requirement. Proponents argue that the dropout rate from school will decrease if school dropouts are denied a license to drive automobiles. Among those who disagree with this view are teen-agers who become parents prior to age 18 and dropout of school to work and support their family. They argue that a car is necessary for them to travel to work and assume the responsibility of parenthood. They claim that their right to fair employment is jeopardized and the denial of their opportunity to meet their family obligations is a violation of their rights.

Those who favor denial of driver's licenses for dropouts are primarily concerned with:

(A) Punishing those who drop out of schools before graduation.

(B) Preventing teen-agers who drop out of school from taking jobs away from adults who would otherwise have a job.

(C) Reducing the tendency of some high school students to view motherhood or fatherhood as a status symbol.

(D) Reduction of teen-age reckless driving.

(E) Reducing the attractiveness of dropping out of school with encouragement to remain in school.

22. Those in the passage who oppose the denial of driver's licenses for dropouts are concerned with:

(A) The violation of the constitutional rights of school dropouts.

    (B)  The burden on society to support teen-age dropouts and their children.

    (C)  The opportunity for teen-age mothers and fathers to assume responsibility for their financial obligation to be self-supporting.

    (D)  Finding enough people in society who are willing to work at necessary but low-paying jobs.

    (E)  The rights of people to own property, including automobiles, if they have the means to do so.

23.  Some statements could be classified as conceptual, others are factual, and still others are expressions of opinions. Furthermore, some statements are expressions of principles and others are statements of laws (like the law of gravity or legal canons). In a discussion about the location of the capital of the United States John argued that Washington, D.C. would never be located where it is today because it is not centrally located and is vulnerable to attack. He said if it was located in a more central location and in a mountainous region it could be reached less easily and would be in a safer location.

John stated a rationale for the location of capitals and also drew a conclusion. The remarks by John could be classified as:

    (A)  Concepts and Facts      (D)  Concepts and Opinions

    (B)  Facts and Laws           (E)  Principles and Opinions

    (C)  Principles and Facts

24.  Mary said that the basis on which John recommended the location of capitals was too limited. She argued that safety and convenience were less important than the "image" or accessibility of a city. She stated that Chicago is neither centrally located nor "safe" but would be a better location than Springfield as a capital.

The remarks by Mary could be classified as:

    (A)  Concepts and Facts      (D)  Facts and Laws

(B)   Facts and Opinion         (E)   Principles and Facts

(C)   Concepts and Principles

25.   Bill asked a question about the difference between cities that are
      and capitals and those that are not. He asked what the real
      difference was. Ann answered by stating that capitals can be
      classified in a different category than other cities because they
      have certain attributes. She said they are cities where laws are
      made, where public budgets are established, where priorities for
      public action are determined, where elected officials represent
      their constituents in official session. Thus, the distinction be-
      tween capitals and non-capitals can be made because the func-
      tions that set them apart can be clearly identified.

      The answer given by Ann was primarily a response that provided
      Bill with a _____ .

      (A)   Conception of "capital."

      (B)   Set of facts about the location.

      (C)   Set of principles to determine the best location.

      (D)   Statement of social laws about capitals.

      (E)   Statement of opinion about the purpose.

## STOP

If time still remains, you may go back and check your work.
When the time allotted is up, you may go on to the next section.

# Section 6

> **TIME:** 30 Minutes
> 25 Questions
>
> **DIRECTIONS:** Eachquestion or group of questions is based on a passage or set of statements. Select the best answer choice.

Questions 1 – 5 refer to the following passage.

Two women, Debbie and Joy, and two men, Al and Jeff, are doctors. One is a dentist, one a surgeon, one an optometrist, and one a general practitioner. They are seated around a square table with one person on each side.

1) Al is across from the dentist.
2) Jeff is not across from the surgeon.
3) The optometrist is on Debbie's left.
4) Joy is the general practitioner.
5) The surgeon and general practitioner are married to each other.
6) The general practitioner is not on Joy's left.
7) The general practitioner is across from the optometrist.


1.    Which statement is repeated information?

   (A)  1                          (D)  7

   (B)  5                          (E)   none of these

   (C)  6


2.    Which of the following must be false?

   I.    Al is the dentist.

   II.   The surgeon and general practitioner are women.

   III.  The dentist is across from the surgeon.

(A)  I

(D)  I and II

(B)  II

(E)  II and III

(C)  III

3.   Which of the following must be true?

   I.   Two women sit next to each other.

   II.   Two men sit across from each other.

   (A)  I only

   (B)  II only

   (C)  both I and II

   (D)  either I or II, but not both

   (E)  neither I nor II

4.   Which of the following must be true?

   I.   Jeff is the optometrist.

   II.   The surgeon and general practitioner sit next to each other.

   (A)  I only

   (B)  II only

   (C)  both I and II

   (D)  either I or II, but not both

   (E)  neither I nor II

5.   Which of the following is true?

   (A)  Jeff is the general practitioner.

   (B)  Al is the surgeon.

   (C)  Joy is the dentist.

   (D)  Debbie is the optometrist.

   (E)  none of the above.

Questions 6-10 refer to the following passage.

Mr. Green is hiring five persons to do sheetrocking and foundation work on a building site. He must have a minimum of two sheetrockers. Nine persons have applied for the jobs: David, Fred, and Charles are sheetrockers, while Glenn, Stan, Dennis, Ralph, Brent, and Lawrence are foundation workers.

1)  Mr. Green is unwilling to hire Ralph and Brent to work together because they argue all the time.
2)  Stan and Dennis are buddies and will only work together.
3)  Charles won't work with Glenn because of their failure in a limited partnership effort.

6.  If David, Fred, and Charles are hired, the team of foundation workers can consist of

    (A)  Only Stan and Dennis

    (B)  Stan and Dennis or Ralph and Brent

    (C)  Ralph and Lawrence or Brent and Lawrence

    (D)  Stan and Dennis, or Ralph and Lawrence, or Brent and Lawrence

7.  Mr. Green has the greatest number of choices for hiring as foundation workers if the sheetrockers he chooses are

    (A)  David, Fred, and Charles

    (B)  David and Fred

    (C)  David and Charles

    (D)  Fred and Charles

8.  If Glenn is hired, the other persons hired must be

    (A)  David, Fred, Stan and Charles

    (B)  David, Fred, Charles, and either Ralph, Brent, or Lawrence

    (C)  David and Fred, together with either Stan and Dennis or Ralph and Lawrence

(D) David and Fred, together with either Stan and Dennis, Ralph and Lawrence, or Brent and Lawrence

9. If David is hired and Fred is not, which of the following statements must be true?

   I. Stan and Dennis are hired

   II. Either Ralph or Brent is hired, but not both

   (A) I only           (C) both I and II

   (B) II only          (D) neither I nor II

10. Mr. Green can put together the rest of his crew in the greatest number of ways if he hires

   (A) Stan and Dennis      (C) Ralph

   (B) Charles            (D) Brent

Questions 11-16 refer to the following statements.

A, B, and C are 3 chemical elements.

If A reacts with A, the result if B.
If A reacts with C, the result if A.
If B reacts with any element, the result is always B.
If C reacts with C, the result is C.
The order of the reaction makes no difference.

11. Which of the following must be true?

   I. If A reacts with any other element, the result is never A.

   II. If C reacts with any element, the result is that element.

   III. If B reacts with B, the result is A.

   (A) I           (D) I and II

   (B) II          (E) II and III

   (C) III

543

12. If the result is B, then

    I.    B had to be in the reaction.

    II.   C had to be in the reaction.

    (A)  I                              (D)  both I and II

    (B)  II                             (E)  neither I nor II

    (C)  either I or II, but not both

13. If the result of A and C reacts with the result of B and C, then the result is

    (A)  A                              (D)  A or C

    (B)  B                              (E)  cannot be determined

    (C)  C

14. Which of the following must be false?

    I.    Whenever an element reacts with itself, the result is the original element.

    II.   If the result is C, then C had to be in the reaction.

    (A)  I                              (D)  both I and II

    (B)  II                             (E)  neither I nor II

    (C)  either I or II, but not both

15. If the result is A, then

    I.    A had to be in the reaction

    II.   B could not be in the reaction

    III.  C had to be in the reaction

    (A)  I                              (D)  II and III

    (B)  I and II                       (E)  I, II, and III

    (C)  I and III

16. If the result of A and A reacts with the result of C and C, then the result is

   (A)  A            (D)  A or B
   
   (B)  B            (E)  cannot be determined
   
   (C)  C

Questions 17-18 refer to the following statement.

"The sum of behavior is to retain a man's dignity without intruding upon the liberty of others," stated Sir Francis Bacon. If this is the case, then not intruding upon another's liberty is impossible.

17. The conclusion strongly implied by the author's argument is that

   (A)  retaining one's dignity is impossible without intruding upon another's liberty

   (B)  retaining dignity never involves robbing others of liberty

   (C)  dignity and liberty are mutually exclusive

   (D)  there is always the possibility of a "dignified intrusion"

   (E)  B.F. Skinner's *Beyond Freedom and Dignity* takes its cue from Bacon

18. The author's argument would be weakened if it was pointed out that

   I.   Bacon's argument has been misinterpreted out of context

   II.  neither liberty nor dignity can be discussed in absolute terms

   III. retaining dignity always involves a reduction of liberty

   (A)  I, II, and III        (D)  II and III only

   (B)  III only             (E)  I and II only

   (C)  I only

19. The current trend toward specialization is the opposite of what is needed. Diverse, complex, and interrelated are all terms that describe today's world problems. Only a generalist who sees the broad picture can begin to understand these problems. Unless a broad, liberal education is provided in our schools, the world will crumble as we each work in our own narrow vocations and professions.

Each of the following, if true, would weaken the conclusion drawn above, except:

(A) Many of the world's problems can be solved only by highly specialized experts working in their area of expertise.

(B) A few generalists can coordinate the work of many specialists.

(C) Specialization does not entail losing sight of the broad picture.

(D) Increasingly complex problems require a growing level of expertise and this requires specialization.

(E) Liberal education is today more highly specialized.

Questions 20-22 refer to the following passage.

David would be much better off if he would put aside his fripperies and shoulder his responsibilities. He is the heir to one of the biggest mining concerns in the country, yet he wastes his time and energy on such things as auto racing, support for the arts, and saving whales — saving them for what, I don't know. No one can be a captain of industry unless he pursues his goal with single-minded devotion. If David wants to become a titan, as his father and grandfather were, he must apply his talents to important things.

20. The argument would be weakened by pointing out that:

(A) 92% of all heirs to great fortunes dissipate them.

(B) A shareholder group is planning to challenge David's control of his largest mining company.

(C) The inflation rate is falling.

(D) Under David's control, the mining empire built by his ancestors has retained its value.

(E) Other captains of industry were people of diverse interests.

21. Based on what you know of the author from this statement, which of the following would he be likely to disapprove?

   I. David taking an economics course.

   II. Organizations dedicated to encouraging the dramatic arts.

   III. Heirs of great fortunes becoming mountaineers.

   IV. Balloon races.

   (A) I and II        (D) III only

   (B) II only        (E) II, III and IV

   (C) II and III

22. The argument does not assume which of the following?

   I. Versatility is necessary to a captain of industry.

   II. Industry needs single-minded people to lead it.

   III. David is not particularly talented in the areas of conservation, sports, and the arts.

   (A) I only        (D) II and III

   (B) II only        (E) I, II and III

   (C) I and III

Question 23 refer to the following passage.

Women are equals to men in every activity, including tennis. It's true that Bobby Riggs beat Margaret Court, but he played like a woman and she played like a man.

23. The main problem with this argument is

   (A) it is biased toward feminists

    (B)   it assumes that Margaret Court is the best woman tennis player

    (C)   it confuses people with playing styles

    (D)   it assumes that all women ought to play the same way

    (E)   it assumes that women are equal to men, and thus constitutes circular reasoning

Questions 24 – 25 refer to the following statements.

"The department store owned by my competitor sells green necklaces that glow in the dark. Customers of mine wearing those necklaces must be giving business to the competition."

24.   This statement could best be strengthened by

    (A)   deleting **that glow in the dark**

    (B)   changing **sells** to **has sold**

    (C)   changing **the competition** to **my competitor**

    (D)   inserting **only** as the first word in sentence one

    (E)   changing **wearing** to **owning**

25.   The author foolishly assumes that

    (A)   the customers might find the necklaces attractive

    (B)   customers are not buying other products from the competition

    (C)   customers will wear the necklaces in daylight

    (D)   a department store should not sell necklaces

    (E)   the competition is outselling the author

### STOP

If time still remains, you may go back and check your work.

# TEST 4

## ANSWER KEY

### Section 1 — Verbal Ability

| | | | | | | | |
|---|---|---|---|---|---|---|---|
| 1. | (D) | 11. | (B) | 21. | (A) | 31. | (B) |
| 2. | (D) | 12. | (A) | 22. | (D) | 32. | (D) |
| 3. | (C) | 13. | (D) | 23. | (C) | 33. | (E) |
| 4. | (D) | 14. | (B) | 24. | (D) | 34. | (E) |
| 5. | (C) | 15. | (A) | 25. | (D) | 35. | (B) |
| 6. | (E) | 16. | (E) | 26. | (A) | 36. | (C) |
| 7. | (D) | 17. | (A) | 27. | (D) | 37. | (D) |
| 8. | (E) | 18. | (B) | 28. | (E) | 38. | (D) |
| 9. | (E) | 19. | (C) | 29. | (A) | | |
| 10. | (D) | 20. | (A) | 30. | (E) | | |

### Section 2 — Verbal Ability

| | | | | | | | |
|---|---|---|---|---|---|---|---|
| 1. | (A) | 11. | (C) | 21. | (D) | 31. | (E) |
| 2. | (C) | 12. | (B) | 22. | (C) | 32. | (C) |
| 3. | (D) | 13. | (B) | 23. | (E) | 33. | (A) |
| 4. | (B) | 14. | (D) | 24. | (C) | 34. | (B) |
| 5. | (E) | 15. | (B) | 25. | (A) | 35. | (D) |
| 6. | (D) | 16. | (E) | 26. | (A) | 36. | (A) |
| 7. | (B) | 17. | (E) | 27. | (E) | 37. | (E) |
| 8. | (E) | 18. | (B) | 28. | (B) | 38. | (B) |
| 9. | (A) | 19. | (A) | 29. | (C) | | |
| 10. | (A) | 20. | (A) | 30. | (E) | | |

### Section 3 — Quantitative Ability

| | | | | | | | |
|---|---|---|---|---|---|---|---|
| 1. | (A) | 3. | (B) | 5. | (B) | 7. | (A) |
| 2. | (B) | 4. | (C) | 6. | (A) | 8. | (B) |

| 9. | (C) | 15. | (D) | 21. | (B) | 27. | (D) |
|----|-----|-----|-----|-----|-----|-----|-----|
| 10. | (D) | 16. | (A) | 22. | (B) | 28. | (E) |
| 11. | (C) | 17. | (C) | 23. | (C) | 29. | (D) |
| 12. | (B) | 18. | (A) | 24. | (A) | 30. | (A) |
| 13. | (C) | 19. | (D) | 25. | (B) | | |
| 14. | (B) | 20. | (D) | 26. | (B) | | |

## Section 4 — Quantitative Ability

| 1. | (C) | 9. | (A) | 17. | (C) | 25. | (B) |
|----|-----|----|-----|-----|-----|-----|-----|
| 2. | (A) | 10. | (C) | 18. | (A) | 26. | (D) |
| 3. | (D) | 11. | (A) | 19. | (D) | 27. | (B) |
| 4. | (B) | 12. | (D) | 20. | (B) | 28. | (E) |
| 5. | (A) | 13. | (C) | 21. | (A) | 29. | (A) |
| 6. | (C) | 14. | (B) | 22. | (D) | 30. | (C) |
| 7. | (D) | 15. | (B) | 23. | (C) | | |
| 8. | (B) | 16. | (E) | 24. | (E) | | |

## Section 5 — Analytical Ability

| 1. | (A) | 8. | (A) | 15. | (D) | 22. | (C) |
|----|-----|----|-----|-----|-----|-----|-----|
| 2. | (A) | 9. | (C) | 16. | (A) | 23. | (E) |
| 3. | (E) | 10. | (E) | 17. | (D) | 24. | (B) |
| 4. | (C) | 11. | (D) | 18. | (C) | 25. | (A) |
| 5. | (D) | 12. | (D) | 19. | (D) | | |
| 6. | (B) | 13. | (C) | 20. | (D) | | |
| 7. | (E) | 14. | (E) | 21. | (E) | | |

## Section 6 — Analytical Ability

| 1. | (C) | 8. | (D) | 15. | (E) | 22. | (E) |
|----|-----|----|-----|-----|-----|-----|-----|
| 2. | (D) | 9. | (A) | 16. | (B) | 23. | (C) |
| 3. | (A) | 10. | (A) | 17. | (A) | 24. | (D) |
| 4. | (C) | 11. | (B) | 18. | (E) | 25. | (B) |
| 5. | (B) | 12. | (E) | 19. | (E) | | |
| 6. | (D) | 13. | (B) | 20. | (E) | | |
| 7. | (B) | 14. | (A) | 21. | (D) | | |

# DETAILED EXPLANATIONS
# OF ANSWERS

## Section 1—Verbal Ability

1. (D)
EMPHASIZE and CONCEAL are antonyms, with EMPHASIZE meaning to stress and CONCEAL meaning to remove from view. DISAVOW and NEGATE are synonyms meaning to deny. CAMOUFLAGE means to disguise, which is the best choice, since his stoutness is being somewhat disguised or covered over by his erect bearing and quickness of movement.

2. (D)
CONDITION is a prerequisite which must be satisfied. PHENOMENON refers to appearances. EVOLUTION is the slow change from one state to another. CHARACTER is an accumulation of qualities which distinguish an individual at any one time. DISPOSITION is the correct choice because it is the predominating habit of one's mind developed over time. The word "ages" implies recurring action over a period of time.

3. (C)
SEJUNCTIONED, SEGREGATED, RESCINDED and SCISSIONED are all synonyms referring to separation. ASCRIBED is the correct choice because it gives to someone something which is not apparent, but inferred from action. All emotions are inferred from behavior.

4. (D)
MORAL refers to knowledge of right and wrong while PIOUS suggests deeds only. RELIGIOUS includes both thought and deed. The statement could be paraphrased as "A man may know right and wrong without his behavior reflecting this knowledge, but he cannot have the thought and do the deeds without knowing right and wrong."

"Therefore, the correct choice is PIOUS-RELIGIOUS.

5.　(C)

IRRESOLUTE, CAPRICIOUS and VACILLATING are synonyms referring to inconsistency. RECIDIVIST is not relevant. AUTHORITARIAN and DOCTRINAIRE are the correct choice because they suggest the concentration of power which results in the making and enforcing of these rules. DOGMATIC is a belief which follows and is the result of the making and enforcing of rules.

6.　(E)

DISPARITY and TRANSCENDENCY refer to quantity. MISOGAMY implies celibacy. CONCORD suggests agreement. VARIANCE is that state which precedes action. "To remain" implies the speaker is at a stationary point with a possibility to turn back.

7.　(D)

ACCLIMATED has no relevance to the passage. ACCOMMODATE and RECONCILE are synonyms referring to bringing into agreement. DETERRED suggests turning aside due to fear. "Eagerly" contradicts this. "Although" is the key word implying the following phrase will be the opposite of the preceding clause. Therefore, DISSUADED, referring to advice given, is the correct choice.

8.　(E)

BENEVOLENCE refers to the "will" to do good; while PHILANTHROPY indicates the act of giving, specifically money, on a large scale, thereby creating a cause and effect relationship. INTOLERANCE, not TOLERANCE, would have created the cause/effect relationship with BIGOTRY. LENITY and VIRULENCE are near antonyms in definition, with lenity referring to indulgence while virulence describes extreme bitterness. SPORADIC means to occur occasionally, while HAUNT suggests reappearing continually. AMIABILITY and COMPLAISANT both refer to being generally agreeable. PENURIOUS suggests extreme frugality resulting in HOARDING, a cause and effect relationship.

9. (E)
    DESIRE is defined as a longing or craving which is a more intense form of WANT, just as AVIDITY is defined as a consuming greed. Therefore, DESIRE and AVIDITY denote a maximum degree of WANT and GREED. PENCHANT and PARTIALITY are nearly synonymous, both meaning to incline to an attachment to something. PROPENSITY is an antonym of SUPINENESS, with propensity referring to an irresistible attachment to a thing; while supineness suggests the opposite, "apathetic passivity." A whole/part relationship is suggested in DISDAIN and INATTENTION. Disdain suggests looking upon something with scorn. Inattention implies a lack of concentration. ASPIRE and SEEK are synonymous, both implying the searching for and laboring to attain.

10. (D)
    ABYSS is the lowest point as contrasted with APEX which is the highest point. BOTTOM is the lowest point as contrasted with PINNACLE which is the highest point. EAST and WEST are antonyms relating to direction. HORIZONTAL and PARALLEL are antonyms. Horizontal is defined as operating in a plane parallel to the base line while parallel indicates "extending in the same direction" but not necessarily in the base line. ACROSS and BESIDE is a whole/part relationship with across encompassing beside. OVER and UNDER are antonyms with over designated as a situation in a position higher than another; while under is described as a position lower or below something.

11. (B)
    FRIENDLY and AFFABLE are synonymous as AMICABLE and CONGENIAL are synonymous. FUN and SMILE are cause and effect. Fun provides amusement or enjoyment producing the smile. HILARIOUS and DELIGHT are cause and effect, with hilarious being an exhilaration of the spirit which is expressed in emotion called delight. SPEAK and CONVERSATION are a part-whole relationship. Speak means to utter, as conversation is an oral exchange. TACITURN and OUTSPOKEN are antonyms, taciturn meaning to incline not to talk, while outspoken means to be inclined to speak.

12.  (A)
TIMIDITY is encompassed in COWARDICE even as GALLANTRY is encompassed in COURAGE. Both are an act of the will, resulting in action. POLTROONERY and FORTITUDE are antonyms, with poltroonery referring to cowardice and fortitude suggesting strength of mind to bear pain with courage. PUSILLANIMITY and CHIVALRY are antonyms. Pusillanimity refers to cowardice and chivalry to martial valor, marked with honor. ANXIETY and SOLICITUDE are synonyms referring to a state of mind resulting in uneasiness. AGITATION and PERTURBATION are synonymous, again referring to a troubled mind.

13.  (D)
PRIDE and HAUGHTINESS are synonyms referring to an attitude of superiority as is VAINGLORY and POMPOSITY. ARROGANCE and SUBMISSION are antonyms with arrogance meaning a feeling of superiority and submission referring to a feeling of humility. ABASEMENT and CRESTLESS are antonyms of action versus inaction. Crestless refers to one of low birth and abasement suggests the lowering of another in rank or esteem. AFFABILITY and SUPERCILIOUS are antonyms of exhibited action. Affability infers graciousness while supercilious implies crudeness. DIPLOMATIC and INCONSONANT are also antonyms. Diplomatic indicates a good natured disposition while inconsonant suggests an unsympathetic, unfeeling personality.

14.  (B)
EQUATOR and MISSISSIPPI RIVER is a contrast between the real and imaginary. Mississippi River is a geographical feature that is REAL as the equator is a geographical feature that is IMAGINARY. SKIES and ROADS both belong to the category of visible and discrete. TELEVISION and TELEPHONE fit in the description of skies and roads. VITAMINS and FOOD are a part to whole relationship as vitamins are a part of food. OXYGEN and BREATH are a part to whole relationship with oxygen being a part of breath.

15.  (A)
WANTED and NEED are synonyms, both meaning to "require,

failure to possess." INDIGENCE and EXIGENCY are synonyms which also mean "a reduced circumstance, requiring much." DESIRE and LUST have a part to whole relationship as lust encompasses desire and exacts satisfaction. DEPRIVE and CRAVE are antonyms; deprive suggests withholding something and crave implying a great longing for something. THIRST and HUNGER are a part to whole relationship; both are a part of the body's basic needs. COVET and NECESSARY are antonyms.

16. (E)
   INFER and DEDUCE are synonymous like ALLUDE and HINT. SHY and CONSPICUOUS are antonyms of actions. Shy suggests being easily frightened, disposed to avoid a person or thing. Conspicuous denotes the desire to attract attention. OBSTREPEROUS and BOISTEROUS are synonyms implying loud action. INTELLIGENT and SAGACIOUS are synonyms implying the ability to know. SELF-CONSCIOUS and ASSERTIVE are antonyms.

17. (A)
   Choices (B) and (E) are stated within the passage. But the passage states in sentence one that the patient has serious forgetfulness —particularly of recent events—implying that events from childhood may or may not be remembered.

18. (B)
   Sentence 6 states "Judgment, concentration, orientation, writing, reading, speech, motor behavior, and naming of objects may also be affected."

19. (C)
   Sentence 5 states "As the disease progresses, memory loss and such changes in personality, mood, and behavior as confusion, irritability, restlessness, and agitation are likely to appear."

20. (A)
   Choice (B) is stated; (C), (D) and (E) are not mentioned. In the passage, the use of the phrase "long-term care institution" indicates that the Alzheimer sufferer's life is not necessarily shortened due to the disease.

21.  (A)
Paragraph three states "the submarine's greatest advantage was being able to operate beneath the ocean surface where detection was difficult."

22.  (D)
This information is stated in sentence four.

23.  (C)
Paragraph four says a hydrophone was "used to detect screw noises and sounds."

24.  (D)
The last paragraph describes the modification which streamlined the submarine. All other choices are either stated or not mentioned.

25.  (D)
The last sentence states "...increased greatly with improved electronic equipment."

26.  (A)
Since Bushnell was the inventor, he was indirectly responsible for the sinking of the first ship.

27.  (D)
SONAR is the acronym of sound, navigation and ranging.

28.  (E)
REFECTION is the antonym of FATIGUE. The root of fatigue means "hunger" while refection refers to the nourishment of the body. Exhaustion and prostration are degrees of fatigue.

29.  (A)
ABSOLUTE is the antonym of NONEXISTENCE. Absolute

denotes the essence of existence which is the opposite of "does not exist." Nullity and void are synonymous, referring to "having no value" while existing. Abeyance denotes temporary inactivity. Amorphism suggests without form but does not deny the existence.

30. (E)

ANTITHESIS and REFUTATIVE refer to ideas. ADAPTING suggests modification "to make fit" while FOIL implies to prevent from attaining. Only COALESCENCE means to unite into a whole as compared to CONTRAST which means to compare similar objects to set off their dissimilar qualities.

31. (B)

ADJUNCT and ACCESSORY refer to an addition but carry the added meaning of the addition being nonessential. CURTAIL implies to make less of while ADHERENT refers to being connected by contract. Only SEVERANCE (to remove or cut off) is the opposite of APPENDAGE, which is an attachment to something larger and more important.

32. (D)

PERMEATE and PENETRATE are synonymous, referring to diffusing or spreading out. CURRENCY refers to general usage while ADVANTAGE implies superiority of position. PREVALENCE is defined as dominant, with its opposite SUBORDINATE denoting lower in class or rank.

33. (E)

MISCEGENATION implies a mixture of races. HYBRID is heterogeneous in origin. JUNCTION refers to the point in time of the joining. ADULTERANT is the result of adding impurities. Only HOMOGENEOUS, meaning of the same kind, is the antonym of INTERMIXTURE (mixture versus purity or sameness).

34. (E)

ANALYSIS and CATALYSIS are synonyms of RESOLUTION. OBDURATE and DISLOYAL indicate an act of the will. Only

SYNTHESIS, meaning to put together, is an antonym of RESOLU-TION which means to dissolve.

35. (B)

GRADATION is a synonym of HARMONY as both refer to an ordered scale, regularity. COLLATERAL implies position, EUPHONY suggests music and SUBORDINATE implies rank. Only ANOMALY is the opposite of HARMONY (regularity versus irregularity).

36. (C)

All choices are synonymous to PRECEDENCE except CONSE-QUENCE, which means to follow rather than be first.

37. (D)

DIFFUSION is a synonym of DISPERSION, both meaning "to scatter." EDIT is to shorten, EDUCE is to draw out, while RADIA-TION infers diffusion. Only COMPILATION, bringing together, is an antonym of DISPERSION, to scatter.

38. (D)

All choices are synonyms of GENERIC, with SPECIFIC being the antonym, meaning "belonging to one class as distinguished from all others," as opposed to the meaning of generic: "symbolic of whole or majority." It is distinctiveness versus conformity.

## Section 2–Verbal Ability

1. (A)

A "storm of INDIGNATION" arises when CORRUPTION is known. (B) is incorrect because people do not PROTEST COOPERA-TION. Choices (C) and (D) do not fit the context of the sentence, and (E) is contradictory, "a storm of INDIFFERENCE."

2. (C)

Writers who want to emphasize certain ideas often use repetition

of key words or phrases for this effect. In this case the key word is PERILS, mentioned in the first clause. The correct answer is (C), because the key word, PERILS, is repeated. While each of the alternatives does make sense, none fits the sentence as does (C).

3.    (D)
The key to this problem lies in noticing the negative which appears early in the sentence: "...not...(but)..." is the usual and logical pattern of usage. Here, "...not personal qualities but public services..." is the accurate statement. None of the other terms which appears first in the alternative pairs permits the meaning to stay intact by offering a contrast. Since it is the public services which undergird our lives rather than personal qualities, per se, which enable independence, the feeling of personal independence and self-sufficiency is really more illusion than fact.

4.    (B)
The LATTER refers to the frame. The FRAME is REMOVED without disturbing the OTHER frames. (A) is incorrect because it is not the BEE which is HANDLED without disturbing the "other bees." (C) is incorrect because it is not the HIVE which is TAKEN without disturbing the "other hives"; (D) is wrong because it is not the VESSEL which is DESTROYED without disturbing the "other vessels."

5.    (E)
School boards must plan for the future, and to do so, need to obtain accurate information about the number and kinds of students who will be attending their school(s). All of the terms presented first in the pairs includes the idea of identifying a future state of affairs (ANTICIPATE, PREDICT, FORETELL, PROJECT, and FORECAST). Only one of the second terms given continues this. Thus, the answer is (E) due to the word SUCCEEDING.

6.    (D)
The key to this problem is to identify, among the first terms given, that term most closely associated with corruptibility, which is (D) POWER. This term may include WEALTH, FAME, PRESTIGE, and

STATUS. But more important, POWER means the AUTHORITY to do or to act. None of the other terms includes this idea of authority to do or to act. A person who has authority or power to act will find out if he is corruptible only when the opportunity to use his power in dishonest ways is present, and he declines to do so. One can DESIRE to be corruptible, be TEMPTED to be corruptible, have a PURPOSE or a need to be corruptible, but these are to no avail.

7. **(B)**
(B) is the correct alternative. An enthusiastic audience, by virtue of the clapping or other noise they produce could make even a vigorous rapping for order a futile attempt on the part of the chairman. (A) is wrong because boredom or weariness on the part of an audience would not make it impossible to get their attention. A bored and weary audience is not a loud, noisy group. (C) is incorrect because the phrase "he soon gave up the attempt" implies that the chairman was unsuccessful in getting the attention of the audience. In (C) the audience is "interested." His quick rapping would be successful. (D) is wrong because a chairman cannot be timid when calling for order. (E) is also incorrect because a chairman would not rap lightly when calling for order.

8. **(E)**
The first term in the analogy given identifies a characteristic which is <u>not</u> possessed by the kind of person identified by the second term. A SOCIOPATH is a person who is antisocial, a person who is <u>not</u> characterized by SOCIABILITY. Likewise, in alternative (E), a NEUROTIC person suffers many anxieties and is not characterized by CALMNESS. Alternatives (B) and (D) are wrong because the first term gives a characteristic related to the second. A PSYCHIC has great SENSITIVITY, and PSYCHOSIS is identified by the presence of ILLUSIONS. Alternative (C) SPACE:CLAUSTROPHOBIA is wrong because the first term identifies the entity.

9. **(A)**
The key relationship here is multiplicity. Many grains of SAND may form a DUNE. The answer is (A) because many TREES may form a FOREST. (B) is wrong because many ROCKS do not form a boulder and (E) is wrong because many TWIGS do not form a LOG. CLAMOR and TUMULT, (D), are interchangeable terms and

SHOWER:DELUGE, (C), present a relationship of intensity. A light rain or shower, when intensified, becomes a deluge.

10.  (A)
   The analogy here is that of simple to complex. In math, a VARIABLE is less complex than an EQUATION. The correct answer is (A), OXYGEN:WATER. OXYGEN is a simpler element than WATER, which contains both hydrogen and oxygen. PARAMECIA and AMOEBA (B) are both simple one-celled life forms. In alternative (C), ANALYSIS:SUMMARY, the first term identifies a more complex process than the second term. Here the relationship is complex to simple. Alternative (D) CLAY:SCULPTURE presents an analogy of use: CLAY is used to SCULPTURE. Alternative (E) FURNACE:HEAT is an analogy of function; a FURNACE produces HEAT.

11.  (C)
   A QUILL is a precursor of a FOUNTAIN PEN. In the correct alternative, (C), a TRUCE is a precursor of PEACE. The relationship in (A), RURAL:URBAN is one of opposites and in (B) YOUNG:OLD is one of progression. A young person, in time, progresses in age and becomes old. A quill does not progress in time to become a fountain pen. The relationship in (D) SOLO:QUARTET is a numerical one, specifically a one-to-four relationship. In alternative (E), both a MANGLE and an IRON serve the same purpose, but a mangle is specifically designed to iron certain kinds of items.

12.  (B)
   An ARC is one part, component, or segment of the CIRCUMFERENCE. The correct answer is (B), an HOUR is one part of or segment of a DAY. MOON:EARTH (A) are a satellite and planet. Their relationship is, as in alternative (C), one of size. CABINS are small and MANSIONS are large, but both are places to live; again, both are examples of the same entity — homes. (D), EXERCISE and REST are both components of a healthy lifestyle, rather than one being a component of the other. The relationship in alternative (E) is one of like terms.

13. (B)

EXPURGATE (Latin, *ex* -out; *purgate* -to cleanse) means "to remove passages considered obscene, etc., from a book or writing." The English word "purge" also is related to "expurgate." CENSOR (Latin, *censere* -to judge) is to examine literature, mail, etc., and remove or prohibit anything considered obscene or objectionable. These are synonymous terms. The terms in alternative (B) are also synonymous. The word ARCANE (Latin, *arcanus* -hidden) is an adjective which means secret. Alternatives (A), (C), and (D) present pairs of words which are intended to be perceived as similar, although no relationship exists other than sound. (A) EXPUNGE means "to erase", not WASH; (C) FRENETIC means "frantic", not FRENCH; (D) PHRENETIC is another spelling for FRENETIC, and still means "frantic."

14. (D)

This is an analogy of purpose. The purpose served by PHYLUM is that of CLASSIFICATION. The correct answer, (D), contains the same relationship. The purpose of a MEDAL is to HONOR the recipient. Alternative (A) CAT:FELINE presents an animal and its class; alternative (B) COMMITMENT:VOW presents synonyms; alternative (C) LIE:DECEIT presents an example of the second term through the first term. Alternative (E) CONTROL:HARNESS is a relationship of function — the function of a harness is to control.

15. (B)

This is an analogy of function. The metal RIBS of an UMBRELLA give its shape. The corresponding analogy is (B). The STUDS of a WALL form a frame which gives the wall its shape. Incorrect alternatives are (A), LEGS hold a TABLE up but do give the table its shape; (C), a SHELF is placed within a CLOSET; and (D) and (E), in which instances the HINGE and KNOB are extraneous to the DOOR and DRAWER, respectively.

16. (E)

This is an analogy of purpose. One DECODES in order to UNDERSTAND. The correct answer is (E), one SOWS in order to REAP, or harvest. Alternative (A) is an analogy of likeness. To DETONATE is

synonymous with EXPLODE. Alternative (B) is an analogy of whole-to-part. STUDY may include a RESEARCH component. Alternative (C) is wrong because the analogy here is that of opposition. To DESTROY is the opposite of to BUILD. Alternative (D) is wrong because the second term does not identify the purpose of the first term.

17. (E)

The author discusses the French heritage in America through the entire article. (A) is incorrect. Even though the British forced the French out of Nova Scotia, they were allowed to settle in the American colonies; (B) and (C) are incorrect as the author mentions these two different groups of Frenchmen. (D) is incorrect as the odyssey spoken of by the author was Longfellow's *Evangeline*.

18. (B)

The Acadians were run out of Nova Scotia. The author also discusses "Other persecuted Huguenots." (A) is incorrect, as the Acadians were French. (C) and (E) are incorrect. The Acadians were stable and dispersed themselves in the society of the American colonies and settled in Louisiana. (D) is incorrect because nothing can be inferred about happiness.

19. (A)

(A) is the correct answer as the author's views are favorable or auspicious toward America's French heritage. (B) unfortunate, would be a negative reaction and an incorrect response. (C) inevitable, may be inferred by the reader since the French were relocated and settled in the colonies, but cannot be inferred from the author's viewpoint as expressed. (D) unlikely, cannot be inferred from the selection; and (E) foreboding, is incorrect because it refers to negative things.

20. (A)

The social and political freedoms made the colony attractive to different religious beliefs. The encouragement of individual endeavors, as well as good land, made for prosperity. (B) is incorrect since nothing could be inferred about the attitude of the older Penn. (C) is incorrect. There were other proprietary colonies that were not nearly

as successful. (D) is incorrect. Even though the colonists allowed the Indians to babysit, they still cared for their children. (E) is incorrect. Rapid growth does not have much to do with success.

21.  (D)

In the final paragraph the author states that the Holy Experiment encouraged individuals' morality and freedom of conscience. Even though English-Colonial collaboration (A), a bicameral legislation (B), and a treaty with the Indians (C) were important factors in the development of the Pennsylvania colony, they were considered as part of the "Holy Experiment." (E) is incorrect because other proprietary colonies were not founded on the same premise.

22.  (C)

The colony was open to all religions and nationalities. All other answers are characteristics of the Pennsylvania colony.

23.  (E)

In paragraph four the author states that "...unlike the other colonies, it was not troubled by the Indians. Penn had bought their lands and made a series of peace treaties that were scrupulously fair and rigidly adhered to." The author did not make comparisons that are referred to in answers (A), (B), (C), and (D).

24.  (C)

Religious toleration, bicameral legislature, and forward-looking penal code all added to a progressive (i.e., republic) form of government. (A) is incorrect. In terms of today Penn would be considered a politician; in his terms he was a humanitarian. (B) is incorrect because although there were treaties with the Indians, this was only one of several factors which contributed to the government's being a progressive one. (D) is incorrect because there were no restrictions on immigration. In relation to alternative (E), the "Great Law" and the "First and Second Frames of Government" were never overturned.

25.  (A)

Even though the author never calls Pennsylvania a melting pot,

because of the guarantee of freedoms several nationalities as well as several religious sects settled in the colony, making it a "melting-pot" society.

26. (A)
(B) Jews; (C) Baptists; (D) Mennonites; and (E) Quakers were all mentioned as members in the settlement.

27. (E)
(E) is the correct answer. He uses facts to show growth. The colony was awarded in 1681 and by the summer of 1683 there were 3000 settlers. (A) is incorrect, syllogism is the presentation of a major and a minor premise, and a conclusion drawn from the two premises. (B) is incorrect. An analogy is the "inference that certain resemblances imply further similarity." (C) is an incorrect answer. A literary allusion is to compare a point with some concept or period in literature. (D) is incorrect. The author made no attempt to quote other authors.

28. (B)
CAPRICIOUS is an adjective meaning erratic, subject to sudden impulsive changes. Its opposite is (B) STEADFAST, meaning fixed, or constant. The alternatives all identify personal qualities unrelated to the term CAPRICIOUS or the term STEADFAST. (A) STUFFY means dull. (C) SCURRILOUS means abusive or offensive. (D) SAGACIOUS means shrewd or astute, and (E) SYBARITIC means sensualistic or hedonistic (given to pleasure).

29. (C)
To CORROBORATE is to confirm or to support. The Latin stem *robur*, strength, is found in the word. The opposite of confirm or strengthen is (C) CONTRADICT, literally, to speak against something, to be contrary to something. The other alternatives move away from the idea of contradict. Specifically, (A) ABROGATE is to abolish or annul; (B) DISCLAIM is give up any claim. (D) DIS-PROVE is to prove something false; and (E) DOUBT is to tend to disbelieve.

**30. (E)**

To REPUDIATE (Latin, *repudium* -separation) is to separate oneself from something, specifically, to disown or to disavow. One might disown a relative, or disavow an idea. Its opposite is (E), ADOPT, which is to take as one's own, as to take a child into one's family or to choose or accept an idea. Incorrect alternatives include (A), ADORE (to love greatly); and (B) AGREE (to be in accord with) which is close to adopt but does not include the idea of taking on as one's own. (C) ADVOCATE (to speak or write in favor of something), and (D) ADMIRE (to esteem highly) are wrong because one can advocate or admire an idea without choosing to take it on as one's own.

**31. (E)**

A UNIFORM thing does not vary from others, in form, rate, or degree. It is like all others of the same class. Its opposite is (E) VARIOUS, which means differing one from another; of several kinds. ASYMMETRICAL, (A), is wrong because it refers to balance, specifically, lack of balance in size, shape, or position; CONFUSION, (B), is wrong because it refers to a state of disorder; CHAOS, (C), also refers to a state of disorder. DISASSEMBLED, (D), is wrong because it means separated into component parts.

**32. (C)**

An ADDICT (Latin, *addicere* -to give assent) is a giving up of oneself to a strong habit. Its opposite is (C), WEAN, to withdraw (a person) as from a habit. These are transitive verbs or verbs which take an object. One is addicted to something and weaned from something. The other alternatives, to stop, (A), to take away, (B), and to change in attitude to indifference, (E), lack the idea of the subject's withdrawing from something.

**33. (A)**

To UNDERMINE is to weaken or injure, especially by subtle or insidious means. Its opposite is (A), REINFORCE, meaning to strengthen, support, or buttress. To REESTABLISH, (B), means to rebuild. To RESTORE, (C), is to return to a former state. Both (B) and (C) carry the idea of rebuilding or restoring an entity which has been destroyed or injured. These are "after the fact" remedies, so to speak.

A structure can be reinforced at any state of being. To CONSOLI-DATE, (D), is to combine several things into one, thereby achieving greater strength. UNDERMINE and REINFORCE can apply to a single structure. To CORROBORATE, (E), is to support by confirming rather than by buttressing.

34. (B)

The opposite of RELIGIOUS is (B), SECULAR (Latin *secularis*, meaning worldly). A MALEVOLENT, (A) is a person who wishes harm or evil to others. (C) EVIL, is the antonym for good; while (E), UNRIGHTEOUS is the antonym for righteous. IMPIETY, (C) means irreverent.

35. (D)

A GLUTTONOUS individual is one who eats to excess, while an ABSTEMIOUS (D) person is one who is moderate or temperate in eating or drinking. The word glutton comes from the Latin word for swallow (*gluttiere*). A person with a VORACIOUS appetite (A) craves large amounts of food; a FASTIDIOUS person (B) is one who is not easily pleased; an ASCETIC (C) is one who is self-denying; and an AUSTERE (E) person is one who is stern, harsh, or morally strict.

36. (A)

RUDE is an adjective meaning crude, rough, or unrefined. Its opposite is (A) URBANE, polite in a smooth, polished manner. DEBONAIR, (B), is wrong because it means genial; PLEASANT, (C), is wrong because it means agreeable. FRIENDLY, (D), is wrong because its opposite is unfriendly, and while an unfriendly person may be rude, unfriendliness is not a prerequisite for rudeness. Friendly people can be crude as well. CONFIDENT, (E), is wrong because its opposite is uncertain or unsure of oneself. A rude person may be very confident and sure of himself.

37. (E)

The word UNINTELLIGIBLE means "not able to be understood; not clear." Its opposite is (E), APPARENT, which means "evident, obvious, readily seen." (A) EXPLICABLE (able to be explained) falls

short of the idea of not understandable, as do (B), SOLVABLE, and (C), RECOGNIZABLE. Alternative (D), RATIONAL means "based on reason," or "able to reason." An idea may be based on reason yet remain unintelligible to people. Also, a person may be a rational (sane) person and still find certain ideas unintelligible.

38.  (B)

RESERVED comes form the Latin word "back," *re* and "keep," *servare*. As an adjective in English, reserved means "undemonstrative," "self-restrained," or "distant." Its opposite in the list given is (B), AFFABLE, which means "friendly," or "sociable." Alternative (A), CHIVALROUS, means gallant or courteous; alternative (C), INGRATIATING, means to "bring oneself into another's favor"; alternative (D), CULTIVATED, means "developed," as in a "developed mind," and alternative (E), WELL-BRED, means "showing good breeding," "courteous," or "considerate."

# Section 3—Quantitative Ability

1.  (A)

Replacing $x$ and $y$ with 1, we have $f(1,1) = [(2 \times 1) + 1]/1^2 = 3$. In the second case, $x = 1$, $y = 2$, $f(1,2) = [(2 \times 1) + 2]/2^2 = 4/4 = 1$. Thus, $f(1,1) > f(1, 2)$.

2.  (B)

Given $\overset{\frown}{AB} = \overset{\frown}{BC}$ then $\alpha = 35°$ and $\beta = 70°$. Therefore,

$$3\alpha = 105° > 70° = \beta.$$

3.  (B)

60% of X + 2 is 36.

$$
\begin{aligned}
{}^{60}/_{100}\,(x + 2) &= 36 \\
x + 2 &= 60 \\
x &= 58.
\end{aligned}
$$

4.　(C)

The sum of the interior angles in a triangle is 180°. Therefore,

$$
\begin{aligned}
X + 2X + 3X &= 180° \\
6X &= 180° \\
X &= 30° \\
3X &= 90°
\end{aligned}
$$

5.　(B)

The three even numbers (consecutives) are 2X, 2X + 2, and 2X + 4.

$$
\text{Average} = \frac{2X + (2X + 2) + (2X + 4)}{3}
$$

$$
= (6X + 6)/3 = 2X + 2
$$

$$
2X + 2 > 2X
$$

6.　(A)

Redraw the figure and add the letters $D, E, F$, and $G$. The triangles are:

| | | |
|---|---|---|
| *ABC* | Equilateral | (1) |
| *AGC, CGB, AGB* | Isosceles | (3) |
| *AFC, AFB, AGD, GDC, CEB, CEA* | | |
| *AGE, GEB, BDA, BDC, GFB, GFC* | Scalene | (12) |

The total number of triangles is 16.

7.　(A)

Redraw the graph.

$X$ is a positive number.
$Y$ is a negative number.

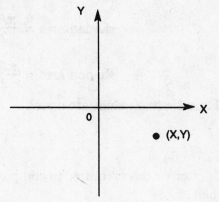

Then $X > Y$ and also $X > 2Y$.

8.  (B)
    First, calculate the hours that the boy sleeps in 3 weeks.

    14 hours/day $\times$ 7 days/week $\times$ 3 weeks = 294 hours.

    Then calculate the hours that the boy does not sleep in a month.

    10 hours/day $\times$ 30 days/month $\times$ 1 month = 300 hours.

9.  (C)
    The perimeter of the shaded area is equal to the perimeter of the square $ABCD$. The perimeter of the square = $4a$.

10.  (D)
    Given that $m > n$, then

    if $\qquad$ $m > 0$ and $n > 0$,
    then $\qquad$ $m^2 > n^2$,

    if $\qquad$ $m < 0$ and $n < 0$,
    then $\qquad$ $m^2 < n^2$

    The answer cannot be determined from the information given.

11.  (C)
    To compare both alternatives, calculate the shaded area.

    shaded area = half of circle (radius $R$) − circle (radius $R/2$)

    $$\text{shaded area} = \frac{\pi R^2}{2} - \pi \left(\frac{R}{2}\right)^2$$

    $$\text{shaded area} = \frac{\pi R^2}{2} - \frac{\pi R^2}{4} = \frac{\pi R^2}{4}$$

    Thus the two values are equal.

12.  (B)
    Let $x$ = days required to complete the job if $A$ and $B$ work together, then

    $$\frac{1}{4} + \frac{1}{6} = \frac{1}{x} \quad \text{or} \quad \frac{5}{12} = \frac{1}{x} \quad \text{so} \quad x = \frac{12}{5} = 2.4 \text{ days}.$$

13. (C)

Redraw the figure. In the triangle *EAD*

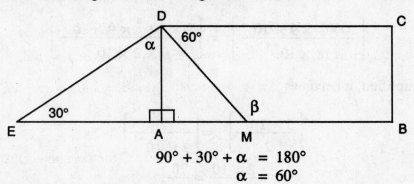

$$90° + 30° + \alpha = 180°$$
$$\alpha = 60°$$

In the quadrilateral *DMBC*

$$60° + \beta + 90° + 90° = 360°$$
$$\beta = 120°$$

Therefore, $\alpha + \beta = 180°$.

14. (B)

$$\cfrac{1}{1 + \cfrac{1}{1 + \cfrac{1}{x}}} = \cfrac{1}{1 + \frac{x}{x+1}} = \frac{x+1}{x+1+x} = \frac{x+1}{2x+1}$$

Since $x > 0$, $2x + 1 > x + 1$, therefore $\dfrac{x+1}{2x+1} < 1$

15. (D)

As an example:

$$x = 1 \qquad (x > 0)$$
$$a = .1 \qquad (a > 0)$$
$$b = .1 \qquad (b > 0)$$

$y = .1 \times 1 + .1 = .2$  Therefore, $x > y$.

If

$$x = 1 \qquad (x > 0)$$
$$a = 2 \qquad (a > 0)$$
$$b = 2 \qquad (b > 0)$$

$y = 2 \times 1 + 2 = 4$. Therefore, $y > x$.

We see that sometimes $x$ is larger than $y$ and sometimes $y$ is larger than $x$.

16. **(A)**

The value of the expression will be

$$\left[\frac{.0003 \times 9 \times 10^{-1}}{18 \times 10^{-4}}\right]^{-1} = \left[\frac{3 \times 10^{-4} \times 9 \times 10^{-1}}{9 \times 2 \times 10^{-4}}\right]^{-1}$$

Simplified, it becomes

$$\left[\frac{3 \times 10^{-1}}{2}\right]^{-1} = \left[\frac{2}{3 \times 10^{-1}}\right]^{1}$$

or

$$\frac{2 \times 10}{3} = \frac{20}{3}.$$

17. **(C)**

Redraw the figure and add the values of the angles.

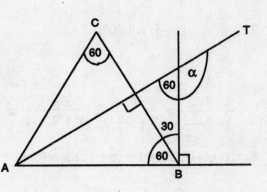

Therefore $\alpha + 60° = 180°$

$\alpha = 120°$

18. **(A)**

First, the number is

$$1 : {}^{8}/_{3} = 1 \times {}^{3}/_{8} = {}^{3}/_{8}$$

The reciprocal of ${}^{3}/_{8}$ is ${}^{8}/_{3}$.

19. **(D)**

If $a * b = 6a - 2bx$ then

$$9 * 6 = (6 * 9) - (2 * 6 * x) = 54 - 12x$$

and we know that $9 * 6 = 6$

$$6 = 54 - 12x$$
$$12x = 54 - 6 = 48$$
$$x = 4$$

572

20.  (D)

Redraw the figure. Note that the diagonal of the square is equivalent to the diameter (2*R*).

Using Pythagoras' Theorem,

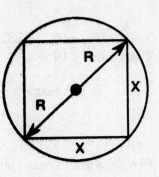

$$X^2 + X^2 = (2R)^2$$
$$2X^2 = 4R^2$$
$$X^2 = 2R^2$$
$$X = R\sqrt{2}$$

Given that the perimeter of the square is 4*x*, as a function of *R* we have
$$4X = 4R\sqrt{2}$$

21.  (B)

The number of people owning cars in 1970 equals

$$^{82}/_{100}\ (130\ \text{million}) = 106.6\ \text{million}$$

Of these, 75% had insurance:  .75(106.6 million) ≈ 80 million.

22.  (B)

First, calculate the number of cars insured in 1955:

$$\text{Number of cars} = ^{70}/_{100}\ (110\ \text{million}) = 77\ \text{million}$$

Of these, 55% were insured:

$$^{55}/_{100}\ (77\ \text{million}) = 42.35\ \text{million}$$

We know that in 1970, about 80 million cars were insured. So, the increase = 80 million – 42.5 million = 37.65 million.

23.  (C)

Cars without insurance in 1970 = 25% * 82% * 130 = 26.65 million.

Cars without insurance in 1955 = 45% * 70% * 110 = 34.65 million.

So, the required ratio $= \dfrac{26.65}{34.65} = .77$

24. **(A)**

Total cars in 1970 = .82 × 130 million = 106.6 million.

Total cars in 1955 = .70 × 110 million = 77 million

$$\% \text{ increase} = \frac{(106.6 - 77)}{77} * 100 = 38.4\%.$$

25. **(B)**

People without cars (1970) = Total People − People with Cars in 1970.

130 million − 106.6 million = 23.4 million.

People without cars (1955) = Total People − People with Cars in 1955.

110 million − 77 million = 33 million

$$\frac{\text{people without cars in 1970}}{\text{people without cars in 1955}} = \frac{23.4 \text{ million}}{33 \text{ million}} = .71.$$

26. **(B)**

$n$ years later, the ages will be

| | |
|---|---|
| father | $40 + n$ |
| son #1 | $6 + n$ |
| son #2 | $3 + n$ |
| son #3 | $1 + n$ |

Therefore

$$6 + n + 3 + n + 1 + n = (80/100) * (40 + n)$$
$$10 + 3n = .8(40 + n)$$
$$10 + 3n = 32 + .8n$$
$$2.2n = 22$$
$$n = 10.$$

27. **(D)**

Rearrange the first equation

$$x = 10 - y - z$$

If we use the smallest values for y and z, we obtain the biggest one for x, that is

$$x = 10 - 5 - 3$$
$$x = 2$$

therefore $\quad\quad\quad x < z$ and also $x < y.$

Now rearrange the expression to analyze proposition III.

$$x + z = 10 - y$$

if $\quad\quad\quad y = 5$ (the smallest one), $x + z = 5$
but if $\quad\quad\quad y > 5 \quad\quad\quad$ then $\quad\quad x + z < 5$
therefore $\quad\quad x + z \leq y.$

28. *(E)*

    $X$ : cost of one pound of pears.
    $Y$ : cost of one pound of peaches.

$$2X + Y = 1.4 \quad\quad\quad (1)$$
$$3X + 2Y = 2.4 \quad\quad\quad (2)$$

(1) times (2)

$$4X + 2Y = 2.8 \quad\quad\quad (3)$$
$$3X + 2Y = 2.4 \quad\quad\quad (2)$$

(3) − (2)

$$X = .4$$

Substitute $X = .4$ in (1) $\quad\quad Y = .6$
therefore, $\quad\quad\quad\quad\quad X + Y = 1.00$

29. *(D)*

    In this case, it is useful to draw a Venn diagram. If we assign $X$ to students that speak French and German then

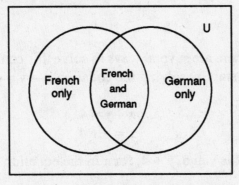

$30 - X =$ students that speak only French
and
$20 - X =$ students that speak only German.

The total students (40) is then fit into the equation:

$$40 = 30 \text{ (French only)} - X + 20 \text{ (German only)} - X \text{ (Both)} + X$$
$$40 = 50 - X, \quad X = 10.$$

30. **(A)**

$$\sqrt{X\sqrt{X\sqrt{X}}} = \sqrt{X\sqrt{X * X^{1/2}}} = \sqrt{X\sqrt{X^{3/2}}}$$

$$= \sqrt{X * X^{3/4}} \qquad \text{(the sum of the exponents}$$
$$1 + {}^3/_4 = {}^7/_4)$$
$$\sqrt{X^{7/4}} = X^{7/8}$$

## Section 4—Quantitative Ability

1. **(C)**
    Since $l$, $m$, and $n$ are lines intersection at point $P$, it follows that angles $BPC$ and $EPD$ are vertical angles. Remember that vertical angles have the same measure. Hence, $x = y$.
    Adding $z$ to both sides of the equation $x = y$, we get, $x + z = y + z$.

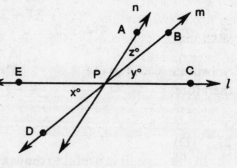

So the two quantities in Columns A and B are equal.

2. **(A)**
    Though there are several ways to solve this comparison problem, one way is to start by solving the equation $x - y = 4$ for $x$ in terms of $y$. Thus,

$$x - y = 4$$
$$x = y + 4$$

Substituting this value, $y + 4$, for $x$ in the equation $2x + y = 6$ yields,

$$2x + y = 6$$
$$2(y + 4) + y = 6$$
$$2y + 8 + y = 6$$

$$3y = 6 - 8$$
$$3y = -2$$
$$y = -^2/_3.$$

So the quantity in Column A is greater.

3.  (D)
    Let $x$ = the price of one shirt in dollars.
        $y$ = the price of one tie in dollars.
Then the centered information can be translated into the following equation:
$$2x + 2y = 80.$$

Dividing both sides of this equation by 2 yields:

$$x + y = 40.$$

This means the price of 1 shirt and 1 tie is $40. Note that the equation $x + y = 40$ is an equation with two unknown variables $x$, and $y$, and we do not know anything about the value of either variable. Thus, the relationship between the two quantities in Columns A and B is indeterminate.

For example, if the price of one shirt, $x$, is $25 and the price of one tie, $y$, is $15, then $x + y = 40$, and $x > y$. That is, the quantity in Column A is greater. But, if the price of one shirt, $x$, is $18 and the price of one time, $y$, is $22, then $x + y = 40$ and $y > x$. That is, the quantity in Column B is greater.

4.  (B)
    The easiest and the most direct approach for attacking this comparison problem is to perform the indicated operations in the quantity given in Column B.

When performing operations in an expression, which has no grouping symbols to indicate the order in which operations are to be performed, we do multiplication and division first as they occur from left to right, and then we do addition and subtraction as they occur from left to right.

Thus, performing the operations indicated in the expression shown in Column B yields,

$$18 \times 3 + 44 - 84 \div 7 = 54 + 44 - 12$$

$$= 98 - 12$$
$$= 88.$$

So the quantity in Column B is greater.

5.    (A)
Since lines $l$ and $m$ meet when extended to the right, we can let point $P$ be their point of intersection as shown in the following figure.

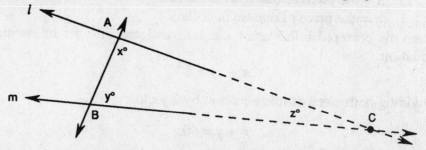

Let $m \angle A$ = measure of angle $A$. Since the sum of the measures of the three interior angles of a triangle is equal to 180°, it follows that

$$x + y + z = 180$$
$$x + y = 180 - Z$$

Since $\angle ACB$ is one of the three angles of triangle $ABC$, it follows that its measure is greater than 0. That is, $m \angle ACB > 0$. But in the above figure, $m \angle ACB = Z$, implies that $Z > 0$.

Thus, $x + y = 180 - Z$ implies that $x + y < 180$.

6.    (C)
Traveling to the airport involves the distance to the airport, the time of travel, and the rate of travel. The relationship between these three quantities is

Distance = Rate × Time.

Let      $d$ = the distance to the airport in miles.
         $t$ = the number of hours of travel in order to arrive at the airport at the right time (or simply, let $t$ = the right time of travel in hours).
         $r$ = rate of travel.

Thus,

$$d = rt, \quad \text{or} \quad t = {}^d\!/_r.$$

Traveling at a rate of (1) 60 mph, the time of travel is equal to ${}^d\!/_{60}$. But,

from the centered information, this time is 1 hour early. That is 1 hour less than *t*. Hence,

$$d/_{60} = t - 1 \quad \text{or} \quad d/_{60} + 1 = t.$$

(2) 30 mph, the time of travel is equal to $d/_{30}$. But, from the centered information, this time is one hour more than the right time of travel, *t*. Hence,

$$d/_{30} = t + 1 \quad \text{or} \quad d/_{30} - 1 = t.$$

Since the right time of travel, *t*, is a constant, it follows that

$$\frac{d}{60} + 1 = \frac{d}{30} - 1$$

$$\frac{d + 60}{60} = \frac{d - 30}{30}$$

$$30\left(\frac{d + 60}{60}\right) = 30\left(\frac{d - 30}{30}\right)$$

$$\frac{d + 60}{2} = d - 30$$

Cross-multiplication yields,

$$d + 60 = 2d - 60$$
$$60 + 60 = 2d - d$$
$$120 = d$$

Thus, the distance to the airport is 120 miles.
    So the quantities in Columns A and B are equal.

7.    (D)
    With the exception of the centered information that *a*, *b* and *c* are integers, no specific information is given about the value of *a*, *b*, or *c*. Hence, the relationship between the two quantities in Columns A and B is indeterminate. For example, if $a = 2$, $b = 3$, and $c = 4$, then $ac = 2(4) = 8$, $bc = 3(4) = 12$, and the quantity in Column B is greater. But, if $a = 2$, $b = 3$, and $c = -4$, then $ac = 2(-4) = -8$, $bc = 3(-4) = -12$, and $ac > bc$, that is, the quantity in Column A is greater.

8.    (B)
    The most direct way to attack this comparison problem is to perform the indicated operation in Column B, and compare the result

with the quantity in Column A. Note that the operation $*$, when it is used on two real numbers, results in adding the two numbers, then subtracting their product from their sum.

Thus,

$$\begin{aligned}
(-4) * 5 &= (-4) + 5 - (-4)\,(5) \\
&= -4 + 5 - (-20) \\
&= 1 + 20 \\
&= 21.
\end{aligned}$$

So, the quantity in Column B is greater.

9.  (A)

By simplifying across the comparisons we get:

$$m\overline{AY} = m\overline{AX} + m\overline{XY}$$
$$m\overline{XZ} = m\overline{XY} + m\overline{YZ}$$

Now, $m\,\overline{AY} > m\,\overline{XZ}$ implies

$$m\overline{AX} + m\overline{XY} > m\overline{XY} + m\overline{YZ}$$

Subtracting $m\overline{XY}$ from both sides of the later inequality yields,

$$m\overline{AX} + m\overline{XY} - m\overline{XY} > m\overline{XY} - m\overline{XY} + m\overline{YZ}$$

Hence, $m\overline{AX} > m\overline{YZ}$. So the quantity in Column A is greater.

10.  (C)

Translating the information in Column A into algebraic expressions yields,

"the difference between $x$ and $y$" : $x - y$

Thus, the difference between $x$ and $y$ divided by 6 is the same is $(x - y) \div 6$, which can be written as $\dfrac{x - y}{6}$.

So the two quantities in Columns A and B are equal.

11.  (A)

Since the more (less) miles the car travels, the higher (lower) number of gallons of gasoline consumed, it follows that this comparison problem can be solved by a direct proportion.

$$\frac{\left\{\begin{array}{l}\text{Number of gallons of}\\\text{gasoline consumed } x\end{array}\right\}}{\left\{\begin{array}{l}\text{Number of miles}\\\text{traveled } x\end{array}\right\}} = \frac{\left\{\begin{array}{l}\text{Number of gallons of}\\\text{gasoline consumed } y\end{array}\right\}}{\left\{\begin{array}{l}\text{Number of miles}\\\text{traveled } y\end{array}\right\}}$$

In this problem, from the centered information and from the quantity in Column A, we have,

$$\frac{20}{400} = \frac{y}{900}.$$

Cross-multiplication yields,

$$400y = (20)(900)$$
$$400y = 18,000$$
$$y = \frac{18,000}{400}$$
$$y = 45.$$

Thus, 45 gallons of gasoline are needed to travel a distance of 900 miles. Thus, the quantity in Column A is greater.

Another way to attack this problem is as follows: From the centered information, the car travels 400 miles on 20 gallons of gasoline. This implies that the car travels a distance of,

$$400 \text{ miles} \div 20 \text{ gallons} = 20 \text{ miles/gallon}.$$

Thus, the number of gallons of gasoline the car consumes in a trip of 900 miles is equal to

$$900 \text{ miles} \div 20 \text{ miles/gallon}$$
$$= {}^{900}/_{20} \text{ gallons} = 45 \text{ gallons}.$$

So the quantity in Column A is greater.

12.  (D)

To answer this comparison question, we need to solve the centered equation for $x$ in terms of $y$ and $z$. Thus,

$$3x + y + z = 15$$
$$3x = 15 - y - z$$
$$= 15 - (y + z)$$
$$x = \frac{15 - (y + z)}{3}$$

$$x = 5 - \frac{(y + z)}{3}$$

Since no information is given about the value of $y$ or $z$, it follows that the relationship between the two quantities in Columns A and B cannot be determined from the information given. For example, if $y = 1$, and $z = 2$, then

$$x = 5 - \frac{(1 + 2)}{3} = 5 - 1 = 4$$

In this case, the quantity in Column B is greater. But if $y = -1$, and $z = -2$, then

$$x = 5 - \frac{(-1 + -2)}{3}$$

$$= 5 - \left(-\frac{3}{3}\right) = 5 - (-1)$$

$$= 5 + 1 = 6.$$

In this case, the quantity in Column A is greater.

13. (C)

The average (arithmetic mean), $\overline{x}$, of a set of numbers is defined as the sum of all the numbers in the set divided by the number of numbers, $n$. That is

$$\overline{x} = \frac{\text{sum of all numbers}}{n}$$

In this problem, calculating the average, $\overline{x}$, of the given numbers, we get,

$$\overline{x} = \frac{40 + 20 + 30 + 24 + 27 + 15}{6}$$

$$= \frac{156}{6} = 26.$$

So the two quantities in Columns A and B are equal.

14. (B)

Since the sun's rays make the same angles with the horizontal for the triangles involving the tree and the meter stick, and since both the tree and the meter stick are assumed to make right angles with the horizontal, $\triangle ABC$ and $\triangle DEF$ are similar, as indicated in the following figure.

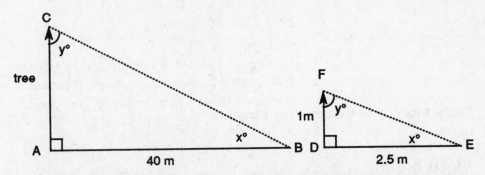

Recall that two triangles are similar if and only if corresponding angles are congruent (have the same angle measure) and corresponding sides are proportional.

Thus, angle $C$ is congruent to angle $F$, angle $A$ is congruent to angle $D$, and angle $B$ is congruent to angle $E$. Also, if $AB$ represents the length of side $\overline{AB}$, then

$$\frac{AB}{DE} = \frac{AC}{DF} = \frac{BC}{EF}$$

Hence, using the proportion $\frac{AC}{DF} = \frac{AB}{DE}$ , yields

$$\frac{AC}{1} = \frac{40}{2.5}$$

Cross-multiplication yields,

$$2.5(AC) = 40$$

$$AC = \frac{40}{2.5} = 16$$

Thus, the tree is 16 meters high.

So the quantity in Column B is greater.

15.   **(B)**

The easiest and most direct way to answer this comparison problem is to solve the centered equation, $y/_3 + y/_2 = 6$, for $y$. Note that on the left-hand side of this equation, we are adding two fractions. Hence, we need to find the least common denominator of $y/_3$ and $y/_2$. The least common denominator is 6. Thus,

$$\frac{y}{3} + \frac{y}{2} = 6$$

or

$$\frac{2y + 3y}{6} = 6$$

Cross-multiplication yields,

$$2y + 3y = 36$$
$$5y = 36$$
$$y = \frac{36}{5} = 7\frac{1}{5}.$$

So the quantity in Column B is greater.

16. (E)

This question requires the calculation of the percent of the mark down of the sale price. We can start by letting $x\%$ = the required percent.

Since the original price of the car is \$1,195 and the mark down is \$300, it follows that the sale price of the car is equal to \$1,195 − \$300 = \$895. Thus, we need to find what percent 300 is of 850. This can be found by a direct proportion as follows:

$$\frac{\text{mark down } x}{\text{sale price } x} = \frac{\text{mark down } y}{\text{sale price } y}$$

Since percent means the number of parts per 100 parts, we have,

$$\frac{x}{100} = \frac{300}{895}$$

Cross-multiplication yields,

$$895\,x = (300)(100)$$
$$x = \frac{(300)(100)}{895} = 0.335$$

Thus, $x\% = 0.335 \times 100\% = 33.5\%$.

Another way of attacking this problem is to divide 300 by 895, then multiply the result by 100%. This yields,

$$x\% = \left(\frac{300}{895}\right) 100\%$$
$$= 33.5\%.$$

Yet a third way to solve this problem is to test each of the percents given in the answer choices as possible answers. This can be done by calculating the given percent of \$895. If the result is \$300, the given percent is correct, otherwise, the given percent is the wrong answer. Thus,

(A) 29.3%:  (.293)(\$895) ≅ \$262 ≠ \$300

(B) 8.4%: $(.84)(\$895) \cong \$75 \neq \$300$

(C) 37.7%: $(.377)(\$895) \cong \$377 \neq \$300$

(D) 25.1%: $(.251)(\$895) \cong \$225 \neq \$300.$

(E) 33.5% $(.335)(\$895) \cong \$300.$

17. (C)

Since $n$ and $k$ are even integers, it follows that $(n - 1)$ and $(k + 1)$ are odd integers; $(n + k)$ is an even integer (even + even = even); and $2n$ and $2(n + k)$ are even integers (2 times any integer yields an even integer).

Now, let us check the integers given in the answer choices as possible answers:

(A) $n + k + 1$. Since $n + k$ is an even integer, $n + k + 1$ is an odd integer.

(B) $(n - 1)(k + 1)$. Since $(n - 1)$ is odd and $k + 1$ is odd, $(n - 1)(k + 1)$ is odd (odd $\times$ odd = odd).

(C) $2(n + k + 1)$. Since 2 times any integer, odd or even, is always an even integer, $2(n + k + 1)$ is even.

(D) $(n - 3)(k + 1)$ cannot be an even integer since $(n - 3)$ is odd and $(k + 1)$ is odd (odd x odd = odd).

(E) $2(n + k) + 1$. Since $2(n + k)$ is even, it follows that $2(n + k) + 1$ is odd.

18. (A)

Let $m \angle A$ represent the measure of angle $A$. Since $l$, $m$, and $n$ are lines intersecting at point $P$, angle $APB$ is a straight angle. Recall that the measure of a straight angle is equal to 180°. That is,
$$m \angle APB = 180°.$$
Thus,
$$x + y + \frac{a}{2} = 180$$
$$x + y = 180 - \frac{a}{2}$$

585

Now, we would like to check if any of the quantities given in the answer choices (B), (C), (D) and (E) can be equal to $x + y$. To do so, note that,

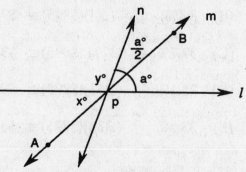

$$x + y = 180 - \frac{a}{2}$$

$$= \frac{360 - a}{2}$$

Thus, if any of the quantities given in the answer choices (B), (C), (D) and (E) are correct, that quantity must be equivalent to $\frac{360-a}{2}$. Thus,

(B) $\dfrac{a}{2} - 180 = \dfrac{a - 360}{2}$

(C) $90 - \dfrac{a}{2} = \dfrac{180 - a}{2}$

(D) $a - 180$

(E) $180 - a$

Obviously, none of these quantities are equivalent to the quantity $\frac{360-a}{2}$.

19. **(D)**
The most direct way to solve this problem is to perform the indicated operations in the given equation and solve it for $x$. Thus,

$$x - (4x - 8) + 9 + (6x - 8) = 9 - x + 24$$
$$x - 4x + 8 + 9 + 6x - 8 = 9 - x + 24$$
$$(x + 6x - 4x) + (8 - 8 + 9) = (9 + 24) - x$$
$$(7x - 4x) + 9 = 33 - x$$
$$3x + x = 33 - 9$$
$$4x = 24$$
$$x = 6.$$

20. **(B)**
Let $x =$ the number of hours it takes $Q$ to wallpaper the house by himself. Then $Q$ wallpapers $1/x$ of the house in 1 hour. Since it takes $R$,

$S$, and $Q$ eight hours to do the job if they work together, it follows that $R$, $S$ and $Q$ complete $1/_8$ of the house in 1 hour. If $R$ and $S$ work together, they complete the job in 12 hours, hence, they can wallpaper $1/_{12}$ of the house in 1 hour.

Putting things together, $R$, $S$ and $Q$ wallpaper $1/_8$ of the house in 1 hour. $R$ and $S$ wallpaper $1/_{12}$ of the house in 1 hour. $Q$ can wallpaper $1/_x$ of the house in 1 hour. Thus, if all three of them work together, they can wallpaper $(1/_{12} + 1/_x)$ of the house in 1 hour. But, we know that all 3 of them wallpaper $1/_8$ of the house in 1 hour. Thus,

$$\frac{1}{x} + \frac{1}{12} = \frac{1}{8}$$

Solving this equation for $x$ yields the number of hours it takes $Q$ to wallpaper the house by himself.

Now,

$$\frac{1}{x} + \frac{1}{12} = \frac{1}{8}$$

$$\frac{12 + x}{12x} = \frac{1}{8}$$

Cross-multiplication yields,

$$8(12 + x) = 12x$$
$$96 + 8x = 12x$$
$$96 = 12x - 8x$$
$$96 = 4x$$
$$x = 24$$

**Questions 21 – 25:**
Refer to the tables for questions 21 – 25. Table 1 represents the amount of money (to the nearest dollar) spent by 50 state university students in the school's book store during the month of August, 1988 on textbooks. The table is broken down by the students class rank, and Table 2 represents the amount of money spent by the same 50 students in the school's book store during the month of August, 1988 on items other than textbooks.

21.  (A)
There are several ways to measure the variation (spread) of data. The simplest is to subtract the least number from the greatest number. This difference is called the range. For example, the greatest and the

least amounts of money spent by members of the sophomore class in the school's book store on items other than textbooks are $17 and $11 respectively, as shown in Table 2. Thus, the range for the amount of money spent by the group of 10 students of the sophomore class on items other than textbooks is $17 - $11 = $6.

Assuming that the data in Tables 1 and 2 represents a random sample of the student body, we can answer this question by computing the range of the amount of money spent by each of the class ranks in the school's book store on items other than textbooks. Thus, from Table 2, the following information can be obtained:

**Amount of money spent on items other than textbooks**

| Class Rank | Greatest Amount | Least Amount | Range |
|---|---|---|---|
| Freshman | $14 | $ 5 | $ 9 |
| Sophomore | 17 | 11 | 5 |
| Junior | 24 | 13 | 11 |
| Senior | 32 | 16 | 16 |
| Graduate | 26 | 7 | 19 |

This table shows that the graduate class has the greatest relative variation in the amount of money spent in the school's book store on items other than textbooks.

22. **(D)**

The average (arithmetic mean), $\bar{x}$, of a set of numbers is equal to the sum of the numbers divided by the number of numbers, $n$. That is,

$$\bar{x} = \frac{\text{sum of numbers}}{n}$$

Thus, this question can be answered by calculating the average of the amounts of money spent in the school's book store on textbooks only. These amounts are listed in the column headed "Senior" in Table 1. They are: 166, 189, 190, 157, 203, 177, 180, 164, 188, and 170. The sum of these numbers is given also in Table 1 as 1778. Since there are 10 numbers, it follows that,

$$\bar{x} = \frac{1778}{10} = 177.8$$

Thus, the best approximation of the average amount of money spent by any Senior class student is $178.

23.     (C)

The total amount of money spent by any student in the school's book store is equal to the sum of the amount of money spent on textbooks, which can be obtained from Table 1, and the amount of money spent on items other than textbooks, which can be obtained from Table 2.

Thus, to answer this question, we need to determine the average total amount of money spent in the school's book store by the Senior class students, and the average total amount spent by the Graduate class students.

From Table 1 the total amount of money spent by the group of ten Senior class students on textbooks is equal to $1,778 and the total amount of money spent by the group of 10 Graduate students is equal to $1,153. From Table 2, the total amount of money spent by the same group of 10 Senior class students on items other than textbooks is equal to $241, and the total amount of money spent by the same group of ten Graduate students is equal to $152. Thus, for the

(i)  Senior class students,

$$\bar{x} = \frac{1778 + 241}{10} = \frac{2019}{10} = 201.9 \cong 202$$

(ii) Graduate class students,

$$\bar{x} = \frac{1153 + 152}{10} = \frac{1305}{10} = 130.5 \cong 131$$

Hence, the difference between the average amount of money spent in the school's book store in August by a Senior student and the average amount of money spent by a Graduate student is equal to

$$\$202 - \$131 = \$71.$$

24.  (E)

To answer this question, we need to determine the average total amount of money spent by any Freshman class student in the school's book store on textbooks and on items other than textbooks, then multiply the result by the number of Freshman class students enrolled in the school during the month of August.

As before, the average total amount of money spent by any Freshman class student can be approximated by dividing the total amount of money spent by the group of 10 Freshman class students on

textbooks and on other items by 10. From Table 1, the amount of money spent by the 10 Freshman class students is equal to $1861 and from Table 2, the amount of money spent by the 10 Freshman class students on items other than textbooks is equal to $114. Thus, the average,

$$\bar{x} = \frac{\text{Total amount}}{10}$$

$$\bar{x} = \frac{\$1861 + \$114}{10} = \frac{\$1975}{10} = \$197.50$$

Multiplying the average amount of money spent by any Freshman class student by the number of Freshman students enrolled in the school yields,

Total amount spent by the Freshman class students
= (3000) ($197.50) = $592,500.

25. (B)

To answer this question, we need to approximate the total amount of money spent in the school's book store on items other than textbooks by the entire student body, the total amount of money spent on items other than textbooks by the Freshman class students. Finally the required percent will be the result of dividing the amount spent by the Freshman class students by the total amount spent by the entire student body.

We can start by calculating the total amount of money spent on items other than textbooks by the Freshman class students. From Table 2, the sum of all the amounts spent by the group of the 10 Freshmen class students is equal to $114. Thus, average, $\bar{x}$, of the amount of money spent by a Freshman class student on items other than textbooks is given by

$$\bar{x} = \frac{\$114}{10} = \$11.40$$

Since there were 3,000 Freshman students, it follows that the total amount of money spent on items other than textbooks by these students is equal to

$$(3000)(\$11.4) = \$34,200.$$

Next, we calculate the total amount of money spent by the entire student body on items other than textbooks. The average of the total amount of money spent by any student in the school can be approxi-

mated by the average, $\bar{x}$, of the total amount spent by any one of the group of 50 students shown in Table 1. Thus,

$$\bar{x} = \frac{\text{sum of all amounts spent by the 50 students}}{50}$$

$$= \frac{114 + 140 + 180 + 241 + 152}{50}$$

$$= \frac{827}{50} = \$16.54.$$

Thus, the total amount of money spent by the entire student body of 10,000 students is equal to,

$$(10,000)\ (\$16.54) = \$165,540.$$

Hence, the required percent =

$$\frac{34,200}{165,400} \cong 21\%$$

26. **(D)**

Since the woman's age is derived from her son's age, let us assign the value $w$ for the son's age at the present time. Then the mother's age now is $6w$.

Next year, that is, 1 year from now:
the son's age will be $w + 1$
the mother's age will be $6w + 1$.

However, next year, it is given that the woman's age will be the square of her son's age. Thus,

$$6w + 1 = (w + 1)^2$$

which means that this equation can be used to find the woman's age.

Note that none of the equations given in answer choices (A), (B), (C), and (E) are equivalent to the equation,

$$6w + 1 = (w + 1)^2.$$

27. **(B)**

Let $m \angle A$ = the measure of angle $A$, $m(\overset{\frown}{ABC})$ = the measure of arc $\overset{\frown}{ABC}$. Since angle $DBC$ is formed by a tangent to circle $O$, $\overset{\leftrightarrow}{BD}$, and a chord, $\overline{CB}$, intersecting at the point of tangency, $B$, it follows that,

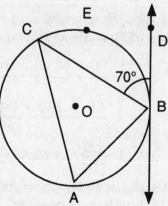

$$m\angle DBC = \frac{1}{2}m(\overset{\frown}{BEC})$$
$$70 = \frac{1}{2}m(\overset{\frown}{BEC})$$
$$m(\overset{\frown}{BEC}) = (70)(2)$$
$$m(\overset{\frown}{BEC}) = 140$$

Since $\angle BAC$ is an inscribed angle in the arc *BAC*, and since arc $\overset{\frown}{BEC}$ is intercepted by angle *BAC*, it follows that

$$m\angle BAC = \frac{1}{2}m(\overset{\frown}{BEC})$$
$$= \frac{1}{2}(140)$$
$$= 70°.$$

28.  (E)

To test whether a number, $N$, is prime, we need to test if $N$ is divisible by any of the prime numbers $\{2, 3, 5, 7, 11, 13, ...\}$ up to the largest natural number, $k$, whose square is less than or equal to the number we are testing, $N$. If $N$ is divisible by any of the prime numbers $P \le k$, where $k^2 \le N$, then $N$ is not a prime number. If $N$ is not divisible by any of the prime numbers $P \le k$, where $k^2 \le N$, then $N$ is a prime number. For example, to test whether 29 is a prime number, we need to test if 29 is divisible by any of the prime numbers starting with 2 and up to 5, that is, we test if 29 is divisible by 2, 3, or 5, since $6^2 = 36$ is $> 29$. Since 29 is not divisible by any of these primes, 29 is a prime number.

Since all the prime numbers, except 2, are odd, it follows that the difference between any two consecutive prime numbers is 2. Thus, each of the pairs of numbers given in the answer choices as possible answers are two consecutive odd numbers.

Thus, to answer this question, we need to test if any of the pairs of numbers given in the answer choices is a pair of prime numbers. Testing these pairs of numbers yields,

(A)   27 and 29. Since $6^2 = 36$, and since $36 > 27$, and $36 > 29$, we need to test if 27 or 29 is divisible by any of the prime numbers less than or equal to 5. That is, if 27 or 29 is divisible by 2, 3, or 5. Since 27 is divisible by 3, then 27 and 29 is not a pair of consecutive prime numbers.

(B)  31 and 32. Again, $6^2 = 36$, $36 > 31$ and $36 > 33$. Hence, we need to test if 31 or 33 is divisible by any of the prime numbers less than or equal to 5. That is, if 31 or 33 is divisible by any of the primes 2, 3, and 5. Since 33 is divisible by 3, then 31 and 33 is not a pair of two consecutive prime numbers.

(C)  35 and 37. Since 35 is divisible by 5, then 35 and 37 is not a pair of prime numbers.

(D)  37 and 39. Since 39 is divisible by 3, then 37 and 39 is not a pair of prime numbers.

(E)  41 and 43. Since $7^2 = 49$, $49 > 41$, and $49 > 43$, it follows that we need to test if 41 or 49 is divisible by any of the prime numbers less than or equal to 6. That is, if 41 or 49 is divisible by any of the primes 2, 3, and 5. Since 41 is not divisible by any of these three primes and 43 is not divisible by any of these three primes either, it follows that 41 and 43 is a pair of consecutive prime numbers.

29.  (A)
The most direct approach to solve this problem is to solve the equation,
$$v = \pi b^2 \left(r - \frac{b}{3}\right)$$
for $r$. Thus,
$$v = \pi b^2 \left(r - \frac{b}{3}\right)$$
$$v = \pi b^2 r - \pi b^2 \left(\frac{b}{3}\right)$$
$$v = \pi b^2 r - \frac{\pi b^3}{3}$$
$$v = \frac{3\pi b^2 r - \pi b^3}{3}$$

Cross-multiplication yields,
$$3v = 3\pi b^2 r - \pi b^3$$
$$3v + \pi b^3 = 3\pi b^2 r$$

593

$$\frac{3v + \pi b^3}{3\pi b^2} = r$$

$$r = \frac{3v}{3\pi b^2} + \frac{\pi b^3}{3\pi b^2}$$

$$r = \frac{v}{\pi b^2} + \frac{b}{3}$$

Note that the right-hand side of this equation is the quantity given in answer choice (A).

Checking all the quantities given in answer choices (B), (C), (D) and (E), we find out that none of those quantities are equivalent to the quantity,

$$\frac{v}{\pi b^2} + \frac{b}{3}.$$

30.  (C)

Let $x =$ the number of inches that must be cut from each dimension so that the ratio of the shorter side to the longer side is $^2/_3$.

Cutting off $x$ inches from the shorter side, which is 24 inches, its length will be

$$(24 - x) \text{ inches.}$$

Cutting off $x$ inches from the larger side, which is 33 inches, its length will be

$$(33 - x) \text{ inches.}$$

Since the ratio of the shorter side to the larger side is $^2/_3$, it follows that,

$$\frac{24 - x}{33 - x} = \frac{2}{3}$$

Solving this equation for $x$ yields the required one length. Thus,

$$\frac{24 - x}{33 - x} = \frac{2}{3}$$

Cross-multiplication yields,

$$3(24 - x) = 2(33 - x)$$
$$72 - 3x = 66 - 2x$$
$$-3x + 2x = 66 - 72$$
$$-x = -6$$
$$x = 6.$$

## Section 5–Analytical Ability

1. (A)   2. (A)   3. (E)   4. (C)

These questions require that the two categories of merit and discretionary raises be separated so the criteria for distribution of each is clear. Secondly, the sequence of deciding merit pay first as a prerequisite to the discretionary increases needs to be understood. Given these parameters, it then can be shown that the chairman can recommend a wide range of salary increases within these guidelines. For example, he could give all the merit and discretionary money to one person (item 1). He could give three faculty $1000 each of the merit money and make them eligible for the discretionary money and then give each $\frac{1}{3}$ of the discretionary money ($700 each). This would give them each $1700 and then divide the remaining $600 of merit money equally between the two remaining faculty (item 2). He could deny salary increases to as many as 1-4 faculty if he distributes the raises among 4, 3, 2, or 1 faculty (item 3). Since he cannot distribute any discretionary money unless he gives at least $1000 to each faculty member who receives discretionary funds, he must provide raises of $1700 as minimum raises for his highest paid faculty. These raises will leave only $600 to be divided between the two lowest paid faculty which would give each of them $300 and create the lowest possible difference of $1400 (item 4).

5. (D)   6. (B)   7. (E)   8. (A)

The solution can be found to items 5 - 8 by organizing a table in which the days of the week and the letter and number designations of employees are placed in compliance with the criteria listed. Study each condition stipulated in the passage and construct the following table:

| | |
|---|---|
| Monday | A B E 1 2 5 |
| Tuesday | A B C D E 1 2 3 4 5 |
| Wednesday | A B C D E 1 2 3 4 |
| Thursday | A B C D 1 2 3 4 5 |
| Friday | C D E 3 4 5 |

9. (C)   10. (E)   11. (D)   12. (D)

The questions in these four items can be answered by looking for conditions that eliminate the choices offered. Each of the incorrect

answers contains an element that does not comply with the requirements for the meeting. For example, in item 9 the question calls for a
meeting to be held on Friday. Since the passage states that M-2 cannot
meet on Friday, A, B, and D are eliminated. Choice (E) includes E-3
who cannot attend meetings at H. Thus, the remaining choice, (C)
seems to be the correct answer. A similar analysis of the board
members in (C) reveals that all of them could attend the meeting. This
procedure should be used with each of the remaining items based on
this passage.

13. (C)   14. (E)   15. (D)   16. (A)
Each question based on this passage requires separate analysis.
The best approach is to calculate the correct response, rather than to
eliminate the incorrect responses. A clear understanding of the variables to be employed in these calculations is the best way to begin. The
essential variables are that (1) 20 people were fined; (2) 15 speeders
were fined; (3) 10 people were put in jail; and (4) a scale of fines was
employed. In question 13, 5 non-speeders could have been among
those jailed which would leave 5 speeders to complete the total of those
jailed. In question 14, it is possible that only speeders were jailed which
would make the maximum speeders in jail 10. In question 15, in order
to collect $845 in fines, you should first multiply 5 (the number of non-
speeders) × $35 to determine the amount the non-speeders paid in
fines. This amounts to $175 which can be subtracted from $845 which
will leave $670 (the amount to be collected from the speeders). If all
15 speeders had been jailed, their combined fines would have been
$750. For each speeder who was not jailed the fine was $10 less. Since
the difference between $750 and $670 is $80 then 8 speeders were not
jailed. That leaves 7 speeders who were jailed. Question 16 calls for
multiplying $10 \times \$50 + 5 \times \$40 + 5 \times \$35 = \$875$.

17.  (D)
The viewpoint in this narrative asserts that people want to be
employed up to their highest level of preparation and ability and that
people who are not employed according to these criteria will be
discontent. The other options may be true but they are not the view
expressed in the passage. The basis on which this passage is based is
found in option (D).

18. (C)

The assertion in the passage is that social engineering or manipulation of social institutions can not succeed. Social forces have their own timetable and any effort to alter these trends is futile. The opposite position to this assertion is found in choice (C) which places confidence in the ability of man to understand his society and to successfully take steps to alter it.

19. (D)

Among the various fallacies of reasoning provided as choices in item 19, with the brevity of this tourist's visit to Paris and the obviously limited exposure she could have had in that short time to the complex topics she spoke about, she was drawing conclusions on the basis of too few instances. This is called "over-generalizing."

20. (D)

The concern for retirees having a reasonable standard of living and the preservation of freedom for both elderly and the other adults in society are the main considerations in this item. The alternative that protects both of these considerations is the best response. Item D meets these criteria better than the other choices. Choices (A) and (C) intrude on the lifestyles of younger adults, and choices (B) and (D) detract from options for the elderly.

21. (E)   22. (C)

Though diverse arguments favoring denial of driver's licenses for youth can be posited, the core argument raised in this passage relates to school attendance. The opposition to this denial can also be cast from different views but the main argument presented here is from the youth who marry young, have children, and want to earn a living as responsible parents. The answer to these questions requires careful reading of the passage and recognizing the main ideas without being distracted by peripheral arguments.

23. (E) 24. (B)   25 (A)

Though one might recognize that John's statement is his opinion, more confidence in selecting (E) as the correct response can be

mounted by eliminating the other responses, as well. Concepts are categories into which objects/ideas are placed because of common features, facts are based on evidence and truths, principles are guiding rules for action, and laws are either natural or social findings or creations. None of John's remarks would fit well into these labels. Mary countered John's remark about location by citing facts about states where centrality was not the basis for location. She simply provided factual information to add to the discussion. Bill commented further by classifying capitals into categories according to certain criteria. This procedure of categorizing is a conceptualizing process. Concepts are abstractions into which terms can be placed as they meet criteria for being classified. Terms such as chair, house, car, and cats are concepts that are useful for discourse because we attribute certain common features to each and we can communicate with this mutual understanding. Bill was using the term "capital" in this same sense.

# Section 6–Analytical Ability

Questions 1 – 5
From statement 1, place Al across from the dentist.

Al

Dentist

(Al is now obviously not the dentist.)
From statement 7, you could tentatively place the general practitioner and the optometrist.

Al

Optometrist (?)      General Practitioner (?)

Dentist

Statement 4 tells you that Joy is the general practitioner. Now you can deduce that Al must be the surgeon, and since Jeff is not across from the surgeon (statement 2), then Jeff must be the optometrist.

The final placement can be made from statement 3, because Debbie must be the dentist, and the optometrist (Jeff) must be on Debbie's left.

**Al**
**Surgeon**

**Jeff**                                                    **Joy**
**Optometrist**                          **General Practitioner**

**Debbie**
**Dentist**

1. **(C)**

   Statement 4 says that Joy is the general practitioner, therefore you already knew that the general practitioner could not be on Joy's left (statement 6).

2. **(D)**

   I is false from statement 1. II is false from statement 5. III is true. Since statement 7 tells you that the general practitioner is across from the optometrist, the dentist must be across from the surgeon. This question could have been answered easily from the diagram.

3. **(A)**

   I must be true by looking at the diagram.

4. **(C)**

   It is evident that both I and II are true, by referring to the diagram.

5. **(B)**

   Once again, this is evident from the diagram. You could have eliminated (A), (C), and (D) easily from statements 3 and 4.

Questions 6 – 10

   Construct a table showing which sheetrockers can work with which foundation workers. Four teams of sheetrockers are possible, with the following possibilities for foundation workers in each case. The first letter of their last name is used to build the combinations.

|     |                        |
| --- | ---------------------- |
| DFC | SD, RL, BL             |
| DF  | GSD, GRL, GBL, SDR, SDL |
| DC  | SDR, SDB, SDL          |
| FC  | SDR, SDB, SDL          |

**6. (D)**

By inspection of the table, notice that choice (B) has an impossible combination.

**7. (B)**

By inspection of the table, notice that this offers five possible combinations. The others offer only three.

**8. (D)**

Charles won't work will Glenn; he can only work with David and Fred. The three possibilities for the other two sheetrockers are given in choice (D).

**9. (A)**

The sheetrockers are David and Charles. Stan and Dennis appear in all teams, but one team can be made up with neither Ralph nor Brent.

**10. (A)**

The table shows that Stan and Dennis appear in eleven possible teams, Charles in nine, and Ralph and Brent in five each.

Questions 11 – 17

To help answer questions 11 – 17, you may have constructed the following chart.

|   | A | B | C |
| - | - | - | - |
| **A** | B | B | A |
| **B** | B | B | B |
| **C** | A | B | C |

11. (B)
     II only must be true. From the chart you will observe that I is false (when A reacts with C, the result is A) and III is false (when B reacts with B, the result is B). Only II is true.

12. (E)
     If the result is B, then A may have been reacting with A, which is neither I nor II. The key words in the statements are "had to be." B and C could be in the reaction but did not necessarily have to be.

13. (B)
     The result of A and C is A. The result of B and C is B. When A reacts with B, the result is B.

14. (A)
     Only statement I is false; when A reacts with A, the result is B.

15. (E)
     The only way A may be the result is if A reacts with C. Thus A and C both had to be in the reaction, and therefore B could not be. Statements I, II, and III are true.

16. (B)
     The result of A and A is B. The result of C and C is C. Thus the result of B and C is B.

17. (A)
     Bacon advocates retaining dignity without intruding upon liberty. The author implies that retaining dignity is impossible without intruding upon another's liberty by stating that not intruding upon liberty is impossible. (B), (C), and (D) contradict the author's argument, and (E) presents an irrelevant issue.

18. (E)
     I and II only. The author both relies on his interpretation of Bacon's statement and discusses liberty and dignity in absolute terms; I and II subvert such reliance. III supports, reiterates in fact, the author's argument.

19. (E)

All other options weaken the argument.

20. (E)

Choice (A) would tend to bolster the speaker, by citing dire consequences in similar cases and making possible an analogy to the present case. Choice (B) points out the imperative necessity of following the speaker's advice. Choice (C) is irrelevant, and so does not weaken the speaker's case. Choice (D) is somewhat closer, but could be explained in several ways. The clear propriety of Choice (E) — which weakens by providing counter-examples — makes it the correct choice.

21. (D)

Statement I would be approved by the speaker, since such an action would be consistent with his goal. The speaker has stated only that he disapproves of David's involvement with the arts, not of the arts in general. Therefore we do not know whether the speaker disapproves of the arts in general and cannot say that he does. Statement III seems in line with the speaker's dislikes — he is hardly less likely to consider mountain climbing as frivolous for heirs of great fortunes than he was to consider David's activities fripperies. There is no basis on which to characterize Statement IV.

22. (E)

The argument does not assume any of the statements. Statement I contradicts the thesis completely. Statement II is not assumed; the speaker says that single-mindedness is necessary to be an industrial leader, not that industry needs single-minded people. Industry might be much better off if its leaders had diverse interests; nevertheless, people who have diverse interests are unable (according to the speaker) to become leaders. Statement III is not assumed. The speaker casts no aspersions on David's talents, and explicitly acknowledges that he is a talented person.

23. (C)

The attempt to explain away the defeat of Margaret Court by

Bobby Riggs proves, at best, that a woman's style of play is superior to that of a man's, not that women themselves are equal or superior to men in tennis. Choice (A) is incorrect, since the argument is not biased — even if the author is biased, this has nothing to do with the validity of the argument itself. Choice (E) is incorrect, since equality of the sexes is what the argument seeks to prove. The other choices are simply irrelevant.

24. (D)

Making only the first word of sentence 1 does not solve all of the logical problems in the passage, but does strengthen the passage by indicating that customers with green necklaces must have brought them from the competition.

25. (B)

The author does not realize that customers not wearing green necklaces may have bought other items from the competition.

# GRE
# GENERAL TEST 5
## ANSWER SHEET

### SECTION 1

1. Ⓐ Ⓑ Ⓒ Ⓓ Ⓔ
2. Ⓐ Ⓑ Ⓒ Ⓓ Ⓔ
3. Ⓐ Ⓑ Ⓒ Ⓓ Ⓔ
4. Ⓐ Ⓑ Ⓒ Ⓓ Ⓔ
5. Ⓐ Ⓑ Ⓒ Ⓓ Ⓔ
6. Ⓐ Ⓑ Ⓒ Ⓓ Ⓔ
7. Ⓐ Ⓑ Ⓒ Ⓓ Ⓔ
8. Ⓐ Ⓑ Ⓒ Ⓓ Ⓔ
9. Ⓐ Ⓑ Ⓒ Ⓓ Ⓔ
10. Ⓐ Ⓑ Ⓒ Ⓓ Ⓔ
11. Ⓐ Ⓑ Ⓒ Ⓓ Ⓔ
12. Ⓐ Ⓑ Ⓒ Ⓓ Ⓔ
13. Ⓐ Ⓑ Ⓒ Ⓓ Ⓔ
14. Ⓐ Ⓑ Ⓒ Ⓓ Ⓔ
15. Ⓐ Ⓑ Ⓒ Ⓓ Ⓔ
16. Ⓐ Ⓑ Ⓒ Ⓓ Ⓔ
17. Ⓐ Ⓑ Ⓒ Ⓓ Ⓔ
18. Ⓐ Ⓑ Ⓒ Ⓓ Ⓔ
19. Ⓐ Ⓑ Ⓒ Ⓓ Ⓔ
20. Ⓐ Ⓑ Ⓒ Ⓓ Ⓔ
21. Ⓐ Ⓑ Ⓒ Ⓓ Ⓔ
22. Ⓐ Ⓑ Ⓒ Ⓓ Ⓔ
23. Ⓐ Ⓑ Ⓒ Ⓓ Ⓔ
24. Ⓐ Ⓑ Ⓒ Ⓓ Ⓔ
25. Ⓐ Ⓑ Ⓒ Ⓓ Ⓔ
26. Ⓐ Ⓑ Ⓒ Ⓓ Ⓔ
27. Ⓐ Ⓑ Ⓒ Ⓓ Ⓔ
28. Ⓐ Ⓑ Ⓒ Ⓓ Ⓔ
29. Ⓐ Ⓑ Ⓒ Ⓓ Ⓔ
30. Ⓐ Ⓑ Ⓒ Ⓓ Ⓔ

31. Ⓐ Ⓑ Ⓒ Ⓓ Ⓔ
32. Ⓐ Ⓑ Ⓒ Ⓓ Ⓔ
33. Ⓐ Ⓑ Ⓒ Ⓓ Ⓔ
34. Ⓐ Ⓑ Ⓒ Ⓓ Ⓔ
35. Ⓐ Ⓑ Ⓒ Ⓓ Ⓔ
36. Ⓐ Ⓑ Ⓒ Ⓓ Ⓔ
37. Ⓐ Ⓑ Ⓒ Ⓓ Ⓔ
38. Ⓐ Ⓑ Ⓒ Ⓓ Ⓔ

### SECTION 2

1. Ⓐ Ⓑ Ⓒ Ⓓ Ⓔ
2. Ⓐ Ⓑ Ⓒ Ⓓ Ⓔ
3. Ⓐ Ⓑ Ⓒ Ⓓ Ⓔ
4. Ⓐ Ⓑ Ⓒ Ⓓ Ⓔ
5. Ⓐ Ⓑ Ⓒ Ⓓ Ⓔ
6. Ⓐ Ⓑ Ⓒ Ⓓ Ⓔ
7. Ⓐ Ⓑ Ⓒ Ⓓ Ⓔ
8. Ⓐ Ⓑ Ⓒ Ⓓ Ⓔ
9. Ⓐ Ⓑ Ⓒ Ⓓ Ⓔ
10. Ⓐ Ⓑ Ⓒ Ⓓ Ⓔ
11. Ⓐ Ⓑ Ⓒ Ⓓ Ⓔ
12. Ⓐ Ⓑ Ⓒ Ⓓ Ⓔ
13. Ⓐ Ⓑ Ⓒ Ⓓ Ⓔ
14. Ⓐ Ⓑ Ⓒ Ⓓ Ⓔ
15. Ⓐ Ⓑ Ⓒ Ⓓ Ⓔ
16. Ⓐ Ⓑ Ⓒ Ⓓ Ⓔ
17. Ⓐ Ⓑ Ⓒ Ⓓ Ⓔ
18. Ⓐ Ⓑ Ⓒ Ⓓ Ⓔ
19. Ⓐ Ⓑ Ⓒ Ⓓ Ⓔ
20. Ⓐ Ⓑ Ⓒ Ⓓ Ⓔ
21. Ⓐ Ⓑ Ⓒ Ⓓ Ⓔ

22. Ⓐ Ⓑ Ⓒ Ⓓ Ⓔ
23. Ⓐ Ⓑ Ⓒ Ⓓ Ⓔ
24. Ⓐ Ⓑ Ⓒ Ⓓ Ⓔ
25. Ⓐ Ⓑ Ⓒ Ⓓ Ⓔ
26. Ⓐ Ⓑ Ⓒ Ⓓ Ⓔ
27. Ⓐ Ⓑ Ⓒ Ⓓ Ⓔ
28. Ⓐ Ⓑ Ⓒ Ⓓ Ⓔ
29. Ⓐ Ⓑ Ⓒ Ⓓ Ⓔ
30. Ⓐ Ⓑ Ⓒ Ⓓ Ⓔ
31. Ⓐ Ⓑ Ⓒ Ⓓ Ⓔ
32. Ⓐ Ⓑ Ⓒ Ⓓ Ⓔ
33. Ⓐ Ⓑ Ⓒ Ⓓ Ⓔ
34. Ⓐ Ⓑ Ⓒ Ⓓ Ⓔ
35. Ⓐ Ⓑ Ⓒ Ⓓ Ⓔ
36. Ⓐ Ⓑ Ⓒ Ⓓ Ⓔ
37. Ⓐ Ⓑ Ⓒ Ⓓ Ⓔ
38. Ⓐ Ⓑ Ⓒ Ⓓ Ⓔ

### SECTION 3

1. Ⓐ Ⓑ Ⓒ Ⓓ Ⓔ
2. Ⓐ Ⓑ Ⓒ Ⓓ Ⓔ
3. Ⓐ Ⓑ Ⓒ Ⓓ Ⓔ
4. Ⓐ Ⓑ Ⓒ Ⓓ Ⓔ
5. Ⓐ Ⓑ Ⓒ Ⓓ Ⓔ
6. Ⓐ Ⓑ Ⓒ Ⓓ Ⓔ
7. Ⓐ Ⓑ Ⓒ Ⓓ Ⓔ
8. Ⓐ Ⓑ Ⓒ Ⓓ Ⓔ
9. Ⓐ Ⓑ Ⓒ Ⓓ Ⓔ
10. Ⓐ Ⓑ Ⓒ Ⓓ Ⓔ
11. Ⓐ Ⓑ Ⓒ Ⓓ Ⓔ
12. Ⓐ Ⓑ Ⓒ Ⓓ Ⓔ

# Answer Sheet

13. Ⓐ Ⓑ Ⓒ Ⓓ Ⓔ
14. Ⓐ Ⓑ Ⓒ Ⓓ Ⓔ
15. Ⓐ Ⓑ Ⓒ Ⓓ Ⓔ
16. Ⓐ Ⓑ Ⓒ Ⓓ Ⓔ
17. Ⓐ Ⓑ Ⓒ Ⓓ Ⓔ
18. Ⓐ Ⓑ Ⓒ Ⓓ Ⓔ
19. Ⓐ Ⓑ Ⓒ Ⓓ Ⓔ
20. Ⓐ Ⓑ Ⓒ Ⓓ Ⓔ
21. Ⓐ Ⓑ Ⓒ Ⓓ Ⓔ
22. Ⓐ Ⓑ Ⓒ Ⓓ Ⓔ
23. Ⓐ Ⓑ Ⓒ Ⓓ Ⓔ
24. Ⓐ Ⓑ Ⓒ Ⓓ Ⓔ
25. Ⓐ Ⓑ Ⓒ Ⓓ Ⓔ
26. Ⓐ Ⓑ Ⓒ Ⓓ Ⓔ
27. Ⓐ Ⓑ Ⓒ Ⓓ Ⓔ
28. Ⓐ Ⓑ Ⓒ Ⓓ Ⓔ
29. Ⓐ Ⓑ Ⓒ Ⓓ Ⓔ
30. Ⓐ Ⓑ Ⓒ Ⓓ Ⓔ

## SECTION 4

1. Ⓐ Ⓑ Ⓒ Ⓓ Ⓔ
2. Ⓐ Ⓑ Ⓒ Ⓓ Ⓔ
3. Ⓐ Ⓑ Ⓒ Ⓓ Ⓔ
4. Ⓐ Ⓑ Ⓒ Ⓓ Ⓔ
5. Ⓐ Ⓑ Ⓒ Ⓓ Ⓔ
6. Ⓐ Ⓑ Ⓒ Ⓓ Ⓔ
7. Ⓐ Ⓑ Ⓒ Ⓓ Ⓔ
8. Ⓐ Ⓑ Ⓒ Ⓓ Ⓔ
9. Ⓐ Ⓑ Ⓒ Ⓓ Ⓔ
10. Ⓐ Ⓑ Ⓒ Ⓓ Ⓔ
11. Ⓐ Ⓑ Ⓒ Ⓓ Ⓔ
12. Ⓐ Ⓑ Ⓒ Ⓓ Ⓔ
13. Ⓐ Ⓑ Ⓒ Ⓓ Ⓔ
14. Ⓐ Ⓑ Ⓒ Ⓓ Ⓔ
15. Ⓐ Ⓑ Ⓒ Ⓓ Ⓔ

16. Ⓐ Ⓑ Ⓒ Ⓓ Ⓔ
17. Ⓐ Ⓑ Ⓒ Ⓓ Ⓔ
18. Ⓐ Ⓑ Ⓒ Ⓓ Ⓔ
19. Ⓐ Ⓑ Ⓒ Ⓓ Ⓔ
20. Ⓐ Ⓑ Ⓒ Ⓓ Ⓔ
21. Ⓐ Ⓑ Ⓒ Ⓓ Ⓔ
22. Ⓐ Ⓑ Ⓒ Ⓓ Ⓔ
23. Ⓐ Ⓑ Ⓒ Ⓓ Ⓔ
24. Ⓐ Ⓑ Ⓒ Ⓓ Ⓔ
25. Ⓐ Ⓑ Ⓒ Ⓓ Ⓔ
26. Ⓐ Ⓑ Ⓒ Ⓓ Ⓔ
27. Ⓐ Ⓑ Ⓒ Ⓓ Ⓔ
28. Ⓐ Ⓑ Ⓒ Ⓓ Ⓔ
29. Ⓐ Ⓑ Ⓒ Ⓓ Ⓔ
30. Ⓐ Ⓑ Ⓒ Ⓓ Ⓔ

## SECTION 5

1. Ⓐ Ⓑ Ⓒ Ⓓ Ⓔ
2. Ⓐ Ⓑ Ⓒ Ⓓ Ⓔ
3. Ⓐ Ⓑ Ⓒ Ⓓ Ⓔ
4. Ⓐ Ⓑ Ⓒ Ⓓ Ⓔ
5. Ⓐ Ⓑ Ⓒ Ⓓ Ⓔ
6. Ⓐ Ⓑ Ⓒ Ⓓ Ⓔ
7. Ⓐ Ⓑ Ⓒ Ⓓ Ⓔ
8. Ⓐ Ⓑ Ⓒ Ⓓ Ⓔ
9. Ⓐ Ⓑ Ⓒ Ⓓ Ⓔ
10. Ⓐ Ⓑ Ⓒ Ⓓ Ⓔ
11. Ⓐ Ⓑ Ⓒ Ⓓ Ⓔ
12. Ⓐ Ⓑ Ⓒ Ⓓ Ⓔ
13. Ⓐ Ⓑ Ⓒ Ⓓ Ⓔ
14. Ⓐ Ⓑ Ⓒ Ⓓ Ⓔ
15. Ⓐ Ⓑ Ⓒ Ⓓ Ⓔ
16. Ⓐ Ⓑ Ⓒ Ⓓ Ⓔ
17. Ⓐ Ⓑ Ⓒ Ⓓ Ⓔ
18. Ⓐ Ⓑ Ⓒ Ⓓ Ⓔ

19. Ⓐ Ⓑ Ⓒ Ⓓ Ⓔ
20. Ⓐ Ⓑ Ⓒ Ⓓ Ⓔ
21. Ⓐ Ⓑ Ⓒ Ⓓ Ⓔ
22. Ⓐ Ⓑ Ⓒ Ⓓ Ⓔ
23. Ⓐ Ⓑ Ⓒ Ⓓ Ⓔ
24. Ⓐ Ⓑ Ⓒ Ⓓ Ⓔ
25. Ⓐ Ⓑ Ⓒ Ⓓ Ⓔ

## SECTION 6

1. Ⓐ Ⓑ Ⓒ Ⓓ Ⓔ
2. Ⓐ Ⓑ Ⓒ Ⓓ Ⓔ
3. Ⓐ Ⓑ Ⓒ Ⓓ Ⓔ
4. Ⓐ Ⓑ Ⓒ Ⓓ Ⓔ
5. Ⓐ Ⓑ Ⓒ Ⓓ Ⓔ
6. Ⓐ Ⓑ Ⓒ Ⓓ Ⓔ
7. Ⓐ Ⓑ Ⓒ Ⓓ Ⓔ
8. Ⓐ Ⓑ Ⓒ Ⓓ Ⓔ
9. Ⓐ Ⓑ Ⓒ Ⓓ Ⓔ
10. Ⓐ Ⓑ Ⓒ Ⓓ Ⓔ
11. Ⓐ Ⓑ Ⓒ Ⓓ Ⓔ
12. Ⓐ Ⓑ Ⓒ Ⓓ Ⓔ
13. Ⓐ Ⓑ Ⓒ Ⓓ Ⓔ
14. Ⓐ Ⓑ Ⓒ Ⓓ Ⓔ
15. Ⓐ Ⓑ Ⓒ Ⓓ Ⓔ
16. Ⓐ Ⓑ Ⓒ Ⓓ Ⓔ
17. Ⓐ Ⓑ Ⓒ Ⓓ Ⓔ
18. Ⓐ Ⓑ Ⓒ Ⓓ Ⓔ
19. Ⓐ Ⓑ Ⓒ Ⓓ Ⓔ
20. Ⓐ Ⓑ Ⓒ Ⓓ Ⓔ
21. Ⓐ Ⓑ Ⓒ Ⓓ Ⓔ
22. Ⓐ Ⓑ Ⓒ Ⓓ Ⓔ
23. Ⓐ Ⓑ Ⓒ Ⓓ Ⓔ
24. Ⓐ Ⓑ Ⓒ Ⓓ Ⓔ
25. Ⓐ Ⓑ Ⓒ Ⓓ Ⓔ

# TEST 5

## Section 1

**TIME:** 30 Minutes
38 Questions

**DIRECTIONS:** Each of the given sentences has blank spaces which indicate words omitted. Choose the best combination of words which fit into the meaning and structure within the context of the sentence.

1.  His life was described as a lonely bachelor life spent in caring for his property and in adding to it by _____ living.

    (A)  parsimonious

    (B)  exorbitant

    (C)  prodigal

    (D)  paltry

    (E)  prudent

2.  The taxi driver had lugged the parcel for the woman and then proving himself a _____ example of his species — had broken a ten dollar bill for her.

    (A)  singular

    (B)  amoral

    (C)  malfeasant

    (D)  subjugated

    (E)  officious

3.  Sophia thought that, after such a sin, the least Amy could do was to show _____ .

    (A)  callosity

    (B)  obduracy

    (C)  contrition

    (D)  trepidation

    (E)  phlegmacy

4. The direct, _____ influence of Protestantism has been to isolate and individualize man.

   (A) sensible

   (B) immediate

   (C) licentious

   (D) capitulated

   (E) obeisant

5. Considering the stages, treatment of the _____ of depression was begun; however, colleagues proposed to treat all aspects of the depression.

   (A) emergence

   (B) appearance

   (C) phases

   (D) symptoms

   (E) condition

6. Tempers were _____ and _____ in the fiery furnace of domestic tribulation.

   (A) pliant...malleable

   (B) spectacular...visible

   (C) tenacious...evanescent

   (D) aphonic...tumultuous

   (E) fulminating...mellifluence

7. "Fate went its way uncompromisingly to the end." This is the _____ of this interesting, dignified apology of one of Austria's Elder Statesmen.

   (A) leitmotiv

   (B) portraiture

   (C) roulade

   (D) theme

   (E) subject

**DIRECTIONS:** In the following questions, the given pair of words contains a specific relationship to each other. Select the best pair of the choices which expresses the same relationship as the given.

8. THEORY:SPECULATION::

   (A) deposition:refutation

   (B) hypothetical:absolute

   (C) diagnosis:obtuseness

   (D) supposition:surmise

   (E) feasibility:inconceivable

9. SERVICE:CHEVRON::

   (A) rank:coronet

   (B) decent:libertine

   (C) chaste:virtuous

   (D) lascivious:licentious

   (E) liturgics:atheism

10. TORQUE:JEWELRY::

    (A) debauch:wanton

    (B) virgin:original

    (C) affectation:sincerity

    (D) humanism:heterodoxy

    (E) procacity:comity

11. CUBISM:ART::

    (A) plant life:biology

    (B) jocund:amusement

    (C) Wall Street:Stock Exchange

    (D) plagiarist:mercature

    (E) sequester:urbanity

12. SPOONERISM:TRANSPOSITION::

    (A) Alpha:Omega

    (B) spree:carousal

    (C) stolid:agitation

    (D) colon:semicolon

    (E) stitch:clothing

608

13. LATENCY:EXPOSITION::

    (A) pleonasm:verbiage

    (B) indigent:poverty

    (C) argonaut:astronaut

    (D) indigested:structured

    (E) incoherence:immiscibility

14. QUADRANT:CIRCLE::

    (A) twenty-five:one hundred

    (B) diameter:circumference

    (C) triangle:hypotenuse

    (D) perpendicular:horizontal

    (E) radius:circumference

15. AGGRANDISE:AUGMENTATION::

    (A) declension:ascent

    (B) abatement:extenuation

    (C) adjunct:detruncate

    (D) increment:dilatation

    (E) vincture:segregation

16. PORIFERAN:SPONGES::

    (A) paladin:cause

    (B) pillory:ridicule

    (C) gulf:chasm

    (D) congratulate:felicitous

    (E) stalwart:invigorate

---

**DIRECTIONS**: Each passage is followed by questions based on its content. After reading the passage, choose the best answer to each question. Answer all questions based on what is stated or implied in that passage.

---

The torpedo is a self-propelled underwater weapon having either a high-explosive or a nuclear warhead. Conventional warheads are loaded with up to 1000 pounds of HBX explosive.

Underwater explosion of the torpedo warhead increases its destructive effect. When a projectile explodes, a part of its force is absorbed by the surrounding air. Upon explosion of the torpedo warhead, the water transfers almost the full force of the explosion to the hull of the target ship.

Fleet-type and Guppy submarines are fitted with 10 tubes, 6 in the bow and 4 in the stern. Spare torpedoes are carried in ready racks near the tubes. On war patrol, a submarine of this type usually puts to sea with a load of 28 torpedoes aboard.

Torpedoes are propelled by gas turbines or electric motors. Turbine types have maximum speeds of 30 to 45 knots, with a maximum effective range of as much as $7\frac{1}{2}$ miles. Electric torpedoes usually have less speed and range than turbine types, but from the submariners point of view, they have the advantage of leaving no visible wake.

17. The passage states that submarines can carry extra torpedoes in "ready racks" near the ten tubes. A Guppy putting to sea with a full load of conventional torpedoes would carry additional explosives on these racks weighing up to:

   (A)  1,800 pounds      (D)  18,000 pounds

   (B)  28,000 pounds     (E)  38,000 pounds

   (C)  56,000 pounds

18. The passage infers that gas turbined torpedoes are least preferred because:

   (A)  a visible wake is left behind.

   (B)  their speed and range exceed that of the electric torpedo.

   (C)  they are of less weight.

   (D)  no sound is created upon firing.

   (E)  destruction of the target is less than that caused by the electric torpedo.

610

19. The passage compares conventional warheads to nuclear warheads by stating that:

   (A) nuclear warheads are guided by electric turbines while conventional warheads are guided by gas turbines.

   (B) nuclear warheads have less weight than conventional warheads.

   (C) conventional warheads are less likely than nuclear warheads to destroy the smaller target.

   (D) the explosive force of both conventional and nuclear warheads is in part absorbed by air if exploded above the water.

   (E) nuclear warheads have a greater degree of accuracy when aimed at an underwater target than does the conventional warhead.

20. The passage suggests that although the torpedo is self-propelled, the function of the turbine is to:

   (A) give direction to the torpedo.

   (B) provide additional power and speed.

   (C) deliver the explosive without sound.

   (D) maintain a balanced weight and force for the Guppy.

   (E) inflict greater damage on a moving target.

Juan Ponce de Léon was the first Spaniard to touch the shores of the present United States. As Columbus had not remotely realized the extent of his momentous discovery, so de Léon never dreamed that his "island" of Florida was a peninsular extension of the vast North American Continent. After coming to the New World with Columbus in 1493, he had led the occupation of Puerto Rico in 1508 and governed it from 1509 to 1512. In 1509, he started a colony at Caparra, later abandoned in favor of San Juan. He was one of the first of the adelantados—men who "advanced" the Spanish Empire by conquest, subjugation of the Indians, and establishment of quasi-military government.

611

In 1513, the aging King Ferdinand awarded de Léon a patent to conquer and govern the Bimini Islands, in the Bahamas, of which the Spaniards had heard but not yet seen. According to a persistent legend, there de Léon would find the marvelous spring whose waters would restore lost youth and vigor. So many wonders had the Spaniards already encountered in the Western Hemisphere that only a cynic would have doubted the existence of such a spring.

In March 1513, de Léon sailed off confidently from Puerto Rico for the Bahamas. Landing briefly at San Salvador, Bahamas, he wound through uncharted islands until he sighted an extensive coastline. He had no reason to suspect that it was anything more than an island, but he followed the coast for a day without rounding its end or finding a suitable landing place. He named the "island" *La Florida,* probably because of the season—*Pascua Florida,* or the Easter festival of flowers. The name came to be applied by the Spanish to the entire present Southeastern United States and beyond.

Then near the 30th parallel, not far from the site of St. Augustine, de Léon landed at the mouth of the St. Johns River. Determined to be the first to circumnavigate the "island," he turned south, traced the coast around the tip of the peninsula, passed through the treacherous waters of the Florida Keys, and moved up the western coast, perhaps reaching Tampa Bay. After 7 weeks, he gave up hopes of circling the northern tip of his "island"; it was incredibly large—bigger even than Cuba—and he may have suspected that he had discovered the long sought mainland. If so, it all belonged to his King, for he had earlier planted the Spanish flag and claimed Florida and all lands contiguous to it for Ferdinand.

Of gold and restorative waters, de Léon had seen nothing; of hostile Indians, predecessors of the Seminoles, he had seen too much. Returning to Puerto Rico in September 1513, he reprovisioned and then spent the next 6 weeks back in the Bahamas fruitlessly searching for the fountain of youth. Before the year was out, he sailed for Spain empty-handed. Ferdinand rewarded him, however, with new patents to the "islands" of Bimini and Florida, but he was to bear the expense of conquest.

Not until 1521 was de Léon able to return to take possession of his grant. By that time, his search for the fountain of youth took on a more immediate importance—for he was 61 years of age. At large cost he

equipped 2 ships, enlisted 200 men, and set out to found a permanent base from which an exhaustive search could be conducted for the fabled fountain. Not only did he fail to find the fountain, but he also lost his life. Almost as soon as he landed on the western shore of Florida, probably near Tampa Bay, Indians attacked, killed scores of men, and mortally wounded de Léon himself. The expedition hastily retreated to Cuba, where the "valiant Lion," as his epitaph was to read, died.

21. According to the passage, Ponce de Léon believed the land he had discovered was:

    (A) part of the Bahamas.

    (B) the new island of Florida.

    (C) the mainland of the United States.

    (D) Cuba.

    (E) Puerto Rico.

22. Although Ponce de Léon was an explorer, the passage suggests that his main goal was to:

    (A) conquer and govern the Bimini Islands.

    (B) locate the fountain of youth.

    (C) circumnavigate Florida.

    (D) claim his royally awarded patents.

    (E) subdue the Seminole Indians.

23. Ponce de Léon was classified as an "adelantado" because he:

    (A) was a great explorer.

    (B) was the first Spaniard to see the shores of the United States.

    (C) was awarded patents by the king for the Bahamas and Florida.

    (D) conquered and ruled by military force.

    (E) claimed Florida for the king of Spain.

24. The statement "awarded de Léon a patent" is found in paragraph two. One can infer from the selection that "awarding a patent" means to:

    (A) recognize de Léon's inventions.

    (B) finance future explorations for de Léon.

    (C) give de Léon the indisputable right to explore, conquer and govern any land in the name of the king of Spain.

    (D) give de Léon the right to claim conquered lands for himself.

    (E) commission de Léon to further explore the Southeastern United States.

25. It is implied that de Léon's motivation for exploration was derived from:

    (A) receiving patents and grants.

    (B) his loyalty to the king of Spain.

    (C) his desire for the restorative waters.

    (D) his desire for gold.

    (E) his passion for conquest and military rule.

26. The passage suggests that de Léon's 1521 expedition resulted in:

    (A) an encounter with unfriendly natives.

    (B) his disappointment in not fulfilling his lifelong quest.

    (C) his discovery of restorative waters.

    (D) his having produced promising results for future explorers.

    (E) his having been mortally wounded in battle and his subsequent death.

27. Ponce de Léon advanced the Spanish Empire by conquests, subjugation of the original inhabitants, and military rule. The passage suggests:

   (A) Ponce de Léon was an explorer, soldier and government administrator.

   (B) his expeditions were followed by military forces.

   (C) his expeditions were comprised only of soldiers.

   (D) each explored location served as the point of departure for the next expedition.

   (E) Ponce de Léon was subject to no man although he claimed all discovered lands for his king.

---

**DIRECTIONS:** Each of the following questions provides a given word in capitalized letters followed by five word choices. Choose the best word which is most <u>opposite</u> in meaning to the given word.

---

28. CALORIC:

   (A) fervor

   (B) modicum

   (C) temperature

   (D) zero

   (E) frigidity

29. FLAVOR:

   (A) insipid

   (B) sentient

   (C) tactility

   (D) naris

   (E) taste

30. CACOPHONY:

   (A) linguistics

   (B) discord

   (C) raucous

   (D) concord

   (E) monody

31. ATAXIA:

   (A) destine

   (B) orgulous

   (C) hauteur

   (D) lucidity

   (E) ambiguity

32. SKEW:
    (A) slant
    (B) contraposition
    (C) convolution
    (D) obliquity
    (E) parallel

33. ACRIMONY:
    (A) pungency
    (B) insipid
    (C) acridity
    (D) mordancy
    (E) savoriness

34. RAUCOUS:
    (A) stridulation
    (B) percussion
    (C) susurrus
    (D) vociferation
    (E) ejaculation

35. SCINTILLATION:
    (A) gleam
    (B) lucidity
    (C) nimbus
    (D) tenebrific
    (E) obscuration

36. SPECTACLE:
    (A) phenomenon
    (B) perspective
    (C) ostentation
    (D) precarious
    (E) eclipse

37. OCCLUSION:
    (A) conduction
    (B) impediment
    (C) quiescence
    (D) preclusion
    (E) perforation

38. VELOCITY:
    (A) extricate
    (B) towage
    (C) languor
    (D) kinematics
    (E) circuition

## STOP

If time still remains, you may go
back and check your work.
When the time allotted is up, you
may go on to the next section.

# Section 2

**TIME:** 30 Minutes
38 Questions

**DIRECTIONS:** Each of the given sentences has blank spaces which indicate words omitted. Choose the best combination of words which fit into the meaning and structure within the context of the sentence.

1. The phenomenon called the "self-fulfilling prophecy" occurs when one holds and acts on a belief that is not true; for example, parents who believe a child is destined to turn out "no good" and treat the child as if he were no good, often have their fears realized: false _____ becomes _____ .

   (A) belief...reality

   (B) fear...truth

   (C) anxiety...fact

   (D) presumption...certain

   (E) dread...proven

2. Teenagers in part-time jobs today are relatively well-paid: _____ , workers in the fast-food segment of the workforce earn up to $5.00 per hour.

   (A) additionally

   (B) however

   (C) therefore

   (D) because

   (E) for example

3. Living out the _____ consequences of choices made, he realized the meager nature of his existence: his life was not to be so _____ as he had once assumed it would be.

   (A) surprising...intricate

   (B) unexpected...exciting

   (C) inevitable...full

   (D) boring...predictable

   (E) happy...unusual

4. Educators may be divided into two general groups based on their thinking in relation to prerequisites: the first group would set them high in order that time and money not be _____ expended; the second would set them low in order that those who might be able to benefit not be _____ .

   (A) pointlessly...tempted

   (B) wastefully...charged

   (C) carelessly...failed

   (D) unnecessarily...enrolled

   (E) needlessly...denied

5. The computer is a/an _____ tool, for if one neglects to save a file, it cannot be recalled.

   (A) ominous

   (B) complicated

   (C) essential

   (D) difficult

   (E) unforgiving

6. Those in power continue to enrich themselves at public expense and this with clear conscience, because they live by a legal rather than a moral ethic: An action is _____ provided there is no law specifically _____ it.

   (A) good...prohibiting

   (B) wrong...enforcing

   (C) ethical...stopping

   (D) unethical...legalizing

   (E) sound...allowing

7. I admire his ability; it's just his manner that I find _____ .

   (A) appealing

   (B) interesting

   (C) hard

   (D) lacking

   (E) compelling

DIRECTIONS: In the following questions, the given pair of words contains a specific relationship to each other. Select the best pair of the choices which expresses the same relationship as the given.

8.   GRASS:EROSION::

(A)  root:tree

(B)  air:tire

(C)  clouds:rain

(D)  dam:water

(E)  breeze:flag

9.   FACADE:BUILDING::

(A)  grill:car

(B)  tongue:shoe

(C)  sheath:knife

(D)  picture:frames

(E)  head:body

10.  SYMPHONY:FUGUE::

(A)  book:novel

(B)  diary:entry

(C)  essay:topic sentence

(D)  novel:short story

(E)  prologue:appendix

11.  SYCOPHANT:SINCERITY::

(A)  pedant:detail

(B)  skeptic:certitude

(C)  gambler:luck

(D)  mercenary:money

(E)  fugitive:flight

12.  GAZPACHO:SOUP::

(A)  wine:dinner

(B)  yeast:bread

(C)  paella:fish

(D)  bratwurst:sausage

(E)  sauce:spaghetti

13.  IGNORANT:KNOWLEDGE::

    (A)  fast:hungry         (D)  despair:hope

    (B)  old:antique         (E)  good:better

    (C)  syllable:word

14.  DIAPHANOUS:GAUZE::

    (A)  labyrinth:confusion     (D)  timbre:sound

    (B)  cement:gravel        (E)  metal:gold

    (C)  meter:prosody

15.  MARINATE:BEEF::

    (A)  visit:friend         (D)  swim:lap

    (B)  paste:wallpaper      (E)  eat:cake

    (C)  study:book

16.  LEGERDEMAIN:MAGICIAN::

    (A)  eyesight:gunslinger     (D)  oven:baker

    (B)  lecture:professor     (E)  peacoat:sailor

    (C)  chaps:cowboy

---

**DIRECTIONS:** Each passage is followed by questions based on its content. After reading the passage, choose the best answer to each question. Answer all questions based on what is stated or implied in that passage.

---

The atmosphere is the medium in which air pollutants are emitted and transported from the source to the receptor. Although this sounds simple on the surface, it is perhaps the most complex and least understood facet of air pollution. Many variables influence the character of a given chemical species from the time it leaves the source until

it reaches the receptor. A few examples will suffice to illustrate the complexity of the situation.

First, consider emission. Pollutants can be emitted from a point source such as a power plant, a line source such as a highway, or an area source such as a city or large industrial complex. The emission point may be close to the ground (e.g., the tailpipe of a car) or over a thousand feet in height (e.g., high stacks of a power plant). Thus, elevation alone has a tremendous influence on how rapidly the pollutant will be dispersed and diluted before it reaches a receptor. The relative size of the pollution source is an obvious variable. Time of emission is important because meteorological conditions vary throughout the day. The atmosphere is more stable at night, and less dilution occurs then. During the day, sunlight plays an important part in transforming the chemical species of pollutants.

Second, consider the transport phenomenon. Many attempts have been made to characterize the vertical and horizontal dispersion of pollution from point and line sources. Many mathematical equations and models have been developed. Each has deficiencies because of the variability of sources, source strength, topography, and other factors. From the receptor standpoint, this is the important phase because, if the pollutants are not adequately dispersed and diluted, atmospheric insults will occur.

There are many factors to consider and it should be kept in mind that a nearby source does not necessarily imply that damage will result.

17. The author discussed several variables that affect the transporting of pollutants. Which of the following is not a variable mentioned by the author:

(A) relative size of the pollution source

(B) daytime

(C) elevation

(D) atmosphere

(E) nighttime

18. Which of the following best states the author's main point:

(A) The atmosphere is the medium in which air pollutants are emitted and transported.

(B) Scientists have a high degree of accuracy when calculating the pollutant dispersion.

(C) A nearby pollutant source may be an indication that change will result.

(D) There are many alternatives that influence the character of pollutants.

(E) Both highway emission and large complex emission are the largest sources of atmospheric pollutants.

19. The author mentions "vertical and horizontal dispersion of pollution from point to line source" because:

(A) there must be a horizontal movement as well as a vertical movement before there can be atmospheric and vegetation damage.

(B) there are deficiencies in the mathematical formulas because of the variabilities of sources, source strength, topography and other factors.

(C) if the pollutants are not adequately dispersed and diluted, atmospheric insults will occur.

(D) although it may sound simple on the surface, it is perhaps the most complex and least understood facet of air pollution.

(E) there are many factors to consider and vertical and horizontal dispersion are the most important.

The two-man crosscut saw was evidently known by the Romans though little used by them. It was not until the middle of the 15th century that the crosscut saw came into fairly common use in Europe. Records exist of the crosscut being used for cutting logs in the United States between 1635 and 1681. About 1880, Pennsylvania lumbermen began felling trees with the crosscut. Before that time all trees had been

ax-felled and crosscut into lengths.

Until the 15th century, the two-man crosscut saw was of a plain tooth pattern. The M tooth pattern seems to have been developed and used in south Germany in the 1400s. Even as late as 1900 most of the European crosscuts still used the plain tooth pattern with a few exceptions of M tooth being used. Not until fairly recently was the saw with a raker or "drag" developed.

In the case of plain, M, and Great American tooth patterns, each tooth both cuts the wood and clears out the shavings. In the case of the champion, lance, and perforated lance tooth, however, cutter teeth cut the wood fibers and the rakers remove the scored wood from the cut.

By the time crosscut use was at its peak, a large number of tooth patterns had been developed, each presumably suited to a particular set of conditions.

Saws can be divided into two types: two-man and one-man. Generally speaking, a one-man saw is shorter, but its defining characteristic is that it is asymmetric. Both one- and two-man crosscuts can be used by either one or two persons.

At one time, one-man crosscuts were made in lengths from 3 to 6 feet. Two-man saws were made in lengths from 4 to 12 feet for the Pacific Northwest, and 16 feet for the California redwoods. If a longer saw were needed, two shorter saws were sometimes brazed together.

There are two basic saw patterns for the two-man saw: the felling pattern for felling trees and the bucking pattern for cutting up trees once they are on the ground. Each has characteristics suited to its use.

The felling saw has a concave back and is relatively light and flexible. It is light so less effort is needed to move it back and forth when felling a tree. It is flexible to conform to the arc a sawyer's arms take when sawing, and it is narrow tooth-to-back enabling the sawyer to place a wedge in the cut behind the saw sooner than with a wide saw.

The bucking saw has a straight back; it is much thicker tooth-to-back than the felling saw, so it is heavier and stiffer. A bucking saw traditionally is run by one person, so it is a fairly stiff saw to help prevent buckling on the push stroke. The more weight put on a saw, the faster it will cut, so the weight of a bucking saw is an asset.

20. The author refers to asymmetric in order to:

    (A) inform the reader that both the one-man and two-man crosscut saws can be used by either one or two persons.

    (B) reveal that there are different lengths of crosscut saws.

    (C) introduce the two saw patterns for the two-man saw.

    (D) define the basic characteristic of the shorter one-man crosscut saw.

    (E) describe the large tooth, small tooth formation.

21. After reading the selection, the title that best fits is:

    (A) The Crosscut Saw and the American Development

    (B) The Crosscut Saw and the Development of the Lumber Industry

    (C) The Crosscut Saw, A European Gift

    (D) The Crosscut Saw, A European Development

    (E) The Crosscut Saw

22. The author mentions plain, champion and lance as examples of:

    (A) tooth formation in crosscut saws.

    (B) types of crosscut saws.

    (C) generations of crosscut saws.

    (D) crosscut saw improvements developed in Germany.

    (E) crosscut saw improvements developed in America.

23. From the comments about the Romans and the crosscut saw, it can be concluded:

    (A) the felling saw was used more widely by the Romans because of the additional slavepower needed to run it.

    (B) the Romans spread its use throughout Europe.

(C)   the Romans introduced the perforated lance tooth.

(D)   the Romans made little use of the saw.

(E)   at the end of the Roman Empire, a number of tooth patterns had been developed.

24.   From the author's description of the bucking saw, it can be inferred that the saw:

(A)   has the lance tooth pattern.

(B)   is from four to twelve feet long.

(C)   was introduced to America from Germany.

(D)   was perfected on the European continent.

(E)   is traditionally a two-man saw.

25.   According to the author there are two basic patterns for the two-man saw, one saw has a concave back and is light and flexible:

(A)   to conform to the arc a sawyer's arms take when sawing.

(B)   and is traditionally operated by one person which makes it easier to saw through large trees.

(C)   and the more weight put on the saw the faster it will cut.

(D)   since the large number of teeth cleans the cut of shavings.

(E)   with a champion tooth pattern.

26. The crosscut saw has several tooth patterns, but the "M" tooth pattern was introduced first in:

(A)   Rome                     (D)   Germany

(B)   United States            (E)   France

(C)   England

27. According to the selection, all of the following are true of the crosscut saw except:

    (A) it was not until the late nineteenth century that the crosscut saw was used to fell trees.

    (B) the "M" tooth pattern was developed in Europe in the fifteenth century.

    (C) generally the longer crosscut saws, those of sixteen feet, were developed for thick forests in the Pacific Northwest.

    (D) the two basic two-man crosscut patterns are the felling saw and the bucking saw.

    (E) the Great American tooth pattern is designed so each tooth both cuts the wood and clears out the shaving.

---

**DIRECTIONS:** Each of the following questions provides a given word in capitalized letters followed by five word choices. Choose the best word which is most opposite in meaning to the given word.

---

28. REPULSIVE:

    (A) elegant

    (B) beauteous

    (C) alluring

    (D) pleasant

    (E) amicable

30. FACTIOUS:

    (A) convoluted

    (B) cooperative

    (C) curved

    (D) cunning

    (E) cowardly

29. DISSEMBLE:

    (A) betray

    (B) put together

    (C) resemble

    (D) agree

    (E) resolve

31. CALCULATING:

    (A) rash

    (B) daring

    (C) risky

    (D) quixotic

    (E) wild

32. INFAMOUS:

 (A) idolized

 (B) ignominious

 (C) unknown

 (D) illustrious

 (E) gracious

33. CALAMITY:

 (A) favor

 (B) advantage

 (C) value

 (D) benefit

 (E) boon

34. ALLEVIATE:

 (A) intensify

 (B) interfere

 (C) irritate

 (D) aggravate

 (E) obviate

35. CONSUMMATE:

 (A) perfect

 (B) hungry

 (C) unsuccessful

 (D) crude

 (E) complete

36. CENSURE:

 (A) court

 (B) accept

 (C) flatter

 (D) adulate

 (E) commend

37. BEMOAN:

 (A) laugh

 (B) exult

 (C) commiserate

 (D) acclaim

 (E) eulogize

38. MELANCHOLY

 (A) sociability

 (B) serenity

 (C) complacency

 (D) impulsiveness

 (E) exhilaration

## STOP

If time still remains, you may go
back and check your work.
When the time allotted is up, you
may go on to the next section.

# Section 3

**TIME:** 30 Minutes
30 Questions

**NUMBERS:** All numbers are real numbers.

**FIGURES:** Position of points, angles, regions, etc. are assumed to be in the order shown and angle measures are assumed to be positive.

**LINES:** Assume that lines shown as straight are indeed straight.

**DIRECTIONS:** Each of the following given set of quantities is placed into either column A or B. Compare the two quantities to decide whether:

(A)   the quantity in Column A is greater

(B)   the quantity in Column B is greater

(C)   the two quantities are equal

(D)   the relationship cannot be determined from the information given.

**NOTE:** Do not choose (E) since there are only four choices.

**COMMON INFORMATION:** Information which relates to one or both given quantities is centered in the two columns. A symbol which appears in both columns will indicate the same item in Column A and Column B.

**EXAMPLES:**

|  | Column A | Column B |
|---|---|---|
| 1. | $5 \times 4$ | $5 + 4$ |

Explanation: The correct answer is (A), since $5 \times 4 = 20$, and $5 + 4 = 9$.

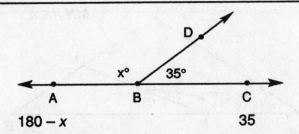

2.        $180 - x$                          35

Explanation: The correct answer is (C). Since Angle *ABC* is a straight angle, its measurement is 180°.

| Column A | Column B |
|---|---|
| 1.  The difference between $a + b$ and $a - b$ | $b$ |

*ABCD* and *A′B′C′D′* are squares of side $a$

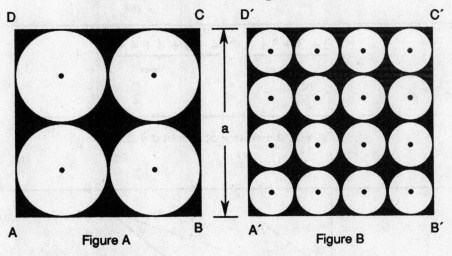

Figure A                     Figure B

2.   Shaded area of Figure A.        Shaded area of Figure B.

Worker A completed a job in 10 days, worker B in 8 days and worker $C$ in 5 days.

3.   Time that it takes A and          Time that it takes worker C
     B together

| <u>Column A</u> | <u>Column B</u> |
|---|---|

$MN \parallel CA$

**4.**      $x + y$            $180°$

---

$$x < 0$$
$$y < 0$$

**5.**      $x - y$            $0$

---

$$n = p^2, \; p > 1$$

**6.**      $n$            $p$

---

$$\underbrace{3 + 3 + 3 + ...}_{m \text{ times}} > \underbrace{4 + 4 + 4 + 4 + ...}_{p \text{ times}}$$

**7.**      $\dfrac{m}{p}$            $2$

---

$$a + 1; \; a + 4; \; a + 3; \; a + 6; \; a + 5; \; 10$$

**8.**      $a$            $2$

---

**9.**      $\alpha$            $30°$

| Column A | Column B |
|----------|----------|

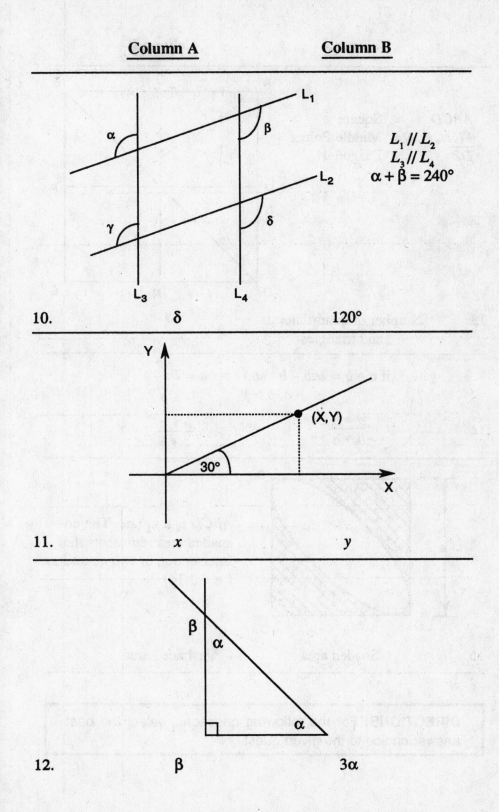

$L_1 \mathbin{//} L_2$
$L_3 \mathbin{//} L_4$
$\alpha + \beta = 240°$

| | |
|---|---|
| **10.** $\delta$ | 120° |

| | |
|---|---|
| **11.** $x$ | $y$ |

| | |
|---|---|
| **12.** $\beta$ | $3\alpha$ |

| Column A | Column B |
|---|---|

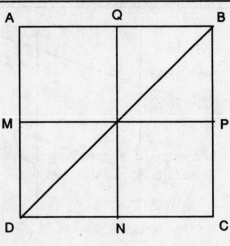

$ABCD$ = Square
$M, N, P, Q$ = Middle Points
$\overline{DB}$ = Diagonal

**13.** Number of quadrilaterals and triangles    |    17

---

if $a * b = 2ab - b$  and  $b * a = 2a - 1$
$a, b > 1$

**14.** $\dfrac{a * b}{b * a}$    |    $\dfrac{b * a}{a * b}$

---

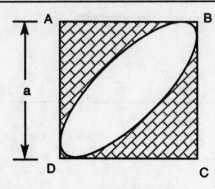

$ABCD$ is a square. The un-shaded area represents the intersection of two quadrants. ($\pi = 3.14$)

**15.** Shaded area    |    Unshaded area

---

**DIRECTIONS:** For the following questions, select the best answer choice to the given question.

16. One wall has 40% of the total bricks needed. If we need 1200 more bricks to complete the wall, how many bricks will the wall have?

    (A) 1500

    (B) 1800

    (C) 2000

    (D) 2400

    (E) 3000

17. In a group of 30 people the average height is 6 ft and 2 inches. Therefore we can assume that:

    I.   Everyone is 6 ft and 2 inches

    II.  Most of the people are 6 ft and 2 inches

    III. Not all could be taller than 6 ft and 2 inches

    (A) Only I

    (B) Only II

    (C) Only III

    (D) I and II

    (E) I, II, and III

18. If $^a/_x - ^b/_y = c$ and $xy = ^1/_c$, then $bx = ?$

    (A) $1 - ay$

    (B) $ay$

    (C) $ay + 1$

    (D) $ay - 1$

    (E) $2ay$

19. In which of the following alternatives can we simplify $a$ without changing the expression?

    (A) $\dfrac{x/a}{a/x}$

    (B) $\dfrac{x + a}{x - a}$

    (C) $\dfrac{ax - a}{a}$

    (D) $\dfrac{x^a}{2^a}$

    (E) $ax + a$

20. Which of the following numbers is the smallest?

(A) $-.6$

(D) $^{-666}/_{1000}$

(B) $-.66$

(E) $^{-3}/_5$

(C) $^{-2}/_3$

Questions 21 – 25.
Adapted from *Scholastic Update*, 5/5/89. Vol. 121, N. 17.

## TWO GIANTS

|  | China | Soviet Union |
| --- | --- | --- |
| Area (sq. mi) | 3.7 million | 8.7 million |
| Population | 1.1 billion | 289 million |
| Percentage Under 15 | 39% (1960) | 31% (1960) |
|  | 25% (1990) | 25% (1990) |
| Percent Who Live in Cities | 19% (1960) | 49% (1960) |
|  | 21% (1990) | 68% (1990) |
| Life Expectancy | 60 (1970) | 70 (1970) |
|  | 69 (1990) | 72 (1990) |
| Infant Mortality | 81 (1970) | 26 (1970) |
| (deaths per 1000 births) | 32 (1990) | 22 (1990) |
| Birth Rate | 37 (1970) | 18 (1970) |
| (births per 1000 pop.) | 18 (1990) | 18 (1990) |
| Citizens per Doctor | 1,757 | 267 |
| Students (Ages 9-15) per teacher | 42 | 25 |
| Literacy | 70% | 99% |
| Gross National Product (GNP) | $315 billion | $2 trillion |
| Percent of GNP to Military | 7% | 11.5% |
| Exports to U.S. | $9.3 billion | $470 million |
| Imports from U.S. | $5.03 billion | $1.5 billion |

21. What is the annual per capita income in China (approximately)?

(A) $2,864

(D) $3,000

(B) $286.4

(E) $315

(C) $300

22. How many persons are older than 15 years old in China (1990)?

    (A) 825 million

    (B) 8.25 billion

    (C) .0825 billion

    (D) 671 million

    (E) 216.75 million

23. How many new borns will die in the Soviet Union (1990)?

    (A) 11,444

    (B) 114,000

    (C) 1,144,444

    (D) cannot be determined

    (E) 114,444

24. What is the ratio of doctors between Soviet Union and China respectively? (approximately)

    (A) .578

    (B) 1.729

    (C) .152

    (D) 6.58

    (E) .263

25. What is the population density of the Soviet Union and China respectively (people/sq. mi.)?

    (A) 33.2 and 297.3

    (B) 297.3 and 33.2

    (C) .03 and .003

    (D) 289 and 1,100

    (E) 1,100 and 289

26. $\dfrac{2^{-4} + 2^{-1}}{2^{-3}}$

    (A) $9/2^7$

    (B) $9/2^{-1}$

    (C) $1/2$

    (D) $2^{-3}$

    (E) $9/2$

27. $\dfrac{1-\frac{1}{1-x}}{1-\frac{1}{1-\frac{1}{x}}} = ?$

 (A) $x$

 (B) $1/x$

 (C) $-1/x$

 (D) $-x$

 (E) $1$

28. In College Bookstore $a + b$ books are selling for $1,000. Myron buys 12 books and for each one has a discount of $1. How much does Myron need to pay?

 (A) $[(a + b) - 1] \times 12$

 (B) $[(a + b)/1000 - 1] \times 12$

 (C) $[(1000/(a + b)) - 1] \times 12$

 (D) $[a + b] \times 12$

 (E) $(a + b)$

29. If $x : y = 1 : 2$ and $y : z = 2 : 3$

 I. $x : y : z = 1 : 2 : 3$

 II. $x : z = 2 : 6$

 III. $x/_y : y/_z = 3 : 4$

 (A) Only I

 (B) Only II

 (C) Only III

 (D) I and II

 (E) I, II, and III

30. What is the value of $x$?

 (A) 20°

 (B) 40°

 (C) 60°

 (D) 90°

 (E) 30°

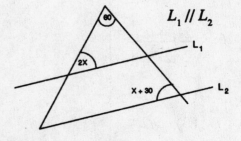

$L_1 // L_2$

## STOP
If time still remains, you may go back and check your work.
When the time allotted is up, you may go on to the next section.

# Section 4

**TIME:**    30 Minutes
              30 Questions

**NUMBERS:** All numbers are real numbers.

**FIGURES:** Position of points, angles, regions, etc. are assumed to be in the order shown and angle measures are assumed to be positive.

**LINES:** Assume that lines shown as straight are indeed straight.

**DIRECTIONS:** Each of the following given set of quantities is placed into either column A or B. Compare the two quantities to decide whether:

(A)   the quantity in Column A is greater

(B)   the quantity in Column B is greater

(C)   the two quantities are equal

(D)   the relationship cannot be determined from the information given.

**NOTE:** Do not choose (E) since there are only four choices.

**COMMON INFORMATION:** Information which relates to one or both given quantities is centered in the two columns. A symbol which appears in both columns will indicate the same item in Column A and Column B.

**EXAMPLES:**

| Column A | Column B |
|----------|----------|
| 1.          $5 \times 4$ |    $5 + 4$ |

Explanation: The correct answer is (A), since $5 \times 4 = 20$, and $5 + 4 = 9$.

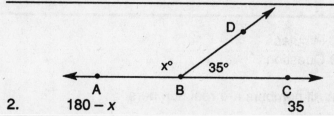

2.     $180 - x$                              $35$

Explanation: The correct answer is (C). Since Angle *ABC* is a straight angle, its measurement is 180°.

| Column A | Column B |
|----------|----------|

1.       5% of 45 is x                    45 is 5% of $x$

2.    Area of a circle:                Area of a rectangle:
      diameter 16                      length, 64, width $\pi$

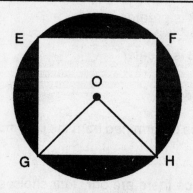

Square *EFGH* is inscribed in circle $GO \perp OH$. Area of triangle $GOH = 12.5$

3.    Area of shaded part of figure              $9\pi$

$x$ is not equal to 0

4.                    $\dfrac{1}{x}$                              $x$

$x > 1$

5.            $\dfrac{1}{\dfrac{1}{x(x)}}$          $\dfrac{\dfrac{1}{x(x-1)}}{\dfrac{x}{x-1}}$

|  | Column A | Column B |
|---|---|---|
| 6. | $(^5/_9)^2$ | $(^9/_5)^{-2}$ |

$$x > 0, y > 0$$

|  | Column A | Column B |
|---|---|---|
| 7. | $\sqrt{\dfrac{y}{2}}\sqrt{\dfrac{2y}{x}}$ | $\dfrac{y\sqrt{x}}{x}$ |

|  | Column A | Column B |
|---|---|---|
| 8. | $x$ | $y$ |

$$2, 5, 11, x, 47, 95, \ldots$$

|  | Column A | Column B |
|---|---|---|
| 9. | $x$ | $(11 + 47)/2$ |

|  | Column A | Column B |
|---|---|---|
| 10. | $\dfrac{2x - \frac{y-5}{6}}{\frac{y-5}{3} - 4x}$ | $-0.5$ |

| 11. | The area of a circle with radius $x$ | The circumference of a circle with radius $x$ |
|---|---|---|

$$x > y$$

|  | Column A | Column B |
|---|---|---|
| 12. | $|x|$ | $|y|$ |

$$x > 1$$

|  | Column A | Column B |
|---|---|---|
| 13. | $(\sqrt{x})^{-2}$ | $x^{-2}$ |

|     | Column A | Column B |
| --- | --- | --- |
| 14. | 15% of 12 | 12% of 15 |
| 15. | $x$ in $x^2 - 10x + 21 = 0$ | $y$ in $y^2 + 10x + 21 = 0$ |

**DIRECTIONS:** For the following questions, select the best answer choice to the given question.

16. Which of the following has the smallest value?

(A) $^1/_{0.2}$

(B) $^{0.1}/_2$

(C) $^{0.2}/_1$

(D) $^{0.2}/_{0.1}$

(E) $^2/_{0.1}$

17. A square is inscribed in a circle of area $18\pi$. What is the length of a side of the square?

(A) 6

(B) 3

(C) $3\sqrt{2}$

(D) $6\sqrt{2}$

(E) Cannot be determined

18. If the triangle $ABC$ has angle $A = 35°$ and angle $B = 85°$, then the measure of the angle $x$ in degrees is:

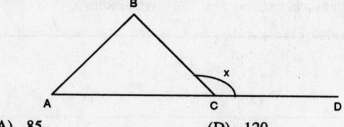

(A) 85

(B) 90

(C) 100

(D) 120

(E) 180

Questions 19 – 20 refer to the following table:

### Payroll Summary of R.S.E.T.T. Company, 1989

| Position Title | Number in Position | Total Amount Paid to Employees in the Position |
|---|---|---|
| Vice President/Manager | 5 | $ 110,000 |
| Team Leader/Coordinator | 25 | 350,000 |
| Assembly Line Worker | 500 | 600,000 |
| Total | 530 | $1,060,000 |

19. What is the ratio of wages earned by a vice president/manager to the wages earned by an assembly line worker?

    (A)  60 to 11          (D)  55 to 3

    (B)  11 to 6           (E)  None of these

    (C)  10 to 6

20. What percent (to the nearest tenth) make up the wages paid to the vice presidents/managers?

    (A)  5.2              (D)  11.4

    (B)  9.5              (E)  42

    (C)  10.4

Questions 21– 22 refer to the following table:

### Table of Weight Distribution of a 70,000-Gram Man
### (Weights of some organs given)

| Organ | Wgt in Grams | Organ | Wgt in Grams |
|---|---|---|---|
| Skeleton | 10,000 | Muscles | 30,000 |
| Blood | 5,000 | Intestinal tract | 2,000 |
| Liver | 1,700 | Lungs | 1,000 |
| Brain | 1,500 | | |

21. If 40 percent of the weight of the blood is made up of cells, what percent (to the nearest tenth) of the total body weight is made up of blood cells?

(A) 7.1

(D) 2.8

(B) 3.6

(E) 9.9

(C) 1.4

22. Which expression represents the total body weight if the weight of the skeleton is represented by $S$ grams?

(A) $7S$

(D) $S + 6$

(B) $70000S$

(E) Cannot be determined

(D) $60s$

Question 23 refers to the following table:

|  | % Cholesterol | % Fat | % Carbohydrates |
|---|---|---|---|
| Food A | 10 | 20 | 30 |
| Food B | 20 | 15 | 10 |
| Food C | 20 | 10 | 40 |

23. Which of the following diets would supply the most grams of cholesterol?

(A) 500 grams of A

(B) 250 grams of B

(C) 150 grams of A and 200 grams of B

(D) 200 grams of B and 200 grams of C

(E) 350 grams of C

24. Jay and his brother Ray own a janitorial service. Jay can do a cleaning job alone in 5 hours and Ray can do the same job in 4 hours. How long will it take them to do the cleaning job together?

(A)  5 hours

(B)  1 hour

(C)  4 hours

(D)  $2\,{}^{2}/_{9}$ hours

(E)  $4\,{}^{1}/_{2}$ hours

25. The length of a rectangle is $6L$ and the width is $4W$. What is the perimeter?

(A)  $12L + 8W$

(B)  $12L^{2} + 8W^{2}$

(C)  $6L + 4W$

(D)  $20\,LW$

(E)  $24\,LW$

26. Three times the first of three consecutive odd integers is three more than twice the third. What is the second of the three consecutive odd integers?

(A)  7

(B)  9

(C)  11

(D)  13

(E)  15

27. A fraction has a value of ${}^{2}/_{5}$. If the numerator is decreased by 2 and denominator increased by 1, then the resulting fraction is ${}^{1}/_{4}$. What is the value of the numerator of the original fraction?

(A)  2

(B)  3

(C)  4

(D)  5

(E)  6

28. What is the smallest positive number that leaves a remainder of 2 when the number is divided by 3, 4 or 5?

    (A) 22

    (B) 42

    (C) 62

    (D) 122

    (E) 182

29. Suppose the average of two numbers is $WX$. If the first number is $X$, what is the other number?

    (A) $WX - X$

    (B) $2WX - W$

    (C) $W$

    (D) $WX - 2X$

    (E) $2WX - X$

30. The sum of three consecutive odd integers is always divisible by (I) 2, (II) 3, (III) 5, or (IV) 6.

    (A) I only

    (B) II only

    (C) III only

    (D) I and III only

    (E) IV only

## STOP

If time still remains, you may go back and check your work.
When the time allotted is up, you may go on to the next section.

# Section 5

TIME: 30 Minutes
25 Questions

DIRECTIONS: Each question or group of questions is based on a passage or set of statements. Select the best answer choice.

Questions 1-4 refer to the following information.

Five children, A, B, C, D and E attend nursery school. There are 5 different play activities, 1, 2, 3, 4, and 5. All children will engage in 4 or more activities each day and must spend at least 20 minutes on any one activity once they begin it. No more than 3 children can be at any one activity at the same time. A and B cannot play together. C and D must always play together. The children are at school from 9 a.m. to 12 noon and take a 30 minute rest from 10:15 to 10:45 daily.

1.  Which of the following schedules would allow an appropriate assignment for D to be made?

    (A)  Activity 1 (9-9:30) A, C, D, E

    (B)  Activity 1 (9-9:30) A, C, E

    (C)  Activity 1 (10-10:30) A, C, D

    (D)  Activity 1 (9-9:30) B, E

    (E)  Activity 1 (9-9:30) A, B, C

2.  What is the maximum amount of time any child could spend on any single activity?

    (A)  50 minutes          (D)  80 minutes

    (B)  60 minutes          (E)  90 minutes

    (C)  70 minutes

645

3. Which of the following groupings conforms to the conditions for organizing the children into activities during the period from 11:00 – 11:30?

    (A)   A, B, and C – Activity 5; D and E Activity – 4

    (B)   A, C, D, and E – Activity 4; B – Activity 3

    (C)   A and C – Activity 2; B, D, and E – Activity 3

    (D)   A, C, and D – Activity 2; B and E – Activity 1

    (E)   B, C, and E – Activity 4; A and D – Activity 2

4. Which of the following groupings conforms to the requirements for grouping the students?

    (A)   A, B, C                    (D)   A, D, E

    (B)   A, C, D                    (E)   A, C, D, E

    (C)   A, C, E

You have been provided a string that is 31.4 inches long. Your assignment is to form the string into an enclosed geometric shape that will create the largest area within the sides of the figure you create. Questions 5 – 8 are based on this information.

5. Which of the following geometric shapes will include the largest area?

    (A)   Triangle                  (D)   Hexagon

    (B)   Square                    (E)   Rectangle

    (C)   Circle

6. If the string is formed into a circle, what is the approximate radius of the circle?

    (A)   10 inches                 (D)   16.7 inches

    (B)   5 inches                  (E)   12.5 inches

    (C)   7.5 inches

7. If the length of the string is doubled and formed into a square, how much larger area would be enclosed than if a square was formed with the original length of 31.4 inches?

   (A) The area would double.

   (B) The area would triple.

   (C) The area would quadruple.

   (D) The area would be eight times larger.

   (E) The area would be six times as large.

8. If the string was formed into an equilateral triangle, approximately how many square inches would be enclosed in the area of the triangle?

   (A) 35          (D) 50

   (B) 40          (E) 55

   (C) 45

Questions 9-11 refer to the following passage.

In a class on microcomputers, 31 students enrolled and only 25 stations were available in the class. The instructor grouped the class into 4 sub-groups of 6 students and 1 group of 7 students. This would allow 6 students to share five computers in 4 of the groups (groups A, B, C, and D) and 7 students to share 5 computers in 1 group (Group E). Student numbers from 1 to 31 were assigned and the groups were organized according to these numbers. Group A included students 1 – 6; Group B included students 7 – 12 and so forth. Within each group a rotation plan was set up so that at each session different students shared a computer.

9. During a semester with 15 class meetings, how many times would student 1 share a computer with another student?

   (A) 2          (D) 5

   (B) 3          (E) 6

   (C) 4

10. During a semester with 15 class meetings, what is the highest number of class meetings that student 29 would work alone on his computer?

(A)  8                      (D)  11

(B)  9                      (E)  12

(C)  10

11. What is the least number of times any student would be assigned to work alone on his/her computer?

(A)  6                      (D)  9

(B)  7                      (E)  10

(C)  8

Questions 12-16 refer to the following passage.

A pendulum swings back and forth (1 cycle) every 30 seconds over a circular plate. The numbers, 1 to 10, are positioned clockwise around the edge of the plate every 36 degrees. The six letters, A to F are positioned clockwise every 60 degrees and the A and 1 are in the same position. The plate rotates clockwise once every 45 seconds. The pendulum begins swinging directly over the position occupied by 1 and A at the same instant the plate begins to rotate. The rotation of the plate and the swinging of the pendulum are both constant. Questions 12 – 16 are based on this information.

12. After 15 seconds, the pendulum will be directly over:

(A)  A                      (D)  D

(B)  B                      (E)  E

(C)  C

13. How many cycles will the pendulum swing (after the initial position) before it is directly over A and 1 again?

(A)  3                      (D)  7

(B)  4                      (E)  8

(C)  5

14. After the pendulum swings one cycle, what letter or number will it be above?

(A)  3

(B)  C

(C)  4

(D)  B

(E)  5

15. After the plate completes one rotation, where will the pendulum be in relation to the plate?

(A)  Over the center of the plate

(B)  Over the C

(C)  Over the number 8

(D)  Over the F

(E)  Over the D and number 6

16. How many cycles will the pendulum swing before it is directly over the letter F?

(A)  1

(B)  $1^1/_2$

(C)  2

(D)  $2^1/_2$

(E)  3

17. Some parents are convinced that private schools are superior to public schools. They argue that children in private schools receive more attention, that they have classmates with higher average ability, and that teachers care more about individual children. Which of the following, if true would most emphatically weaken the arguments listed above?

(A)  Public schools can usually pay teachers more than private schools can pay.

(B)  The facilities in public schools are more complete.

(C)  Public schools enroll a more diverse student population but each is taught to his/her own level.

649

(D) Students in public school with similar entry potential to those in private schools achieve as well as their private school counterparts in college and employment.

(E) Private schools deny admission to some of the students who enroll in public schools and add cultural diversity that helps public school students adjust better to society.

18. To think freely about an issue or event one must have the knowledge and information required to be in command of the important facts and the background to interpret those facts. Ignorance makes us "unfree." One crucial source of information in the United States is the Press. However, newspapers sometimes report different "facts" and diverse views. Our belief or trust in a given newspaper furthers our freedom because we are confident the information they provide is reliable. If we don't believe the information in a given newspaper, we are not truly free to decide. Thus, those who control the Press can control our minds. That is why a controlled Press is an obstacle to democracy.

Which of the following statements is the most defensible conclusion to draw about a newspaper (newspaper X) with a reputation for accuracy, integrity, and forthrightness?

(A) People who subscribe to newspaper X will be better informed.

(B) People who read newspaper X will cast more intelligent votes.

(C) Newspaper X has disproportionate power to influence opinion.

(D) Newspaper X probably makes a positive contribution to the political process.

(E) Newspaper X probably abuses its power.

19. Which of the following statements most nearly characterizes a newspaper (newspaper Y) whose reports are biased, lacking documentation, and often inaccurate?

(A) Newspaper Y will likely be popular because people seek exaggeration in the news.

(B) People who subscribe to newspaper Y receive only a distorted view of the news.

(C) The editors of newspaper Y underestimate the intelligence of the American people.

(D) Those who accept the information as reported in newspaper Y lack critical thinking skills.

(E) Newspaper Y may influence readers just as much as other newspapers whose views are more truthful.

20. Which of the following inferences is most defensible to draw regarding newspapers?

(A) Since no newspaper reporter can know all the facts all the time, newspapers should rarely be trusted as a source of important information.

(B) If the general populace relies on newspapers for information, the populace is usually misinformed.

(C) People develop trust in newspapers when they report opinions with which the readers agree.

(D) Despite their drawbacks, newspapers remain as the best source of reliable information about important events.

(E) Newspapers provide an important service and readers should learn which newspapers provide the "truth" by critically evaluating and comparing newspapers over time.

21. In a certain community, the covenants described rules for home-owners. Among the requirements were the following:

1. All homeowners' cars must be parked in enclosed garages.

2. No business can be run from a person's home.

3. No external structures may be erected without permission of the architectural committee.

One resident of the community was a race car driver who owned

several personal automobiles and race cars. He also converted part of his 3-car garage into an area to work on his cars. He usually parked 3 or 4 cars in his driveway. The homeowners association informed him he was in violation of the covenants and he answered their charge with the following statements. Which of his statements is a defensible argument?

(A) My home is fully paid for.

(B) The cars are expensive and do not detract from the neighborhood.

(C) I am gone much of the time racing cars.

(D) My work on cars in the garage is just a hobby. The business part of maintaining cars is done elsewhere.

(E) Other residents leave cars in their driveway, also.

22. Research conducted on group discussions was directed at answering certain questions. Some of these questions included: (1) Is there an optimal size for small group discussions? (2) What techniques are most useful for discussion leaders to use? and (3) What do people remember best from discussion groups? Regarding the last question, they found that people remembered best the statements that they themselves made. They also found that people retained information that confirmed their biases and forgot those statements that opposed their own views.

Which of the following conclusions is supported by the above passage?

(A) People are usually persuaded to believe new ideas when a group discussion format is used.

(B) People retain information better from a discussion than they do from reading.

(C) People tend to leave discussions with their preconceived ideas altered.

(D) Persuasion is the major goal of most discussion groups.

(E) People usually retain their own ideas rather than adopt the ideas of others.

23. The statement about techniques for group leadership that was supported by the above passage is:

    (A) Discussion leaders should use a democratic style of leadership.

    (B) Discussions that focus on the biases of the group will be more stimulating.

    (C) No special leadership technique was recommended.

    (D) Effective discussion leaders are good persuaders.

    (E) Everyone should be encouraged to say something during a discussion so they will more likely retain something from the discussion.

24. The true scientist does not thrive on truth. The true scientist thrives on doubt. Skepticism is the hallmark of the pioneer in the world of science. "Truth" through the ages has been found lacking by those courageous enough to challenge it. The flat earth, the unreachable moon, and limit of speed (the sound barrier) have all been challenged by doubters. The scientist would rather spend a lifetime chasing doubt than spend it believing things that are not true.

    Which of the following statements is most consistent with the main idea of this passage?

    (A) Scientists are negative thinkers.

    (B) Truth does not exist for the scientist.

    (C) Truth is not important to the scientists.

    (D) Skepticism and Scientific Inquiry are compatible.

    (E) The findings of scientists lack practical applications

25. Psychologists report that proper feedback promotes good feelings and motivates people to continue their task. However, feedback may be positive or negative. It also may be responsible or irresponsible. Which of the following is an example of negative/irresponsible feedback?

(A)   You tried hard but you can do better and get more answers correct if you concentrate.

(B)   You have improved considerably from last week.

(C)   You have severely disappointed me, I can't understand where you misplaced your brains.

(D)   You have not performed up to the standard I would expect from you — we need to confer and help you improve.

(E)   You are failing this course and unless you improve, you will need to repeat it.

# STOP

If time still remains, you may go back and check your work.
When the time allotted is up, you may go on to the next section.

# Section 6

**TIME:** 30 Minutes
25 Questions

**DIRECTIONS:** Each question or group of questions is based on a passage or set of statements. Select the best answer choice.

Questions 1 – 4 refer to the following statements.

An elementary education department head has six faculty members that must be assigned offices. The available offices are numbered 121, 122, 123, 124, 125, and 126. These offices are arranged in a row, and are separated only by dividers. One of the problems with this office space is that the dividers allow for interruptions of smoke and sound from the other spaces.

1) Mr. Bell is a salesman and his work requires extensive phone use.

2) Mr. Philips and Mr. Kersh often talk with one another about their work and prefer adjacent offices.

3) Miss Askew, the senior employee, is entitled to Office 125, which has a panoramic view of the ocean.

4) Mr. Fleniken is a computer analyst and needs silence in the offices adjacent to his own.

5). Mr. Harriman, Mr. Philips, and Mr. Fleniken all smoke. Miss Askew is allergic to tobacco smoke and needs non-smokers in the offices next to her own. Unless specified, all employees maintain silence while in their offices.

1. The best location for Mr. Philips is in Office

    (A) 121        (D) 124

    (B) 122        (E) 126

    (C) 123

2.  The best employee to occupy the office furthest from Mr. Kersh would be

    (A)  Mr. Harriman          (D)  Mr. Fleniken

    (B)  Mr. Bell              (E)  Mr. Philips

    (C)  Miss Askew

3.  The three employees who smoke should be placed in Offices

    (A)  121, 122, and 123      (D)  122, 123, and 124

    (B)  121, 122, and 124      (E)  122, 123, and 126

    (C)  121, 122, and 126

4.  Which of the following events would be the most likely to result in a request for a change in office assignment?

    (A)  Mr. Bell deciding that he needs silence in the offices next to his.

    (B)  Mr. Kersh contracting laryngitis.

    (C)  Mr. Fleniken giving up smoking.

    (D)  Mr. Harriman taking over the duties formerly assigned to Mr. Bell.

    (E)  Miss Askew installing a noisy teletype machine in her office.

Questions 5 – 7 refer to the following statements.

1)  A police lineup contained four men, one of whom was a thief.

2)  The lineup is graduated by height, with the tallest man on the left and the shortest on the right (from the witness's viewpoint).

3)  There are two men between Charles and David.

4)  Jeff is the to left of Glenn.

5)  The thief is third from the left.

6)  David is to the right of the thief.

5. Who is the thief?

   (A) David

   (B) Glenn

   (C) Jeff

   (D) Charles

   (E) Cannot be determined

6. Who is the tallest?

   (A) David

   (B) Glenn

   (C) Jeff

   (D) Charles

   (E) Cannot be determined

7. Which of the following statements would, if added to the first six, be inconsistent with one or more of them?

   I. The man on the far right is taller than Glenn.

   II. The witness named David as the thief.

   III. Jeff is between Charles and Glenn.

   (A) I only

   (B) I and II

   (C) II and III

   (D) II only

   (E) I, II, and III

Questions 8 – 10 are based on the following information.

Jeff's Variety Store has in stock four types of ribbon — A, B, C, and D. Each ribbon comes in two sizes — large and small. There is available one of each of the eight different kinds. The ribbons are solid colored as follows:

1) There are exactly four colors of ribbon — red, white, green, and blue.

2) Every color appears among the small ribbons and three colors among the large ribbons.

3) The color of a specific type of small ribbon — A or B or C or D — cannot be the same as the color of that same type of large ribbon.

4) The large B ribbon is not the color of the small D ribbon.

5) The C ribbons are not blue.

6) The large C and D ribbons are both red.

7) The small B ribbon is white.

8. Which ribbon's color is not determinable by the information given?

   (A) small C

   (B) small D

   (C) large B

   (D) large A

   (E) All of the above are determinable by the information given.

9. The B-type ribbons must be of which two colors?

   (A) red and white

   (D) blue and white

   (B) green and blue

   (E) red and blue

   (C) white and green

10. All four of the colors may be found in which combined pair?

    (A) B's and D's

    (D) B's and C's

    (B) A's and B's

    (E) None of the above

    (C) A's and C's

Questions 11 – 15 refer to the following statements.

Debbie, Mary, Joy, and Jeff have a Physics final on Friday and they all would like to study together at least once before the test.

Debbie can study only on Monday, Tuesday, and Wednesday nights, and Thursday afternoon and night.

Mary can study only on Monday, Wednesday and Thursday nights, and Tuesday afternoon and night.

Joy can study only on Wednesday and Thursday nights, Tuesday afternoon, and Monday afternoon and night.

Jeff can study the afternoons and nights of Tuesday, Wednesday, and Thursday, and on Monday afternoon.

11. If the group is to study twice, then the days could be

   (A)   Monday and Wednesday

   (B)   Tuesday and Thursday

   (C)   Wednesday and Thursday

   (D)   Monday and Friday

   (E)   Tuesday and Wednesday

12. If three of them tried to study together when all four could not,

   (A)   this would be possible twice.

   (B)   it would have to be on Wednesday night.

   (C)   Jeff could not attend the three-person groups.

   (D)   this could be accomplished on Monday and Tuesday only.

   (E)   this would not be possible.

13. If Debbie decided to study every night,

   (A)   she would never be able to study with Jeff.

   (B)   she would never be able to study with Joy.

   (C)   she would have at least two study partners each night.

   (D)   she would have to study alone on Monday night.

   (E)   she would study with only Mary on Thursday night.

14. If the test were moved up to Thursday morning, which of the following must be true?

   I.   The complete group would not be able to study together.

II.   Debbie could never study in the afternoon.

III.  Mary and Joy could study together three times.

(A)  I only                      (D)  II and III only

(B)  I and II only               (E)  I, II, and III

(C)  I and III only

15.   Dennis wants to join the study group. If the larger study group is to be able to study all together then Dennis will have to be available on

(A)  Wednesday night            (D)  Monday night

(B)  Thursday afternoon         (E)  Wednesday afternoon

(C)  Tuesday night

Questions 16 – 19 refer to the following information:

1)   A is the brother-in-law of B.

2)   C is the sister-in-law of E.

3)   F and G have a daughter named H. (F is the father, G the mother.)

4)   E is the sister of B. They have no other siblings.

5)   Neither A nor C have any siblings.

6)   H is married to D and they have a son named I.

7)   D is the child of C.

8)   No one has been married more than once.

16.   A is married to

(A)  E                          (D)  H

(B)  C                          (E)  None of these.

(C)  G

17. I's grandfather is

    (A) A                    (D) D

    (B) B                    (E) None of these.

    (C) C


18. The mother-in-law of H is

    (A) E                    (D) A

    (B) C                    (E) B

    (C) G


19. Which of the following has no blood relative mentioned?

    (A) A                    (D) D

    (B) B                    (E) I

    (C) C


Questions 20 – 21 refer to the following:

   "We have nothing to fear but fear itself? Nonsense. Even the bravest of us may become terrified in the face of any number of gravely threatening situations."


20. To accept this author's argument, we must agree that becoming afraid is

    (A) an occasional trait of the fearless.

    (B) fearful.

    (C) a common and acceptable human quality.

    (D) nonsense.

    (E) allowable only in gravely threatening situations.


21. The author's argument might be weakened by pointing out that

(A)   a less fearful attitude may minimize the threat of a situation.

(B)   fear promotes more accurate responses to threatening situations.

(C)   any blanket generalization is highly vulnerable to criticism.

(D)   who we fear is more important than what we fear.

(E)   brave people often admit that they have been afraid.

Questions 22 – 23 refer to the following passage.

There are many reasons for recognizing or refusing to recognize a foreign government, but none of them are legal reasons. For there to be a legal reason, the recognizing power would have to be able to say, "This government is the lawful government of the territory; therefore, we recognize it as the government." But this would be like saying, "You are my deputy; therefore, I appoint you my deputy," or "This ship is called the Queen Mary; therefore, I name her the Queen Mary."

22.   The author would be less happy with his argument if he realized that

(A)   what you call a ship has nothing to do with legal reason.

(B)   lawyers and statesmen often debate the problem of when to recognize a foreign government.

(C)   you cannot appoint a deputy unless you are legally empowered to do so.

(D)   there is no real difference between lawful and unlawful governments; it is all a question of power, not right.

(E)   whether a government is lawful does not depend on whether another government chooses to recognize it.

23.   Which of the following would support the author's argument?

I.    The reasons for recognizing foreign governments always have to do with expediency and not principle.

II.   The law is not applicable between governments, but only

662

within a given government.

III. It is incoherent to say, "you are married; therefore, I pronounce you man and wife."

(A) I only        (D) I and II only

(B) II only       (E) I, II, and III

(C) III only

Questions 24 – 25 refer to the following:

Henderson was the person who first noted the great ironies in the sunlit room, how history had been shaped by these people, how often their fates had been determined by the thinnest chance and circumstance. He looked across the room and spoke of the strange tides that had separated them, swept them all along, and now had...

24. Question 24 refers to the missing portion of the preceding paragraph. Choose the phrase that best completes the passage.

(A) drowned them.

(B) led to their destruction.

(C) filled them with fear.

(D) made them laugh again.

(E) brought them together again.

25. Which of the following statements about humanity would the author most strongly agree with?

(A) Each individual is the master of their fate.

(B) We are all passive observers of history.

(C) Free will does not exist.

(D) Human history is shaped by a combination of choice and chance.

(E) Individuals play an insignificant role in the eternal scheme of things.

## STOP
If time still remains, you may go back and check your work.

# TEST 5

# ANSWER KEY

## Section 1 — Verbal Ability

| | | | | | | | |
|---|---|---|---|---|---|---|---|
| 1. | (A) | 11. | (A) | 21. | (B) | 31. | (D) |
| 2. | (A) | 12. | (B) | 22. | (B) | 32. | (E) |
| 3. | (C) | 13. | (D) | 23. | (D) | 33. | (E) |
| 4. | (A) | 14. | (A) | 24. | (C) | 34. | (C) |
| 5. | (C) | 15. | (B) | 25. | (C) | 35. | (D) |
| 6. | (A) | 16. | (A) | 26. | (B) | 36. | (E) |
| 7. | (A) | 17. | (D) | 27. | (D) | 37. | (E) |
| 8. | (D) | 18. | (A) | 28. | (E) | 38. | (C) |
| 9. | (A) | 19. | (D) | 29. | (A) | | |
| 10. | (D) | 20. | (B) | 30. | (D) | | |

## Section 2 — Verbal Ability

| | | | | | | | |
|---|---|---|---|---|---|---|---|
| 1. | (A) | 11. | (B) | 21. | (E) | 31. | (A) |
| 2. | (E) | 12. | (D) | 22. | (A) | 32. | (D) |
| 3. | (C) | 13. | (D) | 23. | (D) | 33. | (E) |
| 4. | (E) | 14. | (E) | 24. | (B) | 34. | (D) |
| 5. | (E) | 15. | (B) | 25. | (A) | 35. | (D) |
| 6. | (A) | 16. | (B) | 26. | (D) | 36. | (E) |
| 7. | (D) | 17. | (D) | 27. | (C) | 37. | (B) |
| 8. | (D) | 18. | (A) | 28. | (C) | 38. | (E) |
| 9. | (A) | 19. | (C) | 29. | (A) | | |
| 10. | (D) | 20. | (D) | 30. | (B) | | |

## Section 3 — Quantitative Ability

| | | | | | | | |
|---|---|---|---|---|---|---|---|
| 1. | (D) | 3. | (B) | 5. | (D) | 7. | (D) |
| 2. | (C) | 4. | (C) | 6. | (A) | 8. | (C) |

| | | | | | | | |
|---|---|---|---|---|---|---|---|
| 9. | (C) | 15. | (B) | 21. | (B) | 27. | (D) |
| 10. | (C) | 16. | (C) | 22. | (A) | 28. | (C) |
| 11. | (A) | 17. | (C) | 23. | (E) | 29. | (E) |
| 12. | (C) | 18. | (D) | 24. | (B) | 30. | (E) |
| 13. | (A) | 19. | (C) | 25. | (A) | | |
| 14. | (A) | 20. | (C) | 26. | (E) | | |

# Section 4 — Quantitative Ability

| | | | | | | | |
|---|---|---|---|---|---|---|---|
| 1. | (B) | 9. | (B) | 17. | (A) | 25. | (A) |
| 2. | (C) | 10. | (C) | 18. | (D) | 26. | (D) |
| 3. | (A) | 11. | (D) | 19. | (D) | 27. | (E) |
| 4. | (D) | 12. | (D) | 20. | (C) | 28. | (C) |
| 5. | (A) | 13. | (A) | 21. | (D) | 29. | (E) |
| 6. | (C) | 14. | (C) | 22. | (A) | 30. | (B) |
| 7. | (C) | 15. | (A) | 23. | (D) | | |
| 8. | (A) | 16. | (B) | 24. | (D) | | |

# Section 5 — Analytical Ability

| | | | | | | | |
|---|---|---|---|---|---|---|---|
| 1. | (D) | 8. | (C) | 15. | (E) | 22. | (E) |
| 2. | (E) | 9. | (B) | 16. | (D) | 23. | (C) |
| 3. | (D) | 10. | (D) | 17. | (D) | 24. | (D) |
| 4. | (B) | 11. | (E) | 18. | (D) | 25. | (C) |
| 5. | (C) | 12. | (B) | 19. | (E) | | |
| 6. | (B) | 13. | (A) | 20. | (E) | | |
| 7. | (C) | 14. | (B) | 21. | (D) | | |

# Section 6 — Analytical Ability

| | | | | | | | |
|---|---|---|---|---|---|---|---|
| 1. | (C) | 8. | (D) | 15. | (A) | 22. | (E) |
| 2. | (D) | 9. | (C) | 16. | (A) | 23. | (C) |
| 3. | (A) | 10. | (A) | 17. | (B) | 24. | (E) |
| 4. | (D) | 11. | (C) | 18. | (B) | 25. | (D) |
| 5. | (B) | 12. | (D) | 19. | (A) | | |
| 6. | (D) | 13. | (C) | 20. | (C) | | |
| 7. | (A) | 14. | (D) | 21. | (A) | | |

# DETAILED EXPLANATIONS
# OF ANSWERS

## Section 1—Verbal Ability

1.    (A)
      (B) Implies expensive living which is contradicted by the phrase "lonely bachelor life ... caring for his property ... adding to it." (C) refers to wasteful living. (D) suggests that life is unimportant. (E) denotes economical living. Only (A) implies frugality to the point it is no longer a virtue but a fault.

2.    (A)
      (B) and (C) suggest vice and disreputable. (D) refers to being forced to perform the act. (E) denotes a dutiful action. Only (A) implies indifference from every other instance of its kind; stresses individuality.

3.    (C)
      (A), (B) and (E) reflect a lack of feelings. (D) reveals excitement of feelings due to fear. (C) is the correct choice, "sin" is the contextual clue. It reflects a sorrow that arises out of love of God and a realization one has failed to respond to his grace.

4.    (A)
      (B) refers to brevity of time which is inferentially contradicted. (D) and (E) refer to submission. "Individualized man" contradicts this concept. (C) suggests a lack of restraint. (A) is the correct choice, implying the obvious through its effects. The contextual clues are "isolates" and "individualized" which are the effects in a cause/effect relationship.

5.    (C)
      (C) is the correct choice, referring to viewing of a stage or stages

from every possible point. (A), (B), (D), and (E) are synonyms referring to only appearance.

6.  (A)
    (B) combines visibility with appearance. Emotions are not seen, only behavior resulting from those emotions. (C) combines cohesion with disappear. They are not relevant. (D) combines silence with tumult. They are not relevant. (E) combines violence with music. They also, are not relevant. (A) is the correct choice. PLIANT and MALLE-ABLE are synonyms meaning flexible.

7.  (A)
    (B) refers to music. (D) and (E) refer to literature. (C) refers to music. Only (A) refers to a repeated phrase associated with a particular person or mood.

8.  (D)
    Although (A), (B), (C) and (E) are all antonymous relationships, they contain nuances of meaning. (A) DEPOSITION:REFUTATION suggests evidence versus contrary evidence. (B) HYPOTHETICAL: ABSOLUTE denotes certainty versus uncertainty. (C) DIAG-NOSIS:OBTUSENESS is defined as discrimination versus indiscrimination. (E) FEASIBILITY:INCONCEIVABLE relates to possible versus impossible. (D) is the correct choice. SUPPOSITION: SURMISE have the same relationship as theory and speculation as well as the same meaning.

9.  (A)
    (B) and (D) have a synonymous relationship, all related to a specific lifestyle and attitude. (C) is an antonymous relationship again referring to a lifestyle and attitude. (E) possesses an antonymous relationship referring to the study of worship (liturgic) versus the denial of the existence of God. (A) the correct choice, contains a cause and effect relationship as do the lead words, SERVICE and CHEVRON.

10.  (D)

(A) and (B) both contain a synonymous relationship with DEBAUCH:WANTON referring to waste and corruption. VIRGIN:ORIGINAL suggests something fresh and unspoiled. (C) denotes sincerity versus a lack of sincerity. (E) relates to courtesy versus discourtesy. The correct choice is (D) which belongs to the member:class relationship as do the lead words.

11.  (A)

(D) and (E) both are contained in an antonymous relationship. PLAGIARIST:MERCATURE refer to stealing versus buying. SEQUESTER:URBANITY denotes seclusion versus sociality. (C) relates to the whole/part relationship. (B) is a synonymous relationship implying fun. (A) is the correct choice. It is a part:whole relationship. PLANT LIFE is a part of the study of life: BIOLOGY, as CUBISM is a style of ART.

12.  (B)

(A) and (C) have an antonymous relationship with ALPHA:OMEGA referring to the beginning and the end. (C) AGITATION is a highly emotional state while STOLID suggests a lack of emotion. (D) and (E) function as part-to-part relationships. (D) COLON:SEMICOLON are part of punctuation. (E) STITCH is the least part of CLOTHING. (B) is the correct choice. SPREE and CAROUSAL are synonymous meaning an unrestrained outburst of activity. The key words SPOONERISM and TRANSPOSITION are synonymous, referring to the rearranging of the initial sounds of two or more words.

13.  (D)

(A), (B), (C), and (E) have synonymous relationships. (A) refers to a redundancy. (B) suggests poverty (C) are both navigators, ARGONAUT being a navigator in water; ASTRONAUT is a navigator of space. (E) denotes a lack of cohesiveness. Only (D), the correct choice, has an antonymous relationship as do the lead words.

14.   (A)

(B) and (E) possess a part-to-part relationship. DIAMETER: CIRCUMFERENCE are parts of a circle, as is the RADIUS. (C) is a whole:part relationship with the HYPOTENUSE being a part of a TRIANGLE. (D) is antonymous, with PERPENDICULAR and HORIZONTAL being opposites in direction. (A), the correct choice, reflects that a QUADRANT is one-fourth of a CIRCLE, the ratio being 1:4; therefore 25:100 is also a 1:4 ratio.

15.   (B)

(A), (C), and (E) have an antonymous relationship. DECLEN-SION:ASCENT refer to non-increase versus increase. ADJUNCT: DETRUNCATE suggests added versus non-added; while VINC-TURE:SEGREGATION imply junction versus disjunction. (B), the correct choice, is synonymous in both relationship and meaning.

16.   (A)

(C), (D), and (E) are synonymous relationships. (B) is cause:effect with RIDICULE being the effect of PILLORY. (A) is the correct choice. PALADIN is a part of the whole, CAUSE; as PORIFERAN is a part of the whole, SPONGES.

17.   (D)

Paragraph three states that the submarine can hold a total of twenty-eight torpedoes; which is eighteen more than the number of tubes. Paragraph one states that each torpedo weighs up to 1,000 pounds in explosives. $18 \times 1,000 = 18,000$.

18.   (A)

Paragraph four states that the electric has the advantage of no visible wake, implying gas turbines leave a wake which is a disadvantage.

19.   (D)

Paragraph two states "projectile explodes" and does not differentiate between conventional or nuclear warheads.

669

20.  (B)
  Paragraph four. Electric torpedoes usually have less speed and range than turbine types (inferring the turbine does increase speed and power).

21.  (B)
  (A) and (E) are stated in paragraph three. Paragraph 6 refers to de Léon's retreat to Cuba thus negating (D). (C) is a negative statement found in paragraph one, "never dreamed that his island of Florida was … North American continent." (B) is the correct choice. It is stated in paragraph one, sentence two.

22.  (B)
  (A) is stated in paragraph two. (C) states in paragraph four "determined to be first to circumnavigate the island." The article states de Léon was awarded a patent for the Bahamas and much later received new patents for the Bahamas and Florida; therefore (D) is incorrect. Paragraph five states that de Léon had seen too much of the hostile Indians. Hence (E) is incorrect. (B) is the correct answer. Paragraph five refers to de Léon fruitlessly searching for the fountain of youth.

23.  (D)
  (A) is implied, therefore incorrect. (B), (C) and (E) are true statements relating to de Léon, however paragraph one states he was an *adelantado* because he "advanced the Spanish Empire by conquest, subjugation of Indians and establishment of quasi-military government."

24.  (C)
  (A) is unrelated to the passage. (B) is a negative statement, paragraph five explicitly states de Léon was to bear the cost of the conquest. Paragraph four states that when the Spanish flag was planted the lands were claimed for the king. It is therefore a negative statement and incorrect. (C) is the correct choice. Key contextual words are "conquer" and "govern."

25.  (C)

(A), (B), and (D) are positive statements describing de Léon. (E) is stated in paragraph one, when it is stated "he was one of the first *adelantodos*." (C) is the correct choice. Throughout the selection, phrases such as "Only a cynic would have doubted its existence." "Fruitlessly searching for the fountain of youth." "His search for the fountain of youth took on a more immediate importance."

26.  (B)

(A) and (E) are stated. (C) and (D) are negative statements. (B) is the correct choice. "Fruitlessly searching," "failed" indicated he was disappointed in not fulfilling his quest.

27.  (D)

(A) is stated in the description of *adelantado*. (B) is inferred. (C) is a negative statement. (D) is the correct choice. de Léon governed Puerto Rico, then used it as a point of departure for his expedition to the Bahamas.

28.  (E)

(A) and (B) refer to the degree of hotness or coldness. (D) denotes the point at which the temperature scale begins. (C) is the identification of the degree of hotness/coldness. (E) FRIGIDITY (coldness) is the opposite of caloric (heat).

29.  (A)

(B) refers to sense impressions in general. (C), (D), (E) suggest the avenues through which sense perception occurs. (A) INSIPID (lacking in taste) is the opposite of FLAVOR (something which affects the taste).

30.  (D)

(B) and (C) are synonymous, defined as harsh sounds. (A) is the study of human speech. (E) relates to the rhythm of a piece of music. (D) CONCORD (harmony) is the opposite of CACOPHONY (harsh sound).

31.  (D)
     (B) and (C) are exhibited attitudes. (A) refers to one's situation or event being predetermined. (E) is a synonym of ataxia, which also means confusion. (D) LUCIDITY is the opposite of ATAXIA.

32.  (E)
     (A) and (D) are synonymous of SKEW. (B) refers to inversion. (C) is defined as being coiled. (E) PARALLEL is defined as "extending in the same direction, not meeting" which is the opposite of SKEW, which means a deviation from a straight line.

33.  (E)
     (A) and (C) are synonymous to ACRIMONY, meaning "sharpness." (B) refers to the lack of taste. (D) suggests a harsh taste, but not necessarily a sharp taste. (E) SAVORINESS, meaning pleasantness, is the opposite of ACRIMONY.

34.  (C)
     (A), (D) and (E) are all types of noise even as RAUCOUS is a type of noise. (B) is the impact of the noise on the ear. (C) SUSURRUS, meaning a whispering sound, is the opposite of RAUCOUS.

35.  (D)
     (A) is defined as a small bright light. (B) refers to the luminosity from that light. (C) suggests the luminous vapor surrounding the light. (E) denotes an inadequate amount of light. (D) TENEBRIFIC (causing darkness) is the opposite of SCINTILLATION (rapid changes of brightness).

36.  (E)
     (A) refers to the observable fact or event. (B) refers to the ability to view things in their true importance. (C) suggests an unearned display. (D) is defined as doubtful. (E) ECLIPSE, to remove from view, is the opposite of SPECTACLE which is defined as "something exhibited to view as unusual or notable."

37. (E)

(A) and (C) are antonyms. CONDUCTION referring to motion while QUIESCENCE refers to lack of motion. (B) is a synonym of OCCLUSION with both suggesting obstruction. (D) is defined as prevention. (E) PERFORATION (hole made by piercing or boring) is the opposite of OCCLUSION.

38. (C)

(A) and (E) indicate the direction of motion. (D) is a branch of dynamics that deals with the aspects of motion. (B) refers to the position of the object in motion. (C), LANGUOR, meaning inactivity is the opposite of VELOCITY meaning speed.

## Section 2—Verbal Ability

1. (A)

The answer is (A): false BELIEF, when acted upon, becomes REALITY. Alternative (B) FEAR...TRUTH is wrong because it is belief which is acted upon, not fear; (C) ANXIETY...FACT is wrong because it is belief which is acted upon, not anxiety; (D) PRESUMPTION...CERTAIN is wrong because the presumption itself does not become certain; it remains contrary to fact. The fact that a child turns out to be "no good" does not mean he was, in fact, "no good" as an infant. (E) DREAD...PROVEN is wrong because, as in (D), the first term itself is not what is proven.

2. (E)

Alternative (E) FOR EXAMPLE is correct. The second part of this sentence gives supporting information in the form of an example for the assertion made in the first part of the sentence. Alternative (A) is wrong because the second part of the sentence does not add new information or another assertion. Alternative (B), HOWEVER, is wrong because this word would be followed by information which contradicts or in some way contrasts with the assertion made in the first part of the sentence. Alternatives (C) THEREFORE, and (D) BE-CAUSE, are wrong because they both are used to signal cause-effect relationships, and the second part of the sentence is neither a cause nor an effect of the first part of the sentence.

3.　(C)

The correct answer is (C), INEVITABLE...FULL. The consequences of choices made may be SURPRISING (A), UNEXPECTED (B), BORING (D), or HAPPY (E), but they are always inevitable. This is the reason that (C) inevitable is the only acceptable first term given. In relation to the second term, the missing word must be one which contrasts with "meager," meaning "poor, not full or rich." (C) FULL is the only one of the second terms given which does contrast with "meager."

4.　(E)

The first terms given for each pair are synonyms with each other. Each fits the meaning of the sentence. The key, then, to this problem will be with the second term. The last clause, including the second blank, can be assumed to carry an idea which contrasts with the idea expressed before it. The sentence as a whole identifies two opposing views. The opposing ideas are: (1) set prerequisites high so student and teacher time is not wasted on students who will not be successful; and (2) set prerequisites low so all those who can possibly benefit will have a chance. The answer is (E) NEEDLESSLY...DENIED. Alternatives (A), (B), (C), and (D) are wrong because they do not carry through the opposing thought.

5.　(E)

The second half of this sentence cites an example to support the assertion made in the first part of the sentence. The computer is UNFORGIVING because if one neglects to save a program, that program is lost. It cannot be recalled. The other alternatives: (A) OMINOUS (threatening), (B) COMPLICATED, (C) ESSENTIAL, and (D) DIFFICULT do not express the idea of no reprieve for a mistake made as does (E) UNFORGIVING.

6.　(A)

Alternative (B) WRONG...ENFORCING is wrong because law does not enforce wrong actions; (C) ETHICAL...STOPPING is wrong because law does not stop behaviors, law merely prohibits certain behaviors; (D) UNETHICAL...LEGALIZING is wrong because law does not legalize unethical behavior; (E) SOUND...AL-

LOWING is wrong because laws do not allow or disallow sound actions; they prohibit certain actions.

7.  (D)
    The correct answer is (D) LACKING or wanting, because the sentence requires a word with a negative meaning. The word "just" is a secondary clue that the second part of the sentence is to contrast in meaning with the first part. The word chosen will also have to be sensible as a modifier for ability, since an implication exists as follows: "It's just his manner I find lacking (not his ability). (A), (B), and (E) do not provide the necessary contrast by presenting a word negative in meaning, and (C) does not present a word which can also modify "ability."

8.  (D)
    The relationship in this analogy is one of effect. GRASS retards or stops EROSION. The corresponding alternative is (D). A DAM retards or stops WATER. Alternatives (A), (B), (C), and (E) are inaccurate because ROOTS do not retard or stop a TREE, AIR does not retard a TIRE, CLOUDS do not retard RAIN, and BREEZES do not stop a FLAG.

9.  (A)
    A FACADE is the front or main face of a BUILDING. The corresponding analogy is (A) GRILL:CAR. A grill is the front or main face of a car. In relation to the other alternatives, a TONGUE is on the top of a SHOE, a SHEATH is around a KNIFE, a PICTURE is in a FRAME, and a HEAD is on top of the body.

10. (D)
    A SYMPHONY and a FUGUE identify two different genre (types or kinds) of music. Alternative (D), NOVEL:SHORT STORY identifies two genre or kinds of literature, and is the correct answer. Alternatives (B) and (C) are inaccurate because the second term in each is a subset of the first term. An ENTRY is found in a DIARY and a TOPIC SENTENCE is found in an ESSAY. Alternative (E) is

inaccurate because each term given is a part of the same whole. Each is a part of a book, for example.

11. (B)

A SYCOPHANT (one who seeks favor by flattering people of wealth or fame) lacks SINCERITY. The correct answer is (B) SKEPTIC:CERTITUDE. A skeptic (one who doubts) lacks certitude. Other analogies used were: (A) a PEDANT is concerned with DETAIL; (B) a GAMBLER relies on LUCK; (D) a MERCENARY acts in order to make MONEY; and (E) a FUGITIVE is in FLIGHT.

12. (D)

GAZPACHO is a cold SOUP made of various vegetables. The key relationship in this analogy is that the first term is one kind of the entity identified by the second term. The correct answer is (D). BRATWURST is one kind of SAUSAGE. None of the other alternatives fits the A is one kind of B analogy. In (C) PAELLA is a dish that has various kinds of FISH in it, but is not a kind of fish.

13. (D)

To be IGNORANT is to lack KNOWLEDGE. This relationship is also present in alternative (D) DESPAIR:HOPE. To despair is to lack hope. The relationship in alternative (A) FAST:HUNGRY is one of cause and effect. Alternative (B) OLD:ANTIQUE is an analogy of degree. An item must be considered "very" old to be "antique." Alternative (C) SYLLABLE:WORD presents a part to whole analogy. Alternative (E) GOOD:BETTER is an analogy of degree.

14. (E)

This analogy is one of category and example. GAUZE is an example of a DIAPHANOUS material. The answer (E) METAL:GOLD also expresses this same relationship. Gold is an example of a metal. Alternative (A) LABYRINTH:CONFUSION is a cause and effect analogy. Alternative (B) CEMENT:GRAVEL is a whole to part analogy. Alternative (C) METER:PROSODY is a part to whole analogy. Alternative (D) TIMBRE:SOUND is also a part to whole analogy. Timbre is a quality of sound.

15. (B)

One MARINATES a piece of BEEF in preparation for cooking and eating it. (B) is the correct answer; one PASTES WALLPAPER in preparation for hanging it. The element of preparation is lacking in the incorrect alternatives. One simply VISITS a FRIEND (A), STUDIES a BOOK (C), SWIMS a LAP (D), or EATS a CAKE (E).

16. (B)

LEGERDEMAIN (sleight of hand) is the stock-in-trade of the MAGICIAN. A LECTURE (B) is the stock-in-trade of a PROFES-SOR. The incorrect alternatives identify one of many personal characteristics (A), articles of clothing (C) and (E), and pieces of equipment (D), associated with different vocations.

17. (D)

(D) is not a variable. The author only mentions the atmosphere as it is affected by the time of day. (A) is a variable. The author states, "the relative size of the pollution source is an obvious variable. The author states, "during the day, sunlight plays an important part in transforming the chemical species of pollutants." (C) is a variable. The author speaks of the "tremendous influence" of elevation. (E) is a variable. The author explains the night is more stable, and less dilution occurs.

18. (A)

(A) is the correct answer. This is the introductory concept in the first sentence. (B) is incorrect, as the formula developed by mathematicians have deficiencies as pointed out by the author in paragraph three. (C) is incorrect. The author makes a statement to the contrary in the last sentence of the selection. (D) is incorrect. The word alternative is misused. (E) is incorrect. The author does not point out the largest sources of air pollutants.

19. (C)

(C) is the correct choice. The author makes this point in the final sentence of paragraph three. (A) and (E) are incorrect. The author does not mention either concept. (B) is incorrect. The author only mentions

it to indicate the difficulty in accurate calculations. (D) is incorrect. The author is discussing the atmosphere being the "medium in which air pollutants are emitted and transported from the source to the receptor."

20. (D)

(D) is the correct answer. The author makes this point in the fifth paragraph.

21. (E)

(E) is the correct answer. The author, even though briefly, has written a history of the crosscut saw. (A), (C), and (D) are incorrect. The nations are only named to help build the history of the development of the crosscut saw. (B) is incorrect. The lumber industry is only mentioned by the author to help build the history of the saw.

22. (A)

(A) is the correct answer. The plain tooth pattern is the original. The champion and lance patterns are cutter teeth, which not only cut the wood, but also remove the scored wood from the cut. (B) and (C) are incorrect. The types of crosscut saws (B) are one-man and two-man saws. Of the generation saws (C), the felling saw and the bucking saw are the only ones mentioned. (D) and (E) are incorrect. The author does not mention where the improvements were made.

23. (D)

(D) is the correct answer, as stated by the author in the first line.

24. (B)

(B) is the correct answer. In paragraph six the author states that the two-man saws were made in lengths from four to twelve feet. When describing the bucking saw in the final paragraph, the author describes it as traditionally being run by one person, and making (E) incorrect. Nothing in the passage could allow the reader to infer that the bucking saw has (A) only a lance tooth pattern, (C) was introduced from Germany, or (D) perfected on the European continent.

25. (A)

(A) is the correct answer. The author makes this point in the eighth paragraph. (B) is incorrect. In the author's explanation of the use of the felling saw there is no mention of it being a one-man or two-man saw. (C) is incorrect. This is a characteristic of the heavier bucking saw. (D) and (E) are incorrect. The author makes no comment as to the number of teeth or the tooth pattern.

26. (D)

(D) is the correct answer. The author mentions this in paragraph two of the selection.

27. (C)

All are characteristics of the crosscut saw except (C). The 16 foot crosscut saw was developed for the large redwoods in California.

28. (C)

The adjective REPULSIVE means "disgusting" or "causing strong dislike or aversion." Its opposite is (C) ALLURING, meaning "to attract," to tempt with something desirable. The other alternatives are wrong because they do not include the idea of "attract." (A) ELEGANT means "richness or grace of manner or dress"; (B) BEAUTEOUS means "having beauty"; (D) PLEASANT means "agreeable"; and (E) AMICABLE means "friendly."

29. (A)

DISSEMBLE is a verb meaning "to conceal (the truth, one's feelings, etc.) under a false appearance. Its opposite is BETRAY, meaning "to fail to uphold," to expose treacherously. The concealing of DISSEMBLE and the exposing of betray both occur with an element of "false appearance" or "treachery." (B) PUT TOGETHER (assemble) has as its opposite the word "disassemble." Alternative (C) RESEMBLE, means "to be like or similar to." The opposite of (D) AGREE is to "disagree" or to "not be in accord with." (E) RESOLVE means to break up into separate parts," "to analyze," or solve (a problem).

**30. (B)**

A faction is a group of dissenters who work in common against the main body or organization. FACTIOUS means "produced by intending to produce faction." The opposite of factious (adj.) is (B) COOPERATIVE. The other alternatives have no relationship to the word factious. (A) CONVOLUTED means "coiled, or complicated"; (C) CURVED means "a line having no straight part"; (D) CUNNING means "crafty"; and (E) COWARDLY means in the manner of a coward" or "lacking courage."

**31. (A)**

The antonym for CALCULATING (shrewd or cunning) is (A) RASH (too hasty in acting or speaking; reckless). Alternative (B) DARING is wrong because it has to do with the courage or bravery a person has rather than hastiness or lack of planning; (C) RISKY is wrong because it has to do with exposure to work, not with hastiness in action; (D) QUIXOTIC is wrong because it means "idealistically romantic" and has more to do with purpose of action taken rather than kind (hastiness); (E) WILD is wrong because it means "lacking social or moral restraint." A rash action may be reckless but is not necessarily dissolute, or bad.

**32. (D)**

The antonym for INFAMOUS (notorious; having a bad reputation) is (D) ILLUSTRIOUS (distinguished; outstanding; famous). (A) IDOLIZE is wrong because it means "to admire excessively." An infamous person and an honorable person might both be idolized by different persons. (B) IGNOMINIOUS (Latin *in* -without, and *nomen* -name) means literally "without name," "without reputation," "shamed," or "disgraced." This word is close in meaning to "infamous." (C) UNKNOWN is wrong because not to be known, or not to have a reputation at all is not the opposite of having a negative reputation. (E) GRACIOUS is wrong because it means "having charm or courtesy," and an infamous person may just as well have these characteristics as not.

**33. (E)**

A CALAMITY is a great misfortune or disaster. Its opposite is a

welcome benefit or blessing, a BOON as in alternative (E). Both words share the quality of intensity, great misfortune and great benefit. Alternatives (A), (B), (C) and (D) do not have this element of intensity. (D) BENEFIT refers to anything contributing to improvement, great or small; (B) ADVANTAGE focuses on the idea of superiority rather than great benefit; (C) VALUE means have worth *per se*; and (A) FAVOR refers to any kind of obliging act.

34.  (D)
    ALLEVIATE (Latin *ad* -to, and *levis* -light) means "to lessen or relieve pain" and to decrease. Its opposite is (D) AGGRAVATE (Latin *ad* -to, and *gravis* -heavy) which means "to make worse." Alternative (A) INTENSIFY means "to make stronger"; (B) INTERFERE means "to meddle"; (C) IRRITATE means "to provoke to anger or annoy"; and (E) OBVIATE means "to make unnecessary," or "to do away" with or prevent by effective measures.

35.  (D)
    CONSUMMATE (adj.) comes from the Latin words *con* meaning "together" and *summa* meaning "sum." Today consummate as an adjective means "complete," or "perfect." Its opposite is (D) CRUDE meaning "unfinished"; in a raw or natural condition. Alternatives (A) PERFECT and (E) COMPLETE are wrong because they are synonyms for the word CONSUMMATE. Alternative (B) HUNGRY, is unrelated to consummate in meaning, as is (C) UNSUCCESSFUL.

36.  (E)
    To CENSURE is to condemn as wrong. This word is derived from the Latin word *censere*, which means "to judge." (E) COMMEND is the correct antonym. To commend is to recommend or to praise. Alternative (A) COURT is wrong because it means "to pay attention to so as to get something"; alternatives (C) FLATTER and (D) ADULATE both have an element of insincerity; to "flatter" is "to praise insincerely," and to "adulate" is to "favor upon." Alternative (B) ACCEPT lacks the intensity of commend or praise; it simply means "to approve."

37. (B)

To BEMOAN is to lament. The correct antonym is (B) EXULT, which means to rejoice greatly. (A) LAUGH is "to express mirth." One can rejoice greatly without laughing; (C) COMMISERATE is "to feel or show pity for." This alternative is wrong because it simply unrelated in meaning; (D) ACCLAIM means "to announce with loud approval." One can rejoice greatly without announcing anything in any manner; (E) EULOGIZES a person, for example. No object is needed in order to rejoice greatly.

38. (E)

The noun MELANCHOLY is derived from the Greek words for "black" (*melas*) and "bile" (*chole*), and it means "sadness and depression of spirits." Its opposite is (E) EXHILIRATION, which means "stimulated, lively, gay," and comes from the Latin prefix *ex* -interns, and *hilaris* -glad. (Our word "hilarity" also comes from this Latin root.) Alternatives (A), (B), (C), and (D) are wrong because they fail to include the idea of lively and gay. (A) SOCIABILITY means "liking the company of others"; (B) SERENITY means "undisturbed or calm"; (C) COMPLACENCY means "self-satisfied" or "smug"; and (D) IMPULSIVENESS is "acting upon impulse."

# Section 3—Quantitative Ability

1. (D)

The difference between $a + b$ and $a - b$ is:

$$a + b - (a - b) = a + b - a + b$$
$$= 2b$$
$$\text{if} \quad b > 0 \quad \text{then} \quad 2b > b$$
$$\text{if} \quad b = 0 \quad \text{then} \quad 2b = b$$
$$\text{if} \quad b < 0 \quad \text{then} \quad 2b < b,$$

hence the answer cannot be determined.

2. (C)

In Figure A each circle has a radius of $a/_4$. The shaded area =

Area of the square − Area of the four circles

In Figure A:

$$\text{Shaded area} = a^2 - 4[\pi(\tfrac{a}{4})^2]$$

$$= a^2 - \frac{4\pi a^2}{16} = a^2 - \frac{\pi a^2}{4} = a^2(1 - \tfrac{\pi}{4})$$

In Figure B each circle has a radius of a/8.

$$\text{Shaded area} = a^2 - 16[\pi(\tfrac{a}{8})^2]$$

$$= a^2 - \frac{16\pi a^2}{64} = a^2 - \frac{\pi a^2}{4} = a^2(1 - \tfrac{\pi}{4})$$

The shaded areas are equal.

3.     (B)
Let $x$ = time that it takes A and B together to complete the job. Then,

$$\frac{1}{10} + \frac{1}{8} = \frac{1}{x} = \frac{9}{40} = \frac{1}{x} = x = \frac{40}{9} = 4.\overline{4}$$

$$4.\overline{4} < 5$$

4.     (C)
Redraw the figure. Because $\overline{MN} \parallel \overline{CA}$, $\angle MNB = \angle CAB$, $x + \angle MNB = 180°$. Therefore $x + y = 180°$.

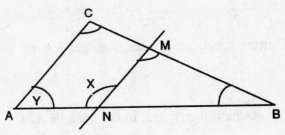

5.     (D)
As a first example, let $x = -3$ and $y = -4$.

$$x - y = -3 - (-4) = 1 > 0.$$

As a second example, let $x = -4$ and $y = -3$.

$$x - y = -4 - (-3) = -1 < 0.$$

6.  (A)

Since $n = p^2$, where $p > 1$, it is always such that $p^2 > p$. Therefore, $n > p$.

7.  (D)

We can rewrite the statement as

$$3m > 4p,$$

therefore

$$^m/_p > ^4/_3,$$

but not necessarily bigger than 2.

8.  (C)

We can rewrite the succession as

$$x, x + 3, x + 2, x + 5, x + 4, 10$$

where $x = a + 1$.

If we take the differences these are

$$3, -1, 3, -1, \dots$$

Therefore
$$10 - (x + 4) = 3$$
$$- (x + 4) = -7$$
$$x = 3.$$
Putting $x$ into the equation we get $3 = a + 1$, or $a = 2$.

9.  (C)

Redraw the figure. In the triangle $ABC$

$$20° + 40° + x° = 180$$
$$x = 120°$$

In the triangle $ECD$

$$30° + x + \alpha = 180°$$
$$30° + 120 + \alpha = 180°$$
$$\alpha = 30°$$

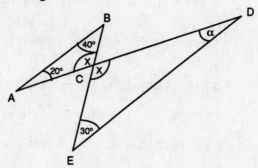

**10. (C)**

Given that $L_1 // L_2$, $\alpha = \gamma$. Given that $L_3 // L_4$, $\beta = \delta$. But $\alpha = \beta$, so, $\alpha = \beta = \gamma = \delta$. From $\alpha + \beta = 240°$, we have $\alpha = \beta = \gamma = \delta = 120°$.

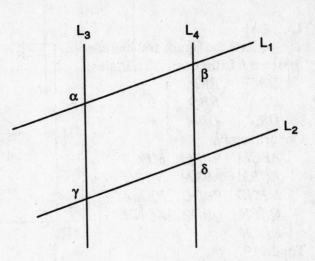

**11. (A)**

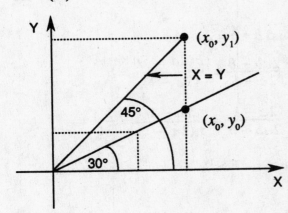

Redraw the graph and put in another line $x = y$. Comparing both points $(x_0, y_0)$ and $(x_0, y_1)$ we can see that

$$x_0 = y_1$$
$$y_1 > y_0$$
$$\text{so, } x_0 > y_0.$$

**12. (C)**

Redraw the figure. We have

$$\alpha + \alpha + 90° = 180°$$
$$2\alpha = 90°$$
$$\alpha = 45°$$

and

$$\alpha + \beta = 180°$$
$$\beta = 180° - 45°$$
$$\beta = 135°.$$

Also, $3a = 45 \times 3 = 135°$.

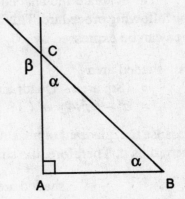

13. (A)
Redraw the figure and include the letter $R$ in the center. Triangles:

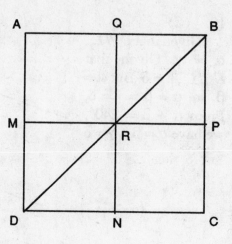

| | |
|---|---|
| DBC | RBP |
| DBA | RBQ |
| DRN | DRM |

$\Big\}$ 6

Quadrilaterals:

| | | |
|---|---|---|
| ABCD | NRBC | MPCD |
| AQRM | ABRM | NCBQ |
| MRND | PRDC | PBAM |
| QBPR | QRDA | AQND |
| RPCN | | |

$\Big\}$ 13

Total: 19.

14. (A)
Given $a * b = 2ab - b$ and $b * a = 2a - 1$,

$$\frac{a * b}{b * a} = \frac{2ab - b}{2a - 1} = \frac{b(2a - 1)}{(2a - 1)} = b$$

and

$$\frac{b * a}{a * b} = \frac{2a - 1}{2ab - b} = \frac{2a - 1}{b(2a - 1)} = \frac{1}{b}.$$

Because

$$b > 1, \quad b > \frac{1}{b}.$$

15. (B)
First, evaluate the shaded area with the following procedure: This half-shaded area can be expressed by

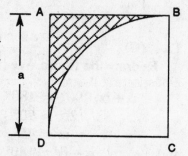

half-shaded area
$$= \text{(Sq. area} - \text{Quadrant area)}$$
$$= a^2 - \pi a^2/4 = a^2 (1 - \pi/4)$$

because the quadrant represents one-fourth of the area of a circle with the radius $a$. Therefore, the shaded area in the problem will be

$$\text{shaded area} = 2a^2(1 - \pi/4) = .43a^2.$$

The unshaded area can be expressed by

$$\text{unshaded area} = \text{(Sq. area} - \text{Shaded area)}$$

686

$$= a^2 - 2a^2 (a - \pi/4)$$
$$= a^2(\pi/2 - 1) = .57a^2.$$

Therefore, the unshaded area > the shaded area.

16.  (C)
If 40% of the bricks are already put in the wall and we need 1200 more, then 1200 bricks = 60% of the total bricks. Letting

$$x = \text{Total bricks,}$$
$$1200 = {}^{60x}/_{100}.$$
$$x = {}^{12000}/_{6}$$
$$x = 2000.$$

17.    (C)
The average of the heights can be 6 ft and 2 inches when no one is this height. Therefore, only statement III is correct.

18.  (D)
We need to find the expression for $bx$ as a function of $y$, where

$$\frac{a}{x} - \frac{b}{y} = c \text{ and } xy = \frac{1}{c}$$

Using the first expression ${}^a/_x - {}^b/_y = c$, we get

$$\frac{ay - bx}{xy} = c = ay - bx = cxy$$

Substituting the second expression in the right side, we have

$$ay - bx = c \cdot {}^1/_c$$
$$= ay - bx = 1$$
$$= bx = ay - 1.$$

19.  (C)
We can simplify $a$ in alternative (C) as shown below.
$$\frac{ax - a}{a} = \frac{a(x - 1)}{a} = x - 1$$
In all of the other choices, simplification of $a$ changes the expression.

20. **(C)**

   If we express all the numbers as decimals, we have

   (A)    $-.6000$

   (B)    $-.6600$

   (C)    $-.\overline{6} = -.6666...$

   (D)    $-.6660$

   (E)    $-.6000$

   We note that the smallest one is $-^2/_3$ or $-.\overline{6}$.


21. **(B)**

   The annual per capita income is:

$$\frac{\text{Gross National Product (GNP)}}{\text{Population}}$$

   In this case

$$\frac{\$ 315 \text{ billion}}{1.1 \text{ billion (citizens)}} = 286.4 \; (\$ / \text{citizen})$$


22. **(A)**

   In 1990 the percentage under 15 in China will be 25%, therefore 75% will be older than 15. Then

$$\frac{75}{100} (1.1 \text{ billion}) = .825 \text{ billion}$$

$$\text{or } 825 \text{ million}$$

23. **(E)**

   To solve the problem we need to know

   a)    Population

   b)    Birth rate, and

   c)    Infant Mortality

$$
\begin{aligned}
\text{New Born in 1990} &= \text{Birth Rate} \times \text{number of citizens} \\
&= {}^{18}/_{1000} \times 289{,}000{,}000 \\
&= 5.202 \times 10^6. \\
\text{New Born that will die} &= \text{Infant Mortality Rate} \times \\
&\quad \text{New Born in 1990} \\
&= {}^{22}/_{1000} \times 5.202 \times 10^6 \\
&= 1.14444 \times 10^5 = 114{,}444.
\end{aligned}
$$

24.　**(B)**

First, calculate the number of doctors in each country.

Soviet Union:

$$\frac{289 \text{ million (citizens)}}{267 \text{ (citizens / doctor)}} = 1.082397 \times 10^6 \text{ doctors}$$

China:

$$\frac{1.1 \text{ billion (citizens)}}{1757 \text{ (citizens / doctor)}} = 626,067 \text{ doctors}$$

$$\frac{\text{No. of Drs., USSR}}{\text{No. of Drs., China}} = \frac{1.082397 \times 10^6}{626,067} \approx 1.729$$

25.　**(A)**

First, calculate the population density in each country.

Soviet Union:

$$\frac{289 \text{ million (citizens)}}{8.7 \text{ million sq. mi.}} = 33.2 \text{ citizens / sq. mi.}$$

China:

$$\frac{1.1 \text{ billion (citizens)}}{3.7 \text{ million sq. mi.}} = \frac{1100 \text{ million (citizens)}}{3.7 \text{ million sq. mi.}}$$

$$= 297.3 \text{ citizens / sq. mi.}$$

26.　**(E)**

$$\frac{2^{-4} + 2^{-1}}{2^{-3}} = \frac{\frac{1}{2^4} + \frac{1}{2}}{\frac{1}{2^3}} = \frac{2^4\left(\frac{1}{2^4} + \frac{1}{2}\right)}{2^4 \frac{1}{2^3}}$$

$$= \frac{1 + 2^3}{2} = \frac{9}{2}.$$

27.　**(D)**

$$\frac{1 - \frac{1}{1-x}}{1 - \frac{1}{1-\frac{1}{x}}} = \frac{1 - \frac{1}{1-x}}{1 - \frac{x}{x-1}} = \frac{(1-x)\left(1 - \frac{1}{1-x}\right)}{(1-x)\left(1 - \frac{x}{x-1}\right)} = \frac{1 - x - 1}{1 - x + x} = -x$$

28. **(C)**
    $a + b$ books $= \$1000$.
    Let 1 book $= x$.

$$x = \frac{1000}{a + b} \ (\$/\text{book})$$

Myron bought each one for $1 less. He paid

$$\frac{1000}{a + b} - 1 \ (\$/\text{book})$$

Therefore for 12, he paid

$$\left(\frac{1000}{a + b} - 1\right) \times 12.$$

29. **(E)**

| | |
|---|---|
| If | $x : y = 1 : 2$ |
| and | $y : z = 2 : 3$ |
| then | $x : y : z = 1 : 2 : 3$ |
| and | $x : z = 1 : 3$ |
| or | $x : z = 2 : 6.$ |
| Given | $x : y = 1 : 2,$ |
| | $\dfrac{x}{y} = \dfrac{1}{2}$ |
| and | $y : z = 2 : 3,$ |
| | $\dfrac{y}{z} = \dfrac{2}{3}.$ |
| Therefore | $\dfrac{x}{y} : \dfrac{y}{z} = \dfrac{1}{2} : \dfrac{2}{3},$ |
| | $\dfrac{x}{y} : \dfrac{y}{z} = \dfrac{1}{2} \times \dfrac{3}{2}$ |
| | $\dfrac{x}{y} : \dfrac{y}{z} = \dfrac{3}{4}.$ |

Therefore all the propositions I, II, and III are true.

30. **(E)**
    Redraw the figure as below since $L_1 \mathbin{/\!/} L_2$.
$$2x + x + 30° + 60° = 180°$$
$$3x + 90° = 180°$$
$$3x = 90°$$
$$x = 30°.$$

## Section 4—Quantitative Ability

1.   (B)
Observe that 5% of 45 is $x$ may be written as $0.05(45) = x$ or $x = 2.25$. Similarly, 45 is 5% of $x$ may be written as $45 = 0.05x$ or $x = 45/0.05 = 900$. Hence, the quantity in Column B is greater.

2.   (C)
Note that the diameter = twice the radius. So, the radius of the circle in Column A is 8 since the diameter is 16.
Thus,
$$\text{Area of circle} = \pi r^2 = \pi(8)^2 = 64\pi \text{ and the}$$
$$\text{Area of rectangle} = \text{length} \times \text{width} = 64\pi.$$

Hence, the quantities in both columns are equal.

3.   (A)
The quantity in Column A is determined by a series of steps. First, observe that radii $OG$ and $OH$ are equal legs of right triangle $GOH$. Since the area of the right triangle is 12.5 one can easily obtain the length of each leg of the triangle as follows:

$$\text{Area of } GOH = (1/2) (\text{leg})(\text{leg}) = (1/2) (\text{leg})^2 = 12.5$$
$$(\text{leg})^2 = 25 \Rightarrow \text{leg} = 5.$$

Next, find the area of the square by using the Pythagorean Theorem to obtain the length of side $GH$, the hypotenuse of the right triangle, as follows:
$$(GH)^2 = (\text{leg})^2 + (\text{leg})^2 \Rightarrow (GH)^2 = 50$$
$$\text{or } GH = \sqrt{50} = 5\sqrt{2}.$$
Then, the area of the square is $(GH)^2 = 50$.
Now, find the area of the circle as follows: Area $= \pi r^2 = (5)^2\pi = 25\pi$.
Finally, the area of the shaded part of the figure is approximately as follows:

$$\text{Shaded area} = 25\pi - 50 = 25(3.14) - 50 = 78.5 - 50 = 28.5.$$

Comparing this value with the value in Column B, $9\pi = 9(3.14) = 28.26$, indicates that the quantity in Column A is larger.

4. (D)

Note that if $x > 1$ or $-1 < x < 0$, then any number $x$ is greater than $1/x$. But, if $x < -1$ or $0 < x < 1$, then any number $x$ is less than $1/x$. So, one cannot tell which quantity in the columns is greater.

5. (A)

One must first simplify each of the complex fractions. Thus,

$$\frac{1}{\frac{1}{x(x)}} = \frac{1}{1}\frac{x(x)}{1} = x^2 \text{ and } \frac{x(x-1)\frac{1}{x(x-1)}}{x(x-1)\frac{x}{x-1}} = \frac{1}{x^2}$$

Since $x > 1$ then $x^2 > 1/x^2$. So, what is in Column A is greater than in Column B.

6. (C)

Note that $(5/9)^2 = 25/81$ and $(9/5)^{-2} = 9^{-2}/5^{-2} = (1/9)^2 (5/1)^2 = (1/81)$ $(25) = 25/81$. Hence, the quantities in the two columns are equal.

7. (C)

Simplify the expression in Column A as follows:

$$\sqrt{\frac{y}{2}}\sqrt{\frac{2y}{x}} = \sqrt{\frac{2yy}{2x}} = \sqrt{\frac{y^2}{x}} = \frac{y}{\sqrt{x}}.$$

But,

$$\frac{y}{\sqrt{x}} = \frac{y}{\sqrt{x}}\frac{\sqrt{x}}{\sqrt{x}} = \frac{y\sqrt{x}}{\sqrt{x^2}} = \frac{y\sqrt{x}}{x}$$

So, the quantity in Column A is equal to the quantity in Column B.

8. (A)

Since the triangle on the right is a right triangle then using the Pythagorean Theorem one can write

$$x^2 + 5^2 = 10^2$$
$$x^2 = 100 - 25$$
$$x^2 = 75$$
$$x = \sqrt{75}$$

Similarly, since the triangle on the left is a right triangle, the same theorem enables one to write

$$5^2 + 6^2 = y^2$$
$$25 + 36 = y^2$$
$$61 = y^2$$
$$\sqrt{61} = y$$

So, since $\sqrt{75}$ is greater than $\sqrt{61}$ it is clear that $x$ in Column A is greater.


9.    (B)
An examination of the sequence of numbers shows that the second number, 5, is 2(first number) + 1 = 2(2) + 1; the third number, 11, is 2(second number) + 1 = 2(5) + 1; the fourth number, $x$, is 2(third number) + 1 = 2(11) + 1 = 22 + 1 = 23; etc. In Column B, the result of (11 + 47)/2 = 58/2 = 29. So, the quantity in Column B is greater.


10.   (C)
Simplify the expression in Column A. The LCD for the rational expressions in the numerator and denominator is 6. So,

$$\frac{6(2x) - 6\left(\frac{y-5}{6}\right)}{6\left(\frac{y-5}{3}\right) - 6(4x)} = \frac{12x - y + 5}{2y - 10 - 24x}$$

$$= \frac{12x - y + 5}{-2(12x - y + 5)} = \frac{1}{-2} = -.05.$$

Hence, the quantity in Column A is equal to the quantity in Column B.


11.   (D)
Recall that the area of the circle is $\pi x^2$. Also, recall that the circumference of the circle is $2\pi x$. Because nothing is said about the radius $x$ it is impossible to determine whether the area of the circle or the circumference is greater. The problem lies in the fact that, if $x > 1$, then $x^2$ is larger than $x$. On the other hand, if $x < 1$, then $x^2$ is smaller than $x$. In either case the comparison is affected. So, there is not enough information to make the comparison.

12. **(D)**

Assume that $x > y > 0$. Then, $|x| > |y|$. On the other hand, assume that $0 > x > y$. This means that both $x$ and $y$ are negative. Then, when the absolute value is taken then the direction of the inequality is changed, so $|x| < |y|$. Hence, from the information given in the problem it is impossible to compare the quantities in the columns.

13. **(A)**

Note that $\sqrt{x} = x^{1/2}$. Thus, one can write

$$\left(\sqrt{x}\right)^{-2} = \left(x^{1/2}\right)^{-2} = x^{(1/2)(-2)} = x^{-1} = 1/x \ .$$

Also, the expression in Column B, $x^{-2}$, can be written as $x^{-2} = 1/x^2$. Now compare $1/x$ with $1/x^2$. But, since $x > 1$ it follows that $1/x$ will always be greater than $1/x^2$. So, the quantity in Column A is greater.

14. **(C)**

In Column A, 15% of $12 = .15 \times 12 = 1.8$. In Column B, 12% of 15 $= .12 \times 15 = 1.8$. Hence, the quantities are equal.

15. **(A)**

Solve for $x$ in Column A by factoring as follows:

$$x^2 - 10x + 21 = 0 \quad \text{or} \quad (x-3)(x-7) = 0.$$

So, $x - 3$ and $x - 7 = 0$. Solving each of these first degree equations leads to $x = 3, 7$. Similarly, solve for $y$ in Column B by factoring as follows:

$$y^2 + 10y + 21 = 0 \quad \text{or} \quad (y+3)(y+7) = 0.$$

So, $y + 3 = 0$ and $y + 7 = 0$. Solving each of these first degree equations leads to $y = -3, -7$.

A simple comparison of each of the values for $x$ and $y$, respectively, reveals that no matter which value of $x$ or $y$ is chosen, $x$ is always greater than $y$, and hence, Column A is greater.

16. **(B)**

Note that $\dfrac{.1}{2} = \dfrac{.1 \times 10}{2 \times 10} = \dfrac{1}{20}$ for response (B).

For Choice (A), $\dfrac{1}{.2} = \dfrac{1 \times 10}{.2 \times 10} = \dfrac{10}{2} = 5$ which is larger than $\dfrac{1}{20}$.

For Choice (C), $\dfrac{.2}{1} = \dfrac{.2 \times 10}{1 \times 10} = \dfrac{2}{10} = \dfrac{1}{5}$ which is larger than $\dfrac{1}{20}$.

For Choice (D), $\dfrac{.2}{.1} = \dfrac{.2 \times 10}{.1 \times 10} = \dfrac{2}{1} = 2$ which is larger than $\dfrac{1}{20}$.

For Choice (E), $\dfrac{2}{.1} = \dfrac{2 \times 10}{.1 \times 10} = \dfrac{20}{1} = 20$ which is larger than $\dfrac{1}{20}$.

17. (A)

The formula for the area of a circle is $A = \pi r^2$. Since the area of the circle is $18\pi$, then it is true that

$$\pi r^2 = 18\pi \quad \text{or} \quad r^2 = 18 \quad \text{or} \quad r = \sqrt{18} = 3\sqrt{2}.$$

Then, the diameter of the circle is $2r = 2(3\sqrt{2}) = 6\sqrt{2}$. The diameter of the circle bisects the inscribed square into two equal triangles which are $45° - 45° - 90°$ triangles. Since the diameter of the circle is also the hypotenuse of each of the triangles, $6\sqrt{2}$, and the sides $x$ of each are equal, one can write the following using the Pythagorean Theorem:

$$x^2 + x^2 = \left(6\sqrt{2}\right)^2$$
$$2x^2 = 36(2)$$
$$x^2 = 36$$
$$x = 6,$$

the length of a side of the square.

So, the correct answer choice is (A). The other answer choices are obtained by failing to find the correct diameter of the circle or failing to use the Pythagorean Theorem correctly.

18. (D)

The measure of the exterior angle $x$ of triangle $ABC$ is equal to the sum of the measures of the two remote interior angles, $A$ and $B$, respectively. Thus,

$$\text{angle } x = 35° + 85° = 120°.$$

Another approach is to remember that the sum of the angles in triangle $ABC$ is $35 + 85 + \text{angle } C = 180$ degrees. Hence, angle $C = 60$ degrees. Then, since angle $C$ and angle $x$ are supplementary angles it follows that angle $x$ must be 120 degrees since angle $C$ is 60 degrees.

19. (D)

First, find the average wages earned by a vice president/manager by dividing 5 into $110,000, which yields $22,000. Similarly, find the average wages earned by an assembly line worker by dividing 500 into $600,000 which is $1,200. Then, the ratio is given by

$$\frac{22,000}{1,200} = \frac{220}{12} = \frac{55}{3}$$

which also can be written as 55 to 3.

20. (C)

Since the total amount of the payroll for the company is $1,060,000 and the wages paid to vice presidents/managers amount to $110,000, then the percent of wages paid to this position group is found as follows:

$$\frac{110,000}{1,060,000} = \frac{11}{106} = 0.104 \text{ or } 10.4\%$$

21. (D)

Since 40% of the weight of blood is made up of cells, then the weight of the cells is 0.4 times 5000 grams or 2000 grams. So, to find the percent of the total body weight that is made up of blood cells, form the following ratio and change the result to a percent.

$$\frac{2,000}{70,000} = \frac{1}{35} = 0.028 = 2.8\%$$

22. (A)

To find the solution one needs to set up a proportion. Thus, let $x$ denote the total body weight in grams and $S$ denote the weight of the skeleton. Then, the following proportion can be formed.

$$\frac{\text{weight of skeleton}}{\text{total body weight}} = \frac{10000 \text{ grams}}{70000 \text{ grams}} = \frac{S}{x}$$

Thus,

$$\frac{1}{7} = \frac{S}{x} \Rightarrow x = 7S,$$

which is response (A).

The other answer choices are obtained by forming incorrect ratios and proportion or errors in the calculations.

**23. (D)**

Since food A has 10% cholesterol, then 500 grams of food A will supply 50 grams of cholesterol which is answer choice (A). Since food B has 20% cholesterol, then 250 grams will supply 50 grams of cholesterol. 200 grams of food B will supply 40 grams of cholesterol; 350 grams of food C will supply 70 grams of cholesterol; and 200 grams of food C will supply the same number of grams of cholesterol. Thus, answer choice (D) will supply $40 + 40 = 80$ grams while answer choice (C) will supply only $15 + 40 = 55$ grams and answer choice (E) will supply 70 grams.

**24. (D)**

The traditional way to solve this problem is to set up and solve an equation. Consider what part of the job could be done in 1 hour by each person. Thus, Jay could do 1/5 of the job in 1 hour and Ray could do 1/4 of the job in the same amount of time. What is unknown is the part of the job they could do together in 1 hour, which can be represented by $1/x$. The $x$ represents the amount of time the brothers can do the job together.

The sum of the amount of the job each brother can do in 1 hour equals the amount of the job they can do together in 1 hour. Hence, the equation is given by:

$$\frac{1}{5} + \frac{1}{4} = \frac{1}{x}$$

Solving for $x$ you calculate as follows:

**Side Notes**

$$\frac{1}{5} \cdot \frac{4}{4} + \frac{1}{4} \cdot \frac{5}{5} = \frac{1}{x}$$

Finding the LCD

$$\frac{4}{20} + \frac{5}{20} = \frac{1}{x}$$

Add like fractions on left side of equation

$$\frac{9}{20} = \frac{1}{x}$$

Cross multiply

$$9x = 20$$

Divide by 9 on both sides of the equation.

$$\frac{9x}{9} = \frac{20}{9}$$

$$x = \frac{20}{9} \text{ or } 2\frac{2}{9} \text{ hours}.$$

To understand why answer choice (A) is incorrect one should consider another approach to the solution of the problem. The approach is referred to as a "logical" or "reasonable" method. It is logical to believe that since Ray can complete the job in 4 hours by himself, he should finish the job in less than 4 hours with the help of his brother. Hence, answer choice (A) can not be correct. Answer choice (C), 4 hours, is found to be incorrect by the same reasoning as given above. Answer choice (E), $4\frac{1}{2}$ hours, is incorrect because of the same reasoning as given for answer choice (A). Finally, answer choice (B), 1 hour, is also incorrect. To see this one needs to assume for a moment that Jay could also do the cleaning job in 4 hours rather than the required 5 hours. Then together the brothers should be able to complete the job in one-half of the time or just 2 hours. Thus it is logical that answer choice (B) does not represent enough time for both to do the job using the assumption.

25. (A)
   In order to find the perimeter of the rectangle it is important first to understand the definition, that is, perimeter equals to the sum of the dimension of the rectangle. Hence for the given rectangle,

$$\text{Perimeter} \ = \ 6L + 4W + 6L + 4W \quad \text{(Add like terms)}$$
$$= \ 12L + 8W$$

Answer choice (E), $24LW$, is incorrect because it represents the area of the rectangle, which is the product of the length and width. Answer choice (C), $6L + 4W$, is incorrect because it represents only one-half of the perimeter of the rectangle. Answer choice (D), $20LW$, is incorrect because this response is obtained by simply adding the coefficients of $L$ and $W$ which is an incorrect application of algebra. Finally, answer choice (B), $12L^2 + 8W^2$, is incorrect because it is obtained by using the definition of the perimeter of a rectangle incorrectly as follows: perimeter $= 2L(6L) + 2W(4W)$.

26. (D)
   Let $x$ = first odd integer, $x + 2$ = the second consecutive odd integer, and $x + 4$ = the third consecutive odd integer. Then, the following equation can be written based on what is given in the problem. Solve the equation

$$3x = 2(x + 4) + 3$$
$$3x = 2x + 8 + 3$$
$$3x - 2x = 11$$
$$x = 11,$$

the first odd integer.

So, the second consecutive odd integer is $x + 2 = 11 + 2 = 13$.

27. (E)

If a fraction has a value of 2/5 one can write an equivalent fraction for 2/5 as $2x/5x$. Thus, the original numerator may be represented by $2x$ and the original denominator by $5x$. So, in accordance with the problem one can write:

$$\frac{2x - 2}{5x + 1} = \frac{1}{4}$$

or by cross multiplying $8x - 8 = 5x + 1$. Now solving the last equation yields the value of $x$ in the representation, $2x$, of the original numerator of the fraction. Thus,

$$8x - 8 = 5x + 1$$
$$8x - 5x = 1 + 8$$
$$3x = 9$$
$$x = 3.$$

So, the original value of the numerator is $2x = 2(3) = 6$.

28. (C)

First find the least common multiple (LCM) of 3, 4, and 5 which is simply $3 \times 4 \times 5 = 60$. Since 3 divides 60, 4 divides 60, and 5 divides 60, then one needs only to add 2 to 60 in order to guarantee that the remainder in each case will be 2 when 3, 4, and 5, respectively, are divided into 62.

29. (E)

Since $X$ is the first number, then let $y$ represent the second number in the average of two numbers. Thus, from what is given in the problem one can write:

$$\frac{X + y}{2} = WX,$$

the average. Solving for $y$ gives the other number. Hence,

$$X + y = 2WX$$
$$y = 2WX - X,$$

the second number.

30. (B)

One can represent the three consecutive odd numbers as follows: $2x + 1$, $2x + 3$, and $2x + 5$, respectively. The sum of these numbers is:

$$(2x + 1) + (2x + 3) + (2x + 5) = 6x + 9.$$

Clearly 2, 5 and 6 do not divide $6x + 9$ exactly (without a remainder). Hence, answer choices (A), (C), (D), and (E) are incorrect. So, answer choice (B) is correct, that is, the value 3 does divide the sum $6x + 9$ as follows:

$$(6x + 9)/3 = 3(2x + 3)/3 = 2x + 3,$$

the quotient.

# Section 5—Analytical Ability

1. (D);  2. (E);  3. (D);  4. (B)

The answers to these four questions requires careful reading of the constraints described in the passage. After understanding these constraints, then the incorrect choices can be eliminated from each question. Since the factor that eliminates incorrect responses is usually easier to detect, it will usually be more expedient to eliminate the incorrect answers than to find the correct answer first. In item 1, for example, choice (A) is deleted because 4 pupils are assigned to this time; Choice (B) separates C and D who must be together, choice (C) includes the rest time, and choice (E) also separates C and D. Choice (D) is acceptable for it would leave pupils A, C, and D to engage in another activity together at this time. This process of elimination works well for items 1, 3, and 4. Item 2 can be answered by subtracting time allocations from the total of 180 minutes at the nursery school. The rest period requires 30 minutes and at least 3 other activities must be engaged in for 20 minutes each. This total of 90 minutes must be subtracted from the total available, leaving 90 minutes.

Test 5

5. (C);   6. (B);   7. (C);   8. (C)

There are several ways to answer this series of questions. One might calculate the area of the square (which would be about $8 \times 8 = 64$) which is only one of the three shapes for which sufficient information is given to do so. The second most obvious shape is a circle. The length of the string would form a circle whose diameter is 10 inches (31.4/3.14) and whose radius is 5 inches. Since $\pi r^2 = 25\pi =$ about 78 square inches is larger than the square, the circle appears to be the largest. One might infer from this (correctly) that a smooth edge with no corners encloses a larger area than one with corners. Experimenting with various lengths for the rectangle, the triangle, and the hexagon should soon make it evident that the circle is the best answer. This is not so much a mathematical question as it is one that calls for logical inference from the data provided. Item 6 was answered in the previous discussion and 7 can be answered with a brief calculation. If the original square had sides of about 8 inches, then a string twice as long would form sides of about 16 inches. 8 squared is 64 and 16 squared is 256, or 4 times as much area. Item 8 calls for a triangle whose sides are each about $10\frac{1}{2}$ inches. The area of a triangle is $\frac{1}{2}$ the base (about 5.25 inches) times the height (about 9 inches) or about 45. Again, this is not so much a mathematical question as it is one of estimating logically. Sketching the geometric figures in this question should help. Approximate answers are all you need to determine to select the correct response.

9. (B);   10. (D);   11. (E)

Student 1 is in a group with 6 students sharing 5 computers. During each class meeting 4 students will have their own computer and 2 students will share a computer. After 5 class meetings, each student will have shared once and had his own computer the other 4 times. 5 class meetings represent $\frac{1}{3}$ of the course and thus, student 1 will share a computer each of 3 sets of 5 class meetings. Student 29 is in a group with 7 students. The rotation of students and computer stations does not come out evenly since there are $5 \times 15$ or 75 stations available and $7 \times 15$ or 105 student-stations needed. The extra 30 student stations will be divided among 7 students which means 5 students will share during 4 class meetings and 2 students will share during 5 class meetings. the answer to Item 10 is $15 - 4 = 11$ and Item 11 is $15 - 5 = 10$.

701

12. (B);   13. (A);   14. (B);   15. (E);   16. (D)

The answers to these five items can be most easily determined by drawing a circle and placing letters and numbers on the edge according to the directions. The diagram below illustrates how to do this. Draw arrows around the outer edge of the circle in the direction the plate will rotate and make a note that the plate rotates every 45 seconds. For each of the questions (12 –

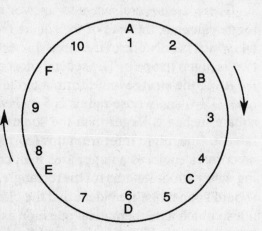

16), place a mark on the circle that indicates where the pendulum will be at the time indicated in the question. Next, determine how far the plate will rotate during that same time period. This will enable you to align the end of the pendulum over the appropriate place over the plate and answer each of these questions. Question 16 requires you to rotate the plate until the letter F is in line with the direction the pendulum swings. Record the length of time it requires for each time the letter F is properly placed. When you continue with this movement of both objects you will find the pendulum will be at the opposite end of the plate from the letter F until it has completed $2^1/_2$ cycles.

17.   (D)

The central consideration in this narrative is the extent to which private schools bring about better results with their pupils than do public schools. Issues about salaries, facilities, or even individual attention are peripheral to the main argument posed. The deciding factor must be the one that addresses the results of public vs. private schools. Thus, the one statement that is most persuasive in favor of public schools and is therefore less supportive of the argument presented in the paragraph is choice (D).

18. (D);   19. (E);   20. (E)

In questions 18, 19, and 20 it is important to recognize that the interaction between newspapers and readers calls for actions on the part of both and that the intent of newspapers and the actual results are

not necessarily the same. For instance, in question 18 Choice (A) suggests that *merely subscribing* to a newspaper will make readers better informed. Choice (B) assumes readers are also voters, and choices (C) and (E) are conclusions based on insufficient evidence. Only choice (D) remains as a viable choice. Questions 19 and 20 call for similar reasoning to avoid attributing undue influence to newspapers or reader reaction that is speculative.

21.   (D)
The only defensible argument is one that is in compliance with the covenants. Since no ban on hobbies is mentioned, choice (D) is a possible defense. All other choices are either rationalizations or irrelevant.

22. (E);   23. (C)
The "mind set" of discussers in group discussions is the dominant idea on which the questions about this passage are raised. Thus, item 22 is choice (E) and item 23 was not addressed in the passage. No discussion techniques were even addressed — choice (C).

24.   (D)
The paragraph emphasizes the importance of raising questions and pursuing answers, rather than accepting information as true just because it is the popular or traditional position to take. Thus, skepticism and inquiry are presented as companions that motivate scientists to engage in research and experimentation.

25.   (C)
The critical information to look for in these responses is to first identify those responses that are negative. Choice (B) is positive and can be eliminated as a possible choice. Next, those responses that include helpful or accurate information can be eliminated, because these are responsible statements that accompany negative feedback. Choices (A), (D), and (E) all provide helpful or informative information. Choice (C) is both negative and lacking useful or informative information.

# Section 6–Analytical Ability

Questions 1 – 4.

This question is best answered by constructing a drawing to examine the assignment of office space.

There are six offices numbered consecutively in a row and separated by a divider. Miss Askew as senior employee will be in office 125.

| Office | Office | Office | Office | Office | Office |
|--------|--------|--------|--------|--------|--------|
| 121 | 122 | 123 | 124 | 125 | 126 |
| | | | | Askew | |

Ms. Askew is in office 125 as a senior member. She may have no smoker near her thus only Mr. Bell or Mr. Kersh may be adjacent to her. Mr. Kersh cannot be in office 126 because he needs to talk with Mr. Philips. This would place Mr. Bell in 126 and Mr. Kersh in 124.

| Office | Office | Office | Office | Office | Office |
|--------|--------|--------|--------|--------|--------|
| 121 | 122 | 123 | 124 | 125 | 126 |
| | | | Kersh | Askew | Bell |

Since Mr. Philips and Mr. Kersh often talk with one another he should have office 123.

| Office | Office | Office | Office | Office | Office |
|--------|--------|--------|--------|--------|--------|
| 121 | 122 | 123 | 124 | 125 | 126 |
| | | Philips | Kersh | Askew | Bell |

Mr. Fleniken needs quiet and cannot be near Mr. Philips who often talks with Mr. Kersh. He should be assigned office 121 and Mr. Harriman will take the remaining office 122.

| Office | Office | Office | Office | Office | Office |
|--------|--------|--------|--------|--------|--------|
| 121 | 122 | 123 | 124 | 125 | 126 |
| Fleniken | Harriman | Philips | Kersh | Askew | Bell |

This chart can be used to answer the questions.

1.    (C)
Observe the summary chart.


2.    (D)
Since he is a programmer and needs silence.


3.    (A)
Observe the summary chart.


4.    (D)
Mr. Harriman is a smoker and because of this cannot be near Miss Askew. Because of her seniority she must stay in #125. This would cause a complete change of assignments.


5.    (B)
Since there are only four men (1), and Charles and David are on the outside (3), and Jeff is to the left of Glenn (4), the order must be (from left to right) Charles, Jeff, Glenn, David. The man third from the left is Glenn; therefore, Glenn is the thief.


6.    (D)
The tallest man is on the left (2). Since there are only four men, and two of them are between Charles and David, Charles and David must be on the outside (3). Since David is to the right of the thief (6) he cannot be on the left side of the line and therefore Charles must be the tallest.


7.    (A)
Statement I would be inconsistent with (2), which states that heights shall be in descending order from left to right. Statement II does not contradict any of the given statements; the fact that a witness identified David as the thief is not inconsistent with the fact that Glenn is the thief. Statement III is perfectly consistent, and may in fact be deduced from the given statements (see the explanation to question 5 where the lineup order is established).

Questions 8 – 10.

Draw two grids, each labeled with the ribbon and color types. The boxes in these two grids will summarize all of the type-color size combinations available.

|   | **small size** | | | |   | **large size** | | | |
|---|---|---|---|---|---|---|---|---|---|
|   | red | white | green | blue |   | red | white | green | blue |
| A |   |   |   |   | A |   |   |   |   |
| B |   |   |   |   | B |   |   |   |   |
| C |   |   |   |   | C |   |   |   |   |
| D |   |   |   |   | D |   |   |   |   |

The rules of the scheme will enable us to eliminate some of the possibilities. The eliminated possibilities will be marked by x. A circle will designate those that are acceptable. All other possibilities will be left blank.

Rules 6 and 7 tell us to make a circle in the small B white box, in the large C red box, and in the large D red box. Then place an x in every other remaining small B, large C, and large D box, since these lettered types have a definite known color. No other small ribbon is white, nor is any other large ribbon red, since by Rule 2 every small ribbon has a unique color — also large A and large B must be colored differently from each other and cannot be red because only three colors appear among the large ribbons.

|   | **small size** | | | |   | **large size** | | | |
|---|---|---|---|---|---|---|---|---|---|
|   | red | white | green | blue |   | red | white | green | blue |
| A |   | x |   |   | A | x |   |   |   |
| B | x | 0 | x | x | B | x |   |   |   |
| C |   | x |   |   | C | 0 | x | x | x |
| D |   | x |   |   | D | 0 | x | x | x |

Now Rule 3 tells us that large B cannot be white, nor any small C or small D be red. Small A is red because some small ribbon has to be red. Thus, small A is not green or blue.

|   | **small size** | | | |   | **large size** | | | |
|---|---|---|---|---|---|---|---|---|---|
|   | red | white | green | blue |   | red | white | green | blue |
| A | 0 | x | x | x | A | x |   |   |   |
| B | x | 0 |   | x | B | x |   |   |   |
| C | x | x |   |   | C | 0 | x | x | x |
| D | x | x |   |   | D | 0 | x | x | x |

Since no C is blue, small C is green, forcing small D to be blue. By rule 4, large B cannot be blue. Thus large B is green.

|   | small size | | | | | large size | | |
|---|---|---|---|---|---|---|---|---|
|   | red | white | green | blue |   | red | white | green | blue |
| A | 0 | x | x | x | A | x |   | x |   |
| B | x | 0 | x | x | B | x | x | 0 | x |
| C | x | x | 0 | x | C | 0 | x | x | x |
| D | x | x | x | 0 | D | 0 | x | x | x |

Because we can deduce no more from the rules, we can now use the grid to solve the questions.

8.  (D)
Only the large A row still has blanks.

9.  (C)
The type B ribbons are white or green.

10.  (A)
The type B and the type D ribbons together exhibit all four of the colors.

Questions 11 – 15.
Begin by building the chart.

|   | Mon. | Tues. | Wed. | Thurs. |
|---|---|---|---|---|
| Debbie | N | N | N | AN |
| Mary | N | AN | N | N |
| Joy | AN | A | N | N |
| Jeff | A | AN | AN | AN |

N = night
A = afternoon

11.  (C)
Wednesday and Thursday. You can see from an examination of the chart that Wednesday and Thursday are the only two days this is possible.

On Monday Jeff could not study at night and the others could not study in the afternoon. On Tuesday Joy could not study at night and the others could not study in the afternoon.

12.   (D)

This could be accomplished on Monday and Tuesday only. Remember from Question 11 that they could all study together on Wednesday and Thursday. This leaves Monday and Tuesday. Choice (A) is incorrect because they could study together more than twice on those two days. On Tuesday Debbie, Mary, and Jeff could study at night and Mary, Joy and Jeff could study in the afternoon. Another study lesson for Debbie, Mary, and Joy would be available Monday night.

13.   (C)

She would have at least two study partners each night. An examination of the chart indicates that on Monday she could study with Mary and Joy; on Tuesday with Mary and Jeff; and on Wednesday and Thursday with the entire group. Choices (A) and (B) are false because Debbie could study with Jeff and Joy on Wednesday and Thursday nights. Choice (D) is false because she could study with Mary and Joy and choice (E) is false because she would study with the entire group.

14.   (D)

II and III only. I is false, because they could all study together on Wednesday. II is true because the only afternoon Debbie could study was Thursday. III is true because Joy and Mary could study together on Monday, Tuesday, and Wednesday. Therefore, II and III are true.

15.   (A)

Wednesday night. Since the four could study together on Wednesday and Thursday night, Dennis would have to be available on one of those nights. The only choice given is Wednesday night.

Questions 16 – 19.

The key is to set up a diagram. The critical facts here are that E and B are siblings and that A and C each have no siblings. The only way

for A to be the brother-in-law of B, and C to be the sister-in-law of E is for A to be married to E and B to C. So we get:

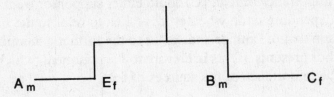

Add in the rest of the facts:

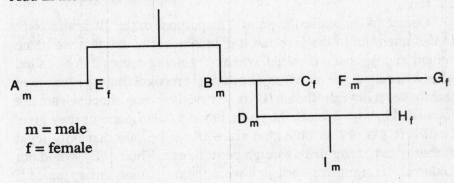

m = male
f = female

16. (A)
A is married to E.


17. (B)
I has two grandfathers, but only one is listed (F is the other).


18. (B)
D's mother, C.


19. (A)
A is the only one with no siblings, parents, or children.


20. (C)
By agreeing that fear is acceptable, we can also agree that fearing fear is nonsense. (D), the only other choice that corresponds at all with the argument of the passage, is a weak choice because the author is arguing that fearing fear is nonsense and that fear itself is acceptable.

21. (A)

Choices (B) and (E) support the author's argument by stressing further the importance of fear. (C) could either support or weaken the argument, depending upon whether it is taken to refer to the blanket generalization that the author attacks, or to the further generalization that the author presents. (D) is irrelevant to the argument, which does not stress the importance of the sources of fear.

22. (E)

Choice (A) is beside the point. The purpose of the illustration was to call attention to the fact that it is incoherent to say that we name something by what it is called, when our naming causes it to be called what it is called; the author thinks that it is recognizing a government that makes it lawful. Choice (B) is obviously wrong, since we are not interested in who debates the point, but in what arguments they give. Choice (C) is not an objection since it can be said that only legal authority can recognize a foreign government. Choice (D) would not undercut the argument, though it would make it unnecessary, since if it is all a question of power then legal reason would never enter the picture in the first place. (E) directly attacks the analogy on which the argument is made; to concede (E) would destroy it.

23. (C)

I does not support the argument, since the author is concerned not with the reason that people in fact have or give for recognizing or failing to recognize foreign governments, but only with the kinds of reasons that might be given in principle. II makes the author's argument superfluous, since if it were true there would be no legal reason for any matters between powers, including the question of recognition. III is an illustration of just the sort that the author gives and therefore (C) is correct.

24. (E)

In completing the missing portion of this passage, we are looking for a phrase that will balance out the original action of the tides, which involved separating the people in the room. The correct answer is Choice (E), which contrasts the original action of separation by the tides, with their present occupation of bringing the people back

together again. The other choices do not make logical sense.

25. (D)

The author of the passage first mentions how history has been shaped by these people, but at a later point he mentions the fact that often the fates of the people involved were out of their hands — determined by chance and circumstance. Hence, the author does not view the human experience as one of total free will or one of complete passivity, but rather as being shaped by an interplay of choice and chance. The correct answer is thus Choice (D).

# GRE
# GENERAL TEST 6
## ANSWER SHEET

### SECTION 1

1. Ⓐ Ⓑ Ⓒ Ⓓ Ⓔ
2. Ⓐ Ⓑ Ⓒ Ⓓ Ⓔ
3. Ⓐ Ⓑ Ⓒ Ⓓ Ⓔ
4. Ⓐ Ⓑ Ⓒ Ⓓ Ⓔ
5. Ⓐ Ⓑ Ⓒ Ⓓ Ⓔ
6. Ⓐ Ⓑ Ⓒ Ⓓ Ⓔ
7. Ⓐ Ⓑ Ⓒ Ⓓ Ⓔ
8. Ⓐ Ⓑ Ⓒ Ⓓ Ⓔ
9. Ⓐ Ⓑ Ⓒ Ⓓ Ⓔ
10. Ⓐ Ⓑ Ⓒ Ⓓ Ⓔ
11. Ⓐ Ⓑ Ⓒ Ⓓ Ⓔ
12. Ⓐ Ⓑ Ⓒ Ⓓ Ⓔ
13. Ⓐ Ⓑ Ⓒ Ⓓ Ⓔ
14. Ⓐ Ⓑ Ⓒ Ⓓ Ⓔ
15. Ⓐ Ⓑ Ⓒ Ⓓ Ⓔ
16. Ⓐ Ⓑ Ⓒ Ⓓ Ⓔ
17. Ⓐ Ⓑ Ⓒ Ⓓ Ⓔ
18. Ⓐ Ⓑ Ⓒ Ⓓ Ⓔ
19. Ⓐ Ⓑ Ⓒ Ⓓ Ⓔ
20. Ⓐ Ⓑ Ⓒ Ⓓ Ⓔ
21. Ⓐ Ⓑ Ⓒ Ⓓ Ⓔ
22. Ⓐ Ⓑ Ⓒ Ⓓ Ⓔ
23. Ⓐ Ⓑ Ⓒ Ⓓ Ⓔ
24. Ⓐ Ⓑ Ⓒ Ⓓ Ⓔ
25. Ⓐ Ⓑ Ⓒ Ⓓ Ⓔ
26. Ⓐ Ⓑ Ⓒ Ⓓ Ⓔ
27. Ⓐ Ⓑ Ⓒ Ⓓ Ⓔ
28. Ⓐ Ⓑ Ⓒ Ⓓ Ⓔ
29. Ⓐ Ⓑ Ⓒ Ⓓ Ⓔ
30. Ⓐ Ⓑ Ⓒ Ⓓ Ⓔ
31. Ⓐ Ⓑ Ⓒ Ⓓ Ⓔ
32. Ⓐ Ⓑ Ⓒ Ⓓ Ⓔ
33. Ⓐ Ⓑ Ⓒ Ⓓ Ⓔ
34. Ⓐ Ⓑ Ⓒ Ⓓ Ⓔ
35. Ⓐ Ⓑ Ⓒ Ⓓ Ⓔ
36. Ⓐ Ⓑ Ⓒ Ⓓ Ⓔ
37. Ⓐ Ⓑ Ⓒ Ⓓ Ⓔ
38. Ⓐ Ⓑ Ⓒ Ⓓ Ⓔ

### SECTION 2

1. Ⓐ Ⓑ Ⓒ Ⓓ Ⓔ
2. Ⓐ Ⓑ Ⓒ Ⓓ Ⓔ
3. Ⓐ Ⓑ Ⓒ Ⓓ Ⓔ
4. Ⓐ Ⓑ Ⓒ Ⓓ Ⓔ
5. Ⓐ Ⓑ Ⓒ Ⓓ Ⓔ
6. Ⓐ Ⓑ Ⓒ Ⓓ Ⓔ
7. Ⓐ Ⓑ Ⓒ Ⓓ Ⓔ
8. Ⓐ Ⓑ Ⓒ Ⓓ Ⓔ
9. Ⓐ Ⓑ Ⓒ Ⓓ Ⓔ
10. Ⓐ Ⓑ Ⓒ Ⓓ Ⓔ
11. Ⓐ Ⓑ Ⓒ Ⓓ Ⓔ
12. Ⓐ Ⓑ Ⓒ Ⓓ Ⓔ
13. Ⓐ Ⓑ Ⓒ Ⓓ Ⓔ
14. Ⓐ Ⓑ Ⓒ Ⓓ Ⓔ
15. Ⓐ Ⓑ Ⓒ Ⓓ Ⓔ
16. Ⓐ Ⓑ Ⓒ Ⓓ Ⓔ
17. Ⓐ Ⓑ Ⓒ Ⓓ Ⓔ
18. Ⓐ Ⓑ Ⓒ Ⓓ Ⓔ
19. Ⓐ Ⓑ Ⓒ Ⓓ Ⓔ
20. Ⓐ Ⓑ Ⓒ Ⓓ Ⓔ
21. Ⓐ Ⓑ Ⓒ Ⓓ Ⓔ
22. Ⓐ Ⓑ Ⓒ Ⓓ Ⓔ
23. Ⓐ Ⓑ Ⓒ Ⓓ Ⓔ
24. Ⓐ Ⓑ Ⓒ Ⓓ Ⓔ
25. Ⓐ Ⓑ Ⓒ Ⓓ Ⓔ
26. Ⓐ Ⓑ Ⓒ Ⓓ Ⓔ
27. Ⓐ Ⓑ Ⓒ Ⓓ Ⓔ
28. Ⓐ Ⓑ Ⓒ Ⓓ Ⓔ
29. Ⓐ Ⓑ Ⓒ Ⓓ Ⓔ
30. Ⓐ Ⓑ Ⓒ Ⓓ Ⓔ
31. Ⓐ Ⓑ Ⓒ Ⓓ Ⓔ
32. Ⓐ Ⓑ Ⓒ Ⓓ Ⓔ
33. Ⓐ Ⓑ Ⓒ Ⓓ Ⓔ
34. Ⓐ Ⓑ Ⓒ Ⓓ Ⓔ
35. Ⓐ Ⓑ Ⓒ Ⓓ Ⓔ
36. Ⓐ Ⓑ Ⓒ Ⓓ Ⓔ
37. Ⓐ Ⓑ Ⓒ Ⓓ Ⓔ
38. Ⓐ Ⓑ Ⓒ Ⓓ Ⓔ

### SECTION 3

1. Ⓐ Ⓑ Ⓒ Ⓓ Ⓔ
2. Ⓐ Ⓑ Ⓒ Ⓓ Ⓔ
3. Ⓐ Ⓑ Ⓒ Ⓓ Ⓔ
4. Ⓐ Ⓑ Ⓒ Ⓓ Ⓔ
5. Ⓐ Ⓑ Ⓒ Ⓓ Ⓔ
6. Ⓐ Ⓑ Ⓒ Ⓓ Ⓔ
7. Ⓐ Ⓑ Ⓒ Ⓓ Ⓔ
8. Ⓐ Ⓑ Ⓒ Ⓓ Ⓔ
9. Ⓐ Ⓑ Ⓒ Ⓓ Ⓔ
10. Ⓐ Ⓑ Ⓒ Ⓓ Ⓔ
11. Ⓐ Ⓑ Ⓒ Ⓓ Ⓔ
12. Ⓐ Ⓑ Ⓒ Ⓓ Ⓔ

13. Ⓐ Ⓑ Ⓒ Ⓓ Ⓔ
14. Ⓐ Ⓑ Ⓒ Ⓓ Ⓔ
15. Ⓐ Ⓑ Ⓒ Ⓓ Ⓔ
16. Ⓐ Ⓑ Ⓒ Ⓓ Ⓔ
17. Ⓐ Ⓑ Ⓒ Ⓓ Ⓔ
18. Ⓐ Ⓑ Ⓒ Ⓓ Ⓔ
19. Ⓐ Ⓑ Ⓒ Ⓓ Ⓔ
20. Ⓐ Ⓑ Ⓒ Ⓓ Ⓔ
21. Ⓐ Ⓑ Ⓒ Ⓓ Ⓔ
22. Ⓐ Ⓑ Ⓒ Ⓓ Ⓔ
23. Ⓐ Ⓑ Ⓒ Ⓓ Ⓔ
24. Ⓐ Ⓑ Ⓒ Ⓓ Ⓔ
25. Ⓐ Ⓑ Ⓒ Ⓓ Ⓔ
26. Ⓐ Ⓑ Ⓒ Ⓓ Ⓔ
27. Ⓐ Ⓑ Ⓒ Ⓓ Ⓔ
28. Ⓐ Ⓑ Ⓒ Ⓓ Ⓔ
29. Ⓐ Ⓑ Ⓒ Ⓓ Ⓔ
30. Ⓐ Ⓑ Ⓒ Ⓓ Ⓔ

16. Ⓐ Ⓑ Ⓒ Ⓓ Ⓔ
17. Ⓐ Ⓑ Ⓒ Ⓓ Ⓔ
18. Ⓐ Ⓑ Ⓒ Ⓓ Ⓔ
19. Ⓐ Ⓑ Ⓒ Ⓓ Ⓔ
20. Ⓐ Ⓑ Ⓒ Ⓓ Ⓔ
21. Ⓐ Ⓑ Ⓒ Ⓓ Ⓔ
22. Ⓐ Ⓑ Ⓒ Ⓓ Ⓔ
23. Ⓐ Ⓑ Ⓒ Ⓓ Ⓔ
24. Ⓐ Ⓑ Ⓒ Ⓓ Ⓔ
25. Ⓐ Ⓑ Ⓒ Ⓓ Ⓔ
26. Ⓐ Ⓑ Ⓒ Ⓓ Ⓔ
27. Ⓐ Ⓑ Ⓒ Ⓓ Ⓔ
28. Ⓐ Ⓑ Ⓒ Ⓓ Ⓔ
29. Ⓐ Ⓑ Ⓒ Ⓓ Ⓔ
30. Ⓐ Ⓑ Ⓒ Ⓓ Ⓔ

19. Ⓐ Ⓑ Ⓒ Ⓓ Ⓔ
20. Ⓐ Ⓑ Ⓒ Ⓓ Ⓔ
21. Ⓐ Ⓑ Ⓒ Ⓓ Ⓔ
22. Ⓐ Ⓑ Ⓒ Ⓓ Ⓔ
23. Ⓐ Ⓑ Ⓒ Ⓓ Ⓔ
24. Ⓐ Ⓑ Ⓒ Ⓓ Ⓔ
25. Ⓐ Ⓑ Ⓒ Ⓓ Ⓔ

## SECTION 6

1. Ⓐ Ⓑ Ⓒ Ⓓ Ⓔ
2. Ⓐ Ⓑ Ⓒ Ⓓ Ⓔ
3. Ⓐ Ⓑ Ⓒ Ⓓ Ⓔ
4. Ⓐ Ⓑ Ⓒ Ⓓ Ⓔ
5. Ⓐ Ⓑ Ⓒ Ⓓ Ⓔ
6. Ⓐ Ⓑ Ⓒ Ⓓ Ⓔ
7. Ⓐ Ⓑ Ⓒ Ⓓ Ⓔ
8. Ⓐ Ⓑ Ⓒ Ⓓ Ⓔ
9. Ⓐ Ⓑ Ⓒ Ⓓ Ⓔ
10. Ⓐ Ⓑ Ⓒ Ⓓ Ⓔ
11. Ⓐ Ⓑ Ⓒ Ⓓ Ⓔ
12. Ⓐ Ⓑ Ⓒ Ⓓ Ⓔ
13. Ⓐ Ⓑ Ⓒ Ⓓ Ⓔ
14. Ⓐ Ⓑ Ⓒ Ⓓ Ⓔ
15. Ⓐ Ⓑ Ⓒ Ⓓ Ⓔ
16. Ⓐ Ⓑ Ⓒ Ⓓ Ⓔ
17. Ⓐ Ⓑ Ⓒ Ⓓ Ⓔ
18. Ⓐ Ⓑ Ⓒ Ⓓ Ⓔ
19. Ⓐ Ⓑ Ⓒ Ⓓ Ⓔ
20. Ⓐ Ⓑ Ⓒ Ⓓ Ⓔ
21. Ⓐ Ⓑ Ⓒ Ⓓ Ⓔ
22. Ⓐ Ⓑ Ⓒ Ⓓ Ⓔ
23. Ⓐ Ⓑ Ⓒ Ⓓ Ⓔ
24. Ⓐ Ⓑ Ⓒ Ⓓ Ⓔ
25. Ⓐ Ⓑ Ⓒ Ⓓ Ⓔ

## SECTION 4

1. Ⓐ Ⓑ Ⓒ Ⓓ Ⓔ
2. Ⓐ Ⓑ Ⓒ Ⓓ Ⓔ
3. Ⓐ Ⓑ Ⓒ Ⓓ Ⓔ
4. Ⓐ Ⓑ Ⓒ Ⓓ Ⓔ
5. Ⓐ Ⓑ Ⓒ Ⓓ Ⓔ
6. Ⓐ Ⓑ Ⓒ Ⓓ Ⓔ
7. Ⓐ Ⓑ Ⓒ Ⓓ Ⓔ
8. Ⓐ Ⓑ Ⓒ Ⓓ Ⓔ
9. Ⓐ Ⓑ Ⓒ Ⓓ Ⓔ
10. Ⓐ Ⓑ Ⓒ Ⓓ Ⓔ
11. Ⓐ Ⓑ Ⓒ Ⓓ Ⓔ
12. Ⓐ Ⓑ Ⓒ Ⓓ Ⓔ
13. Ⓐ Ⓑ Ⓒ Ⓓ Ⓔ
14. Ⓐ Ⓑ Ⓒ Ⓓ Ⓔ
15. Ⓐ Ⓑ Ⓒ Ⓓ Ⓔ

## SECTION 5

1. Ⓐ Ⓑ Ⓒ Ⓓ Ⓔ
2. Ⓐ Ⓑ Ⓒ Ⓓ Ⓔ
3. Ⓐ Ⓑ Ⓒ Ⓓ Ⓔ
4. Ⓐ Ⓑ Ⓒ Ⓓ Ⓔ
5. Ⓐ Ⓑ Ⓒ Ⓓ Ⓔ
6. Ⓐ Ⓑ Ⓒ Ⓓ Ⓔ
7. Ⓐ Ⓑ Ⓒ Ⓓ Ⓔ
8. Ⓐ Ⓑ Ⓒ Ⓓ Ⓔ
9. Ⓐ Ⓑ Ⓒ Ⓓ Ⓔ
10. Ⓐ Ⓑ Ⓒ Ⓓ Ⓔ
11. Ⓐ Ⓑ Ⓒ Ⓓ Ⓔ
12. Ⓐ Ⓑ Ⓒ Ⓓ Ⓔ
13. Ⓐ Ⓑ Ⓒ Ⓓ Ⓔ
14. Ⓐ Ⓑ Ⓒ Ⓓ Ⓔ
15. Ⓐ Ⓑ Ⓒ Ⓓ Ⓔ
16. Ⓐ Ⓑ Ⓒ Ⓓ Ⓔ
17. Ⓐ Ⓑ Ⓒ Ⓓ Ⓔ
18. Ⓐ Ⓑ Ⓒ Ⓓ Ⓔ

# TEST 6

## Section 1

---

**TIME:** 30 Minutes
38 Questions

**DIRECTIONS:** Each of the given sentences has blank spaces which indicate words omitted. Choose the best combination of words which fit into the the meaning and structure within the context of the sentence.

---

1. In preparing a recommendation for his student, the professor _____ his statements in order to express his reservations.

   (A) lengthened

   (B) qualified

   (C) wrote

   (D) formed

   (E) constructed

2. _____ is a key variable in relation to achievement; talent, support, effort, and practice are all important, but the fact remains: those who _____ to succeed go the furthest.

   (A) Potential...need

   (B) Desire...want

   (C) Heredity...train

   (D) Training...struggle

   (E) Education...hope

3. A teacher must learn to be _____ to all students, but unduly _____ with none.

   (A) civil...rude

   (B) objective...hostile

   (C) friendly...familiar

   (D) accepting...pleased

   (E) interesting...attentive

4.  Young people who have never experienced serious illness or harm often have an exaggerated sense of _____ that leads them to believe that the really bad things in life only happen to other people.

    (A)  judgment

    (B)  happiness

    (C)  life

    (D)  well-being

    (E)  concern

5.  He knew that all available evidence indicated the invalidity of the theory in question; nevertheless, he personally _____ it.

    (A)  researched

    (B)  supported

    (C)  investigated

    (D)  repudiated

    (E)  explored

6.  The reason that restaurants have their waitresses and others introduce themselves by their first names is that the _____ of familiarity may _____ the customer's inclination to be critical of the service rendered or the meal received.

    (A)  appearance...reduce

    (B)  affliction...retard

    (C)  reality...prohibit

    (D)  growth...limit

    (E)  pleasure...deny

7.  Perhaps one reason for the lesser number of female writers is that women traditionally have lacked the _____ independence and the _____ necessary to permit them to concentrate their efforts on writing.

    (A)  literary...talent

    (B)  intellectual...ability

    (C)  social...reputation

    (D)  emotional...intelligence

    (E)  financial...leisure

---

**DIRECTIONS:** In the following questions, the given pair of words contains a specific relationship to each other. Select the best pair of the choices which expresses the same relationship as the given.

---

8.  REQUEST:ULTIMATUM::

    (A) mar:ruin                (D) branch:tree

    (B) couplet:sonnet          (E) surfeit:gluttony

    (C) page: book


9.  NERVOUS:POISE::

    (A) angry:sensibility       (D) energetic:enthusiasm

    (B) frightened:confidence   (E) calm:laziness

    (C) empathetic:rationality


10. OXIDATION:RUST::

    (A) burning:napalm          (D) ignorance:education

    (B) hunger:starvation       (E) poverty:alcoholism

    (C) investment:dividends


11. RAIN:PRECIPITATION::

    (A) copper:metal            (D) wind:abrasion

    (B) ice:glacier             (E) heat:evaporation

    (C) oil:shale


12. COCOON:BUTTERFLY::

    (A) apple:pie               (D) adolescent:adult

    (B) blossom:fruit           (E) wood:house

    (C) awareness:understanding

13. RETINUE:FOLLOWER::

   (A) animal:menagerie

   (B) state:federation

   (C) word:vocabulary

   (D) detritus:debris

   (E) tune:medley

14. HARDHEARTED:EMPATHY::

   (A) ambivalent:decisiveness

   (B) assertive:independence

   (C) competitive:adversary

   (D) creative:dogmatism

   (E) avenge:friendship

15. MINUTE:HOUR::

   (A) meter:kilometer

   (B) alto:choir

   (C) state:federation

   (D) student:class

   (E) boxcar:train

16. ANGER:RAGE::

   (A) stubborn:recalcitrant

   (B) quarrelsome:pugnacious

   (C) hot-tempered:irascible

   (D) lucid:perspicuous

   (E) failure:fiasco

---

**DIRECTIONS:** Each passage is followed by questions based on its content. After reading a passage, choose the best answer to each question. Answer all questions based on what is stated or implied in that passage.

---

We believe that our Earth is about 4.6 billion years old. At present we are forced to look to other bodies in the solar system for hints as to what the early history of the Earth was like. Studies of our Moon, Mercury, Mars, and the large satellites of Jupiter and Saturn have provided ample evidence that all of these objects were bombarded by bodies with a wide variety of sizes shortly after they had formed. This

same bombardment must have affected the Earth as well. The lunar record indicates that the rate of impacts decreased to its present low level about 4 billion years ago. On the Earth, subsequent erosion and crustal motions have obliterated the craters that must have formed during this epoch. Since it is generally believed that life on Earth began during this period, the bombardment must have been part of the environment within which this event occurred.

17.  Which of the following bodies was not studied to give evidence that the Earth was bombarded in its conceptual history?

    (A)  Mars

    (B)  Mercury

    (C)  Earth's moon

    (D)  Jupiter

    (E)  Satellites of Saturn

18.  Bombardment of the Earth at one time by various-sized bodies is:

    (A)  indicated by subsequent erosion patterns.

    (B)  documented fact.

    (C)  proven by the lunar record.

    (D)  a necessary environmental factor for the formation of life forms.

    (E)  inferred from what happened on certain other planetary bodies.

19.  Which of the following best states the author's main point?

    (A)  The Earth is an old body having its beginning about 4.6 billion years ago.

    (B)  During its early history, the Earth was bombarded by bodies.

    (C)  Mercury, Mars, Jupiter and Saturn were in place before Earth.

    (D)  It is because of the Earth's atmosphere that it shows no after-effects of the bombardment.

(E)   The Earth's moon actually protected the Earth from much
body bombardment.

Life in colonial times was harsh, and the refinements of the mother
country were ordinarily lacking. The colonists, however, soon began
to mold their English culture into the fresh environment of a new land.
The influence of religion permeated the entire way of life. In most
Southern colonies, the Anglican church was the legally established
church. In New England, the Puritans were dominant; and, in Pennsylvania, the Quakers. Especially in the New England colonies, the local
or village church was the hub of community life; the authorities strictly
enforced the Sabbath and sometimes banished nonbelievers and dissenters.

Unfortunately, the same sort of religious intolerance, bigotry, and
superstition associated with the age of the Reformation in Europe also
prevailed in some of the colonies, though on a lesser scale. In the last
half of the 17th century, during sporadic outbreaks of religious
fanaticism and hysteria, Massachusetts and Connecticut authorities
tried and hanged a few women as "witches." Early in the 17th century,
some other witchcraft persecution occurred in Virginia, North Carolina, and Rhode Island. As the decades passed, however, religious
toleration developed in the colonies.

Because of the strong religious influence in the colonies, especially in New England, religious instruction and Bible reading played
an important part in education. In Massachusetts, for example, the law
of 1645 required each community with fifty households to establish an
elementary school. Two years later the same colony passed the
"Deluder Satan" law which required each town of one hundred
families to maintain a grammar school for the purpose of providing
religious, as well as general, instruction. In the Southern colonies, only
a few privately endowed free schools existed. Private tutors instructed
the sons of well-to-do planters, who completed their educations in
English universities. Young males in poor families throughout the
colonies were ordinarily apprenticed for vocational education.

By 1700, two colleges had been founded: Harvard, established by
the Massachusetts Legislature in 1636; and William and Mary, in
Virginia, which originated in 1693 under a royal charter. Other cultural
activities before 1700 were limited. The few literary products of the

colonists, mostly historical narratives, journals, sermons, and some poetry, were printed in England. The *Bay Psalm Book* (1640) was the first book printed in the colonies. Artists and composers were few, and their output was of a relatively simple character.

20.  Which of the following cannot be inferred or understood from the article about the "Deluder Satan" Act?

  (A)  It was adopted to train lay ministers.

  (B)  It was adopted to train grammar school students in the reading and interpretation of the Bible.

  (C)  It was adopted to promote religious instruction in the grammar school.

  (D)  It was adopted to insure all students in a community had access to similar opportunities in grammar level education.

  (E)  It was adopted to further general education to the grammar school level.

21.  The author mentions the *Bay Psalm Book* because it was:

  (A)  required reading in the Massachusetts grammar school.

  (B)  the basis upon which women were tried for witchcraft.

  (C)  the first book printed in the colonies.

  (D)  the basis for the Anglican church in America.

  (E)  outlawed in Massachusetts as blasphemous.

22.  The impetus for free, public-supported schools came from:

  (A)  the New England colonies.

  (B)  Pennsylvania.

  (C)  Massachusetts.

  (D)  the Southern colonies.

  (E)  private tutors.

23. Which of the following is <u>not</u> a true evaluation of life in the early colonies?

    (A)  There was religious toleration from Massachusetts to Virginia.

    (B)  Life was harsh.

    (C)  The comforts found in England were lacking.

    (D)  Local literary works were limited to historical narratives, journals, sermons, and some poetry.

    (E)  Artists and composers were few.

24. According to the author, those students taking advantage of the apprenticeship programs came from:

    (A)  New York        (D)  Virginia

    (B)  the aristocracy    (E)  poor families

    (C)  plantations

25. It can be inferred from the article that private tutors were educators among the aristocracy in:

    (A)  Pennsylvania     (D)  New York

    (B)  the Middle colonies   (E)  the Southern colonies

    (C)  the New England colonies

26. According to the selection, which of the following was not a result of religious bigotry?

    (A)  There was an outbreak of religious fanaticism and hysteria.

    (B)  The Puritan colony had the best record for religious tolerance.

    (C)  Massachusetts and Connecticut tried to hang women as witches.

    (D)  Witchcraft persecution took place in a few other states.

    (E)  The 17th and 18th centuries were the two worst eras for religious intolerance.

27.  Which of the following cannot be acknowledged from the selection about Harvard University?

    (A)  It originated under a royal charter.

    (B)  It was the first college in America.

    (C)  It was one of two colleges operating by 1700.

    (D)  It was created by the Massachusetts Legislature.

    (E)  It was founded in 1836.

---

**DIRECTIONS:** Each of the following questions provides a given word in capitalized letters followed by five word choices. Choose the best word which is most <u>opposite</u> in meaning to the given word.

---

28.  OSCILLATE:

    (A)  moor

    (B)  stabilize

    (C)  balance

    (D)  vacillate

    (E)  undulate

29.  RESERVED:

    (A)  affable

    (B)  saved

    (C)  given

    (D)  unexpected

    (E)  reticent

30.  ILLUSORY:

    (A)  evident

    (B)  meaningful

    (C)  soluble

    (D)  obvious

    (E)  factual

31.  PREVENT:

    (A)  invite

    (B)  permit

    (C)  encourage

    (D)  demand

    (E)  urge

32. BELLICOSE:

    (A) pulchritudinous

    (B) obdurate

    (C) anorexic

    (D) seraphic

    (E) pacific

33. SCRUPULOUS:

    (A) meticulous

    (B) painstaking

    (C) careless

    (D) honest

    (E) forgetful

34. EMOLIENT:

    (A) attenuate

    (B) absorbent

    (C) adherent

    (D) abrasive

    (E) audacious

35. ALLEGIANCE:

    (A) disapprobation

    (B) treachery

    (C) incompatibility

    (D) dissension

    (E) disputation

36. LUGUBRIOUS:

    (A) joyous

    (B) energetic

    (C) rapid

    (D) facile

    (E) healthy

37. EULOGISTIC:

    (A) officious

    (B) censorious

    (C) depressed

    (D) incomprehensible

    (E) obstinate

38. BANEFUL:

    (A) respected

    (B) beautiful

    (C) reckless

    (D) beneficial

    (E) honorable

**STOP**

If time still remains, you may go
back and check your work.
When the time allotted is up, you
may go on to the next section.

# Section 2

TIME:    30 Minutes
           38 Questions

**DIRECTIONS:** Each of the given sentences has blank spaces which indicate words omitted. Choose the best combination of words which fit into the the meaning and structure within the context of the sentence.

1.    The acquisition of exact knowledge is apt to be _____ , but it is essential to every kind of excellence.

   (A)  wearisome                 (D)  amorphous

   (B)  equable                      (E)  eccentric

   (C)  erratic

2.    Since the calendar year originally contained only 355 days, an extra month was occasionally _____ .

   (A)  contingent                 (D)  superadded

   (B)  introduced                 (E)  intercalated

   (C)  incidental

3.    The overgrown boatdock reeked not of ordinary salt air but stronger, _____ of seaweed, damp and dead fish.

   (A)  malodorous               (D)  pungent

   (B)  rankling                     (E)  redolent

   (C)  poignant

4. His frightful condition of internal strain and instability was _____ to human nature, being a condition of chronic terror that at last became unbearable.

   (A) invidious

   (B) compatible

   (C) alluring

   (D) abhorrent

   (E) congenial

5. There was something _____ about it, and in intangible ways one was made to feel that the worst was about to come.

   (A) ominous

   (B) tutelary

   (C) nymphonic

   (D) celestial

   (E) mythical

6. Strange things happen on a racetrack where human _____ and equine aristocrats fashion bonds beyond the comprehension of the outside world.

   (A) aristocrats

   (B) avarice

   (C) greed

   (D) covetousness

   (E) derelicts

7. The _____ policy of Walpole was regarded by the people as a national humiliation.

   (A) pliant

   (B) impartial

   (C) pacific

   (D) malleable

   (E) histrionic

---

**DIRECTIONS:** In the following questions, the given pair of words contains a specific relationship to each other. Select the best pair of the choices which expresses the same relationship as the given.

---

8.  COMPULSORY:REQUIRED::
    - (A) commitment:vows
    - (B) normal:aberrant
    - (C) freedom:democracy
    - (D) voluntary:mandatory
    - (E) education:intelligence

9.  FRACTIONS:DECIMALS::
    - (A) phonics:word recognition
    - (B) French:English
    - (C) health:physical activity
    - (D) volumes:library
    - (E) harmony:music

10. KEEL:DECK::
    - (A) glasses:see
    - (B) sugar:syrup
    - (C) rock:geology
    - (D) index:glossary
    - (E) grass:lawn

11. RECREATION:SWIM::
    - (A) perspire:run
    - (B) suffocate:breath
    - (C) gymkhana:driving skill
    - (D) gyron:airfoil
    - (E) flourish:thrive

12. MIRAGE:ILLUSION::
    - (A) film:movie
    - (B) print:newspaper
    - (C) teach:facilitate
    - (D) enigma:mystery
    - (E) astronauts:exploration

13. ANXIETY:STRESS::
    - (A) aphanite:rock
    - (B) Apollo:mythology
    - (C) brevity:conciseness
    - (D) insult:invective
    - (E) destroy:inutile

14. SUN:STARS::

   (A) piranha:fish        (D) shrub:tree

   (B) plank:block        (E) emotion:mood

   (C) ovicidal:chemical

15. DONNISH:PEDANT::

   (A) redolent:ammonia      (D) pedagogic:teacher

   (B) jocund:pessimist       (E) esoteric:simpleton

   (C) salacious:minister

16. VIE:RIVAL::

   (A) requiem:death       (D) fugue:composition

   (B) lurid:ruddy         (E) compete:emulate

   (C) hallmark:unique

---

**DIRECTIONS:** Each passage is followed by questions based on its content. After reading a passage, choose the best answer to each question. Answer all questions based on what is stated or implied in that passage.

---

A cave is a natural opening in the ground extending beyond the zone of light and large enough to permit the entry of man. Occurring in a wide variety of rock types and caused by widely differing geologic processes, caves range in size from single small rooms to interconnecting passages many miles long. The scientific study of caves is called speleology (from the Greek words *spelaion* for cave and *logos* for study). It is a composite science based on geology, hydrology, biology, and archaeology, and thus holds special interest for earth scientists of the U.S. Geological Survey.

Caves have been natural attractions since prehistoric times. Prolific evidence of early man's interest has been discovered in caves scattered throughout the world. Fragments of skeletons of some of the

earliest manlike creatures (Australopithecines) have been discovered in cave deposits in South Africa, and the first evidence of primitive Neanderthal man was found in a cave in the Neander Valley of Germany. Cro-Magnon man created his remarkable murals on the walls of caves in southern France and northern Spain where he took refuge more than 10,000 years ago during the chill of the Ice Age.

17.  The passage implies from its definition of cave that:

    (A)  all caves do not have the same characteristics.

    (B)  the opening must be large enough to admit man.

    (C)  not all openings into the earth are classified as caves.

    (D)  there must be a natural opening in the ground.

    (E)  it must extend beyond the zone of light.

18.  It can be inferred that the U.S. Geological Survey is primarily interested in caves because of:

    (A)  the clues they reveal about early man and his environment.

    (B)  the evidence needed to learn about primitive Neanderthal man.

    (C)  the murals on the walls.

    (D)  the interconnected passages.

    (E)  the wide variety of rock types.

19.  The term *speleology* is defined as:

    (A)  the study of early man.

    (B)  the study of water.

    (C)  the study of life.

    (D)  the study of caves.

    (E)  the study of earth, water, life and early man.

20.  The passage describes evidence of the Neanderthal man's habitat as being in Germany; while evidence of the Cro-Magnon man has been found in France and Spain. The Cro-Magnon man selected Spain and France due to:

(A)  a shortage of available food near to the Neanderthal man.

(B)  more temperate weather than found in Germany.

(C)  more nomadic space needed for both the Neanderthal and Cro-Magnon man.

(D)  its proximity to South Africa and his ancestors.

(E)  his preference of the plains to the mountains.

Americans traveling in Europe have for many years been impressed by the large areas around cities that are devoted to small garden plots.

To the casual observer these appear to be simply clusters of miniature truck gardens with scattered fruit trees. More discerning travelers are impressed by the obvious care lavished on these plots. Gardens are weed-free, crops are bountiful, fruit trees are carefully pruned, hedges are clipped, huts and tool sheds — if present — are usually neat and well-tended, and every square foot is carefully utilized. Many garden areas have a festive air, with flags flying.

Try as he will, the traveler will find little reference to these garden areas in guidebooks, on guided tours, or in tourist information bureaus. There are few readily available sources of information for the American on the small garden movement in Europe.

Names given to these areas in Europe vary from the general (such as "garden colonies"), to the manner in which they are allocated ("allotment gardens"), or the facilities they include (such as "hut colonies," which refer to the tool sheds or small houses on garden plots in some countries). Often these collections of individual garden plots are referred to as "workers' gardens." Many simply are called "small gardens" or "small-garden areas."

For centuries people have needed to live in cities and towns in order to find jobs — yet have desired the greenery, the cleaner air, and the

opportunity to garden that rarely are available except in rural or rural-urban fringe areas.

Living space has always been at a premium in cities and towns; there has been little green space — and even less space for gardens. During the Middle Ages, when cities were walled for protection, there was little open space of any type within the walls, and gardens flourished in front of city gates.

Similar crowded conditions occurred several hundred years later when the industrial revolution forced rapid city growth. Ground space was at a premium so that houses were squeezed together side by side, pushed behind into alleys and inner courtyards, or forced up — into five- and six-story buildings with several apartments on each floor.

Many rooms had no outside light. Ventilation was almost nonexistent. Added to this were other poor health conditions, including a general lack of sanitary facilities, inadequate heating, and meager and unwholesome food — all compounded by the terrible crowding as the workers and their families swarmed into the cities. Lack of air, lack of sunlight, and unsanitary, overcrowded conditions were a way of life for most working people.

One of the measures provided to relieve people living in such unhealthy conditions in England was a law in 1819 that provided for leasing land for small gardens to the poor and unemployed. Later, other countries in Europe promulgated laws regarding provision of small-garden areas for city people.

Gardens for working people, the poor, and the unemployed were provided as a health measure by city governments, philanthropists, and some factory owners. Gardens also became a way to help ensure social stability by providing a link to the countryside that the workers had left, as well as a means of improving the quality of life.

By the mid-1800's the small-garden movement had appeared in most European countries, either as an independent effort to meet the local conditions, or influenced by work in neighboring countries. The movement continued to grow into the early 20th century and began to be considered as a factor in planning urban areas.

21. The first garden plots were established:

    (A) to relieve overcrowding.

    (B) to provide enjoyment for the people.

    (C) to relieve unhealthy living conditions.

    (D) to provide extra food for the troops during Medieval times.

    (E) to keep the people occupied.

22. Small houses found on the garden plots are primarily used:

    (A) for weekend lodging.

    (B) for tool and gardening storage.

    (C) for harvest collecting.

    (D) for tourist identification of the small gardens.

    (E) for government regulations.

23. Information supplied within the passage would answer which of the following questions?

    (A) Legal precedence for small gardens was set in what nation?

    (B) The "party spirit" surrounding gardens is related to what festival?

    (C) How are garden sizes determined?

    (D) How may additional information be acquired concerning small gardens in Europe?

    (E) How did neighboring countries influence the spread of small gardens throughout Europe?

24. The passage infers that during the Middle Ages little open space existed within the walls of a city due to:

    (A) Vast populations crowded within the walls.

    (B) Dwellings crowded together.

(C) Building walls requiring extensive resources.

(D) The difficulty of defending walled cities.

(E) The peoples' preference to sleep only within the walls.

25. The passage implies that the first garden plot tenders shared the bounty of the garden plot with the landowners as:

(A) a result of finding work.

(B) a result of the abundance of produce.

(C) evidence of a landowner-tenant relationship.

(D) a result of the peoples' gratitude.

(E) a result of a church requirement.

26. The passage suggests that "necessity is the mother of invention" because:

(A) unhealthy living conditions gave birth to the garden plot.

(B) the Industrial Revolution was a major cause of crowded living conditions.

(C) small walled cities of the Middle Ages was the point of conception for the garden plot.

(D) survival during all ages has depended upon health and nutrition.

(E) modern technology has reduced the need for garden plots.

27. The passage implies an existing correlation between cultural stability and small garden tending which is reflected by:

(A) care lavished upon the gardens.

(B) efficiently utilized gardens.

(C) a festive air surrounding the gardens.

(D) a continuation of their cultural heritage.

(E) improved welfare of the people.

DIRECTIONS: Each of the following questions provides a given word in capitalized letters followed by five word choices. Choose the best word which is most <u>opposite</u> in meaning to the given word.

28. CIPHER:

    (A) estimate

    (B) digit

    (C) series

    (D) calculate

    (E) plenary

29. RECURRENCE:

    (A) infinity

    (B) reiterate

    (C) repetition

    (D) succinct

    (E) terse

30. SYNCHRONISM:

    (A) coincidence

    (B) sequelant

    (C) periodic

    (D) modulation

    (E) capriciousness

31. MUTATION:

    (A) variation

    (B) deviation

    (C) alteration

    (D) innovation

    (E) monotonous

32. CESSATION:

    (A) perpetuation

    (B) innovation

    (C) abeyance

    (D) methodicalness

    (E) latent

33. EXIGUITY:

    (A) paucity

    (B) eccentric

    (C) decimation

    (D) array

    (E) reduction

34. **ABRUPT:**
    (A) inaffable
    (B) extempore
    (C) insolence
    (D) perpetuity
    (E) momentary

35. **DESULTORY:**
    (A) desuetude
    (B) fitfulness
    (C) erratic
    (D) random
    (E) rhythm

36. **VERSATILITY:**
    (A) inclination
    (B) vacillation
    (C) fluctuation
    (D) vicissitude
    (E) constancy

37. **ENERVATION:**
    (A) strenuous
    (B) stress
    (C) flaccidity
    (D) prevaricate
    (E) languor

38. **PREPONDERANCE:**
    (A) influence
    (B) prevalence
    (C) dominance
    (D) auspices
    (E) impotence

**STOP**

If time still remains, you may go back and check your work.
When the time allotted is up, you may go on to the next section.

# Section 3

TIME:   30 Minutes
         30 Questions

**NUMBERS:** All numbers are real numbers.

**FIGURES:** Position of points, angles, regions, etc. are assumed to be in the order shown and angle measures are assumed to be positive.

**LINES:** Assume that lines shown as straight are indeed straight.

**DIRECTIONS:** Each of the following given set of quantities is placed into either column A or B. Compare the two quantities to decide whether:

(A)   the quantity in Column A is greater

(B)   the quantity in Column B is greater

(C)   the two quantities are equal

(D)   the relationship cannot be determined from the information given.

**NOTE:** Do not choose (E) since there are only four choices.

**COMMON INFORMATION:** Information which relates to one or both given quantities is centered in the two columns. A symbol which appears in both columns will indicate the same item in Column A and Column B.

**EXAMPLES:**

| Column A | Column B |
|----------|----------|
| 1.     5 × 4 | 5 + 4 |

Explanation: The correct answer is (A), since $5 \times 4 = 20$, and $5 + 4 = 9$.

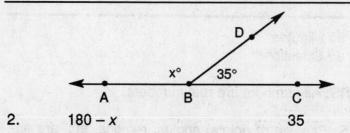

2.          $180 - x$                                    $35$

Explanation: The correct answer is (C). Since Angle *ABC* is a straight angle, its measurement is 180°.

|     | **Column A** | **Column B** |
|-----|--------------|--------------|

$$x - y \neq 0$$

1.          $x + y$                          $\dfrac{x^2 - y^2}{x - y}$

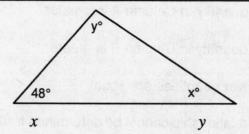

2.          $x$                                  $y$

3.          $5.4048$              $0.105 + 0.5 - 3.1029 + 8$

A farmer calculates that out of every 100 seeds of corn he plants, he harvests 48 ears of corn. In a year, his harvest was 72,000 ears of corn.

4.     Number of seeds planted              85,000

$x$, $y$, and $z$ are integers

5.          $x - y$                              $z - x$

|              | **Column A** | **Column B** |
|--------------|--------------|--------------|

A class' average (arithmetic mean) on a
reading test was 27.5 out of 40. The 19 girls
in the class scored a total of 532 points.

| 6. | Total points scored by the 11 boys in the class. | 287 |

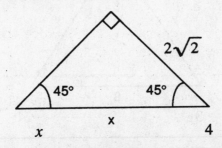

| 7. | $x$ | 4 |

$C$ represents a Celsius temperature and $F$ represents
the equivalent in Fahrenheit temperature.
$$C = \frac{5}{9}(F - 32).$$

| 8. | 65°F | 20°C |

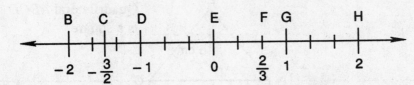

| 9. | $\frac{2}{3}$ | The coordinate of the midpoint of segment $\overline{DH}$ |

$$a < b$$

| 10. | $a^2$ | $b^2$ |

If 288 is added to a certain number $n$, the
result will be equal to three times the amount
by which the number exceeds 12.

| 11. | $n$ | 276 |

| <u>Column A</u> | <u>Column B</u> |
| --- | --- |

$a$ is a real number and $0 < a < 1$.

| 12. | $a$ | $a^2$ |
| --- | --- | --- |

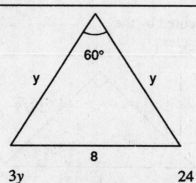

| 13. | $3y$ | 24 |
| --- | --- | --- |

An automatic coin counter at a bank indicates that
$65 in dimes and quarters was processed.
There were 389 coins.

| 14. | Number of quarters | 215 |
| --- | --- | --- |

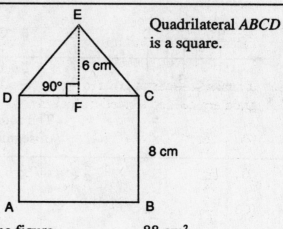

Quadrilateral *ABCD* is a square.

| 15. | Area of the figure | 88 cm² |
| --- | --- | --- |

---

**DIRECTIONS:** For the following questions, select the best answer choice to the given question.

---

738

16. Tilda's car gets 34 miles per gallon of gasoline and Naomi's car gets 8 miles per gallon. When traveling from Washington, D.C. to Philadelphia, they both used a whole number of gallons of gasoline. How far is it from Philadelphia to Washington D.C.?

(A)  21 miles

(B)  32 miles

(C)  68 miles

(D)  136 miles

(E)  170 miles

17. In the figure shown, line r is parallel to line l. Find the measure of angle RBC.

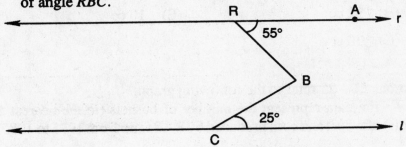

(A)  30°

(B)  80°

(C)  90°

(D)  100°

(E)  110°

18. If it takes s sacks of grain to feed c chickens, how many sacks of grain are needed to feed k chickens?

(A)  $\dfrac{ck}{s}$

(B)  $\dfrac{k}{cs}$

(C)  $\dfrac{cs}{k}$

(D)  $\dfrac{c}{sk}$

(E)  $\dfrac{sk}{c}$

19. The following ratio

$$40 \text{ seconds} : 1\frac{1}{2} \text{ minutes} : \frac{1}{6} \text{ hour}$$

can be expressed in lowest terms as

(A)  4 : 9 : 60    (D)  $^2/_3$ : $1^1/_2$ : 10

(B)  4 : 9 : 6    (E)  60 : 9 : 4

(C)  40 : 90 : 60

20.  A doctor has 40 cc of 2% tincture of iodine. If the iodine is boiled, alcohol is evaporated away and the strength of tincture is raised. How much alcohol must be boiled away in order to raise the strength of the tincture to 8%?

(A)  34 cc    (D)  24 cc

(B)  32 cc    (E)  10 cc

(C)  30 cc

Questions 21 – 25 refer to the following graph.
        The data represent the number of bushels (to the nearest 5 bushels) of wheat and corn produced by RAS farm from 1975 to 1985.

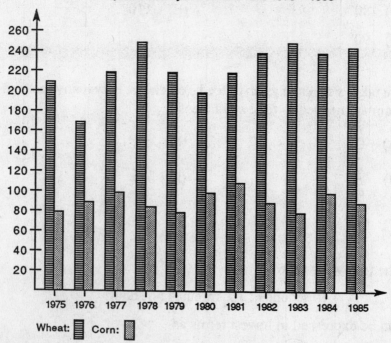

Number of bushels (to the nearest 5 bushels) of wheat and corn produced by farm RQS from 1975 – 1985

21. In which year was the least number of bushels of wheat produced?

    (A) 1976

    (B) 1978

    (C) 1980

    (D) 1982

    (E) 1984

22. In which year did the greatest decline in corn production occur?

    (A) 1978

    (B) 1980

    (C) 1982

    (D) 1983

    (E) 1985

23. During which year or years did the corn production decrease while the wheat production increased?

    (A) 1978 only

    (B) 1978 and 1985 only

    (C) 1982 and 1985 only

    (D) 1982, 1983 and 1985 only

    (E) 1978, 1982, 1983, and 1985

24. The ratio of wheat production in 1985 to that of 1975 is

    (A) 6 : 7

    (B) 8 : 5

    (C) 7 : 6

    (D) 8 : 7

    (E) 5 : 6

25. During which year was the combined production of wheat and corn a maximum?

    (A) 1978

    (B) 1981

    (C) 1983

    (D) 1984

    (E) 1985

26. If $m$ and $n$ are consecutive integers, and $m < n$, which one of the following statements is always true?

    (A) $n - m$ is even

    (B) $m$ must be odd

    (C) $m^2 + n^2$ is even

    (D) $n^2 - m^2$ is odd

    (E) $n$ must be even

27. If $a/b < 0$ and $c/d > 0$, which of the following statements is true?

    (A) $\dfrac{a}{b} \cdot \dfrac{c}{d} < 0$

    (B) $\dfrac{a}{b} \cdot \dfrac{c}{d} > 0$

    (C) $\dfrac{a}{b} + \dfrac{c}{d} < 0$

    (D) $\dfrac{a}{b} + \dfrac{c}{d} > 0$

    (E) $\dfrac{a}{b} = \dfrac{c}{d}$

28. Which of the following equations can be used to find a number $n$, such that if you multiply it by 3 and take 2 away, the result is 5 times as great as if you divide the number by 3 and add 2?

    (A) $3n - 2 = 5 + (n/_3 + 2)$

    (B) $3n - 2 = 5(n/_3 + 2)$

    (C) $3n - 2 = {}^{5n}/_3 + 2$

    (D) $5(3n - 2) = {}^n/_3 + 2$

    (E) $5n - 2 = {}^n/_3 + 2$

29. In the five-pointed star shown, what is the sum of the measures of angles $A$, $B$, $C$, $D$, and $E$?

    (A) 108°

    (B) 72°

    (C) 36°

    (D) 150°

    (E) 180°

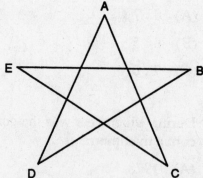

30. Pete and Lynn travel on bicycles from the same place, in opposite directions, Pete traveling 4 mph faster than Lynn. After 5 hours, they are 120 miles apart. What is Lynn's rate of travel?

    (A)  20 mph

    (B)  9 mph

    (C)  10 mph

    (D)  12 mph

    (E)  14 mph

## STOP
If time still remains, you may go back and check your work.
When the time allotted is up, you may go on to the next section.

# Section 4

**TIME:**   30 Minutes
           30 Questions

**NUMBERS:** All numbers are real numbers.

**FIGURES:** Position of points, angles, regions, etc. are assumed to be in the order shown and angle measures are assumed to be positive.

**LINES:** Assume that lines shown as straight are indeed straight.

**DIRECTIONS:** Each of the following given set of quantities is placed into either column A or B. Compare the two quantities to decide whether:

(A)   the quantity in Column A is greater

(B)   the quantity in Column B is greater

(C)   the two quantities are equal

(D)   the relationship cannot be determined from the information given.

**NOTE:** Do not choose (E) since there are only four choices.

**COMMON INFORMATION:** Information which relates to one or both given quantities is centered in the two columns. A symbol which appears in both columns will indicate the same item in Column A and Column B.

**EXAMPLES:**

| Column A | Column B |
|---|---|
| 1.        $5 \times 4$ | $5 + 4$ |

Explanation: The correct answer is (A), since $5 \times 4 = 20$, and $5 + 4 = 9$.

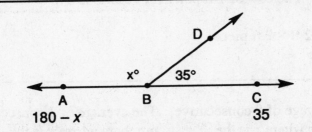

| | |
|---|---|
| A | C |
| 2. 180 – x | 35 |

Explanation: The correct answer is (C). Since Angle *ABC* is a straight angle, its measurement is 180°.

| | <u>Column A</u> | <u>Column B</u> |
|---|---|---|
| 1. | 30% of 40 | 40% of 30 |

$$K(I) = I^2 + 1, \quad L(I) = 1 - I^2,$$
$$I > 0$$

| | | |
|---|---|---|
| 2. | $K(I) - L(I)$ | $K(I) + L(I)$ |

$$m < 0, \ n < 0, \text{ and } m > n$$

| | | |
|---|---|---|
| 3. | $\dfrac{m}{n}$ | $\dfrac{n}{m}$ |

If we define $(a, b) = a + 3b$
and $(2, 3) = (3, x)$

| | | |
|---|---|---|
| 4. | 2 | x |

$$y = x - 2$$

| | | |
|---|---|---|
| 5. | $y + 3$ | $x - 1$ |

| | Column A | Column B |
|---|---|---|

The cost of 1 ft per 1 ft of fabric is \$4.

| 6. | Cost of 2 ft × 2 ft piece of fabric | 10 |
|---|---|---|

| 7. | The average of 5 consecutive numbers where $x$ is the central number | The average of 3 consecutive numbers where $x$ is the central number |
|---|---|---|

$p > 0,\ q > 0,$ and $p \neq q$

| 8. | $p + q$ | $\dfrac{p^2 - q^2}{q - p}$ |
|---|---|---|

$A$ is bigger than $P$ and $B$ is not less than $P$

| 9. | $A$ | $B$ |
|---|---|---|

$n > 2$

| 10. | half of $n$ square | $\dfrac{n}{2}$ |
|---|---|---|

$b < 0,\ y \neq a$

| 11. | $\dfrac{ab - by}{y - a}$ | $b$ |
|---|---|---|

In a Boeing 747 with 320 seats, 73 women are traveling and 20% of the seats are empty.

| 12. | Men that are traveling | 185 |
|---|---|---|

| 13. | $4 - \dfrac{1}{\dfrac{1 + \frac{1}{2}}{1 - \frac{1}{2}}}$ | 2 |
|---|---|---|

| Column A | Column B |
| --- | --- |

The sum of three consecutive even
numbers is 42

14.            First number                 11

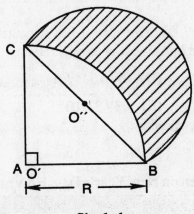

$O'$ is the center of quadrant
$O''$ is the center of semi-circle

15.            Shaded area               $R^2$

---

**DIRECTIONS:** For the following questions, select the best answer choice to the given question.

---

16. Reduce the following expression, $a > b > 0$

$$\left[(\sqrt{a+b})^2 - \sqrt{(a-b)^2}\right]$$

(A) $2a$               (D) $a$

(B) $2(a-b)$       (E) $b$

(C) $2b$

17. One year ago Pat was three times his sister's age. Next year he will be only twice her age. How old will Pat be in five more years?

(A) 8              (D) 13

(B) 12           (E) 15

(C) 11

18. $\left[\left(\dfrac{x}{y}\right)^{-1} - \left(\dfrac{y}{x}\right)^{-1}\right]^{-1} = ?$

    (A) $xy$

    (B) $1/xy$

    (C) $x^2 - y^2$

    (D) $y^2 - x^2$

    (E) $xy/(y^2 - x^2)$

19. Which is the smallest number?

    (A) $5 \cdot 10^{-3} / 3 \cdot 10^{-3}$

    (B) $.3 / .2$

    (C) $.3 / 3 \cdot 10^{-3}$

    (D) $5 \cdot 10^{-2} / .1$

    (E) $.3 / 3 \cdot 10^{-1}$

20. At my party 21 hugs were given on New Year's Day. How many people were at this party?

    (A) 7

    (B) 6

    (C) 9

    (D) 4

    (E) 11

Refer to the table on page 749 for questions 21 – 25.

21. What is the highest percentage growth country in South America?

    (A) 4.67%

    (B) 3.68%

    (C) 4.55%

    (D) 46.7%

    (E) .467%

22. What country has the lowest infant mortality?

    (A) United States

    (B) Iran

    (C) Sweden

    (D) Netherlands

    (E) Sweden and Netherlands

## Questions 21 – 25 refer to the following table:

**Birth Rates and Death Rates per 1,000 Population and Infant
Mortality per 1,000 Live Births in Selected Countries, 1957**

| Country | Birth rate | Death rate | Infant mortality | Country | Birth rate | Death rate | Infant mortality |
|---|---|---|---|---|---|---|---|
| **North America** | | | | Norway | 18.2 | 8.6 | 21 |
| Alaska | 35.1 | 5.9 | 39 | Poland | 27.5 | 9.5 | 77 |
| Canada | 28.3 | 8.2 | 31 | Portugal | 23.7 | 11.4 | 89 |
| Costa Rica | 39.2 | 10.1 | 92 | Rumania | 24.2 | 9.9 | 81 |
| Dominican Republic | 40.9 | 8.6 | 74 | Spain | 21.7 | 10.0 | 48 |
| El Salvador | 48.9 | 13.8 | 87 | Sweden | 14.6 | 9.9 | 17 |
| Guatemala | 49.4 | 20.6 | 89 | Switzerland | 17.7 | 10.0 | 23 |
| Honduras | 43.1 | 10.4 | 55 | United Kingdom | 16.5 | 11.5 | 24 |
| Mexico | 46.9 | 12.9 | 69 | England and Wales | 16.1 | 11.5 | 23 |
| Panama | 40.4 | 9.4 | 56 | Scotland | 19.0 | 11.9 | 29 |
| Puerto Rico | 32.4 | 7.0 | 51 | Northern Ireland | 21.5 | 10.9 | 29 |
| Trinidad and Tobago | 36.7 | 9.3 | 55 | Yugoslavia | 23.5 | 10.5 | 101 |
| United States | 25.3 | 9.6 | 26 | | | | |
| | | | | **Asia** | | | |
| **South America** | | | | Ceylon | 36.5 | 10.1 | 67 |
| Argentina | 23.8 | 8.2 | 58 | Hong Kong | 37.9 | 7.5 | 56 |
| Chile | 35.4 | 11.9 | 112 | India | 24.2 | 11.8 | 100 |
| Ecuador | 45.5 | 15.2 | 113 | Iran | 37.8 | 8.3 | — |
| Peru | 36.6 | 9.0 | 94 | Israel | 27.9 | 6.5 | 33 |
| Uruguay | 11.4 | 7.0 | 73 | Japan | 17.2 | 8.3 | 39 |
| Venezuela | 46.7 | 9.9 | 67 | Jordan | 39.7 | 8.6 | 74 |
| | | | | Malaya | 45.5 | 11.3 | 78 |
| | | | | Singapore | 42.9 | 7.3 | 43 |
| **Europe** | | | | Syria | 24.3 | 5.6 | 54 |
| Austria | 16.8 | 12.7 | 44 | Formosa (Taiwan) | 41.4 | 8.5 | 34 |
| Belgium | 16.9 | 12.4 | 35 | | | | |
| Bulgaria | 19.5 | 9.4 | 72 | | | | |
| Czechoslovakia | 18.9 | 10.0 | 31 | **Africa** | | | |
| Denmark | 16.7 | 9.3 | 23 | Union of South Africa | | | |
| Finland | 20.1 | 9.4 | 28 | (Europeans) | 25.6 | 8.8 | 31 |
| France | 18.5 | 12.0 | 29 | Mauritius | 43.1 | 13.0 | 66 |
| Germany (western) | 17.0 | 11.3 | 36 | | | | |
| Greece | 19.2 | 7.6 | 44 | **Oceania** | | | |
| Hungary | 17.0 | 10.6 | 59 | Australia | 22.9 | 8.8 | 21 |
| Ireland | 21.2 | 11.9 | 33 | Hawaii | 20.2 | 5.8 | 24 |
| Italy | 18.2 | 10.0 | 50 | New Zealand (total) | 26.2 | 9.3 | 24 |
| Luxembourg | 15.7 | 12.1 | 37 | Europeans | 24.8 | 9.3 | 20 |
| Netherlands | 21.2 | 7.5 | 17 | Maoris | 46.3 | 10.1 | 58 |

Britannica Book of the Year (1959), Encyclopedia Britannica, Inc.

23. What is the percentage of infants in the total death rate in the
United States?

   (A)  68.5%          (D)  26%

   (B)  .685%          (E)  27.1%

   (C)  6.85%

24. If the United States had 200 million (citizens), how many births were there in 1957?

   (A)  $5.06 \times 10^6$          (D)  $5.06 \times 10^4$

   (B)  $5.06 \times 10^5$          (E)  $5.06 \times 10^3$

   (C)  $5.06 \times 10^7$

25. According to the table, if the U.S. had 200 million people in 1957 what was the population in 1958?

   (A)  205.06 million          (D)  204.00 million

   (B)  203.14 million          (E)  210.00 million

   (C)  194.80 million

26. $\dfrac{x+y}{y} = a$ ; $\dfrac{y}{x} = ?$

   (A)  1          (D)  $a - 1$

   (B)  $a$          (E)  $1/(a - 1)$

   (C)  $1/a$

27. I filled $^2/_3$ of my swimming pool with 1800 ft³. What is the total capacity of my swimming pool?

   (A)  2400 ft³          (D)  3600 ft³

   (B)  2700 ft³          (E)  3200 ft³

   (C)  3000 ft³

28. 20% of the U.S. citizens have traveled out of the USA more than two times. 70% have not traveled out of the USA. Therefore

   I.    10% have traveled one time

   II.   10% have traveled one or two times

   III.  80% have traveled less than two times

(A)  Only I

(D)  II and III

(B)  Only II

(E)  I and III

(C)  Only III

29.  If $z = x^a$, $y = x^b$ then $z^b y^a = ?$

(A)  $x^{(ab)^2}$

(D)  $x^{2ab}$

(B)  $x^{ab}$

(E)  $x$

(C)  $x^0$

30.  Peter has five rulers of 30 cm each and three of 20 cm each. What is the average height of Peter's rulers?

(A)  25

(D)  26.25

(B)  27

(E)  27.25

(C)  23

## STOP

If time still remains, you may go back and check your work.
When the time allotted is up, you may go on to the next section.

# Section 5

---

**TIME:** 30 Minutes
25 Questions

**DIRECTIONS:** Each question or group of questions is based on a passage or set of statements. Select the best answer choice.

---

Questions 1-5 refer to the following passage.

The traditions in a primitive tribe were based on height, age, and male/female characteristics. Eight members of this tribe are designated by letters A through H and can be characterized as follows. Natives A, B, C, and D are males and the remaining natives are females. A is taller than B and both are shorter than C. D is taller than C. E is taller than B, and F, H, and G are shorter than B in that order. D is older than A. B and E are the two youngest and E is older than B. C and G are younger than A and older than H and F. C is older than G and F is younger than H.

1. The last natives allowed to sit down in the hut are the youngest male and female members of the tribe. Who are the last two natives entitled to sit?

   (A)  A and E          (D)  H and B

   (B)  G and B          (E)  E and B

   (C)  D and A

2. Hunting is always done in groups of three and the first hunting of the season must include the two adult males who are the oldest and youngest and the tallest female. Which of the following natives comprise the hunting party that meets these requirements?

   (A)  A, D, and F          (D)  A, D, and G

   (B)  B, D, and H          (E)  B, D, and E

   (C)  C, D, and H

3.  The order in which the members of the tribe are allowed to eat is alternated between the men and women. The oldest always precedes the youngest within the male and female categories. Who will be the first and last to eat?

    (A)  D and B

    (B)  A and E

    (C)  D and F

    (D)  D and E

    (E)  D and G

4.  It is the responsibility of the youngest male and youngest female to bring in the firewood except on the first day of hunting when the youngest boy is in the hunting party and the second youngest male brings in the firewood. On the first day of hunting, who will bring in the firewood?

    (A)  A and E

    (B)  C and E

    (C)  A and F

    (D)  C and F

    (E)  B and E

5.  Hunting for wild fruit and berries is done by the two oldest women and the two youngest males. Four people always do this chore so they can work in pairs. Which of the following groups will hunt fruit and berries?

    (A)  B, C, G, and H

    (B)  A, B, G, and H

    (C)  C, D, E, and F

    (D)  A, C, E, and G

    (E)  B, C, E, and G

Questions 6-8 refer to the following passage.

A merchant listed the wholesale price on his merchandise with a letter code that was changed each year. The code word for his system was CITYSQUARE. This code word contains 10 non-repeating letters which each stand for a number from 0 to 9. He used the last digit of each year to modify the code annually. In a year ending with the number 8 (such as 1988) the 8th letter in the code word represented 0, the 9th letter represented 1, the 10th letter represented 2 and so forth. He listed the wholesale price to the nearest cent, omitted the decimal and used

a single digit for the year. This system allowed employees who knew the code to interpret prices but customers did not know the wholesale price.

6.   If an item was purchased wholesale in 1987 for 87 cents, which of the following provides this information?

(A)   SY 7

(B)   AU 7

(C)   .SY 7

(D)   SY 87

(E)   AU 87

7.   If the merchant labeled an item CYR 9, how much did he pay for the item and when did he purchase it?

(A)   25 cents in 1989

(B)   $1.59 in 1989

(C)   $25.00 in 1989

(D)   $2.50 in 1989

(E)   $1.50 in 1989

8.   If the merchant wanted to compare the cost of an item over a period of 3 years and the letter C represented the number 5 in the first year of comparison, what number would the letter C represent in the third year?

(A)   3

(B)   2

(C)   7

(D)   8

(E)   Depends on the year the comparison began

Questions 9-12 refer to the following passage.

Six women went shopping and each bought one item. They bought a dress, slip, tie, belt, scarf, and pantyhose. Their names were Sally, Betty, Dorothy, Paula, Thelma, and Susan. They could be described as bold, slim, short, depressed, tall, and perky. No one purchased an article with the same letter as her first name and no one could be

described with a word that began with the same letter as her first name. Susan was considered bold and Sally was perky. Dorothy bought a slip and the person who was short bought a dress. Betty was slim and bought a tie. Paula bought a scarf.

9.  What did the tallest lady purchase?

    (A)  Belt

    (B)  Slip

    (C)  Scarf

    (D)  Dress

    (E)  Pantyhose

10. How would you describe the lady who bought the belt?

    (A)  Perky

    (B)  Slim

    (C)  Tall

    (D)  Depressed

    (E)  Short

11. Who bought the dress?

    (A)  Susan

    (B)  Sally

    (C)  Thelma

    (D)  Paula

    (E)  Betty

12. Who was depressed and what did she buy?

    (A)  Paula, dress

    (B)  Thelma, scarf

    (C)  Dorothy, slip

    (D)  Paula, scarf

    (E)  Thelma, scarf

Questions 13-16 refer to the following information.

A golf coach needed to select his team of 5 players from 8 who were finalists for his team. The players are Art, Bob, Chuck, Dan, Ed, Fred, George, and Hal. Due to ability under various conditions, temperament, and team morale the following conditions must be met in the team selection.

1.   If Dan is on the team, then Fred must also be on the team.

2.   Hal and Ed cannot both be on the team.

3.   George and Chuck cannot be on the team unless both are on the team.

4.   Art cannot be on the team if Dan is on the team.

13.  Which of the following team selections conforms to the requirements of team membership?

   (A)  Art, Bob, Chuck, Ed, and George

   (B)  Art, Bob, Chuck, Dan, and Fred

   (C)  Dan, Ed, Fred, George, and Hal

   (D)  Art, Bob, Chuck, Dan, and Ed

   (E)  Dan, Ed, Fred, George, and Hal

14.  If Dan is on the team, which of the following must occur?

   (A)  Fred and Art must be on the team

   (B)  Fred will not be on the team

   (C)  Art will be on the team

   (D)  Fred must be on the team and Art must not be on the team

   (E)  Hal and Ed will also be on the team

15.  Which of the following is the largest number of players (or player) the coach can select whose selection would not require either the inclusion or exclusion of at least one other player?

   (A)  Bob                  (D)  Bob and Hal

   (B)  Fred                 (E)  Fred and Bob

   (C)  Fred and Art

16.  If the coach selects Dan, Hal, George, and Chuck, which of the

following lists all the players who could not be chosen for the fifth player?

(A)   Fred and Art                    (D)   Art and Bob

(B)   Art, Bob, and Ed               (E)   Fred, Art, Ed

(C)   Fred, Bob and Ed

17.   An important distinction between a paradox and a contradiction is that a contradiction occurs when two ideas cannot co-exist and a paradox occurs when "apparent" contradictory ideas do co-exist. For example the views by some that the Earth is flat and the view of others that the Earth is round are contradictory views since both cannot be true. If one is true the other must be false. A basic principle on which employment contracts are negotiated is that people will work their best when they are well paid and that poorly paid people are less motivated to work. But some people who are poorly paid work extremely hard. In fact, some well-paid people may even work with less diligence as their income increases. Though the arguments favoring higher pay for harder work may be true in many instances, paradoxically some people are motivated by factors other than money and "seem" to contradict this basic principle.

Which of the following statements is the most significant inter-pretation of the information provided in this passage?

(A)   The Earth was once thought to be flat.

(B)   Contradictory propositions are logically incongruent.

(C)   Paradoxes cannot logically co-exist.

(D)   Some people are not motivated by money.

(E)   Paradoxes and contradictions cannot co-exist.

18.   Two of the psychological mechanisms often used to enable people to justify their behavior are rationalization and projec-tion. Rationalization is more commonly recognized than is projection. Projection includes the tendency to see one's own faults in someone else. Engaging in this practice allows people to

project their own faults to another person and avoid facing that fault as their own. The excessively thrifty person who calls others misers and the person who drives carelessly and blames others for their poor driving habits are examples.

Which of the following is an example of this form of projection?

(A) The taxpayer who complains about government spending.

(B) The voter who disagrees with legislative actions.

(C) The talkative person who claims others dominate the conversation.

(D) The speeder who gets arrested and claims others were going faster.

(E) Parents who brag excessively about their children.

19. An *ad hominem* argument is a technique used to win an argument by attacking the person instead of the issue. This approach is found throughout everyday life including children's play, social discussions and in the formalized courts of law. If, for example, a person who had once been an alcoholic was arguing for more severe laws against driving while intoxicated, which of the following remarks by the opposition is an *ad hominem* retort?

(A) Everyone knows that people vary in their ability to drink and drive.

(B) Bartenders and party hosts must share some of the responsibility for drunk drivers.

(C) Drunk driving is not as big a problem as the lack of adequate highways to prevent accidents.

(D) You wouldn't expect a former drunk to be able to present a reasonable viewpoint.

(E) Drugs are a bigger problem than alcohol on the highways.

20. Analogies provide a useful way to link new learning to previous knowledge or to bring theories to a more understandable level. Analogies are always imperfect representations of the real thing,

however. There is also danger in trying to use an analogy in lieu of proof and thus, drawing an unwarranted conclusion. Which of the following is an analogy that attempts to lead someone to a conclusion though the evidence is insufficient?

(A)   A penny saved is a penny earned.

(B)   No man is an island.

(C)   Opposites attract but they don't bond.

(D)   Experience is the best teacher.

(E)   Where there is smoke there is fire.

21.   A farmer observed that after his rooster crowed the sun came up. This is an example of the *post hoc* fallacy. When one event precedes another, it is tempting to assume the latter event is caused by the former. In some of the instances where two events occur together, it is obviously fallacious to attribute a cause-effect relationship. For instance, just because the cows we observe in the pasture have two front legs and two back legs, we would not conclude that the front legs caused the back legs. However, not all events are so clearly lacking a causal relationship. Research in leper colonies unveiled the fact that victims of this malady typically grew blind. The conclusion was drawn that leprosy caused blindness. After studying the disease more closely it was found that the nerves that react to dust and other intrusions that causes eyes to blink grew insensitive and the eyes did not cleanse themselves through the normal blinking process. A simple operation could be performed that made the eyes blink while chewing food. This finding preserved the eyesight of those who previously would have been blinded by leprosy. Scientists, politicians, juries, and many others who must make important decisions must be fully aware of the *post hoc* fallacy or they will make serious errors of judgement.

Which of the following is the most defensible inference to draw from the above passage?

(A)   Haste makes waste.

(B)   Cause-effect relationships are often assumed, not proven.

(C) Cause-effect relationships are most often based on emotion rather than evidence.

(D) Logic and science are not helpful in proving cause-effect relationships.

(E) Most doctors treat illness without knowing the cause.

22. A community in which an unusually high percentage of the population was retired needed support for schools. In the discussion about how to appeal to the community to raise taxes for schools, concern was expressed about resistance to taxation from their retired citizens. Their chief concerns were that many were new residents in the community, that they might feel they had done their part when they were younger, and that they did not have the higher incomes they did when working and should not be expected to contribute to the schools in their retirement years.

Which of the following points of view is most likely to be an effective basis on which to get support from the retired citizens for school support?

(A) Even newcomers to a community have an obligation to support local institutions.

(B) Younger citizens are also facing heavy financial obligations.

(C) The quality of life in the community for everyone depends partly on the behavior of each generation, including school-age children.

(D) Retirees have more discretionary money than the average working member of the community.

(E) If retirees did not plan to support they community, they should not have moved into it in the first place.

23. Written language has its origin in paintings and drawings. Facts and events were originally depicted visually by drawings, diagrams, and other visual records. The earliest forms of visual representation have undergone abbreviation which, in turn led to letters and alphabets. The task of the philologist is to study the

relationship between the visual forms and the development of new forms of expression and written communication.

Which of the following statements is not supported by this passage?

(A) Pictures and drawings preceded written language.

(B) Letters developed from abbreviations of drawings.

(C) Language had a civilizing effect on people.

(D) Philology is the study of the development of visual forms and their relationship to language.

(E) Early history was recorded visually.

24. The regulations and expense to invent, patent, and market new ideas and products imposes a heavy burden on inventors. The cost is often absorbed by large corporations with research and development facilities they provide. Corporations also help creative people contribute to society without them suffering the loss of income or security of the private inventor. The realities of this arrangement are that many good ideas are never brought into the marketplace and the cost of products to the public is high because of the development costs. However, protection provided by patents and safety to the public to avoid placing harmful products on the market is important to maintain. Thus, as is often the case, rules and regulations have their favorable and unfavorable consequences.

Which of the following changes is most justifiable to encourage more individual and private inventions of new products?

(A) Eliminate the requirement of obtaining patents for individuals.

(B) Impose a higher registration fee on corporations

(C) Waive safety regulations temporarily for individuals.

(D) Increase the government provisions for assistance with patents, marketing, and development for private inventors.

(E) Require large corporations to subsidize private inventors.

25. Married couples with no children often work two jobs for 5 or more years to purchase the American dream, a home of their own. They often find that after purchasing a home they must both continue working to meet the financial obligations they have incurred. Their desire to have children, their careers, and their acquisition of a home are often not compatible.

    If this passage reflects today's reality, which of the following statements most nearly describes the future in respect to home ownership and raising a family?

    (A) Fewer married people will be able to purchase a home and have children.

    (B) Fewer couples will have children.

    (C) Fewer couples will purchase a home.

    (D) Fewer women will have careers.

    (E) More men will forego their careers.

## STOP

If time still remains, you may go back and check your work.
When the time allotted is up, you may go on to the next section.

# Section 6

TIME:   30 Minutes
        25 Questions

DIRECTIONS: Each question or group of questions is based on a passage or set of statements. Select the best answer choice.

Questions 1-6 refer to the following passage.

Strawberries are grown in Arkansas, Alabama, Mississippi, and Florida. Blueberries are grown in Nevada, Alabama, Mississippi, and Arizona. Boysenberries are grown in Arkansas, Nevada, Utah, Mississippi, and Florida. Blackberries are grown in Arizona, Nevada, Utah, and Colorado. Raspberries are grown in Arizona, Mississippi, Alabama, and Arkansas. Gooseberries are grown in Alabama, Mississippi, Florida, and Utah.

1.  The berry that grows in most states is

    (A) strawberry          (D) blackberry

    (B) blueberry           (E) all are the same

    (C) boysenberry

2.  The state that has the most different kinds of berries growing in it is

    (A) Arkansas            (D) Nevada

    (B) Alabama             (E) Utah

    (C) Mississippi

763

3.    If one wanted to grow boysenberries, gooseberries, and black-berries, then one should live in

(A)  Alabama            (D)  Nevada

(B)  Arizona            (E)  Utah

(C)  Mississippi

4.    Which of the following must be true?

I.    Arizona is the only state to grow gooseberries, but not boysenberries.

II.   Alabama is the only state to grow strawberries, but not boysenberries.

(A)  I only

(B)  II only

(C)  both I and II

(D)  either I or II, but not both

(E)  neither I nor II

5.    Blackberries can be grown in

(A)  Utah, where boysenberries cannot be grown

(B)  Nevada, where strawberries cannot be grown

(C)  Arkansas, where boysenberries cannot be grown

(D)  Mississippi, where blueberries cannot be grown

(E)  Arizona, where raspberries cannot be grown

6.    If someone wanted to make preserves from both blueberries and blackberries that were freshly picked, then the person would have to live in

(A)  Arkansas or Utah

(B)  Alabama or Arizona

(C)  Arizona or Nevada

(D) Mississippi of Colorado

(E) Florida or Utah

Questions 7 – 10 refer to the following information.

Jeff, Dennis, Stan, Roger, and Glenn have an average height of six feet. Roger is taller than Jeff. Glenn is shorter than Stan. Dennis is shorter than Roger. Glenn is taller than Dennis. Roger is shorter than Stan. Dennis is the shortest of the five.

7. The tallest boy is

(A) Jeff

(B) Glenn

(C) Roger

(D) Stan

(E) cannot be determined

8. Jeff is not necessarily

I.   taller than Dennis

II.  taller than Glenn

(A) I only

(B) II only

(C) either I or II

(D) both I and II

(E) neither I nor II

9. Which of the following must be true?

I.   Stan is taller than Jeff.

II.  Roger is taller than Glenn.

III. Glenn is taller than Jeff.

(A) I

(B) II

(C) III

(D) I and II

(E) II and III

10. If Fred joins the group and is taller than Glenn, but shorter than Jeff, then which of the following must be true?

    I.   Roger is taller than Fred.

    II.  Jeff is taller than Glenn.

    (A)  I only                    (D)  both I and II

    (B)  II only                   (E)  neither I nor II

    (C)  either I or II

Questions 11 – 14 refer to the following information.

Five children in a family of six children have dimples. Three children in the family are girls. Four children in the family have brown eyes.

11. Which of the following must be true?

    I.   All of the girls have dimples.

    II.  At least one girl has brown eyes.

    (A)  I                         (D)  both I and II

    (B)  II                        (E)  neither I nor II

    (C)  either I or II, but not both

12. Which of the following must be false?

    I.   All the brown-eyed girls have dimples.

    II.  No children with dimples have brown eyes.

    (A)  I                         (D)  both I and II

    (B)  II                        (E)  neither I nor II

    (C)  either I or II, but not both

13. Which of the following can be deduced from the statements?

    (A) None of the girls have dimples.

    (B) Three of the blue-eyed children have dimples.

    (C) One girl has no dimples.

    (D) All of the girls have brown eyes.

    (E) None of the above.

14. Which of the following must be false?

    (A) One of the children does not have dimples.

    (B) Three of the children are boys.

    (C) All of the boys have brown eyes.

    (D) Three children have blue eyes.

    (E) None of the above.

Question 15 – 16 refer to the following information.

(1) A college student must take four subjects.

(2) The subjects he may choose from are English, History, Math, Biology, Chemistry, Physics.

(3) The student must take either Biology or Chemistry, but not both.

(4) The student cannot take Math and Physics together.

15. If a student takes Biology, which other course(s) must he take?

    I.   Physics

    II.  History

    III. Math

    (A) I only                    (D) I and II only

    (B) II only                   (E) II and III only

    (C) III only

16. How many different combinations of courses are available for the student to choose from?

    (A) 2

    (B) 3

    (C) 4

    (D) 5

    (E) more than 5

17. Which of the following comes closest to being a factual statement?

    (A) Lawyer: "Our whole political system is corrupt."

    (B) Financial expert: "The price of gold is bound to increase."

    (C) Doctor: "Cigarette smoking may be hazardous to your health."

    (D) Upholsterer: "These are the most comfortable chairs we make."

    (E) Coin collector: "Fewer than ten of these silver coins were minted in the year 1947."

18. It is immoral to blame people for what they do. They are simply behaving as they have been conditioned to behave and have no choice in the matter. Blaming them will never change their behavior.

    The author undercuts his own argument by

    (A) adopting dubious psychological theories

    (B) undermining morality

    (C) attacking human freedom

    (D) arguing emotionally

    (E) doing what he argues against

Questions 19 – 21 refer to the following information.

(1) Four bureaucrats habitually pass their responsibilities on to one another.

(2) Whenever one bureaucrat is delegated a responsibility by another, he cannot immediately pass it directly back.

(3) A bureaucrat, finding no other bureaucrat to accept a responsibility, must keep the responsibility.

(4) The bureaucrats consistently follow the same pattern of delegating and receiving responsibility to and from the same people.

(5) They never send responsibilities to or receive responsibilities from any bureaucrat outside their group of four.

(6) Each of the four bureaucrats has, at some time, either sent a responsibility to or received a responsibility from each of the others.

19. Which of the following **may** be true?

   I.   At least one bureaucrat does not delegate responsibility.

   II.  At least one bureaucrat is not delegated responsibility.

   III. It is possible for a responsibility to be passed on to each bureaucrat in turn, and then to be sent back to its original delegate.

   (A)  I only

   (B)  II only

   (C)  II and III only

   (D)  I and II only

   (E)  I, II, and III

20. Which of the following is **necessarily** true?

   I.   If there is one bureaucrat who is not delegated responsibility, then there is another who does not delegate responsibility.

   II.  Exactly one of the four bureaucrats always delegates responsibility, while another does not delegate responsibility.

III. Three of the bureaucrats, A, B, and C, sometimes pass on a responsibility in the order A to B to C back to A.

(A) I only

(B) III only

(C) I and II only

(D) I and III only

(E) None of the above is necessarily true.

21. Which is possible in the responsibility exchange activities of the four bureaucrats?

(A) Two bureaucrats may make a direct exchange of responsibilities.

(B) One bureaucrat may delegate two different responsibilities, one to each of two other bureaucrats.

(C) A fifth bureaucrat may occasionally join the other four in delegating and receiving responsibilities.

(D) Two bureaucrats are so unfriendly that each sees to it that a responsibility of one bureaucrat never reaches the other.

(E) Each of the four bureaucrats must always participate in the giving or receiving or responsibilities.

Questions 22 – 23 refer to the following passage.

I cannot overemphasize the need to steer our company away from the path of insolvency. For over 94 years now, our firm has not missed one dividend, nor refused to honor one of our interest payments. We have been in the forefront of American industry, and have carried the banner of capitalism. If our firm were to collapse,

22. In providing the missing portion, choose the completion that is best in keeping with the passage.

(A) How would we support our families?

(B) Who would take the blame?

(C)   Can the entire economy be far behind?

(D)   Then we would cease to pay dividends.

(E)   I would resign as Chairman of the Board.

23.   Based on the preceding paragraph, which of the following assumptions about the speaker is most justified?

(A)   He has foresight.

(B)   He is anti-Communist.

(C)   He is honest in his dealings with creditors.

(D)   He is proud of his company.

(E)   He is at least ninety-four years old.

24.   Ralph:   All Italians enjoy spaghetti.

     James:   I must disagree. I have known some Italians who love baked potatoes.

James's response shows that he has interpreted Ralph's remarks to mean that

(A)   Italians do not like potatoes.

(B)   only Italians eat potatoes.

(C)   most people cannot appreciate good spaghetti.

(D)   only Italians enjoy spaghetti.

(E)   Italians enjoy only spaghetti.

25.   By far the best long-distance runners are those who train in mountainous areas. Anyone who can acclimate himself to the thin air of high altitudes and the rugged terrain should have no trouble disposing of those competitors who practice in air-conditioned gymnasiums.

Which question would the author find most difficult to answer?

(A)   Why would anyone want to build a gymnasium?

(B)  Isn't it easier to run at lower altitudes?

(C)  How is it that the top four long-distance runners in the world have trained solely in gymnasiums?

(D)  Why don't U.S. Olympic long-distance runners train in mountainous areas?

(E)  Isn't there more danger involved in mountain running than in gymnasium running?

# STOP

If time still remains, you may go back and check your work.

# TEST 6

# ANSWER KEY

## Section 1 — Verbal Ability

| | | | | | | | |
|---|---|---|---|---|---|---|---|
| 1. | (B) | 11. | (A) | 21. | (C) | 31. | (B) |
| 2. | (B) | 12. | (D) | 22. | (C) | 32. | (E) |
| 3. | (C) | 13. | (D) | 23. | (A) | 33. | (C) |
| 4. | (D) | 14. | (A) | 24. | (E) | 34. | (D) |
| 5. | (B) | 15. | (A) | 25. | (E) | 35. | (B) |
| 6. | (A) | 16. | (E) | 26. | (B) | 36. | (A) |
| 7. | (E) | 17. | (D) | 27. | (A) | 37. | (B) |
| 8. | (A) | 18. | (E) | 28. | (B) | 38. | (D) |
| 9. | (B) | 19. | (B) | 29. | (A) | | |
| 10. | (C) | 20. | (A) | 30. | (E) | | |

## Section 2 — Verbal Ability

| | | | | | | | |
|---|---|---|---|---|---|---|---|
| 1. | (A) | 11. | (C) | 21. | (C) | 31. | (E) |
| 2. | (E) | 12. | (D) | 22. | (B) | 32. | (A) |
| 3. | (E) | 13. | (E) | 23. | (A) | 33. | (D) |
| 4. | (A) | 14. | (A) | 24. | (D) | 34. | (D) |
| 5. | (A) | 15. | (D) | 25. | (C) | 35. | (E) |
| 6. | (E) | 16. | (E) | 26. | (D) | 36. | (E) |
| 7. | (C) | 17. | (C) | 27. | (D) | 37. | (A) |
| 8. | (A) | 18. | (A) | 28. | (E) | 38. | (E) |
| 9. | (A) | 19. | (D) | 29. | (A) | | |
| 10. | (D) | 20. | (B) | 30. | (C) | | |

## Section 3 — Quantitative Ability

| | | | | | | | |
|---|---|---|---|---|---|---|---|
| 1. | (C) | 3. | (B) | 5. | (D) | 7. | (C) |
| 2. | (D) | 4. | (A) | 6. | (A) | 8. | (B) |

| 9. | (A) | 15. | (C) | 21. | (A) | 27. | (A) |
|----|-----|-----|-----|-----|-----|-----|-----|
| 10. | (D) | 16. | (D) | 22. | (C) | 28. | (B) |
| 11. | (B) | 17. | (B) | 23. | (E) | 29. | (E) |
| 12. | (A) | 18. | (E) | 24. | (C) | 30. | (C) |
| 13. | (C) | 19. | (A) | 25. | (D) | | |
| 14. | (B) | 20. | (C) | 26. | (D) | | |

## Section 4 — Quantitative Ability

| 1. | (C) | 9. | (D) | 17. | (B) | 25. | (B) |
|----|-----|-----|-----|-----|-----|-----|-----|
| 2. | (D) | 10. | (A) | 18. | (E) | 26. | (E) |
| 3. | (B) | 11. | (A) | 19. | (D) | 27. | (B) |
| 4. | (B) | 12. | (B) | 20. | (A) | 28. | (B) |
| 5. | (A) | 13. | (B) | 21. | (B) | 29. | (D) |
| 6. | (A) | 14. | (A) | 22. | (E) | 30. | (D) |
| 7. | (C) | 15. | (B) | 23. | (C) | | |
| 8. | (A) | 16. | (C) | 24. | (A) | | |

## Section 5 — Analytical Ability

| 1. | (E) | 8. | (A) | 15. | (E) | 22. | (C) |
|----|-----|-----|-----|-----|-----|-----|-----|
| 2. | (E) | 9. | (B) | 16. | (B) | 23. | (C) |
| 3. | (D) | 10. | (A) | 17. | (B) | 24. | (D) |
| 4. | (B) | 11. | (C) | 18. | (C) | 25. | (A) |
| 5. | (A) | 12. | (D) | 19. | (D) | | |
| 6. | (A) | 13. | (A) | 20. | (E) | | |
| 7. | (D) | 14. | (D) | 21. | (B) | | |

## Section 6 — Analytical Ability

| 1. | (C) | 8. | (B) | 15. | (B) | 22. | (C) |
|----|-----|-----|-----|-----|-----|-----|-----|
| 2. | (C) | 9. | (A) | 16. | (C) | 23. | (D) |
| 3. | (E) | 10. | (D) | 17. | (E) | 24. | (E) |
| 4. | (B) | 11. | (B) | 18. | (E) | 25. | (C) |
| 5. | (B) | 12. | (B) | 19. | (E) | | |
| 6. | (C) | 13. | (E) | 20. | (E) | | |
| 7. | (D) | 14. | (D) | 21. | (B) | | |

# DETAILED EXPLANATIONS
# OF ANSWERS

## Section 1–Verbal Ability

1.  **(B)**
    The professor (B) QUALIFIED (delimited) his statements in order to express his reservations. (C) WROTE, (D) FORMED, and (E) CONSTRUCTED are not specific enough. Alternative (A) is unrelated logically to the thought.

2.  **(B)**
    The first blank identifies a key variable in relation to achievement and the second blank reiterates the importance of this same variable. The key phrase here is "…but the fact remains…." The answer is alternative (B), because DESIRE and WANT are synonymous. To want is to desire. The synonymous relationship required by the sentence is not present in the choices given in the other alternatives.

3.  **(C)**
    The blanks in this sentence require words which refer to the same emotion or quality, with the first being desirable and the second being not desirable (unduly ____). The word "but" precedes a qualifying thought, as well. The correct answer is alternative (C) FRIENDLY…(unduly) FAMILIAR. Alternatives (A), (B), (D), and (E) would be acceptable in the sentence if the word "but" were replaced with an "and," which would not require a contrary thought.

4.  **(D)**
    The first lines explain how the state of being described by the word in the blank comes to exist. Never experiencing serious illness or harm leads to a sense of WELL-BEING, which is the term in alternative (D). An "exaggerated" sense of well-being gives a person a false sense of security. The alternatives present words which are not compatible with this thought.

5.  (B)

The key to this problem lies in recognizing the fact that the word "nevertheless" precedes information that is contrary to the thought presented in the first part of the sentence. Evidence which indicates invalidity of a theory is the opposite of SUPPORT. The correct answer is (B) for this reason. Alternatives (A) RESEARCHED, (C) INVESTIGATED, and (E) EXPLORED make sense, but do not express an idea contrary to the thought. Alternative (D) REPUDIATED is wrong because repudiate (to disavow) agrees with the thought presented rather than contradicts it.

6.  (A)

The correct answer is (A) APPEARANCE...REDUCE. The persons in question remain strangers to each other but on the surface they share a first-name basis. (B) is wrong because having a waitress give a customer her first name is not an AFFLICTION (cause of suffering) which would RETARD (slow) a person's criticism. (C) is wrong because the familiarity in the situation described is merely apparent, not a REALITY. Alternative (D) is wrong because the time necessary for meaningful familiarity to grow is not present in the situation described. (E) is wrong because no degree of familiarity would completely DENY a customer the ability to criticize.

7.  (E)

The correct answer is alternative (E). Writers are particularly helped by FINANCIAL independence and personal LEISURE, or money and time, in order to focus their efforts on writing. The key phrase here is "...in order to focus their efforts on writing." Freedom from the need to work for a livelihood and from other responsibilities gives the writer time. With this, he can focus his efforts on writing. TALENT, ABILITY, REPUTATION, and INTELLIGENCE are all helpful also, but a writer without any one of these could still focus his efforts on writing.

8.  (A)

This is an analogy of intensity. An ULTIMATUM is an intensified REQUEST. This relationship also exists in alternative (A) MAR:RUIN. To mar is to make imperfect. To ruin is to destroy something. A vase

776

might be marred by a scratch, but would be ruined by dropping it on the floor and breaking it. Analogies of intensity have to do with quality. The foils used in the alternatives have to do with quantity. In alternative (B) COUPLET:SONNET, a couplet is made up of two lines while a sonnet is made up of 14 lines. This is an increase in quantity rather than an increase in quality. Increases in quantity are also apparent in alternative (C) PAGE:BOOK and (D) BRANCH:TREE. Alternative (E) SURFEIT:GLUTTONY is incorrect because both indicate an over-indulgence, particularly of food or drink. There is no increase in intensity from one to the other.

9.    (B)
     To be NERVOUS is to lack POISE. This relationship also exists in alternative (B) FRIGHTENED:CONFIDENCE. To be frightened is to lack confidence. Alternative (A) ANGRY:SENSIBILITY is not right because sensibility (the capacity for physical sensation) can be present simultaneously with anger. Alternative (C) EMPATHETIC: RATIONALITY is incorrect because a person can be rational and also be empathetic. Alternative (D) ENERGETIC:ENTHUSIASM is incorrect because an energetic person does have enthusiasm. Alternative (E) CALM:LAZINESS is incorrect because a calm person may or may not lack laziness.

10.   (C)
     The process of OXIDATION causes RUST. This relationship is also found in alternative (C). INVESTMENT causes or results in DIVIDENDS. This relationship is not present in the other alternatives. The first term given is not a cause of the second term given.

11.   (A)
     RAIN is a form of PRECIPITATION. The analogy is one of example:class. The correct answer is (A) COPPER:METAL. Copper is an example of a metal. The analogy in alternative (B) ICE:GLACIER is wrong because a glacier is made up of ice, but ice is not necessarily an example of a glacier. In relation to alternative (C) OIL:SHALE, oil is found in shale, but is not an example of shale. Alternative (D) WIND:ABRASION has the relationship of cause:effect. Wind is a cause of abrasion. This relationship also exists in alternative (E)

777

HEAT:EVAPORATION, as heat is a cause of evaporation.

**12. (D)**

A COCOON undergoes a metamorphosis which results in a changed form and appearance. This situation also exists in relation to alternative (D) ADOLESCENT:ADULT. Alternatives (A) APPLE:PIE and (E) WOOD:HOUSE both require external actions to effect the change. In relation to alternative (B) BLOSSOM:FRUIT, pollination is an external happening without which step the fruit does not appear. Alternative (C) AWARENESS:UNDERSTANDING is incorrect because awareness does not always result in understanding.

**13. (D)**

A RETINUE is a group of FOLLOWERS. The corresponding analogy is found in alternative (D) DETRITUS:DEBRIS, since an accumulation of debris is referred to as detritus. The first term in the analogies refers to a collection of those things or items referred to by the second term. In each of the remaining alternatives, the reference to the whole follows instead of precedes reference to the part.

**14. (A)**

A person who is HARDHEARTED lacks EMPATHY. The same relationship is evident in alternative (A) AMBIVALENT:DECISIVENESS, as a person who is ambivalent lacks decisiveness. This relationship does not exist in the alternative pairs given.

**15. (A)**

This analogy is one of part to whole, but also includes the idea of progression. A certain number of MINUTES must elapse before an HOUR has passed. Likewise, in alternative (A) METER:KILOMETER, a certain number of meters is required to be in place before a kilometer can be said to exist. Alternative (B) CHOIR may have any number of ALTOS or even no altos and can still exist. Alternative (C) FEDERATION may have any number of STATES, and alternative (E) TRAIN may have any number of BOXCARS.

**16. (E)**

RAGE is a heightened form of ANGER. In the correct alternative, which is (E) a FIASCO is a heightened form of FAILURE. A fiasco is a "complete, ridiculous failure." The other alternatives each present synonymous pairs of words. Although the second term in each pair may appear more serious, in meaning it is the same.

**17. (D)**

The author mentions the study of the satellites of Jupiter but not Jupiter.

**18. (E)**

The author infers this when he states, "This same bombardment must have affected the Earth as well." (A) and (B) are incorrect since it was not a stated fact. (C) is incorrect. The author has attempted to use this observation to show the Earth could not have been missed. (D) is incorrect. The author notes that it was during this period that life began.

**19. (B)**

The entire selection is an attempt to show that the Earth was bombarded during its early history. (A) is incorrect. The author speculates it began 4.6 billion years ago but this is not the main point. (C) is incorrect. The author does not claim these bodies were in place prior to Earth. (D) is incorrect. The author only discusses the possibility. (E) is incorrect. The moon reveals a bombardment, but the author does not infer this.

**20. (A)**

The author does not mention the training of lay-ministers. Reading the Bible (B) and promoting religious instructions (C) strongly influenced the schools in New England. The Massachusetts Legislature did pass the law (D) to require all householders to provide education for the students. The act was also passed to further general education (E).

**21. (C)**

(C) is the correct answer, as stated by the author in the final paragraph of the selection.

22.   (C)

In 1645 and again in 1647 the Massachusetts Legislature passed laws requiring communities to support education first for elementary school and then for the grammar school.

23.   (A)

There was religious "intolerance" as the author describes in paragraph two. (B) and (C) are incorrect. Both are found in the second paragraph. (D) and (E) are incorrect and found in the last paragraph.

24.   (E)

The author indicates this answer in the last sentence of paragraph three.

25.   (E)

In paragraph three, line eight, the author notes, "private tutors instructed the sons of well-to-do planters,..." This sentence follows a sentence that discusses the Southern colonies.

26.   (B)

The author does not mention this in the article. It can be clearly inferred from the selection that the Puritans were not tolerant. (A), (C), and (D) are well mentioned in paragraph two. (E) can be clearly inferred from paragraph two.

27.   (A)

The final paragraph states that William and Mary was created by royal charter and Harvard was established by the Massachusetts Legislature in 1636.

28.   (B)

To OSCILLATE is to swing to and fro. The opposite of oscillation is stabilization. To STABILIZE (B) is to keep from changing; to make steady. (A) MOOR is wrong because it means "to tie down"; (C) BALANCE is wrong because it means to bring into proportion or

harmony. (D) VACILLATE and (E) UNDULATE are both wrong because these words are synonyms for the term given, oscillate.

29.  (A)
RESERVED means "self-restrained" or "reticent." Its opposite is (A) AFFABLE, meaning "friendly." Alternative (B) SAVED, is a synonym for "reserved" when it means "kept in reserve," or "set apart." (E) RETICENT (quiet) is also a synonym for "reserved." Alternative (C) GIVEN (accustomed to be habit) and (D) UNEXPECTED (unforeseen) are unrelated to the meaning of "affable."

30.  (E)
ILLUSORY means an "unreal or misleading appearance or image." Its opposite is (E) FACTUAL, meaning "of or containing facts; real, actual." Alternative (A) EVIDENT, is wrong because both an illusory image and a factual image could be evident, that is, easy to see or perceive. Alternative (B) MEANINGFUL (what is meant or intended to be significant) could also apply to both illusory and factual events. Alternative (C) SOLUBLE (able to be solved) is unrelated in meaning to illusory. Alternative (B) OBVIOUS (easy to understand) is wrong because it may apply to both illusory (misleading) and factual occurrences.

31.  (B)
To PREVENT is to stop someone from doing something or to keep something from happening. The antonym in this case is (B) PERMIT, which means "to allow to be done," "to consent to." Alternatives are (A) INVITE (to ask to come somewhere or do something); (C) ENCOURAGE (to give support to); (D) DEMAND (to require); and (E) URGE (to advocate). They are unrelated to the meaning needed.

32.  (E)
BELLICOSE (adj.) comes from the Latin *bellicus*, meaning "war." In English, bellicose has come to mean "quarrelsome," or "warlike." Its opposite is another word with a Latin root, PACIFIC, which comes from the Latin word for peace, which is *pax*. In English, pacific means "peaceful," "calm," or "tranquil." Alternative (A) PULCHRITUDI-

NOUS (Latin *pulcher*, beauty) means beautiful, (B) OBDURATE (Latin *durus*, hard) means "hard-hearted" or "stubborn; (C) ANO-REXIC (Greek, *an*, without and *orexis*, desire) means an obsession with loss; a loss of desire to eat; and (D) SERAPHIC means "angelic." None of these words carries a meaning related to peacefulness.

33. (C)

   A SCRUPULOUS person is one who is careful of details, or precise in the manner he does about work. The antonym is (C) CARELESS (not paying enough heed; neglectful). Alternatives (A), (B), and (D) are wrong because they are similar in meaning to the term given. Alternative (E) is simply unrelated to the meaning needed.

34. (D)

   EMOLIENT means "softening," or "soothing." It is an adjective. The opposite of "emolient" is (D) ABRASIVE, which means "causing abrasion by rubbing or scraping away." Incorrect alternatives refer to an ability to absorb (B); the state of being present (A); the state of supporting (C); and the state of being bold and daring (E).

35. (B)

   ALLEGIANCE is loyalty or devotion. Its opposite is (B) TREACH-ERY, which is betrayal of trust or disloyalty. The alternatives are wrong because they include in their meanings ideas which are only a part of disloyalty. (A) DISAPPROBATION means "disapproval"; (C) INCOMPATIBILITY means "an ability to reconcile two points of view; (D) DISSENSION and (E) DISPUTATION carry meanings of dissenting, disagreeing, or quarreling.

36. (A)

   LUGUBRIOUS (adj.) comes form the Latin *lugere*, "to mourn," and means "very sad" or "mournful." The opposite in the list given is (A) JOYOUS. The incorrect alternatives are (B) ENERGETIC (having energy; vigorous); (C) RAPID (moving or occurring with speed); (D) FACILE (done easily); and (E) HEALTHY (having good health). None of the alternatives has the meaning of joyous.

**37. (B)**

The Greek word in this case, *eulegein* means "to speak well of." A EULOGISTIC speech is one in which a person or thing is praised highly. The antonym of eulogistic is (B) CENSORIOUS, (Latin *censere*, to judge) meaning "harshly critical." The alternatives are incorrect because they do not express the idea of a critical response. (A) OFFICIOUS (offering unwanted advice or services); (C) DEPRESSED (sad, dejected); (D) INCOMPREHENSIBLE (not understandable); and (E) OBSTINATE (determined to have one's way) do not include the idea of critical attitudes or actions.

**38. (D)**

BANEFUL means "harmful" or "ruinous." Its opposite is (D) BENEFICIAL, which means "favorable," "producing benefits," or "advantageous." The alternatives are not related in meaning to beneficial. (A) RESPECTED (held in esteem, honor, or regard); (B) BEAUTIFUL (having beauty); (C) RECKLESS (heedless, rash); and (E) HONORABLE (worthy of honor) are unrelated to the meaning needed.

## Section 2–Verbal Ability

**1. (A)**

AMORPHOUS, ECCENTRIC and ERRATIC are all synonyms meaning inconsistent, sporadic. EQUABLE suggests a uniform methodical occurrence. WEARISOME is the correct choice, indicated by the key words "exact," "and," "but," and "essential."

**2. (E)**

CONTINGENT and INCIDENTAL refer to chance and superfluous. INTRODUCED suggests to bring forth for the first time; while SUPERADDED implies to add to something already complete. The passage implies the necessity of repeating the addition of an extra month, therefore eliminating contingent, incidental, superadded, and introduced. The correct choice is INTERCALATED meaning "to insert among existing elements."

3.  (E)

PUNGENT, POIGNANT and RANKLING refer to a sharp, irritating sensation; while MALODOROUS suggests an offensive odor. The key word of "reek" indicates a strong disagreeable odor which is emitted continuously by seaweed, damp and dead fish. Therefore, REDOLENT is the correct choice, meaning "diffusing a strong odor."

4.  (A)

COMPATIBLE, CONGENIAL and ALLURING are nuances of an emotion which is pleasant and sought; while ABHORRENT is an antonym of the same emotion. INVIDIOUS means "so alien as to arouse antogonism." The term "frightful" is the key to the correct choice of invidious.

5.  (A)

TUTELARY, MYTHICAL, CELESTIAL and NYMPHONIC are synonymous with shades of meaning referring to heavenly beings related to pagan gods. "Worst" is the key word suggesting the perception of an event as evil. OMINOUS is the correct choice, being defined as "foreshadowing of evil."

6.  (E)

"Strange" eliminates ARISTOCRATS which would have been a bond between equals. AVARICE, GREED and COVETOUSNESS are behaviors, therefore unable to form a bond. DERELICTS is the correct choice, suggesting bonds being developed between opposites.

7.  (C)

PLIANT and MALEABLE are synonymous and reflect the ability to bend or be flexible. HISTRIONIC refers to the dramatic. IMPARTIAL suggests an equality among all. Flexibility, dramatic and impartiality are positive characteristics of a policy. Only PACIFIC could be perceived as weak.

8.  (A)

COMMITMENT and VOWS are a synonymous relationship. NORMAL and ABERRANT are antonyms. FREEDOM and DE-

MOCRACY are a cause and effect relationship. VOLUNTARY and MANDATORY are antonyms. EDUCATION and INTELLIGENCE are cause and effect relationship. COMPULSORY and REQUIRED also have a synonymous relationship. Therefore (A) is the correct choice.

9.  (A)
    PHONICS and WORD RECOGNITION have a part-to-part relationship. FRENCH and ENGLISH have a whole-to-whole relationship. VOLUMES and LIBRARY have a part-to-whole relationship. HEALTH and PHYSICAL ACTIVITY also have a part-to-whole relationship. HARMONY and MUSIC have a part-to-whole relationship. FRACTIONS and DECIMALS are part of the unidentified subject of mathematics as phonics and word recognition are a part of the unidentified subject of reading.

10.  (D)
    GLASSES and SEE are a cause and effect relationship as SUGAR and SYRUP are also cause and effect. ROCK and GEOLOGY; INDEX and GLOSSARY; and GRASS and LAWN are all part-to-whole relationships. Index and glossary are parts of a book, as KEEL and DECK are parts of a boat. It is a part-to-part relationship.

11.  (C)
    PERSPIRE and RUN have a cause and effect relationship. SUFFOCATE and BREATH are antonymous in relationship. GYRON and AIRFOIL are synonymous in their relationship as are FLOURISH and THRIVE. (C) is the correct choice. GYMKHANA has a whole-to-part relationship with DRIVING SKILL as SWIM is a part of the whole of RECREATION.

12.  (D)
    FILM and MOVIE have a part-to-part relationship as do PRINT and NEWSPAPERS. TEACH and FACILITATE have a cause and effect relationship as do ASTRONAUTS and EXPLORATION. MIRAGE and ILLUSION are synonyms as ENIGMA and MYSTERY are synonyms.

13.  (E)

ANXIETY and STRESS have a cause and effect relationship just as DESTROY is a cause and the effect is found in INUTILE. APHANITE and ROCK as well as APOLLO and MYTHOLOGY have a member-class relationship. BREVITY and CONCISENESS have a synonymous relationship. INSULT and INVECTIVE contain a part-to-whole relationship.

14.  (A)

PLANK and BLOCK possess a synonymous relationship as do EMOTION and MOOD. SHRUB and TREE belong to a member-to-member category. OVICIDAL and CHEMICAL are cause and effect. SUN and STARS as well as PIRANHA and FISH are in a member-class relationship.

15.  (D)

PEDAGOGIC is an adjective correctly describing a TEACHER, just as DONNISH is an adjective correctly describing a PEDANT. The remaining selections contain adjective which incorrectly describe the nouns following them.

16.  (E)

REQUIEM and DEATH are a relationship of purpose. LURID and RUDDY belong to an antonymous relationship. HALLMARK and UNIQUE are synonymous as are FUGUE and COMPOSITION. Only COMPETE and EMULATE have both a synonymous relationship with VIE and RIVAL plus a synonymous definition.

17.  (C)

Choices (A), (B), (D) and (E) are stated in paragraph one. (C), the correct choice, is implied by the qualifying characteristics for categorizing ground openings into caves which is explicitly stated. Any opening not meeting the specific requirements would be classified as something other than a cave.

18.  (A)

(A) is the correct choice. It can be inferred from the sentence which

defines speleology as "... a composite science based on geology, hydrology, biology and archaeology."

19. (D)

Choice (D) is stated in paragraph one, sentence three.

20. (B)

(B) is the correct choice, inferred from the last sentence of paragraph two. "... he took refuge more than 10,000 years ago during the chill of the Ice Age." The key contextual clues are "refuge" and "chill of the Ice Age."

21. (C)

Paragraph 9 explicitly states "One of the measures provided to relieve people living in such *unhealthy conditions*..."

22. (B)

Paragraph 4 supports choice (B) by the following phrase: "'hut colonies' which refer to the toolsheds or small houses on garden plots in some countries."

23. (A)

Choice (A) can be answered by information given in paragraph 9: "in England was a law in 1819 that provided for leasing land...."

24. (D)

Paragraph 6 infers that walled cities were only large enough to protect the people, due to the difficulty of defending them, therefore the gardens were outside the gate and wall.

25. (C)

Paragraph 9 reads "provided for leasing land for small gardens..." and paragraph 10 uses the term "were provided by philanthropists" inferring a landowner-tenant relationship.

26. (D)

Paragraph 10 speaks of "improving the quality of life." Population, to a degree, is regulated by famine, war and disease. Small gardens reduced famine and disease.

27. (D)

Paragraph 10 states "to help ensure social stability by providing a link to the countryside that the workers had left." This implies that the workers' cultural heritage would be found in the countryside.

28. (E)

CALCULATE and ESTIMATE are synonymous, both meaning to reckon, referring to dealing with the problematical process. DIGIT is identified as any of the Arabic numbers while SERIES indicates the sum of an infinite sequence of numbers. (E) PLENARY is the opposite of CIPHER; empty versus full.

29. (A)

REITERATE and RECURRENCE are synonymous, referring to the repeating of something said. SUCCINCT and TERSE express the quality of what has been said. REPETITION has the more general meaning of "performing again by either the same or different agents." Only (A) INFINITY is the opposite of recurrence; the turning back versus endlessness.

30. (C)

COINCIDENCE suggests events occurring at the same time. SEQUEANT is defined at the result of. CAPRICIOUSNESS, a sudden unpredictable change, is the antonym of MODULATION, meaning regulating according to measure. (C) PERIODIC, occurring at regular intervals, is the opposite of SYNCHRONISM, meaning "to happen at the same time."

31. (E)

INNOVATION suggests making a change which may be either temporary or permanent, while ALTERATION refers to making something different without changing it into something else. VARI-

ATION denotes having many forms and types but not the changing of those forms or types. DEVIATION implies turning aside from a standard. Only (E) MONOTONOUS, which is defined as "unvarying," is the opposite of MUTATION which is defined as a permanent change in hereditary material.

32. (A)
   LATENT and ABEYANCE both imply temporary inactivity. INNOVATION and METHODICALNESS are antonyms. Innovation suggests change, methodicalness refers to habitually proceeding with no change but in a predetermined manner. (A) PERPETUATION is the opposite of CESSATION. Perpetuation denotes "to continue forever," cessation is defined as "to stop."

33. (D)
   DECIMATION and REDUCTION are synonyms, both inferring the act of diminishing in number. PAUCITY and EXIGUITY are also synonyms describing a smallness in number. ECCENTRIC has no reference to quantity but only alludes to deviating from an established pattern. (D) ARRAY is the opposite of exiguity, since array infers a "gathering or collecting" of an amount.

34. (D)
   INAFFABLE and INSOLENCE refer to attitude. EXTEMPORE and MOMENTARY are synonymous referring to "instantly." ABRUPT, sudden termination, is the opposite of (D) PERPETUITY, meaning "everlasting."

35. (E)
   FITFULNESS, ERRATIC and RANDOM all denote the lack of a definite plan, lacking in regularity. DESUETUDE as a result of irregularity is discontinued from use. Only (E) RHYTHM, an ordered, recurrent strong continuation is the opposite of DESULTORY.

36. (E)
   INCLINATION and FLUCTUATION both infer uncertain movement, while VACILLATION suggests to waver in the mind. VICIS-

SITUDE implies the result of change while (E) CONSTANCY, meaning unchanging, is the opposite of VERSATILITY, which means to change readily.

37. (A)

STRESS and PREVARICATE both denote extreme effort. LANGUOR, ENERVATION and FLACCIDITY are synonymous and imply a lack of effort. Only (A) STRENUOUS, defined as "vigorous, active" is the opposite of ENERVATION.

38. (E)

INFLUENCE describes an act of the will by producing an effect without apparent force. PREVALENCE and DOMINANCE are synonyms while AUSPICES refers to the act of being prosperous. (E) IMPOTENCE is the opposite of PREPONDERANCE which means superiority.

## Section 3—Quantitative Ability

1. (C)

Consider the quantity $\dfrac{x^2 - y^2}{x - y}$. It can be written as

$$\frac{x^2 - y^2}{x - y} = \frac{(x - y)(x + y)}{(x - y)}$$

since $x - y \neq 0$, we can divide both the numerator and the denominator by $(x - y)$. This yields

$$\frac{x^2 - y^2}{x - y} = \frac{(x - y)(x + y)}{(x - y)} = x + y$$

Thus, no matter what the values of $x$ and $y$ are, as long as $x - y \neq 0$, the two quantities in columns A and B are equal.

2. (D)

Since the sum of the measures of the three interior angles of a triangle is equal to $180°$, it follows from the center information that

$$x + y + 40 = 180$$
$$x + y = 180 - 40$$
$$x + y = 140$$

Since no information is given about the value of $x$ or $y$, the relationship between the two quantities given in Columns A and B cannot be determined.

3.   **(B)**

The easiest and the most direct way to compare the two quantities in Columns A and B is to perform the indicated operations in the quantity given in Column B. This involves addition and subtraction of decimals.

In general, adding and subtracting decimals is a three-step process:

(i)    List all the numbers vertically lining up the decimal points.
(ii)   Add the numbers as if they were whole numbers.
(iii)  Insert the decimal point in the sum directly below the decimal points in the numbers being added or subtracted.

In this problem, $0.105 + 0.5 + 8 = 8.605$, since

$$
\begin{array}{r}
0.105 \\
0.500 \\
\underline{8.000} \\
8.605
\end{array}
$$

Hence, $0.105 + 0.5 - 3.1029 + 8 = 8.605 - 3.1029 = 5.5021$ since

$$
\begin{array}{r}
8.6050 \\
\underline{-3.1029} \\
5.5021
\end{array}
$$

So the quantity in column B is greater.

4.   **(A)**

Since the more seeds the farmer plants, the more ears of corn he harvests, it follows that a direct proportion can be used to solve this problem.

791

$$\frac{\text{Number of seeds}}{\text{Number of seeds}} = \frac{\text{Number of ears}}{\text{Number of ears of}}$$
$$\frac{\text{planted } x}{\text{planted } y} = \frac{\text{of corn harvested } x}{\text{corn harvested } y}$$

In this problem,

$$\frac{100}{y} = \frac{48}{72,000}$$

Cross-multiplication yields,

$$48y = (100)(72,000)$$
$$y = \frac{(100)(72,000)}{48}$$
$$= 150,000$$

So the quantity in Column A is greater.

5.    (D)

Since no specific information about the value of $x$, $y$, or $z$ is given, the relationship between the two quantities in Columns A and B cannot be determined from the information given. For example, if $x = 1$, $y = 2$, and $z = 3$, then $x - y = 1 - 2 = -1$, and $z - x = 3 - 1 = 2$. Thus, the quantity in Column B is greater. But, if $x = 3$, $y = 2$, and $z = 1$, then $x - y = 3 - 2 = 1$, and $z - x = 1 - 3 = -2$, which makes the quantity in Column A greater.

6.    (A)

The average (arithmetic mean), $\bar{x}$, of a set of scores is equal to the sum of all scores divided by the number of all scores, $n$. Thus,

$$\bar{x} = \frac{\text{sum of all scores}}{n}$$

In this problem, there are 19 girls and 11 boys in the class, so $n = 19 + 11 = 30$. Thus,

$$\bar{x} = \frac{\text{sum of all scores}}{n}$$

$$27.5 = \frac{\text{sum of all scores}}{30}$$

Cross-multiplication yields

$$\text{sum of all scores} = (27.5)(30)$$
$$= 825.$$

Note that,

$$\text{sum of all scores} = \text{sum of the scores of all}$$
$$19 \text{ girls} +$$
$$\text{sum of all scores of 11 boys}$$

Hence, $825 = 532 + \text{sum of scores of all 11 boys}$ which yields

$$\text{sum of scores of all 11 boys} = 825 - 532$$
$$= 293$$

So the quantity in Column A is greater.

7. **(C)**

Label the vertices of the triangle A, B and C, and let $\overline{AB}$ represent the length of side $AB$

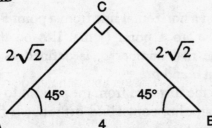

From the centered information, triangle $ABC$ is a right isosceles triangle. Hence, $\overline{CA} = \overline{CB} = 2\sqrt{2}$.

Since ABC is a right triangle, by Pythagorean Theorem (if $a$ and $b$ are the lengths of the shorter sides (legs) of a right triangle and $c$ is the length of the longer side (hypotenuse), then $a^2 + b^2 = c^2$) it follows that

$$(\overline{AB})^2 = (\overline{AC})^2 + (\overline{BC})^2$$
$$(\overline{AB})^2 = (2\sqrt{2})^2 + (2\sqrt{2})^2$$
$$= 4(2) + 4(2)$$
$$= 8 + 8$$
$$= 16$$

Taking the square root of both sides of the equation $(AB)^2 = 16$, yields $\overline{AB} = 4$.

So the quantities in both columns are equal.

8. (B)

From the centered information, we can convert a Fahrenheit temperature to a Celsius temperature or vice versa by simply using the formula

$$C = \frac{5}{9}(F - 32)$$

In this problem, to compare the quantities in Columns A and B, convert 65°F to a Celsius temperature. Thus,

$$C = \frac{5}{9}(F - 32)$$
$$C = \frac{5}{9}(65 - 32)$$
$$= \frac{5}{9}(33) = 18\frac{1}{3}.$$

Thus, 65°F is equivalent to $18\frac{1}{3}$°C.

So the quantity in Column B is greater.

9. (A)

The distance on a horizontal line from a point $P$, that corresponds to a real number $a$, to a point $Q$ that lies on the same line and corresponds to the real number $b$, is defined as the non-negative difference between $a$ and $b$.

Let $AB$ denote the distance from the point $A$ to the point $B$ where $A$ and $B$ lie on the same horizontal line. In the above figure, the distance from $F$ to $H$ is given by

$$FH = 2 - \frac{2}{3} = \frac{4}{3}$$

and the distance from $F$ to $D$ is equal to the non-negative difference of $-1$ and $\frac{2}{3}$, which is equal to

$$-(-1 - \frac{2}{3}) = -(-\frac{5}{3})$$
$$= \frac{5}{3}$$

Thus, if $P$ is the midpoint of segment $\overline{DH}$ that corresponds to the real number $x$, then the distance from $D$ to $P$ is equal to the distance from $P$ to $H$. That is,

$$DP = DH$$
$$x - (-1) = 2 - x$$
$$x + 1 = 2 - x$$
$$2x = 1$$
$$x = \frac{1}{2}$$

So the quantity in Column A is greater.

**10. (D)**

Since $a < b$, it follows that one might conclude that $a^2$ is greater than $b^2$. This is not the case.

Since no other information is given about the value of $x$ or $y$, the relationship between the two quantities is indeterminate. For example, if $a = -3$ and $b = -2$, then $a < b$, $a^2 = -(3)^2 = 9$, and $b^2 = (-2)^2 = 4$. In this case, $a^2 > b^2$. But if $a = 3$ and $b = 4$, then $a < b$, $a^2 = (3)^2 = 9$, and $b^2 = (4)^2 = 16$. In this case $a^2 < b^2$.

**11. (B)**

To determine the value of $n$, one needs to translate the centered information into an algebraic equation with one variable, $n$, then solve it for $n$.

Thus,

$$288 + n = 3(n - 12)$$
$$288 + n = 3n - 36$$
$$288 + 36 = 3n - n$$
$$2n = 324$$
$$n = 162.$$

So the quantity in Column B is greater.

**12. (A)**

This comparison problem can be attacked by recalling that when both sides of an inequality are multiplied by the same negative number, the inequality changes direction, and when multiplying both sides by the same positive number, the inequality does not change direction. That is,

If $x < y$ and $c < 0$, then $cx > cy$, and if $x > y$ and $c < 0$, then $cx < cy$. But if $x < y$ and $c > 0$, then $cx < cy$ and if $x > y$ and $c > 0$, then $cx > cy$.

In our problem, since $0 < a < 1$, it follows that

$$a < 1 \quad \text{and} \quad a > 0.$$

Thus, multiplying both sides of the inequality

$$a < 1$$

by the same positive number $a$ $(a > 0)$, does not change the direction of the inequality. Hence,

$$a < 1$$
$$a \cdot a < a \cdot 1$$
$$a^2 < a \quad \text{or} \quad a > a^2.$$

Thus, the quantity in Column A is greater.

13. (C).

Label the vertices of the triangle $A$, $B$ and $C$, let $m \angle A$ denote the measure of angle $A$, and $\overline{AB}$ denote the length of side $AB$.

From the central information, $\overline{AC}$ = $y$ and $\overline{BC} = y$, hence, triangle $ABC$ is an isosceles triangle. This means that $m \angle A = m \angle B$.

Because the sum of the measures of the three interior angles of a triangle is equal to $180°$, it follows that

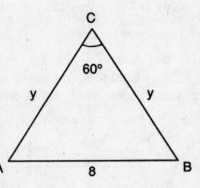

$$m \angle A + m \angle B + m \angle C = 180$$
$$m \angle A + m \angle B + 60 = 180$$
$$m \angle A + m \angle B = 180 - 60$$
$$m \angle A + m \angle B = 120$$

since $m \angle A = m \angle B$, it follows that

$$m \angle A = 60° \text{ and } m \angle B = 60°.$$

Thus, triangle $ABC$ is an equilateral triangle. That is, all of its sides have equal lengths. Hence, $y = 8$ and $3y = 3(8) = 24$.

So the quantities in Columns A and B are equal.

14. (B)

The easiest and the most direct approach to attack this problem is to express the centered information in an algebraic equation in one variable and solve for the variable. To do so, let $q$ be the number of quarters processed, then the number of dimes processed will be $(389 - q)$.

Since each quarter is 25¢ and each dime is 10¢, it follows that the total amount of money processed is equal to $25q + 10(389 - q)$. Also, the total amount of money processed is \$65. Thus, expressed in an

algebraic equation, the centered information states that

$$25q + 10(389 - q) = 6500$$
$$25q + 3890 - 10q = 6500$$
$$15q = 6500 - 3890$$
$$15q = 2610$$
$$q = {}^{2610}/_{15} = 174.$$

Thus, the number of quarters processed was 174, and so the quantity in Column B is greater.

15. (C)

The centered figure can be divided into 2 non-overlapping figures, the square *ABCD* and the triangle *CDE*. Thus, the area of the given

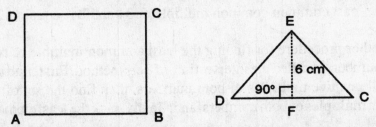

figure is equal to the sum of the areas of the square and the triangle. Since the side of the square is 8 cm, it follows that its area is equal to (8 cm) (8 cm) = 64 cm².

Recall that the area of a triangle is equal to $^1/_2 bh$, where *b* is the base of the triangle (any one of its sides) and *h* is the altitude of the triangle (the perpendicular segment drawn from the vertex opposite the base of the triangle to the base itself or to the line containing the base).

In this problem, side $\overline{CD}$ can be the base, *b*, of triangle *DCE* and $\overline{EF}$ is its altitude. Since the length of the base of the triangle is the same as the length of the side of the square, it follows that *b* = 8 cm, and

$$\text{Area of triangle } DCE = {}^1/_2\, bh$$
$$= {}^1/_2\, (8 \text{ cm}) (6 \text{ cm})$$
$$= 24 \text{ cm}^2$$

But, area of centered figure = area of squares + area of triangle

$$= 64 \text{ cm}^2 + 24 \text{ cm}^2$$
$$= 88 \text{ cm}^2$$

So the two quantities in Columns A and B are equal.

16.   (D)

Tilda's car gets 34 miles per gallon of gasoline, and Naomi's car gets 8 miles per gallon. Since each of them used a whole number of gallons of gasoline in traveling from Washington, D.C, to Philadelphia, it follows that the distance between the two cities must be a multiple of the two numbers 34 and 8.

The least common multiple of two (or more) whole numbers is the smallest non-zero whole number that is a multiple of both (all) of the numbers.

The least common multiple of 34 and 8 can be found by factoring each of 34 and 8 into their prime factors expressed in exponential form as follows:

$$8 = 2 \cdot 2 \cdot 2 = 2^3$$
$$34 = 2 \cdot 17.$$

Then the least common common multiple of 34 and 8 is equal to $2^3 \cdot 17 = 136$.

Another procedure for finding the least common multiple of two whole numbers is called the intersection-of-sets method. First, find the set of all positive multiples of both numbers, then find the set of all common multiples of both numbers, and, finally, pick the least element in the set.

In this problem, multiples of 8 are:

8, 16, 24, 32, 40, 48, 56, 64, 72, 80, 88, 96, 104,
112, 120, 128, 136, 144, 152, 160, 168, ...

Multiples of 34 are:

34, 68, 102, 136, 170, ...

The intersection of the multiples of 8 and 34 is the set

{136, 272, 408, ...}

Because 136 is the smallest common multiple of 8 and 34, it follows that the least common multiple of 34 and 8 is 136. Thus, the distance from Washington D.C., to Philadelphia is 136 miles.

Yet another way to attack this problem is to check if any of the answer choices is a common multiple of both 34 and 8. Checking the answer choices given yields,

(A)  21 is not a multiple of 34 or 8.

(B)  32 is a multiple of 8, but not of 34.

(C)  68 is a multiple of 34, but not of 8.

(D)  136 is a multiple of both 34 and 8.

(E)  170 is a multiple of 34, but not of 8.

17.  (B)
    Extend $\overline{RB}$ to meet line $l$ at point $E$, then angle $ARB$ and angle $CER$ are alternate interior angles. Since $r$ is parallel to $l$, it follows that the measure of angle $ARB$ is equal to the measure of angle $CER$. Thus, the measure of angle $CER = 55°$.

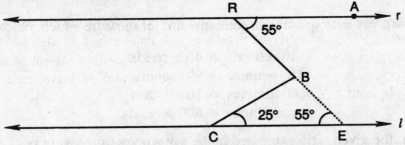

Since angle $RBC$ is an exterior angle of triangle $BEC$, and the measure of an exterior angle of a triangle is equal to the sum of the measures of the two non-adjacent interior angles of the triangles, it follows that the measure of angle $RBC$ is equal to the sum of the measures of angle $BEC$ and angle $BCE$. Thus

$$\text{measure of angle } RBC = 55° + 25°$$
$$= 80°.$$

18.  (E)
    Obviously, the more (less) chickens we have, the more (less) sacks of grains needed. Thus, this problem can be solved by using a direct proportion as follows:

$$\frac{\text{Number of sacks of feed } x}{\text{Number of chickens } x} = \frac{\text{Number of sacks of feed } y}{\text{Number of chickens } y}$$

Since it takes $s$ sacks of grain to feed $c$ chickens it follows that the correct proportion to use is:

$$\frac{s}{c} = \frac{y}{k}$$

where $y$ is the required number of sacks of grain needed to feed $k$ chickens. Solving this proportion for $y$ in terms of $s$, $c$, and $k$ yields,

$$\frac{s}{c} = \frac{y}{k}$$

$$cy = sk$$

$$y = \frac{sk}{c}$$

19.　(A)

One of the simplest and most direct methods for attacking this problem is as follows:

1.　Express each quantity in the same unit of measure which yields,

$$40 \text{ seconds} = 40 \text{ seconds}$$
$$1\frac{1}{2} \text{ minutes} = 90 \text{ seconds}$$
$$\frac{1}{6} \text{ hour} = \frac{1}{6} \times 60 \text{ minutes} = 10 \text{ minutes}$$
$$= 10(60) = 600 \text{ seconds.}$$

Thus, the given ratio expressed in the same units of measure is

$$40 \text{ seconds} : 90 \text{ seconds} : 600 \text{ seconds}$$

2.　Since a ratio, $a : b$ can be written as $^a/_b$, it follows that the ratio

$$40 \text{ seconds} : 90 \text{ seconds}$$

can be written as

$$\frac{40 \text{ seconds}}{90 \text{ seconds}} = \frac{40}{90}$$

Similarly, the ratio

$$90 \text{ seconds} : 600 \text{ seconds}$$

can be written as

$$\frac{90 \text{ seconds}}{600 \text{ seconds}} = \frac{90}{600}$$

Thus, removing the common unit, seconds, from the ratio obtained in

step (1) above yields the ratio

$$40 : 90 : 600$$

3. Dividing by the highest common factor of 40, 90, and 600, which is 10, we obtain,

$$4 : 9 : 60$$

**20. (C)**

Since we have evaporation occurring in this problem, we shall be using subtraction.

Let $x$ = the number of cc of alcohol evaporated. Then $(40 - x)$ = the number of cc in the resulting solution.

A diagram as in the following figure is helpful.

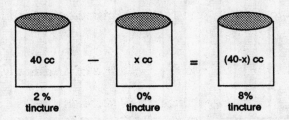

2% of 40 cc = the number of cc of iodine in original solution.
0% of $x$ cc = number of cc of iodine in the alcohol evaporated.
8% of $(40 - x)$ cc = number of cc of iodine in the resulting solution.

Using this relationship,

(Iodine in original solution) – (Iodine in evaporated solution)
$\quad$ = (Iodine in resulting solution).

We get,
$$(0.02)(40) - 0(x) = (0.08)(40 - x)$$
$$0.8 - 0 = 3.2 - 0.08x$$
$$0.08x = 3.2 - 0.8$$
$$0.08x = 2.4$$
$$x = {}^{2.4}/_{.08} = 30$$

Thus, 30 cc of alcohol must be evaporated in order to raise the strength of the tincture to 8%.

**21. (A)**

This is simply a graph-reading question. To determine the least number of bushels of wheat produced, locate the shortest bar of wheat

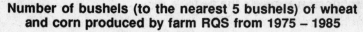

**Number of bushels (to the nearest 5 bushels) of wheat and corn produced by farm RQS from 1975 – 1985**

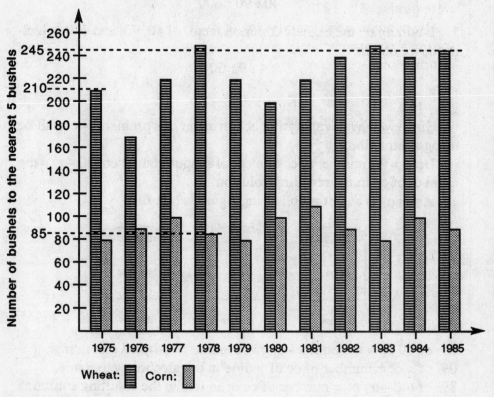

Wheat: ▨  Corn: ▨

production for the years 1976, 1978, 1980, 1982, and 1984. The reason for considering these years is because they are listed as possible answers. By inspection of the graph, we find that the shortest bar representing wheat production is the one representing the wheat production for 1976. Thus, the least number of bushels of wheat was produced in 1976.

22.  (C)

As in problem 21, this is a matter of reading the part of the graph which represents the corn production. One needs only to look for the corn production of each of the years given in the answer choices and the production of the years immediately preceding each of them. For example, to find the number of bushels of corn produced in 1978, we locate the bar of corn production for 1978, then draw a horizontal line from the top of the bar to the vertical axis. The point where this

horizontal line meets the vertical axis represents the number of bushels of corn produced in 1978. The graph shows that 85 bushels of corn were produced in 1978.

Now, reading the graph for the years given as possible answers and for the years immediately preceding them, we obtain the following information:

| Year | Number of Bushels of Corn Produced | |
|------|-----------------------------------|---|
| 1977 | 100 | |
| 1978 | 85 | A decline of 15 bushels |
| 1979 | 75 | |
| 1980 | 100 | An increase of 25 bushels |
| 1981 | 110 | |
| 1982 | 90 | A decline of 20 bushels |
| 1982 | 90 | |
| 1983 | 75 | A decline of 15 bushels |
| 1984 | 100 | |
| 1985 | 90 | A decline of 10 bushels |

Thus, the greatest decline in corn production occurred in 1982.

23.  (E)

This question can be answered by reading both parts of the graph, (wheat production graph and corn production graph), for each of the years listed in the answer choices and for the years immediately preceding them. For example, in 1978, there was a decline in corn production, because the bar representing corn production in 1978 is shorter than the bar representing corn production in 1977. Also, in 1978, there was an increase in wheat production because the bar representing wheat production in 1978 is longer than the bar representing wheat production in 1977. By inspecting the given graphs in this fashion, we find out that corn production decreased and wheat production increased in each of the years 1978, 1982, 1983 and 1985.

24.  (C)

From the graph representing wheat production, the number of bushels of wheat produced in 1975 is equal to 210 bushels. This

number can be found by locating the bar on the graph representing wheat production in 1975 and then drawing a horizontal line from the top of that bar to the vertical axis. The point where this horizontal line meets the vertical axis represents the number of bushels of wheat produced in 1975. This number on the vertical axis is 210. Similarly, the graph indicates that the number of bushels of wheat produced in 1985 is equal to 245 bushels.

Thus, the ratio of wheat production in 1985 to that of 1975 is 245 to 210, which can be written as $^{245}/_{210}$. Simplifying this ratio to its simplest form yields,

$$\frac{245}{210} = \frac{5 \cdot 7 \cdot 7}{2 \cdot 3 \cdot 5 \cdot 7} = \frac{7}{2 \cdot 3}$$

$$= \frac{7}{6} \text{ or } 7:6$$

25. (D)

This question requires reading the graphs, listing the number of bushels of wheat and the number of bushels of corn produced in each of the years listed as possible answers in the answer choices (A) through (E), and then adding the number of bushels of wheat produced each year to the number of bushels of corn produced in the same year. The largest number obtained represents the maximum combined production. Thus, reading the graphs yields the following information:

| Year | Number of Bushels of Wheat Produced | Number of Bushels of Corn Produced | Total |
|------|-------------------------------------|-------------------------------------|-------|
| 1978 | 250 | 85 | 335 |
| 1981 | 220 | 110 | 330 |
| 1983 | 250 | 75 | 325 |
| 1984 | 240 | 100 | 340 |
| 1985 | 245 | 90 | 335 |

Thus, from the above table, the combined production of wheat and corn was at a maximum in 1984.

26. (D)

If $m$ and $n$ are consecutive integers, and $m < n$, it follows that

$$n = m + 1$$

Now, we can check each of the answer choices (A) through (E) as follows:

(A)  $n - m = (m + 1) - m = m + 1 - m = 1$, which is odd. Thus, the statement in answer choice (A) is false.

(B)  Since no specific information is given about the integer $m$, $m$ can be an odd integer or an even integer. So, the statement is answer choice (B) is false.

(C)  $m^2 + n^2 = m^2 + (m + 1)^2 \quad = m^2 + m^2 + 2m + 1$
$$= 2m^2 + 2m + 1$$
$$= 2(m^2 + m) + 1$$

Since 2 times any integer (even or odd) yields an even integer, it follows that $2(m^2 + m)$ is an even integer, and hence, $2(m^2 + m) + 1$ is an odd integer. Hence, the statement in answer choice (C) is false.

(D)  $n^2 - m^2 = (m + 1)^2 - m^2 \quad = m^2 + 2m + 1 - m^2$
$$= 2m + 1$$

Again, since 2 times any integer (even or odd) yields an even integer, it follows that $2m$ is an even integer and $2m + 1$ is always an odd integer. Hence, the statement in answer choice (D) is correct.

(E)  Since $m$ and $n$ are any pair of two consecutive integers, it follows that $m$ can be an even integer or an odd integer. Since $n = m + 1$, it follows that if $m$ is odd, then $n$ is even and if $m$ is even, then $n$ is odd. Thus, the statement in answer choice (E) is false.


27.  (A)
Recall that for all real numbers $p, q, r$, and $s$, if $p/_q < 0$, and $r/_s > 0$, then

$$\frac{p}{q} \cdot \frac{r}{s} < 0$$

(negative × positive = negative.)
In this problem, we have $a/_b < 0$, and $c/_d > 0$, thus,

$$\frac{a}{b} \cdot \frac{c}{d} < 0.$$

So answer choice (A) is the correct answer.

Answer choice (B) is wrong because $a/b < 0$, and $c/d > 0$ imply that $a/b \cdot c/d$ cannot be greater than 0 (negative × positive = negative). Answer choice (C) is wrong because the quantity $a/b + c/d$ can either be positive or negative depending on the values of $a, b, c$ and $d$. For example, if $a = -1, b = 2, c = 4$ and $d = 3$ then

$$\frac{a}{b} = -\frac{1}{2} < 0, \quad \frac{c}{d} = \frac{4}{3} > 0 \text{ and}$$

$$\frac{a}{b} + \frac{c}{d} = -\frac{1}{2} + \frac{4}{3} = \frac{5}{6} > 0.$$

However, if $a = -5, b = 2, c = 1$, and $d = 2$, then

$$\frac{a}{b} = -\frac{5}{2} < 0, \quad \frac{c}{d} = \frac{1}{2} > 0, \text{ and}$$

$$\frac{a}{b} + \frac{c}{d} = -\frac{5}{2} + \frac{1}{1} = -2 < 0.$$

Answer choice (D) is wrong for the same reasons stated in answer choice (C).

Answer choice (E) is wrong on the basis that it is impossible to have a real number which is positive and negative at the same time.

28.  (B)

Translating the given information into algebra yields the equation that can be used to find the required number, $n$.

$$3n - 2 = 5((n + 3) + 2)$$
$$3n - 2 = 5(n/3 + 2)$$

This equation is the same as the equation given in answer choice (B).

Inspecting all the equations given in answer choices (A), (C), (D), and (E), we find out that none of them is equivalent to the equation $3n - 2 = 5(n/3 + 2)$.

29.  (E)

Let $m \angle A$ represent the measure of angle $A$. Though there are several ways to attack this question, one way is to recall that the sum of the measures of the three interior angles of a triangle is equal to $180°$, and the measure of an exterior angle of a triangle is equal to the sum of the measures of the two non-adjacent interior angles of the triangle.

We can now start by considering triangle $ACL$. Of course,

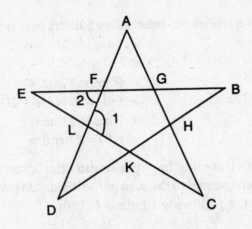

$$m \angle A + m \angle C + m \angle 1 = 180°, \dots \qquad (1)$$

But $\angle 1$ is an exterior angle to triangle $LEF$, thus,

$$m \angle 1 = m \angle E + m \angle 2.$$

Substituting this in equation (1) yields,

$$m \angle A + m \angle C + m \angle E + m \angle 2 = 180°, \dots \qquad (2)$$

However, $\angle 2$ is an exterior angle to triangle $FBD$, thus,

$$m \angle 2 = m \angle B + m \angle D$$

Substituting this result in equation (2) yields,

$$m \angle A + m \angle C + m \angle E + m \angle B + m \angle D = 180°$$

Thus, the sum of the measures of angles $A, B, C, D,$ and $E$ is equal to 180°.

30. (C)
   Certainly, the easiest and the most direct way to answer this question is to translate the given information into an algebraic equation in one unknown variable, then solve it for that variable.
   In this problem, the distance traveled, the time of travel and the rate of travel are involved. The relationship between these three quantities is given by

$$\text{Distance} = \text{Rate} \times \text{Time}$$

So, let $r$ be Lynn's rate of travel in miles per hour. Then Pete's rate of

travel will be $(r+4)$ miles per hour. After 5 hours of travel, the distance traveled by

Pete is
$$d_1 = \text{Rate} \times \text{Time}$$
$$= (t+4)\, 5 = (5t+20) \text{ miles}$$
Lynn is
$$d_2 = \text{Rate} \times \text{Time}$$
$$= r(5) = 5r \text{ miles}$$

Since they are traveling in opposite directions, the total distance, $d$, traveled by both is equal to the sum of the distances traveled by both. A diagram as in the following figure is helpful.

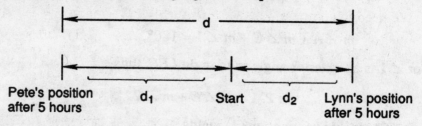

Pete's position after 5 hours    $d_1$    Start    $d_2$    Lynn's position after 5 hours

Now, total distance after 5 hours of travel is,

$$d = d_1 + d_2$$
$$= (5r+20) + 5r$$
$$= 5r + 20 + 5r$$
$$= 10r + 20$$

But, we also know that they are 120 miles apart after 5 hours of travel. Thus,

$$10r + 20 = 120$$
$$10r = 120 - 20$$
$$10r = 100$$
$$r = 10$$

This means Lynn is traveling at the rate of 10 mph.

# Section 4—Quantitative Ability

1. **(C)**
   30% of 40 = 30/100 × 40 = 12.
   40% of 30 = 40/100 × 30 = 12

2. **(D)**
   $K(I) + L(I) = I^2 + 1 + 1 - I^2 = 2$ and
   $K(I) + L(I) = I^2 + 1 + 1 - (1 - I^2) = 2I^2$
   We need to compare 2 with $2I^2$ (Remember $I > 0$).
   If $I > 0$, but less than 1, $2 > 2I^2$.
   If $I > 1$, $2I^2 > 2$.

3. **(B)**
   Since $m < 0$, $n < 0$, $^m/_n$ and $^n/_m > 0$. Also, $m > n$ gives us $^m/_n < 1$,
   $^n/_m > 1$ (remember $m, n < 0$) therefore $^n/_m > ^m/_n$.

4. **(B)**
   Given that
   $$(a, b) = a + 3b$$
   $$(2, 3) = 2 + 3 * 3 = 11$$
   $$(3, x) = 3 + 3x$$

   and
   $$(2, 3) = (3, x)$$
   $$11 = 3 + 3x$$
   $$x = {}^8/_3 > 2.$$

5. **(A)**
   $$y = x - 2$$

   Add 3 to both sides:
   $$y + 3 = x + 1$$

   For any value of $x$, we always have $x + 1 > x - 1$, thus,
   $$y + 3 > x - 1.$$

6.   (A)

1 ft.² of fabric costs \$4. 2 ft. per 2 ft. or 4 sq. ft. will cost \$16, and $16 > 10$.

7.   (C)

Let five consecutive numbers where $x$ is the central number be: $x - 2, x - 1, x, x + 1, x + 2$. Then

$$\text{Average} = \frac{x - 2 + x - 1 + x + x + 1 + x + 2}{5} = x$$

In the second case, let three consecutive numbers be: $x - 1, x, x + 1$. Then

$$\text{Average} = \frac{x - 1 + x + x + 1}{3} = x$$

So, both averages are equal.

8.   (A)

$$\frac{p^2 - q^2}{q - p} = \frac{(p - q)(p + q)}{-(p - q)} = -(p + q)$$

and $p + q > -(p + q)$ since $p + q > 0$.

9.   (D)

The statement says

$$A > P$$
$$B \geq P$$

Therefore it can be $A > B, A = B, A < B$.

10.   (A)

Half of $n$ square $= \left(\dfrac{n}{2}\right)^2$ if $n > 2$ then $n/_2 > 1$, therefore $\left(\dfrac{n}{2}\right)^2 > \dfrac{n}{2}$.

11.   (A)

$$\frac{ab - by}{y - a} = \frac{b(a - y)}{(y - a)} = \frac{b(a - y)}{-(a - y)} = -b$$

given $b < 0$; $-b > b$.

12. **(B)**

Men = $x$;  Women = 73.

Empty seats = $^{20}/_{100}$ (320) = 64

Women + Men + Empty seats = 320

$$73 + x + 64 = 320$$
$$x = 183 < 185$$

13. **(B)**

$$\cfrac{1}{4 - \cfrac{1+\frac{1}{2}}{1-\frac{1}{2}}} = \cfrac{1}{4 - \cfrac{\frac{3}{2}}{\frac{1}{2}}} = \cfrac{1}{4 - 3} = 1.$$

14. **(A)**

We can define an even number as $2x$, and the following numbers will be $2x + 2$ and $2x + 4$. Therefore

$$2x + 2x + 2 + 2x + 4 = 42$$
$$6x + 6 = 42$$
$$6x = 36$$
$$x = 6.$$

Remember that the first number was $2x$, which is 12 if $x = 6$.

15. **(B)**

Redraw the figure. Assigning $M, N$ and $P$ the respective areas, then

area = $\dfrac{R^2}{2}$.

By using the Pythagorean theorem

$$R^2 + R^2 = x^2$$
$$R\sqrt{2} = x$$

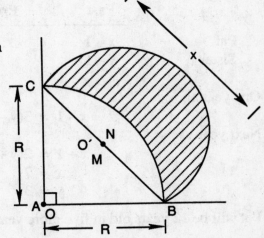

$$\text{Area } M = \frac{R^2}{2}.$$

$$\text{Area } N = \text{Area Quadrant} - \text{Area } M$$

$$= \frac{\pi R^2}{4} - \frac{R^2}{2} = R^2\left(\frac{\pi}{4} - \frac{1}{2}\right)$$

$$\text{Shaded Area} = \text{Area } P = \text{Semicircle Area} - \text{Area } N$$

$$= \frac{\pi\left(\frac{R\sqrt{2}}{2}\right)^2}{2} - R^2\left(\frac{\pi}{4} - \frac{1}{2}\right)$$

$$\text{Area } P = \frac{\pi R^2}{4} - \frac{\pi R^2}{4} + \frac{R^2}{2}$$

$$\text{Area } P = \frac{R^2}{2}$$

16.  (C)

$$\left(\sqrt{a+b}\right)^2 = a+b, \quad \sqrt{(a-b)^2} = a-b \text{ since } a > b.$$

So,

$$\left[\left(\sqrt{a+b}\right)^2 - \sqrt{(a-b)^2}\right] = [(a+b) - (a-b)]$$
$$= [a+b-a+b]$$
$$= 2b$$

17.  (B)

|        | Past    | Present | Future  |
|--------|---------|---------|---------|
| Pat    | $x-1$   | $x$     | $x+1$   |
| Sister | $y-1$   | $y$     | $y+1$   |

One year ago...

$$x-1 = 3(y-1)$$

Next year...

$$x+1 = 2(y+1)$$
$$x = 7$$
$$y = 3$$

Pat will be 12 years old in five more years.

18. **(E)**

$$\left[\left(\frac{x}{y}\right)^{-1} - \left(\frac{y}{x}\right)^{-1}\right]^{-1} = \left[\left(\frac{y}{x}\right)^{1} - \left(\frac{x}{y}\right)^{1}\right]^{-1}$$

$$= \left[\frac{y}{x} - \frac{x}{y}\right]^{-1} = \left[\frac{y^2 - x^2}{xy}\right]^{-1}$$

$$= \left[\frac{xy}{y^2 - x^2}\right]^{1} = \frac{xy}{y^2 - x^2}$$

19. **(D)**

To find the smallest number we will calculate each one

(A) $\dfrac{5 \cdot 10^{-3}}{3 \cdot 10^{-3}} = \dfrac{5 \cdot 10^{-3}}{3 \cdot 10^{-3}} = \dfrac{5}{3} = 1.6$

(B) $\dfrac{.3}{.2} = \dfrac{.3}{.2} = 1.5$

(C) $\dfrac{.3}{3} \cdot 10^{-3} = \dfrac{.3}{3 \cdot 10^{-3}} = \dfrac{.3 \cdot 10^3}{3} = \dfrac{3 \cdot 10^2}{3} = 100$

(D) $5 \cdot \dfrac{10^{-2}}{.1} = \dfrac{5 \cdot 10^{-2}}{.1} = \dfrac{5 \cdot 10^{-2}}{10^{-1}} = 5 \cdot 10^{-1} = .5$

(E) $\dfrac{.3}{3} \cdot 10^{-1} = \dfrac{.3}{3 \cdot 10^{-1}} = \dfrac{.3 \cdot 10}{3} = \dfrac{3}{3} = 1$

The correct answer is (D).

20. **(A)**

$x$ : Number of persons

| Person | Number of hugs |
|--------|----------------|
| 1 | $x - 1$ |
| 2 | $x - 2$ |
| 3 | $x - 3$ |
| $\vdots$ | |
| $x$ | $x - x$ |
| Total | $x^2 - (1 + 2 + \ldots + x)$ |

$$\text{Total} = x^2 - \frac{x(x+1)}{2}$$

$$\text{Total} = x^2 - \frac{x^2}{2} - \frac{x}{2}$$

$$\text{Total} = \frac{x^2}{2} - \frac{x}{2}$$

The total is 21.
Therefore

$$\frac{x^2}{2} - \frac{x}{2} = 21$$

$$\frac{x^2 - x}{2} = 21$$

$$x^2 - x = 42 = 0$$

where $x_1 = 7$; $x_2 = -6$. The number of persons = 7.
You can solve also with probability theory.

21.   (B)
We need to calculate the percentage growth of each country in South America. In general:

$$\text{Percentage growth} = \left[\frac{\text{Birthrate}}{1000} - \frac{\text{Deathrate}}{1000}\right] \times 100\%$$

$$\text{Percentage growth of Argentina} = \left[\frac{23.8}{1000} - \frac{8.2}{1000}\right] \times 100\% = 1.56\%$$

$$\text{Percentage growth of Chile} = \left[\frac{35.4}{1000} - \frac{11.9}{1000}\right] \times 100\% = 2.35\%$$

$$\text{Percentage growth of Ecuador} = \left[\frac{45.5}{1000} - \frac{15.2}{1000}\right] \times 100\% = 3.03\%$$

$$\text{Percentage growth of Peru} = \left[\frac{36.6}{1000} - \frac{9.0}{1000}\right] \times 100\% = 2.76\%$$

$$\text{Percentage growth of Uruguay} = \left[\frac{11.4}{1000} - \frac{7}{1000}\right] \times 100\% = .44\%$$

$$\text{Percentage growth of Venezuela} = \left[\frac{46.7}{1000} - \frac{9.9}{1000}\right] \times 100\% = 3.68\%$$

The answer is 3.68%.

22.   (E)
Looking at the table, the countries that have the lowest infant mortality are Sweden and The Netherlands, each one with 17. Note that Iran is not 0.


23.   (C)
In the U.S. we had 9.6 deaths per 1000 citizens and an infant mortality rate of 26 per 1000 births and also 25.3 births per 1000 citizens. Therefore,

$$\text{Total death} = 9.6/1000 \text{ citizens}$$
$$\text{Infant death} = 26/1000 \times 25.3/1000 \text{ citizens}$$
$$\text{Infant death} = .668/1000 \text{ citizens.}$$

Let $x$ be the desired percentage, then

$$x = \frac{0.668}{9.6} \times 100\%$$

$$= 6.85\%$$


24.   (A)
We had 25.3 births per 1000 citizens, therefore

$$200 \text{ million (citizens)} = \frac{25.3 \text{ births}}{1000 \text{ citizens}} = 5.06 \times 10^{6} \text{ (Births)}$$


25.   (B)
To calculate the population in 1958 we need to consider the birth rate and also the death rate:

$$\text{Percentage growth of U.S.} \left( \frac{25.3}{1000} - \frac{9.6}{1000} \right) \times 100 = 1.57\%$$

$$
\begin{aligned}
\text{Population 1958} &= \text{Population 1957} + \\
&\quad 1.57\% \text{ Population 1957} \\
&= 1.0157 \text{ (Population 1957)} \\
&= 1.0157 \times 200 \text{ million} \\
&= 203{,}140{,}000 \\
&= 203.14 \text{ million}
\end{aligned}
$$

26. (E)
   What is an expression for $y/x$ as a function of $a$ if $\dfrac{x+y}{y} = a$ ?

$$\frac{x+y}{y} = a$$

$$\frac{x}{y} + \frac{y}{y} = a$$

$$\frac{x}{y} + 1 = a$$

$$\frac{x}{y} = a - 1$$

$$\frac{y}{x} = \frac{1}{a-1}$$

27. (B)
   Let $x$ be the total capacity of the swimming pool, then $\frac{2}{3}x = 1800$.

$$x = \frac{1800 \cdot 3}{2} = 2700 \text{ ft}^3$$

The correct answer is (B).

28. (B)
   20% have traveled more than two times. 70% have never traveled. Therefore 10% have traveled one or two times.

29. (D)
   If $\qquad\qquad z = x^a$ and $y = x^b$
   
   then $\qquad\quad z^b = (x^a)^b / b$
   
   $\qquad\qquad\quad z^b = (x^a)^b$
   
   $\qquad\qquad\quad z = x^{ab}$
   
   and $\qquad\qquad y = x^b / a$
   
   $\qquad\qquad\quad y = (x^b)a$
   
   $\qquad\qquad\quad y = x^{ba} = x^{ab}$
   
   so $\qquad\quad z^b y^a = x^{ab} x^{ab} = x^{ab+ab}$
   
   $\qquad\qquad\quad z^b y^a = x^{2ab}$

30. (D)

$$\text{Average} = \frac{5 \times 30 + 3 \times 20}{8}$$

$$\text{Average} = \frac{150 + 60}{80} = \frac{210}{8} = 26.25$$

# Section 5–Analytical Ability

1. (E);    2. (E);    3. (D);    4. (B);    5. (A)

These questions can be answered by developing a chart listing males, females, and the rank order according to height and age. The chart that follows is based on the information provided in the passage.

| Males | Females | Height (Rank order) | Age(Rank order) |
|-------|---------|---------------------|-----------------|
| A | | D | D |
| B | | C | A |
| C | | A | C |
| D | | E | G |
| | E | B | H |
| | F | F | F |
| | G | H | E |
| | H | G | B |

After constructing this chart, all questions can be answered by referring to the appropriate columns and information in this chart.

6. (A);    7. (D);    8. (A)

This series of questions requires an understanding of the code and the procedures for revising the code annually. It also requires attention to details such as (1) omitting decimals and (2) using only the last digit to indicate the year (an 8 means 1988 and a 7 means 1987). To answer these questions, write the code CITYSQUARE and then place numbers over (or under) the letter according to the year. For example, if the year is 1987, then the diagram that would clarify the code is the following:

4 5 6 7 8 9 0 1 2 3

C I T Y S Q U A R E

After preparing this diagram according to the information provided for each question, the correct choice can be found in the diagram.

9. (B);   10. (A);   11. (C);   12. (D)

Prepare a chart and place the information given directly in the chart to enable you to begin deriving the additional information to complete the chart. In the chart below, information that you can obtain directly is shown in capital letters and the explanation that follows describes the procedures to determine the remaining information.

| Name | Description | Purchase |
|------|-------------|----------|
| SALLY | PERKY | belt |
| BETTY | SLIM | TIE |
| DOROTHY | tall | SLIP |
| PAULA | depressed | SCARF |
| THELMA | short | dress |
| SUSAN | BOLD | pantyhose |

Based on the given information, Sally had to purchase a belt or dress, Susan had to purchase a dress or pantyhose, Thelma had to either purchase a dress or belt. Paula was either depressed or tall; Dorothy was tall; therefore Paula was depressed and the only characteristic left was "short" which had to apply to Thelma. Thus Thelma purchased a dress. That left a belt for Sally to purchase and the pantyhose for Susan.

13. (A);   14. (D);   15. (E);   16. (B)

The items based on this passage can be answered by comparing the choices with the conditions stipulated for team membership. You can either select the right answer or eliminate the wrong answers. The safest procedure is to do both. In item 13 choice (A) conforms to the conditions stated. However, to avoid overlooking a detail, a cross-check of the other choices will reveal that they do not work. Each of the remaining choices can be eliminated for the following reasons: Choice (B) has Art and Dan on the team; Choice (C) has George but not Chuck; Choice (D) has Art and Dan; and Choice (E) includes Hal and Ed. It is through this process that each of the correct answers can be determined.

17.   (B)

This passage calls for an understanding of the difference between a paradox and a contradiction. Both terms describe two or more events

or ideas whose co-existence is impossible (in the case of contradictions) or apparently contradictory (in the case of paradoxes). Choice (B) is the answer that is clearly correct, although the other statements in another context might be defensible.

18.  (C)
The crucial concept in this passage is the recognition of a behavior in which one's faults are not recognized but are seen as the faults of others. Choices (A) and (B) are statements of disagreement but there is no implication that the speaker is guilty of the same fault. Choice (D) is not denying his own violation as much as he is claiming others should also be arrested. Choice (E) is a behavior that doesn't necessarily suggest they object to the way others do the same thing. Choice (C) is clearly a case of someone complaining about others' actions when that same action is a characteristic of the person speaking.

19.  (D)
The important clue in this passage and choices given, is to look for an attack on the person rather than addressing the issue under discussion. Only choice (D) provides an *ad hominem* argument.

20.  (E)
The question called for here is to find a statement that attempts to lead someone to a conclusion by analogy. The phrase "where there is smoke there is fire" is used to accuse or judge people by the appearance of wrongdoing, often by their association with places or people. Thus a person who associates closely with known criminals or who has close friends who are drug addicts may be considered a criminal or drug addict and others "prove" this in their own minds with the phrase, "where there is smoke there is fire."

21.  (B)
The *post hoc* fallacy is a frequent illogical conclusion because enough cases to verify a relationship are often difficult to obtain. Relationships between people are among those that illustrate the difficulty of drawing valid conclusions. We might say things like "mixed marriages do not work" or "slow drivers cause as many

accidents as speeders" but there are many exceptions that seem to show the opposite is true. It has taken many years of study to link smoking to cancer and statements made about this correlation 30 years ago did not have the validity they have today. Conclusions drawn from insufficient evidence abound and choice (B) is the answer that is the most defensible in the light of the information provided in the passage.

22. (C)

Arguments that persuade others to cooperate with a program or idea are more likely to be effective if some benefit to the target group can be identified. An appeal to the retirees on the grounds that they will have a better community if the younger generation is well-educated will carry more power than arguments that are mere persuasion, attempts to browbeat them or opinions that are aimed at making them feel guilty. The alternative that avoids the counter-productive arguments mentioned here and provides some positive regard for the retirees is choice (C).

23. (C)

Choices (A), (B), (D), and (E) are all statements that can be identified in the passage and they are all directly supported in the passage. Choice (C) may be a conclusion historians or philologists might like to draw but it is not supported in the narrative provided.

24. (D)

The issue in this topic is how to preserve the safeguards necessary with new inventions so that ideas, environment, health, and economic concerns are not damaged and still make it possible for new ideas that will benefit society to come from the most diverse sources, including individuals with limited resources. The choice that most nearly protects these diverse interests without imposing unfair, illegal, or unconstitutional constraints is (D).

25. (A)

This question requires a projection based on goals that might be met in contrast to goals that conflict with one another to the extent that achieving one goal eliminates the possibility of the others. If the

information in the passage is correct, then an increasing number of married couples will be faced with the decision to obtain homes or children, but not both. Choice (A) is the correct answer.

## Section 6—Analytical Ability

With the information given for questions 1 to 6, a chart may be constructed.

| Berry | AR | AL | MS | AZ | NV | CO | FL | UT |
|-------|----|----|----|----|----|----|----|----|
| | | | | | | **States** | | |
| Strawberry | X | X | X | — | — | — | X | — |
| Blueberry | — | X | X | X | X | — | — | — |
| Boysenberry | X | — | X | — | X | — | X | X |
| Blackberry | — | — | — | X | X | X | — | X |
| Raspberry | X | X | X | X | — | — | — | — |
| Gooseberry | — | X | X | — | — | — | X | X |

1.  (C)
From the chart, it can be seen that boysenberries grow in five states.

2.  (C)
Mississippi has five varieties of berries.

3.  (E)
In Utah you can grow boysenberries, blackberries, and gooseberries.

4.  (B)
Alabama is the only state the grows strawberries, but does not grow boysenberries.

5.  (B)
Blackberries grow in Nevada, but strawberries do not.

6. **(C)**
Arizona and Nevada grow both blackberries and blueberries.


**Questions 7 – 10**
Using greater than (>) and less than (<) symbols will help place the boys in some order.

| | |
|---|---|
| Roger is taller than Jeff | R > J |
| Glenn is shorter than Stan. | G < S |
| Dennis is shorter than Roger. | D < R |
| Glenn is taller than Dennis. | G > D |
| Roger is shorter than Stan. | R < J |
| Dennis is the shortest of the five. | |

Now putting this information together gives the following relation-ships:

$$S > R > J > D$$
$$S > — G — > D$$

Notice that some of the boys cannot be placed in exact order. This is not necessary to answer the questions.


7. **(D)**
From the diagram, Stan is obviously the tallest.


8. **(B)**
I is false, because Jeff is necessarily taller than Dennis. II is true, because Jeff and Glenn cannot be compared by the information given, therefore Jeff is not necessarily taller than Glenn.


9. **(A)**
From the chart, I is the only true statement, because Stan is taller than Jeff.


10. **(D)**
If Fred joints the group and is taller than Glenn, but shorter than

Jeff, then the order of the boys must be

$$S > R > J > F > G > D$$

**Answers 11 – 14**

**11. (B)**
 II is true. Since four of the six children have brown eyes and three of the six are girls, then at least one girl has brown eyes. All of the girls do not have to have dimples.

**12. (B)**
 II must be false. Since five of the six children have dimples and four of the six children have brown eyes, then some of the dimpled children must have brown eyes. Statement I, "all the brown-eyed girls have dimples," could be true.

**13. (E)**
 None of the statements can be deduced from the information given.

**14. (D)**
 "Three children have blue eyes" must be false. Since four children have brown eyes, that would total seven children. There are only six children in the family.

**Answers 15 – 16**
 We shall take note of the guidelines in preparing the final Possible Combinations table:

|  | B | M | C | E | H | P |
|---|---|---|---|---|---|---|
| Combination 1:<br>Biology and Math | X | X | O | X | X | O |
| Combination 2:<br>Biology but not Math | X | O | O | X | X | X |

|  | B | M | C | E | H | P |
|---|---|---|---|---|---|---|
| Combination 3:<br>Math but not Biology | O | X | X | X | X | O |
| Combination 4:<br>Neither Math nor Biology | O | O | X | X | X | X |

From the above table, we see that the possible combinations are B, M, E, H or B, E, H, P or M, C, E, H or C, E, H, P.

**15. (B)**

From the table above, we can see that, for Combinations 1 and 2, "History" is marked with an X.

**16. (C)**

The table describes four different combinations.

**17. (E)**

The answer to this question is clearly choice (E). Only the coin collector makes a factual statement — on the number of coins of a specific type minted in a certain year. The remaining people present opinions, which, however qualified, cannot be established empirically.

**18. (E)**

Though the author argues that blaming people is immoral and futile, he blames those who blame others, thus doing just what he argues against. Choice (D) is incorrect, since the author does not appeal to emotion. Choices (A), (B), and (C), even if true, would not constitute undercutting the argument.

**Answers 19 – 21**

Let us denote the four bureaucrats by small circles, each labeled with a letter A, B, C, or D. Responsibility transmitted from one bureaucrat to another is to be designated by an arrow → pointing toward the one receiving the responsibility, and originating from the

one delegating responsibility. Thus, if A passes a responsibility on to B, we write

A O - - - - - - - - - - - - - - - - - - - - - - - - →O B

We distinguish between two cases:

Case 1: A small cycle of responsibility passing is possible, as in this picture.

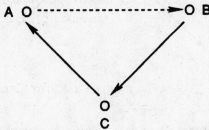

Case 2: Suppose that no such cycle of

A - - - - - → B - - - - - → C - - - - - → A

delegation is possible. Then only the following situation arises:

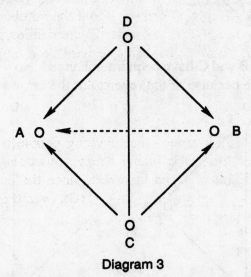

Diagram 3

We are now prepared to determine the correct choices by referring to Diagrams 1, 2, 1a, 2a, and 3.

The following possibilities for including the last bureaucrat (D) are indicated in the diagram below.

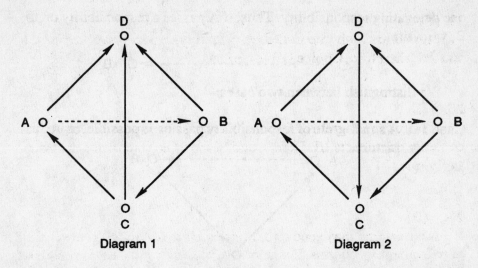

Diagram 1                    Diagram 2

If we now reverse all of the arrows in the above diagrams, the circular pattern — A to B to C back to A — remains essentially the same.

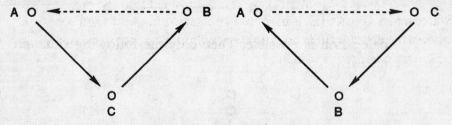

The roles of B and C have been interchanged. However, two new diagrams emerge because of the reversal of the arrows at D.

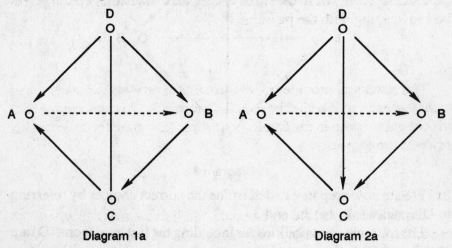

Diagram 1a                    Diagram 2a

These exhaust the four possibilities in Case 1.

**19. (E)**

I and II are both true in Diagram 3. III is true in both Diagrams 2 and 2a. Therefore, Choice (E) is correct.

**20. (E)**

II is true in Diagram 3. Diagrams 1 and 1a contradict I. Diagram 3 certainly contradicts III. Hence, one of the three statements is necessarily true.

**21. (B)**

A bureaucrat may send two different responsibilities, one to each of two other bureaucrats. Diagram 1a, 2a, and 3 indicate this possibility. Choice (A) is incorrect since it contradicts Statement 2 which forbids a direct exchange of responsibilities. Choice (C) is incorrect since Statement 5 forbids an outside bureaucrat. Choice (D) is incorrect because such an unfriendly situation could not exist in line with Statement 6. Choice (E) is incorrect because Statement 3 indicates that, when a bureaucrat finds no other bureaucrat to accept a responsibility, he must keep the responsibility.

**22. (C)**

The statement in the narratives all indicate the price of the speaker for the company. They also indicate that the company is the banner of capitalism. Thus, while the other choices are plausible, option (C) is best in keeping with the passage.

**23. (D)**

The statement provides no evidence about the author's age, foresight, honesty, or whether he is anti-Communist. His statement about his company being in the forefront of American industry indicates his pride in the company.

**24. (E)**

James interpreted Ralph's remark "all Italians enjoy spaghetti" to mean that "Italians enjoy only spaghetti." This explains why he disagrees with Ralph and claims that he knows some Italians who like baked potatoes — i.e., a food other than spaghetti.

25.   (C)
    Although the author may be of the opinion that the best training is done in mountainous areas, he may still appreciate the many benefits that a gymnasium offers. Similarly, there could be several reasons why the U.S. Olympic team doesn't train in mountainous areas — e.g., monetary. The answers to Choices (B) and (E) do not present any problem to the author. Only Choice (C) would seem to undermine the crux of the author's assertion that the best long distance runners are those who train in mountainous areas.